EASTERN
EUROPE

EASTERN EUROPE

Politics, Culture, and Society since 1939

EDITED BY

Sabrina P. Ramet

Indiana University Press

BLOOMINGTON AND INDIANAPOLIS

This book is a publication of

Indiana University Press
601 North Morton Street
Bloomington, Indiana 47404-3797 USA

www.indiana.edu/~iupress

Telephone orders 800-842-6796
Fax orders 812-855-7931
Orders by e-mail iuporder@indiana.edu

The paper used in this publication meets the minimum
requirements of American National Standard for Information
Sciences—Permanence of Paper for Printed Library
Materials, ANSI Z39.48-1984.

Manufactured in the United States of America

Library of Congress Cataloging-in-Publication Data

Eastern Europe : politics, culture, and society since 1939 / edited by
Sabrina P. Ramet.
p.   cm.
Includes bibliographical references (p.   ) and index.
ISBN 0-253-33470-5 (hardcover : alk. paper). — ISBN 0-253-21256-1
(pbk. : alk. paper)
1. Europe, Eastern—History—20th century. I. Ramet, Sabrina P.,
date.
DJK49.E16   1998
947'.0009'04—dc21   98-26834

1 2 3 4 5   03 02 01 00 99 98

For Zachary Irwin,
my dear friend

CONTENTS

ACKNOWLEDGMENTS

All of the chapters except 15 and 16 were written specifically for this book. Chapter 15 was originally published in *Survival*, Vol. 35, No. 2 (Summer 1993)—in that incarnation, under the sole authorship of Daniel N. Nelson. Chapter 16 was originally published in T. Hara, ed., *Slavic Eurasia in Transition: Multiple Analyses* (Sapporo, Japan: Slavic Research Center of Hokkaido University, 1994). I am grateful to the editors of these publications for permission to reuse this material.

I am grateful to Indiana University Press for having asked me to assemble this volume, to the Press's anonymous readers for helpful comments on successive drafts of the chapters, and to my spouse, Chris Hassenstab, for her continued enthusiasm for my work.

EASTERN
EUROPE

Introduction

SABRINA P. RAMET

I

This book provides an introduction to East European politics and history since 1939. Like Gaul, it is divided into three parts. In Part I, Gale Stokes provides historical background, explaining how the events of the past have set the stage for the problems and challenges of the present.

Part II presents chapters on the individual countries of Eastern Europe. Their chief aim is to familiarize readers with the major political developments in each country since 1939; within this political context, the country chapters also take up salient economic, cultural, and religious issues. I have chosen 1939 as the starting point in order to place the region's postwar development in the context of the destruction it experienced during World War II, but more particularly, because the task of economic rebuilding which was inextricably bound up with the initial communist economic programs was shaped by the destruction and damage caused by the war.

Part III takes up particular policy areas for fuller discussion. Chapters 11, 12, and 13 (on gender, religion, and film) consider the period since 1945, contrasting communist policies in these spheres with the situation since the collapse of communism. By contrast, chapters 14 and 15 (on economics and security) focus on the period since 1989, discussing the dramatic changes in these spheres associated with the transition from socialism to uncertain pluralism. Chapter 16 (on democracy and tolerance) argues that the central task of the fledgling systems of Eastern Europe should be to develop political cultures based on tolerance.

Readers will quickly see that three of the chapters deal with "defunct" states: the German Democratic Republic, Czechoslovakia, and Yugoslavia. Some may wonder why these chapters are not titled, instead: The Eastern Provinces of the Federal Republic of Germany, the Czech and Slovak Republics, and Yugoslavia and Its Successors. The reason is that these now-defunct states existed for most of the period under review in this book, and the processes of their breakup and the emergence of new political realities can appropriately be considered within the existing framework. For that matter, it would be incongruous to see an extended discussion of SED General Secretaries Ulbricht and Honecker within a chapter labeled "the Eastern Provinces of the Federal Republic of Germany."

The selection of countries is "traditional," excluding, thus, Greece, Austria, Finland, and any of the former Soviet republics. For most of the period under review, the eight societies included herein shared some common challenges and tasks, while experiencing conditions rather different from the noncommunist or Soviet republics.

II

The chapters of this book emphasize six central themes, growing out of a Hegelian-holistic view of political reality. On this view, political developments do not occur in a vacuum but reflect and are influenced by developments in other spheres and in turn influence and affect those spheres. Among such interconnected spheres are economics, religion, culture, gender relations, and a society's view of itself.

The first theme underpinning this book is *party politics and elite factionalism*, including an assessment of who benefited and who did not at each stage, what problems arose and when, intra-elite factionalism and agendas, dissidents and opposition, and the way in which the media figured in party politics. Closely associated is the theme of *economics and economic policy*, including the seemingly never-ending discussions about "reform" which surfaced throughout the region in the early 1960s and continued until the collapse of communism in 1989. Communist ideology assumed the priority of economics over politics, holding that political systems naturally served the interests of specific economic strata, i.e., the ruling class. In order to reverse the ascendancy of wealth over power, the communist regimes sought to capture the reins of government and establish a monopoly over the means of coercion, thereby asserting control over "the commanding heights of the economy." Communist governments nationalized banks, enterprises, farms, housing, and other properties, confiscated land from Churches, and reorganized the econ-

GERMANY

East
Prussia

• Wilna

SOVIET
UNION

Berlin
★

Warsaw
★

GERMANY

• Breslau

Kraków
•

POLAND

• L'viv

SLOVAKIA
★ Bratislava

Vienna
•

Budapest
★

HUNGARY

• Cluj

ITALY

Zagreb
•

ROMANIA

YUGOSLAVIA

Belgrade
★

Bucharest
★

• Split

Sofia
★

Ruse
•

BULGARIA

ALBANIA

Skopje
•

Tiranë
★

TURKEY

GREECE

MAP 1
CENTRAL AND
EASTERN EUROPE
March – August 1939

omy as a planned system. In a word, they aspired, as Gale Stokes has aptly noted,[1] to establish a *hyperrational polity*. Ironically, this meant that despite the communist belief in the primacy of economics over politics, in practice the communist regimes endeavored to establish the primacy of politics over economics.[2]

In communist Eastern Europe, politics and economics were closely linked. Thus, the most coercive politics tended to go hand in hand with the most coercive economics, whereas programs of economic liberalization and reform led directly to pressures for, and eventually programs of, political liberalization and reform.

SOVIET
UNION

GERMANY   GENERALGOUVERNEMENT

Berlin
★

REICHSPROTECTORATE   Warschau   GERMAN-
of BOHEMIA-   OCCUPIED
MORAVIA
              Breslau   Krakau

                                    Lemberg

                    SLOVAKIA
                    ★ Bratislava
        Vienna

              Budapest
              ★   Kolozsvár
           HUNGARY   •   ROMANIA

ITALY

        ★ Zagreb

                                    Bucharest
           CROATIA   ★
    ITALIAN-   GERMAN-
    OCCUPIED   • Split OCCUPIED
    CROATIA   SERBIA
                              Sofia   Ruse
                               ★

      ITALIAN-
      OCCUPIED   • Skopje BULGARIA
      MONTENEGRO   ★
                   Tiranë

      ITALIAN-   TURKEY
      OCCUPIED   GREECE
      ALBANIA

        MAP 2
     CENTRAL AND
   EASTERN EUROPE
    October 1943 – 1945

The next two themes which receive attention throughout this book, *nationalism and religion*, are also closely linked. The communist regimes saw them as closely associated and considered both to be enemies of socialism. Insofar as communism aspired to reshape human consciousness and to create the "new socialist woman" and "new socialist man," nationalism and religion had to be either suppressed or harnessed. The formula chosen varied from state to state. In Romania, to take an extreme example, nationalism became wedded to communist ideology early in the long reign of Nicolae Ceauşescu (general secretary of the Romanian Communist Party, 1965–89), while the Romanian Orthodox

MAP 3
**CENTRAL AND
EASTERN EUROPE**
November 1955 – October 1990

Church was made the object of doting attention in exchange for its complete capitulation to the communist state. Elsewhere, the control exercised by the state over the Church was not as extreme. But even in the German Democratic Republic, where certain courageous pastors achieved genuine popularity through their support for independent pacifist and environmentalist groups, many pastors and at least one bishop (Friedrich-Wilhelm Krummacher, onetime Bishop of Greifswald) were later revealed to have had inappropriate contacts with the *Stasi* (the State Security Service), sometimes acting as informants.[3] And even in ecclesias-

MAP 4
CENTRAL AND
EASTERN EUROPE
1996

tical organizations whose ministers did not consciously cooperate with the state, it was common practice for the East German regime to bug the confessionals.

Control of the religious organizations was toughest in Romania, Bulgaria, and Czechoslovakia, while in Albania, religion was declared illegal altogether in 1967. Conditions for religious organizations were somewhat more liberal in Hungary and in the Orthodox and Muslim parts of Yugoslavia (i.e., Serbia, Macedonia, Montenegro, and, albeit inconsistently, Bosnia), but only in Poland, the GDR, and the Catholic parts of Yugoslavia (Slovenia and Croatia) were religious organizations permitted by the state to adopt critical stances on certain topics vis-à-vis the local regime.

No necessary correlation existed between a regime's religious policy and its nationalities policy, but in practice, communist regimes which promoted an "accommodative" religious climate tended at the same time to be cooptive of nationalism.[4] Beneficiaries of this combination of policies would include the Evangelical Church in the GDR from 1969 to 1989, the Serbian Orthodox Church after 1984, the Macedonian Orthodox Church after 1967, the major religious organizations in Hungary from 1976 to 1989, and the Bulgarian and Romanian Orthodox Churches from soon after the war until 1989. By contrast, communist policies which assumed a "confrontational" attitude toward religious organizations tended, at the same time, to be hostile toward nationalism. The situation of the Catholic Church in Poland until 1989, the Catholic Church in Croatia for most of the period from 1945 to 1990, the Catholic Church in Soviet Lithuania, and the Greek-Rite Catholic Church in Ukraine from 1946 to 1989 serve to illustrate this dynamic. The alternative combinations of policies were, in communist times, the exception. Only in the cases of the Greek-Rite Catholics of Romania and of religious organizations in Albania generally was a confrontational religious climate associated with a regime policy cooptive of nationalism, while only in the case of the Muslims of socialist Yugoslavia was an accommodative religious climate associated with a regime policy that was hostile toward nationalism.

When the communists first took power in Eastern Europe, they tended to view nationalism as "bourgeois nationalism," a threat pure and simple, and they fought to stamp out any of its manifestations, whether in literature, in music, in the religious sphere, or in politics. In Tito's Yugoslavia, the standard and oft-repeated formula was "Every nationalism is dangerous"—and the Titoists went so far as to embrace the principle that no one was allowed to criticize nationalist excesses in other republics; one was permitted to criticize only the nationalism of one's own republic. Thus, it was permitted for a Croat to criticize Croatian nationalism, and for a Serb to criticize Serbian nationalism—but not for a Croat to criticize a Serb and vice versa.

Communist antagonism toward nationalism had the unintended result of driving nationalists into the arms of democratic dissidents and, thus, of facilitating a wedding of liberalism and nationalism. It was, however, a marriage of convenience; since the demise of communism, the more extreme nationalists have displayed open contempt for democratic practices.[5] A sociological study conducted among German young people in 1989 confirmed that there was ". . . a close correlation between nationalist identification and authoritarian, intolerant attitudes. Fifteen to twenty percent of all youth . . . [were said to] exhibit 'authoritarian,

nationalistic, and xenophobic' orientations, with a much higher percentage who showed antagonistic feelings toward people who thought or
lived differently."[6] This theme is explored in some detail in the final chapter of this book.

The fifth theme which the contributors to this book take up concerns
gender relations and women's equality, including a discussion of policies
under the communists as well as since the collapse of communism in
1989–90. Feminist scholars have developed the argument that the entire
fabric of any political system is closely interconnected with the prevailing
system of gender hierarchy. As German feminist Frigga Haug has argued,
"the level of emancipation of a society can be read in the level of emancipation of [its] women."[7]

While feminists of the left seek to transcend liberal democracy, re-
monstrating against its acceptance (sometimes even sacralization) of gender inequality,[8] Marxists traditionally sought to transcend feminism.
Their view was that emancipation was an all-engulfing project, and that
women would be liberated as a by-product of class emancipation. This,
in turn, meant that communists displayed an ingrained hostility toward
feminists, whom they often accused of "objectively" working against the
interests of women's equality. Since only the communist party could offer
a genuine path to true equality, including gender equality, any group acting outside communist frameworks was, ipso facto, working against the
achievement of equality.

The feminists of Yugoslavia and East Germany contributed to the
demise of communist rule in their respective countries. But to their great
disappointment, feminists in those two areas found they were more marginalized *after* communism than they had been under communist rule.
Indeed, as Hana Havelkova has observed in connection with the Czech
case, "It may be one of the paradoxes of history that reaction to the
communist experience brings forth in ideology, political thinking, and
economic practice extremely conservative elements, more conservative
than was the trend in precommunist Czech society."[9] Although the communists had insisted on controlling the processes of socialization and
change, they shared the feminists' view that women and men should be
equal. In the post-communist societies of Eastern Europe, the ruling elites
not only do not agree that gender equality would be desirable but in fact
frequently advocate women's return to "traditional" roles.[10]

The points of contact between nationalism and gender equality, and
between religion and aspirations toward gender equality, as well as those
between economic interests and the maintenance of a system in which
one gender is assigned to work menial jobs at substandard wages, should
be apparent.

The sixth and final theme addressed by the contributors to this volume is *culture and cultural policy*; in this regard, the contributors take

stock of cultural policy under the communists, and note the contribution made by literary figures, musicians, artists, and filmmakers to the social dialogue.

The communist governments in Eastern Europe were well aware of the importance of controlling cultural life, and communist ascendancy had a profound effect on the literary, artistic, and musical output in the areas under communist rule. This was especially true during the Stalinist era—an era which, nominally, ended with the death of Stalin in March 1953, but which, in practical terms, continued in Poland until 1956, in Czechoslovakia and Hungary until 1968, in the GDR until 1971, and in Romania, Bulgaria, and Albania until the bitter end in 1989.

The communists were, of course, concerned not only with what they liked (i.e., what they believed would promote their programs of socialization and their developmental programs), but also with what they did not like, and this meant that Boris Pasternak's *Dr. Zhivago* and George Orwell's novels, *Animal Farm* and *1984*, were nowhere available, either in translation or in their original languages. Stravinsky's *Rite of Spring*, the ballet score that had provoked a near-riot on the occasion of its world premiere in Paris in 1913, was banned in Poland for more than a decade. Composers whose music was too complicated became suspect, and they often found it difficult to have their works performed. Polish composer Andrzej Panufnik, for example, was denounced by a committee of "political and cultural activists" in 1952 for having produced a "formalistic" and "decadent" piece of music. The piece in question had just won first prize in a contest judged by Panufnik's fellow composers, but the sharp dissonances in the score troubled the commissars, who preferred highly tonic and triumphant music, preferably programmatic music with a clear (and "positive") line.[11]

Literature and music, like the other arts, were subjugated to the doctrine of "socialism realism" throughout the region, including in Yugoslavia. First promulgated in the Soviet Union in 1932, in an article appearing in *Literaturnaia gazeta* (The Literary Gazette), the doctrine held that artists, composers, and writers were obligated to concern themselves with "the task of educating workers in the spirit of Communism"[12] and to display unbridled optimism in the "glorious future" assured by communist hegemony. As Soviet chief of ideology Andrei Zhdanov told the 1934 Soviet writers' conference, "[socialist] literature must be able to show our heroes, must be able to glimpse our tomorrow."[13]

In Czechoslovakia the ascendancy of socialist realism in the 1950s produced such novels as A. Zapotocký's *Red Glow over Kladno* (1951) and V. Rezač's *The Offensive* (1951), which dealt with the theme of socialist construction. Stalin's personal taste in music stressed mass songs and other massive productions. Accordingly, composers in Czechoslovakia emphasized cantatas and mass songs, producing such obviously panegyric and political works as V. Dobias's cantata, *Build up the Motherland, and You Will Strengthen Peace!*, his mass song, *Join Our Brigade*, and J. Seidel's oratorio-cantata, *People, Be Vigilant!*[14] Elsewhere in the region, early postwar trends in music followed a parallel course.

Socialist realism also influenced the theater and the film industry, with partisan themes occupying a prominent place in the early postwar plays and films produced in Albania, Bulgaria,[15] and Yugoslavia.[16] In general, plays were expected to treat "useful" themes, as in the case of the Albanian plays *Doctor Aleksi* by Ibrahim Uruci, which deals with "the rectification of erring intellectuals," and *"Quiet" Lina* by Arsinoi Bino, which takes up the approved theme of female emancipation.[17]

When "cultural producers" strayed from the party line, there was always the risk of suppression of the offending piece and censure of its producer. In the GDR, for example, the opera, *The Trial of Lukullus*, by Paul Dessau and Bertolt Brecht, was criticized (in 1951) for pacifist and formalist tendencies, while the libretto of Hanns Eisler for the planned opera, *Faust*, excited intense ideological polemics.[18] Here, as elsewhere, culture was viewed as part of the arsenal of the ruling elite—thus, as a means to be exploited in the continuing struggle against capitalism and bourgeois values. In the Yugoslav case, after an early socialist-realist phase and a subsequent phase in which ". . . nature and love lyrics were cultivated,"[19] a local style of painting known as "naïve art" became popular. The "naïve" artists glorified peasant life, but not in the stylized heroic cast of socialist realism, and looked to the countryside for inspiration, especially to mundane scenes of everyday life.

The plastic arts were similarly enlisted in the task of glorifying socialism and the communist one-party state. Communist policy vis-à-vis the plastic arts was fashioned in harmony with Gyorgii Plekhanov's dictum ". . . that there is no such thing as a work of art completely devoid of ideological content, and also that not every idea can serve as a theme for a work of art, or truly inspire the artist. Only that which promotes communion between men [sic] can be the basis of a work of art [in socialist conditions]."[20] Artists were therefore instructed to take up "approved" themes (such as the evils of capitalism and imperialism, the struggle for peace, and solidarity with peoples fighting for freedom from Western colonialism) and to portray them in harmony with the doctrine of socialist realism, thereby rendering socialist heroes larger than life and purely good, and depicting capitalist-imperialist enemies as purely evil, scheming, greedy, and egotistical. With time, the constraints on the arts slackened, but for as long as they ruled in the region, the communists never lost their sense of the political uses of art.[21]

Likewise when it came to film, political judgments became crucial during the political life span of communism, as shown in Herbert Eagle's chapter. In the late 1940s and early 1950s, the East European film industry came under the pale of Zhdanovism,[22] and in the cases of directors who fled to the West, their names were erased from the history of socialist cinema, their works suppressed, their contributions ignored and denied.[23]

Even rock musicians were enlisted in the task of praising the leader. The Yugoslav group *Indeksi*, for example, praised Comrade Tito in song in the mid-1960s, singing,

> We knew that the sun was smiling on us,
> because we have Tito for our marshal![24]

Meanwhile, in neighboring Romania, rock groups were encouraged to sing songs with titles like "The Party, Ceaușescu, Romania," "Communist Years," and "Glory to Our First President." Somehow, it is difficult to imagine young people rocking to such songs.

But the communist effort to control culture eventually failed, because while the communists could finance as much cultural output as they liked, and buy off a certain sector of the cultural elite, there were always writers, artists, and musicians (such as Hungary's Coitus Punk Group) who refused to be coopted, who refused to collaborate. Such individuals ultimately played a small but conspicuous role in the process of dismantling communism, brick by brick or, perhaps, song by song.

Notes

1. Gale Stokes, *The Walls Came Tumbling Down: The Collapse of Communism in Eastern Europe* (New York and Oxford: Oxford University Press, 1993), 5, 8–9.

2. By contrast, the inheritors of the liberal tradition, believing in the primacy of political rights and political institutions, end by allowing economic interests to dominate the political system.

3. See *Der Spiegel* (Hamburg), 26 July 1993, 58; and *Welt am Sonntag* (Hamburg), 23 April 1995, 5.

4. See Sabrina Ramet, "Politics and Religion in Eastern Europe and the Soviet Union," in George Moyser, ed., *Politics and Religion in the Modern World* (London and New York: Routledge, 1991), 78–88.

5. For examples, see Sabrina P. Ramet, ed., *The Radical Right in Central and Eastern Europe* (University Park: Penn State Press, forthcoming).

6. Paul Hockenos, *Free to Hate: The Rise of the Right in Post-Communist Eastern Europe* (New York and London: Routledge, 1994), 56.

7. Frigga Haug, "Über die Frauenfrage als Systemfrage," in *Das Argument* (Berlin), Vol. 32, No. 2 (March–April 1990), 263.

8. An example of this tendency is Zillah Eisenstein, who argues that liberal feminism is inherently an oxymoron which crumbles under the pressures of its own internal self-contradictions. See Zillah R. Eisenstein, *The Radical Future of Liberal Feminism*, with a new preface and postscript by the author (Boston: Northeastern University Press, 1993).

9. Hana Havelkova, " 'Patriarchy' in Czech Society," in *Hypatia*, Vol. 8, No. 4 (Fall 1993), 95.

10. For details, see Sabrina Petra Ramet, *Social Currents in Eastern Europe: The Sources and Consequences of the Great Transformation*, 2nd ed. (Durham: Duke University Press, 1995), Chap. 18.

11. Liner notes by Andrzej Panufnik (Twickenham, 1971) on *Andrzej Panufnik: Heroic Overture, Nocturne, Tragic Overture, Autumn Music* (Unicorn Records, RHS 306, 1971).

12. Constitution of the Soviet Writers' Union (1934), as quoted in Matthew Cullerne Bown, *Art under Stalin* (New York: Holmes & Meier, 1991), 90.

13. Quoted in Bown, *Art under Stalin*, 90.

14. "Czechoslovakia," in *Great Soviet Encyclopedia*, 3rd ed., Vol. 29 (New York: Macmillan, 1982), 255, 257.

15. Regarding Bulgaria, see Ronald Holloway, "Bulgaria: The Cinema of Poetics," in Daniel J. Goulding, ed., *Post New Wave Cinema in the Soviet Union and Eastern Europe* (Bloomington: Indiana University Press, 1989), 229–230.

16. Regarding Yugoslavia, see Daniel J. Goulding, "Yugoslav Film in the Post-Tito Era," in Goulding, ed., *Post New Wave Cinema*, 249, 254.

17. Peter R. Prifti, *Socialist Albania since 1944: Domestic and Foreign Developments* (Cambridge: MIT Press, 1978), 121, 122.

18. Heinz Alfred Brockhaus and Konrad Niemann, eds., *Musikgeschichte der Deutschen Demokratischen Republik, 1945–1976*, Vol. 5 (East Berlin: Verlag Neue Musik, 1980), 66–67.

19. "Yugoslavia," in *Great Soviet Encyclopedia*, 3rd ed., Vol. 30, 732.

20. Gyorgii Plekhanov, "On Art for Art's Sake" (1912), in Berel Lang and Forrest Williams, eds., *Marxism and Art: Writings in Aesthetics and Criticism* (New York: David McKay, 1972), 90.

21. For further discussion of the politics of art, see Arnold Hauser, *The Social History of Art*, Vol. 4: *Naturalism, Impressionism, the Film Age* (New York: Vintage Books, 1951); Timothy W. Luke, *Shows of Force: Power, Politics, and Ideology in Art Exhibitions* (Durham: Duke University Press, 1992); and Paul Sjekocha and Igor Mead, *Unofficial Art in the Soviet Union* (Berkeley and Los Angeles: University of California Press, 1967).

22. David Paul, "Hungary: The Magyar on the Bridge," in Goulding, ed., *Post New Wave Cinema*, 176.

23. Peter Hames, "Czechoslovakia: After the Spring," in Goulding, ed., *Post New Wave Cinema*, 107.

24. Quoted in Sabrina Petra Ramet, *Balkan Babel: The Disintegration of Yugoslavia from the Death of Tito to Ethnic War*, 2nd ed. (Boulder: Westview, 1996), 95.

PART ONE

❏

Historical Background

2

Eastern Europe's Defining Fault Lines

GALE STOKES

The term "Eastern Europe" as it is used in this book refers to a strip of thirteen countries (at the time of writing) that runs north and south in an uneven band several hundred miles wide, from the Baltic Sea to the Aegean.[1] The region's approximately 140 million people speak even more languages than the number of countries involved, comprise five major religious groups, three of which are Christian, and have experienced a variety of national histories that in some cases go back more than a thousand years. All the peoples of the region can be considered in a fundamental sense to be Europeans, and yet in another way they have historically been separate from the great transformations that characterized Western Europe. The Renaissance, the Reformation, the scientific revolution, the Enlightenment, the creation of limited government, and the French Revolution all had their reflections and impacts in the region, but they were not generated there. On the other hand, despite a strong linguistic connection to Russia and a cultural linkage to Orthodox Christianity, the region did not participate directly in the unique Russian historical trajectory either. Even though the Soviet Union dominated Eastern Europe over most of the post–World War II era, historically the region was not subject to direct Russian control.

Eastern Europe consists of "the lands between," as Alan Palmer styled them.[2] Linked by many important connections to cultures to the east, to the south, and to the west, the East European peoples were not fully part of any of them. Three fundamental historical fault lines that divided the European continent define the region.[3] These are (1) the line that separates Orthodox Christians from Catholics; (2) the line that separates the Ottoman cultural area from that influenced by the great Christian empires, primarily Habsburg Austria, but also Prussia and Russia; and (3) the line that divides the socioeconomic conditions of Western Europe from those of Eastern Europe. In addition, Eastern Europe has been one of the most important laboratories of the quintessentially modern political ideology, nationalism—a fact made especially salient by the region's extremely confused ethnic situation. Eastern Europe is a shatterzone whose ethnic map in 1900, if indeed one could be drawn, would resemble the cracked bottom of a dried mud puddle. A discussion of these three fault lines and of the consequences of ethnicity and nationalism in Eastern Europe constitutes the introduction to this volume.

Neolithic settlements have been uncovered in the area we now call Eastern Europe. Anthropological finds confirm the presence there of prehistoric peoples, and Greek and Roman ruins dot Southeastern Europe in particular. But the history of the region as a specifically European entity began with the migration of the Slavs in the sixth century and the conversions to Christianity at the end of the first millennium. Originally, the Christian Church was one unit, Jesus and his disciples, and for the first three hundred years of its existence internal theological and political struggles had merely local interest. But in the fourth century of our era the Roman Empire, which dominated the Mediterranean world, adopted Christianity as its official religion. The newly authoritative position of Christianity made it imperative to define the faith accurately. Over the next two hundred years, by means of several ecumenical Church councils, the Christian emperor and his bishops defined the character of the Trinity and settled a number of theological issues. In doing so they lost the easternmost portion of the Church, such as the Copts, but in return they provided the Church a coherence and a mission that it had lacked previously.

At about the same time these Christological controversies were being worked out, the Roman Empire collapsed under the weight of its own size and under the pressure of the Germanic peoples on its periphery. The traditional date given for "the fall of Rome" is 476, but in fact the process took place over several centuries. Furthermore, it was not the entire empire that collapsed, but only the western part centered in Rome. The eastern half of the empire, the center of which was Constantinople (today Istanbul), survived as the Byzantine Empire until its final conquest by the Ottoman Turks in 1453. The consequences of this bifurcation were enormous. In the West a single Christian patriarch in Rome faced a disintegrating political situation, whereas in the East several patriarchs (in Jerusalem, Antioch, Alexandria, and, eventually, Constantinople) attended a rich and powerful state. Over time the Roman Church filled the political vacuum in which it found itself and became the organizational and spiritual heir to the Roman Empire. The Pope ruled over a hierarchical Church organization modeled on that empire; canon law took its lead from Roman law; and the Church adopted the language of the empire, Latin. Eventually, when strong secular kings arose in northern Europe, the struggle between pope and king became a fruitful source of western political theory and practice, while monastic movements and Church councils periodically produced both moral cleansings and crises of authority within the Church.

In the East, however, where there was no political vacuum, the Christian Church worked in "harmonious concert" with the Byzantine emperors, retaining at the same time a strong sense of community. Patriarchs maintained their local authority. When new peoples converted to the Byzantine rite, they were permitted to have their own national Churches, to use their own languages in the liturgy, and even to write their holy works in their own alphabets. Monasticism in the East remained a personal matter, a going into the desert for purification, and never developed the organizational dimension that characterized the western Church. Neither did the eastern Church recognize any Church councils after the seventh ecumenical council in the year 787. The different spirits of the diverging Churches are captured in their names and in the style of their affirmations of faith. The western Church called itself the Catholic, or universal, Church and began its creed "I believe," that is, I, the believing citizen of this hierarchically organized religious successor to the Roman Empire, believe. The eastern Church called itself the Orthodox Church since it perceived its goal as preserving the faith of the early Church fathers intact. It began its affirmation of faith "we believe," that is, we, the members of this community banded together as believers in the ancient faith, believe.

Between approximately 800 and 1200 the two centers of Christianity, Rome and Byzantium, competed to convert the pagans of northern and eastern Europe to their brands of Christianity. The ragged line separating those who chose Orthodoxy from those who chose Catholicism is roughly equidistant between Rome and Constantinople. Thus the Greeks, Bulgarians, Serbs, Romanians, Ukrainians, and Russians became Orthodox, while the Croats, Slovenes, Hungarians, Czechs, Slovaks, and Poles became Catholic. Among the latter peoples, educated persons learned and used Latin well into the nineteenth century, as did educated persons throughout the Catholic west. Among the former peoples, however, almost no one knew Latin, since the eastern Churches did not use that language in their liturgies. Because the Renaissance was fueled in good measure by the rediscovery of Latin texts from the Roman past, Orthodox lands did not participate in that awakening. Naturally the Reformation, which was fundamental not only in a religious sense but in fomenting the conflicts that led to the beginnings of the European state system in the seventeenth century, could not occur in the Orthodox east either, although abortive reform movements did occasionally arise. Neither did the scientific revolution, the Enlightenment, the industrial revolution, nor the French Revolution arise in the East. Russian history in particular, which consisted in good measure of the imposition of Russian imperial rule on the region that eventually became the Soviet Union, followed a radically different trajectory from the West. One of the most important reasons was its cultural isolation from the creative discontinuities of western development brought about by its adherence to Orthodoxy.

The Orthodox peoples of Southeastern Europe did not experience the same kind of historical development as did the Orthodox Christians of Russia because between the fourteenth and the sixteenth centuries Southeastern Europe came under the rule of the Ottoman Empire. This created the second major fault line running through Eastern Europe, a division between the cultural and political area of the Ottoman Empire to the south and that of the three European empires—the Russian, the Prussian, and, especially, the Austrian—to the north. The Ottomans originated as one of many warrior societies of Turkic origin populating the Anatolian peninsula. In the thirteenth century a particularly able leader, Osman, gathered a successful group of fighters around himself and took control of much of western Anatolia. Early in the fourteenth century his successors began to achieve military success in Southeastern Europe. Well organized under able leadership, the Ottoman troops were more than a match for the medieval states of the Bulgarians, Serbs, and Bosnians. In 1453 the Ottomans captured Constantinople, thus completing the fall of the second Rome, and by the sixteenth century, under the leadership of their greatest sultan, Süleyman the Law Giver, they had conquered all of Southeastern Europe and even besieged Vienna. Beaten back from Vienna, the Ottomans settled into Hungary and Southeastern Europe. As time went by, conquests in North Africa and the Near East extended their empire from the border of Morocco to the edges of Persia. The Ottomans ruled over Hungary for only one hundred and fifty years, but they dominated Serbia and Bulgaria for approximately five hundred years and ruled in some parts of the Balkans, such as Bosnia and Macedonia, into the twentieth century.

The Ottoman Empire was a Muslim empire of conquest, "the divinely protected, well-flourishing, absolute domain of the House of Osman," as they styled it.[4] It succeeded as a patrimonial state, that is, one in which the state and all within it was in theory the property of the prince, or in this case the sultan. This occurred in part because the Ottoman Empire experienced ten successive generations of able rulers from Osman through Süleyman. These rulers commanded a new-style standing army, the *janissaries*, that was well trained and well armed, and a cavalry of feudal knights, called *sipahis*, whom the sultan rewarded with estates in conquered territory. The administrators of the empire were the sultan's slaves, literally. Often these persons had been recruited as young boys from Balkan peoples, converted to Islam, rigorously trained, and then permitted to rise as far in the sultan's service as their talents allowed. One of the strengths of the Ottoman Empire at its peak was this administration, in which ability, not family background or wealth, was the secret to personal success.

The Ottoman sultans ran their empire according to the precepts of the Qur'an as interpreted by the holy law, the Sheri'a, and by the chief justice of the realm, the Seyh-ül Islam, who could and did advise the sultan as to the ethical and legal consequences of his actions. Because of Islamic law, the sultan considered himself the direct ruler of all the people in his realm and took steps to permit even ordinary subjects to remonstrate with him and his court about injustices. Paradoxically, the Islamic character of the Ottoman Empire was the reason that Southeastern Europe did not become Muslim. According to the Qur'an, before God vouchsafed his final revelation to Mohammed, he had made earlier revelations to Adam, Abraham, Moses, and Jesus, as told in the Old and New Testaments. Muslims, therefore, consider Jews and Christians to be "peoples of the book" whose religions, while incomplete, are revelations of God nevertheless.

The Ottomans never made a concerted effort to convert the Christians or Jews of Southeastern Europe to Islam. Of all the peoples on the Balkan peninsula only the Albanians, who are today 70 percent Muslim, and some Bosnians converted over time. Instead the Ottomans established the millet system, whereby the Orthodox Christians, and eventually the Jews as well, maintained their religious organizations and were permitted to adjudicate civil differences among their own believers. The Greek, Bulgarian, Serbian, and Romanian Orthodox Churches survived the Ottoman period and remain today living parts of national sensibilities in each of those countries. Jews expelled from Spain in 1492 established strong communities in the Ottoman Empire, especially in Thessaloníki and Sarajevo, where Ladino speakers survived until World War II.

The Habsburg lands absorbed the main thrust of the Ottoman push into Central Europe. The Habsburg family established itself around Vienna in the thirteenth century. In the fifteenth and sixteenth centuries, by a series of fortunate marriages, it created by far the most extensive medieval holdings of any European dynasty. Charles V (1500–1558) was not only the senior member of a family with claims to Austria, Hungary, and Bohemia in Central Europe and holder of the crown of the Holy Roman Empire of the German Nation, but he also ruled over Burgundy, Milan, Naples and Sicily, the Netherlands, Spain, the Spanish new world, and the Philippines, among other places. Despite this extensive realm, Charles and his brother Ferdinand, who administered the Central European, or Austrian, part of this family realm, were not able to push the Ottomans out of Hungary. The Habsburgs accomplished this only at the end of the seventeenth century, by which time the Ottoman Empire had begun to decline. The Treaty of Karlowitz in 1699 drew a new line between the Ottomans and Habsburgs that left Croatia, Vojvodina, Hungary, and Transylvania in Habsburg hands, whereas Bosnia, Serbia, Romania, Bulgaria, and Greece remained in Ottoman hands. This east-west line divided the peoples of East Central Europe from those of Southeastern Europe. The decline of the Ottomans opened what became known as "The Eastern Question," which was, basically, which great power would step into the power vacuum developing in the Balkans: Russia or Austria.

The new Habsburg realm confirmed at Karlowitz included two of the three major kingdoms of medieval East Central Europe, Bohemia and Hungary. Both had become Christian about the year 1000, and both had a complex medieval history. The Czechs, who live primarily in Bohemia and Moravia, particularly celebrate the Protestant movement of Jan Hus. Early in the fifteenth century, one hundred years before Martin Luther, Hus inspired a successful insurgency of reforming Czech Christians against the Roman church and its German defenders. The Hungarians, who do not speak an Indo-European language, entered Central Europe at the beginning of the tenth century and established themselves in the plains surrounding the middle course of the Danube River.[5] Becoming Christian in the year 1000 under King Stephen, the Hungarians created a state and society based on a strong feudal aristocracy. The Habsburgs established a claim to the Hungarian crown in 1526, when the Ottomans defeated the Hungarian nobility at the battle of Mohacs and killed Louis, their reigning monarch. Ferdinand of Austria had married Louis's sister, while Louis had married Ferdinand's sister, under an arrangement that permitted the surviving monarch to succeed to the other's throne. Since Louis was also king of Bohemia, Ferdinand now claimed that crown as well.

The Habsburgs were not able to dominate the Czech lands completely until 1620. In that year they defeated rebellious Czech forces at the battle of White Mountain and assumed hereditary control of Bohemia and Moravia. Control of the lands of the Holy Crown of St. Stephen, as the Hungarian holdings were known, came with the Treaty of Karlowitz. The Habsburgs were able to Germanize Bohemia and Moravia by dispossessing the Czech nobility in favor of deserving members of the Habsburg aristocracy, but in Hungary their Germanization policy failed. The Hungarian nobility retained its privileges and sustained aristocratic and gentry cultures that dominated Hungary up to World War II.

The third of the great medieval states of Central Europe was Poland.

After its dynastic union with Lithuania in the fourteenth century, Poland became the largest kingdom in Europe. The main characteristic of this kingdom, or commonwealth as it became known in the seventeenth and eighteenth centuries, was the success of its landowning class in establishing its rights and privileges over those of the king. While Poland's neighbors, particularly Prussia and Russia, were becoming more powerful by rationalizing their military and administrative structures, the Polish nobles kept their king weak and their administration minimal. The Polish nobles considered themselves the freest men in Europe, and they were, but they also ruled over what increasingly became the weakest state in Europe. At the end of the eighteenth century their powerful neighbors—Russia, Prussia, and Austria—simply divided up Poland among themselves in three "partitions," leaving no Polish state at all by the time of Napoleon.

While Austria was establishing its hegemony in East Central Europe, Southeastern Europe remained a peripheral area of the great Ottoman state that dominated the Near East. For the Balkan peoples, the model of culture and politics, and the center of economic intercourse, lay to the south in Istanbul. They were able to maintain their Orthodox Christian traditions, but even in this case the orientation was southward, since the ecumenical patriarch was located in Istanbul. The orientation of the peoples of East Central Europe, on the other hand, was toward Vienna, Berlin, and points west. This cultural divide between those peoples oriented toward the Ottomans and those oriented toward the Habsburgs, which cuts across the north-south line dividing Orthodox Christians from Catholics, constitutes the second historical fault line dividing Eastern Europe.

A third fault line of economic differentiation runs approximately along the Elbe River and thence south and west to Trieste. After the year 1000, the time by which most of Europe had been converted to Christianity, economic divisions between the territories east and west of that line begin to emerge. Western Europe experienced a demographic and economic boom in the twelfth and thirteenth centuries. Population grew; new methods of cultivation using the three field system and the deep plow increased agricultural production and inspired the retreat of serfdom; towns emerged as trading centers; and commerce boomed. East of the Elbe River, however, all of these tendencies were attenuated. Population densities were much lower, making commerce more difficult; towns grew up primarily as military and administrative centers rather than as autonomous trading units; and agricultural technology spread much more slowly. In the fourteenth century population declined throughout Europe, in part because of the Black Death, but when the demographic climb started again in the fifteenth and sixteenth century, an entirely new element entered the picture. Starting about 1450 the Portuguese and Spanish took to the seas, exploring the west coast of Africa, discovering a sea route to India and Asia, and landing in North America. The Atlantic-facing communities of Europe entered a completely new era of commercial possibilities. By stripping the New World of its gold and silver and by bringing home luxury products from Asia, they began the process that created the world trading system of capitalism.

Central Europeans, not advantageously situated geographically, did not participate directly in this economic boom or in the elaboration of property rights that accompanied it, although the economic changes produced by the successes of the Atlantic-facing communities had a great effect on them. In Poland the main impact came through the grain trade. Since medieval times Polish landowners had exported grain through the Hanseatic system of ports, particularly from Danzig to the Netherlands. In the fifteenth and especially sixteenth centuries this trade became the dominant fact of the Polish economy. The Vistula River became the great highway by which the Polish nobility took its grain to the German and Dutch merchants who had made Danzig (today Gdańsk) a great trading city. Since the Polish nobility was already strong, the opportunity for profits in the grain trade encouraged them to insure the labor supply they needed to produce the grain by imposing serfdom on the Polish peasants. Whereas in Western Europe serfdom had been eliminated as a legal category by the sixteenth century, in Poland it was imposed at that time. This outcome was not solely the result of the grain trade, as is demonstrated by the fact that Russia, which did not participate heavily in that trade, also imposed serfdom at the same time, but the sociological outcome was to rigidify the Polish social structure and to condemn its agriculture to a backward style of extensive grain production. While the French port cities, the Netherlands, England, and North America were developing new and productive commercial devices, Poland was saddling itself with a backward social and agricultural system that greatly widened the already large economic gap between it and Western Europe.

Hungary felt the impact of the Atlantic opening too. One of Hungary's main exports in late medieval times was live cattle, which were driven to markets in southern Germany. As those German towns became increasingly linked into the new world economy, their need for Hungarian cattle greatly lessened and the Hungarians had to look to Vienna or even to the Ottomans for markets. In both cases this cut them off from integration into the changing western economies. When Hungary became part of the Habsburg lands in the eighteenth century, it assumed the role of an agricultural producer. Hungary finally began its industrialization only late in the nineteenth century.

Bohemia, much of which actually lies to the west of the Elbe-Trieste line, was the only place in East Central Europe that became more or less integrated into the West European trade system. Already in the middle ages Bohemia had exported textile products, primarily linens, and in the early modern period it exported wool products successfully as well. Whereas the Habsburgs assigned Hungary an agricultural role, they considered Bohemia one of their main industrial and commercial centers. In the eighteenth century, Bohemia was among the first parts of Europe to turn to the mechanization of textile production, as even noblemen introduced proto-industrial production facilities into the countryside. Early in the nineteenth century mechanized cotton production took off, so that by World War I Bohemia and Moravia were the most industrialized parts of Eastern Europe, on a par with many parts of the West.

The economic picture in Southeastern Europe, of course, was quite different. The Romanian lands supplied Istanbul with grain produced on large estates by tenant peasants, while Bulgaria developed a small-scale commerce and a modest textile industry supplying Ottoman needs. Greece had the most varied economy. It had its wretched peasants and primitive mountain people, as did the rest of the Balkans, but Greek shipowners were able to take advantage of the opening of the Black Sea in 1774 to prosper during the Napoleonic wars. Upper-class Greeks living in Istanbul, the so-called Phanariots, ruled the Romanian lands as administrators in the eighteenth century and dominated the Orthodox millet, often including the national churches of the Bulgars, Romanians, and Serbs. With these exceptions, by the time of the French Revolution, the Balkans were economically in an even more undeveloped state than most of East Central Europe.

The transformation of Eastern Europe into the region with which we are familiar today began with the French Revolution and the entire nexus of ideas and institutions that grew out of it. Of these the most important has been nationalism. England was the first country in which a community spirit encompassing the people as a whole became the justifying idea behind the state, and France was the second. The French Revolution provided the world with a wealth of texts identifying the nation as the sovereign. Under Napoleon, the doctrines of the Enlightenment spread throughout Europe. In both England and France, the sense of nation matured within the boundaries of an already existing state. But the notions of liberty, equality, and fraternity, coupled with the idea of popular sovereignty, entered an Eastern Europe in which no states existed that could be considered "national." Instead, four multinational empires based on variations of the medieval principles of kingship, nobility, and loyalty ruled over a vast variety of religious, ethnic, and traditional groups. Until the ideas of the Enlightenment and the French Revolution began to spread in Eastern Europe, most of the peoples there did not grant much saliency to their ethnic or linguistic background. Educated Christians spoke Latin, French, German, or Greek, and the important differentiating characteristic was religion.

The conclusion of the Napoleonic period brought political reaction to Central Europe under the leadership of Clemens von Metternich in Vienna, Prussian conservatives in Berlin, and Nicholas I in Russia. But underneath the apparently calm surface maintained by these leaders, small groups of intellectuals of varying social backgrounds began to investigate the implications of Enlightenment ideas. Often basing their efforts on the work of Germans, such as Herder, rather than on French or English authorities, they undertook to codify their languages, to discover and transcribe folk poetry, and to study history. Slavic speakers in both Russia and Eastern Europe started to become aware that their languages were related. In some places this created a Panslavic enthusiasm, while in others, nascent nationalists developed a fear of domination by the Russians or Poles. In Croatia, for example, the Illyrian movement of the 1840s suggested that all speakers of Serbian, Croatian, and Bulgarian were South Slavs who had a fundamental cultural unity, while among the Czechs Karel Havliček became convinced that the Slavs were not one nation. He argued that the Czechs were better off supporting the multinational but Western-oriented Habsburg empire than they would be pursuing a long-range goal of Slavic unity that risked subjugation to Russia.

The revolutions of 1848 opened an opportunity to liberal and nationalistically minded Germans and Hungarians, as well as to the Slavs. Since educated Slavs in Eastern Europe were few in number, poorly organized, and without a state apparatus, the best they could do in the revolutionary situation was to hold a conference in Prague and reject affiliation with the Germans and Hungarians. Some Slavs, particularly the Serbs and Croats, even joined forces with the Habsburgs. The Hungarians, however, with an ancient tradition of an independent aristocratic state behind them, went much further. Under the leadership of the revolutionary Lajos Kossuth, the Hungarians declared their independence from the Habsburgs and set out on their own path of national development. Within little more than a year, however, the Habsburgs rallied and, with the military help of the reactionary Russian tsar Nicholas I, reincorporated Hungary into their lands.

The failure of the revolutions of 1848 ushered in a ten-year period of reaction in Central Europe, but it did not end the growth of a sense of nation among the educated strata of the non-Germanic peoples of Central Europe. In the 1860s, their aspirations received an enormous boost, both psychologically and practically. Italian and German unification more than offset the failure of the Polish revolt of 1863. In 1867 the Hungarians were able to achieve autonomy. By the *Ausgleich* of that year, Austria and Hungary became separate realms linked together only by the person of the ruler and by common policies in foreign affairs, military governance, and finances. From that moment on the two halves of the Dual Monarchy followed separate paths in their domestic politics, although they continued to act as one state in international affairs.

The terms *Hungary* and *Austria* hide the important fact that both elements were themselves multinational medieval agglomerations of great variety. Therefore, during the rest of the century both Austria and Hungary faced not only their mutual conflict, but also growing political movements based on nationality inside their own realms. In the Austrian lands perhaps the most important of these was the regeneration of the Czechs, who assumed by the end of the nineteenth century a key role in the Austrian parliament. Polish nobility from Galicia also found a way to achieve political importance, but they were less nationalists than they were traditionalists who socially dominated their backward region and found a way to make their local dominance pay off in Vienna. In Hungary the most difficult ethnic problems concerned the Croats, who had a special relationship with the Hungarian crown since the year 1102, and the Romanians, who constituted a majority in the traditionally Hungarian region of Transylvania. Themselves increasingly nationalistic, the Hungarians pursued a policy of Magyarization (forcing Hungarian language and culture on populations whose mother tongue was not Hungarian) that alienated these and other ethnic groups under their rule.

Jews played a significant role in both the Austrian and Hungarian halves of the Dual Monarchy. By the end of the nineteenth century they even began to develop their own brand of nationalism, which they called Zionism. Despite the emergence of anti-Semitic politicians and parties in Austria (the mayor of Vienna from 1897 to 1910 was explicitly anti-Semitic), Jews played a key cultural and economic role in Vienna. In Budapest, the aristocratic Hungarian leadership pursued an assimilationist policy that permitted rich and successful Jews to enter the nobility, so that the most successful Jewish community in Eastern Europe became the Hungarian one, especially that of Budapest. In other parts of Eastern Europe, especially in Romania, however, anti-Semitism grew more widespread at the end of the nineteenth century.

While national movements were coalescing in Habsburg lands, new national entities were emerging in the Ottoman region as well. The "Eastern Question" had originally been which of the Great Powers, Russia or Austria, would take the place of "The Sick Man of Europe" (the Ottoman Empire) in the Balkans. But during the nineteenth century a third possibility arose—that the Ottoman Empire would be replaced by national states. The first people to revolt successfully against the Ottomans were the Serbs, who achieved autonomy within the Ottoman Empire by 1830. The Serbian uprisings were probably based more on Ottoman models of political behavior than they were on French Revolutionary traditions or nationalism, but they provided an administrative basis for the growth of a Serbian state. By 1878, Serbia achieved full statehood and began adopting European standards rather than Ottoman ones, turning, that is, from a southward orientation of cultural and political dependency to a northward-facing orientation. Serbs adopted a constitution, formed political parties, created a court system, built a bureaucracy, and, of course, adopted the legitimating notion of nationalism.

Greeks too achieved their independence through revolution, although in the Greek case that independence (also achieved in 1830) came only with substantial international involvement, so that throughout the nineteenth century Greece, while adopting forms of western public life, came under the strong influence of foreign states, particularly England.

The Romanians achieved their independence in 1859 by clever tactical politics. The two main Romanian regions, Wallachia and Moldavia, were borderlands of the Ottoman Empire, ruled in the eighteenth century by Greek surrogates from Istanbul. In the early nineteenth century they came under the domination of Russia, which paradoxically introduced the first elements of Western-style rule there. After Russia's defeat in the Crimean War, the Great Powers decided that rather than reimposing either the eighteenth-century Greek representatives of the Ottomans or the nineteenth-century Russian administrators, they would permit the Moldavians and Wallachians to elect their own local princes, while remaining under Ottoman rule. But the Romanians outfoxed the Powers by electing the same man as prince in both regions, thereby in effect uniting Moldavia and Wallachia into one country. In 1878 the Treaty of Berlin recognized Romania as an independent state.

In Bulgaria a movement of renascence that began in the 1830s was in full flower by the 1870s. When war broke out between the Russians and the Ottomans in 1877, it was the Bulgarians who benefited most. In 1878 the Russians forced the defeated Ottomans to recognize Bulgarian independence in the Treaty of San Stefano. This treaty created a large Bulgaria, including the entire territory known as Macedonia. But the Great Powers found the creation of a strong Russian client astride the Balkan peninsula unacceptable and forced the Russians to back down. By the Treaty of Berlin, Bulgaria gained its independence, but lost Macedonia. Therefore, the very origin of the Bulgarian state was flawed by disappointment and a sense of loss. Three times since then—in the Balkan Wars, in World War I, and again in World War II—the Bulgarians regained Macedonia, but each time only temporarily. Since Greece and Serbia also entertained aspirations to Macedonia, it remained a volatile part of Europe.

The first stirrings of Albanian nationalism came only near the end of the nineteenth century, and an independent Albania came into existence in 1912. This new country included only about 60 percent of the Albanians living on the Balkan peninsula. The rest remained in Serbia, Bosnia, Montenegro, and Macedonia, all of which at the end of World War I became parts of Yugoslavia. During the interwar years, Albania became a client of Italy, and after World War II it retreated into almost complete isolation from both Eastern and Western Europe.

World War I and the collapse of the Habsburg Empire brought independent national states to life in Central Europe. The origins of World War I are complex and long debated. Certainly the ambitions of Germany to exercise power on a world scale and its fears of being encircled by enemies were important to the specific way in which the war broke out. Both Russia and Austria also entertained fears about their Great Power status. But the one problem that no amount of negotiation could have solved was the underlying contradiction between nationalism and the medieval principle of *Kaisertreue*, or loyalty to the emperor. The Habsburg realm relied on *Kaisertreue* to draw the disparate Austro-Hungarian Empire together. The nationality principle held that for popular sovereignty to have full meaning in the post–French Revolutionary world, the state should be organized for the protection of the nation. Putting this principle into effect obviously would mean the end of the Habsburg Empire. The specific arena in which this confrontation between the old and the new turned into actual politics was the conflict between Serbia and Austria.

After becoming independent in 1878, Serbia became an Austrian client, but in 1903 it began to pursue an independent policy. Austria-Hungary reacted in 1905 by restricting Serbian imports, and in 1908 it seized Bosnia and Herzegovina, parts of which the Serbs coveted. An emotional wave of anti-Austrian nationalism bubbled to the surface of Serbian public life. The success Serbia enjoyed in the Balkan Wars of 1912–1913, in which it and Greece seized the lion's share of Macedonia, greatly enhanced its prestige among all the non-Germanic peoples of Austria-Hungary, especially among the Serbs and Croats. Serbia's success also correspondingly intensified Austro-Hungarian fears that the Serbian example was intensifying the centrifugal forces in the empire. When some very young Serbs from Bosnia assassinated the heir to the Habsburg throne in Sarajevo, Austria-Hungary decided to act. The Germans, seeing in the Serbian-Austrian conflict a way to overcome their frustrations through war, encouraged the Austrians to act decisively, giving the Austrians what historians have called "a blank check" to take whatever action they felt appropriate. When the Serbs did not accept the resultant Austrian ultimatum unconditionally, the war started.

No one expected the Great War to destroy all four of the ancient states that had dominated Eastern Europe for so long, but that is what happened. A secular Turkey under the leadership of Kemal Ataturk replaced the Ottoman Empire, while Bolshevik revolution brushed the Russian Empire aside and established the Soviet Union. The defeated German Empire was replaced by a frail democratic republic, which suffered various insults before giving way to Hitler's Third Reich. And a string of independent states stretching from the Baltic to the Adriatic took the place of the Austro-Hungarian Empire.

Even though the victory of the allies in World War I in a sense vindicated the nationality principle over *Kaisertreue*, all the new and changed states of Eastern Europe that came into existence in 1918, with the exception of Hungary, were very diverse ethnically. Poland reemerged from more than a century of nonexistence and, after a successful war with the new Bolshevik regime, pushed its eastern border far into Belarus and Ukraine. Poland, especially urban areas such as Warsaw, also contained a significant number of Jews and Germans. Czechoslovakia, a completely new state that had never existed before, comprised two ruling groups, Czechs and Slovaks, but it also contained large and compact German, Hungarian, Ukrainian, and Jewish minorities. The Romanians doubled their territory by seizing Transylvania, where the underprivileged Romanian peasantry constituted a majority, but Transylvania was traditionally Hungarian and had a compact and prosperous German community. The Romanians also took Bukovina and Bessarabia, both of which were dominated culturally by significant Jewish and Ukrainian populations. The most diverse state was Yugoslavia, where no national group constituted a majority. There the successful efforts of the Serbs to dominate the new country set the other peoples on edge, particularly the Croats, and established a pattern of ethnic conflict that has endured.

The interwar years in Eastern Europe were dominated by several conflicts the East Europeans could have controlled if they had found the wisdom, and several major developments over which they had no control. The issues over which the East Europeans had some control were territorial questions, economic relations, and internal political organization. The issues over which they had no control were the international economic situation, the rise of the Nazis, and the power of the Soviet Union. If ever these lands were "in between," it was during the 1930s and 1940s. It is difficult to blame the East Europeans for not being able to focus on policies that might have brought stability to the region during the 1920s and 1930s. The problems they faced in organizing new countries out of the heterogeneous remnants of ancient states were enormous; very few had any experience in the politics of accommodation; many of them were excited and rash in the first flush of national self-determination; and, with the exception of Bohemia and Moravia, all of them were economically undeveloped. At first, it seemed that political parties designed to appeal to the peasantry, such as the Bulgarian Agrarian National Union under the original leadership of Alexandûr Stamboliski, or the Croatian Peasant Party under Stjepan Radić, might find original solutions to the problems faced by the main social class of the region. But the success of the intelligentsia and state class in seizing and maintaining power, the corrosive power of nationalism, the erratic personalities of the peasant leaders, and the antimodern thrust of their programs doomed these efforts to failure.

At least two of the new East European countries were extremely dissatisfied with their fate. The Bulgarians had entered the war on the side of the Germans in order to seize Macedonia. Having lost, many of them, including terrorist emigrés from Macedonia, nursed violent grievances through the 1920s. The victorious allies forced the Hungarians to accept the Treaty of Trianon by which they lost many of the traditional lands of the Crown of St. Stephen, such as Croatia, Slovakia, and Transylvania, to their newly independent or expanded neighbors. Bitter rejection of Trianon tainted Hungary's entire interwar psychology.

Challenged by the difficult task of integrating varied administrative procedures inherited from the departed empires into a single state system, disrupted by ethnic controversy, debilitated by weak economies, misguided by attempts to protect infant industries through tariff measures, wracked by bitter border disputes, and lacking a useful democratic past, these first approximations of modern democracies in Eastern Europe were destined to fail. But even had the East Europeans been more successful in the interwar years in their efforts to cope with new and difficult problems, they probably would have failed anyway in the fifteen years between 1933 and 1948 under the extraordinary pressures placed on them first by the depression, and then by the expansionist policies of Germany and the Soviet Union.

During the 1920s the revisionist powers, Hungary and Bulgaria, along with Austria, looked to Mussolini's Italy for help and guidance, but in the 1930s Hitler's Germany took over that role for all of Eastern Europe. East European countries could not emerge from the Great Depression by themselves, but during the 1930s they found that the Western democracies were not inclined to help them through credits or acceptance of their agricultural products. Hitler's Germany, however, attracted East European trade with credits and outright purchases. By the end of the 1930s Germany had become Eastern Europe's largest trading partner.

In the political arena, East European politicians, who by the time of Hitler tended toward authoritarian solutions in any event, realized by the mid-1930s that they could expect little support from the Western democracies. If France would not react to such an obvious threat to its vital self-interest as Hitler's occupation of the Rhineland in 1936, the chances that the West would protect its East European allies from Hitler's initiatives were negligible. The final proof of this came in the crisis of September 1938, when Prime Ministers Neville Chamberlain and Eduard Daladier met with Adolf Hitler and Benito Mussolini in Munich and agreed, without the participation of Czechoslovak Prime Minister Edvard Beneš, to permit Nazi Germany to occupy the ethnically German parts of Czechoslovakia. This British and French act of appeasement only encouraged Hitler and demonstrated that, for the West, Eastern Europe was, as Chamberlain put it regarding Czechoslovakia, "a far away country . . . [of which] we know little."[6] It is little wonder that Slovakia, Hungary, Romania, and Bulgaria reached their accommodations with Hitler and entered World War II as Germany's allies.

Eventually, of course, the West did react against Hitler. When the Nazis occupied Bohemia and Moravia in 1939, the British unilaterally guaranteed the integrity of Poland, so that when Hitler invaded that country on 1 September 1939, the British and French declared war. Just as in World War I, Germany and its central European allies could not sustain the massive costs of their aggression. By 1943 the tide of war had changed, and in 1944 the Red Army entered Eastern Europe from one direction while the Americans, British, and Free French invaded France from the other. In May 1945 the victorious allied armies converged over the prostrate body of a crushed and defeated Germany, and within a short time the cold war began. This is not the place to enter into the details of the imposition of Stalinist rule in Eastern Europe, which was one of the main causes and consequences of that cold war, but, in general, it can be said that unlike Western Europe, the countries of Eastern Europe lost the opportunity for restructuring in a democratic way that the great caesura of 1945 afforded Germany, France, and Italy. Whereas the defeated Germans took the creative and constructive steps of ending their long-standing enmity with France and of joining with the other Western states in a voluntary and pluralistic European Community, East Europeans were forced to submit to coercive dictatorships that closed the door to debate and reconciliation. Forty years later the negative consequences of closing off Eastern Europe to a generation of reconciliation and remembrance have become apparent.

Eastern Europe constitutes a specific arena of European historical development defined by three long-standing and fundamental fault lines and strongly influenced by nationalism and ethnic diversity. A religious fault line separates Orthodox Christianity from Catholicism and its Protestant heirs. Russia and the Orthodox east pursued a very different historical trajectory than did the Catholic countries. Crosscutting this more or less north-south line is the roughly east-west line separating the Ottoman Empire and the European empires, particularly the Habsburgs. Whereas Greeks, Serbs, Bulgarians, and Romanians looked south and east for cultural and political models for hundreds of years, central Europeans looked toward Rome, Vienna, and Berlin. The third fault line, the economic one, ran southeast along the Elbe River and then south to Trieste, but lay several hundred miles to the west of the Orthodox/Catholic line. It separated the commercial and developing West from the agricultural and backward East. In the generation following World War II, it sometimes seemed that these ancient fault lines had been erased by the homogenizing internationalism of Stalinism and communism, not to mention by industrialization and modernization, but after 1989 it has become clear that they were not.

Notes

1. Poland, Hungary, the Czech Republic, Slovakia, Romania, Bulgaria, Greece, Albania, Slovenia, Croatia, Bosnia and Herzegovina, Yugoslavia, and Macedonia.

2. Alan W. Palmer, *The Lands Between: A History of East Central Europe since the Congress of Vienna* (London: Weidenfeld & Nicolson, 1970).

3. For a recent explication of a similar argument, see Dennis Hupchick, *Culture and History in Eastern Europe* (New York: St. Martin's, 1994). See also Jenö Szücs, "The Three Historical Regions of Europe," *Acta Historica Academiae Scientiarum Hungaricae*, Vol. 29/2–4 (1983), 131–84.

4. Peter Sugar, *Southeastern Europe under Ottoman Rule, 1354–1904* (Seattle: University of Washington Press, 1977), 3.

5. Hungarian, or Magyar, is a Finno-Ugric language. Although the only other European languages related to it are Finnish and Estonian, Hungarian is approximately as close to those languages as English is to Persian (the latter are both Indo-European languages).

6. Keith Feiling, *The Life of Neville Chamberlain* (London: Macmillan, 1946), 372.

PART TWO

Countries

3

Czechoslovakia

SHARON L. WOLCHIK

Political developments in the twentieth century in what was until 1 January 1993 Czechoslovakia have reflected the impact of developments in the broader international environment as well as the country's ethnic composition. The history of Czechoslovakia has been shaped to a large degree by its position as a small power at the heart of Europe. As such, the lands that came to comprise Czechoslovakia were often ruled by or were a part of larger powers, and the actions of larger, more powerful neighbors often played an important role in determining the fate of the peoples who lived in the area that became Czechoslovakia.

The Czechoslovak republic was created as an independent state in 1918 in the aftermath of the breakup of the Austro-Hungarian Empire after World War I. Led by President Tomáš Masaryk, the country was the only one of the new democracies created in the region in 1918 that maintained a democratic form of government until it was ended by outside forces. Because the country, particularly the Czech Lands, had a more developed economy and more experience with self-organization and limited self-rule than many of its neighbors, as well as very high literacy rates and a sizable middle class, the preconditions for maintaining democratic government were better than elsewhere. The political values and the progressive economic and social policies adopted by the country's leaders also helped to defuse popular discontent.

The 1938 incorporation of the Sudeten Lands by Germany ended the country's interwar experience with democracy. This step was soon followed by German occupation of Bohemia and Moravia and the cre-

ation of a pseudo-independent Slovak state under Hitler's tutelage in
1939. After the liberation of the country in May 1945, Czechoslovakia
enjoyed a brief period of modified pluralism. In February 1948, this too
ended, when the coalition government was replaced by one clearly dominated by the Communist Party.

The end of communist rule in 1989 signaled a return to democratic
government once again. However, as in the interwar period, when ethnic
tensions provided the pretext for outside actors to break up the state,
ethnic conflict dominated the political agenda of post-communist
Czechoslovakia and eventually resulted in the end of the federation.
Leaders of the two new states that have replaced Czechoslovakia espouse
democratic principles. The transition to the market and a democratic
government has gone more smoothly in the Czech Republic than in Slovakia. However, both governments continue to face problems related to
the legacy of communism and to the fact that the transition from communist rule is a long-term process even in the best of circumstances.

The history of the state has also been conditioned by its ethnic
makeup. The first Czechoslovak republic contained sizable Ukrainian,
German, Hungarian, Jewish, and gypsy or Roma minorities in addition
to the dominant Czechs and Slovaks. The expulsion of the Sudeten Germans and many Hungarians after World War II and the decimation of
most of the Jewish population by the Holocaust simplified the ethnic
composition of the country. However, relations among the country's various ethnic groups continued to be important political issues during the
communist period. And, as will be discussed below, ethnic issues led to
the demise of the Czechoslovak federation when the new democratic political framework proved incapable of containing the conflict between
Czech and Slovak leaders over many fundamental questions related to
the transition from communist rule.[1]

THE AFTERMATH OF WAR AND RECONSTRUCTION

Although Czechoslovakia was liberated in large part by Soviet troops,
democratic forces continued to play some role in the country's government until February 1948. President Edvard Beneš, who headed the government in exile in London during the war, returned to the country and
once again served as his country's leader. Other non-communist political
leaders also played important roles in politics. However, although other
political parties continued to exist and operated freely during this period,
the Communist Party of Czechoslovakia enjoyed special privileges. Members of the party held key ministries in the government, including those
of the interior, information, education, and agriculture, which enabled
the party to garner public support.

The party also benefited from the provisions of the Košice agreement of 1945 which served as the basis for the new government. According to this agreement, Czechoslovakia's party system was simplified, limiting the number of parties permitted to two in Slovakia (the Communist Party of Slovakia and the Slovak Democratic Party) and four in the Czech Lands (the Communist Party of Czechoslovakia, the National Socialist Party, the Social Democratic Party, and the Czechoslovak People's Party). In addition, all parties were in effect governmental parties. There was no true opposition.

Legal throughout the interwar period, the Communist Party had a sizable domestic base of support in Czechoslovakia. Drawing on the country's strong social democratic and progressive traditions and on the fact that there was a sizable urban working class, particularly in the Czech Lands, the party succeeded in rebuilding its own organization and also gained the support of larger groups of people, in part as the result of its sponsorship of measures to help the economy recover from the war, which had a good deal of popular support. In the 1946 elections, the Communist Party gained 37.9 percent of the vote, the largest share obtained by any party.[2] The communists also benefited from their association with the liberating Soviet troops and the proximity of Soviet forces.[3]

The latter proved to be decisive in February 1948, when a government crisis resulted in the resignation of the democratic ministers from the coalition and their replacement by a government clearly dominated by the Communist Party. The catalyst for the establishment of a communist government was a crisis which the Communist Party provoked over control of the police. The resignations of the non-communist ministers in the government, which were designed to force the dissolution, backfired. Faced with the threat of civil unrest, President Beneš accepted the resignations of the non-communist ministers and opened the way for the formation of a government controlled by Klement Gottwald and the Communist Party. In the May 1948 elections, voters in Czechoslovakia were able to choose only those candidates approved by the party.

The end of the period of modified pluralism in Czechoslovakia immediately after World War II in part reflected the decline in support for the Communist Party from its high point in 1946 and the increased militancy of party leaders as their plan to come to power by the ballot box faded. International developments were also becoming less favorable. As the wartime alliance between the Soviet Union and the Western allies deteriorated, Stalin's policy of encouraging Central and East European communist leaders to find their own roads to socialism was replaced by an insistence on conformity in domestic institutions and policies and support for Soviet objectives abroad.

COPYING THE SOVIET MODEL

After the February 1948 coup, Czechoslovakia's new leaders moved rapidly to change the country's political and economic institutions, social structure, political values and attitudes, cultural policies and orientation, and foreign policy commitments. Earlier emphasis on the need to establish a Czechoslovak form of socialism was forgotten as the country's leaders attempted to emulate the Soviet model of political organization, economic development, and social transformation. As in other Central and East European countries that became communist after World War II, this process involved the attempt to destroy old institutions and allegiances and establish new ones.

Perhaps because of the country's previous experience with democracy, the Communist Party's leadership moved quickly and harshly to discredit prominent non-communist politicians and business leaders and destroyed their power bases. They also took steps to solidify their own organizational network and, in the purges and show trials of the late 1940s and 1950s, rid it of "traitors," including communist leaders who had remained in the country during the war and thus had a domestic base of support, as well as Jews and other minorities.

In the organizational realm, the Communist Party leadership copied the essentials of the Soviet model as it existed at the time. Although most pre-1948 government institutions were retained, their work was redirected to different areas. The country's new leaders took measures to ensure the Communist Party's monopoly of political power. The Communist Party became the only effective political party in the country. Although the People's Party in the Czech Lands, the Slovak Party of Freedom, and the Slovak Revival Party were allowed to exist, these were clearly subordinated to the Communist Party and served largely to mobilize segments of the population that would not be likely to become members of the Communist Party to support official objectives. People loyal to the Communist Party were chosen to fill government positions, and government organs were subordinated to the directives of the Communist Party organization at each level. The country's once-rich associational life was simplified, as all voluntary organizations were unified in single mass organizations whose task was to mobilize their members to carry out the objectives of the party. Czechoslovakia's new leaders also established a system of censorship to control information and ensure that only those views compatible with the new official ideology, Marxism-Leninism, were allowed to be disseminated.

In the economic realm, the new leaders adopted a central planning system designed to allow central authorities to control all economic decisions from production to distribution. They also adopted ambitious goals to industrialize the country rapidly by mobilizing all available labor resources and establishing a system of binding five-year plans. Steps were taken to complete the nationalization of the economy begun under the previous government, and to collectivize agriculture. In this way, virtually all private ownership of economic assets was eliminated. Economic plans emphasized heavy industry to the detriment of Czechoslovakia's traditional focus on light industry. The country's trade was also reoriented toward the Soviet Union and other European communist countries.[4]

The leadership also attempted to change the structure of society, as well as people's values and attitudes. Policies that severely restricted inheritance rights were supplemented by those that prohibited the children of the bourgeoisie from attending university as regular students and gave priority to applicants who came from peasant or worker backgrounds. Wage policies were manipulated to increase the status of manual laborers and agricultural workers. The leadership also instituted propaganda campaigns to upgrade public images of industrial workers and agricultural workers, as well as women.

As part of the effort to change citizens' values and attitudes, the regime mounted campaigns against religion. Those citizens who continued to practice their religion openly often lost their jobs, and their children were barred from studying. These campaigns were particularly severe in Slovakia, where more people practiced their religion on a regular basis and where religion, particularly the Catholic Church, had had a more important political role in the interwar period. The majority of the population identified themselves as Roman Catholics in the Czech Lands as well. However, as in many more developed countries, levels of religious observation were not as high at the beginning of the communist period as in Slovakia. There were also strong Protestant minorities in both countries. The influence of Protestantism was particularly strong in the Czech Lands. The Protestant Hussite tradition, begun by Jan Hus, who led an early effort to reform the church in the fifteenth century, was an important element of the Czech national movement, despite the fact that the population was forcibly recatholicized in the seventeenth century. Although fewer in number, protestants also played an important role in early efforts to create a Slovak nation.[5]

Leisure, the arts, and education were also politicized, as the leadership sought to direct all activity toward political ends. The impact of this orientation became evident in the cultural sphere very quickly. Throughout their history, Czechs and Slovaks had seen themselves as part of Europe. Prague was an important cultural center at various points, and many Czechs and Slovaks made important contributions to European culture. Czech culture, in particular, developed in close association with German culture, and Czechs as well as Slovaks defined themselves in terms of European values.

After 1948, communist leaders forced Czechs and Slovaks to turn East culturally. Contact with the West was forcibly interrupted. In areas as diverse as popular music and translations of literature, only products from the Soviet Union or other communist countries were allowed. As in the rest of the region, culture was also subordinated to political ends. Socialist realism, i.e., the effort to depict reality in terms that were supportive of the building of socialism, came to be the ruling dogma in the cultural sphere. Artists and others who worked in culture became employees of the state, and only those who were recognized by the state as artists were allowed to be active in the cultural sphere.

The impact of these policies on culture was predictable. Cut off from the West and forced to subordinate their art to political ends, artists and other cultural figures produced works of great mediocrity. There were exceptions to this pattern. Artists and other cultural figures would later use periods of ideological thaws to expand the boundaries of the permissible. In the late 1960s, creative intellectuals would be among the forces that helped to bring about reform in the system. During the Gottwald and early Novotný era, however, most intellectuals produced what the regime required.[6]

As in other communist countries, Czechoslovakia's communist rulers came increasingly to rely on coercion to implement the far-reaching changes they advocated. The purges within the party, which began in 1949 and continued with staged show trials of supposedly guilty party officials, were among the most severe in the region and came to involve numerous top party officials, including Rudolf Slánský, the secretary-general of the party.[7]

In Czechoslovakia, the Stalinist system outlived both the death of Stalin in March 1953 and the process of de-Stalinization that took place in the Soviet Union after 1956. In contrast to the situation in Poland and Hungary, where popular pressure led to political crises, the Stalinist system was not seriously challenged in Czechoslovakia at this time. Workers' protests in Plzeň in 1953 were quickly suppressed by the police. Although the Czechoslovak leadership paid lip service to the need to de-Stalinize, in fact the system continued to function in much the same fashion once Antonín Novotný came to be top party leader after Gottwald's death in 1953.

Novotný and other communist leaders in Czechoslovakia again paid lip service to the need to de-Stalinize after Khrushchev's Secret Speech in 1956. The top state and party positions were divided; Czech and Slovak leaders talked about the need to reorient the economy in such a way as to give greater attention to consumer products and light industry; and there were numerous discussions of the need to adhere to principles of socialist legality.[8] However, very little changed in the way the system operated.

In part, the reluctance of the Novotný leadership reflected the lack of pressure outside the party for reform. In contrast to the situation in Poland and Hungary, where economic decline mobilized large sectors of the population to push for change, in Czechoslovakia the country's

higher level of economic development provided a buffer against the impact of Stalinist economic patterns of organization and policies. It would
not be until the early 1960s that Czechoslovakia's economy would begin
to falter and provide an incentive to reform. In addition, in contrast to
the situation in Poland and Hungary, where there were strong anticommunist traditions among intellectuals, in Czechoslovakia many intellectuals were favorably disposed to the party at the outset of communist rule.
They were, therefore, less likely to challenge the party. There was also no
strong anti-Soviet or anti-Russian tradition in Czechoslovakia to fuel the
desire for change. Finally, the ethnic division of the country mitigated
against opposition to the system, as the leadership could play the two
groups off against each other.

The persistence of Stalinism also reflected the leadership's resistance
to change. Implicated in the purges and show trials that continued in
Czechoslovakia until 1954, Novotný and other top leaders had little desire to see the issue of the abuses of the system opened up to public discussion.

Pressure to examine the trials and the abuses of socialist legality
mounted in Czechoslovakia, particularly after a temporary thaw in the
Soviet Union following the Twenty-second party congress was reflected
in a slight relaxation of ideological pressure in Czechoslovakia. In 1962,
Novotný agreed to the creation of a commission to review the trials of
Slovak communist leaders in the 1950s. However, the party leadership
successfully resisted efforts to make the conclusions of this commission
public or to take action to discipline those responsible. The issue of the
political trials would thus continue to be an issue throughout the 1960s.
It would only be in the context of the 1968 reforms that the issue would
be examined openly.[9]

THE PRAGUE SPRING: RETHINKING
THE BASIS OF SOCIALIST SOCIETY

Both international and domestic factors contributed to the theoretical
renewal that eventually culminated in the political reforms of 1968. This
process, which came to be known as the Prague Spring, or the effort to
create "Socialism with a Human Face," had its roots in several areas of
life in Czechoslovakia. These included a severe decline in the performance of the economy in the early 1960s; new strains in Czech-Slovak
relations; and the reawakening of a critical spirit on the part of Czechoslovakia's intellectuals. New signals from Moscow in the early 1960s
contributed to this process. In the late 1960s, divisions within the party
allowed the process to come out into the open and assume a directly
political character.

One of the most important catalysts for change came from the economy. By the early 1960s, Stalinist economic policies had taken their toll on Czechoslovakia's economy. The problems associated with central planning and unbalanced investment elsewhere in the region also led to declining economic performance in Czechoslovakia. By 1963, the economy experienced a negative growth rate.

In an effort to stem this decline, the party authorized a team of economic experts headed by Ota Šik, who was a member of the party's Central Committee, to devise a plan to improve economic performance. The difficulties that their plan encountered because of bureaucratic and political obstacles led this team to argue that economic reform would be impossible without political reform.[10]

Other intellectuals affiliated with the party also became more critical in the mid 1960s. Beginning with the writers, who were the first to challenge the regime, other intellectuals, including philosophers, sociologists, and historians, began pushing the limits on expression and questioning established dogmas. Critical tendencies also became evident among students and leaders of the mass organizations.[11] Confined largely to the elite level, these reformulations of the basis of socialist society provided the theoretical base for the political reforms that came into the open in 1968.

Creative intellectuals and artists also took advantage of the more open intellectual climate after the Twenty-second Party Congress in the Soviet Union to challenge the limits on expression. During this period nonconformist works by Josef Škvorecký, Ivan Klíma, Ladislav Fuks, Ludvik Vaculík, Vladimír Paral, and Bohumil Hrabal were published. In contrast to the techniques and themes sanctioned by socialist realism, these works examined problematic aspects of life and themes that had been proscribed since 1948. Josef Topol, Pavel Kohout, and Milan Kundera also published works that explored unconventional themes. The revival of interest in Franz Kafka, evident in a 1963 international conference on his work, both symbolized and contributed to these developments.[12]

The mid to late 1960s also saw a flowering in the theater and film. Václav Havel, as well as other dramatists, including Milan Uhde, Alena Vostrá, and Ladislav Smoček, contributed to the development of the theater of the absurd.[13] In the world of film, the 1960s saw the burst of creativity that came to be called the New Wave. Encouraged by the fact that certain films that did not fit the accepted model were shown in the early 1960s, young cinematographers and film directors such as Miloš Forman, Ivan Passer, Jaroslav Papousek, Vera Chytilová, Jan Nemec, Ester Krumbachová, Jiří Menzel, Elmar Klos, Jan Kadar, and Evald Schorm achieved world acclaim.[14] Once censorship effectively ceased to exist in March 1968, this resurgence of creative activity spread to other areas of culture as well.[15]

The issue of the political trials also came to the fore again in the mid 1960s. Dissatisfied with the results of the official investigation to date, intellectuals pushed for a more probing investigation into the abuses of justice that had occurred and rehabilitation of the innocent victims of the show trials and purges. In the context of the effort to rethink the basis of socialist society, efforts to rehabilitate the victims led to proposals to institutionalize guarantees of citizens' rights and prevent further abuses. In 1968 in particular, this attempt to come to terms with the Stalinist past became an important part of the reform movement and was reflected in the Action Program of the party, adopted in April 1968.[16]

Increasing Slovak dissatisfaction with Slovakia's position in the state also contributed to the growth of support for reform in the 1960s. The reduction in the powers of Slovak national organs and the fate of Slovak Communist Party leaders who were executed or jailed in the purges of the 1950s on charges of "bourgeois nationalism" fueled Slovak dissatisfaction. Slovak desires for greater control over decision-making in Slovakia were also expressed more openly. In the more open political climate of the mid 1960s, Slovak intellectuals and experts drew attention to the fact that the region's living standard continued to be lower than that of the Czech Lands, despite substantial progress in narrowing the gap, and to what was perceived to be continued domination from Prague.[17]

In the late 1960s, the movement for reform came to be reflected within the Communist Party itself. Deep divisions between those centered around Novotný, who favored maintaining the status quo, and those, including Alexander Dubček, who supported more radical change, came to a head in late 1967. After Dubček replaced Novotný as head of the party in January 1968, the reform moved very quickly into the political realm. The reform movement also acquired a mass dimension.

The leadership's call for greater public involvement in the process of reform and open discussion of the need for far-reaching changes in the way the political system as well as the economy operated were followed by a wave of popular interest in politics. Censorship in effect ceased to exist in March 1968. With its end, the country embarked on a freewheeling debate of a kind not seen since 1948. At the elite level, this process was aimed at correcting the abuses of the system and achieving a form of humane socialism appropriate to a country at Czechoslovakia's level of development with strong roots in European culture. Best exemplified in the Action Program adopted in April 1968, the leadership's vision of the reform included a larger political role for nonparty groups and citizens, greater parity for the Slovaks, and an open confrontation with the mistakes of the past. However, the Communist Party was to retain its leading role, and there was to be no provision for parties outside the Communist Party to become a true opposition.[18] Czechoslovakia was also to remain a member of the Warsaw Pact and CMEA.

As the reform progressed, citizens who were at first suspicious of the reformist leaders began to become involved in the process and to call for reforms that went beyond those advocated by the Communist Party leadership. Part of the strategy of Dubček and other reformers affiliated with the party was to change the basis of support for the regime. Instead of relying on a mixture of coercion and improvement in the standard of living to insure that citizens would obey the regime, they sought to develop legitimacy based on popular support. As public involvement increased, Dubček and other reformers were caught between the need to refrain from harsh measures to limit discussion in order to maintain the trust they were trying to cultivate on the part of the citizenry and the growing reservations about the course of the reform expressed by the Soviet leadership and those of the country's communist neighbors.

In the end, Dubček and his followers were unable to reassure their Soviet allies. After a series of increasingly difficult meetings with the Czechoslovak leadership in the summer of 1968 failed to alter the direction of the reform, Warsaw Pact troops led by the Soviet Union invaded Czechoslovakia on 21 August 1968. Dubček and the Czechoslovak party leadership were flown to Moscow where they were coerced into agreeing to the stationing of Soviet troops on Czechoslovak soil.

The actions of Dubček during 1968 have been the subject of a good deal of controversy. Head of the Slovak Communist Party at the time of his selection to replace Novotný, Dubček was an unlikely reformer. He had been educated in Moscow and worked his way up through the ranks of the party. In the late 1960s, he as well as several other Slovak communist leaders became convinced of the need to improve Slovakia's status within the state. As the reform process continued, Dubček came to symbolize the hopes of Czechs and Slovaks for a form of socialism appropriate to a developed, Western country. Often seen as Gorbachev's precursor, Dubček tried to promote change within the framework of a socialist system. Despite repeated warnings from the Soviet leadership in the summer of 1968 about Soviet concerns that the reforms were getting out of hand, Dubček did not believe that the Soviets would invade to stop the process. According to the firsthand account of Zdeněk Mylnař, who accompanied the top leadership to Moscow as a functionary of the party, Dubček suffered a nervous breakdown while the Czechoslovak leadership was in Moscow in August 1968.

There was little armed resistance to the invasion. However, many leaders and citizens attempted to salvage what was possible from the reform in the latter months of 1968 and early 1969. Dubček's supporters were able to convene an Extraordinary Fourteenth party congress under the eyes of the occupying forces. Underground radio stations also attempted to keep up the hopes of the population; many people engaged in other forms of passive resistance. These activities were punctuated by more radical protests, most notably the self-immolation of Jan Palach, a young Czech student, in January 1969.[19] However, when Dubček was replaced as the head of the party by Gustáv Husák in April 1969, it was clear that the reform was over.

"NORMALIZATION": TURNING BACK THE CLOCK

Under the leadership of Husák, the conservative elements of the Czechoslovak Communist Party began in 1969 to eliminate all possible vestiges of the 1968 reforms. These steps included a massive personnel purge that removed some 500,000 supporters of the reform from positions of influence in political, economic, and intellectual life. The activities of the mass organizations were brought back under the leadership of the Communist Party. Student organizations and publications were disbanded and intellectuals were warned of the need to adhere to positions approved by the party leadership. Censorship was restored, and the party attempted to reassert its leading position in all areas of life.

The effects of this process, which came to be known as "normalization," and the legacy of 1968 conditioned political and economic life in Czechoslovakia until the end of communist rule. Fearful of any resurgence of the events of 1968, the conservative leaders of Czechoslovakia prohibited any discussion of reform or significant change for nearly twenty years. The personnel purges also removed many of the most talented experts and intellectuals from any possibility of influencing public policy. As a result, the leadership found itself poorly equipped to deal with the economic and political problems it faced in the 1970s and 1980s.

A Slovak lawyer who was himself tried for political reasons in the 1950s, Husák served on the Legal Commision of the Communist Party Central Committee responsible for the promotion of legality in state organs in the late 1960s and originally supported the reform movement. He is often seen as having taken a middle-of-the-road position within the hardline leadership that came back to power after the invasion of August 1968. However, while it may be the case that he prevented certain of his colleagues, including those who called upon the Soviet Union to invade, from carrying out harsher measures, he presided over the purge of the reformers and sanctioned if not advocated the harsh political control that characterized political life in Czechoslovakia for most of the next two decades. In contrast to the more innovative policies that the Kádár leadership used to come to terms with the population after the 1956 revolution in Hungary, Husák's long tenure as head of the party was characterized by a bureaucratic, repressive approach to public issues.

Although the Husák leadership succeeded in ensuring political stabil-

ity in Czechoslovakia in the 1970s and 1980s, it faced increasingly serious problems. To a large extent, these problems resembled those that
existed in other European communist states at the time and that would
eventually lead to the demise of communist rule in the area.

Although Czechoslovakia did not experience the acute economic crises that characterized the last decades of communist rule in Poland and
led to the gradual adoption of market reforms in Hungary, the country
experienced chronic economic difficulties. As a result of the inefficiencies
and distortions associated with central planning that had led reformers
in the 1960s to call for decentralization and political change, the economy had marked difficulties in competing on the world market. Coupled
with adverse weather conditions and the delayed impact of the oil shortage after 1979, these factors led to a particularly severe economic slump
in the early 1980s, when industrial production increased very little and
real wages and the standard of living stagnated. Economic performance
improved somewhat in the 1980s, but economic planners and officials
continued to regard economic performance as unsatisfactory in the late
1980s.[20]

Declining economic performance also posed political difficulties for
the Husák and Jakeš leaderships. Throughout much of the 1970s, Husák's strategy of rule seemed to work well. Thus, while neighboring Poland experienced numerous upheavals, in Czechoslovakia improvements
in the standard of living and the selective use of coercion were successful
in keeping citizens quiet.

The founding of Charter 77 in 1977 and activities of dissident intellectuals demonstrated that this strategy was not a complete success.
Persecuted for their actions and subjected to police surveillance, imprisonment, and other forms of harassment, independent activists nonetheless continued to protest the violation of human rights in Czechoslovakia.

Despite the harsh penalties that nonconformists faced, intellectuals
and other activists continued to challenge the regime during this period.
Many of the country's leading cultural figures were involved in the reform movement in the 1960s. After the invasion, most were prevented
from openly taking part in the country's cultural life. Many emigrated or
were forced to leave the country, and many of those who remained
earned a living by working as manual laborers. However, many artists,
musicians, and other creative intellectuals continued to write "for the
drawer" or for *samizdat* (independent) publications. Although samizdat
publications, including series such as the *Edice petlice* (or Padlocked Edi-
tions), were typed in limited numbers of copies and circulated clandes-
tinely, many were widely read and became well known beyond
opposition circles. Artists, musicians, playwrights, and actors staged illegal exhibitions and performances in provincial cities or private apartments.[21] Creative intellectuals also played a major role in the develop-

ment of the dissident community in the late 1970s. Musicians and artists, including those who were no longer able to work in their professions, continued to experiment with new forms and develop their art in ways that contradicted the political messages of the regime. As in other areas of popular culture, Western artists and singers became very popular in the musical and artistic underground that developed after the end of the reform era. The persecution of a group of young musicians, the Plastic People of the Universe, who played nonconformist music, was one of the catalysts for the foundation of Charter 77.[22]

Dissident groups, particularly the Charter, also came to serve as a focus of a second, independent intellectual community, where issues that were not discussed at all in the official world and divergent opinions could be aired. In samizdat essays, dissident intellectuals provided alternative analyses of social, political, and economic problems and explored topics not dealt with by official publications or sources. One of the more important of these was the essay "The Power of the Powerless" by Václav Havel, in which Havel argued that "living in truth," or according to one's own moral compass, was a form of power available to all citizens irrespective of the form of the state in which they lived.[23] Other intellectuals, such as Václav Benda and Radím Palouš, explored the notion of the "parallel polis" and other political topics.[24]

Although many officials of the Catholic Church continued to be subservient to the regime, religious groups and certain elements of the Catholic Church hierarchy also began to be more active in the 1980s. The elderly Cardinal František Tomášek in particular spoke out on controversial issues, such as the stationing of missiles in Czechoslovakia in the early 1980s. Mass processions and pilgrimages to religious shrines in Moravia and Slovakia also began and grew from approximately 100,000 per year in the early 1980s to 800,000 in 1988.[25]

Their small numbers and the fact that many were intellectuals and most from the Czech Lands, as well as the very real personal risks involved in being openly identified as a dissident, kept the Chartists and other activists from having a direct impact on public policy or politics for much of the 1970s and 1980s. However, they played an important role in fostering independent thought and in undermining support for the communist regime. In November 1989, activists associated with the Charter took the lead in negotiating the end of communist rule. Many also became prominent figures in the country's new noncommunist government.

PERESTROIKA AND GLASNOST: THE BEGINNING OF THE END

Important as the activities of dissident activists were in maintaining a moral reference point in Czechoslovakia, the main threat to communist

rule came from continued economic difficulties and from the policies
Gorbachev espoused in the Soviet Union. In the first area, economic
problems made it increasingly difficult for the leadership to ensure citizens' support through material improvements. Forced by the late 1980s
to admit that the economic system was in serious difficulty, the leadership
began to be more open in discussing the problem and also called on citizens to accept austerity measures.

Developments in the Soviet Union also threatened the conservative
policies of the Czechoslovak leadership. Husák and Miloš Jakeš, who
replaced him as head of the party in December 1987, gave lip service to
the need to emulate Gorbachev's policies of *perestroika* and *glasnost*.
However, clearly fearful of a repetition of 1968, the leadership kept strict
limits on political debate and reacted harshly to the efforts of dissidents
to expand their activities.

The impact of Gorbachev's policies on developments in Czechoslovakia was most evident in the economic area. Spurred by its own domestic problems and the introduction of *perestroika* in the Soviet Union, the
party leadership adopted a new plan to improve economic performance
in January 1987. In contrast to measures adopted between 1969 and
that time, the new plan specifically called for reform; it also called for
decentralization of the economy and the introduction of certain market
features. However, the principles adopted were very general, and the
timetable set out for their implementation gradual. Relatively few of the
measures of this general plan for reform were enacted before the end of
the communist system. The plan was also criticized within Czechoslovakia and abroad because it did not go far enough in introducing the market to solve the problems it was designed to address.[26]

There was no parallel in Czechoslovakia to the dramatic political
developments that characterized the Gorbachev period in the Soviet
Union. However, under the surface stability of the system, important
changes occurred between 1987 and 1989. These reflected increasing divisions within the leadership of the Communist Party and an increased
willingness on the part of the population to challenge the regime.

One of the most important of the changes that occurred in Czechoslovakia during the last two years of communist rule was an increase in
the number of dissident groups and in the willingness of citizens to protest or question the actions of the leadership. Although the numbers of
independent groups never reached those in Poland, Hungary, or the Soviet Union after Gorbachev came to power, several new groups were
formed and larger numbers of citizens became willing to identify themselves with the initiatives organized by independent activists. Several features of this development proved important in 1989. First, many of those
who joined the ranks of the dissidents were young people. Secondly, by
the late 1980s, support for independent initiatives had also grown in Slo-

vakia, where activists were in many cases able to continue to work in the official system at some level while engaging in nonconformist activities. The increased willingness of many in official positions throughout the country to support opposition initiatives was a further change that was to prove significant in 1989. The support that many figures in the official cultural and media worlds gave to petitions calling for the release of Havel after he was imprisoned in retaliation for his participation in a commemoration of Palach's suicide in January 1989 was a marker of the extent of the disaffection of these groups by that time. Finally, the increased numbers of ordinary citizens who were willing to respond to activists' calls to join mass demonstrations further illustrated the desire for change that existed among many groups in the population.[27]

These changes at the mass level were paralleled by and to some extent reflected changes at the top of the party. The election of Jakeš to replace Husák as head of the party in December 1987 did not immediately signal any dramatic departures from previous policies. Jakeš had been responsible for overseeing the personnel purges in the party that had occurred after the invasion, and was an unlikely candidate to become a reformer. However, his selection signaled the beginning of a broader process of change within the party leadership. By March 1989, very few of the members of the Presidium of the party had been in their posts for longer than a year. The new leaders did not differ markedly from their predecessors in terms of previous experience or background. However, most were somewhat younger. They were, therefore, both less committed to maintaining the policies of normalization at all costs and also had less experience in dealing with popular challenges. Both of these factors proved to be decisive in the period between 1987 and 1989, because the vacillation of the leadership allowed the dissident movement to grow. The changes discussed above also weakened the party's ability to deal with the crisis it faced in November 1989.

Thus, although external factors, including the impact of Gorbachev's policies in the Soviet Union and the fall of the hardline Honecker regime in East Germany, played a critical role in leading to the fall of communism in Czechoslovakia, serious economic and political problems helped to undermine support for the system in the decades preceding its demise. Changes within the political leadership and among the population also contributed to the willingness of large numbers of people to openly challenge the regime in 1989. They also helped to shape the fall of the old system and establishment of the new.

THE VELVET REVOLUTION: RE-CREATING DEMOCRACY

The collapse of the communist system in Czechoslovakia began on 17 November 1989, when police brutally beat peaceful student demonstra-

tors in Prague. Outraged by these events and emboldened by developments in Poland and Hungary and the fall of the hardline Honecker
regime in East Germany, hundreds of thousands of Czechs and Slovaks
took to the streets to demand an end to communist rule. These events,
which came to be known as the "Velvet Revolution" in reference to their
peaceful nature, ushered in a process of negotiation between two umbrella organizations formed by dissidents, the Civic Forum in Prague and
Public Against Violence in Bratislava, and the communist authorities.
The process quickly led to the fall of the communist government.
Twenty-three days after the protests began, the communist leadership
resigned. The election of dissident playwright Havel as president by a
parliament still dominated by the Communist Party and his inauguration
in late December 1989 capped the victory of the democratic forces.[28]

In contrast to the situation in Poland and Hungary, where the end of
communism occurred as the result of extended roundtable negotiations
between the opposition and reformist elements and the Communist Party
leadership, in Czechoslovakia the communist system collapsed very suddenly. Although there were important changes in the political leadership,
and open support for dissident activities increased in the last two years
of communist rule,[29] the country's new rulers came to power without any
real experience in politics. They were linked to each other by ties forged
during what were in many cases decades of living as outcasts in their own
society. But most, including Havel, were little known to ordinary citizens,
aside from the negative picture painted by the old regime. These aspects
of the collapse of communism in Czechoslovakia were important, for
they conditioned the situation the country's new political leaders faced
once coming to power. They also influenced the political resources available to political leaders to address these issues.

In the early days after the fall of communism, there was a high degree
of consensus on the main goals of the revolution. These were often summarized as "Democracy, the Market, and Back to Europe." As events
were to show, however, agreement on these terms provided little guidance once it became necessary to enact concrete public policies to put
them into action. This formula also said nothing about the issue that
eventually led to the demise of Czechoslovakia—the sometimes different
understanding of these terms by members of different ethnic groups.

In Czechoslovakia as in other formerly communist states, the end of
communist rule was quickly followed by the repluralization of politics.
The umbrella and student organizations formed to lead the revolution
were soon joined by a plethora of political parties, interest groups, and
voluntary associations. Many organizations that had existed during the
interwar period, when Czechoslovakia had a rich web of voluntary associations that were replaced by unified mass organizations subordinate to

the Communist Party after 1948, were re-created. These were joined by many new parties and groups.

The speed of this process was reflected in the fact that over sixty political parties had registered by late February 1990; twenty-three of these competed in the June 1990 parliamentary elections. In political orientation, the new groups spanned the political spectrum and included, in addition to right and left of center secular and Christian parties, far right groups such as Miroslav Sladek's Republican Party; ethnically based parties such as the Slovak National Party and Coexistence, a coalition of groups representing the Hungarian and Ukrainian populations in Slovakia; and the Association for Moravia and Silesia—Movement for Self-Governing Democracy. They also included a number of nonpartisan social movements and groups, such as the Party of the Greens and the Beer Drinkers' Party. Many of these groups did not receive the 3 to 5 percent of the vote necessary to seat deputies in the legislature, but a sizable number remained viable political forces.

The June 1990 parliamentary elections legitimated the ad hoc government that was formed immediately after the collapse of communism. Civic Forum and Public against Violence emerged as the victors with 50 percent and 37 percent of the vote to the Federal Assembly's House of Nations and 53.2 percent and 33 percent of the vote to the House of Peoples. In the Czech Lands, the Communist Party of Bohemia and Moravia emerged as the second strongest party with approximately 13 percent of the vote. In Slovakia, Public Against Violence was followed by Ján Čarnogurský's Christian Democratic Movement, which received 19 percent of the vote.[30]

As the result of this process, citizens in Czechoslovakia gained new opportunities to be active in public life. Together with the end of censorship and diversification of the media, the repluralization of politics made it possible for citizens to make their views known to political leaders, organize with others who held similar political views, and mobilize public opinion to put pressure on political leaders to address their concerns.

The country's new leaders also began the complicated and lengthy process of rewriting the country's constitution and reforming its legal code to remove the distortions of the communist period. New laws were passed to restore private ownership; create the legal basis of a market economy; and remove barriers to foreign investment. The country's new legislators also adopted measures to restore property confiscated by the communist regime to its previous owners or their heirs and to reduce the economic power of the Communist Party.

Parliamentary leaders also began the process of coming to terms with the legacy of communism. One of the more controversial aspects of this process came to be known as "lustrace," or letting the light shine in. This process, which amounted to a form of vetting, was intended to prevent those who had collaborated with the secret police from holding high public office. However, it remained controversial, as it was impossible to verify the accuracy of the secret police files or control the many distortions the files undoubtedly contained.[31]

The new leadership also began reforming the bureaucracy. This process involved not only personnel changes, but also the attempt to reorient the style of work of public officials in order to make them more responsive to citizens' needs. In many cases, old officials were retained, as many had given largely lip service to the communist system and it proved impossible in any case to replace them on a mass scale.

At the same time, political life in post-communist Czechoslovakia continued to be characterized by a number of problems. The re-creation of democratic institutions and values proved to be a complicated, lengthy process. Political life in the first three years after the end of communism also shared a number of characteristics with other post-communist systems experiencing the politics of transition. These were evident in the development of the party system, which remained fluid and uninstitutionalized for the most part. With few exceptions, the new or newly re-created political parties formed after 1989 had difficulties in extending their organizational roots beyond the largest cities. In reaction to the requirement that they be active in politics and join the Communist Party if they wished to advance in their careers or have a chance of influencing political decisions, many citizens refused to join any political party after 1989. Levels of party identification were also very low. Most citizens in the Czech Lands and in Slovakia did not have the benefit of this mechanism which serves in more established democratic systems to simplify political decision-making and moderate political conflict. As a result, citizens' political preferences remained volatile, and many citizens in both parts of the country were available to be mobilized.

In contrast to the situation in early 1990, many citizens lost interest in politics. Levels of trust in political leaders and institutions also declined in both Slovakia and the Czech Lands. President Havel was to some degree immune from this trend, particularly in the Czech Lands, although his support declined precipitously in Slovakia between mid 1991 and the June 1992 elections. However, other political institutions, including the federal and republic governments and parliaments, did not fare as well.[32]

Popular dissatisfaction with the results of the transformation continued to grow during 1991 and 1992, particularly in Slovakia. By September 1991, for example, 61 percent of respondents in the Czech Republic were rather or very dissatisfied; 78 percent in Slovakia were in that category. Equally telling, only 3 percent of the population in each republic was very satisfied.[33]

GOOD ESSAY TOPIC

An additional feature of transitional politics that stood out during this period was the lack of well-developed links between representatives and their constituencies. This situation was due in part to the lack of incentives to establish such connections in an electoral system that relies on party lists, in part to the limited resources available to legislators to travel outside the capital, and in part to their limited office staffs. Coupled with the preoccupation of most political leaders with "high politics," including economic reform, constitutional change, and political restructuring, and the corresponding neglect of local and "low politics," including social questions and problems, this pattern in turn contributed to the growing sense among many groups in the population that politics had little to do with the concerns of ordinary people. In this situation, support also grew for antidemocratic or nationalistic forces in both parts of the country. In the Czech Lands, this trend was evident in the sizable degree of support for Miroslav Sladek's extreme right wing Republican Party, particularly in those regions with very high unemployment rates, such as Northern Bohemia. In Slovakia, growing disaffection with the results of economic as well as political change led to increased support for the Slovak National Party, which advocated independence for Slovakia, and for Vladimír Mečiar's Movement for a Democratic Slovakia, which took an ambivalent position on the issue of independence prior to the June 1992 elections, but strongly challenged the government's economic policies.

Political life in the first three years of the post-communist period in Czechoslovakia shared a number of further characteristics with other post-communist European states. Thus, although the forms of politics were democratic ones, the country's newly reoriented political institutions often functioned in ways that contradicted the aims of democratization. To some degree this tendency reflected the difficulties facing any newly established political system. But it also reflected the impact of forty years of communist rule on the attitudes and behaviors of those who became the countries' new leaders as well as the difficulty of acting rationally in a situation characterized by a high degree of uncertainty in many areas.[34]

It soon became evident that re-creation of democratic institutions does not automatically guarantee that all groups in society will have equal access to the political system or that the needs and concerns of particular groups will find their way onto the political agenda. Women and minorities, particularly the Romanies, or gypsies, continued to be marginalized in post-communist as well as in communist Czechoslovakia.[35]

The recruitment and training of new political leaders also continued to be problematic. In the years just after 1989, creative intellectuals, including many who had been dissidents, played a critical role in politics.

Havel's election as president was accompanied by a broader influx of
writers, set designers, artists, and actors into positions in the legislative
and bureaucratic elite. Economist Václav Klaus's selection as prime minister, on the other hand, reflected the importance intellectuals with more
applied, technical specializations played in the composition of the government.[36]

The choice of Havel as president reflected his stature as the de facto
leader of the opposition as well as the political capital his long opposition
to the communist regime brought in the period immediately after the end
of communist rule. Although Havel became a well-known figure in his
own country only after November 1989, he soon came to enjoy higher
levels of trust than most other politicians, particularly in the Czech
Lands.[37] Insisting that politics was not an area of life incompatible with
morality, Havel played a major role in determining the composition of
the first government created after the June 1990 elections and in the
major political decisions of the day. As the political system became more
stable and as other political organizations and leaders became more important, Havel's influence on day-to-day decision making declined. His
inability to prevent the dissolution of the federation, despite his vigorous
efforts to do so, is perhaps the best illustration of the limits of his influence. However, Havel continued to play an important role as the symbol
of the federation. Havel's powers as president of the Czech Republic are
more circumscribed. However, he continues to raise important issues for
the public and politicians and has intervened successfully at times to influence political developments.[38]

Many creative intellectuals lost their political positions as the result
of the 1992 parliamentary elections. The development of more hierarchically structured party organizations, coupled with popular reactions
against intellectuals, have reduced the direct role intellectuals play in the
exercise of political power. This phenomenon was particularly evident in
Slovakia, where many intellectuals were in favor of preserving the federation.[39]

RE-CREATION OF A MARKET ECONOMY

After early hesitation due to divisions within the new leadership, the government installed after the ouster of the communist system and legitimated by the June 1990 elections eventually adopted a plan designed to
re-create a market economy in Czechoslovakia. Advocated by Klaus,
then finance minister, a program of economic changes designed to rapidly
reintroduce the market was adopted by the republic and federal governments in September 1990. This program built on the legal changes already enacted, which legalized private property and established the legal
basis for a market economy. The country's new leaders also liberalized

prices and ended government subsidies to many unprofitable firms. Some 85 percent of prices were freed on 1 January 1991.[40] Regulations governing foreign investment were liberalized and officials took steps to attract outside investors. They also began to reintegrate Czechoslovakia into the world market and reorient its trade patterns away from its former heavy reliance on trade with the Soviet Union and other European socialist countries. This process was hastened by the collapse of the CMEA and later of the Soviet Union itself.[41]

Privatization of economic enterprises was an important part of this program of economic change. This process occurred in part as the result of the founding of new economic enterprises. Many small economic concerns were auctioned to private individuals in 1990 and 1991. Foreign investors also contributed to privatization. The success of this aspect of privatization is evident in the fact that the private sector grew to account for approximately 20 percent of GDP in Czechoslovakia by December 1992.[42]

The centerpiece of Czechoslovakia's privatization efforts was the controversial "voucher" or "coupon" privatization plan proposed by Klaus. Designed to create a political constituency for reform as well as to serve economic objectives, voucher privatization proved to be far more successful than most envisioned. Approximately 80 percent of those eligible participated, many after private investment funds promised very high returns on investment.[43] Critics of the program acknowledge that it received widespread support from the population, but charge that the method left newly privatized firms without the capital needed to modernize.[44]

The Slovak government also adopted the program designed to quickly re-create a market economy, but the move to the market proved to be far more costly in Slovakia than in the Czech Lands. Thus, while unemployment rates averaged 2 to 3 percent in the Czech Lands in 1991 and 1992, in Slovakia they ranged from 12 to 13 percent.[45]

These trends reflected the fact that much of Slovakia's industrialization had occurred during the communist period. In contrast to the situation in the interwar period, when the Slovak economy stagnated despite attempts to foster development of the region, the policies adopted by the communist government succeeded in industrializing Slovakia and narrowing the developmental gap between the two parts of the country. However, because industrialization occurred as the result of the implementation of the Stalinist model of economic organization and development, it reflected the inefficiencies and characteristic problems associated with that model. Many of Czechoslovakia's most inefficient large industries were concentrated in Slovakia, as was a good part of the country's sizable arms industry. As a later section of this chapter discusses in greater detail, the different impact of the move to the market in the Czech

Lands and in Slovakia was one of the factors that contributed to the breakup of the Czechoslovak federation.

CULTURAL DEVELOPMENTS

The end of communist rule had an immediate impact on Czechoslovakia's cultural life. The political restrictions that had prevented many of the country's most talented cultural figures from being active in their own country were lifted, and many of those banned from public view for two decades suddenly reappeared. Cultural life was also enriched by the return of some of the many writers and other creative intellectuals who had emigrated or been exiled.

To some extent, these changes were a continuation of developments in the late 1980s, when officials of the writers' union began to reevaluate banned writers and reestablished links to émigré writers. Similar signs of change were evident in the area of film and theater in 1988 and in early 1989.[46]

With the end of communist rule, cultural life was also pluralized. The official writers' union and other cultural unions lost their monopoly on cultural life, as a variety of new organizations were formed. The publishing of banned books and performance of banned plays and films offered the public a cultural feast. In 1990 alone, for example, over five hundred books by banned writers that previously had been available only in samizdat were published. There was also a proliferation of new independent publishing houses.

As in other areas of life, the end of the communist rule has also raised new issues in the area of culture. Although the end of censorship has allowed artists and other intellectuals to create freely, it did not lead to the creative explosion many anticipated. The changed function of culture, now that it no longer has to serve as a surrogate form of politics, and the dramatic increase in the price of tickets led to a decline in attendance at cultural performances on the part of citizens of the country. The financing of culture has also emerged as an important problem as state subsidies have decreased. No longer able to count on a guaranteed income, many creative intellectuals have turned to other fields, such as politics or business, to make a living. Those who remain face many of the same difficulties as their counterparts in other market economies.[47]

BACK TO EUROPE

Czechoslovakia's new leaders took steps very soon after coming to power to reassert the country's independence in foreign policy. Czech and Slovak leaders negotiated the withdrawal of Soviet troops from their soil, a process completed on 26 June 1991. They also reoriented the country's external economic relations, which had been very heavily concentrated in the Soviet Union and other European communist states prior to 1989.

Havel and Foreign Minister Jiří Dienstbier also reestablished cordial relations with the United States, which dated to the interwar period but had been disrupted for nearly 40 years. President Havel captured the imagination of many Americans during his 1990 visit to the United States, and the United States supported the return to democracy and the market with a variety of assistance and aid programs in the early 1990s.[48]

The centerpiece of Czechoslovakia's foreign policy between 1990 and 1993 was clearly Europe. The country's new leaders sought to reclaim what they perceived to be Czechoslovakia's rightful place on the European stage and to normalize the country's relationships with its immediate neighbors. They also sought to join European and Euro-Atlantic institutions. The country was accepted as a member of the Council of Europe and signed an association agreement with the EC.

President Havel and Foreign Minister Dienstbier originally took the lead in arguing for the creation of European institutions to fill the security gap caused by the collapse of the Warsaw Pact. Dienstbier urged that the CSCE process be institutionalized, and succeeded in situating the newly established secretariat in Prague. As the situation deteriorated in the Soviet Union and armed conflict erupted in Yugoslavia, both Havel and Dienstbier came to emphasize the importance of NATO membership.

Czechoslovakia participated in the founding of several regional groupings. The most important of these, the Visegrad agreement, which originally included Poland, Hungary, and Czechoslovakia, called for cooperation in a wide variety of areas, ranging from scientific research on common problems to trade issues. The most important achievement of the Visegrad agreement, which included both successors to the Czecho-slovak federation after 1993, was the creation of a free trade zone that went into effect in March 1993.

THE UNDERSIDE OF FREEDOM: SOCIAL AND PSYCHOLOGICAL COSTS

The end of communist rule brought the citizens and leaders of Czechoslovakia many benefits. However, the elimination of the tight political control and the opening of the country's borders also exacerbated old social problems and created new ones. The large-scale changes involved in shifting from a rigidly controlled polity and a highly centralized economy also entailed social and psychological costs.

The impact of these changes was evident in a number of ways, including the rapid increase in crime, particularly in major cities.[49] Drug abuse also increased, as foreign suppliers were able to ply their trade more easily.[50] The opening of the country's borders also led to an increase

in prostitution, particularly in regions bordering Germany, with a likely
increase in the incidence of AIDS in the country. Pornography and sex
shops also proliferated. After the elimination of censorship, it also became possible to talk openly about many other social ills that previously
had either been taboo as subjects of public discussion or were discussed
primarily by specialists in limited circulation journals. These included
wife and child abuse, alcoholism, juvenile delinquency, and other forms
of social deviance. The tensions and disruptions that accompanied the
shift to the market and the wide-scale change that occurred in nearly
every area of life exacerbated many of these problems.[51]

The transition to democracy and the re-creation of the market also
carried with them psychological and emotional costs. It is clear that the
end of communist rule was welcomed by many Czechs and Slovaks; the
creation of a market economy and the elimination of political interference at the workplace and in other areas of life also brought benefits for
many citizens. However, the liberalization of prices, the elimination of
job security, and the growth in unemployment created greater hardship
for many groups of the population. The strains created by living in a
situation in which everything from the organization of day care to the
expectations of one's employers changed had political as well as social
implications.

THE VELVET DIVORCE

Ethnic issues dominated the political agenda in the first three years of the
post-communist period in Czechoslovakia and complicated the tasks of
constitutional revision and economic reform. In contrast to the situation
in parts of the former Soviet Union and Yugoslavia, tensions between
Czechs and Slovaks did not result in armed conflict. However, as in the
interwar period, when the dissatisfaction of the Sudeten Germans and
many Slovaks provided the pretext for the breakup of the republic, conflicts between Czechs and Slovaks posed the main threat to the stability
and eventually led to the breakup of the state.

The end of censorship and repluralization of political life that followed the collapse of communist rule in 1989 once again allowed open
expression of tensions among the various ethnic groups in the multiethnic Czechoslovak state. Leaders of many of these groups organized to
articulate and defend the interests of their groups in ways that were not
possible during the communist period. In Moravia, demonstrations in
1991 demanding a greater share of the Czech Republic's budget reflected
the shift in Moravian identity from a secondary, cultural identity to one
with more direct political content.[52] Representatives of the approximately 600,000 Hungarians and 40,000 Ukrainian / Ruthenians in Slovakia organized to call for greater attention to their cultural and

educational needs.[53] Activists also emerged among the estimated 115,000 to one and a half million Romany, or gypsy, population.[54]

It was tensions between Czechs and Slovaks that led to the breakup of the Czechoslovak federation in January 1993. Early coordination of actions by leaders of Civic Forum in the Czech Lands and Public Against Violence in Slovakia soon gave way to more open conflict between Czech and Slovak politicians. As I have argued more fully elsewhere,[55] the main points of contention centered around constitutional and economic issues. Czech and Slovak representatives proved unable to agree on a formula for dividing the powers of the federal and republic governments. Czech and Slovak leaders also disagreed over the extent to which the republic or federal government should control economic life and held different perspectives on the government's economic reform program.[56]

The results of the June 1992 elections posed the question of the future of the federation very sharply. Slovakia's new leader, Vladimír Mečiar, and his supporters argued after the elections that they did not want an end to a common state with the Czechs, but rather a confederation that would consist of two sovereign republics. Klaus and many Czech leaders, on the other hand, pointed to the impossibility of having both two independent states and a unified state. They also argued that such an arrangement would allow Slovakia to drain money from common resources and endanger the re-creation of a market economy.

Relations between Czechs and Slovaks were also complicated by a number of less tangible, but important symbolic issues. Although most Slovaks did not want to see the state divided, the perception that the federation did not serve Slovak interests was widespread. On the other side, there was often a good deal of incomprehension in Bohemia and Moravia concerning Slovaks' aims and perspectives. The subtext of the conflict, in other words, included perceptions of power relations by both Czechs and Slovaks that were colored by the history of relations between the two groups.[57]

The roots of the conflict between Czechs and Slovaks reflected the historical differences between the two groups and the legacy of policies adopted during the communist period. Although they are not as obvious as those that separate many other ethnic groups, there are important differences in the perceptions, values, and orientations of Czechs and Slovaks that reflect historical differences in the cultures, levels of development, and political experiences of the two groups.[58] Many of these result from the fact that Slovaks and Czechs were part of two larger states prior to the formation of a common Czechoslovak state in 1918.[59] The Czech Lands, particularly Bohemia, became one of the industrialized centers of the Habsburg Empire and developed a social structure similar to those of other industrial urbanized areas of Europe. Slovakia, on the other hand, remained one of the least developed and most agrarian regions of the empire.[60] Efforts to industrialize Slovakia and to reduce the disparity in levels of development and social structure in the two regions during the interwar period failed, in part as the result of the world depression.[61]

Tensions between Czechs and Slovaks also reflected the legacy of the communist period. Despite the near equalization of the material conditions of life that occurred under communism,[62] the importance of ethnicity as a source of tension and political conflict did not decrease. Because most of Slovakia's development occurred during the communist period, the move to the market was much more painful in Slovakia than in the Czech Lands.

The political situation in the first two years after the collapse of communism also created fertile ground for the growth of ethnic tensions and nationalism. Coupled with the hardship and dislocations that accompany large-scale economic change, growing popular dissatisfaction and increasing distrust of most political leaders and institutions also provided incentives for political leaders to use nationalism as a tool to gain or to keep influence and power in the new system.

Political leaders, particularly those in Slovakia, played a key role in mobilizing the population around ethnic issues in order to increase their own support prior to the June 1992 elections. However, the situation is more complex than it appears at first glance. Most citizens in both Slovakia and the Czech Lands continued to prefer a common state even as their political leaders negotiated the end of the federation. But there were important and growing differences in the attitudes and political preferences of Czechs and Slovaks prior to the split. Numerous public opinion polls found, for example, that respondents in Slovakia were more likely than those in the Czech Lands to want the state to retain responsibility for ensuring employment for all citizens. They were also less supportive of a radical and rapid move to the market and of privatization than Czechs.[63]

As the result of the June 1992 elections, Klaus and Mečiar, neither of whose parties won a majority of the popular vote in their region, negotiated the end of the federation. Popular opinion in both the Czech Lands and Slovakia continued to be against the breakup of the state even as the negotiations proceeded, but the main political forces supporting the continuation of a common state did very poorly in the June elections in both regions.

THE CZECH REPUBLIC AND
THE SLOVAK REPUBLIC

Political and economic developments in the two states that replaced Czechoslovakia on 1 January 1993 reflected many of the differences in perspective and in objective conditions that led to the breakup of the federation. Leaders in both new states pledged to continue to support democratic government and the move to the market, as well as to become more active players on the European stage. However, political and economic developments soon began to diverge.

In February 1993, the currency union between the two new states ended. Trade between the two plummeted by 30 to 40 percent in the first few months after the breakup of the common state. Although political and economic officials took great pains to minimize the economic disruption of the split, in fact both economies suffered in 1993. The Czech economy recovered more quickly from these disruptions, as trade with Germany increased markedly to take up the slack created by the decline in trade with Slovakia.

Although it did not do as well as experts predicted, the Czech economy experienced its first growth since 1989 in 1993. Foreign investment, which had been heavily concentrated in the Czech Republic prior to 1993, continued to grow in that country and totaled 455 million USD for the first three quarters of 1993.[64] Privatization continued, and, despite delays, a second wave of voucher privatization took place in March 1994. By July 1993, the private sector accounted for 23 percent of total employment. Unemployment continued to be less than 3 percent, although experts and government officials predicted that it would increase to 6 to 8 percent. Inflation rose only slightly from 17 percent in 1992 to approximately 20 percent in 1993 despite the imposition in January of a value added tax (VAT) which resulted in a 8.5 percent increase in prices for that month.[65] The Czech crown remained a very stable currency until 1997 when financial scandals and charges of corruption shook confidence in the crown.

Economic conditions were more difficult in Slovakia after the split. Although it had come to power in part due to its strong critique of the previous government's economic policies, the Mečiar government did not move dramatically away from those policies in 1993. In an effort to obtain the confidence of foreign investors, Mečiar's government retained a tight monetary policy and kept inflation in check, after the initial jump in early 1993 that accompanied the introduction of a VAT. In July 1993, the leadership devalued the Slovak crown by 10 percent. Unemployment increased somewhat to 13 percent in mid 1993.[66] From the perspective of international financial organizations, including the IMF, the most worrisome aspect of economic developments in Slovakia after independence was the increase in the budget deficit, estimated at 16 billion Slovak crowns (USD 480 million) in July 1993.[67]

Mečiar's government also took steps to increase foreign investment in Slovakia, which was far lower than in the Czech Lands prior to independence. Generous tax holidays and other incentives were enacted in early 1993 to encourage investment from abroad. These measures, however, had not yet resulted in any significant increase in foreign investment by the end of 1993.[68]

Although Mečiar talked about the need to create a "social market" in Slovakia rather than a strictly market economy, his government in fact continued to pursue many of the policies of its predecessor in order to satisfy external lenders, such as the cuts in social entitlements required by the IMF. Although certain actions, such as the decision to rely primarily on "traditional" forms of privatization, slowed privatization of state enterprises significantly after the June 1992 elections, the private sector continues to grow. The share of GDP produced by the private sphere has increased from 21 percent in 1992 to an estimated 35 percent in 1993.[69] Slovakia has also made progress in reorienting its trade toward other European countries and signed a new association agreement with the EC on 15 June 1993.

Political developments also diverged in the two newly separate states. In the Czech Lands, support for Prime Minister Klaus remained high until the late 1990s. Social welfare reform, financial crises, and corruption scandals eventually led to Klaus's resignation and the formation of a new government in 1997. Support for moderate leftist parties, such as the Social Democrats, continued to grow; however, the Communist Party of Bohemia and Moravia split, thus fragmenting the approximately 13 percent of popular support the party earned in the 1992 elections.[70]

A significant problem emerged in connection with minority rights and human rights in the Czech Republic in the 1990s. The migration of many Romanies or gypsies from Slovakia in anticipation of Slovak independence from other parts of the region, including Romania, exacerbated the already tense relations between Czechs and Romanies. Efforts on the part of local councils and later Parliament to use residence laws that would have restricted the rights of Romanies were rescinded, but popular perceptions of Romanies continue to be exceedingly negative among Czechs. In 1997, outside governments and organizations criticized the Czech government for its treatment of the Roma. The Czech Republic's leaders also faced the need to deal with their newly increased Slovak minority. In contrast to the Romanies, most Slovaks who chose to emigrate to or stay in the Czech Lands were well educated. Many had positions in the intellectual or academic world in Prague. The issues involved in satisfying the demands of this group, therefore, have been quite different from those that arose in connection with other minority groups.

In Slovakia, political developments in the period since independence have been more contentious. Early expectations that Mečiar might try to drastically control the press and other media or restrict the rights of his opponents proved to be unfounded. The press in particular continued to be very critical of the government. Certain officials of Slovakia's government displayed an extreme sensitivity to public criticism, however, and interpreted any discussion of problems or critiques as attacks on Slovakia.[71] Political considerations also reentered the academy, as certain well-known liberal scholars were not allowed to teach in their departments and others faced pressure to resign from their academic positions.

Political life in Slovakia after the split was also complicated by issues related to the 600,000-strong Hungarian minority. In 1993, disagreements arose over the issue of the right of Hungarian women to drop the ending used in Slavic languages from their last names and the use of Hungarian street signs in predominantly Hungarian areas of Slovakia. The Hungarian minority also called for the right to use Hungarian in official dealings in villages and cities with sizable Hungarian populations as well as for greater attention to the training of Hungarian-speaking teachers for elementary and secondary schools in Hungarian districts.[72]

The Mečiar government faced increasingly sharp divisions within the ranks of the HZDS and in its coalition with the SNS. The dispute between Mečiar and then Foreign Minister Milan Kňažko concerning the orientation of Slovakia's foreign policy in early 1993 was followed by continued conflict between the HZDS and its sometimes coalition partner, the Slovak National Party, as well as by further conflicts between Mečiar and other leading figures in the HZDS.

This conflict and growing fears that Mečiar would take drastic steps to limit constitutional rights led to Mečiar's ouster as prime minister in March 1994. Galvanized by a speech by Slovak President Michal Kovač, Mečiar's opponents united to unseat him by a vote of no confidence and formed a grand coalition government to replace him.

This government, whose members ranged from the Party of the Democratic Left, the successor to the former Slovak Communist Party to Jan Čarnogurský's right-of-center Christian Democratic Movement Party, demonstrated a remarkable degree of consensus. Clearly a caretaker government until the 30 September–1 October 1994 elections, it, nonetheless, adopted a number of important policies designed to restore Slovakia's good name abroad, normalize relations with Hungary and defuse tensions between Slovaks and Hungarians within Slovakia, and reembark on the road to the market.[73]

Many of these policies were overturned after the 1994 elections, when Vladimir Mečiar once again became Prime Minister in coalition with the Slovak National Party and the newly formed Association of Slovak Workers. Under Mečiar's leadership, tensions once again increased between the Slovak and Hungarian communities. Relations between the government and President Kovacs mounted, and the government came under repeated criticism by outside governments and international organizations for acts that violated the spirit if not the letter of democracy.

Both the Czech and Slovak Republics continued to follow the main

HZDS Peoples' Party the Movement Democratic Slovakia
SNS Slovak National Party

tenets of Czechoslovakia's foreign policy after the split. The Czech Republic's leaders immediately reaffirmed their commitment to the Western orientation of the former Czechoslovak state's foreign policy. Then Prime Minister Klaus forcefully expressed his country's desire to join NATO and the EC and highlighted the ways in which the Czech Republic was a "Western" rather than "Central" European country. In the early months of 1993, Czech officials downplayed the importance of the Visegrad agreement, but they continued to participate in its deliberations and also joined the reformulated Central European Initiative.[74]

The foreign policy of independent Slovakia reflects a good deal of continuity with the policies of the Czechoslovak federation. The Mečiar leadership affirmed its desire to continue to cooperate with Hungary and Poland as well as with the Czech Republic within the framework of the Visegrad agreement. It also renegotiated Slovakia's association agreement with the EC on 15 June and secured Slovakia's acceptance into the Council of Europe, despite reservations about the treatment of the Hungarian minority. The Mečiar government was also able to secure a loan from the IMF, as well as assistance from the World Bank. The new coalition that replaced Mečiar's government secured additional assistance from the IMF and World Bank. Both the Czech and Slovak Republics have joined the Partnership for Peace. The differences between the two countries were highlighted in 1997. The Czech Republic was among the post-communist countries proposed as part of the first wave of NATO expansion. The country's leaders were also invited to begin accession talks with the EU. Slovakia, by way of contrast, was not included in either group of countries.

CONCLUSION

As developments in Czechoslovakia since World War II and now the Czech and Slovak Republics illustrate, the legacy of the communist era continues to be felt. The transition to democracy and the market has not been a simple one, even in a country with favorable preconditions for such a transition. Although the reintroduction of democratic political institutions and the basics of a market economy were achieved rather quickly, the tasks of "creating democrats," or people with democratic political values and attitudes,[75] and functioning market economies that will lead to prosperity clearly will take longer than the few years that have elapsed since the end of communist rule. The case of Czechoslovakia also illustrates the social and psychological costs that accompany such large-scale, rapid economic and political changes, as well as the impact of these changes in the social and cultural spheres. These are evident in the growth of social problems and ills as well as in changes in cultural life since 1989. They are also reflected in the fact that Czechoslovakia's political framework proved unable to contain the political conflict between Czechs and Slovaks that ultimately led to a breakup of the state. Developments in the two new republics created in 1993 demonstrate the continued impact of previous history and levels of economic development, as well as the importance of the international environment. After separation, political leaders in the Czech Lands and in Slovakia moved in somewhat different directions; they also face different problems. However, many of the fundamental issues remain the same. As in other post-communist countries, leaders and citizens of both the Czech and Slovak republics must continue to come to terms with the impact of the communist past and with the demands of the international community as well as with the sometimes unanticipated results of the political, social, economic, and cultural transitions that are still under way.

Notes

1. See Sharon L. Wolchik, *Czechoslovakia in Transition* (New York: Pinter, 1991), Chap. 1, for a more detailed overview. See also Wolchik, "The Right in Czechoslovakia," in Joseph Held, ed., *Democracy and Right-Wing Politics in Eastern Europe in the 1990s* (Boulder: East European Monographs, 1993).

2. Richard Boyles Burkes, *The Dynamics of Communism in Eastern Europe* (Westport, Conn.: Greenwood, 1976), 215.

3. See Wolchik, *Czechoslovakia in Transition*, Chap. 1; also Zdeněk Suda, *Zealots and Rebels: A History of the Ruling Communist Party of Czechoslovakia* (Stanford: Hoover Institution Press, 1980), 178–84.

4. See Josef Korbel, *Twentieth Century Czechoslovakia: The Meanings of Its History* (New York: Columbia University Press, 1977) 38–41 and 261–268; Radomír Luža, "Czechoslovakia between Democracy and Communism," in Victor Mamatey and Luža, eds., *A History of the Czechoslovak Republic, 1918–1948* (Princeton: Princeton University Press, 1973), 387–415; and Paul Zinner, *Communist Strategy and Tactics in Czechoslovakia, 1918–1948* (New York: Praeger, 1963), 1226–28 for discussion of these measures in 1945–48 and after 1948.

5. See Peter A. Toma and Milan J. Reban, "Church-State Schism in Czechoslovakia," in Bohdan R. Bociurkiw and John W. Strong, eds., *Religion and Atheism in the USSR and Eastern Europe* (London: Macmillan, 1975); and Pedro Ramet, "Christianity and National Heritage among the Czechs and Slovaks," in Pedro Ramet, ed., *Religion and Nationalism in Soviet and East European Politics*, rev. and exp. ed. (Durham: Duke University Press, 1989).

6. See Wolchik, *Czechoslovakia in Transition*, Chap. 5.

7. See Jiří Pelikan, *The Czechoslovak Political Trials, 1950–1954* (Stanford: Stanford University Press, 1971), 37–147; H. Gordon Skilling, *Czechoslovakia's Interrupted Revolution* (Princeton: Princeton University Press, 1976), Chap. 13.

8. See Suda, *Zealots and Rebels;* and Korbel, *Twentieth Century Czechoslovakia.*

9. See Pelikan, *Czechoslovak Political Trials.*

10. See Skilling, 57–63; Andrzej Korbonski, "Bureaucracy and Interest

Groups in Communist Societies: The Case of Czechoslovakia," in *Studies in Comparative Communism,* Vol. 4, No. 1 (January 1971) 57–79; and Martin Myant, *The Czechoslovak Economy, 1948–1988* (Cambridge: Cambridge University Press, 1989). See also Wolchik, *Czechoslovakia in Transition,* Chap. 4.

11. See Skilling, 72–82; Vladimir Kusin, *The Intellectual Origins of the Prague Spring: The Development of Reformist Ideas in Czechoslovakia, 1956–1967* (Cambridge: Cambridge University Press, 1971); Golia Golan, *The Czechoslovak Reform Movement: Communism in Crisis, 1962–1968* (Cambridge: Cambridge University Press, 1971); Wolchik, "Demography, Political Reform, and Women's Issues in Czechoslovakia," in Margherita Rendel, ed., *Women, Power, and Political Systems* (New York: St. Martin's, 1981), 135–50; and Alena Heitlinger, *Women and State Socialism: Sex Inequality in the Soviet Union and Czechoslovakia* (Montreal: McGill-Queen's University Press, 1979).

12. A. French, *Czech Writers and Politics, 1945–1969* (Boulder: East European Monographs, 1982), 194–243; William Harkins, "The Czech Novel since 1956: At Home and Abroad," in William Harkins and Paul Trensky, eds., *Czech Literature since 1956: A Symposium* (New York: Bohemia, 1980); Harkins, "Vladimir Paral's Novel Catapult," in Harkins and Trensky; Antonin Liehm, "Milan Kundera: Czech Writer," and "Some Observations of Czech Culture and Politics in the 1960s," in Harkins and Trensky; and Peter Kussi, "Havel's 'The Garden Party' Revisited," in Harkins and Trensky.

13. See Paul Trensky, *Czech Drama since World War II* (White Plains: M. E. Sharpe, 1978), Chaps. 3–4; Trensky, "The Playwrights of the Krejca Circle," in Harkins and Trensky; and French, *Czech Writers and Politics,* 182–192.

14. See Antonin Liehm, *Closely Watched Films: The Czechoslovak Experience* (White Plains: International Arts and Science Press, 1974).

15. See Josef Skvorecky, *All the Bright Young Men and Women: A Personal History of the Czech Cinema* (Toronto: Peter Martin Associates, 1971); Antonin Liehm, "Miloš Forman: the Style and the Man," in David Paul, ed., *Politics, Art, and Commitment in the East European Cinema* (London: Macmillan, 1983), 211–224; and David Paul, *Politics, Art, and Commitment,* 1–27.

16. See Robin Remington, *Winter in Prague: Documents on Czechoslovak Communism in Crisis* (Cambridge: MIT Press, 1969) for an English translation of this document.

17. See Carol Skalnik Leff, *National Conflict in Czechoslovakia: The Making and Remaking of a State, 1918–1987* (Princeton: Princeton University Press, 1988); Skilling, 49–56; Kusin, *The Intellectual Origins of the Prague Spring,* and *Political Grouping in the Czechoslovak Reform Movement 1968* (New York: Columbia University Press, 1972).

18. See Komunisticka strana Ceskoslovenska, *Akcni program kommunisticke strany ceskolovenska priaty na plenarim zasedani uv KSC dne 5, dubna 1968* (Prague, 1968); and Remington, *Winter in Prague.*

19. See Skilling, 764–772; Barbara Jancar, *Czechoslovakia and the Absolute Monopoly of Power: A Study of Political Power in a Communist System* (New York: Praeger, 1971); and Joseph Wechsberg, *The Voice* (Garden City: Doubleday, 1969).

20. See Myant, *The Czechoslovak Economy;* Joseph Brada, "Czechoslovak Economic Performance in the 1980s," in *Pressures for Reform in the East European Economies,* Joint Economic Committee, United States Congress (Washington: U.S. Government Printing Office, 1989); and Wolchik, *Czechoslovakia in Transition,* Chap. 4 for more detailed overviews of economic performance in the 1980s.

21. See A. Heneka, František Janouch, Vilem Prěcan and Jan Vladislav, *A Besieged Culture* (Stockholm: Charter 77 Foundation, 1985); French, *Czech Writers and Politics*, 335–364, 379–397; and Wolchik, *Czechoslovakia in Transition*, 284–291.

22. See Timothy W. Ryback, *Rock around the Bloc: A History of Rock Music in Eastern Europe and the Soviet Union* (New York: Oxford University Press, 1990). See also Sabrina Petra Ramet, ed., *Rocking the State: Rock Music and Politics in Eastern Europe and Russia* (Boulder: Westview, 1994).

23. Vacláv Havel, "The Power of the Powerless," in Havel, *Selected Writings, 1965–1990* (New York: Knopf, 1991), 125–214.

24. See H. Gordon Skilling, *Samizdat and an Independent Society in Central and Eastern Europe* (Columbus: Ohio State University Press, 1989).

25. See Peter Martin, "Church-State Relations," in Radio Free Europe, *Czechoslovak Situation Report*, No. 22 (22 December 1988), 19–24; Paul Wilson, "Religious Movement in Czechoslovakia, Faith or Fashion?" in Ladislav Matejka, ed., *Cross Currents: A Yearbook of Central European Culture*, Vol. 7 (Ann Arbor: Michigan Slavic Materials, 1988), 109–119; and Wolchik, *Czechoslovakia in Transition*, 212–215.

26. See Karel Dyba, "Reforming the Czechoslovak Economy: Past Experience and Present Dilemmas," paper presented at Woodrow Wilson International Center for Scholars, Washington, 1989; Karel Dyba and Karel Kouba, "Czechoslovak Attempts at Systemic Change," in *Communist Economies*, Vol. 1, No. 4, 1989, 313–325; Myant, *The Czechoslovak Economy*, 250–252; and Wolchik, *Czechoslovakia in Transition*, 245–248.

27. See Wolchik, *Czechoslovakia in Transition*, Chaps. 1 and 5.

28. See Timothy Garton Ash, *The Magic Lantern: The Revolution of '89 Witnessed in Warsaw, Budapest, Berlin, and Prague* (New York: Random House, 1990); John F. Bradley, *Czechoslovakia's Velvet Revolution: A Political Analysis* (Boulder: East European Monographs, 1992).

29. See Wolchik, *Czechoslovakia in Transition*, Chap. 1.

30. See Wolchik, "The Repluralization of Politics in Czechoslovakia," in *Journal of Communist and Post-Communist Studies*, 1994, and "The Re-emergence of the Political Right," for analyses of the 1990 elections.

31. See Paulina Bren, "Lustration in the Czech and Slovak Republics," *RFE/RL Research Report*, Vol. 2, No. 29 (16 July 1993), 16–22, for a detailed discussion of these issues.

32. See Wolchik, "The Repluralization of Politics," for references to sources that document these trends. See also AISA, "Výzkum politických postoju," 15.–24. dubna 1992 (Prague: AISA, May 1992), 8.

33. Ivan Gabal, director of the Presidential Office for Political Analysis, as reported in "Poll Views Czech, Slovak Attitudes on Issues," Foreign Broadcast Information Service—East European Report—91-185, 24 September 1991, 13–14.

34. See Wolchik, "The Repluralization of Politics"; and Valerie Bunce and Maria Csanadi, "Uncertainty in the Transition: Postcommunism in Hungary," manuscript, 1992, for an analysis that highlights the importance of these factors.

35. See Wolchik, "Women and the Politics of Transition," paper presented at the World Institute for Development Research of the United Nations University, Helsinki, 1993; and "Women and Politics in Czechoslovakia," paper presented at International Research and Exchange Conference, Prague, 1992; "Women's Issues in Czechoslovakia in the Communist and Post-Communist Periods," in Barbara Nelson and Najma Chowdhury, eds., *Women and Politics*

Worldwide (New Haven: Yale University Press, 1994); and Barbara Einhorn, *Cinderella Goes to Market: Citizenship, Gender, and Women's Movements in Eastern Central Europe* (London: Verso, 1993).

36. See Wolchik, *Czechoslovakia in Transition*, Chap. 2 for a discussion of the social backgrounds of government ministers elected in 1990.

37. See Sharon L. Wolchik, "The Czech Republic: Hável and the evolution of the presidency since 1989," in Raymond Taras, ed., *Postcommunist Presidents* (Cambridge: Cambridge University Press, 1997).

38. See James McGregor, "The Presidency in East Central Europe," *RFE/RL Research Report*, Vol. 3, No. 2, 14 January 1994, 23–31, and Sharon L. Wolchik, "The Czech Republic: Hável and the evolution of the presidency since 1989," in Raymond Taras, ed., *Postcommunist Presidents* (Cambridge: Cambridge University Press, 1997).

39. See Timothy Garton Ash, "Prague: Intellectuals and Politicians," *The New York Review of Books*, Vol. 42, No. 1, 12 January 1995, 34–40; Petr Pithart, "Intellectuals in Politics: Double Dissent in the Past, Double Disappointment Today," *Social Research*, Vol. 60, No. 4, Winter 1993, 751–761; and Caroline Bayard, "The Changing Character of the Prague Intelligentsia," *Telos*, No. 94 (Winter 1992–93), 131–144 for discussions of the political roles of intellectuals.

40. Karel Kříž, "Cenové zemětřesení," *Lidové noviny*, 29 December 1990, 1, 3.

41. See Wolchik, *Czechoslovakia in Transition*, Chap. 4, for a more detailed discussion of these policies in the early post-communist period. See also Wolchik, "Czechoslovakia's 'Velvet Revolution,'" in *Current History*, Vol. 89, No. 551 (December 1990), 413–416, 435–437; and Joseph Brada, "The Mechanics of the Voucher Plan in Czechoslovakia," *RFE/RL Research Report*, Vol. 1, No. 17 (24 April 1992).

42. See Ben Slay, ed., "Roundtable: Privatization in Eastern Europe," in *RFE/RL Research Report*, Vol. 2, No. 32 (13 August 1993).

43. See Wolchik, *Czechoslovakia in Transition*, Chap. 4; and Joseph Brada, "The Mechanics of the Voucher Plan in Czechoslovakia," for an analysis of the voucher privatization plan.

44. See Brada, "The Mechanics of the Voucher Plan"; and Slay, ed., "Roundtable: Privatization in Eastern Europe."

45. "Slovak Monthly Economic Monitor," in *Plan Econ Report*, Vol. 9, Nos. 13–14 (30 April 1993).

46. See Jiří Pehe, "Growing Ferment in Czechoslovak Culture," in Radio Free Europe, *Czechoslovak Situation Report*, No. 23 (30 November 1989), 37–43.

47. See Cierna, 1990, 17 and Srsnová, 1990, 14; see Wolchik, *Czechoslovakia in Transition*, Chap. 5, for an overview.

48. Wolchik, report from the "Task Force on Czechoslovakia," The Atlantic Council, Washington, D.C., 1991.

49. Wolchik, *Czechoslovakia in Transition*, 106–107.

50. John Kramer, "Drug Abuse in Eastern Europe," in James Millar and Sharon Wolchik, eds., *The Social Legacy of Communism* (Washington, D.C.: Woodrow Wilson Press; Cambridge and New York: Cambridge University Press, 1994).

51. See Wolchik, "Women and the Politics of Transition," for an earlier discussion of these issues.

52. The high level of support for the Movement for Self-Governing Democracy, Association for Moravia and Silesia, which won 7.9 percent of the vote to

the House of the People and 9.1 percent to the House of Nations in the June 1990 parliamentary elections and 4.9 percent of the vote to the House of the People and 4.2 percent of the vote to the House of Nations in the June 1992 elections, reflects the new political significance of this identity.

53. See Wolchik, *Czechoslovakia in Transition*, 94–95, 180–195, for an analysis of the activities of these groups in the early post-communist period.

54. The 1990 census indicates that there are 115,000 gypsies in Czechoslovakia. Dr. Peter Hunčik, formerly an adviser to President Havel, estimates that there are approximately 400,000 gypsies. See "Obyvatelstvo ČSFR podle národností a náboženského vyznání," *Dokumentační přehled*, ČTK, 32 (1991): H-1; see Wolchik, *Czechoslovakia in Transition*, 182–183, for a discussion of varying estimates of the gypsy population.

55. Sharon L. Wolchik, "The Politics of Ethnicity in Czechoslovakia," in *East European Politics and Societies* (Winter 1994).

56. See Peter Martin, "Economic Reforms and Slovakia," *Report on Eastern Europe*, Vol. 2, No. 27 (5 July 1991), for an overview. See also interview with Slovak Prime Minister Ján Čarnogurský on 14 May 1991, as reported in "Čarnogurský Interviewed on Slovak Economy," Foreign Broadcast Information Service—East European Report-91-095 (16 May 1991), 13–14.

57. See Katherine Verdery, *National Ideology under Socialism: Identity and Cultural Politics in Ceausescu's Romania* (Berkeley: University of California Press, 1991), for an analysis that highlights the importance of this dimension. See also Anthony D. Smith, "The Ethnic Sources of Nationalism," in *Survival*, Vol. 35, No. 1 (Spring 1993), 48–62; and Benedict Anderson, *Imagined Communities: Reflections on the Origin and Spread of Nationalism* (London: Verso, 1983).

58. See Archie Brown and Gordon Wightman, "Czechoslovakia: Revival and Retreat," in Archie Brown and Jack Grey, eds., *Political Culture and Political Change in Communist States* (London and New York: Holmes & Meier, 1979); Pavol Frič, Zora Bútorová, and Tatiana Rosová, "Relations between Czechs and Slovaks in the Mirror of Research," Bratislava, 1991; Centrum pre výzkum spoločenských problémov, and Marian Timoracký, *Aktuálne problémy Česko-Slovenska* (Bratislava, November 1990); Zora Bútorová and Martin Bútora, "Ostražitosť vôči Židom," *Přítomnost*, No. 4, 1992, 10–11, and AISA, "Výzkum politických postoju 15.-24. dubna 1992" (Prague, 1992).

59. See Josef Alan, "Česko-slovenské vztahy po pádu komunistického panství," in Fedor Gál, et al., *Dnešní krize česko-slovenských vztahu* (Prague: Sociologické nakladatelství, 1992), 8–17, for an overview of these differences. See also Jiří Musil, "Česká a slovenská společnost. Skica srovnaci studie," *Sociologický časopis*, Vol. 29, No. 1, 1993, 9–24, and Eva Broklová, "Češi a Slovaci, 1918–1938," *Sociologický časopis*, Vol. 29, No. 1, 1993, 25–42.

60. See Václav L. Beneš, "Czechoslovak Democracy and Its Problems," in Mamatey and Luža, eds., *History of the Czechoslovak Republic*, 43; Owen Johnson, *Slovakia, 1918–1938: Education and the Making of a Nation* (New York: Columbia University Press, 1985), 77; and Wolchik, *Czechoslovakia in Transition*, 7–8.

61. See Zora P. Pryor, "Czechoslovak Economic Development in the Interwar Period," in Mamatey and Luža, eds., *History of the Czechoslovak Republic*, 188–215; and Alice Teichová, *The Czechoslovak Economy 1918–1980* (London and New York: Routledge, 1988), 17–86.

62. See Wolchik, "Regional Inequalities in Czechoslovakia," in Daniel J. Nelson, ed., *Communism and the Politics of Inequalities* (Lexington: Lexington Books, 1983), 249–270; and *Czechoslovakia in Transition*, 186–195.

63. AISA, "Výzkum politických postojů," 15.-24. dubna 1992 (Prague: AISA, May 1992), 8. V. Krivý and I. Radičová, "Atmosféra dôvery a atmosféra nedôvery?" *Sociologické aktuality*, No. 2, 1992, 12–13.

64. Information provided by the U.S. Department of Commerce's Eastern European Business Information Service.

65. See "Czech Economic Monitor," in *Plan Econ Report*, Vol. 9, Nos. 26–27 (23 July 1993); and "The Czech Economy: A Second Spring," in *The Economist*, 13 November 1993.

66. The Economist Intelligence Unit, "The Business Outlook II: Slovakia," in *Business Eastern Europe*, 20 September 1993, 5.

67. See Sharon Fisher, "Economic Developments in the Newly Independent Slovakia," *RFE/RL Research Report*, Vol. 2, No. 30 (23 July 1993); and Economist Intelligence Unit, "The Business Outlook II: Slovakia," for further information.

68. Fisher, "Economic Developments," 45.

69. See Slay, "Roundtable: Privatization in Eastern Europe"; and "Slovak Monthly Economic Monitor," in *Plan Econ Report*, Vol. 9, Nos. 13–14 (30 April 1993).

70. Institut pro výzkum veřejného mínění, "Popularita politiků," Prague, March 1992; "Žebříček popularity politiků," Prague, May 1992; and "Žebříček popularity politiků," July 1992.

71. See "The Slovak Government versus the Media," *RFE/RL Research Report*, Vol. 2, No. 6 (5 February 1993).

72. See Fedor Gál and Peter Hunčík, "Legislation and the Problem of the Hungarian Minority in Slovakia," in Pavol Frič, Fedor Gál, Peter Hunčík, and Christopher Lord, *The Hungarian Minority*, report published by the Institute of Social and Political Science, Charles University, Prague, 1993.

73. See Sharon L. Wolchik, "Slovakia after Independence," paper presented at the 1994 meeting of the Conference on European Problems, Magdeberg, Germany, June 1994.

74. See Alfred Reisch, "The Central European Initiative: To Be or Not to Be?" in *RFE/RL Research Report*, Vol. 2, No. 34 (27 August 1993); and Milada Anna Vachudová, "The Visegrad Four: No Alternative to Cooperation?" in *RFE/RL Research Report*, Vol. 2, No. 34 (27 August 1993) for further discussion of these issues.

75. Ivan Havel, interview, March 1990, Prague.

4

Hungary

LÁSZLÓ KÜRTI

The Republic of Hungary is not a country which can easily be categorized. It is a European country, and yet its unique language (related to Finnish and to the Khanty and Mansi languages spoken in Siberia) and its complex history connect it to non-European (Asiatic) traditions and civilizations. Hungary is today a pluralist democracy, but its multiparty system dates only from 1990, when the communists were voted out of office. The country's population is barely ten million; and yet, there are another five million Hungarians scattered elsewhere in Europe (chiefly in southern Slovakia, Romanian Transylvania, and Serbian Vojvodina), in the Americas, and even in Australia. Hungary is small, no larger than the state of Connecticut, but it has notched some notable intellectual achievements in the sciences, music, and film.

WORLD WAR II AND ITS AFTERMATH

Following World War I, the Austro-Hungarian Monarchy came to an end, and Habsburg rule over Hungary, which had continued uninterrupted since the early sixteenth century, except for a brief moment in 1848–49, was terminated. As a result of the Treaty of Trianon (1920), Hungary was stripped of two-thirds of its territory, losing important coal and mining resources, and giving up territory to Czechoslovakia, Romania, and Yugoslavia. Hungarians bitterly resented these territorial losses which, in turn, fueled rightist aristocratic and religious circles during the reign of Miklós Horthy (1920–1944). As a by-product of Trianon, Hungary's population became ethnically more homogeneous and, as refugees from the successor states flooded the urban and industrial centers of post-Trianon Hungary, its economy was on the upswing. Peasants from the extraordinarily poverty-stricken underdeveloped northern and western counties—so beautifully rendered by Hungary's foremost writer, Gyula Illyés, in his autobiographical novel *People of the Puszta*—also traveled to the newly emerging factory towns. As Hungary's tragic working-class poet, Attila József, wrote, "Poverty is our national sickness." These writers captured the gloom of a desolate working-class existence, and it was not without justification that interwar Hungary was called "the country of three million beggars."

Although still referred to as a "kingdom," a land without a king, governed by Regent Horthy, Hungary's position vis-à-vis the Third Reich was ambiguous, to say the least, particularly in its early years. Apart from the brief periods of the prime ministerships of Count Pál Teleki (1939–1941), Miklós Kállay (1942–1944), and General Géza Lakatos (September 1944–October 1944), who attempted to maintain detached or nonaligned status, the governments of Hungary at the time were largely pro-Nazi. Economically, too, there was little doubt that Hungary had joined forces with Nazi Germany when Premier Gyula Gömbös (1932–1936) took office. Their close alliance could be detected in the dynamic growth of metallurgy, production of agricultural and electrical equipment, and especially in the area of aluminum processing. This new militarization of Hungarian industry was legally accepted in the government patent, issued during the Győr Program of 5 March 1938, that followed the Austrian *Anschluss*.

There were other signs on the horizon that neo-fascist and extreme rightist religious circles were slowly gaining the upper hand. United in nationalist, anti-Semitic, and racist organizations such as the Union of Awakening Hungarians (EME), Party of the Defenders of the Magyar Race (MFP), Hungarian National Defense League (MOVE), and Hungarian Arrow Cross Party (MNYSZ), these groups reflected the fact that the ruling political tapestry was indeed quite monochromatic in composition.

The only viable opposition was a literary-artistic intelligentsia, uniting leftists, socialists, trade unionists, but, more importantly, the country's radical populists. Many of the radical populists came from peasant and working-class backgrounds; more significant, however, was their active antigovernment stance concerning Hungary's agricultural (i.e., peasant) population. Perhaps the most well-known act of these "populists," as they were called, was the creation of a literary genre (known as "*szociográfia*"—sociography), fusing history, sociology, anthropology, and literature, which focused especially on the plight of the peasantry in a radically different fashion. As the country was becoming more and more

involved with German expansionism and the war, the populists organized a conference in 1943, known as the "Szárszó" meeting.[1] While
pressing issues of poverty and unemployment were discussed, center
stage was taken by those who discussed Hungary's fate after the war.
From these debates, the "third road" alternative gained popularity—an
idea stressing Hungary's specific historical and cultural strength in rejecting both Soviet communism and German fascism and instead directing
its energies into liberal democracy. Many interpretations have been offered for the significance of the Szárszó meeting, but the events of the
1980s and 1990s proved that neither of the authoritarian "roads" were
suitable or long lasting.

Despite the populists' efforts, the right became victorious, a historical move which was not unique to Hungary but occurred throughout the
region as a whole; as the deadlock of the world-market system became
evident, fascism rose as a "revolutionary tendency directed as much
against conservatism as against the competing revolutionary force of socialism."[2]

The Hungarian government, working with the small military elite
organized under the Hungarian Independence Movement (*Magyar Füg-
getlenségi Mozgalom*), attempted in vain to sign a last-minute armistice
with the Soviet Union on 11 October 1944.[3] On 15 October after the
arrest of the regent, the country came under the terror of the Arrow Cross
and the *Hungarista* (Hungarist) commandos led by the extreme reactionary Ferenc Szálasi. On 19 March 1944, the German army occupied Hungary, sealing Hungary's fate.

Jews, communists, and leftist sympathizers were rounded up and
taken away. Many social democrats and communists throughout the
country were killed in the next few months, among them many successful
organizers and underground leaders, adding to an already long list of
casualties whose names were later appropriated by the Stalinists for en-
listment in the cause of building communism after World War II.

STALINISM AND STATE SOCIALISM

The war devastated Hungary and as a result of its alliance with Germany
the government was required to pay reparations. The foundations of totalitarian rule in Eastern Europe were laid down immediately after World
War II, during a period of economic reconstruction, and the rebuilding
of a country devastated by war; for the first two years there was a brief
experimentation with parliamentary democracy.[4] As the consolidation of
the system was achieved, new and dynamic socioeconomic and political
processes were put into effect. On 1 August 1946, the "bourgeois currency," the *pengo*, was replaced by the *forint*, still the coin of the realm.
On 4 November 1945, the country voted in its first free elections after

the war with astounding results. The Smallholders Party (the peasant party) won 57 percent while the Soviet-backed Communist Party took only 17 percent of the votes. It had begun to seem as if Hungary, despite occupation by the Soviet army, would be allowed to establish a truly democratic multiparty system while maintaining its relative independence.

After World War II, the installation of an official workers' movement and the elimination of previous relations of production dramatically altered the fate of workers and citizens alike, a direct consequence of Soviet domination and Stalinist dictatorship in the new communist Eastern Europe (the "Soviet Bloc"). This brief period of transition was the time for Stalin and his *apparatchiki* (party bureaucrats) to make their move to construct a Bolshevik-style Soviet system in Hungary. As the result of intellectual agitation and political pressures, between May 1945 and December 1947 the Communist Party increased its membership from 150,000 to 864,000, providing a massive show of support and a popular base for its legitimacy. After two years of struggle, political and religious factions were eliminated and the newly created communist Hungarian Workers' Party (*Magyar Dolgozók Pártja* or MDP) became the country's only party. A twentieth-century witch-hunt was organized to arrest and delegitimize religious leaders of the various churches. One such show-trial involved József Cardinal Mindszenty, the last primate of Hungary, against whom so-called "evidence" of counterespionage and antistate activities was produced. Mindszenty was imprisoned, remaining behind bars until the 1956 revolution, when he was freed and took refuge at the American Embassy in Budapest. Later he was allowed to emigrate to the West where he died. (As an interesting footnote to history, it should be mentioned that Mindszenty was reburied in Hungary after the József Antall government took office in 1990.)

In the first years of communist rule, the secret political police (known best by its Hungarian abbreviations AVH and AVO) was one of the most important tools in cementing Stalinism in Hungary, much as the *Stasi* was in East Germany, the *Cheka* or later the *KGB* in the Soviet Union, and the *Securitate* in Romania.[5]

The masters of the new state attached great importance to the political values held by the population, and hence the emphasis they placed on education, culture, and political socialization. Between 1945 and 1949, young people—those under 24, nearly three million of a population of nine-and-a-half million in Hungary—were courted by competing party interests in dozens of youth organizations.[6] Despite the enforced high numbers, only about eight percent were card-carrying members of these parties. Gender-based division was an added feature—interestingly enough, not only the religious but the socialist trade unions separated girls' and boys' organizations.

However, it soon became clear that the communists were not about to allow the proliferation of youth organizations and, following the Soviet model of the *Komsomol*, a single organization was to be created. The young János Kádár—Hungary's leader between 1956 and 1988—appeared on the scene in a speech at the Csepel Works with a radical proposition to eliminate "reactionary" and "rightist" factions by propagating a single-party system.[7] Consequently, in March 1950, all alternative youth organizations became illegal and were thenceforth fused into a single youth group: the Workers' Youth Association (*Dolgozó Ifjúsági Szövetség*, or DISZ). Founded on 16 June 1950, its founding declaration explained the organization's purpose:

> The Workers' Youth Association is a nonparty mass organization uniting the widest spectrum of working youth into a revolutionary association. It is the vanguard of the Hungarian working-class and the people, led indirectly by the Hungarian Workers' Party. All activities of the DISZ are determined by the victorious world-view of the working class, marxism-leninism.[8]

In tandem with this political reorganization, industrial enterprises, private businesses, banks, railroads, and schools were nationalized; large landed estates were taken away from aristocrats and redistributed among peasants. By 1949, when the First Five-Year Plan was introduced, Stalinism and state control had been fully established throughout the economy and society.

Together with the formation of an idealized socialist labor force, the building of centrally planned "socialist cities" (called Stalintowns and Lenintowns) was of prime importance for the new government. Workers living in these new towns enjoyed salaries above the national average and contributed, no doubt, to their speedy economic recovery. Many became legendary symbols of socialist reconstruction and victory during the 1950s and 1960s. Socialist slogans popular in those years proclaimed: "In this country only those who labor will have a place. Work! This country is yours; you are building it for yourselves." As more factory-towns were built, thousands of young couples were recruited from the countryside. Single men and women, and those who could not afford to build their own houses, were lured to these industrial centers with offers of guaranteed accommodations; many, however, received only beds in workers' hostels and only the trusted elite enjoyed free, comfortable housing. Such privileges set the residents of these factory-towns apart from other people living in the countryside, which was suffering from hunger, privation, and the drive toward collectivization.

The conflict between the towns and villages was exacerbated as young industrial workers were urged to form "village-brigades" (*falujáró brigádok*) to assist in rebuilding the devastated countryside and to provide labor for the harvest and, undoubtedly, to reeducate the masses of "untrustworthy peasants." A Stalinist euphoria resulted, according to the contemporary ironic saying, in "salami tactics," planning first the elimination of the radical opposition and then of members of the moderate opposition.

In accordance with this ideological agenda, the infrastructure was also reorganized according to the principle known as "socialist urban planning."[9] Paved roads were built, and electric and water lines were repaired and extended to include the new *lakótelepek*, apartment complexes. Schools, day nurseries, kindergartens, and medical facilities were also erected; free education and medical supplies were introduced as basic rights of citizens of the Stalinist socialist state. Outstanding workers and their families received premium vacations, allowing them to spend leisure time on the former estates of aristocrats that now functioned as the factory's own vacation resorts, such as those of Lake Balaton, where not only leisurely activities but political education were the order of the day.

To boost industrial production, extra work shifts and forced labor methods were implemented on the model of the Soviet Stakhanovite industrial movement. Men and women in production received their respective medals; the two most common were the "Hero of Socialist Labor" (*Szocialista Munka Hóse*) and the "Red Flag Medal of Work" (*Munka Vörös Zászló Érdemrendje*). Posters, films, poems, and songs adhered to the precepts of "socialist realism." As an example of "socialist realism" I quote here a fashionable Stakhanovite song crafted to a folk melody:

> The Stakhanov movement is growing day-by-day,
> Our inventors help to materialize the five-year plan.
> We'll get ahead for the Soviets are sending us machinery
> And the workers of the world will benefit greatly.[10]

During the Stalinist era, Hungarian artists and composers were expected to conform to the doctrine of socialist realism—a doctrine imposed on Soviet cultural life in 1933–34. In line with this doctrine, artists and composers in socialist countries were expected to direct their attention

> . . . towards the victorious progressive principles of reality, towards all that is heroic, bright, and beautiful. . . . Socialist realism demands an implacable struggle against folk-negating modernistic directions that are typical of the decay of contemporary bourgeois art, against subservience and servility towards modern bourgeois culture.[11]

This doctrine, employed as a weapon of control by Hungary's cultural commissars, contributed to the isolation of Hungarian art and music after 1945. Béla Bartók (1881–1945) had left the country in 1941, and his works remained out of favor in Stalinist-era Hungary. The cultural isolation of Hungary reached its apogee in the years 1949–59.[12] The film industry was nationalized in 1948 and likewise obliged to follow the dictates of socialist realism. Between 1954 and 1956, however, film directors István Szöts, Zoltán Fábri, and Félix Máriássy cautiously abandoned socialist realism and expanded the boundaries of the permissible.[13] In the musical realm, the premieres in 1959 of Six Orchestral Pieces (by Endre Szervánszky) and String Quartet Op. 1 (by György Kurtág) marked a "breakthrough" in Hungarian musical development.[14] With the subsequent establishment (in 1970) of the New Music Studio of the Central Artists' Ensemble of the Young Communist League, experimental music found a home in Hungary and Hungarian music became reconnected with the rest of Europe.[15]

Clearly, the establishment of Stalinism and central control over the economy brought fundamental alterations to Hungarian society and culture. Stalinism's program had four principal theoretical foundations: Communist Party rule, representing the interests of the working classes; socialization of the means of production; replacement and supplementation of the market mechanism by central planning; and elimination of private property with the introduction of a socially equal redistribution of goods, services, and national income.[16] As a consequence, Stalinist rule affected the life of every citizen throughout the country.

The creation of the "new society" was in full swing. The Mátyás Rákosi government (1949–1956) realized that the "bourgeois and highly selective system of education" had to be replaced with a new communist educational system favoring working-class and peasant children and youth; by 1953, their ratio in high school was 65 percent and in university an impressive 55 percent.

The new communist value system played down love and camaraderie and emphasized, instead, internationalism and love of the Soviet Union. The Hungarian Stalinist nation-state was legitimized as a "workers' state" whose leaders had acquired mythical proportions, a feat achieved by a large number of well-salaried intellectuals. Both Hungarian Party Chief Rákosi and Stalin were idolized as "fathers," inspiring numerous novels, poems, films, songs, and posters describing their heroic deeds.

Equally extraordinary were the measures taken to curtail women's rights, sexual practices, and family life, and the general subordination of women to men concomitant with the solidification of a masculine gender model. Youth and females were viewed as essentially masculinized workers (munkás), an image reinforced by the blue overalls so visible in the media of the 1950s, and aided by the ungendered Hungarian language. Women's "individualistic" desires and sexual pleasures were thought to require taming by the newly conjured citizen of the Stalinist state, replacing the purportedly selfish, egotistic, bourgeois personality. Young

Women Situation maternity care, abortion outlaw education

women were expected to bear children for Rákosi's homeland, a policy resulting in a redefinition of such women as progressive and socialist, receiving maternity leaves, supplementary consumer goods, and "multiple-child bonuses."[17] Abortion was outlawed, childless families were forced to pay a surtax on their childlessness, and contraception was available only in extreme circumstances in the progression toward a communist utopia. At the same time, women were encouraged to obtain an education—often only at the Marxist-Leninist high school of the Communist Party—and to take an active role in local and state-level politics. A national women's organization was created (following the earlier Soviet pattern of the *zhenotdel*) to address the needs of all women in Hungary. Known as the Hungarian Women's National Council (MNOT), this body played a supportive role but eventually became over-bureaucratized and politicized, lacking any real lasting social impact or efficacy.

Ratkó

These ideological and economic incentives and pressures were extremely successful: by the late 1990s there had been only three years during which Hungary achieved a population boom, 1952–53–54, when children were called "Ratkó kids," after the Stalinist minister of health, Anna Ratkó. The demographic changes during the early 1950s are instructive indices of Stalinist redefinitions of gender roles and the ways in which these patriarchal tendencies simultaneously undermined and elevated the status of women. It may be argued that the Rákosi regime and the Communist Party had embarked on a monstrous course of irrationality in its quest for target plans and quotas in industrial production. The perverse connection between the "number crunching" strategies deployed by Stalinists and applied to both the factory and the womb served the state's utopian goal: the creation of a communist nation-state of Hungary.

In conjunction with these pressure tactics in the sphere of gender roles, cultural life was also drastically reorganized. The era's fashionable epithet was "Fight, struggle" (*harc*) which literally meant fighting against the capitalist west, but translated as faithfully serving and fulfilling party incentives. Another popular slogan of the time, "Forward for the establishment of socialist culture," meant spending as much time as possible in an organized manner with fellow Communist Party and trade union members. Young pioneers were required to greet each other with a firm sounding "Forward" (*Elóre*) which was meant both as an exhortation and a sense of direction about the coming of the future communist society. Mass sports activities soon became the ideal way of educating oneself and keeping fit physically. To be fair to the communist regime, it must be noted that it spent considerable sums for sports and mass physical education. Outstanding athletes and club members were awarded honoraria, such as the "Prize for the Socialist Culture" and most prestigious of all, the state's "Kossuth Prize."

While some intellectuals were relocated to the countryside and to reeducation camps in the central and western parts of the country, "socialist culture and progress" became synonymous with hard-working Stakhanovite men and women unselfishly—and in unison—building a socialist nation-state. The many inherent contradictions notwithstanding, it looked as if youth had been tamed to become the true vanguard of the Communist Party. Remarkably enough, the image of youth and the future were fused into one common mythic theme as exemplified by the Democratic World Federation of Youth anthem, taught in grade schools around the country, extolling the "rhythm of the future."

1956—THE REVOLUTION

No revolutions happen according to prescribed plans and the one in Hungary in 1956 was no exception. However, changes followed rapidly after the Twentieth Congress of the Communist Party of the Soviet Union (held 14–25 February 1956) in which the cult of personality and the errors of Stalinist policies were denounced by Nikita Khrushchev.

Several factors contributed to the rising tensions in Hungary: the rising cost of living, the appearance of Imre Nagy's "national communistic" program, the intellectual ferment created by the journal *Literary Gazette*, together with the university opposition group, the "Petőfi Circle." These youths were at first described as hooligans and reactionary elements by the government's paid intellectuals. In an ironic twist of fate, in the late 1980s these "hooligans" were renamed "true revolutionary youth" by the Antall government, the first freely elected government of the post-1989 period.

June 1956 witnessed the first strike in Hungary, when thousands of workers demanded wage increases, the return of normalcy in working conditions, and a better system of food distribution. However, while this strike was quickly solved through emergency measures, others flared up throughout the country's working-class communities. In July 1956, Rákosi was demoted for his hard-line policies and "personality cult." Many of his loyal followers were singled out by the emerging intellectual opposition from within the party's leading ranks. They were labeled "revisionists," "Rákosi sympathizers," and "reactionary elements," charged with hindering production and the building of communism. By the first weeks of October, several university students gave speeches at the Csepel Works—Hungary's famed working-class center—as well as other industrial districts agitating against the worsening socioeconomic conditions and the unfulfilled promises of the Communist Party. On 23 October when a massive demonstration by students and workers took place in Budapest, the Workers' Party leadership responded by inviting military reinforcement; armed militiamen and Soviet tanks appeared by midday

on 24 October, causing enormous resentment on the part of the revolutionaries. Under heavy pressure the Soviet tanks withdrew and Budapest
was under the control of the "counterrevolutionary forces." The generational and class aspect of the uprising of 1956 is worth noting. As Bill
Lomax explains, ". . . the Hungarian Revolution of 1956 was first and
foremost a social revolution in which the main motivating force—before,
during, and after the uprising of October 1956—was the industrial working class."[18] Indeed, Hungarians had seen no street demonstrations since
1948, especially none in which anti-Stalinist, anti-Soviet, and antigovernment slogans were heard. Paul Kecskemeti observes that a true "peer-
group solidarity" was felt:

> When some children got weapons and went out to fight, this apparently
> started a teen-age epidemic: the others felt they could not remain behind. . . .
> They found that they could easily establish contact with any group—workers
> and peasants as well as government officials, professionals, and army offi-
> cers. . . . As soon as word was out that the first Workers' Council was orga-
> nized—at the Incandescent Lamp Factory on October 24—within three
> days, a network of councils covered the entire country and general strike
> ensued.[19]

Numerous accounts underscore the general countrywide feature of
the 1956 revolution. However, many (often misrepresented) interpretations have been offered with regard to the three weeks of fighting, ram-
page, and killings. Although the events of 1956 were to linger in the
minds of Hungarians for decades to come—during the three weeks 2,500
were killed in the fighting, about 500 were executed, more than 10,000
jailed and black-listed, and some 200,000 emigrated to the West—recovery
was achieved by mid-1957. The prime minister, Nagy, who was called
a turncoat by his fellow communists for accepting that post from the
revolutionary government, was executed in 1958 with several of his colleagues. This, as it will be shown later, was not only an act of barbarism
but also a grave mistake, costing the communists their political survival.

BUILDING STATE SOCIALISM

As a result of the 1956 revolution, the Rákosi–Erno Gerö–Mihaly Farkas
troika had disappeared, while Kádár had emerged both as first secretary
of the newly created Hungarian Socialist Workers' Party (hereafter
HSWP) and leader of the new government. Kádár took no chances: he
was successful in eliminating both the "right" and the "reactionary elements," which interestingly included some comrades he could not trust.
State socialist hegemony was achieved by the formation of the HSWP
and through the repoliticization of working youth by means of the Communist Youth League, the KISZ, replacing all previous political factions

for those under thirty; children between ten and fourteen were assigned to the Young Pioneers, and those younger, to the "Little Drummer" (*Kisdobos*) organization. The only other legally recognized nonparty body was the Patriotic People's Front (HNF), whose leader Imre Pozsgay would become influential later, during the intellectual ferment in the 1980s concerning reforms of state socialism.

Recovery in its generational aspects meant the recovery of "lost youth." By the end of the same year, 170,000 young men and women were enlisted in the KISZ nationwide; in five years, this number had increased to 708,000.[20] Undoubtedly, the mobilization of the young—those between fourteen and thirty—under the aegis of the KISZ provided Hungary's ruling apparatus with an exclusive and even decisive edge in forming a new hegemonic hierarchical system. Moreover, Kádár's "political skill and his understanding of the people and conditions . . . enabled him to gain the cooperation and eventual respect of most Hungarians as well as the international community."[21] This assured his solid rule in Hungary from the end of 1956 until 22 May 1988 when he was dismissed from his post as general secretary of the HSWP.

To continue socialist industrialization and rapid agricultural collectivization, the Kádár government did everything in its power to maintain its image of a modernizing and democratic socialist state. In the period referred to as the new First and Second Five-Year Plan (1957–1965) the Soviet pattern of shop-floor organization, the socialist brigade movement (*szocialista brigadmozgalom*), was put to work organizing each shop and office into small (ten- to fifteen-member) brigades responsible for short-term plans.[22]

A new socialist working class—referred to variously as the "peasant-workers" or the "awkward-class" because of its rootedness in the countryside and its rural mentality—was clearly in the making throughout the country.[23] However, as elsewhere in the Soviet Bloc, decision-making and economic power were concentrated in the hands of the party apparatus—strictly speaking the Political Bureau—and its subservient politically educated managerial class. The new local elite was allowed to thrive, as party cadres, white-collar workers, and private businessmen were given permits to operate small family businesses on the side.

Hungarian society was undergoing a structural transformation in which the gap between the haves and have-nots was becoming more pronounced, a development that ran counter to the official ideology of equal pay for equal work, as Hungarian sociologists remarked.[24] Indeed this is the beginning of the social dimorphism noted by many social scientists, referring to the division of Hungarian society into two competing factions—with the large part of the populace becoming indifferent to the stated goals of the socialist state and hence coming to be known by the phrase "second society."[25]

Overambitious plans, the slow transformation of produced goods and their low value in the world market, and state financing of production units not profitable on their own contributed to a massive crisis by the mid-1960s. The New Economic Mechanism, introduced on 1 January 1968, was supposed to reverse these trends and put Hungarian industry back on track. Among the basic features of the NEM were a softening of central control over industrial and state enterprises, the implementation of indirect methods of state control over the firms, and the establishment of market relations and market prices.[26]

Concomitantly, these changes in technology and labor organization substantially affected the structure of the labor force, to which young people contributed more than ever: by 1973, more than one million of the 4.6 million under the age of thirty worked in Hungarian industry.[27] Obsessed with "winning over the West," Hungary's communists focused on the development of heavy industry and machine-tool technology, which in turn required technical or "polytechnical" training. These sectors were given preference by the regime over a liberal high-school education—a common tendency in Eastern Europe.[28]

Yet even by the end of the Third Five-Year Plan (1965–1970), it was generally acknowledged that the original ideas of the NEM had been useful only to a certain degree in helping Hungarian industry recover from its slump. As Hungary became reincorporated more and more into the world economy, the NEM reforms, despite their modest successes in revolutionizing production and work organization, met with official disfavor and even political counterattack from orthodox politburo members. Thus, "the antireform drive of 1973–74 accidentally coincided with the world economic shock of the oil crisis and its immediate consequences."[29] Among the most devastating effects of these events were price increases (70 percent by 1980), a slowdown in trade with both the East and West, and the accumulation of a large deficit and a huge international debt. In 1979, the Kádár government introduced another wave of economic reforms to combat these external economic shocks and their internal repercussions, an attempt that resulted in more inflation and mounting foreign debt.

INTELLECTUAL UNDERCURRENTS

Facing such enormous political and economic difficulties, the Kádár government consented to several major reform policies. Although in 1963 Kádár granted amnesty to political prisoners who had been convicted of "conspiracy" in the events of 1956 and offered concessions to the peasantry, Hungary's political stability was contingent upon maintaining a minimal level of contentment on the part of the intellectuals. Kádár's government tried to address this latter need with a growing cultural liberalism (especially after 1968) and, on the economic front, allowed Hungarians to establish small privately owned shops.[30] J. F. Brown is among those who have referred to Kádár's package of policies as a "social compact."[31] This "compact" involved a kind of tacit bargain between the state and its citizens, in which the latter were allowed to pursue private material interests in exchange for withdrawal from political life and for deferring to state administrative decisions.

There was also a dramatic easing in Church-state relations about this time. This was associated, to a considerable extent, with the elevation of Bishop László Lekai, in February 1976, to the position of Archbishop of Esztergom. Lekai reversed the confrontational posture of his predecessor, Cardinal Mindszenty, and concentrated on finding a *modus vivendi* with the state. Among other things, ". . . Cardinal Lekai took a seat on the Presidium of the People's Patriotic Front and exhorted the faithful to participate conscientiously in the building of socialism."[32] This strategy, in turn, yielded a series of small concessions to the Catholic Church, and therefore came to be known as the "small steps" policy.[33] The easing of Church-state tensions made a major contribution to the more relaxed atmosphere of the late Kádár era.

This easing of tensions notwithstanding, the Hungarian workers were becoming increasingly contemptuous of the communist regime.[34] Addressing this issue, Brown has listed six interrelated factors contributing to public disenchantment with the Kádárist regime: (1) economic problems; (2) social problems (including disparities in incomes, alcoholism, and drug abuse); (3) generational factors (such as the coming of age of the post-1956 generation); (4) oppositional groups (the emergence of dissident circles); (5) Gorbachev's presence (the impact of his early "perestroika"); and (6) the Romanian factor (the issue of the Hungarian minority in Transylvania).

In fact, these interrelated factors—as well as the collapse of the Brezhnev doctrine following the death of Leonid Brezhnev—ensured the emergence of an opposition to the regime on the part of the population at large. One of the most striking features of the early 1980s was the oppositional stance which artists, musicians, film directors, and educators took by forming dissident circles and publishing *samizdat* (unofficial) literature. Perhaps one of the most important antistate forces during the early 1980s was the amateur underground rock music scene. Young middle- and working-class artists produced illegal concerts and cassettes, singing songs about the police-state mentality and the fear of the Soviet Union and, by so doing, ridiculed the centralized control of the party state. Groups such as Mos-oi (Smile), CPG (Coitus Punk Group), the Albert Einstein Committee, and Beatrice, while differing in style, orchestration, and content, sang of youth disillusioned with the unfulfilled promises of the HSWP and the state.[35]

Until the mid-1980s, there was in Hungary only one minor political group uniting intellectuals. It was known as the "democratic opposition" and later the Network of Free Initiatives. This loose coalition included two factions referred to as the "urbanists" and the "populists."[36] Briefly, that intellectual division, dating back to the 1930s, reflected the tension between a more conservative political stance with regard to Hungary's external relations, and a more liberal one. As mentioned earlier, the populists of the 1980s—like their counterparts in the 1930s—stressed the importance of the country's history and culture as a mobilizing force and advocated a more gradual integration into a privatized, Western-style market economy. On the other hand, the urbanites (the Free Democrats, the Young Democrats, and the Social Democrats of the 1990s) championed a liberal, Western orientation that emphasized civil liberties, stronger political and cultural ties to the West, and complete free-market liberalization. Gábor Demszky, a former dissident elected mayor of Budapest in 1990, has summarized the way in which the opposition recognized the waning of communists' power as part of this "urbanist agenda":

> The question of the very survival of communism increasingly brought Kierkegaard's *Either-Or* to mind. We discovered, in other words, that there was no such thing as the "social market economy": there was either socialism or a market economy. Likewise, there was no "socialist democracy": there was either socialism or democracy.[37]

Although both populists and urbanites have concerned themselves with questions of democracy and a liberalized economic structure, the urbanites' emphasis has clearly been on these issues rather than on notions of "Hungarianness" (*magyarság*) or "Hungarian culture" (*magyar kultúra*) as elements of political unity and power. By the mid-1980s, it seemed that the populists were a winning majority, or at least they were the loudest and most visible oppositional force. As Hungary was experiencing an influx of Hungarian refugees from neighboring Romania, Hungarian popular attention turned favorably toward this group, emerging as the Democratic Forum, an intellectual movement espousing the plight of ethnic Hungarians outside Hungary. The language of this newly emerging elite politics was antistate and overtly populist, and openly addressed what it considered to be the devastating impact of 35 years of communist rule upon Hungarian citizens.

After 1987, when the historic Democratic Forum summit took place at Lakitelek, the Hungarian public was becoming increasingly concerned with ecological disasters, poverty, police brutality, illegally stationed Soviet troops, lack of funding for health and education, and especially the plight of the Hungarian diaspora in neighboring states, issues wholly avoided by the HSWP and the KISZ. It was indeed by virtue of KISZ that the opposition was able to gain the confidence and support both of the national and the international public. By debunking communist slogans ("Eight hours work . . ." and "Forward to building a socialist internationalism," incantations often heard at May Day parades) and confidently claiming the perpetuation of grave human rights violations in Romania and Czechoslovakia, this intellectual movement became an accepted political force by 1988 when one of the first (and largest) peaceful demonstrations took place in Budapest on 27 June 1988. This solidarity march, condemning Nicolae Ceaușescu's genocidal plan for the destruction of thousands of Saxon, Hungarian, and Romanian villages in the Transylvanian region of Romania, was tantamount to a victory procession for the opposition and, at the same time, a funeral dirge for communism.[38] This form of national identity and minority nationalism was accepted as a positive cultural and political force, and most intellectuals united under their seemingly innocent banners.

In the more relaxed political attention of the late 1980s, Churches took up the welfare issue of refugees and their families who stayed behind, thereby emerging as a radical antistate force capable of uniting among these lines. Catholic and Protestant, Evangelical and Baptist Churches in Hungary thereby spoke with one voice to attempt to mobilize and politicize their members. The concerns of the more radical opposition were far more immediate, encompassing human rights abuses, the plight of Hungarian minorities in Romania, the burden of the Warsaw Pact and COMECON, the fear of Big Brother, and the building of the expensive Danube Dam at Bos-Gabcikovo.

As is evident, a fledging civil society was in the making and, consequently, the power of the party state had been continuously eroding throughout the final years of the Kádár era. By 1988, it was evident that the aging ruler would no longer be in office; a replacement was found in the person of the liberal communist Károly Grósz, who was nominated in May of the same year. However, Grósz's rise to power lasted less than a year, at which point the "gang of four" (as the quartet of Miklós Németh, Rezsö Nyers, Pozsgay, and Mátyá Szürös came to be known) took office. The latter group remained in place until the election results of spring 1990 forced its members to step down.[39]

It was 16 June 1989 that must be credited with the significance of launching Hungary's post-communist history. On that day, the entire country mourned and celebrated the belated funeral of Nagy and his colleagues of 1956; the tricolor was draped in black and at midday bells rang out, symbolizing both the resurrection of a post-communist nation and the repossession of its long-awaited (democratic and European) history. Culminating a long and gradual revelation of historical details—achieved mainly through the creation of an important lobby-group called Committee on Historical Justice/Truth—the reinterment of Nagy suc-

ceeded in de-legitimating the very government responsible for this rehabilitation. About the same time, the Hungarian government decided to
let East Germans leave Hungary and cross into Austria.

The funeral ritual at Heroes' Square symbolized not only the significance of historical symbols and dead heroes, but, equally important, the
state's admission of failure and the public mourning of a nation coming
to terms with its own past. After this much-publicized media event, others followed in rapid succession: by the beginning of 1990, Hungary had
become a multiparty democratic state, declaring itself to be a republic; it
abolished the party's control in factories and the appellation "comrades."
Former religious holidays, suppressed under statist rule, were brought
back and, at the same time, the socialist rituals of 4 April (Liberation
Day), May Day, Socialist Constitution Day, and Soviet Revolutionary
Day (7 November) became footnotes to history; and, in turn, 15 March
(1848 Revolution Day), 23 October (1956 Revolution), and 20 August
(St. Stephen's Day) were celebrated and prompted by the Antall government (1990–1994). Streets received their pre-1947 names and statues of
socialist heroes and politicians disappeared—the few that were allowed
to remain thus permitting visitors to obtain a glimpse of Hungary's
thirty-five years of struggle with the ideas of Stalinism and state communism.

By the end of 1989, the Network of Free Initiatives had evolved into
Hungary's most radical democratic party, the Alliance of Free Demo-
crats, and the populists formed their own Hungarian Democratic Forum.
Slogans, such as "God, Nation, Family," espoused a perspective uniting
intellectuals across the political spectrum into the Christian Democratic
Party and the peasant party, known as the Independent Smallholders'
Party.

The elections of 1990 in Hungary were the first free and open elections in the former Soviet Bloc. All the oppositional groups, splitting off
from the original democratic opposition, were engaged in a fierce battle
to gain as many seats as possible in the parliament. From the inception
of the election campaign, it was clear, however, that only a few parties
would be able to gather enough momentum and strength to win over
enough voters. The new parliament thus represented the nationalistic and
religious shift in the political tapestry as three parties with overtly national programs—the Democratic Forum, Smallholders, and Christian
Democrats—garnered 42.93 percent of the total votes.[40] In the early
1990s, with several new factions and parties emerging (such as the Entrepreneurs Party, the Imre Pozsgay–led National Democratic Coalition,
and the Hungarian Life and Justice/Truth), the original percentage of
party seats seemed to hold. What is an interesting change, however, is
that the former intellectual dissidents are today members of parliament,
and holding various municipal and party posts. This added a rather

TABLE 4-1 Results of the Hungarian Parliamentary Elections, 1990

Party	Percentage of Vote	Seats Won
Democratic Forum (MDF)	24.71	164
Free Democrats (SZDSZ)	21.38	92
Smallholders (FKGP)	11.76	44
Socialists (MSZP)	10.89	33
Young Democrats (FIDESZ)	8.94	22
Christian Democrats (KDNP)	6.46	21
Agrarian Alliance	3.15	2
Independent Candidates	—	6
Two-party Candidates	—	2
TOTAL		386

schizophrenic twist to certain politicians' motivation in wanting to jail former communists for greediness, in proposing an amendment for outlawing private radio and television stations, or in forbidding foreigners to buy land in Hungary, aspects which determined the elite's discourse during much of the 1990–1994 period.[41]

National sentiments, however, soon have turned sour: isolated cases of anti-Gypsy and anti-Semitic attacks have occurred;[42] women's reproductive rights received a blow as abortion rights were curtailed; and Europeanness, liberalism, and democracy became empty words with politicians espousing their party interests instead of caring for the emerging class of unemployed (slowly increasing since 1992 from 700,000 to nearly a million by the beginning of 1995), the retired, and the rural producers unable to keep abreast of inflation.[43] All this occurred at a time when joint East-West industrial ventures numbered in the thousands and Hungary's external hard-currency debt had increased—again—to over $26 billion, and when strikes and other expressions of popular discontent were becoming common occurrences.[44]

All this, and perhaps another dosage of elite dissatisfaction with the nationalistic programming of the media by the Antall government (1990–1993) and later by that of Peter Boross (1993–1994), led to a total reversal of political power in 1994. In the elections the Hungarian Socialist Party (MSZP) had a field day: over 50 percent of parliamentary seats were taken by the socialists; the Free Democrats received 18 percent of the seats, a number slightly lower than its 1990 figure. The Democratic Forum lost all its credibility as the populace voted them out of office (see Table 4.2).

It is clear from the election results that the liberal parties retained almost their same position, and while the center-right Christian camp decreased in size (only the Christian Democrats gained slightly), the cen-

TABLE 4-2 Results of the Second Hungarian Parliamentary Elections, 1994

Party	Percentage of Votes	Seats Won
Socialists (MSZP)	32.99	209
Free Democrats (SZDSZ)	19.7	70
Democratic Forum (MDF)	11.7	38
Smallholders (FKGP)	8.8	26
Christian Democrats (KDNP)	7.03	26
Independents	—	1
TOTAL		386

ter-left coalition of the Socialists and the Free Democrats gained a clear majority in the parliament. Although the "return" of the former rulers is not necessarily the continuation of Kádárist rule—as some have feared—there is a continuation of a political tradition which seems inherent in the 1990 and 1994 elections. The result of the spring 1994 national elections sent a clear message: that the nationalistic propaganda of the Antall-Boross governments lacked popular support; and that the extreme right and conservative agenda was only a loud but empty media event.

As the Socialist government steered toward greater privatization and increased economic integration with the world market, culture and the arts suffered losses of state funding. Private sponsorship was inadequate as it seemed that the only persons to provide backing for culture were those who believed they could profit from cultural activities. As a result, there was growing popular discontent and artistic disillusionment.

Hungary's post-communist transition has been a difficult one, although—as of mid-1996—most observers assessed it as largely successful. As of 1994, 52 percent of all earned foreign exchanges (whether from exports or from remittances from Hungarians working abroad) had to be used to repay the long-term debt and to pay interest on that debt.[45] In March 1995, the forint was devalued by 9 percent, and wages fell dramatically in the course of that year.[46] Moreover, by early 1996, privatization had cost Hungary some 1.5 million jobs, and the major stage of privatization was completed only at the end of 1997.[47] Organized crime had also spread, prompting the government to propose the creation of a rapid-reaction anticrime agency.[48] Hardships aside, the Hungarian economy had begun a tentative recovery (as the figures in Table 4-3 reveal). Moreover, the relative success of Budapest's program of economic stabilization was being reflected as early as spring 1996 in the increasing activity of the Budapest Stock Exchange.[49]

CONCLUSION

At the outset I suggested that twentieth-century Hungary cannot be easily labeled. Its situation in 1996 is fragile to say the least. It is a country

TABLE 4-3 Hungarian Economic Indicators, 1994–1996

	1994	1995	1996
GDP growth	2.9%	2.0%	2.5%
Inflation	18.8%	28.2%	23.5%
Cumulative budget deficit	$2.3 bn.	$950 mill.	$1.6 bn.
Current account deficit	$4.1 bn.	$2.4 bn.	$1.7 bn.
Exports	$7.6 bn.	$12.8 bn.	$13.9 bn.
Imports	$11.4 bn.	$15.1 bn.	$15.9 bn.

Source: Euromoney Central European (29 May 1996), on Nexis.

which aspires to become a member of NATO and the European Union; yet it must struggle on a daily basis with its legacy of communism and its newly acquired independence, democracy, and market liberalization. However, there are cracks in the unitary politics of the government coalition as the Socialist Party and the Free Democrats must continue to struggle with the odds of economic, political, and international instabilities. As Hungary is redefining itself as more and more "European" instead of "East European," all around its borders, military and political (Serbia, Bosnia, Croatia, Russia), and economic (Romania, Ukraine, Slovakia, Macedonia) crises and upheavals have been the rule rather than the exception. Even though Hungary joined the Visegrád group—named for the place where it took shape—with Poland and the Czech Republic to organize and balance common economic and trade ties, Hungary's internal stability will depend as much on sound national policies as on its external relations and stability with its neighbors. Although Slovakia and Romania are now members of the Council of Europe, Hungary's relationships with both remain strained. The intensity of homegrown nationalisms in all three countries make it difficult to deal realistically with the plight of various minorities living on their territories, a continual trauma of these states in light of their move to "join Europe."[50]

Under its socialist government, Hungary is facing crises endemic to all of Europe. This new period just might test the boundaries of democracy and market economy in its redefined East-Central European setting once again.

Notes

1. The literature on Hungarian twentieth-century populism is vast. For an overview, see Gyula Illyés, People of the Puszta (Budapest: Corvina, 1967); on populism see Ferenc Erdei, A falukutatástól a népi kollégiumokig (Budapest: Múzsák, 1985).

2. Karl Polanyi, *The Great Transformation: The Political and Economic Origins of Our Time* (Boston: Beacon, 1964), 240.

3. István Szent-Miklóssy, *With the Hungarian Independence Movement, 1943–1947* (New York: Praeger, 1988), 88–93.

4. Ivan T. Berend and György Ránki, *The Hungarian Economy in the Twentieth Century* (London: Croom Helm, 1985), 77–97.

5. The secret police infiltrated all major institutions—schools, municipal administrations, factories, radio, television, newspapers, and political parties—and began a reign of terror over the population. On 27 February 1947, the so-called "conspiracy trials" began during which more than 200 people—the enemies of the socialist state—were sentenced before the "People's Court"; see Charles Gati, *Hungary and the Soviet Bloc* (Durham: Duke University Press, 1986), 27–36.

6. On the history of the youth organizations, see Lajos Gál and Lászlóné Szarvas, *A magyar ifjúsági mozgalom története 1945–1950* (History of Hungarian Youth Movement, 1945–1950) (Budapest: Ifjúsági Lapkiadó Vállalat, 1981).

7. Quoted in the local newspaper *Fogaskerék* (Csepel), 12 February 1948, 1.

8. György Petrus, *A magyar ifjúsági mozgalom története (1950–1956)* (History of the Hungarian Youth Movement, 1950–1956), (Budapest: Ifjúsági Lap és Könyvkiadó, 1984), 41.

9. Paul A. Compton, "Planning and Spatial Change in Budapest," in *The Socialist City: Spatial Structure and Urban Policy*, ed. R. A. French and F. E. I. Hamilton (Chichester: John Wiley & Sons, 1979), 461–492; and Gábor Csanádi and János Ladányi, *Budapest Térbeni-Társadalmi Szerkezetének Változásai* (Budapest: Akadémiai, 1992).

10. Set to the tune of "You can recognize the swineherd," the remainder of this Stakhanovite song continues in the same vein:

While in the capitalist west weapons are being made,
Here, on the Stalin bridge, workers are happily hammering.
Hey! The metro is under construction—how fantastic,
To hell with those who are waiting to make war.

Rakosi will lead us, he thinks of peasants too,
Those who are with us will not suffer.
Hey! Our party is increasing its target plans,
In a free land we'll keep fighting for peace, with its advice.

On the extent of such cultural production in state-supported popular music, see József Bényei, *Rigmusköltészet az ötvenes években* (Rhythmic Poetry in the 1950s) (Debrecen: Kossuth Lajos Tudományegyetem, 1992).

11. Composers' Union of the USSR, as quoted in Boris Schwarz, *Music and Musical Life in Soviet Russia, 1917–1981*, enl. ed. (Bloomington: Indiana University Press, 1983), 114.

12. *Contemporary Hungarian Music in the International Press* (Budapest: Editio Musica Budapest, 1982), 8.

13. David Paul, "Hungary: The Magyar on the Bridge," in Daniel J. Goulding, ed. *Post New Wave Cinema in the Soviet Union and Eastern Europe* (Bloomington: Indiana University Press, 1989), 176.

14. *Contemporary Hungarian Music*, 8.

15. Ibid., 92.

16. Berend and Ránki, *The Hungarian Economy in the Twentieth Century*, 199–200; and J. Wilczynski, *The Economics of Socialism: Principles Governing*

Hungary 91

the Operation of the Centrally Planned Economies under the New System (London: Allen & Unwin, 1982), 2–3.

17. László Kürti, "The Wingless Eros of Socialism: Nationalism and Sexuality in Hungary," in Anthropological Quarterly, Vol. 64, No. 2. (April 1991), 55–67.

18. Bill Lomax, "The Hungarian Working Class in the Hungarian Revolution of 1956," Critique, Vol. 12 (1978–80), 28.

19. Paul Kecskeméti, The Unexpected Revolution: Social Forces in the Hungarian Uprising (Stanford: Stanford University Press, 1961), 117.

20. László Eperjesi, A magyar ifjúsági mozgalom története 1956–1960 (History of Hungarian Youth Movement 1956–1960), (Budapest: Ifjúsági Lopkiadó Vállalat, 1981), 94.

21. Andrew Felkay, Hungary and the USSR, 1956–1988: Kadar's Political Leadership, (New York: Greenwood, 1989), 3.

22. László Kürti, "Hierarchy and Workers' Power in a Csepel Factory," Journal of Communist Studies, Vol. 6, No. 2, (Spring 1990), 61–84; and Kürti, "Red Csepel: Young Workers at a Socialist Firm in Hungary," East European Quarterly, Vol. 23, No. 4, (Winter 1989), 445–468. Some of these characteristics are also described in Michael Burawoy and János Lukács, The Radiant Past: Ideology and Reality in Hungary's Road to Capitalism (Chicago: University of Chicago Press, 1992).

23. See, for example, George Kolankiewicz, "The New 'Awkward Class': The Peasant-Workers in Poland," Sociologia Ruralis, Vol. 20, Nos. 1–2, (Fall 1980), 28–41; and Marc Rakovski, Towards an East European Marxism (London: Allison and Busby, 1978).

24. Zsuzsa Ferge, Hungary: A Society in the Making (White Plains: M. E. Sharpe, 1980); and András Hegedus, The Structure of Socialist Society (London: Constable, 1977).

25. See Elemér Hankiss, Kelet-európai alternatívák (Budapest: Közgazdasági és Jogi Könyvkiadó, 1989), esp. 117–143.

26. The list of studies on the New Economic Mechanism in Hungary, its results and errors, is extensive; see, for example, Berend and Ránki, The Hungarian Economy ; and János Kornai, Visions and Reality, Market and State: Contradictions and Dilemmas Revisited (New York: Routledge, 1990).

27. Csaba Mako and Lajos Hethy, "Worker Participation and the Socialist Enterprise: A Hungarian Case Study," The Quality of Working Life in Western and Eastern Europe, ed. C. L. Cooper and E. Mumford (Westport, Conn.: Greenwood, 1979), 296–326.

28. See, for example, Tamás Kozma, Tudásgyár? Az iskola mint társadalmi szervezet (Factory of Knowledge: School as a Social Institution), (Budapest: Közgazdasági és Jogi Könyvkiadó, 1985).

29. Berend and Ránki, The Hungarian Economy, 246; see also Nigel Swain, Hungary: The Rise and Fall of Feasible Socialism (London: Verso, 1992), 120.

30. Kürti, Red Csepel, 460–461; and Hankiss, Kelet-európai.

31. J. F. Brown, Surge to Freedom: The End of Communist Rule in Eastern Europe (Durham: Duke University Press, 1991), 98–99.

32. Leslie Laszlo, "The Catholic Church in Hungary," in Pedro Ramet, ed., Catholicism and Politics in Communist Societies (Durham: Duke University Press, 1990), 167.

33. Dennis J. Dunn, Detente and Papal-Communist Relations, 1962–1978 (Boulder: Westview, 1979), 141–143; and Joseph Pungur, "Church-State Policy in Communist Hungary, 1948–1990," An Eastern European Liberation Theology, ed. Joseph Pungur (Calgary: Angelus Publishers, 1994), 84–108.

34. These are described in Miklós Haraszti, "The Beginnings of Civil Society: The Independent Peace Movement and the Danube Movement in Hungary," in Vladimir Tismaneanu, ed., *In Search of Civil Society: Independent Peace Movements in the Soviet Bloc* (New York and London: Routledge, 1990), 71–87; Barbara Misztal, "The Exhaustion and Transformation of State Socialism," in *Thesis Eleven*, Vol. 27 (1990), 63–81; and László Urban, "Hungary in Transition: The Emergence of Opposition Parties," in *Telos*, Vol. 79, No. 3 (Winter 1989), 108–118.

35. For a detailed discussion, see László Kürti, "Rocking the State: Youth and Rock Music Culture in Hungary, 1976–1990," in *East European Politics and Societies*, Vol. 5, No. 3 (Fall 1991), 483–513; reprinted, in revised version, under the title, " 'How Can I Be a Human Being?' Culture, Youth, and Musical Opposition in Hungary," in Sabrina Petra Ramet, ed., *Rocking the State: Rock Music and Politics in Eastern Europe and Russia* (Boulder: Westview, 1994), 73–102.

36. On the emergence of intellectual debates in the late 1980s, see Susan Gal, "Bartok's Funeral: Representations of Europe in Hungarian Political Rhetoric," in *American Ethnologist*, Vol. 18, No. 3 (Fall 1991), 440–458; Misha Glenny, *The Rebirth of History: Eastern Europe in the Age of Democracy* (Harmondsworth: Penguin, 1990), 72–75; and Ferenc Miszlivetz, "Central Europe— The Way to Europe," paper presented at the annual meeting of the Hungarian Sociological Association (Budapest, July 1991).

37. Gábor Demszky, "Building a Market Economy in Hungary," in *Uncaptive Minds*, Vol. 4, No. 2 (Summer 1991), 46.

38. On the escalation of Romanian-Hungarian conflict concerning Hungarian minorities in Romania in the 1980s, see László Kürti, "Transylvania—Land Beyond Reason: Toward an Anthropological Analysis of a Contested Terrain," in *Dialectical Anthropology*, Vol. 14, No. 3 (Spring 1989), 21–52; and Trond Gilbert, *Nationalism and Communism in Romania* (Boulder: Westview, 1990).

39. Imre Pozsgay was the foremost critic of the system, especially in 1989 when, turning against his party comrades, he publicly announced that the 1956 revolution was a true popular uprising. This was a daring act from a Politburo member at that time. Yet, in a true twist of irony, Pozsgay, a true reformer, was not able to survive the political changes of 1989–90, and, as a result of the elections, lost all political clout. These changes are detailed in Rudolf L. Tõkés, *Hungary's Negotiated Revolution: Economic reform, social change, and political succession* (Cambridge: Cambridge University Press, 1996).

40. Attila Ágh, "A kezdet vege: Helyzetkép a politikai átmenet elsó szakasza után" [The Beginning of the End: After the First Period of the Political Transition], in *Mozgó Világ*, Vol. 12, No. 3 (1990), 101–112; and Andras Korosenyi, "Pártok és szavazók—Parlamenti valasztasok 1990—ben" [Parties and Voters during the Parliamentary Elections of 1990], in *Mozgó Világ*, Vol. 8 (1990), 39–51.

41. On the internal crisis of the Democratic Forum, see Kata Beke, *Jézus Mária, gyóztünk* [Jesus, we've won!] (Budapest: Belvárosi Könyvkiadó, 1993).

42. For further discussion, see Paul Hockenos, *Free to Hate: The Rise of the Right in Post-Communist Eastern Europe* (New York and London: Routledge, 1994), Chaps. 3–4.

43. For more detail about the nature and complexities of Hungarian unemployment, the following should suffice: According to figures released by the *Országos Munkaügyi Központ*, as of 31 August 1994, the total number of those registered as unemployed came to 551,000, which is slightly higher than the fig-

ure recorded in July (546,000). Of this number, 74,000 are looking for their first jobs: Budapest, for the first time, is leading in the number of unemployed. About one out of every three unemployed is reapplying, while fewer than one in ten is participating in a training program of any kind. Thirty-four percent of unemployed have received unemployment benefits. Some 201,000 receive welfare and social assistance. Some 162,000 have not been provided with any kind of benefits, according to *Népszabadság* (Budapest), 24 September 1994, 5. By the end of September, the total number of unemployed declined to 545,868, according to *Magyar Hírlap* (Budapest), 6 October 1994, 5. Other figures released by independent organizations, such as the Koping-Datorg and Szonda-Ipsos foundations, put unemployment as high as 16 percent. Hungary's minister of labor, however, mentions that "actual" or "existing" unemployment may be as high as one million.

44. According to figures released by the Economic Research Institute, Hungary's external debt increased to $26.5 billion by the end of July 1994. *Népszabadság*, 27 September 1994, 12.

45. *Bangkok Post*, 28 May 1996, on *Nexis*.

46. *Hungarian Radio* (Budapest), 30 March 1996, trans. in *BBC Monitoring Service: Eastern Europe* (1 April 1996).

47. *Hungarian Radio* (9 February 1996), trans. in *BBC Monitoring Service: Eastern Europe* (12 February 1996).

48. MTI (17 May 1996), in *BBC Monitoring Service: Eastern Europe* (18 May 1996).

49. *Reuters News Service*, 4 April 1996, on *Nexis*.

50. I have detailed this in "Globalisation and the Discourse of Otherness in the 'New' Eastern and Central Europe," *The Politics of Multiculturalism in the New Europe: Racism, Identity and Community*, ed. Tariq Modood and Pnina Werbner (London: Zed, 1997), 29–53; and *Beyond Borders: Remaking Identities in the New East and Central Europe*, ed. László Kürti and Juliet Langman (Boulder: Westview, 1997).

5

The German Democratic Republic

BRIGITTE H. SCHULZ

The German Democratic Republic (GDR), a child of the Cold War antagonism between the United States and the Soviet Union, died a few days short of its forty-first birthday. It would certainly serve the interests of parsimony simply to attribute this death to the loss of support by its Moscow parent under the leadership of Mikhail Gorbachev. However, this explanation, though elegant in its simplicity, does not do justice to the historical developments which led to the unification of the GDR with its much larger and more powerful western counterpart, the Federal Republic of Germany (FRG).

This chapter, then, in retelling the story of the rise and fall of the GDR, will seek to address questions which go beyond the fact that the country owed its existence largely to the Cold War. What exactly was this first socialist state on German soil? How did its status as a part of a divided nation affect its policy options? What were some of the internal and external causes of its demise? Why did the East German government fail so completely in instilling in its citizens a sense of loyalty, in spite of decades of political socialization and indoctrination? What was the nature of the opposition which so successfully forced the communist government to surrender its total power and control? Why did this same opposition fail so miserably in leading the East German population into the post-communist era? Were there any achievements made under communism which can be carried over into reunified Germany? Indeed, how is it possible to unite two radically different economic and social systems? What is the ongoing legacy of East German communism?

The problem emerges as to how to impose a theoretical framework that will help to answer these questions. No single paradigm will adequately answer the questions posed here. Applying a traditional power politics model, for example, may help in explaining the radically altered Soviet foreign policy objectives under Gorbachev,[1] but it would not explain other important external factors such as changes in the world economy which had a crucial impact on East German policy options. On the other hand, concentrating solely on *external* determinants would entail the omission of the many *internal* contradictions of East German society which ultimately contributed to the demise of the country as a sovereign entity. Throughout this chapter, which is chronologically organized, I will refer to various theoretical approaches or analytical tools expressed in concepts such as political socialization, political culture, legitimacy, and nation and state building to explore the politics of the East German government.[2]

The Socialist Unity Party of Germany (SED) represented almost an ideal type of "post-totalitarian" regime which completely insulated itself from the growing pressures and demands of an increasingly diversified society.[3] Seeking to understand East German society solely from the standpoint of those who governed and the structures set up by them to enforce their rule tells only half of the story, however. Clearly the Berlin government, like other communist governments in Eastern Europe, enjoyed only limited popular support. How did the population react to the imposition of communist rule? What options were available? Which were exercised and why? Albert O. Hirschman's seminal work on general questions of "exit" and "voice" inform this part of the chapter. According to Hirschman, when conditions become intolerable, people either exercise the option to look for more satisfaction elsewhere (i.e., to "exit"), or they insist on changes by giving "voice" to their demands.[4] As will be shown, "voice" was largely absent in the GDR until the 1980s with the gradual reemergence of a civil society which, like in other East European countries, meant the "appearance of social activity based on free association, not mobilized participation, and the articulation of interests from below as well as above."[5]

Another important piece of the puzzle is found by looking at economic factors. Rapid technological change in the advanced capitalist countries sharply diminished the competitiveness of the East throughout the 1980s. This, coupled with growing hard currency debts, influenced the policy options available to East European governments. The East German economy thus is not seen in isolation, but as an integral part of a rapidly changing global economy. Despite ideologically motivated assertions to the contrary, by the late 1970s centrally planned economies had clearly been reintegrated into the capitalist world system. This intensified the contradictions inherent in a model which insisted on the primacy of politics over economics and contributed significantly to the final collapse. According to Immanuel Wallerstein, this collapse must be seen within the context of an ongoing challenge to the entire modern world system, of which communism was an integral part. Wallerstein argues that the challenge to communism was part of a profound global structural crisis which began with the revolts of 1968 and will end in the demise of the entire capitalist world system in the foreseeable future.[6]

Throughout the chapter particular attention will be paid to the special situation in the GDR as part of a divided country. From the beginning, this had a dramatic effect on the political economy of the GDR, adding an air of uncertainty which even the Wall and a border lined with mines and automatically activated weapons systems could not ameliorate. As will be explained below, it also deprived the East German government of an important tool for state building—i.e., nationalism.

The two German states were united on 3 October 1990. The process of unification will be recounted briefly, both in its domestic and international dimensions. The final section is devoted to the experiences of post-unification Germany.

THE BIRTH OF A STATE IN A DIVIDED AND DEMORALIZED NATION

The end of the Second World War did not mean liberation for Germany collectively, although it did mean such for those who had suffered under Naziism both inside and outside the country. For German society, 1945 meant final defeat and complete collapse at all levels—economic, political, and social. The Hitler dictatorship had left behind a devastated country, both materially and spiritually.

The war years 1939 to 1945 for Germany had meant a megalomaniacal attempt first to rule Europe and then the entire world. The war itself, begun against Poland in 1939, was the culmination of years of preparation under a bellicose fascist dictatorship. A cornerstone of this dictatorship under the National Socialists (the "Nazis") was a strident anti-communism combined with the determination to cleanse Germany and the world of the "red menace."[7] This included attacking and imprisoning Social Democrats and communists, who had fought among themselves rather than against the growing fascist danger. Specially built concentration camps thus housed not only racial "undesirables" such as Romanies and Jews, but also those who opposed fascism on principle.

When the war finally ended, defeated Germany was divided into four separate zones of military occupation. What was to become the GDR constituted the Soviet zone, which was governed by the Soviet Military Administration Germany (SVAG in Russian, SMAD in German) and comprised 108,000 square kilometers with 18.3 million inhabitants. SMAD was supported in its efforts by those German Communist Party

(KPD) members who managed to escape Nazi Germany for Moscow and who returned from this exile with the victorious Red Army. Through a rigorous program of denazification, leading to the dismissal of roughly 520,000 individuals from public posts, SMAD was able to fill most important vacancies with "their" German communists.[8]

It should be understood that the German communists put into power by SMAD were not, despite their later claims, the leaders of a victorious working-class party embarking with revolutionary élan on the construction of socialism. Rather they were, for the most part, a group of men who, like Walter Ulbricht and Wilhelm Pieck, had lived in exile in Moscow for the duration of the Third Reich. These men were hardly visionary revolutionaries. Rather, they were experienced survivors of the murderous internecine party wars that had characterized Stalin's Moscow. Thus, their entire outlook was that of the small-minded, authoritarian bureaucrat with a deep-seated fear of any differences of opinion or independence of ideas. As such they were the advance cohort of a stratum that proliferated and came to dominate East German society culturally as well as politically and economically; what the first permanent representative of West Germany to the GDR, Günther Gaus, was later to characterize as *Kleinbürgertum*—people with neither taste nor vision.[9] All aspects of political, economic, cultural, and even personal life had to be controlled, regulated, standardized, and centralized as far as possible.

Thus from the very beginning, the relationship between the political elite and those it governed was highly problematic. Either explicitly or by simple compliance, the German population had largely supported the Hitler dictatorship with its strident anti-communism and racism. The imposition of Soviet-style economic and political structures took place within a punitive atmosphere which came not only from Red Army personnel but also from the German communists who presented themselves as the only real heroes of the Hitler era. Mutual suspicion and mistrust thus were cornerstones of relations between the communist elites and the spiritually shattered population. While returning KPD members from Moscow saw their fellow Germans as being in dire need of reeducation and proper ideological guidance, the masses considered their new leaders puppets who owed their positions to Stalin and his geopolitical ambitions. Disagreeing with these ambitions was at one's own peril. The Soviets went so far as to reopen some of the old Nazi concentration camps to imprison uncooperative Germans, many of them Social Democrats or even communists who had a different vision for postwar Germany. By the time the camps were closed again in 1950, 130,000 political prisoners had been incarcerated there, of whom roughly 50,000 perished and another 20,000 to 30,000 were deported to camps in the Soviet Union.[10] Surely these were not ideal circumstances for building a new society of any type!

This is not to say that some of the policies pursued by SMAD did not enjoy popular support. For example, the land reform of September 1945, in which all estates over 100 hectares (about 250 acres) were distributed among 500,000 persons, enjoyed broad popular support. In this fashion, 2.1 million hectares were distributed among a half million Germans, while simultaneously destroying the Prussian Junkers (the landed gentry) as a hitherto powerful political class. Even the gradual nationalization of the industrial and banking sectors found relatively high levels of popular consent. For example, in Saxony the question of turning industrial enterprises into "people's property" was approved on 30 June 1946 by 77.6 percent of the votes.[11] The response of the expropriated Junkers and large industrialists was to move to the Western zones then under American, British, and French occupation. This pattern of East-West migration on the part of the disaffected constitutes another important particularity of developments in the GDR, right up to the collapse of communism in the fall of 1989.

The reason agrarian and industrial reforms carried out by the Soviet occupation forces found high levels of popular support is that they roughly conformed to a broad consensus as to the future of the country.[12] SMAD, in its Directive #2 of 10 June 1945, allowed for the formation of political parties, provided that they were explicitly antifascist. By 14 July, four parties had combined into an "antifascist-democratic bloc." In January 1946, the two most explicitly anticapitalist parties, the Social Democratic Party (SPD) and the German Communist Party (KPD), had 512,000 and 437,000 members respectively in the Soviet zone.[13] Both the Christian Democratic Party (CDU) and the Liberal-Democratic Party of Germany (LDPD) were newly created bourgeois parties and their membership was considerably lower, 70,000 and 88,000 respectively.[14] Because both the KPD and the SPD had suffered enormously under the Hitler dictatorship, there was an enormous desire to cooperate in political work. This was much more emphatically expressed by the SPD immediately after the war, but by the time the two parties officially merged into the "Socialist Unity Party" (SED) in April 1946, it had become an expression of the will of SMAD to control political activities in the Soviet zone. The SED increasingly became a Leninist party "of a new type" with the active support of SMAD, while the SPD's role became ever more marginal.[15] What gave the illusion of a unified front, a "democratic bloc" of political parties, was rapidly transformed into a model in which the communists assumed a "vanguard" role. This reduced the input of the other parties merely to paying lip service—an alibi function which these "bloc parties" continued until the collapse of the whole system in the winter of 1989–90.

In the immediate postwar years there was clearly a popular mandate for socialist measures, but within the context of a "special German road

to socialism" rather than the adoption of the Soviet model. Unfortunately, this special road led nowhere for two dialectically related reasons:
first, the imposition of the hierarchical, centralized, authoritarian Bolshevik political model and, second, deteriorating superpower relations
which made the division of Germany all but a certainty by 1948.[16] The
dream of establishing an indigenous socialist order first in the Soviet zone
and then throughout a sovereign Germany ended where the Cold War
began. In May 1949 the British and American zones became the Federal
Republic of Germany, an event much heralded in the West as the dawn
of a new and democratic era on German soil. Five months later, on 7
October 1949 the German Democratic Republic was born, spurned in
most of the world as the illegitimate offspring of the Cold War and deprived of any form of diplomatic recognition outside the Soviet bloc.

To make matters worse, support was not even certain from the Moscow parent. It seems clear that the Soviets did not want a division of
Germany in the first place. The creation of the GDR was seen by Stalin
as a provisional solution caused by growing antagonism between the allies and the beginning of the Cold War. Even after 1949, he continued to
work toward a unified, albeit militarily neutral Germany. Stalin's final
attempt toward this objective came in his famous note to the West German government in March 1952, followed a month later by Soviet consent to free elections in all of Germany. The election was never held
because of continuing fundamental disagreements among the four former
allies. What it showed, however, is that Stalin was willing to sacrifice the
"first socialist state on German soil" long after the GDR was founded,
had it suited his geopolitical ambitions.

The SED's response to this massive insecurity was to become ever
more slavish in its devotion to the Soviet model, in defiance of the general
will of the population. Critics were silenced and excluded from political
life. In 1950–51 150,000 members of the SED were expelled and the
party's top leadership purged of oppositional elements, including many
old communists whose vision for a socialist Germany differed from the
Stalinist one.[17]

Clearly, the imposition of the Stalinist model under conditions of
Soviet hegemony was not supported by popular consent anywhere in
Eastern Europe. The situation in the GDR was enormously more complicated, however, because of the division of Germany and the problem of
national identity. Other communist leaders in Eastern Europe, for example in Poland, were at least able to appeal to nationalist sentiments
among the population in the process of state-building. That option was
not available to the SED leadership for several reasons. First, nationalism
was thoroughly discredited in Germany after the Hitler experience. Second, even had that not been the case, any rekindling of nationalist sentiments would have strengthened those who opposed the division of

Germany and the establishment of two separate German states. Third, since the SED regime insisted that its legitimacy came from socialism, it was hard to find a "usable past" on which to construct a GDR-specific national identity. What to do with some of the beacons of German history such as Luther, Goethe, or Friedrich the Great? Thus, as Peter Jochen Winters has pointed out, it was never possible for the SED to develop among the citizenry a sense of loyalty to the GDR, a "GDR patriotism or even a GDR-specific national consciousness."[18] As will be explained below, the lack of a cohesive national identity also greatly impeded the creation of a civic movement uniting dissident workers and intellectuals in the country three decades later.

Two additional and interrelated elements of insecurity existed for the SED regime which made it unique in postwar Eastern Europe: (1) the entire *raison d'être* of the country was based on "socialism;" i.e., the GDR's legitimacy as a separate political entity was derived completely from the Cold War division of Europe into East and West, and (2) West Germany, the rich and powerful "other Germany" established by the Western allies, claimed to represent *all* Germans and automatically extended full citizenship to all East Germans. This resulted in slavish SED obedience to the Soviet mentors while simultaneously seeking to "insulate" (*abgrenzen*) the population from the influences of the capitalist West. Thus, even after the GDR was founded, its government faced insecurities and dilemmas far exceeding those of other East European communist regimes.

CRISES IN LEGITIMACY AND STATE-BUILDING

At its party congress in July 1952, the SED, under the leadership of Ulbricht, formally announced that conditions now had matured enough in the country to allow for the formal "construction of socialism." This clearly reflected more the SED's desire to integrate the GDR ever more closely into the Soviet bloc than a balanced assessment of the forces inside the country willing to support this radical course. Over the next year the SED, nevertheless, moved ahead with measures such as the growing collectivization of agriculture, more investments in heavy industry, dramatic price hikes in increasingly scarce consumer products, and raising production quotas by 10 percent.

The working class responded with a general uprising throughout the GDR on 17 June 1953. In strikes and demonstrations demands were raised for free trade unions, free elections, and the ousting of Ulbricht. Industrial workers protested the increase in production quotas, while peasants rebelled against the growing collectivization of land. The uprising was crushed by the East German state and secret police with the help of Soviet troops.[19] Although it became "historiographic canon" in the

West that this uprising was essentially antisocialist, there is considerable evidence that it instead rested on the best traditions of the German industrial working-class movement. The uprising was not procapitalist as much as anti-Stalinist and insisted that socialism and freedom are inseparable.[20] By the time the East German working class again participated in mass demonstrations in the winter of 1989–90, this call for a better socialism had been replaced by German nationalism and the demand for unification with the consumer society in the West.

What options are available to a population whose open expression of dissent has been forcibly crushed? In the GDR after 1953, the "voice" option was exercised only by some sectors of the Protestant Church and the intelligentsia. The Lutheran Church, whose membership comprised roughly 90 percent of the East German population, had survived the Hitler dictatorship and now found itself in the unenviable position of once again having to accommodate itself to a hostile and undemocratic political system. During these early years, the profound differences between the vision of the Church and the atheist political establishment were always close to the surface. Bishops such as Otto Dibelius of Berlin were openly hostile to the socialist vision and made little secret of their views that Christians should not serve an openly atheistic communist state. Even Bishop Moritz Mitzenheim of Thuringia, who would later come to be known as the GDR's "Red Bishop," openly opposed the SED's attempts to secularize all aspects of life in the GDR, such as the introduction of the *Jugendweihe* in 1954.[21]

Two of the most influential novels of the early years were J.R. Becher's *Abschied. Einer deutschen Tragödie* (first published in 1940 and reissued throughout the early postwar years) and Hans Marchwitza's *Roheisen* (1955). *Abschied*, which showed all the marks of socialist realism, aspired to show young people "a path out of negativity,"[22] while *Roheisen*, vaunted as *the* model for East German literature shortly after it was published, "sought to portray the industrial reconstruction of the GDR."[23]

Socialist realism also colored the development of architecture and the plastic arts in the GDR, with considerable emphasis being placed on the obligation of artists to depict industrial labor, construction sites, agricultural cooperatives, and socialist brigades in positive ways. Music was likewise politicized, as may be inferred from the titles of some of the musical compositions of Hanns Eisler (1898–1962): "Song of Solidarity," "Song of the Unemployed," "Song of the United Front," and "The Comintern," not to mention his 1937 composition, *Requiem for Lenin*. This same spirit infused the assignment undertaken by lyricist Kurt Barthel (1914–67) and composer Jean Kurt Forest (1909–75) to compose a cantata for Stalin.[24] The regime was also determined to combat the hedonism of American and British pop music of the time, such as the "boogie-

woogie," and devised a response in the form of the "new German folk-
song movement," orchestrated by Minister of Culture Johannes R.
Becher and the aforementioned Eisler (who had collaborated in writing
the national anthem). "These folksongs," SED General Secretary Ulbricht assured his listeners in a 1950 speech, "are an expression of what
is beautiful and new in our society. They inspire our youth and working
people to new and greater heights of achievement."[25]

    In terms of the role played by the East German intelligentsia, it is
important to understand that it differed from that in other East European
countries in fundamental ways. On one hand, most of these hostile to the
very idea of socialism chose the "exit" option early on and moved to
West Germany. On the other hand, the country attracted German socialists such as Wolf Biermann and Stefan Heym from the West who were
convinced that they were moving to the better Germany. "Dissent" on
the part of the intelligentsia in the GDR thus took place within a revisionist Marxian paradigm, advocating socialism but disagreeing with the way
in which the SED went about establishing it.[26] The best known group of
dissenters in the fifties was the so-called "Harich group," which suggested that the wholesale application of Soviet-style socialism to East
Germany was inappropriate and advocated an end to ultra-centraliza-
tion, adoption of a more gradual approach to the socialization of the
economy, and the development of a democratic socialist politics both
within the SED and in society as a whole.

    The "exit" mode, on the other hand, was employed by a consider-
ably larger number of citizens. In 1953 alone, 391,390 East German citizens moved West and by the time the Wall was built in Berlin on 13
August 1961, effectively ending the option to "exit" the country, another
one and a half million had left.[27] Roughly half of those who moved West
were under the age of twenty-five, most of them skilled young males.[28]
The Wall thus became a visible reminder of the SED regime's failure to
create even a modicum of legitimacy and stability in the country. Unde-
terred, the SED called the Wall an "antifascist wall of protection" which
was designed to insulate East Germans from their class enemy. While
most East German citizens had the sense of living in a huge prison after
the Wall was built, the SED sought to realize its rigid Leninist vision for
the construction of a socialist society.[29]

THE MIDDLE YEARS: THE ILLUSION OF STABILITY AND PROGRESS

Once the Wall and deadly minefields along the East German–West German border had effectively cut off any means of exiting, the situation
inside the country stabilized. The government sought new methods of
ruling over the population, which itself sought new patterns of accommo-

dation with the regime. The SED replaced open terror with more subtle forms of intimidation, while the majority pretended to go along with the system. The working class expressed its opposition in a massive "go slow" to which the SED responded with constant but futile exhortations for greater effort and higher levels of achievement. This is an interesting contradiction of Hirschman's model, which postulates that once the exit option no longer exists, people will insist on having more of a "voice." Jeffrey Kopstein goes so far as to argue that it was precisely this *passive* everyday resistance that led to "the long-term creeping immobilization" of the SED regime which, in the end, led to its utter defeat.[30]

Officially, of course, there was no need for protest and dissent because classes had been abolished in the GDR and the SED was the organization which represented the interests of all citizens. While public protests were seen as an essential form of political participation in Western bourgeois countries, in the GDR it was seen as unnecessary and indeed a violation of the basic principles of a socialist society.[31] Freedom of expression thus was only acceptable within the limits determined by the SED, the true vanguard of the working class.

The SED's New Economic System dating from 1963 began decentralizing the economic sphere as individual plants were given much greater autonomy and encouraged to compete and to make a profit. These changes were wrapped in appeals to *material* self-interest, to a socialist version of *homo oeconomicus*. The higher the level of material production and consumption, the more successful "socialism" was presented to be.[32] Greater emphasis was also placed on the use of high technology. Skills and competence rather than simple political reliability became relatively more important. This was necessitated by the demands of an increasingly complex industrial society, and the SED embarked on a tightrope act of trying to allow the flexibility demanded by economic growth and technological change while continuing its insistence on monolithic political rule. In cases of conflict, real or imagined, politics won. How to encourage technological innovation within an authoritarian political model was a fatal dilemma which the SED, like other communist ruling parties, was never able to solve.

Much like during the Hitler era, the Church had begun to accommodate itself to the realities of life under a dictatorship, with the general population actively participating in the process. For example, in 1945–55, only 17.7 percent of adolescents participated in the *Jugendweihe*, the SED's response to the traditional Protestant confirmation of its youths at roughly age fourteen. By the late sixties, over 90 percent chose Jugendweihe over a Church-based confirmation.[33] An ever more secularized society and increasing infiltration of the Church by the SED's state security forces, the *Stasi*, inevitably led to ever more accommodation of the Church with socialism; i.e., it became a *Kirche im Sozialismus* (Church within Socialism). In 1969 it broke its official ties with the Protestant Church of West Germany, again part of its policy of accommodation with the SED state. Communism and Christianity were no longer seen as inherently antagonistic.

The main voices of dissent heard during this period came from within the Marxist camp. Robert Havemann, a professor of chemistry at East Berlin's Humboldt University, became a locus for intellectual and political dissent that continued to his death in the early 1980s. A long-time communist who had been imprisoned by the Nazis, Havemann argued that the rigid, Stalinoid political and economic order was antithetical to socialism and impeded its progress. Only with democracy could socialism hope to carry mankind to a higher level of existence.[34] Predictably, Havemann lost his academic position and was expelled from the party. He continued to be a powerful voice of dissent in the country, however, especially after the Warsaw Pact's crushing of the reform efforts in Czechoslovakia, the so-called Prague Spring. In hindsight, the use of this ruthless force and the GDR's participation in it were the turning point for many in the GDR who had hoped that reforms might eventually also be possible in their own country in order to give socialism a more human face.

In May 1971 Ulbricht was replaced as general secretary of the SED by Erich Honecker, a man who had spent the war years in Nazi concentration camps. This move once again was a reflection of massive party insecurity, both vis-à-vis the general population and the Soviet Union. By the early seventies it had become increasingly clear that Ulbricht's leadership style was outdated and the system as a whole in dire need of reform. There is also considerable evidence that Ulbricht had become too self-confident for Moscow and was beginning to alienate not only Soviet but other East European communist leaders with his brash assertions that the GDR was *the* model for building socialism in advanced industrial societies. While Ulbricht had insisted on ruling through intimidation and bombastic promises and demands, Honecker promised a more conciliatory leadership, especially toward the cultural intelligentsia, and insisted that the SED's goals were determined by a concern for the "welfare of the people" (*Alles zum Wohl des Volkes*). This did not mean a liberalization of party discipline, however, and the concept of democratic centralism was even tightened during the Honecker era.

An important example of how little things really changed under Honecker was the case of Biermann, an outspoken poet and balladeer who had moved to the GDR from West Germany. In 1976, he was deprived of his GDR citizenship and prevented from returning from a concert in West Germany. The "Biermann affair" elicited widespread opposition from both within and without the GDR. A large number of the cultural intelligentsia, most of whom heretofore had not directly defied the regime, signed a statement criticizing the decision.[35] Growing disillusionment resulted, not only among the cultural intelligentsia but, more ominously, also among younger members of the party itself. Rudolf Bahro, who published *Die Alternative* in 1977, was one of those disillusioned party members who dared to go public.[36] His powerful and compelling critique of the internal contradictions of the system made impeccable use of Marxian categories, effectively accusing the SED of having subverted Marx's socialist vision. The response of the *apparat* was immediate and ferocious. In the tradition of Lenin and the Bolsheviks he was accused of being an agent of imperialism, arrested, imprisoned, and subsequently expelled.

The growing dissatisfaction among SED rank and file was undoubtedly a reaction also to the changing nature of the party itself. It was increasingly run by "professionals," i.e., by upwardly mobile technocrats who were using their positions to gain personal power and privilege. For example, by 1970, 92.5 percent of the district party secretaries were university graduates, representing a fundamental transformation of a party which had its roots in Germany's industrial working class and which still claimed to be the sole representative of the proletariat.[37]

GROWING CONTRADICTIONS AND THE REAPPEARANCE OF VOICE

At one level, the SED leadership had reasons to be proud of its achievements. By 1973 relations between the two German states had been "normalized" and the *status quo* of a divided Germany appeared finally accepted. Rapid diplomatic recognition by most of the world's countries meant that by the end of the decade the GDR entertained diplomatic relations with 131 states. The country was also being recognized for its longstanding support of various national liberation movements in the so-called Third World, especially with the end of Portuguese colonialism in Africa in the mid-seventies. This, along with the revolution in Ethiopia, meant for the SED that the global "correlation of forces" had decisively shifted in favor of socialism. That also was the message communicated to the East German population, and each state visit by a foreign head of state was used as evidence that the world had finally accepted the GDR as a legitimate member of the international community. Foreign policy thus became an important tool in domestic politics—i.e., building legitimacy for the SED state. Even in the Olympic Games the GDR had distinguished itself, ranking third behind the Soviet Union and the United States—clearly another indication that "socialism" was on the move.

Furthermore, the GDR continued to be a powerful force within the Council on Mutual Economic Assistance (CMEA, also referred to as Comecon in the West), ranking second only to the Soviet Union. The

"complex integration" within the CMEA was functioning reasonably well from the SED's perspective, and roughly two-thirds of the GDR's exports went to CMEA states (fully half of all exports to the Soviet Union alone).[38] In terms of standard of living, the GDR ranked second to none within the Soviet bloc. Consumer items had become more plentiful and almost all East German households now had television sets, washing machines, and refrigerators.[39]

The SED regime had also proven to be effective in silencing opposition and maintaining law and order, while conditions in neighboring Poland became ever more unruly. Nor was it plagued with an organized dissident movement such as that of *Charter 77* in Czechoslovakia. The SED had also successfully prevented the rise of a dissident leader such as Adam Michnik in Poland, Václav Havel in Czechoslovakia, or György Konrad in Hungary whose voices served as important irritants in their respective socialist societies. This is, paradoxically, where the existence of a separate capitalist German state served as an important stabilizing element because "undesirables" could simply be sent into exile across the border. If they were first thrown into prison in the GDR, they could always be "sold" to the West German government, which was willing to pay up to DM 150,000 per prisoner. Dissidents thus also became one of the most profitable hard currency export items for the SED, since up to 1,500 "undesirables" were sent to the West annually in this fashion.[40] This practice, in effect until the collapse of 1989–90, lasted for twenty-six years, during the course of which the FRG "bought" almost 34,000 prisoners for more than DM 3.5 billion.[41] One wonders what might have happened in Czechoslovakia or Poland had there also been a Western (capitalist) counterpart eager to buy dissidents to prove its "moral superiority!"

For the SED, in any case, this arrangement contributed considerably to the illusion of peace and social contentment. In order to transmit its ideas and values, it successfully maintained mass organizations as important tools for political socialization. For example, over half of the population (8.7 million persons) held membership in the only trade union, the Free German Trade Union (FDGB), which was founded in June 1945 but had long since degenerated into simply a transmission belt for communicating SED directives *to* the working class. Likewise, the "Free German Youth" (FDJ) had 2.3 million members and was the most important tool for recruitment into the SED. It also had been founded in the early days of Soviet occupation, in March 1946, and was closely modeled after the Soviet *Komsomol* youth organization. It was symptomatic, however, that in the late seventies, FDJ membership came primarily from upwardly mobile students rather than from members of the proletariat. The latter constituted only a quarter of the total membership.[42]

For leading party cadres there was specialized training in Marxist-

Leninist theory and practice, amounting to little more than catechism classes in the *status quo*. Eighty percent of the SED's party secretaries had received intensive training lasting a minimum of one year in special party academies.[43] Elections produced a virtually complete turnout and the SED and its bloc parties were consistently reelected with over 99 percent of the votes. Small wonder, then, that an "official" historian of the GDR, Heinz Heitzer, was able to describe the situation at the end of the seventies in the following fashion: "The unity of the party, the working class, and the people was firmer than ever before."[44]

On the surface, this rosy picture was rather correct. As mentioned above, East Germany's "silent majority" had long practiced a pattern of passive resistance at the workplace coupled with a retreat into the private sphere. It was in the privacy of their living rooms that they pretended to live on the other side of the Iron Curtain, watching mainly American programs broadcast on West German television. On weekends, they retreated to little country cabins (*dachas*) and tended to small garden plots. The GDR was, in Gaus's words, a quintessential *Nischengesellschaft* in which people retired to their private "niches" and interacted with official East German society only to the extent necessary for physical survival.[45] After the erection of the Wall, they employed the "silent non-exit" mode, which meant that they exercised neither the "exit" option (which in its illegal variant was deadly or, in the legal variant, meant many years of social and economic dislocation while exit visas were being processed by the government) nor that of "voice."[46] These were the days during which public dissent was expressed by rock groups giving themselves English-language names such as "Silly" or "City." East German youths "voiced" their protest by preferring to listen to Western rock music over officially sanctioned East German music, screened for the purity of its commitment to socialist principles by the GDR's chief ideologist, Kurt Hager.[47]

For the SED, art, to be worthwhile, thus, had to be politically useful. Even opera was subject to this expectation, and accordingly, some of the opera produced in the GDR in the 1960s and 1970s treated such themes as war, revolution, racial prejudice, modern capitalism, and fascism—naturally, in a didactic spirit. One of the GDR's best-known operatic composers was Paul Dessau (1894–1979), whose *Puntila* (first performed in 1966) tells the story "of Puntila, [a] representative of the wealthy class of big land-owners . . . and of his relationship with his chauffeur Matti, representative of the proletariat."[48]

The same constraints also applied to the motion picture industry in the GDR. Of all of the mediums, film was the least able to liberate itself from the tight embrace of socialist realism. Whereas literature, theater, and art were all able to push back the limits of the permissible, filmmakers found that their immense influence was, at the same time, a constraint. As Manfred Garbing noted, "[GDR film] should help to shape the ideological-moral psyche of people according to socialist criteria."[49] Be that as it may, the GDR film industry experienced brief periods of thaw from time to time, one of the most tangible being associated with Honecker's accession to the post of general secretary of the SED in 1971. Artists and filmmakers alike drew encouragement from Honecker's address to the Eighth Party Congress in December 1971, when he declared, "If one comes from a firm socialist position, there can, in my opinion, be no taboos in the realm of art and literature."[50]

Ultimately, socialist realism declined not as a function of liberalization, but because its efficacy was increasingly called into question. By the early 1980s, GDR cultural elites entered into a national debate about aesthetics and the lack of "true heroes" in fiction and film.[51] It was, however, not so much the goals of GDR cultural policy that were changing, as the specific means and strategies authorized. This was clear enough from Honecker's comments in the course of a 1984 address, in which he reminded his listeners, "Our time needs works of art which strengthen socialism, which call into consciousness the beauty and greatness of what has been achieved, often with difficulties."[52]

The beginning of the end for "the first socialist state on German soil" could well be placed in the year 1949. It took four decades, however, until the contradictions at all levels of society led to a rapid deterioration, culminating in the opening of the Wall on 9 November 1989. Three factors were particularly instrumental in the collapse. The first is the state of the East German economy; the second, changes inside the GDR itself, particularly with regard to a redefined role of the Evangelical Church and the birth of an independent "peace" movement; and the third, the most important external factor, the coming to power of radical communist modernizers in the Soviet Union under the leadership of Mikhail Gorbachev.

(1) The East German economy had gotten off to a difficult start. While West Germany became a showcase for capitalism, funded generously by the American Marshall Plan,[53] the Soviets dismantled machinery and entire industrial plants, especially in heavy industry, and shipped them home as reparation for the extensive damage inflicted by Nazi Germany. This was in line with the agreements reached at the allied conference in Potsdam in July 1945; the policy of expropriation and removal was not officially stopped until 1 January 1954. Since reparations were only taken out of the Soviet zone, the East German population felt they alone were being held responsible for the crimes committed by the Nazis in the Soviet Union. This sense of being "victims," of consistently finding themselves on the wrong side and thus punished by history, persists among East Germans to the present.

During its forty-year existence, the GDR was never able to catch up with capitalist West Germany. The only two areas in which it excelled were in providing full employment and incorporating women into the labor force. In 1989, 91 percent of all women between the ages of fifteen and sixty were either working or in training, while the corresponding number for the Federal Republic was only about 50 percent.[54] How one looks upon these differences clearly depends on one's ideological preference: from the logic of capitalist production, employing more people rather than investing in better technology makes little sense, as it dramatically reduces competitiveness on world markets. If, on the other hand, the priority rests with providing jobs for all, including women, then the GDR was clearly superior to West Germany in this regard. The difficulty for the SED was that it sought to provide both full employment *and* competitive products, objectives which ultimately proved irreconcilable.

By the early eighties it became clear that the East German economy was running out of steam. While incredible technological advances were revolutionizing the production process in the capitalist world, all of the centrally planned economies were losing their competitiveness, in terms of both quality and price, on the world market. Newly emerging capitalist competitors such as Asia's "little tigers" produced with the most advanced technology, while little had changed in the labor-intensive production techniques within the CMEA. In an effort to rectify this deficiency, the SED leadership, like its counterparts in other East European countries, had embarked on an economic program in the mid-seventies which called for borrowing hard currency in the West, purchasing Western technology with it, and repaying these loans through hard currency exports. This plan succeeded only to the extent that it brought the country huge hard currency debts to Western lenders, amounting to $14.9 billion by the end of 1981. This debt was reduced to $11.2 billion by 1984, but at a severe cost to domestic consumption and investment.[55] In hindsight it is clear that the East German economy in the early eighties faced imminent collapse, a condition which, paradoxically, was temporarily delayed by a huge hard currency loan from Bonn.[56] Stalin's insistence in the early fifties that a separate socialist world economy had been created in the Soviet bloc clearly had been proven an illusion by the early eighties.[57]

André Gunder Frank argues that it was the fundamental failure to compete in the global economy which directly led to the collapse of 1989. As he put it:

> Had the East German economy not faltered in the 1980's, both absolutely and relative to that of West Germany, there would have been little movement of "democratic" opposition against the regime. The wall and then the regime itself would not have come down.[58]

It is without doubt true that economic failure greatly contributed to the general level of dissatisfaction inside the GDR in the eighties. What Frank ignores, however, is the question as to *why* the GDR was not able to generate new technology *internally*. It is here that politics and economics in communist societies were linked in a deadly symbiosis. A system which rewards above all political loyalty and punishes any type of independent thinking is ill equipped to come up with innovations of any type.[59] Minefields might be good for keeping inhabitants inside the country against their will, but they also allow human innovation and curiosity to atrophy. Staying technologically competitive would have required the Communist Parties of Eastern Europe to eschew their monolithic control over all aspects of political *and* economic life. That is why, ultimately, the economy of the GDR and all other East European countries failed. In this sense, Frank confuses cause and effect.

(2) The birth of the independent "peace movement" which ultimately swept the SED from power coincided with a renewed intensity of the East-West conflict. It was also fueled by many of the issues discussed in the West German Green Party, including increased awareness over ecological devastation and true equality for women. The dissident groups that began to emerge in the late seventies and early eighties had several defining characteristics that separated them from their predecessors. First, they came almost completely from the generation that had grown up under socialism. They had known neither fascism nor war nor the privations of postwar reconstruction. Second, in terms of social category many of those involved began to blur the distinction between worker and intelligentsia. Many of the new activists, while workers, were simultaneously part of an alternative, countercultural intelligentsia; theology students, musicians, artists, writers, filmmakers, etc. who had been able to carve out a precarious niche on the fringes of GDR society. They were *Aussenseiter* who largely owed their subsistence and social security to the system which they despised and had resisted. Third, these younger people had absorbed many of the ideals associated with socialism—peace, fairness, equality, women's rights, freedom, third world solidarity, a rejection of most features of Western capitalism—even if it was a socialism they had never experienced. Fourth, they did not situate their no-less-fundamental critique of "actually existing socialism" within the Marxist paradigm. In their experience Marxism (most of the time interchangeable with the words socialism and communism) was a set of slogans, policy application, dictatorial rule, and political cant they had come to despise. Marx and the ideas of Marxism were not so much wrong as irrelevant.[60]

The new dissidents never worked out a comprehensive program, either collectively or individually. Instead, the various groups represented a collection of ideas. Demands and proposals were made by a larger number of autonomous groupings that often worked in cooperation with similar like-minded groups, thus gradually creating an informal opposition network.[61] This was greatly facilitated by the increasingly bold effort of the Protestant Church,[62] particularly individual pastors, to support the dissident movement. While the Church never assumed the same level of importance as did the Catholic Church in Poland, for example, it did provide moral support as well as physical meeting space for various dissident groups. By the fall of 1989, churches such as the Nikolai Kirche in Leipzig had become central to the effort to force the SED into concessions and, finally, defeat.[63]

It is important to understand that the groups that collectively made up the *Bürgerbewegung* (citizens' movement) never struck deep roots among the masses. The same limitation faced by the SED in the process of state-building—i.e., the lack of a cohesive nationalism—prevented unity with the general population. The dissidents could appeal only to highly abstract moral imperatives and universal principles since they themselves had categorically rejected the legitimacy of nationalism. Although they rejected the bureaucratized and centrally planned economy installed by the SED and its Soviet mentors, the dissidents were also anticapitalist and rejected the rampant consumerism of the West. In many ways, their ideological counterpart was the West German Green Party, which also had its origins in various grassroots movements.[64] The East German dissidents wanted the continuation of the GDR, but in a "new and improved" variety, and were wholly unprepared for the fervent nationalism which emerged once the SED state had collapsed.[65] One of the campaign slogans of the conservative alliance in the election in March 1990 clearly captured the response of the East German masses to those who had been instrumental in bringing down the SED regime: "No more experiments!"

(3) The same social and economic forces that brought about reform efforts in Poland, Czechoslovakia, and Hungary also produced, *mutatis mutandis*, the rise of Gorbachev in the Soviet Union in 1985. What is of concern for the purposes of this chapter is the impact of Gorbachev's reform policies on the entire Soviet bloc in general and East Germany in particular. Once Gorbachev rescinded the Brezhnev Doctrine, thus signaling his willingness to work with a new generation of reform communists, the handwriting was on the wall for the GDR leadership. The SED, experienced with "protecting" its citizenry from Western publications and propaganda through its policy of *Abgrenzung*, now found itself squeezed between two fronts. No longer did the SED slogan *ex oriente lux* ("the light comes from the East") express party sentiments, while the East German population suddenly began to look to the Soviet Union in the hope of bringing about concrete changes in the GDR as well. As early as June 1987, young East Germans chanted "Gorby, Gorby" in East Berlin when they were prevented by police from listening to a rock concert taking place on the other side of the Wall. By November 1988, the SED regime saw itself forced into canceling the German version of the sud-

denly popular Soviet publication *Sputnik* because of its "subversive" influence on GDR citizens.[66] Gorbachev to the end unsuccessfully sought to enlist the SED leadership in his efforts to reform communism in Eastern Europe. His final warning came while attending the forty-year anniversary of the GDR on 7 October 1989. History punishes those who stay inflexible in light of changing circumstances, he admonished an unconvinced SED leadership. One month later that entire old guard would no longer be in power.

THE FINAL COLLAPSE AND THE MARCH TOWARD UNIFICATION

The beginning of the end came on 2 May 1989 when the Hungarian government decided to open its border with Austria. This "Green Border" captured the world's attention throughout the summer of 1989 as tens of thousands of East Germans, officially in Hungary as tourists, chose to exercise the "exit" option in a near stampede.[67] Much of the panic stemmed from the fact that the majority of East Germans were convinced that the SED was absolutely unwilling to make any meaningful changes in the country's political system.

It was at this point that the various groups which constituted the "independent peace movement" began ever more openly to challenge the absolute power of the state. On 10 September, *Neues Forum* was founded as an independent opposition group. Mass demonstrations began to take place every Monday evening in Leipzig, the GDR's second-largest city. The rallying cries centered on an emphatic rejection of the emigration option (*Wir bleiben hier*—we are staying here) as well as an insistence that the political process be democratized (*Wir sind das Volk*—we are the people). With each Monday evening, the crowds got larger and the mood ever more daring. On 9 October the SED decided to put a forceful stop to these demonstrations but in the end was unable to carry through these plans.[68]

The speed with which the SED collapsed in the following weeks was stunning. The aborted effort to crush the growing rebellion culminated in the ouster of Honecker on 18 October to be replaced by Egon Krenz, a high party functionary who had been sent to Beijing a few months earlier. Growing numbers of rank-and-file members resigned in protest over the leadership's unwillingness to agree to meaningful reforms. On 4 November one million East Germans demonstrated in East Berlin, calling for more democracy and freedom. The situation in the country was now clearly completely out of control. The politburo was bitterly divided and on 8 November the entire old guard resigned, making way for reform-minded party members. On 9 November at 6:57 P.M., the information spokesman for the party announced that all East German borders were now open for unimpeded travel by any citizen who so chose. A phase of history ended as tens of thousands of East and West Berliners celebrated the opening of the Wall throughout the night.

It was in the following five short months that the fate of the GDR was decided. The SED, ever more in disarray and now clearly no longer in charge of the country, dismissed Krenz on 13 November and replaced him with Hans Modrow, the Dresden Party leader and a Gorbachev-type reformer. Honecker, along with the other members of the old guard, was expelled from the party on 4 December. Krenz himself resigned from all official party and government functions on 6 December. Two days later the party renamed itself SED/PDS (Party of Democratic Socialism) and Gregor Gysi, an attorney, became its new general secretary.

Under the auspices of the Protestant Church, representatives of the ever more discredited SED/PDS, various opposition groups, the newly created East German Social Democratic Party (SPD)[69] as well as the bloc parties met at a "round table" on 7 December in order to discuss the country's future. They agreed to new elections to take place on 6 May 1990. The SED was clearly not governing under a popular mandate. The citizens movement was too fragmented and neither practically nor ideologically prepared to constitute itself formally into a political party. The CDU, FDP, and LPD, which had collaborated with the SED throughout, now scrambled to disown this complicity and to present themselves as "victims" worthy of popular support.

In the following weeks, as these various groups sought to come up with viable election platforms, the mood inside the country changed dramatically. The population continued to stir. Before the opening of the Wall, opposition to the SED and the Monday demonstrations called for more access to the political process, expressed in the slogan *Wir sind das Volk* (We are *the* people). Now, as the future of the country was being contemplated, a new breed of demonstrator emerged, shouting the nationalist slogan of *Wir sind ein Volk* (We are *one* people). Now that the SED state had collapsed, the desire of the average East German was to become as West German as possible, which meant joining the Western consumer society as quickly as possible. The discussion thus shifted away from what type of East Germany to rebuild and instead to what the terms of unification should be and how quickly they might be implemented. On 29 January 1990 Modrow, as interim head of the government, suggested the election date be moved forward to 18 March in an attempt to stabilize the situation inside the country.

As the country prepared for the election, nearly three dozen different political parties emerged, of which fourteen united into five different alliances. Thus, twenty-four political parties and electoral alliances competed for the 12.2 million eligible voters. Among these various parties and alliances, two broad groups emerged whose defining characteristics ultimately came down to their position on unification with the "other" Germany. The right-of-center *Allianz für Deutschland* (Alliance for Germany), made up of the (East) Christian Democratic Party (CDU), *Deutsche Soziale Union* (German Social Union—DSU), and *Demokratischer Aufbruch* (Democratic Awakening—DA), was most vehement in its demand for unification. After some initial waffling on the issue, the Eastern Social Democrats also joined the pro-unification side, as did the Liberal Party. This camp was also increasingly aided by West German sister parties, including an impressive amount of personal campaigning for the CDU on the part of West German Chancellor Helmut Kohl.[70] The second group was comprised of those forces inside the GDR that were reluctant to underwrite a simple merger of the two German states. They sought to retain as much sovereignty for their country as possible in order to prevent what they saw as a simple surrender to the more powerful Western brother. This camp included the PDS, an amalgam of the various former dissident groups running for the election as *Bündnis 90* (Alliance 90), as well as a newly formed green/feminist coalition.

On 18 March 1990—119 days after the Wall was opened—the East German people participated in the first reasonably free elections held in those regions since 1933. Voter turnout was at 93.22 percent, a clear indication of the level of personal commitment the people of East Germany attached to the event. The election granted a massive victory to the pro-unification forces, with the Christian Democrats winning the largest number of seats. *Bündnis 90* and the green/feminist coalition combined did not even get 5 percent of the votes.

The domestic stage was thus set for a rapid unification of the two Germanies. Two options were available for the unification process itself, and both were written into the *West* German Basic Law (*Grundgesetz*): Article 23 simply called for the incorporation of East into West Germany, while Article 146, recognizing the provisional intent of the *Grundgesetz*, called for its repeal and the creation of a new constitutional framework once the country was reunited. This was clearly intended to give expression to the hopes and expectations of the German people from both sides of the previously divided country. The postelection mood in both parts of the country was overwhelmingly in favor of Article 23, however, and those calling for adherence to Article 146 were looked upon as troublemakers.

Thus the main problem remaining for Lothar de Maizière, the head of the newly elected East German CDU government, was how to negotiate the absorption of his country into West Germany while the GDR was formally a member of the Warsaw Pact and the FRG a member of NATO. De Maizière was clearly the junior partner to Kohl and his foreign minister, Hans Dietrich Genscher, who now became the leaders of the unfolding unification process. The GDR officially ceased to exist on

3 October 1990, when it was incorporated into the Federal Republic
under Article 23 of the West German constitution.

POSTUNIFICATION EASTERN
GERMANY—FROM NATIONALIST DREAM TO
ECONOMIC AND SPIRITUAL NIGHTMARE

Nancy Bermeo has argued that simply having experienced and opposed
dictatorship does not automatically make people pro-democratic. Re-
democratization takes place in the phase *after* a dictatorship itself has
been overthrown. Thus second phase, she argues, is crucial for the future
of democracy itself; i.e., political learning leads to cognitive changes
which are in support of democratic values and ideals.[71] It is experiences
gained *after* the revolution which are thus most important for the future
of democracy in such a society. Seen from this perspective, reunification
under Article 146 would ultimately have contributed more to the cause
of democracy in East Germany. Although the debates about a new all-
German constitution would undoubtedly have been cumbersome and
messy, the process itself would have involved a great deal of necessary
political learning for both sides. It also might have prevented a growing
sense among the East German population of simply having been annexed
by an uncaring and overpowering bigger brother.[72]

Hannelore Horn, in looking at the events in the GDR in 1989–90,
also insists on the importance of the "winding down phase" in any revolution. It is during this phase that experimentation with new conceptions
for state and society takes place and the objectives of the revolution are
consolidated.[73] Lessons from previous revolutions tell us that a certain
level of dissatisfaction and irritation are normal during this phase, as
society embarks on a new and autochthonous path toward the future.
Horn argues that all post-communist societies of Eastern Europe are currently in this phase. In the former GDR, on the other hand, the revolution
abruptly ended with unification, thus depriving the East German population of this crucial experience.

These two theoretical attempts at understanding what happens in the
aftermath of any revolution might begin to explain some of the profound
dissatisfaction among the East German population which has accompanied the postunification era. The GDR simply ceased to exist, as the entire West German political, economic, legal, and social apparatus was
imposed on the Eastern part of the country as though it were a *tabula
rasa.* The fact that the majority of East Germans had voted for this an-
nexation by giving the pro-unification forces an overwhelming share of
their votes was forgotten as more and more people developed a sense of
having been colonized by West Germany.[74]

After unification it also became evident that a heavy price was attached to the "silent non-exit" option exercised by the majority of East Germans between 1953 and 1989. Public life in the GDR was marked by a particular type of human discourse and interaction, one characterized by suspicion and lack of both self-confidence and individuality.[75] Conformity meant the forfeiture of ethics, of permanently living a lie. This "system of lies," which was at the core of all communist societies of Eastern Europe, prompted Havel to write about "his attempt to live a life of truth."[76] Without this willingness on the part of dissidents, the reemergence of civil society would not have been possible anywhere in the Soviet bloc. Now that the "system of lies" has collapsed formally, its legacy at the psychological level and the deformations which it produced in human discourse continue to haunt post-communist societies. Its most obvious manifestation in the former GDR has been the search for scapegoats, for finding and punishing those "responsible" for the many injustices committed during the SED era. In this fashion, the same population which chose the "silent non-exit" mode is seeking to exculpate itself of its complicity in forty years of communist dictatorship.

On the other hand, unification with the "other" Germany enormously complicated the process of psychological healing for East Germans. They simultaneously had to cope with the introduction of a very aggressive political and ruthless economic system, their absolute subordination to *Besserwessis*, the complete negation of the value of their past life experiences, and overcoming the effects of almost six decades of dictatorship on their soil. Rare exceptions notwithstanding, West Germans have not shown much sensitivity to these feelings. Indeed, in conservative West German circles, the old GDR appears to have become the scapegoat for past German sins, for exorcising the demons of the Third Reich. In this new demonology, the forces of evil in German history now were commanded by people named Ulbricht and Honecker, not just Hitler and Himmler. This "relativizing" of twentieth-century German history has meant the construction of a new "usable past" in order to make German nationalism acceptable again, now that the forces of evil have been destroyed.[77]

For East Germans, the practical result of unification was that everything they had learned in the past was now obsolete and how they did everything was negated. Civil servants from the old FRG were exported to the East to teach the *Ossis* how to do things from now on. Even five years after unification, most supervisory and managerial positions in the government bureaucracy were still held by *Wessis*. The same was true for most top positions in research and academic institutions. Since leading positions had previously belonged to loyal members of the SED, a massive purge took place after unification to "purify" the country of ideological undesirables. Replacements were generally chosen in the West, deepening the resentments of those in the East.[78] The GDR's printed and electronic media were likewise either simply taken over by West German enterprises or closed down.

Even "privatization," that magical solution to post-communist woes, has created in East Germans the sense of being deprived of the just fruits of their past labor. While in most other East European countries individual citizens have at least gotten the legal right to purchase, or to receive on a grant basis, stock in former "people's owned enterprises," the East German economy was sold to the highest bidders through a special institution, the *Treuhandanstalt* in Berlin. Although founded under the Modrow communist caretaker government on 1 March 1990 with the charge of overseeing the transition from a centrally planned to a market economy, the *Treuhandanstalt* has become the symbol of Western domination over the old GDR. Charged with selling off 32,400 enterprises in the former GDR, from restaurants to grocery stores to chemical plants, *Treuhand* automatically became an institution of the Bonn government after unification. The East German government under Modrow had claimed that the total value of this property would amount to between DM 1 and DM 1.6 trillion. According to a detailed study undertaken by two West German economists, the official value of net fixed assets in the GDR was 1.745 trillion marks.[79] Calculations made by the Institute for Applied Economic Research in Berlin, which took into account the obsolete and often noncompetitive nature of East German capital stock, put the value of fixed assets at only 576 billion marks.[80]

However, the privatization of the GDR's economy turned into a dramatic loss. By the time the *Treuhand* closed its doors on 31 December 1994, it had received roughly DM 65 billion from the new owners of the privatized enterprises, while spending DM 155 billion for restructuring these enterprises before selling them off.[81] This stunningly low level of return from the privatization of East Germany's industrial stock has led to a lot of criticism of the *Treuhand*. Günter Grass, in his controversial new novel, *Ein Weites Feld*, has made the *Treuhand* the main target of his attack on the nature of German unification. Otto Kohler, a German journalist, points out that the *Treuhand*'s board of directors reads like a "Who's Who" of West German industry. This explains, in his view, the "liquidation" of East German industry with the twin purposes of preventing it from competing with West German companies while simultaneously opening up the East German market for these firms.[82] East Germans thus feel cheated by a West German state that promised them prosperity, not just freedom from the SED dictatorship.

An additional factor contributing to the discontent in the former GDR is the degree of economic decline and deindustrialization which has taken place since unification. Between 1990 and 1992 GDR fell by 33 percent, while production output in the processing industries fell by 64

percent and in agriculture and forestry 50 percent during the same time period.[83] There are a number of factors which contributed to this decline. As explained above, two-thirds of the GDR's exports went to other CMEA countries. When hard currency was introduced to the GDR with the monetary union on 1 July 1990, the country's products now suddenly had to compete with those of other hard currency countries. This, along with the CMEA's subsequent total collapse, caused much of the drop in demand for East German products.

Coupled to this decline in East German industrial production was a gradual adjustment of East German wages to those earned in the western part of the country. As pointed out by Hans-Werner Sinn, an early critic of the process of economic unification, this wage adjustment was pushed by West German trade unions as well as employer organizations in order to protect the *West German* standard of living and economic status quo.[84] Not recognizing the fatal impact this dramatic increase in wages would have on their jobs, East Germans readily concurred. The West German market economy had been introduced literally overnight, as the entire country became part of the West German deutsche mark zone in the night of 30 June to 1 July 1990. For the average consumer this meant that prices instantly reflected West German levels, while wages remained those of the old GDR, about 35 percent of those in the West. Real wages did increase by 94 percent between 1990 and 1992, but employment declined by 37 percent during the same period (from 9.35 million to 5.86 million). Even six years after unification, the employment situation had not improved, with the official unemployment at 15.5 percent while an additional 10 percent of the workforce received its wages from public funds, so-called "work creation measures."[85]

Seventy percent of all those who lost their jobs were women.[86] Particularly unskilled female workers and women over age forty-five have been affected by mass unemployment and their chances of ever finding work again are slim to nonexistent.[87] At the same time, many of the day-care facilities built up under the SED were also closed and other fringe benefits relating to parenthood either dramatically reduced or cut altogether, again to the particular disadvantage of working mothers.[88] This is not to argue, of course, that the SED had effectively ended patriarchal structures in the GDR and offered women opportunities on equal footing with men. Women's status has always lagged behind men's and unification with the capitalist West only intensified existing structures of discrimination. It is little wonder, then, that women have borne a disproportionate share of the social and economic disaster which has followed unification.[89]

While the population in the Eastern part of the country thus faced massive job insecurity, the situation in the Western part also deteriorated with the onset of the most severe recession since the Second World War. This was coupled with an unprecedented level of public deficit spending, reaching DM 1.67 trillion, or 55 percent of GDP, by the end of 1992, caused primarily by unification.[90] It was now clear that the Kohl government had rushed the country into political union without any sense of the grave consequences for the social and economic security of people in both East and West. Since then, the Bonn government has sought to cut back public spending, mainly by reducing the social safety net. The (West) German *Sozialstaat* has been the foundation of much of the German population's sense of solidarity with the (West) German state. The cost of unification, which in the first five years meant a transfer of DM one trillion in public funds to the East, is now used as an excuse to cut back on everything from the age of retirement to job protection measures. The planned introduction of this "savings package" led to the largest postwar demonstration in Bonn on 15 June 1996, when 350,000 Germans took their concerns to the streets.

What the communist government was unable to accomplish in four decades, the experiences since unification have achieved easily: the creation of a separate and distinct East German identity. Suddenly, Germans in both parts of the country have become aware that forty-five years of separation have left their mark, not only on consciousness but also on the language used to express it.[91] With the first euphoria gone, Germans now face themselves across a new divide: one that expresses itself not in minefields but in a vastly different way of seeing the world and of interacting at all levels of society. People in the former GDR feel humiliated by the experiences gained after unification and many are nostalgic for the old East German way of life. West Germans, on the other hand, yearn for a return to the days when their only worry revolved around where their next vacation would be. Massive economic as well as psychological insecurity and the need to find convenient scapegoats have been key reasons for the ugly attacks on foreigners and a general upsurge in xenophobic violence in Germany over the past few years. Unification thus suddenly thrust the question of national identity back into the forefront of political discourse in Germany.

The prospects are thus not bright for Germany, especially in the short and medium term. If nationalist sentiments cannot be generated to compensate for the real sacrifices necessary to bring the East up to Western standards, there is no telling what road the angry mood in both parts of the country will take. On the other hand, should nationalism succeed, it is a road well traveled in Germany and one that has brought untold misery to people on the entire continent. Thus, while a renewed spirit of nationalism would certainly facilitate the successful completion of the unfinished process of unification, it might well turn into a menace for Europe and the world. What began so happily on that long-ago night in November 1989 thus far has not turned into a promise for a better tomorrow. The specter of communism continues to haunt Europe.

Notes

1. For a classic exposition of this model, see Martin Wight, *International Theory: The Three Traditions* (New York: Holmes & Meier, 1992), esp. Chap. 3, 5, and 6.

2. These concepts have been a standard part of the literature on political development. See, for example, the seminal works of Gabriel Almond and Samuel P. Huntington, as well as a penetrating critique of these works in Irene L. Gendzier, *Managing Political Change: Social Scientists and the Third World* (Boulder: Westview, 1985).

3. The model of a totalitarian society is traditionally one in which a centralized political power intrudes into all aspects of political, economic, social, cultural, and intellectual life. For a fuller discussion, see Ernest A. Menze, ed., *Totalitarianism Reconsidered* (Port Washington, N.Y.: Kennikat, 1981). With regard to "post-totalitarianism" in Eastern Europe, see Marcia A. Weigle and Jim Butterfield, "Civil Society in Reforming Communist Regimes," in *Comparative Politics*, Vol. 25, No. 1 (October 1992).

4. Albert O. Hirschman, *Exit, Voice, and Loyalty: Responses to Declines in Firms, Organizations, and States* (Cambridge: Harvard University Press, 1970).

5. Weigle and Butterfield, "Civil Society in Reforming," 3.

6. Immanuel Wallerstein, "The World-System after the Cold War," in *Journal of Peace Research*, Vol. 30, No. 1 (February 1993), 4.

7. Most communist activists were either killed, incarcerated, or driven into exile within the first three months of the Nazi seizure of power. For a detailed account of this period in German history, see Gunter W. Remmling, "The Destruction of the Workers' Mass Movements in Nazi Germany," in Michael N. Dobkowski and Isidor Walimann, eds., *Radical Perspectives on the Rise of Fascism in Germany, 1919–1945* (New York: Monthly Review Press, 1989), 215–230.

8. Hermann Weber, *DDR: Grundriss der Geschichte 1945–1990* (Hamburg: Fackelträger, 1991), 31.

9. Günter Gaus, *Wo Deutschland Liegt: Eine Ortsbestimmung* (Hamburg: Hoffmann und Campe, 1983).

10. Weber, *DDR: Grundriss*, 32.

11. Ibid., 34.

12. As William Graf has convincingly shown, it was precisely this willingness on the part of the German population to support broad anticapitalist measures which informed the reluctance of the United States and Great Britain to lift their respective bans on German political activities and parties in their respective zones of occupation immediately after the war. See William D. Graf, *The German Left since 1945: Socialism and Social Democracy in the German Federal Republic* (Cambridge: Oleaner, 1976), 21–27; and Mike Dennis, *The German Democratic Republic* (London: Pinter, 1988), 13–16.

13. *Vorgeschichte und Entstehung der DDR. Der Anfang vom Ende* (Bonn: Friedrich-Ebert-Stiftung, 1989), 23.

14. Ibid., 17.

15. For a very useful summary of this transformation, based on hitherto secret SED files, see Dietrich Staritz, "Die SED, Stalin und die Gründung der DDR," in *Aus Politik und Zeitgeschichte*, Vol. 91, No. 5 (25 January 1991), 3–11.

16. Norman M. Naimark, "Forty Years after: The Origins of the GDR," in *German Politics and Society*, Issue 17 (Summer 1989), 10–11.

17. Weber, *DDR: Grundriss*, 50–51.

18. Peter Jochen Winters, "Was bleiben wird," in *Deutschland Archiv*, Vol. 22, No. 9 (September 1990), 1313.

19. For an account based on secret SED files of the uprisings, see Armin Mitter, "Die Ereignisse im Juni und Juli 1953 in der DDR: Aus den Akten des Ministeriums fur Staatssicherheit," in *Aus Politik und Zeitgeschichte*, Vol. 91, No. 5 (25 January 1991), 31–41.

20. For a fuller discussion, see Christoph Klessmann, "Opposition und Dissidenz in der Geschichte der DDR," in *Aus Politik und Zeitgeschichte*, Vol. 91, No. 5 (25 January 1991), 55.

21. For an excellent discussion of the evolution of Church-state relations in the GDR, see Mary Fuller, *Anatomy of a Dictatorship: Inside the GDR 1949–1989* (Oxford: Oxford University Press, 1995), especially Chap. 4 ("Render unto Caesar? The Pivotal Role of the Protestant Churches"), 87–125.

22. Quoted in Dennis Tate, *The East German Novel: Identity, Community, Continuity* (New York: St. Martin's, 1984), 39.

23. Ibid., 46.

24. Ibid., 26.

25. David Bathrick, *The Powers of Speech: The Politics of Culture in the GDR* (Lincoln: University of Nebraska Press, 1995), 178.

26. See Günter Minnerup, "East Germany's Frozen Revolution," in *New Left Review*, No. 132 (March/April 1982), 5–32.

27. Weber, *DDR: Grundriss*, 295–305.

28. Ibid., 95.

29. For a discussion and critique of this model, see William W. Hansen and Brigitte H. Schulz, "Was jetzt tun? Leninismus, Sozialismus, und Demokratie," in T. Bergmann, W. Hedeleere, M. Kessler, and G. Schafer, eds., *Leninismus in Theorie und Praxis: Historische Perspektiven* (Mainz: Decaton Verlag, 1994).

30. Jeffrey Kopstein, "Chipping away at the State: Workers' Resistance and the Demise of East Germany," in *World Politics*, Vol. 48, No. 3 (April 1996), 422.

31. For a full discussion of the official SED view, see Roger Woods, *Opposition in the GDR under Honecker, 1971–85* (New York: St. Martin's, 1986), Chap. 1.

32. This degeneration of the socialist/communist vision into naked consumerism in the twentieth century is analyzed and critiqued in Herbert Marcuse's *One-Dimensional Man: Studies in the Ideology of Advanced Industrial Society* (Boston: Beacon, 1964).

33. Fuller, *Anatomy of a Dictatorship*, 97.

34. This argument is a recurring theme in all of Havemann's writings. See, for example, his essays "Sozialismus und Demokratie" and "Der Sozialismus vom morgen," in Robert Havemann, ed., *Ruckantworten an die Hauptverwaltung "Ewige Wahrheiten"* (Munich: R. Piper Verlag, 1971).

35. For an excellent discussion of dissent in the GDR, see David Bathrick, "The Politics of Culture: Rudolf Bahro and Opposition in the GDR," in *New German Critique*, No. 15 (Fall 1978), 3–24.

36. Rudolf Bahro, *The Alternative in Eastern Europe*, trans. from German by David Fernbach (London: NLB, 1978).

37. Weber, *DDR: Grundriss*, 102.

38. Hermann von Berg, "Wirtschaftsprobleme der DDR," in Hermann von Berg, Franz Loeser, and Wolfgang Seiffert, *Die DDR auf dem Weg in das Jahr 2000* (Cologne: Bund Verlag, 1987), 66–75.

39. For more specific statistics, see Weber, *DDR: Grundriss*, 164–165.

40. Timothy Garton Ash, *"Und willst Du mein Bruder sein . . ." Die DDR heute* (Reinbek bei Hamburg: Rowohlt Taschenbuch Verlag, 1981), 18.

41. Peter Ferdinand Koch, *Das Schalck-Imperium lebt: Deutschland wird gekauft* (Munich: Piper GmbH, 1992), 124.

42. Weber, *DDR: Grundriss*, 159–160.

43. Ibid., 155.

44. Heinz Heitzer, *GDR: An Historical Outline* (Dresden: Verlag Zeit im Bild, 1981), Chap. 4 ("The further development of advanced socialist society, 1971–1978"), esp. 225; also Gabriele Eckart, *So sehe ich die Sache: Protokolle aus der DDR* (Cologne: Kiepenheuer & Witsch, 1984).

45. See Gaus, *Wo Deutschland Liegt*, 156–233.

46. The term "silent non-exit" was borrowed from Brian Barry, "Review Article: 'Exit, Voice, and Loyalty,' " in *British Journal of Political Science*, Vol. 4, Part 1 (January 1974), 91.

47. For an interesting selection of translated texts of East German rock music, combined with an elegant analysis, see Olaf Leitner, "Rock Music in the GDR: An Epitaph," in Sabrina Petra Ramet, ed., *Rocking the State: Rock Music and Politics in Eastern Europe and Russia* (Boulder: Westview, 1994), 17–40.

48. Gordon Tracy, "Opera of the 1960s and 1970s in the GDR," in Margy Gerber, et al., eds., *Studies in GDR Culture and Society* (Washington: University Press of America, 1981), 244.

49. Quoted in "Filmwesen," in Zimmermann, ed., *DDR Handbuch*, Vol. 1, 389.

50. Quoted in Sigrun D. Leonhard, "Testing the Borders: East German Film between Individualism and Social Commitment," in Daniel J. Goulding, ed., *Post New Wave Cinema in the Soviet Union and Eastern Europe* (Bloomington: Indiana University Press, 1989), 52.

51. Ibid., 74.

52. Quoted in Ibid., 75. For further discussion of cultural policy in the GDR, see Joachim Streisand, *Kulturgeschichte der DDR* (Cologne: Paul-Rugenstein Verlag, 1981); and Günther Rüther, ed., *Kulturbetrieb und Literatur in der DDR* (Cologne: Verlag Wissenschaft und Politik, 1987).

53. For a detailed account of America's postwar geopolitical objectives and West Germany's role in this, see Melvyn P. Leffler, *A Preponderance of Power: National Security, the Truman Administration, and the Cold War* (Stanford: Stanford University Press, 1992). On the effects of the Marshall Plan on West German economics and society, see Charles S. Maier and Gunter Bischof, eds., *The Marshall Plan and Germany: West German development within the framework of the European Recovery Program* (Oxford: Berg, 1991).

54. Rainer Geissler, "Soziale Ungleichheit zwischen Frauen und Mannern im geteilten und im vereinten Deutschland," in *Aus Politik und Zeitgeschichte*, Vol. 91, No. 14/15 (29 March 1991), 14.

55. Michael C. Kaser, "The Economic Dimension," in Edwina Moreton, ed., *Germany between East and West* (Cambridge: Cambridge University Press, 1987), 132.

56. Koch, *Das Schalk-Imperium*, 22–27. Koch documents how the SED sought to avoid the inevitable through cheating, lying, and actively collaborating with the "class enemies" in the West.

57. See André Gunder Frank, "The Socialist Countries in the World Economy," in Brigitte H. Schulz and William W. Hansen, eds., *The Soviet Bloc and the Third World: The Political Economy of East-South Relations* (Boulder: Westview, 1989), 9–26.

58. André Gunder Frank, "No Escape from the Laws of World Economics," in *Review of African Political Economy*, No. 50 (March 1991), 27.

59. For an account by a leading East German scientist and dissident, see Jens Reich, "Wissenschaft und Politik im deutschen Einigungsprozess," in *Aus Politik und Zeitgeschichte*, Vol. 91, No. 5 (22 February 1991).

60. For a fuller analysis of these groups, see William Graf, William Hansen, and Brigitte Schulz, "From *the* People to *One* People: The Social Bases of the East German 'Revolution' of 1989," in Hermine G. DeSoto and David G. Anderson, eds., *The Curtain Rises: Rethinking Culture, Ideology, and the State in Eastern Europe* (Atlantic Highlands, N.J.: Humanities Press, 1993).

61. For a very useful collection of documents and other relevant information on this topic, see Gerhard Rein, ed., *Die Opposition in der DDR. Entwurfe für einen anderen Sozialismus* (Berlin: Wichern Verlag, 1989).

62. Regarding the confessional distribution, see Roland Smith, "The Church in the German Democratic Republic," in David Childs, ed., *Honecker's Germany* (London: Allen & Unwin, 1985), 68.

63. Karl Cordell, "Political Change in the GDR: The Role of the Evangelical Church," in *International Relations*, Vol. 10, No. 2 (November 1990), 161–166.

64. In May 1993, the party representing a significant remnant of the old GDR *Bürgerbewegung, Bündnis 90* and the West German Green Party indeed merged.

65. Bärbel Bohley, one of the leading dissident figures in the late 1980s, is quoted as reacting to the opening of the Wall by exclaiming: "The people are crazy, and the government has lost its senses." See Detlef Pollack, "Das Ende einer Organisationsgesellschaft," in *Zeitschrift für Soziologie*, Vol. 19, No. 4 (August 1990), 305.

66. In line with its general policy of dishonesty, the official explanation was that the country was suffering from a severe paper shortage and thus could no longer afford to print *Sputnik*. Other Soviet magazines, however, such as those targeting sportsmen, anglers, etc., continued to be produced.

67. By the end of September 1989, more than 25,000 East Germans had gone West via Hungary. Additional numbers sought refuge in West German embassies in Czechoslovakia and Poland. When the Wall was opened, some 40,000 East Germans immediately fled westward. See Weber, *DDR: Grundriss*, 344–345.

68. For an account of this day in Leipzig, see Christoph Links and Hannes Bahrmann, *Wir sind das Volk: Die DDR im Aufbruch—Eine Chronik* (Berlin and Weimar: Aufbau Verlag, 1990), 15–19.

69. The SPD-Ost was founded on 8 October 1989, effectively canceling the "unity" agreement with the communists. See Micha Wimmer, et al., *Wir sind das Volk! Die DDR im Aufbruch*, 2nd ed. (Munich: Wilhelm Heine Verlag, 1990), 60.

70. On the eve of the election, Chancellor Helmut Kohl went so far as to call on East Germans to vote for the construction of a "free and united Germany in a free and united Europe." See *Süddeutsche Zeitung* (Munich), 17/18 March 1990. For an analysis of how the Kohl/CDU-West political bulldozer orchestrated and manipulated the 18 March election, see Gunter Minnerup, "Kohl Hijacks East German Revolution," in *Labor Focus on Eastern Europe*, No. 1 (1990), 4–13.

71. Nancy Bermeo, "Democracy and the Lessons of Dictatorship," in *Comparative Politics*, Vol. 24, No. 3 (April 1992), 273–275. See also Stephanie Lawson, "Conceptual Issues in the Comparative Study of Regime Change and

Democratization," in *Comparative Politics*, Vol. 25, No. 2 (January 1993), 183–203.

72. Unification brought a string of new expressions into the German language, including *Ossi* (an East German), *Wessi* (a West German), and *Besserwessi* (which is a pun on *Besserwisser*, meaning a know-it-all).

73. Hannelore Horn, "Die Revolution in der DDR von 1989: Prototyp oder Sonderfall," in *Aussenpolitik: Zeitschrift für internationale Fragen*, Vol. 44, No. 1 (January 1993), 56–65.

74. Dorothy Rosenberg, "The Colonization of East Germany," in *Monthly Review*, Vol. 43, No. 4 (September 1991). For a challenge to this position, see Brigitte Schulz and William Hansen, "A Critique of Rosenberg's Thesis on Colonialism in East Germany," in *Monthly Review*, Vol. 44, No. 1 (May 1992).

75. Hans-Joachim Maaz, "Psychosoziale Aspekte im deutschen Einigungsprozess," in *Aus Politik und Zeitgeschichte*, Vol. 91, No. 19 (3 May 1991).

76. Václav Havel, *Versuch, in der Wahrheit zu leben* (Reinbek bei Hamburg: Rowohlt Taschenbuch Verlag, 1989).

77. Günter Grass has some interesting observations on this aspect of unification, as well as the rise of nationalism and xenophobia, in "On Loss: The Condition of Germany," in *Dissent*, Vol. 40, No. 1 (Spring 1993), 178–188.

78. For the difficult process of "mental unification" of the two Germanys, see, for example, Michael Lukas Moeller and Hans-Joachim Maaz, *Die Einheit beginnt zu zweit. Ein deutsch-deutsches Zwiegespräch* (Berlin: Rowohlt Verlag, 1991); and Reinhard Bobach, "Mentale Konversion? Kulturelle Aspekte der deutschen *Vereinigung*," in *Deutschland Archiv*, Vol. 26, No. 1 (January 1993), 7–20.

79. Gerlinde Sinn and Hans-Werner Sinn, *Jumpstart: The Economic Unification of Germany* (Cambridge: MIT Press, 1992), 67.

80. Ibid., 67.

81. *Fünf Jahre der Entscheidung. Deutschland nach dem Kriege, 1945–1949* (Frankfurt: Akademische Verlagsgesellschaft, 1969), 22–23.

82. Otto Koehler, *Die grosse Enteignung: Wie die Treuhand eine Volkswirtschaft liquidierte* (Munich: Knaur, 1994).

83. "Structural Changes in Eastern Germany," in *Transition: The Newsletter about Reforming Economies* (Washington: The World Bank), Vol. 4, No. 1 (February 1993), 8.

84. *Der Spiegel* (Hamburg), 17 June 1996, 114.

85. "Institute: Eastern Growth Will Remain Modest," in *The Week in Germany* (New York: German Information Center, 28 June 1996), 5; and *taz* (Berlin), 27 July 1996, 1.

86. See *Süddeutsche Zeitung*, 26 March 1993 and *Der Standard* (Vienna), 21 May 1993.

87. For a detailed analysis of the situation of women in postunification Germany, see Renate Schmidt, Sabine Berghahn, and Andrea Fritzsche, *Nach der Vereinigung Deutschlands. Frauen fordern ihr Recht* (Bonn: Friedrich-Ebert-Stiftung, 1991). For an overview of the situation of the female labor force in the former GDR, see Anneliese Braun, "Welche Perspektiven für die Hälfte der Frauen? Zur Sozialen Lage in den 'neuen Ländern,' " in *Das Argument*, No. 199 (May/June 1993), 381–392.

88. "Erwerbsverläufe der Deutschen in Ost und West in den Jahren 1949 bis 1989," in *DIW Wochenbericht*, Vol. 60, No. 16 (22 April 1993), 207–211.

89. For an interesting analysis of the SED's policy vis-à-vis women, see Ingrid Arbeitlang, "Wie befreiend war die DDR-Frauenförderung? Analyse rech-

tlicher und sozioökonomischer Regelungen," in *Das Argument*, No. 198 (March/ April 1993), 231–240. Arbeitlang's conclusion is that "in the GDR the foundation of patriarchal structures was identical to those of market oriented industrial societies. . . . The understanding of equality did not contain the notion of equal value, but rather the women's acceptance of a patriarchal hierarchy of values" (239). Thus, for the author, the fate of women in postunification Germany is the logical consequence of the continuation of patriarchy in the SED state and society.

90. *Süddeutsche Zeitung*, 12 May 1993.

91. For an interesting account of how the German language itself developed along different paths in East and West Germany, see Horst-Dieter Schlosser, "Deutsche Teilung, deutsche Einheit, und die Sprache der Deutschen," in *Aus Politik und Zeitgeschichte*, Vol. 91, No. 17 (19 April 1991).

6

Poland

JACK BIELASIAK

The 1989 revolutions in Eastern Europe swept away the forms of governance that prevailed over a period of forty-five years under communist rule. The postrevolutionary task was to create institutions, rules of behavior, and codes of political action that redefined the relationship between the authorities and society. The formation of a new political system was not new to the region, which has been an arena of political experimentation during most of its history.

Poland is a primary example. For 125 years the country disappeared from the map of Europe, partitioned by neighboring empires. During that time, its identity and historical continuity were assured by institutional modes vested in society, not the polity. Culture, language, family, Church, tradition were the guardians of Poland. Only with the recovery of independence in 1918 could the nation return to the formation of indigenous political institutions. Since that time, the question that defined the political development of the country centered around the types of governing structures that best served the interests of the nation. After a brief interlude of democracy, the country turned to an authoritarian regime. World War II once again claimed the independence of Poland, which reemerged after 1945 under the dominance of the Communist Party. For the next decades, the state and elements of society engaged in an attempt to define the relationship between rulers and ruled, a struggle punctuated by recurrent crises and confrontations throughout the period of communist rule.

These crises defined the postwar history of Poland by restructuring the relationship between the authorities and the citizenry. They did so by affecting, often altering, the institutional setting that mediates politics through redefinitions of formal organizations and informal roles, political procedures and behavior norms that govern the relations between the state and society, as well as among groups in the polity. For that reason, the political development of Poland can best be understood through the actions of political actors, their strategies for change, the processes of coalition building, and forms of political opposition, especially as defined by the cycle of crises.

BACKGROUND

Between 1795 and 1918, Poland did not exist as an independent state.[1] During this time of partitions among the Russian, Prussian, and Austrian empires, Polish society preserved its identity as a cultural nation by safeguarding its traditional institutions: family, literature, Church were the primary tools in the struggle for independence against the foreign state. The period was punctuated by repeated episodes of heroic rebellion to restore the Polish state to serve the Polish nation. The First World War forced the withdrawal of empires from Eastern Europe, and enabled the restoration of Polish independence in 1918. The newly formed countries of Eastern Europe faced daunting tasks of modernization to secure a strong state, economic viability, social peace, and political stability.

The territory of the new Poland was inhabited by several national groups, besides the majority Polish community which accounted for about two-thirds of the state's population. In addition, significant minorities of Ukrainians, Germans, Byelorussians, and Jews were part of the resurrected country. The first task was the integration of these diverse nations and cultures into a common state identity, a policy that led to substantial conflicts between the majority and minority populations during the interwar years. The situation was aggravated by the economy which was largely agrarian, underdeveloped and dependent, and adversely affected by the Great Depression. Domestic politics were thus permeated with the issues of national and minority rights, economic security, and political expression. The state, through its government and bureaucracy, became the driving force for the resolution of the problems. The fragile structure of democratic institutions was incapable of meeting the challenge, and soon (1926) succumbed to the personalized authoritarian regime of Marshall Jozef Pilsudski.

One the eve of the Second World War, the 23 August 1939 Nazi-Soviet Pact led to the "fourth partition" of Poland. The country was subject to a brutal occupation by Nazi Germany, with subhuman treatment of its population, the annihilation of its Jewish minority—by means of systematic isolation in ghettos, brutal slave labor in concentration camps, and mass murder in extermination camps—and Soviet repression of its intellectual and professional classes, as in the execution of thousands of Polish officers in the Katyn forest.[2] Once again, the population rallied to the defense of the Polish nation through the formation of resistance movements that dramatically affected the postwar political outcome. The prewar authoritarian system was discredited by the failure to safeguard the country. Instead two rival movements advocated new political solutions. The underground Home Army was allied with the Western powers, and represented political parties committed to a democratic future. The Union of Polish Patriots had strong backing from the Soviet Union and advocated a communist future.

The Home Army's attempt at self-liberation during the Warsaw Uprising of August 1944 failed due to lack of Soviet support. Instead the Soviets used the Red Army to establish communist power throughout Eastern Europe. Through coercion, the promise of economic reconstruction, and international acquiescence to a Soviet sphere of influence in Eastern Europe, the communist takeover was completed in the 1944–48 period. Poland altered not only its political but also its physical shape, as territories on the east were incorporated into the USSR, and Poland was compensated by former German territories in the west. The need to secure recognition for the new Oder-Neisse border and the "recovered provinces" in the West became a rallying point for the communists and the population. The geopolitical transformation, on top of the devastations produced by the war, re-created a Poland that shed its former diversity into a near ethnic and religious homogeneity. Although some minority groups were still present, communist policy in the ensuing years sought to deny their ethnic and cultural identity.

On the domestic front, the communists moved to sweep away the vestiges of the old political order through military and coercive measures that bordered on civil war in some rural parts of the country.[3] The principal target was the Peasant Party, whose leader Stanisław Mikołajczyk had substantial support for rebuilding a democratic Poland. In accord with the Yalta agreements, and due to Western backing, Mikołajczyk was included as vice-premier in the postwar coalition government, although as part of a dominant communist majority. Through pressure tactics and overt intimidation, Mikołajczyk and his party were increasingly isolated and finally outmaneuvered in the manipulated elections of 19 January 1947. Thereafter, the communists were in control of the state and moved to establish control over the country.

By 1948 communist political consolidation was completed, but led to a bitter ideological struggle within the ruling party over the relative merits of a strict Soviet model or a milder Polish way to socialism. The intraparty conflict culminated in the denunciation of Władysław Gomułka, the head of the party in the underground during the war, for

Jelada 4)

"nationalist deviationism" and led to his expulsion from the party. The
purge signaled an end to the "national communism" approach in building a new socialist society through gradual changes taking into account
specific Polish traditions, such as the strong influence of religion. Instead
the victorious leadership implemented a policy emulating the Stalinist
model of development. This consisted of a rapid transformation of the
economic and social base through an emphasis on heavy industrialization
and central planning, the collectivization of agriculture, the suppression
of independent cultural norms, the use of coercion and psychological terror, and strict adherence to Moscow's interests on the international front.

During this time, at the height of the Stalinist period in the early
1950s, the communist leadership made a concerted effort to eradicate
trends in Polish tradition and culture that impeded progress toward a
socialist society. These efforts, however, proved less systematic and coercive than in other parts of Eastern Europe, allowing some vestiges of
cultural expression to remain outside the strict standards of Soviet doctrinal orthodoxy. The Church came under attack, and the primate of
Poland, Stefan Cardinal Wyszyński, was imprisoned in September 1953.
Yet, unable to destroy the influence of the Church and religion in Polish
society, the regime sought to establish alternative Catholic organizations
loyal to the government, the best known of which was PAX. In this conflict, the state did not succeed in eroding the hold of religion on the population. On the contrary, the Church became ever more the symbol of the
nation and of its moral independence.

Still, in order to influence the citizenry, organizations such as PAX
were provided with a degree of cultural autonomy unheard of in the hey-
days of Stalinism. The official stance in the cultural realm was that of
"socialist realism," placing a requirement on the creative intelligentsia
to produce works that glorified the accomplishments of the masses, the
working class, and the economic and social breakthrough to a new socialist society. Many writers, composers, painters, and film and theater-
directors succumbed to the requirement of harnessing their creative efforts to the cause of the class struggle and the building of socialism. Polish culture was controlled through strict censorship in literature, theater,
and the arts. Yet alongside the works of socialist realism, there was room
for independent cultural activity as well. Some artists and university professors were allowed to pursue work free of ideological content. This
ambiguity in cultural policy was again clearly evident in the publishing
activity of PAX, which was permitted to print not only prayer books but
also works by prominent Polish and Western authors otherwise unavail-
able in Poland, or elsewhere in Eastern Europe.

Still, the attempted imposition of the Stalinist mode of development
on the Polish nation had profound consequences throughout the history
of socialist Poland. The issues debated during the 1948 intraparty conflict

came to haunt the country again and again through several political crises over the next decades. The crises led to overt defiance of the communist authorities over both the economic priorities and the political course embraced by the state. In the socioeconomic realm, the confrontation was over the policy of favoring capital accumulation and heavy industrialization over investments in consumption, the provision of consumer goods, and a fair wage bill. On the political front, the opposition was to the penetration of party and state institutions into the private lives of the citizenry. Throughout, social groups expressed resentment of the Soviet dominance of the country. Time and time again, these issues were expressed by waves of popular discontent.

THE CRISES OF COMMUNISM

The first attempt at political restructuring occurred in the aftermath of Stalin's death in March 1953 and the ensuing process of de-Stalinization through the region. The new Soviet leadership realized that coercive Stalinist methods could not be sustained, and thus moved to reshape both the relations between the Soviet Union and its East European allies and the course of socialist transformation taking place in the East European states. The shift in the center's policy provided the opportunity for the Polish people to push for further changes.

Two distinct variants of opposition came into being in the mid-1950s. The first was an expression of political and cultural discontent, carried forward primarily by the intellectuals. They sought to restore human dignity to socialist transformation by the introduction of greater freedoms of expression and independence in private lives. Through writings and discussion clubs, the effort led to a cultural thaw that benefited the creative social strata. For example, in August 1955, the poet Adam Ważyk published "Poem for Adults." The title is not a reference to a pornographic message, but to a serious, i.e., adult, theme: a scathing denunciation of Stalinist political and economic practices, and a call for major political reforms allowing greater freedoms to the people of Poland. Similar demands were heard from numerous creative circles, which together produced a chorus of political criticism and renewed cultural independence.

A second wave of discontent was motivated by demands for improved living conditions. The workers' cry was felt most intensely on 28 June in Poznań, where strikes and street demonstrations ended with suppression. Nonetheless, the incident did prod the leadership to institute changes that in turn opened the way for social initiatives. In the workplace, it led to the formation of workers' councils as representative of labor's interests. The self-management movement echoed the faith of the intellectual classes in the reformation of the system.

Both trends of discontent found common ground in demands for greater autonomy from Soviet domination. The popular outcry reached its crescendo in October 1956, in conjunction with the rehabilitation of Gomułka as first secretary of the PUWP, despite initial Soviet opposition to his restoration as head of the ruling party.[4] The people's mood was hopeful, in the belief that the new leadership would bring about major changes. Popular expectations centered not only around improvements in living standards, but also in greater freedoms and substantial autonomy from Soviet domination.

Gomułka's return to power was thus critical in defusing the 1956 political crisis, for it was interpreted by the population as a commitment to de-Stalinization and a Polish way to socialism. Moreover, the successful defiance of Soviets' preferences created a feeling of unity among the leadership, the party, and the nation. The initial transformations gave credence to the optimism of October, as the Catholic Church was allowed to pursue religious practices, Cardinal Wyszyński was released from prison, and peasants were able to decollectivize agriculture.

In the face of events that suggested the erosion of communist power, Gomułka moved quickly to assure the party's dominance. Paradoxically, his popularity among the population was used to reaffirm the "leading role of the party" in society. By the late 1950s, many gains obtained during the October days were revoked, e.g., workers' councils were incorporated into the central system of management and cultural freedoms were curtailed through tighter censorship. Gomułka's rule became the "little stabilization," the rejection of a major transformation of society in favor of the status quo safeguarded by a guarded, authoritarian political style. The little stabilization succeeded in maintaining political order for the next decade, but at heavy costs to the country. The neglect of fundamental social and economic tasks resulted in economic stagnation and a decline in the standard of living. Once more, dissatisfaction among the population rose and precipitated new crises at the end of the 1960s.

The unrests were preceded by a mounting critique of the Gomułka regime. Frustrated by the lack of political initiative to deal with the economic and social needs of the country, intellectuals began to criticize the party-state. Most notable at the time were the activities of discussion clubs, such as the Clubs of the Catholic Intelligentsia (KIK), youth and student organizations engaged in political debates, and the writings in "semi-independent" Catholic publications, such as *Tygodnik Powszechny* and *Znak*. This intellectual effort was directed at first at persuading the communist party leadership to embark on a more reformist and tolerant course. This appeal to revisionism proved futile, as the regimes pursued a repressive cultural policy. In turn, the situation forced a more open and defiant strategy on the part of the intelligentsia. At the beginning of 1964, thirty-four prominent writers, scholars, and artists signed

the "letter of 34" decrying the government's cultural policy and demand-
ing less censorship and more open publications. Soon thereafter, two
young academics, Jack Kuron and Karol Modzelewski, wrote the "Open
Letter to the Party," denouncing the bureaucratic nature of socialism in
Poland and demanding more democratic, self-governing political rule.
The government responded with strong denunciations and arrests.

Nonetheless, the growing ferment among academic, cultural, and artistic circles, along with the enlightenment represented by the Prague
Spring in neighboring Czechoslovakia, produced student protests in
March 1968.[5] While the demonstrations were largely confined to university and intellectual communities, the incidents were used by hardline
party leaders, the "Partisans," to launch a campaign to reinforce their
position in the corridors of power. The thrust of the move escalated into
a major anti-Semitic and anti-intellectual maneuver. The consequence
was an intraparty factional struggle that forced Gomułka to bring
younger, better-educated technocrats into leadership positions to counterbalance the hardline Partisans and safeguard his hold over the party.

The 1968 conflict had a profound effect on the social and political
life of the country. In the first place, it made clear that the party was not
an enlightened, self-reforming organization committed to a humane type
of socialism. The intellectuals' faith in such a revisionist concept was
shattered, contributing to a more overtly oppositionist role for many
members of the community. Second, the incident revealed the isolation
of the diverse social groups in Poland. March 1968 proved to be a conflict among the upper strata of society, between the intelligentsia and the
party elite. The working class remained outside the conflict, concerned
foremost with material issues. Third, the political infighting within the
party broke the immobilism of the little stabilization, forcing several policy initiatives. For example, the state provided further concessions to the
Church to practice its faith. In turn, Catholic bishops were instrumental
in arranging a reconciliation between Poland and West Germany, and the
treaty of December 1970 recognized the existing Oder-Neisse boundaries
between the two countries.

The social and international successes were not matched by economic ones. Gomułka's policies had contributed to severe economic
problems, and drastic action was needed to rectify the situation. A reform
was launched requiring sacrifices on the part of the blue-collar workers,
through an end to state subsidies for food and a price increase of up to
30 percent just ten days before the 1970 Christmas shopping spree. The
workers' response was immediate: strikes and demonstrations erupted in
the shipyards of the Baltic coast, spreading to other industrial centers.[6]

The workers' demands focused on economic matters but went beyond these to seek guarantees for a "voice" in policy issues. The failure
of the post-1956 self-management path directed labor's attention to the

formation of free trade unions capable of protecting worker interests against state demands. (This 1970 attempt to redefine the institutional structure of communism failed, for three primary reasons.)

First, the working class's concern was foremost economic in nature. When price increases were rescinded after a second wave of strikes in early 1971, the primary demands of the working population were attained. Second, the blue-collar element was largely isolated from the other social groups in Poland. The professional class was a beneficiary of the economic reform, and the intelligentsia and the students were more concerned with civil rights. Third, the party leadership was able to use carrot-and-stick techniques of crisis-management that applied coercive measures and promises of future improvements to defuse the crisis.

The transfer of political power from Gomułka to Edward Gierek on 19 December 1970 was an early tactic to contain unrest, just as was the 1956 leadership change in favor of Gomułka. Gierek had been first secretary of the Katowice province since 1957, where he developed a reputation for efficient and dynamic stewardship. Neither the reputation nor the tactic was sufficient during the 1970 crisis, as the people no longer had faith in their leaders, and unrests continued. Only the subsequent change in policy, the reversal on price increases, assured tranquility.

The basic task of the new leadership was to rebuild the social fabric by moving beyond stop-gap measures to calm working class unrest.[7] To that end, Gierek embarked on a "new political style" strategy involving a dual track. One was to improve the economic conditions of the country and on that basis achieve social reconciliation between the regime and the people. The other was to use the anticipated success in economic and social endeavors to consolidate the position of the party in society.

The cornerstone of the policy was a rapid drive for economic modernization, played out during the first half of the decade. The idea was to "build a second Poland" through the renovation of the industrial plant, higher priority to the agrarian sector, and better provision of consumer goods. The drive was heavily dependent on aid from the West, in the form of credits, know-how, technology, and machinery. The Gierek regime opened the economy to outside influence in the belief that the absorption of Western methods of management and Western financing would culminate in higher efficiency and performance of the Polish economy, leading to its status as the "new Japan." Instead, the centralized and bureaucratic nature of the command economy precluded such improvements. While the infusion of Western goods and credits did provide for a temporary amelioration in the living standard, it did so at heavy costs to the economy as a whole. Poland was saddled with an ever-growing debt to Western creditors, which contributed to rapid deterioration of economic conditions in the second half of the decade.

Alongside the economic strategy, Gierek pursued a social strategy of incorporation. This involved a political style that appealed directly to the workers for their help, travels around the country to meet factory crews, consultations with representatives of other social groups, and a renewed state-Church dialogue. Overall, Gierek's new political style was based on a combination of consumer communism and political corporatism to assure social stability.

By the mid-1970s, the perception of success in both areas led to a new course of political consolidation to assure the dominance of the party over society. In this, the regime appeared motivated by the need to emulate the Soviet bloc's emphasis on a higher ideological stage, "developed socialism," that demanded greater commitment to socialist construction. At the same time, Gierek needed to guard against possible repercussions from détente in East-West relations and the 1975 Helsinki Accords' emphasis on human rights. Thus to guard against potential instability and confident in its past success, the Gierek leadership embarked on an ideological offensive to secure the leading role of the party in the country. For that purpose, several steps were taken to secure regime control, including administrative restructuring that reinforced the power of the PUWP over the state administration, the control of the center over regions, and the organizational merger of mass organizations.

Most significant in this context was the revision of the country's constitution. In October 1975, the government proposed a series of amendments—all aimed at strengthening the position of the communist party through formal inclusion of the "leading role of the party" principle, the declaration of Poland's "unshakable fraternal bond" with the Soviet Union, and the linkage of citizens' rights to the performance of their duties to the state—aimed at curbing the rights of practicing Catholics in the atheist state. The consequence was a chorus of opposition involving denunciations by the Episcopate from the pulpit, appeals by intellectuals for freedoms of conscience and expression, an outcry of public opinion, and even criticism in the Sejm, the Polish parliament. In the face of mounting public pressures, the leadership had to withdraw from its heavy-handed approach to impose ideological conformity. The constitutional changes were toned down, but the episode emerged as an indication of the growing schism between the regime and influential sectors of society.

The precarious situation produced by the constitutional crisis at the turn of 1975–76 was dramatically reinforced by an ensuing attempt at economic streamlining. The regime's consolidation policy precluded administrative decentralization as a viable option. Instead, the emphasis was on improved cost efficiency through a decrease in subsidies and an increase in prices. The step was taken without adequate preparations among the public, with devastating results for the regime. The official

announcement of price increases on 24 June 1976 was greeted by immediate workers' strikes and protests, first in Ursus and Radom in central
Poland, then in other parts of the country. Well aware of the December
1970 precedent, when the Gomułka leadership lost power as a result of
workers' actions against price rises, Gierek's team rescinded the price
increases on the following day, 25 June 1976. The communist leadership
was safe for the moment, but the working class was once again able to
alter the policy preferences of the ruling elite.

The Gierek regime, aware of its loss of credibility as a result of the
constitutional debacle and working class defiance, sought to reclaim
some prerogatives by moving against the activists of the June protests
through work dismissals, arrests, and trials. But in the atmosphere of
increased alienation of social groups from the regime, the workers received substantial aid from the intellectual and professional communities. In September 1976, the Committee for the Defense of Workers
(KOR) was formed with the specific aim of providing financial and legal
help to the accused workers. This illegal organization acted as a catalyst
for the formation of closer ties between the intelligentsia and the working
class, and for the proliferation of dissident movements throughout society. In view of its continued mismanagement of the economy, its dependency on Western credits, and its political vulnerability, the Gierek
regime had little choice but to tolerate the new phase in Polish political
life.

In 1977, KOR expanded it activities to cover all sectors of society,
renaming itself as the Committee for Social Self-Defense—KSS "KOR."
Simultaneously, in the late 1970s, numerous dissident associations came
into being, such as the Movement for the Defense of Human and Social
Rights (ROPCiO), the Confederation of Independent Poland (KPN), and
various Catholic and student organizations. The proliferation of social
dissent also affected the activism of the labor class. The 1970 and 1976
worker rebellions made apparent that official trade unions and self-management conferences were inadequate venues for the expression of
worker demands. To rectify the situation, worker activists formed a Free
Trade Union movement in the Baltic cities in 1978—with Lech Wałęsa,
an electrician in the Gdansk shipyard, as a founding member. Similarly,
in the countryside, peasant self-help circles emerged as alternatives to
the official structure of power. The growth of independent movements
contributed to a more activist role of the Catholic Church, fueled in turn
by the selection of Karol Cardinal Wojtyła of Kraków to the papal throne
in October 1978. The pope's visit to his homeland in June 1979 provided
an important stimulus to the confidence of society and dissident circles.

By the end of the decade, for the first time since 1956, a congruence
of dissatisfaction existed among several sectors of society, involving intellectuals, workers, peasants, and priests. Most significantly, the discontent

was being openly expressed through political activism, i.e., the formation of opposition and self-organization associations outside the communist system. While the various social strata were motivated by different primary interests, all had common cause in the expansion of civil rights and freedoms. To such purpose, a new strategy of political change emerged at the time. Former expectations of change from above through reformist acts by the authorities were abandoned in favor of a strategy of change from below, through the actions and pressures of society upon the regime. This program of "new evolutionism"[8] was articulated forcefully by prominent intellectual dissidents, including Adam Michnik and Kuron. Their aim was to devise an alternative "anti-politics" style of social action that was dramatically different from the stagnant politics of the communist party-state. The basis of new evolutionism was the formation of a civil society outside the official polity through the construction of an independent society composed of self-organized groups such as KOR and Free Trade Unions, the establishment of independent publications, and the advocacy of openness in all social endeavors. The fundamental belief was that such an approach would produce meaningful political change, a civil society independent of the communist party-state.

THE SOLIDARITY PERIOD

The activation of society contrasted with the stagnation of the official policy. By the late 1970s, the economy was in shambles: severe shortages of consumer goods prevailed in the streets of cities and towns, long lines in front of stores were a prominent feature of the urban landscape, and an already restive population was becoming more dissatisfied. In 1979, when the country's growth rate became negative, the severity of the economic situation was evident to all.

The government had to act. To salvage the economy, reliance on Western goods had to be lowered, productivity improved, and demand curtailed. Once again, short of a major move to decentralization and marketization, subsidies had to be lowered, wages stabilized, and prices increased. Well aware of workers' reaction to such policy steps, the Gierek leadership launched at the Eighth PUWP Congress a propaganda campaign of austerity, aimed at convincing the population of the need to accept economic setbacks. On 1 July 1980, the government announced price increases of meat products.

Once again, the government's expectations were thwarted by worker reactions.[9] Labor was unwilling to absorb economic costs for past government failures, and factory crews throughout the country went on strike to demand higher wages as compensation for the price rises. Over the next weeks, strikes erupted throughout the country, reaching the Baltic coast in mid-August. There the demands of the workforce moved beyond economic issues to demand social and political concessions. The workers' rebellions in 1956, 1970, and 1976, as well as the self-organization of the 1970s, had a clear effect: long-term benefits to the population depended not only on immediate governmental concessions in the economic sphere, but also on political concessions guaranteeing the independence of the working class.

The organized, disciplined form of workers' action forced the government to accept the 21 Demands of the Gdańsk Interfactory Strike Committee (MKS), under the leadership of Wałęsa, as a settlement for the entire country. The demands called for the establishment of independent trade unions, for the right to strike, for the provision of civil liberties, and for the improvement in living standards. On 31 August 1980, the Gdańsk Accords between the workers and the government recognized the validity of all the demands.

The Accords sanctioned the establishment of the first free trade union in the communist world, which took the name of NZSS SOLIDARNOŚĆ— the Independent, Self-Governing Trade-Union Solidarity. Chapters of the union began to emerge throughout the country, and its membership eventually reached close to ten million, the majority of the working class in Poland.

The formation of Solidarity challenged the monopoly and legitimation of communist rule, since both the party and the trade union claimed to represent the true interests of the working class. The competing claims were solved theoretically in the language of the August Accords by distinguishing between the state and society: the party had a "leading role in the *state*" in contrast to the "leading political force of *society*" defined in the constitution. Solidarity recognized the distinction through its formula of the "self-limiting revolution," disclaiming any interest in sharing state power. The self-limitation provision was meant to relieve Solidarity from responsibility for the problems of the economy, as well as to serve as a guarantee to Soviet interests in safeguarding the organizational primacy of the PUWP in Poland. The August 1980 formula was also a reflection of the new evolutionism strategy to disassociate society and the nation from the party and the state. Solidarity's slogan "Let Poland Be Poland" conveyed the message that the true Poland was to be found among the people, and not the government.

From the very beginning, however, the regime's position was to appropriate the process of change under the guise of a "renewal" policy that recognized past mistakes and aimed at new beginnings. As in past incidents of social unrest, a change in the top political leadership was depicted as a primary example of the new line. Gierek, just like Gomułka in 1970, fell victim to the workers' discontent, and was replaced as first secretary on 6 September 1980 by Stanisław Kania. The new leadership defined renewal as a new phase in the economic and social adjustment of the country, a policy directed from above by the regime. The official concept of renewal was at odds with the position of Solidarity and other independent organizations, which looked upon the post-August period as an opportunity for popular involvement in societal issues.

During the sixteen months of Solidarity's legal existence, the two sides confronted the issue in numerous incidents. On 24 October the regime unilaterally inserted "the leading role of the party" phrase into Solidarity's bylaws, to subordinate the trade union to the communist organization. To prevent such a step, Solidarity had recourse to a general warning strike. The incident came to characterize much of the subsequent period, when the implementation of the provisions signed in Gdańsk was subject to a tug of war between the regime and Solidarity. Issues concerning free Saturdays (from work), the independent status of farmer and student organizations, access to the media, or educational reform repeated the pattern: the regime sought to limit or delay the evolving pluralization of society, and the working class and other groups responded by prodding the government into action through work stoppages, strikes, and protests. This produced a cycle of confrontations that reinforced the level of tension in the country in 1980–1981.

During the 1980–81 Solidarity period two independent spheres of social and political action existed side by side, one embodying the values and interests of society and the nation, the other clinging to the prerogatives of the party-state. For Solidarity and the independent society it symbolized, the entire period was a feast of cultural renewal, the rediscovery of truths, and open political discourse. Publications free from the mantle of communist "truths" proliferated across the country, turning to subjects previously taboo. Most significant in this process was a return to history, and the redemption of historical events and developments denied or slanted by the communist censors. Personalities and events hidden behind closed doors or in underground publications emerged into the open: Marshal Piłsudski, the Home Army, the Warsaw Uprising, Russian-Polish relations graced the pages of journals, magazines, and newspapers. Similar recounting flourished along other dimensions as well, including the devastation of the economy and the environment, the suppression of social traditions, and the treatment of the Church. The cultural blossoming also turned to the West, with the translation of important writers in the literary, historical, and economic fields into Polish. The opening was not restricted to high culture only, as popular music and fiction from the West came to influence the cultural renaissance in Poland.

The existence of two distinct social and political spheres in the country produced a growing stalemate between the regime and Solidarity, subjecting the party itself to pressures for change. In the spring and summer of 1981, the PUWP's rank and file sought to alter the party's power structure through "horizontal linkages" among primary party organizations at the enterprise level, thereby bypassing the vertical top-down controls exercised by the political center. The attempts at democratization of party life provoked strong opposition at home and from abroad. The party bureaucracy reacted strongly in defense of the status quo, by overt resistance to innovations and the formation of orthodox groups in defense of the party's Leninist position. The growing divisions within the PUWP alarmed further the Soviet leaders, who made their dissatisfaction clear through a series of steps that included military maneuvers on the Soviet-Polish border, and an official letter in June 1981 that denounced Kania's methods and his inability to control social unrest. Under the circumstances, the Ninth Extraordinary Party Congress in July 1981 failed to produce the expected breakthrough to move beyond the impasse. Instead, despite heated open debates at the congress and more democratic procedures, no economic reforms were inaugurated to stem the tide of deterioration and establish a new political line of cooperation with Solidarity.

In an effort to move beyond the state-society impasse, Solidarity assumed a more forceful self-management stance in order to take on greater responsibility in economic management. The position was not without controversy among the union's leadership, although the collapse of the economy and social infrastructure led to the endorsement of the policy by the first Solidarity Congress in September and October 1981. At the same time, the delegates appealed to the government for an anticrisis agreement to resolve the problems of the country.

The response of the authorities was motivated more by fear of a further erosion of its power as a result of the self-management drive against the nomenclature system of appointments and controls. The PUWP leadership thus embarked on a policy of consolidation, through a hardline stance in negotiations with Solidarity, through media denunciations of counterrevolutionary activities within the movement, and through preparation for military action. The new spirit was epitomized by the replacement of Kania as head of the PUWP on 18 October by General Wojciech Jaruzelski, who assumed the post while maintaining his positions as prime minister and minister of defense. The clear intent of the change was to replace what was seen by the party's Central Committee as a weak leadership with a strongman capable of defending the position of the party and the state.

THE MARTIAL LAW PERIOD

Ultimately, that task was accomplished by force. The party was too weak to inflict its will on a self-organized society. Instead, Jaruzelski was instrumental in imposing martial law over the country on 13 December 1981 through the use of military and security forces to suppress the Solidarity movement.[10] The arrest of Solidarity and opposition leaders, the banning of the trade union and other independent organizations, and the imposition of strict censorship and other social controls put an end to the sixteen months of open social activism that had characterized Polish life since the rise of Solidarity. While Solidarity as a legal force disappeared from the political life of the country, it reemerged as an underground organization committed to independent trade unionism. The people as a whole became disillusioned with politics, and more cynical about public life and the future. Young people in particular had little faith in the system, and many turned toward alternative music and lifestyles for solace. At the same time, an extensive oppositional culture took root throughout society, finding shelter in churches and private homes, and giving expression to nonofficial values and hopes through literature, theater, art, and even film. Throughout most of the decade, this alternative culture sustained the spirit of the Solidarity movement. Solidarity itself was to emerge into the open once again in 1988, this time to defeat communism and usher in a new period in the life of Poland and Eastern Europe.

In the interim, a new phase in the state-society relationship was inaugurated, defined by the Jaruzelski regime's attempt to impose its "normalization" policy of political order on a reluctant society. The first step was the reestablishment of the state's hegemony by the elimination of independent social organizations. Beyond this immediate political restructuring, long-term normalization depended on economic and social solutions to the problems besieging Poland. In particular, the resolution of persistent material hardships was a prerequisite to the reconciliation of the state and society. In this task, the Polish authorities faced severe obstacles: (1) low economic resources that prevented a consumerist policy to build popular support, (2) a hostile international environment directed against Jaruzelski's regime, (3) the prior use of crisis management techniques, as in the post-1956 little stabilization of Gomułka and the 1970s new political style of Gierek, that eroded public confidence in official programs, and (4), most significantly, the persistence of alternative values in society formed during the new evolutionism and the Solidarity periods.

To overcome these difficulties and "normalize" the country, the regime embarked on a three-fold program of political restoration, economic reconstruction, and social reconciliation. The first of these involved the organizational demobilization of civil society, primarily through dissolution and delegalization of independent associations, including journalist, student, rural, and labor unions. The next step was to engage in institution building through the formation of pro-government associations more pliable to the regime, such as the Movement for

National Rebirth (PRON) and government-sponsored trade unions (OPZZ), whose tasks were to coopt societal groups with grants of special privilege.

The reconstruction of popular support was to be enhanced by adherence to the program of economic transformation, initiated in January 1982. However, the program was stripped of the previously anticipated participation of social forces in economic rebuilding. Instead the reform blueprint was redefined into a narrow, technical plan for enterprise autonomy and administrative decentralization to improve efficiency on the basis of a mixed economy combining central directives and market mechanisms. Without popular support and workers' participation, the reform package fell victim to administrative inertia and bureaucratic resistance. It became clear by the mid-1980s that without societal backing the reform would fail and the economy deteriorate further. The realization led to a "second stage of reform" in 1987 which sought to involve society in the reconstruction effort by reemphasizing the self-management features of enterprise reform. To acquire society's support for the government's economic plan, the regime had recourse to a national referendum. The population, however, would have none of it, and on 29 November 1987, due to a high rate of absenteeism, the referendum was defeated.

The reason was the continued alienation of the major social groups from the regime of Jaruzelski and the normalization process. Economic renewal was perceived as the work of the government without consideration for the will of the people, who did not accept austerity as the necessary precondition to economic recovery. Living standards and production levels remained low and were compounded by a mounting external debt of close to $38 billion and a rapidly growing inflation rate. The popular mood was grim and expectations for improvements absent.

The combination of economic hardship, popular dissatisfaction, and price increases led once more to the inevitable mass protests, expressed in two strike waves in the spring and summer of 1988. The strikes, involving a younger, post-Solidarity generation frustrated by material difficulties and the lack of social advancement, concentrated first on wage improvements. By August, however, demands included the relegalization of the Solidarity trade union as a protective umbrella for the interests of the working class.

Once again, as in 1970, 1976, and 1980, the workers' protest sent a shock wave throughout the system that put an end to the immobility of the normalization years. Jaruzelski's leadership team realized that without popular participation in the reform process, the country was doomed to a downward economic spiral. Efforts at establishing the dominance of the regime over society culminated in an alienated and apathetic public. Only a bold opening of the polity could alter the situation. The government had little choice but to offer, in August 1988, to meet with former Solidarity leaders and negotiate the reemergence of the union as a representative of society.

THE 1989 NEGOTIATED REVOLUTION

That step led to a gradual reconstruction of political power that resulted in the collapse of the communist system in Poland—the first of the 1989 Revolutions in Eastern Europe. The events were a combination of mass action and reform from above. Despite the attempt to suppress civil society by means of normalization policies, the values of self-organization remained part of the popular consciousness, kept alive by an underground society active in illicit publications, visual and art productions in churches and private homes, education in forbidden curricula, and self-organization networks independent of official institutions.

The survival of that spirit enabled its open emergence during the *perestroika* reforms launched in the mid-1980s. The old guard ruling in the Kremlin at the time of the 1981 suppression of Solidarity gave way to a new generation of Soviet leaders who had embraced reform as a necessary solution to the economic problems and social ills of communism. Mikhail Gorbachev emerged as the symbol of this change from above by advocating a strong reformist course not only at home but also in Eastern Europe. The transformation of the Polish system was no longer limited by external pressures to curb societal aspirations. A conjunction of internal and external factors occurred: demands for change on the part of Poland's civil society fit into the reformist program of the Soviet leadership.

The transfer of power in Poland was a process of negotiations and gradual changes that moved in stages: a shift away from the monopoly of communist power, the inclusion of the Solidarity movement into the political process, the formation of a coalition government dominated by Solidarity, and, finally, the establishment of a democratic government.[11]

The opening phase was the Round Table negotiations from February to April 1989, the promised resolution to the August strikes. After some initial controversies as to the participants, the Round Table brought together the regime, Solidarity, and the official trade unions to discuss a wide range of economic, political, and social issues. The fundamental question concerned trade union pluralism, i.e., the legalization of Solidarity. The 5 April 1989 agreement resolved the dilemma by reinstating Solidarity and providing for access to media and organizational resources. In return, Solidarity as a social movement was to become engaged in the reform process, in the hope that such a stance would assure popular acceptance of austerity measures to resolve the long-standing economic problems of the country.

The movement toward co-responsibility by Solidarity was made palatable by provisions for an election to the Polish parliament that involved the participation of Solidarity-backed candidates. The April agreements provided for a "semi-free election" with the outcome guaranteed in favor of the communist party alliance. The formula divided the electoral process into separate compartments, with different degrees of free choice. For the lower legislative house, the Sejm, 65 percent of the seats were guaranteed to the communist coalition, while Solidarity could compete for the remaining 35 percent of legislative posts. To counterbalance this controlled outcome, a second parliamentary chamber was created, the Senate, whose 100 seats were open to full, free contestation. To further safeguard the existing balance of power, a national list of communist luminaries was to run unopposed, although names could be crossed out from it in a negative vote. A similar goal was the refurbished presidency, which was to go to Jaruzelski as a guarantee of communist control over the armed forces and as reassurance of Poland's standing in the communist bloc.

At the time, in early 1989, the response of the Soviet Union and the Warsaw Pact to Polish developments was still uncertain, despite the Gorbachev reforms and the gradual distancing of the Soviet leadership from the Brezhnev Doctrine. For that reason, the agreements could not move toward a full transition from communism to democracy, but aimed at the diffusion of power within the existing political framework. Until a fully democratic polity could be instituted, power-sharing institutions were created on the basis of the semi-free electoral system.

Reality once more prevailed over intent, as the results of the 4 June 1989 election gave a resounding moral victory to Solidarity and accelerated the transition away from communism. The Citizens' Committees which sponsored Solidarity-backed candidates used the popularity of Wałęsa, the Solidarity movement, and prominent dissidents to attain a sweeping victory in the open portions of the elections. In the Sejm, Solidarity won all of the 161 contested seats, i.e., all of its available 35 percent. In the Senate, ninety-nine out of the one hundred legislators were Solidarity affiliated; the one exception was an independent. As dramatic was the defeat of the unopposed national list of prominent communist leaders, thirty-three of whom were crossed out and were unable to enter parliament. The results of the semi-free elections were viewed not only in Poland but throughout the world as a referendum on communist rule, which was roundly defeated by the Polish people.

The result presented the nation with the problem of governance. The lack of legitimacy and support for the ruling communist party was evident, while the Solidarity opposition had obtained overwhelming popular support despite the controlled semi-free election. The problem became more acute as the PUWP's allied parties deserted the communist coalition, denying a majority to the communists. The crisis was resolved under the guise of a formula presented by Michnik, "Our Prime Minister, Their President." The slogan echoed the strategy of the new evolutionism, now openly entering the corridors of power. The proposal provided for a Solidarity prime minister with full governing responsibility, counterbalanced by the presidential office in "their," i.e., communist, hands as a guarantee of Polish alliance with the Soviet bloc. The latter was accomplished by the selection of Jaruzelski to the presidency by a minimum vote of approval in parliament.

A historic moment took place on 12 September 1989, when Tadeusz Mazowiecki, a well-known dissident, former editor of the Catholic monthly *Wiez,* and adviser to Solidarity, formed a coalition government. For the first time since 1948, a non-communist stood at the head of a government in Eastern Europe. Even though the communists retained the portfolios of defense, interior, communications, and foreign trade, the event marked an orderly transfer of power from the hegemony of the communist party to a pluralist government. As significant was the acceptance of Mazowiecki by the Soviet leadership, who openly acquiesced to the termination of a long-standing sine qua non of communist power in Eastern Europe: the maintenance of the leading role of the communist party in politics. The Brezhnev Doctrine was no longer valid, and the Polish transformation served as an example to the other peoples of Eastern Europe whose demands for political change led to the collapse of communism throughout the region in the fall of 1989.

THE POST-COMMUNIST TRANSITION

Poland entered a new political phase, dedicated to the establishment of a democracy. But after forty-five years of communist rule, the country had to reinvent democratic forms of governance, introduce market relations in the economy, and develop new social and cultural attitudes among its people. In contrast to postauthoritarian transitions in other parts of the world, where changes were confined essentially to the political sphere, the former communist countries had to rebuild their economies and shape their societies. The task of transition was thus much more extensive and burdensome, involving considerable dislocations and uncertainties in all aspects of the people's lives.

The advantage of the Mazowiecki government was its ability to command extensive mass support, in marked contrast to its communist predecessors. For the first time in postwar history, a Polish government enjoyed almost universal approval: close to 90 percent in the first months of Mazowiecki's rule. On the basis of this support, the government was able to move rapidly to the implementation of a plan to transform the command economy into a market one. In pursuing rapidly the economic "shock therapy" remedy, Poland was once again at the forefront of change in Eastern Europe. However, it soon became evident that the approach was very costly in economic as well as social and political terms. Political unity could not be maintained for long, resulting in a rapid fragmentation of the political scene and the splintering of the Solidarity movement into competing parties. The economic dislocation and political chaos went hand in hand with major social unrests and popular discontent, in turn affecting the political course of the country.

ECONOMIC "SHOCK THERAPY"

Among the first tasks of the Mazowiecki government was the resurrection of the economy, which under the weight of communist practices operated at crisis levels in the late 1980s, with high inflation rates, mounting foreign debt, and continued shortages of consumer goods. From the very beginning, a market economy was deemed essential, both to remedy the standard of living and to sustain democratic practices.[12] Indeed, an almost idealistic vision of capitalism came to permeate the decision-making process, in the belief that a capitalist economy constructed by political will was the needed panacea for the nation.

The task of economic transformation centered around two primary issues: substantive questions of policy and strategic calculations on the pace of change. Under strong influence from Western experts and international organizations, e.g., the IMF and the World Bank, the Polish government chose to move quickly. Deputy Prime Minister and Finance Minister Leszek Balcerówicz, who gave his name to the "Balcerówicz Plan," rejected a gradual, incremental implementation of change in favor of a shock therapy to be administrated at once and taking effect as soon as 1 January 1990. The argument was that the state of the economy necessitated an immediate infusion of remedy rather than a slow cure.

The shock was administered primarily through a stabilization program of fiscal controls, while a second phase of the reform, privatization, was to emerge in the wake of the stabilization. The primary task was to curb the high rate of inflation and introduce monetary discipline by establishing a supply-demand equilibrium and strengthening the Polish currency. To that end, the government stopped subsidizing most consumer goods as well as many enterprises, held down wages, allowed prices to increase, introduced new taxes, lifted trade restrictions, and in general created a legal and economic environment to facilitate the transition to a market economy.

Despite severe material dislocations to the population and the decline in production, the government was able to proceed with the program due to the political support the Solidarity government enjoyed at the time. The stabilization program did succeed in its main goals, curbing inflation, strengthening the zloty, reducing the budget deficit, and stimulating trade to reduce the debt burden. It did so, however, by increasing the cost of living to most families, creating unemployment, and widening the gap in social differentiation.

Beyond stabilization, the economy had to be privatized so as to create the ownership structure essential to the market economy. The task was formidable, with over 80 percent of the economy in the state sector. The transfer to private ownership was plagued by legal, financial, and social problems about rightful ownership, the rights of the workforce in state enterprises, and the rise in unemployment stemming from a more efficient private sector requiring fewer workers. Privatization thus evolved along two tracks—a "small privatization" located primarily in the retail sector and a "large privatization" concerning the major state factories and enterprises.

The first moved along swiftly, fueled by an entrepreneurial spirit. New ventures in the consumer and service sectors mushroomed, as thousands of new stores, restaurants, and other retail outlets appeared. This activity accounted for much of the growth in productivity during the first year of the Balcerówicz plan. It led to improvements in the availability of consumer goods, but of course at higher prices, thus depriving large sectors of the population on fixed income of the fruits of the consumer revolution. The pace of the large privatization was much slower, due to the need for large capital investments and the danger of major social discontent. Successive governments delayed the task, preventing a comprehensive rapid privatization of the Polish economy as a whole.

Nonetheless, the economic transformation continued to produce severe social dislocations and political discontent. The most severe impact was in the first two years of the Balcerówicz plan, with substantial recession in production, continued inflation, growing unemployment, decline in real wages, and dismemberment of many safety nets. By the end of 1993, the economy showed some improvements on the productivity side, although unemployment reached over 15 percent of the workforce, inflation remained substantial, real wages declined, and social inequality among groups widened. Under the strain of economic hardships, the popular mood shifted away from the prior unconditional support of the first Solidarity government. Only a few months after the launching of shock therapy, political fissures appeared in the Solidarity camp that led to a major transformation of the political landscape.

POLITICAL FRAGMENTATION

The primary task of the transition was to move from the monolithic politics of communism to the pluralist politics of democracy. To this aim, progress occurred in the formal institutions of democratic governance through constitutional amendments that eliminated the "leading role" of the communist party. A more formidable task was the establishment of institutions for political representation and interest articulation, that is of political parties, able to express competitive preferences and alternative options.[13]

In this, the country was handicapped by the legacy of communism, the nature of the opposition movement, and the process of democratic transformation. Communist monopoly prevented the formation of open, diverse organizations competing freely in the polity. Instead, political identities formed around opposition or support to communist rule, expressed in the popular "we" versus "they" image. The result was a politics based on normative value judgments rather than on the expression of particular material and social interests. Solidarity became a nationwide movement of consensus built around its opposition to the authorities, bringing together under its umbrella a diversity of interests cast aside for the common purpose of defeating communism. The semi-free elections of June 1989 represented the very essence of this political bifurcation between the communist state and the Solidarity movement.

The collapse of communist power structures made irrelevant the normative commitment to the anti-communist struggle, despite attempts by some leaders to retain the solidarity and common purpose of the movement as a mechanism for the transformation of society. Moreover, the Balcerówicz program introduced new economic and social conflicts among the population and the political elite, conflicts that needed new channels of expression. The problem was the lack of established political identities, since neither the communist era nor the nascent transitional society provided the framework for a democratic party system. The consequence was a proliferation of political "parties" representing numerous programmatic aspirations and personal ambitions, but without sufficient grounding in mass support.

The first impetus for political proliferation came from the dismemberment of Solidarity over disputes concerning the extent of economic transformation and adherence to the Round Table accords. The split reflected Solidarity's identity as an *opposition* movement to communism, not a party in agreement on economic and political changes. By mid-1990, Solidarity split into two political wings. The Center Alliance (PC) emerged as a vehicle for the presidential candidacy of Wałęsa, while Civic Movement–Democratic Action emerged in response to safeguard the policies of the Mazowiecki government.

In the meantime, the dismemberment of the communist bloc and the disintegration of the PUWP in Poland had made Jaruzelski's hold on the presidency increasingly precarious. The president became marginalized in post-communist politics, finally resigning the post, and thereby precipitating a presidential contest in a fully free election. The principal rivals were Wałęsa as the leader of the Solidarity movement and Mazowiecki as the head of the Solidarity government. Additional candidates represented the parties associated with the former communist regime, as well as an outsider: Stanisław Tymiński, an obscure Canadian-Polish entrepreneur who created Party X to denounce both the Solidarity establishment and the former communist regime. Tymiński succeeded in gathering 23 percent of the vote from among discontented elements in society, particularly among small towns hit hard by the economic reform, thereby forcing Wałesa (40 percent of the vote) into a runoff election. The big defeat was suffered by Mazowiecki, who obtained only 18 percent of the vote in a show of major public discontent with economic shock therapy. In the second round, after rallying together the former Solidarity forces, Wałęsa did succeed in obtaining a major victory, and assumed the post of the first freely elected president in post-communist Poland.

The election of Wałęsa did not stem the tide in the ongoing political fragmentation of the country. On the contrary, the presidential contest signified an end to the predominance of the Solidarity movement in politics and signaled the opening up of competitive politics to other forces—already evident in the "Tymiński phenomenon." The process was fueled by the realization that the legislative chambers formed under the conditions of the "semi-free elections," and still dominated by deputies associated with the communist regime, were increasingly irrelevant to the democratic needs of the new Poland. There was wide agreement that free elections were essential, although a severe conflict emerged in the spring of 1991 concerning the electoral law for the upcoming parliamentary elections. After considerable wrangling by the different political parties, and the president and the Sejm, a law was adopted on 28 June 1991 establishing a pure proportional representation system for the 460 Sejm seats, and a plurality first-past-the-post system for the one-hundred-member Senate.

The consequence was a veritable explosion of competing political parties, groups, and movements bent on exploring the opportunities presented by an unrestricted voting system to the lower parliamentary house. Initially 111 political groups sought to take part in the election, and sixty-seven were actually able to compete, with twenty-nine different electoral lists entering the Sejm as a result of the 27 October 1991 election. A similar breakdown was evident in the Senate, despite the different electoral process. Clearly, the political outcome was the artifact not only of electoral rules, but also of the lack of clear political cleavages that bound sectors of the electorate to particular political parties.

Political dispersement was evident in that no party obtained more than 13 percent of the vote, with eight parties in the 5 percent to 12 percent range. The parties, in and out of parliament, represented a variety of political orientations: post-Solidarity parties that had emerged from the opposition movement, post-communist parties or their former allies that had shed their communist ideology, and several national and Christian parties. The political fragmentation was even more dramatic given the low voter turnout, since only 43 percent of the eligible electorate participated in the first fully free parliamentary election in postwar Poland. Both the low turnout and the high fragmentation testified to the growing apathy and confusion of the population with a political system that remained ill-defined and lacked stable channels for interest representation.

The election produced a highly fractured institution, rendering difficult the maintenance of governing coalitions, leading to extreme multipartism in the Sejm, and reinforcing differences among the parliamentary parties. The divisiveness pertained to a number of political cleavages, so that parties aligned on one issue were often divided on other policy dimensions, making stable alliances most difficult.

The most salient issues concerned the scope of economic transformation and state intervention in the economy.[14] Some post-Solidarity parties, the Democratic Union and the Liberal Democratic Congress, were committed to the Balcerówicz plan's rapid alteration of the economy with minimal state interference. Others, ranging across post-Solidarity, independent, and post-communist groups, aligned behind a slower approach that called for state protectionism and disadvantaged groups or specific sectors such as agriculture. The liberal-statist division became a major point of contention during the parliamentary session, although the exigencies of economic transformation tended to diminish policy options and successive governments adhered to the basic tenets of the original plan. To a large extent the steady course was directed by the need to relieve the country's debt burden and obtain external financial supports, making it vital to heed economic conditionalities imposed by international agencies, i.e., the IMF and the World Bank.

Political divisions were as intense on the clerical-secular and regime dimensions. The first point of contention centered around the extent of religious influence in public and private lives. The Church sought to infuse Catholic values among the population by legislating religious education in public schools, severely limiting the right to abortion, and requiring the media to mirror Catholic values. The program was met with considerable dissatisfaction among the people, especially women who resented Church intervention in their most private lives. Despite the popular mood, advocacy for the Church's stance came from several religious parties, notably the Christian National Union, and several conservative and peasant parties—which were aligned on this issue, but were on different sides of the liberal-statist question. Similarly, advocates of a

Czechoslo

secular state independent of Catholic intervention ranged across the political spectrum, including the liberal post-Solidarity parties, the former communist SDP, and the nationalist KPN.

The regime dimension in the post-1991 parliament evolved around the problem of decommunization, i.e., how to deal with former organizations and supporters of the communist regime. Strong opposition to any *because* reckoning with the past came from the former communists and their erstwhile allies, who were fearful of reprisals for past political activities. A similar stance, for a very different reason, was taken by the Democratic Union, whose policy of a "thick line" as a clear demarcation between the past and the present reflected its primary concern with building a variable economy and democracy unhindered by recriminations about the former communist system. In contrast, most of the conservative and Christian parties were very vocal about the presence of former communists in positions of power and their profiteering from privatization.

The issue differences produced a highly fragmented political scene, reflected more intensely at the top of the system than among the citizenry. The primacy of parliamentary parties was assured by the absence of well institutionalized political organizations with firm roots in identifiable social constituencies. There were few mass political parties that reflected the preferences of specific support groups, and fewer still that were bound by constituency demands. Instead most parties were small institutions with weak discipline, prone to the personal ambitions of elites. The consequence was not only high factionalism, but also considerable dealignment and realignment among the political clubs in the Sejm. Weak party institutionalization signified low party allegiance among deputies, with close to one-fourth of the Sejm membership switching party affiliation during the post October 1991 term. This led to the disintegration of several existing party organizations, the formation of new political parties, and the prevalence of internal differences in the parties.

The overall effect has been substantial political fluidity and extensive multipartism that has affected the formation of governing coalitions. The large number of parties, the ongoing realignments, and the disparate policy preferences along several issue dimensions made it difficult to attain political stability. The tumultuous history of government formation is ample evidence of the problem. The Bielecki government, formed after the 1990 presidential election, resigned as a consequence of the 1991 parliamentary outcome, which was interpreted as an expression of popular discontent with the policies of the post-Solidarity governments. The step, however, led to a prolonged stalemate, with parties weaving in and out of potential coalitions. The government of Jan Olszewski did not come into being until some two months after the October election, and then only as a minority coalition. Almost immediately, policy differences on economic priorities and on decommunization threw the Olszewski cabinet into a constant political struggle. After five months of political infighting, the government fell because of its push on decommunization, specifically over the accusation of some prominent politicians of collaborating with the communist secret police.

The no-confidence vote for the Olszewski government produced a renewed political impasse. President Wałęsa nominated Waldemar Pawlak, the head of the former communist allied peasant party, to head a new government, and the Sejm approved the candidacy on 6 June 1992. Despite that, the political heritage of the PSL became an obstacle to the formation of a new cabinet, since several parties viewed the PSL as a neo-communist organization that could not be supported to govern in a democratic polity. After thirty-three days, Pawlak gave up the attempt to form a ruling coalition.

Instead, the parliamentary leaders sought to form a grand coalition to secure governance and stability. After the defection of the Center Party from the potential eight-party coalition, Hanna Suchocka of the UD was able to form a cabinet, although it too was a minority government whose survival depended on "abstentions" from noncoalition parties. The Suchocka coalition, despite its common lineage in the Solidarity tradition, was characterized by substantial ideological and programmatic differences over economic priorities, religious influence, and reckoning with the communist past. In some instances, the coalition partners advocated diametrically opposed policies.

In such circumstances, the Suchocka government had to remove controversial questions from its purview, and allow the Sejm to take the initiative on significant issues, e.g., abortion rights and financial priorities. This only served to reinforce the diverse preferences of the political parties, often leading to vindictive rhetoric. The policy disputes overcame the earlier consensus, producing renewed crises that culminated in the fall of the Suchocka government and new parliamentary elections.

The national condition had become ever more precarious during the parliamentary term. The rapid economic transformation caused not only disputes among political parties, but also produced major economic hardships among large sectors of the population, which in turn found expression in social disturbances. The public mood became ever more negative as the rapid turn toward a market economy contributed to a rapid rise in unemployment, inflating the number of people living below the poverty line, and widening the gap in income differentials. Public opinion turned against both the economic and social repercussions of shock therapy. Overt opposition was manifested by the growing militancy of the working class and the peasantry. The latter demanded state support for Polish agriculture through antigovernmental demonstrations and protests. The working class sought to limit the ill effects of the private economy by demanding wage and employment guarantees through work stoppages and strikes. The pressures forced the Suchocka government into negotiations that culminated in a "Pact on State Enterprises" to develop more protective employment and income policies. Before the pact could be implemented, the differences between the economic policies of the post-Solidarity Suchocka government and the Solidarity trade union became so acrimonious as to lead to the defection of the union parliamentary deputies from the governing coalition, enabling the non-confidence vote to pass and force the government's collapse in May 1993.

The fragmentation of the Sejm made it difficult to envisage still another governing coalition. Instead, President Wałęsa chose to dismiss the sitting parliament and call for new legislative elections. The experience of the outgoing Sejm contributed to a general view that a new electoral law was needed to assure greater political stability. Most significant was the new requirement for a 5 percent threshold in the national vote for entry into the Sejm. It thus became more difficult to replicate the political dispersement of the 1991 election.

THE ELECTORAL FILTER

Much of the electoral campaign during the summer of 1993 concerned economic policies, with most parties signaling their awareness of the public mood by advocating a slower and more protectionist program. Given the popular discontent, the September results marked a major shift in the political orientation of the country. The elections were a sweeping victory for the parties on the left, i.e., the post-communist SLD alliance, and the PSL, the peasant party previously allied with the communists. Both parties were critical of the shock therapy approach and advocated policies to shelter economic sectors and social groups hard hit by the privatization drive. As significant was the defeat of the parties on the right, which for the most part failed to clear the 5 percent threshold and were thus deprived of representation in the Sejm. Among those were several post-Solidarity entries, such as the Center Party, the Solidarity trade union, and the coalition of former Premier Olszowski. The same fate befell the Christian National Union, which was supported by the Catholic Church, and whose defeat can also be attributed to the saliency of the secular-religious issue among the public. The intervention of the Church on the abortion issue caused a major split in Polish society and alienated a growing number of women from the Church and its political supporters.

The new Sejm was indeed a less fractured institution. In addition to the post-communist coalition and the peasant party, four other political organizations cleared the minimal threshold. Among those was the Democratic Union, representing the mainstay of former Solidarity's political wing, still tied to the Balcerówicz plan. Labor Solidarity, reflecting a so-cial democratic program within the former Solidarity camp, succeeded in improving its position in the new Sejm considerably. On the other hand, the nationalist KPN emerged with fewer deputies than previously; it was joined on the right side of the political spectrum by a new entrant, the alliance formed by President Wałęsa as a vehicle to support economic change and ensure the powers of the presidential office in politics. The upper chamber of the legislature, the Senate, despite an electoral proce-dure based on a plurality vote, showed a similar voting pattern, the domi-nance of the left over the right.

Only four years after the collapse of communism, the Polish elector-ate had dramatically altered its political choice. The country that had given birth to the major opposition movement to communism in the 1980s and had initiated the 1989 revolutions that forced the collapse of the communist system in Eastern Europe, had once again inaugurated a new political course by bringing back into power parties derived from the communist regime. The command of a majority of the Sejm by the SLD and PSL enabled the two parties to form a government. The coali-tion selected Pawlak, who had attempted unsuccessfully to form a gov-ernment in mid-1992, as the new prime minister. The coalition was able to hold together, despite increasing tensions among its partners and a growing rift between the prime minister and presidential offices. The gov-erning coalition was beset by differences in regard to the pace of privati-zation, relations with the Church, and leadership styles, while President Wałęsa and Prime Minister Pawlak entered into a political struggle over the respective powers of their office and appointments to government ministries.

These political tensions led to the forced resignation of Pawlak in February 1995. The partnership between the Democratic Left Alliance and the Peasant Party remained in place as the governing coalition, al-though with the former communist party assuming the senior role. Po-land's tilt toward political rule by the former communist elite, now remade in the guise of social democracy, continued through additional government changes in the cabinet and the presidential office. The new prime minister, Józef Olesky, was able to remain as head of the govern-ment for less than a year, submitting a resignation in January 1996 among charges that he had collaborated with the KGB, the Soviet secret police, and its Russian successor agency. While Olesky denied the charges, the scandal rocked the political establishment, led to a parlia-mentary investigation, and forced yet another turnover at the head of the Polish government. In February 1996, the new president appointed a new government under the leadership of Włodzimierz Cimoszewicz, a former community activist who had challenged Wałęsa in the first free presidential election in December 1990. In less than eight years, since the collapse of communism in 1989, the country had installed eight different governments.

Despite the apparent political instability, the democratic process continued to evolve in post-communist Poland. Strong evidence of the commitment to democratic politics came not only from the parliamentary elections of 1991 and 1993 and the various changes in government, but also through a second wave of elections. First was the presidential contest held at the end of 1995, followed by the mandated 1997 elections to the legislature. The incumbent, Lech Wałęsa, hero of the Solidarity period and a symbol of the opposition to communism, had lost considerable popularity while in the presidential office. His personal style and political interventionism had led many to see Wałęsa as unfit to represent Poland in its highest office. Yet, despite an initial low standing in the polls, Wałęsa was able to use the force of his personality and his past politics to emerge as the most viable candidate among several competitors on the center and right of the political spectrum. His main opponent came from the post-communist left, Alexander Kwaśniewski, a young, presentable, and Western-style politician. In the first round of the presidential contest in November 1995, the two men ran neck and neck, and outdistanced all the other presidential aspirants; Kwaśniewski gathered 35 percent and Wałęsa 33 percent of the vote. Clearly, the second round between the two was going to be close. In the ensuing campaigning during public appearances and television debates, Kwaśniewski appeared as more dynamic and future oriented, while Wałęsa came across as a man of the past. The result of the December second round of voting was a slim victory for Kwaśniewski, who took 51.7 percent of the vote to Wałęsa's 48.3 percent. The changeover in the president's office on 23 December 1995 was a symbolic end to the politics of anticommunism that had defined the struggles of the preceding decades and led to a reemergence of normal politics defined by the representation of the left as part of the Polish political spectrum.

Another political swing occurred as a result of the September 1997 elections to the national legislature, when AWS, the Solidarity Electoral Action coalition, emerged as the predominant political force in parliament. AWS was a movement composed of over thirty parties and organizations rooted in the anticommunist struggle of the 1980s, and grouped around the trade union Solidarity. The purpose of the coalition was to form a counter force to the recent combination of leftist parties with antecedents in the communist past, that is, the SLD and the Peasant Party. To attain that objective, AWS had to bring together under a common umbrella the political parties and leaders that had remained apart in the 1993 elections. At that time, the splintering of the right, conservative side of the political ledger had contributed greatly to its defeat by parties with ties to the former communist regime.

Under the leadership of Marian Krzaklewski, the chair of the Solidarity trade union, AWS was able to forge a political coalition and mount an effective political campaign against the incumbent government dominated by the SLD. On 21 September 1997, Polish citizens went once more to the polls, and the results brought another shift in political fortunes. The main plurality of votes went to Solidarity Electoral Action, with 33.8 percent of the vote, followed by its opponent, the Democratic Left Alliance, with 27.1 percent. The remainder of the vote was shared by three main parties on the left and the right, including the Peasant Party and the Freedom Union.

Since no single party had a majority of seats in the Sejm, yet another coalition government was formed to rule Poland. This time around, the partners came from the other side of the aisle from the leftist outgoing coalition. The government created after the September 1997 elections brought together the center and the right of the political spectrum: the Freedom Union and Solidarity Electoral Action. The latter was the senior partner in government, which was headed by a relatively unknown former university professor, Jerzy Buzek. Still, the government included a number of well-known individuals, several with roots in the Solidarity opposition movement. Also prominent in the ruling coalition, as deputy prime minister and finance minister, was Balcerówicz, famed for the original shock therapy approach to the transformation of the Polish economy.

This last appointment was of symbolic significance, as it signaled the continuity of the economic reform program in Poland—despite the fact that a continuing theme in political discourse was a deep concern with the negative side of economic change. Political parties on the left and the right had denounced the costs of economic adjustment suffered by segments of the population. Paradoxically, both the left and the right sought to gain political terrain by redefining the economic and social course associated with shock therapy. Their principal promise was to bring a milder form of the economic shock, to protect those adversely affected by marketization. Yet, neither the post-1993 leftist coalition nor the post-1997 rightist coalition moved away from the spirit of the Balcerówicz economic program. Clearly, despite the different emphasis in policy statements, all the Polish governments since 1989 have followed the main thrust of the economic transformation process.

After all, Poland had embarked on a major reconstruction program that dismantled the centrally planned system, with all its shortages and failures, to establish a market and private economy that produced important improvements in the consumer sector. Secondly, options for policy change were severely limited by continued international pressures from multinational agencies and Western governments, which viewed Poland as an affirmation of the shift from a command to a market economy. The successive governments were thus unable to deviate too much from the thrust of the transformation program. Besides, despite the initial severe dislocation to important social groups, the Polish economy began to show significant improvements in the mid-1990s: indicators for economic growth and industrial production were among the highest in Europe. Even the problem areas of unemployment and inflation showed improvements, reinforcing the image of the Polish economy as a dynamic success.

The economic performance enabled Poland's governments to pursue a foreign policy agenda aimed at better integration with the West, including joining the European Union and NATO. While there were difficulties with such integration, particularly in regard to Russia's fears about a Western security zone on its borders, the political consensus in Poland was strongly in favor of the Europeanization of Poland's economic, political, and security position. This consensus ranged across the political spectrum of left and right, including the 1995-installed post-communist president and the 1997-inaugurated post-Solidarity government.

There was less agreement on other policy issues, notably on the framework for the new constitution and the concordat between the state and the Catholic Church. One of the major disputes in regard to a new constitutional foundation concerned the respective powers of the executive and legislative branches of government. During his term, Wałęsa was an advocate of a strong presidency, and stood in the way of a dominant parliamentarian system for the new Poland. Kwaśniewski, as the former head of the constitutional commission, appeared less committed to executive dominance. Progress on the constitutional issue was made during his tenure in office, and a new constitution was approved by public referendum in May 1997. Another political controversy centered around the place of religious values in Poland's polity and society. The 1993 concordat between the government and the Vatican granted a privileged position to the Catholic Church in Poland. The ratification of the document by the Sejm proved difficult and was delayed due to political opposition by some parties to a state religion in a democratic Poland. The forceful intervention of the Church in several policy areas, notably restrictions on the right to abortion and in favor of teaching catechism in public schools, had alienated a significant portion of the population, including many who identified with the Catholic religion. The issue of religious and secular value as influences in the political and social life of the country has remained controversial, despite the fact that the concordat was ultimately passed by parliament and then signed into law by President Kwaśniewski in January 1998.

The lessons of Poland's recent political history are self-evident. The post-communist transition is an ongoing process, and the transformations necessary to move beyond hegemonic politics, a command economy, and popular dependency on the state demand prolonged adjustments across political, economic, and sociocultural dimensions. Moreover, the transformations occur in a context of constant change, when people's expectations are fluid, when the societal environment is highly uncertain, and when a political vacuum must be filled by new institutions and new values. In short, the period of post-communist transition is not a time of "normal politics," but a period of system construction that operates according to its own logic and rules.

An evaluation of the path taken must thus take into account the transformative nature of the Polish political system. And the evidence of the first post-communist years shows considerable accomplishments, despite the volatile and fragmented nature of the political scene in the aftermath of communism. The successive parliamentary and presidential elections were instrumental in reducing the political chaos. The electoral contests functioned as a kind of political filter, first by reducing the number of viable political contenders and eliminating parties with little popular support, and second by helping to define the political space in Poland in terms of the victorious parties' policy preferences.[15] Thus, the 1993 and 1995 installation of a post-communist government and president in the country restored the left to a legitimate place in public life. It made clear that the stigma of communism could not prevent the participation of leftist parties and agendas in political discourse, even when the parties in question traced their roots to the former regime. Yet the reassertion of the post-communist left had to find a countermeasure in the reaffirmation of the right. To do so, the latter had to overcome its extreme fragmentation. The formation of a Solidarity-based coalition was the first step in that direction, and translated to the 1997 parliamentary victory of AWS. The outcome suggests the healthy reemergence of "normal politics" in Poland, defined by a clear pattern of left-right politics in public life.

Democracy is about choice, but informed political choice. The hegemonic communist system offered no choice while the fragmentation of post-communism provided chaotic choice. The streamlining of the political system in the mid-1990s introduced informed choice, with constituencies more aware of their interests, and political parties bound by greater responsibilities to programs and constituencies. The formation of new institutions, political actions, and norms of behavior over the past several years points to the establishment of an entrenched pluralist system and a mature democracy in Poland.

Notes

1. Norman Davies, *God's Playground: A History of Poland* (New York: Columbia University Press, 1982).

2. Hugh Seton-Watson, *The East European Revolution,* 3rd ed. (New York: Praeger, 1956), Chaps. 3–8.

3. Zbigniew K. Brzezinski, *The Soviet Bloc: Unity and Conflict* (Cambridge: Harvard University Press, 1967), Chap. 1; and Krystyna Kersten, *The Establishment of Communist Rule in Poland* (Berkeley: University of California, 1992).

4. Adam Bromke, *Poland's Politics: Idealism vs. Realism* (Cambridge: Harvard University Press, 1967), Chaps. 6–9.

5. Jack Bielasiak, "Social Confrontation to Contrived Crisis: March 1968," in *East European Quarterly,* Vol. 22, No. 1, March 1988, 283–309.

6. Jakub Karpinski, *Countdown: The Polish Upheavals* (New York: Karz-Cohl, 1982), Chap. 5.

7. Keith John Lepak, *Prelude to Solidarity* (New York: Columbia University Press, 1988), Chaps. 2, 5, 6.

8. Adam Michnik, "The New Evolutionism," in *Survey,* Vol. 22, No. 2 (Summer/Autumn 1976).

9. Neal Ascherson, *The Polish August* (New York: Viking, 1981); and David Ost, *Solidarity and the Politics of Anti-Politics* (Philadelphia: Temple University Press, 1990).

10. Jack Bielasiak and Maurice Simon, eds., *Polish Politics: Edge of the Abyss* (New York: Praeger, 1984).

11. Walter D. Connor and Piotr Ploszajski, eds., *Escape from Socialism: The Polish Route* (Armonk, N.Y.: M. E. Sharpe, 1992).

12. Jeffrey Sachs, *Poland's Jump to the Market Economy* (Cambridge: MIT Press, 1993).

13. Jack Bielasiak, "The Dilemma of Political Interests in the Post-Communist Transition," in Walter D. Connor and Piotr Ploszajski, eds., *The Polish Road from Socialism* (Armonk, N.Y.: M. E. Sharpe, 1992) and "Institutional Building in a Transformative Society: Party Fragmentation in Poland's Parliament," Lawrence D. Laughingly, ed., *Comparative Legislative Studies* (IPSA, 1993).

14. Stanislaw Gebethner and Krzysztof Jasiewicz, "Poland," in *European Journal of Political Research,* Vol. 24, No. 4 (December 1993), 519–535.

15. Jack Bielasiak, "Substance and Process in the Development of Party Systems in East Central Europe," in *Communist and Post-Communist Studies,* Vol. 30, No. 1, March 1997, 23–44.

7

Yugoslavia

SABRINA P. RAMET

Yugoslavia—literally, "land of the South Slavs"—never entirely lived up to its name. To begin with, it never included the Bulgarians, the most sizable group of "South Slavs." But more to the point, alongside its Serbs, Croats, Slovenes, Macedonians, Montenegrins, and Bosnian Muslims, there were also tangible numbers of non-Slavic peoples—primarily Albanians and Hungarians but until 1945 also significant numbers of Germans, and smaller numbers of Italians, Czechs, Slovaks, Romanians, Turks, Jews, and Gypsies. It was a polyglot country par excellence.

The first Yugoslavia, under the ceremonial crown of the Serbian Karadjordjević dynasty, lasted twenty-three years—from 1918 to 1941. The second Yugoslavia, created by communist Marshal Josip Broz Tito in 1945, lasted forty-six years—exactly twice as long as the first Yugoslavia. In each case, the unity of the country was shattered because of the same problem: the insistence by the Serbs on viewing Yugoslavia as Serbia writ large, and the consequent resentment of the non-Serbs who had outnumbered the Serbs ever since 1918 and who, by 1991 (when the second Yugoslavia officially died), collectively outnumbered the Serbs by a wide margin. The so-called "national question," in short, was always a Serb–non-Serb question; all other dimensions of the question were marginal or derivative.

Both Yugoslavias ended in civil war, pitting Serbs against non-Serbs. And from the jaundiced vantage point of the present, it would be easy to see no further than the ethnic conflicts which have frequently troubled the country. But it is important to remember that for a quarter of a century (roughly 1955 to 1980), Yugoslavia's self-management system was widely admired, and the Yugoslav press proudly enumerated a seemingly endless flow of delegations from ministries of economics and business corporations on all continents, including from such countries as China, Japan, Germany, Peru, the United States, and several countries in Africa. Yugoslavia seemed, for a brief period in the 1970s particularly, to be a special place, which had some insights about democracy at the workplace, a seemingly viable hybrid economy ("market socialism"), and even a handle on building harmony among the diverse peoples inhabiting the country. Then something went wrong.

This chapter traces political and social developments in Yugoslavia from 1941 to 1996. It thus begins with civil war and ends with civil war.

BIRTH BY FIRE

The first Yugoslavia was highly unstable, lurching from Serb-centralism to royal dictatorship to experiments with coalition governments to the beginnings of a Serb-Croat "historic compromise" on the eve of war, when Belgrade conceded wide autonomy to a large Croatian governate (*banovina*) under the Cvetković-Maček agreement. But in April 1941, less than two years after this agreement was signed, Hitler's *Wehrmacht* struck into Yugoslavia, drawing, in tow, sundry Axis allies: the Italians, who annexed southern Slovenia and Dalmatia; the Hungarians, who annexed the Hungarian-inhabited Vojvodina; the Bulgarians, who annexed most of Macedonia; and the Croatian fascists (the *Ustashe* led by Ante Pavelić), who set up a quisling Croatian state in the center of the country. Hitler annexed northern Slovenia to Germany, and assigned Kosovo and the western part of Macedonia to Albania. Part of what little was left of Yugoslavia was placed under direct German military administration, and the fragment that remained was advertised as a revived Serbian state and entrusted to the quisling government of Milan Nedić.

The Albanians of Kosovo and the Hungarians of Vojvodina were by and large gratified by this reassignment since their wishes had been ignored when the borders had been drawn earlier in the century; the Albanians of Kosovo, moreover, had been subjected to severe discrimination by the interwar Belgrade regime, which confiscated large amounts of Albanian-owned land, turning it over to Serbian "colonists," and would not operate state schools in areas populated by Albanians.[1] Likewise, the Macedonians initially gave the invading Bulgarian forces a tumultuous welcome, viewing the Bulgarians as "liberators" from Serbian chauvinism and repression. The extent of Serbian neglect of Macedonia can be gauged from the fact that even in the midst of war, the Bulgarian occupation authorities established 800 new schools in Macedonia and endowed Skopje with a library, a museum, a national theater, and, effective in December 1943, its first university (named after the recently deceased

Tsar Boris).[2] Initially most Croats too welcomed their separation from the Serbs. But as the Pavelić regime showed its colors, and set about the systematic killing of Serbs, Gypsies, and Jews, support for the communist "Partisan" resistance grew among Croats, as well as among other peoples. In addition to the *Ustashe* and the Partisans, there were two other organized fighting forces among the indigenous peoples of "Yugoslavia." The Chetniks, a Royalist Serbian force led by General Draža Mihailović, began as an authentic resistance movement but at least some of the units gravitated, in the course of the war, toward collaboration with the Nazis in order to concentrate their fire on the Partisans. The second fighting force was the Bali Kombëtar, consisting of Albanians who wanted basically one thing—to keep Kosovo part of Albania.[3] In addition, one should mention the Serbian fascist regime headed by Nedić and Milan Aćimović, which functioned as a Nazi quisling regime. The Croatian *Ustashe* hurriedly set up a network of concentration camps, the best known being that at Jasenovac, and incarcerated Serbs, Gypsies, and Jews, as well as antifascist Croats, within their walls.[4] Simultaneously, the *Ustashe* initiated a policy of expelling large numbers of ethnic Serbs from the territory of the puppet Croatian state, and laid plans for the resettlement of some 179,000 Slovenes in Croatia.[5] Several concentration camps were set up by the Nazis, at the same time, on the territory of the quisling Nedić regime, the most famous being those in Belgrade (on the site of the present-day fairgrounds) and in Niš.[6]

The casualties in Yugoslavia during 1941–45 were staggering. Although the subsequent official claim of 1.7 million dead is now generally considered an exaggeration, reliable scholarship has estimated some 1,027,000 war casualties. Of these, about 530,000 were Serbs, 192,000 were Croats, 103,000 were Muslims, and the remainder were from other groups.[7] The *Ustashe,* Chetniks, and Partisans all massacred civilians—in many cases in gruesome ways. Others were killed by one foreign occupation force or another, or by German aerial bombardment, or in a major typhus epidemic which cut through Chetnik ranks early in 1945.

But out of this hell, one force—Tito's Partisans—emerged triumphant. And they mythologized the civil war, highlighting its aspect as a National Liberation Struggle and painting the *Ustashe* and the Chetniks—with some truth—as mirror images of each other. After they had consolidated their power, Tito's communists would use memories of the civil war to demonize noncommunist politics, regularly warning that any attempt to restore a multiparty system would necessarily spark a new civil war.

CONSOLIDATION, 1945–51

At the end of the war, the sundry noncommunist parties reappeared, elected deputies to the parliament, established independent newspapers, and proceeded to take part in debates about the country's future. Tito pretended at first to respect political pluralism, and initially the Popular Front was advertised as a forum in which political actors with a wide diversity of views could take part and to the implementation of whose program the communist party merely contributed. But the communists showed their hand soon enough, with the controlled elections of 11 November 1945 and with the arrests and trials of many innocent people immediately after. Then, in September 1946 came the show trial of Catholic Archbishop Alojzije Stepinac of Zagreb, on concocted charges of collaboration with the *Ustashe,* and about the same time, the passage of the 1946 constitution which was modeled directly on the Stalin constitution in Russia. The communists enjoyed several overwhelming advantages over the noncommunist parties, including control of the chief political offices, control of the armed forces, control of the police and judiciary, and control of the unions. Pluralism died bit by bit, as noncommunist politicians in the Constituent Assembly found themselves unable to speak in session over the din of communist catcalls and shouts, as communists prevented noncommunist parties from establishing regional and local branches or conducting any activities outside of the chief cities, and as the noncommunist papers either ceased to function ("for technical reasons," or because the printers' union "refused" to print them) or were taken over by the Communist Party of Yugoslavia (CPY).

As early as 14 October 1946, Tito specified the limited role that he saw for political "opposition" in the new Yugoslavia. After expressing his opinion that the opposition was "discrediting" itself by its behavior, Tito made it clear that the "opposition" would not be permitted to oppose anything, but would be welcomed only in the capacity of an auxiliary support force.[8] By the following year, there was no longer room for a plurality of parties at all. This process pushed forward relentlessly until in 1948, at the Fifth Congress of the Communist Party of Yugoslavia, the Popular Front was described as contributing to the implementation of the program of the CPY—a reversal of the earlier nominal relationship.

Tito's communists instituted nationalization of the economic wealth, seizing even lands owned by the Catholic and Orthodox Churches, and launched an ultimately abortive five-year plan. The education system was reorganized and standardized (in the process lowering the previously high pedagogical standards maintained in Slovenia to the level sustainable by the rest of the country).[9] In the cultural sector, the Stalinist doctrine of socialist realism was imposed as de rigueur for art, music, and literature.

Tito's consolidation of power closely followed the pattern set throughout Eastern Europe—but for one crucial detail. Elsewhere, the communists cooperated closely with Moscow and Moscow easily placed its agents in control in key offices, and infiltrated police, army, and the party itself. In Yugoslavia, by contrast, the party resisted Moscow's efforts to infiltrate the system; indeed, Aleksandar Ranković, head of the Yugoslav secret police (UDBa) and Tito's right-hand man, systematically obstructed such efforts. Then Stalin summoned Tito to Moscow, and to Stalin's surprise, Tito refused to go, sending Milovan Djilas, at that time chief of propaganda, instead. This "insubordination" earned Tito the hostility of Stalin, who warned ominously, "I will shake my little finger, and there will be no more Tito."

Although Stalin was escalating the pressure, Tito and his associates were caught off guard when, on 28 June 1948, the Soviet-controlled Cominform issued a thunderous condemnation of the CPY, expelled Yugoslavia from its ranks, and imposed a crippling economic embargo on the country. Yugoslavia, which had sundered economic ties with the West and reoriented its trade largely eastward, reeled from the shock. The seven-year plan then in progress dissolved in chaos and had to be abandoned. Tito, Ranković, Djilas, Edvard Kardelj (the Slovenian theorist), and many others in the party went into a state of shock. The rank and file were also in shock.

For several months, Tito and his associates tried to convince themselves that Stalin was misinformed, that it was just a matter of convincing Stalin that they were good communists. After twenty years of glorifying Stalin, it was no easy matter for them to realize that Stalin had turned on them. So for the interim, they continued to sing Stalin's praises and, meanwhile, accelerated the incipient process of collectivization in order to impress their Kremlin idol. Eventually, as Soviet organs continued to subject them to a barrage of criticism and abuse, this position became untenable, and they had to accept the situation for what it was. They had to go to their people, to whom they had been describing Stalin and Stalin's Russia as models for emulation for as long as they had been active, and tell the people that Stalin was wrong now and they, Stalin's creatures, were right. It is no surprise that the country was split down the middle, with some Yugoslavs sympathizing with the Cominform (especially in Serbia and Montenegro), many with Tito, and many not caring one way or the other but wanting only to survive. According to one source, almost 20 percent of the CPY membership sided with Moscow.[10]

The Soviets tried, through agents, to organize a military coup in Yugoslavia, and failing that, began preparations for a military invasion of the country.[11] Eventually, when preparations were nearly complete, Stalin called off the plan when a firm U.S. response to North Korean provocations suggested that the West might fight over Yugoslavia too.

In the meantime, Tito had been forced to retreat on collectivization in order to minimize troubles with the rural population during the fight with Stalin. As a result of subsequent ideological changes, the communists would no longer perceive collectivization as a prerequisite for social-ist society, and as a result, about 85 percent of Yugoslavia's farmland remained under private ownership throughout the postwar period (i.e., until the breakup of the country in 1991), with most of the collectivized land consisting of land expropriated from German landowning families who were driven out of the country at the end of World War II.

TRANSFORMATION, 1950–65

Under the impact of the split with Stalin, Yugoslavia's leaders searched for some way to assert their greater fidelity to Marxism-Leninism, their communist "correctness." Sometime in 1949, they came up with the idea of workers' councils, associating these with a Marxist program for the "withering away of the state." The idea was that these councils would enable workers to manage enterprises for themselves: as a result, the sys-tem came to be known as self-management. It was introduced at selected locations in 1950, on an experimental basis, and two years later, self-management was declared official policy and established on a nationwide basis. _Self-management_ became one of the three central pillars of Titoism.

A second pillar—expressed in the slogan *brotherhood and unity*—had different operational meanings at different times, but always asserted the CPY claim to have articulated a program that was mending the tat-tered relations among the diverse nationalities and building real harmony among Yugoslavia's peoples. Yugoslavia's multiethnic composition was reflected structurally in the federal system itself. Five of the republics were created on behalf of specific national groups—Serbia, Croatia, Slo-venia, Montenegro, and Macedonia. A sixth republic, Bosnia-Herzego-vina, was established because the population in that region was ethnically mixed (Serb, Croat, "undeclared"). Bosnia's Serbs were traditionally Or-thodox Christians; local Croats were mostly Roman Catholics; those reg-istering as "undeclared" were, for the most part, Muslims. The boundaries of these six republics closely followed historic boundaries, some of them dating back centuries. Within Serbia, the autonomous province of Vojvodina and the autonomous region of Kosovo (later like-wise upgraded to provincial status) were created. Vojvodina contained a mixed population of Serbs, Hungarians, Czechs, Slovaks, and other peo-ples. The majority of residents of Kosovo were Albanians, although the proportion of Serbs in Kosovo was larger at that time than it is today.

The system's third pillar—*nonalignment*—related to foreign policy, and emerged in the years after 1955, when Tito began to court Third World leaders such as Egypt's President Gamal Abdel Nasser and India's Prime Minister Jawaharlal Nehru. These "nonaligned" countries held a historic conference at Bandung (Indonesia) in 1955, and, in succeeding

years, these conferences became regular events. Tito played a major role
in prodding along the institutionalization of the Nonaligned Movement.
The movement served Tito well as an arena in which he would appear to
be playing a global role. His dominant role in the Nonaligned Movement
seemed to place him equidistant between Washington and Moscow and
lent weight to his argument that socialist Yugoslavia was playing a positive role in assuring world peace. And this, in turn, contributed to the
legitimization of his system at home.

Ironically, it was Tito's growing contacts with Third World leaders
that kindled Soviet interest in a rapprochement and that stirred Soviet
First Secretary Nikita Khrushchev to fly to Belgrade on 13 May 1955.
Khrushchev read a dramatic apology for past Soviet behavior toward
Yugoslavia at the Belgrade airport and negotiated with Tito a document
that came to be known as the "Belgrade Declaration," which specifically
allowed that socialism could be constructed according to different formulas. Tito and Khrushchev were both interested in denigrating Stalin,
if for somewhat different reasons, and became fast friends—for the time
being—and Khrushchev got what he wanted: introductions to Tito's new
friends in the Third World.

Tito and Khrushchev started to fall out scarcely eighteen months
later, when Soviet tanks subdued the Hungarian Revolution in November 1956. But it was not until the winter of 1957–58 that one could
speak of a second rift, when the communist party, by then renamed the
League of Communists of Yugoslavia (LCY), published its draft program
for its upcoming Seventh Congress (Ljubljana, April 1958). In this program, the LCY defined self-management as the most progressive system
in the world (and hence, as more progressive than the Soviet system). The
Soviets were not pleased.

This second rift was far less serious than the first. Above all, Yugoslavia had considerably diversified its trade by then, with major trading
partners in the West as well as in the Third World.

But by the beginning of the 1960s, the highly centralized economic
system in Yugoslavia was encountering various problems, including distorted and obstructed growth, distorted prices, irregularities in supply,
poor investments, and the proliferation of unprofitable factories built for
reasons of prestige or for other political reasons (hence, known as "political factories"). In 1961, the LCY decided to open the Yugoslav economy
to the world market, to reorganize the financial markets, and to relax
wage controls. Between 1964 and 1965, additional liberalizing measures
were adopted, resulting in the repudiation of the Stalinist concept of au-
tarkic development (which, in the Yugoslav context, had been perversely
applied at the level of each of the six constituent republics), the adoption
of a more realistic exchange rate, the revision of price ratios (boosting
prices of raw materials and agricultural goods), and the expansion of the

role of banks in the Yugoslav market. In addition to these measures, it was also decided to transfer, from the federal government to the constituent republics, much of the responsibility for administering the economy.

Of the original Yugoslav "big five," one (Moše Pijade) had died soon after the war. Another (Djilas) had penned a series of boldly critical articles for *Borba* and, as a result of this indiscretion, had been stripped of his posts and expelled from the party.[12] By the end of the 1950s, if not earlier, it was clear that a major rift was developing between Slovene Kardelj and Serb Ranković. In 1959, Kardelj was shot and wounded by a certain Jovan Veselinov whom Pepca Kardelj, Edvard's wife, would always suspect of having acted on instructions from Ranković.[13] This personal rancor was simultaneously reflected in policy differences (Kardelj favoring more "liberal" policies than did Ranković) and in controversies in the relations between Slovenia and the federation.

Inter-republican discussions concerning the drafting of a new constitution, which had been announced in 1960, had to be deferred for a year because of deep differences, *inter alia* between Slovenia and some of the other republics.[14] In 1962, the Slovenian delegation to the Federal Assembly even refused to endorse the federal economic plan and ostentatiously walked out of the assembly session.[15]

The new constitution was eventually passed in 1963 (postwar Yugoslavia's "third" constitution, if the Basic Law of 1953 is counted as the "second"), setting Yugoslavia on a decentralizing course. Then, in December 1964, the leadership opened a debate concerning nationalities policy at the Eighth Party Congress. The debate revealed that there were in fact serious divisions within the party concerning nationalities policy. *Integralists,* led by Ranković (by then also vice president), argued that the party should endeavor to foster a Yugoslav national identity which would, in time, efface the sundry Serbian, Croatian, Slovenian, and other identities. *Organicists,* led by Kardelj (the party ideologue), argued that there was no need for these regional identities to fade away, that they would in any event be around for the foreseeable future, and that the party should content itself with fostering loyalty to and affection for the Yugoslav political community. Tito, who at one time had subscribed to the views championed by Ranković, was increasingly swayed by the organicists. Yugoslavia's relaxation of economic controls was, thus, accompanied by a relaxation of political controls; and economic decentralization was increasingly accompanied by political decentralization.

LITERARY AND MOTION-PICTURE TRENDS

For a few years after the break with Stalin, socialist-realist tendencies remained influential in literature. But by the latter half of the 1950s, introspective works of fiction were becoming more common, while, in the late 1960s, naturalism exerted its influence.

The postwar Yugoslav motion-picture industry similarly began its work in the shadow of socialist realism. Aleksandar Vučo, director of the federal committee for cinematography, sounded the keynote for the industry in a 1946 article, urging filmmakers:

> Our film art cannot and must not allow itself to have any other interests than the interests of our national authority, no other tasks than that of educating the wide mass of viewers in the spirit of our national and cultural revolution.[16]

Vučo held that the Soviet film industry should serve as a model for Yugoslav cinematography. Later, however, after Stalin's expulsion of Yugoslavia from the Cominform, Vučo reassessed the Soviet contribution in this area and, on the basis of a reanalysis of Soviet films of that era, identified "a progressive degeneration of the Soviet Union's great socialist experiments in film of the 1920s and 1930s toward portrayals on the screen of 'great Russian hegemonic and nationalistic chauvinism.' "[17]

The earliest postwar Yugoslav films gave pride of place to the theme of the antifascist struggle. Indeed, the theme of war and patriotism remained a central preoccupation throughout the Tito era. Prominent patriotic films of that era included *The Ninth Circle* (1960, directed by France Štiglic), *Battle of the River Neretva* (1969, directed by Veljko Bulajić), and *The Užice Republic* (1974, directed by Živorad Mitrović).

But it was only in the late 1970s and early 1980s that the Yugoslav film industry came into its own. Emir Kusturica's films *Do You Remember Dolly Bell?* (1981) and *When Father Was Away on Business* (1985) remain landmarks of Yugoslav cinematography,[18] while the decade running from 1976 to 1986 brought to the fore a new generation of Yugoslav filmmakers who successfully combined elements of realism and surrealism. Among their number were Rajko Grlić, Goran Marković, Srdjan Karanović, and Lordan Zafronović.[19]

REFORM AND CRISIS, 1965-74

The years 1964–66 were years of organizational battle between party conservatives (integralists) and liberals (organicists). As official policy shifted in a liberal direction, conservative bastions in Serbia and Montenegro subverted the plans they were handed and endeavored to obstruct the spirit of the changes. The Macedonian party was split down the middle. Much of the reason for this obstruction was traced back to Ranković and his circle. Liberals began whittling away at Ranković's base, and in spring 1966 finally persuaded Tito of the need to dismiss Ranković.

Then, in July 1966, Ranković and his deputy, Svetislav Stefanović, were released from their posts; Ranković was also expelled from the party central committee.[20]

This eliminated the chief obstruction to the implementation of the liberal program. In the succeeding years, numerous amendments were tagged on to the constitution, chiefly with an eye to strengthening the powers of the republics, at the expense of the federal government.

The decade beginning in 1965 was a time of economic boom. This was fueled in part by the rapid development in this period of touristic resorts, especially along the Dalmatian coast, and in part by Yugoslavia's increasing ability to compete in trade markets. Even at that point in time, the less developed areas (especially Kosovo, Bosnia-Herzegovina, and Macedonia) resented the fact that even in times of boom, far from catching up with the more developed republics, they actually seemed to be falling behind in relative terms. The more developed republics (Croatia especially, but also Slovenia), which were now starting to earn significant foreign currency through tourism, resented the fact that they were required to turn most of it over to the federal government. Everyone felt exploited. This was an early fruit of decentralization.

This general feeling of being exploited, combined with pervasive suspicions arising from the fact that most Yugoslavs spoke the same language but spoke it differently, would shortly ignite an excitation of national feeling among Yugoslavia's national groups, magnifying mutual fears and feelings of being threatened. The Serbs, Croats, Muslims (who were declared an official "nation" in 1968), and Montenegrins spoke the same language and had, therefore, agreed to collaborate on a common dictionary and orthography. This project ran into trouble in 1967, as the participating scholars found they could not agree as to which words were standard, and which were a regional variant. In fact, they could not even agree on the name of the language. Was it Serbo-Croatian (as most of us in the West have long called the language) or Croato-Serbian or Serbian or Croatian or Bosnian (*Bosanski,* as Bosnians called their language until recently) or just plain "Yugoslav"? And if the language should be called Yugoslav, was it Jugoslovenski (as the Serbs would say) or Jugoslavenski (as the Croats would say)? Or were Serbian and Croatian "entirely different languages" as some Croatian scholars started to insist, even though Serbs and Croats experience no particular semantic difficulties in speaking to each other? And for that matter, Serbs liked to write the language in the Cyrillic alphabet (the Serbian alphabet being similar to but not identical with the Russian alphabet), while the Croats wrote their language exclusively in the Latin alphabet, and both groups viewed the choice of alphabet as a political choice. By November 1970, the collaborative project was dead.[21]

Tito was giving the liberals some latitude, to see where their formulas

would lead. Between 1970 and 1971, there was a considerable liberalization in several sectors, including the religious sector, the press, and economic management. Many of the leading liberals at that time were also
advocates of a decentralized political system. Ultimately, the liberal formula ran aground in Croatia, where demands for secession, for a separate army, for a separate currency, and so forth, started to be heard. By
late 1971, Tito had had enough, and he swept many of the leading liberals out of the party in Croatia, Serbia, Slovenia, and Macedonia. In the
higher echelons of the Croatian party alone, 741 persons were dismissed
from office and ejected from the party, with another 280 persons merely
dismissed from office.[22]

The purge of liberals continued into 1973. Understandably, many
observers, both in Yugoslavia and in the West, expected that this presaged a thorough recentralization of the system and a partial return to
"integralism." Instead, Tito surprised the world by confirming all of the
devolutionary measures passed in the preceding years, and by making
some concessions to the developed republics on the question of the reten-
tion of foreign currency. The 1974 constitution—which briefly held the
world record as the longest state constitution (until India's surpassed
it)—struck an unstable balance between federation and confederation.
But as long as Tito was around to serve as the ultimate arbiter of disputes, this instability was not noticed.

THE GOLDEN AGE, 1974–80

It is not only in retrospect that the six years of "late Titoism"—from the
passage of the fourth postwar constitution in 1974 to Tito's death in
May 1980—look like a "golden age." Even at the time, the late Titoist
system compared very favorably with what had preceded it. To begin
with, there was the growth in the cities of a sense of "Yugoslavness."
This did not apply to the villages in any of the republics, but since political agendas and symbologies were essentially defined by the cities (especially the "big three": Belgrade, Zagreb, Ljubljana), this did not seem to
matter.

Moreover, it was in this period that the fruit of the economic boom
in the preceding period started to be felt by ordinary citizens. Purchases
of cars and televisions soared, telephones became customary, and young
people started spending serious money on fashions. It was in this period
too that feminist circles in Belgrade, Zagreb, and Ljubljana started to
establish themselves, convening a major international conference of feminists in Belgrade in 1978. And it was also in this period that popular
culture reached maturity. The year 1974 saw the founding by Goran
Bregović of the innovative rock group White Button (in Sarajevo), which
drew on ethnic melodies and quickly established itself as one of the lead-

ing bands in the country. In 1978, Bora Djordjević's Fish Soup (Belgrade) and the Macedonian group Bread and Salt (Skopje) were launched.[23]

And these were years of stability—economic stability, political stability, even (to a large extent) foreign policy stability for Yugoslavia. But this stability was inherently transient, since it was purchased with uncontrolled borrowing, which sent the Yugoslav foreign debt spiraling upwards.

But there were some danger signs as well, such as Kardelj's irrepressible political experimentation, which manifested itself in a proliferation of bureaucracy (a feature found in other communist systems too, but without the complexity of the Kardeljian system), and the creation of complicated hierarchies of offices with vaguely defined jurisdictions and frequently overlapping or duplicative services. More especially, the changes in economic policy and management between 1974 and 1976 (i.e., culminating with the Basic Law on Associated Labor in 1976) undermined some of the strengths of the system and led directly to the collapse of the Yugoslav economy, which began to be reflected in economic indices in 1978.[24] And finally, even while paying lip service to the constitution, neither the main part of the Serbian leadership nor the army ever really accepted the 1974 constitution, if former SRFY Defense Minister Veljko Kadijević (an ethnic Serb) is to be believed. According to him, they remained unreconciled and worked to subvert that constitution *from the very beginning.*[25]

Toward the end of his life, Tito decided that there was no one who could fill his shoes and that he should, therefore, be succeeded by a collective presidency, the chairmanship of which would rotate among the eight members (one from each of the eight federal units) each year.

In his final years, Tito increasingly focused his attention on foreign affairs, leaving the management of the economy and the political system to others. It was, thus, only too appropriate that his "last hurrah" was played out in Havana, far from home. Castro's Cuba, although closely aligned with the Soviet Union, had acquired membership in the Nonaligned Movement and was due to host the movement's conference in September 1979. Castro planned to use his chairmanship of the conference to push through a resolution endorsing "positive nonalignment"—Castro's code for a pro-Soviet tilt—and underlining the commitment of nonaligned nations to "progressive" politics—again pro-Soviet code. Tito was determined to prevent Castro from succeeding, and spent much of the time in the months preceding the conference flying to foreign capitals in Africa, Asia, and Latin America to build support for a more nonaligned nonalignment. In Yugoslav eyes, the Tito-Castro clash at Havana was a battle of titans, and when Tito prevailed, he returned to an exultant society.

Three months later, Tito was hospitalized, had a leg amputated, and subsequently slipped into a coma. He hovered between life and death for four months, while authorities carefully planned and rehearsed his funeral. When Tito died, there was a huge outpouring of emotion in Yugoslavia. People (especially young people) gathered in crowds on public squares, at bus stations, and at railroad stations to sing the old patriotic song, "Comrade Tito, We Pledge to You that We Will Never Deviate from Your Path," and the newer, but equally patriotic "Jugoslavijo." Tito's death brought the country together. For a few months it seemed that there were no longer Serbs and Croats, Slovenes and Albanians—but only Yugoslavs. It was an inspiring, if transient, phase.

THE PARALYSIS OF THE CENTER, 1980–86

The death of Tito, who had ruled the country for 35 years, was as great a shock to the country as the rift with Stalin had been thirty-two years earlier. For a while the leadership tried to maintain the fiction that in some larger sense, Tito was not dead. The authorities now promulgated the slogan, "After Tito, Tito," and each day newspapers were replete with pictures of Tito, hobnobbing with foreign heads of state and delivering historic speeches. It would be another three to four months before Tito would pass from the pages of the newspapers and be buried psychologically.

Meanwhile, the collective-rotational system that Tito had devised quickly proved incapable of producing either consensus at the center or effective policy. There were two reasons for this: first, the cumbersome collective structure of the system itself, which allowed the federal units veto power at many levels of government; and second, the fact that promotion in the CP had increasingly been based on what the Austrians would have called *Kaisertreue* (loyalty to the emperor—and Tito was a kind of emperor) rather than talent or intellect. Within two years, the paralysis of the center had become generally apparent. This had two chief consequences: the aforementioned paralysis of policy, but also a de facto liberalization, as people increasingly spoke out, organized quasi-oppositional groups, voiced highly divergent views in the press, and found the regime too weak or too divided to do anything to restrain them.

The result was a quickening of the incipient processes of repluralization as pacifist, gay rights, environmentalist, and feminist groups either organized for the first time or became more active. These groups were largely a phenomenon of Belgrade, Zagreb, and Ljubljana. In their wake came human rights groups and, in Belgrade, a committee to defend artistic expression, defiantly chaired by Svetlana Slapšak. New magazines appeared, which reflected the new ambience—magazines such as *Potkulture* (a magazine devoted to sundry subcultures, especially among young people) and *Rock* magazine, a glossy Belgrade publication.

Between the economic downturn and pervasive bottlenecks in the system, party elders were forced to admit that the system was malfunctioning. Accordingly, they appointed two commissions to make recommendations for the reform of the system. Sergej Krajgher, a Slovene, was appointed to head a commission for the reform of the economic system, and Tihomir Vlaškalić, a Serb, was appointed to head a commission for the reform of the political system. The Krajgher Commission filed its report in 1983, and the Vlaškalić Commission finished its report by 1986. The republics endorsed the former, but failed to take the necessary steps to carry out the Krajgher Commission's recommendations, or even to attend meetings to discuss the subject. The report by the Vlaškalić Commission was essentially ignored. In the meantime, the Serbian party organization stunned the other regional party organizations by issuing its own recommendations in October 1984, in the form of a four-part draft reform program. Among other things the Serbs called for strengthening the federal government, rolling back the autonomy and prerogatives of the autonomous provinces of Kosovo and Vojvodina (both located within juridical Serbia), democratizing the electoral system, and beefing up the autonomy of enterprises.

If there had been a mixture of uncertainty and calm resolve after Tito's death, the latter had soon been shattered by Albanian riots in the province of Kosovo in spring 1981. In 1912–13, the emergent Albanian national state had laid claim to Kosovo, the majority of whose population was Albanian. But the Great Powers had intervened to prevent this and, on Russia's initiative, assigned the province to Serbia. After the dismemberment of Yugoslavia during World War II, Tito had needed to apply raw force to coerce the Kosovar Albanians back into the Yugoslav fold. And throughout the Tito era, there was an uncertain peace in Kosovo, originally based above all on police surveillance, but after 1976 increasingly based on broad concessions to the Albanians, who, by the end of the Tito era, comprised 80 percent of Kosovo's population. Above all, the 1970s had seen a steady increase in the numbers of Albanians in positions of authority and responsibility in the province. But Kosovo was the least developed by Yugoslavia's eight federal units (six republics and two autonomous provinces), and the feeling of economic deprivation was easily translated into nationalist terms: the Albanians felt that their economic backwardness was not being taken seriously by Yugoslavia's Slav majority.

So on 1 April 1981, violent riots broke out at the University of Priština, and over the next few days, disorder swept throughout the province. The riots had an anti-Serbian and anti-Yugoslav character—anti-Serbian because most of the non-Albanians in Kosovo were Serbs, anti-Yugoslav because of resentment at the country's failure to treat them, as they saw it, equally. Albanian-inhabited districts in western Macedonia and in southern Montenegro also experienced some unrest. At least a hundred persons were killed in the riots, and about a thousand were injured, many by firearms.

In the succeeding months, the Yugoslav public learned that there had been troubles in Kosovo throughout the 1970s. But now, in the wake of these riots, police started to uncover underground Albanian organizations, some of them secessionist in orientation, some of them basically liberal. Between April 1981 and September 1987, some 5,200 Kosovar Albanians were arraigned on criminal charges relating to these underground organizations.[26]

The Serbs had long retained a quasi-mystical orientation toward the province, chiefly because of a major battle there in 1389 in which a Serbian army had confronted an Ottoman-Turkish army. Interestingly enough, until recent decades, there had always been some Serbian historians who portrayed the battle (which ended with the withdrawal of both armies) as a *Serbian victory* and as late as 1940, Serbian historian Mihailo Dinić gloated over the "Christian victory" over the Turkish Muslim army on the Field of the Blackbirds.[27] But in 1968, historian G. Ostrogorski defined what has come to be the standard interpretation of the battle as a *Turkish* victory, noting that the Serbian state subsequently collapsed, seventy years later.[28] This statement reinforced what has been the dominant interpretation among Yugoslavs in general. It gained political importance, however, only much later—in the course of the 1980s, as a powerful Serbian backlash, focusing on Kosovo, swept a hitherto lesser-known banker-turned-party-official named Slobodan Milošević to power in Belgrade.

The riots of 1981 electrified the Serbian public. Rumors, which blended reality with paranoid fantasy, started to circulate about the alleged harassment of Serbs by Albanians; Serbs also insisted that a fire which had destroyed parts of the Orthodox monastery at Peć had been set by Albanian arsonists; Albanians denied this. In spring 1982, the Serbian Orthodox Church charged into the fray with the publication in the patriarchate's news organ, *Pravoslavlje*, of a long critique of the regime's policy in Kosovo and an appeal for the protection of the local Serbian population and Orthodox Shrines in Kosovo. The article described Kosovo as "the Serbian Jerusalem."[29]

"Kosovo" now began to poison the political atmosphere in Yugoslavia, gradually emerging as the most prominent issue in Serbian political discourse. Where Kosovo's Albanians felt neglected, Serbs became convinced that the Albanians had been pampered. In a survey of 1,000 Belgrade residents in October 1983, for example, about 50 percent of respondents favored reducing economic assistance to Kosovo and the other less developed regions.[30] Between April 1981 and December 1987, nearly 25,000 Serbs and Montenegrins left Kosovo, often for economic

*Albani
genocide*

reasons, usually to live in Serbia proper, reducing the Slavic component
in Kosovo's population, and bringing back stories of violent assaults on
Serbs, the killing of farm animals owned by Serbs, Albanian rapes of
Serbian women, and so forth. In 1982, 1985, and twice in 1986, Kosovar
Serbs drew up widely publicized petitions to federal authorities, complaining, in the January 1986 petition, that the Albanians were pursuing
a policy of "genocide" against non-Albanians.[31]

The new nationalism sent reverberations throughout the system. In
Serbia, Danko Popović's novella, *Knjiga o Milutinu* (1986), created a
huge stir among the public. Looking at the world from the perspective of
a simple Serbian peasant frustrated by the injustice of history, Popović's
novella struck a resonant chord; it was, in fact, a nationalist chord. Other
cultural figures took a different slant. Kosovo, mythologized and sacra-
lized, emerged as a major theme in Serbian poetry, and ever with nationalist effect.[32] Then there was the controversial play, *Pigeonhole,* which
recounted the story of young children growing up in a country destroyed
by war.[33]

In September 1986, the Serbian Academy of Sciences and Arts leaked
a seventy-four-page "Memorandum" to the press. The "Memorandum"
indicted Tito for alleged injustices against Serbs, called Serbs the "real
victims" of Titoist Yugoslavia, and demanded a rectification of these historical injustices.

COUNTDOWN, 1987–91

*Milošević
Coup*

In late 1987, in what amounted to an internal party coup, Milošević,
already second-in-command in the Serbian party organization, edged out
his erstwhile mentor, Ivan Stambolić, and took the leadership post for
himself. He quickly set about bringing the daily newspapers *Politika* and
Politika ekspres, alongside Radio-Television Belgrade, under his personal
control, and radically reoriented politics in Serbia. Beginning with his
ascent to power, there was a strong revival of interest in Serbian history,
followed by a renewed insistence on the Cyrillic alphabet (and a reversal
of Tito's policy of disseminating the Latin alphabet in that republic), followed by an escalating absorption with Kosovo (tinged with the collective pain that nationalist mythology can inspire), followed by the slow
emergence (by 1989) of the first hints of what would, by early 1991,
become a full-scale campaign of vilification of Albanians, Croats, and
Bosnian Muslims. Serbia was quickly engulfed with passion over Kosovo. Pop singers sang songs about Kosovo. Historians wrote books
about Kosovo (in Cyrillic, of course). Television programs and magazines
devoted space to recounting the sufferings of Serbs in Kosovo. It was as
if the entire Serbian people had suddenly come down with a bad case of
"Kosovo fever." So totally was Serbia engulfed with this "fever" that

there was even a perfume named for the six-century-old Battle of Kosovo: "Miss 1389." Hatred of Albanians, Croats, and Muslims was now "discovered" to have historical "sanction." The aforementioned reappraisal of the significance of the battle of Kosovo played directly into the hands of those wishing to build up strong ethnic consciousness on the foundation of the hatred of various "out-groups."

Milošević dramatically changed the conduct of politics in Serbia. Under Tito and his immediate successors, nationalism was consistently seen as "dangerous," the involvement of religious organizations in political and nationalist activities was forbidden, and criticism of the policies of other republics was taboo. Under Milošević, Serbian nationalism was explicitly rehabilitated, the Serbian Orthodox Church was praised for its role in fostering Serbian nationalism, and the Serbian party began to make a regular practice of criticizing other parties. Moreover, where under Tito and his immediate successors the mobilization of the grassroots to effect political change was strictly taboo, now, under Milošević, a Committee for the Protection of Kosovo Serbs and Montenegrins was set up, for the express purpose of organizing popular disturbances. Between 9 July and 4 September 1988, the committee organized a series of rallies, which assembled crowds of more than 100,000 persons at each rally.[34] These rallies destabilized the governments of Vojvodina, Kosovo, and Montenegro and helped to consolidate Milošević's power base.

Milošević used these demonstrations and disturbances to destabilize and overthrow the governments of Vojvodina, Kosovo, and Montenegro, replacing the incumbents with his own followers. He also exploited the commemorations of the 600th anniversary of the June 1389 Battle of Kosovo to raise Serbian nationalism to a fever pitch. As early as June 1988, Milošević succeeded in imposing Serbo-Croatian as the sole official language of Kosovo (ending Tito's policy of allowing two official languages in the province—Serbo-Croatian and Albanian).[35] Subsequently, in February 1989, Milošević pushed through a series of amendments which terminated the provinces' authority to pass their own legislation and scrapped their autonomy in other spheres as well. Village militias, consisting of local Serbian civilians, were set up throughout Kosovo, armed (by the JNA), and trained for combat.[36] Milošević now turned his attention to Bosnia-Herzegovina, dispatching agents of the Serbian security service to that republic in order to gather intelligence and begin the internal subversion of that republic.[37] Since Milošević was president of Serbia, not of Yugoslavia, he clearly lacked a constitutional mandate to authorize such activities in another republic.

Milošević overstepped his mandate in another, more crucial matter—by authorizing the purchase, from the Soviet Union, of huge quantities of military hardware, without the knowledge, much less the consent, of Yugoslav Prime Minister Ante Marković (a Croat).[38] Much of this hardware was destined for (illegal) distribution, by the Serb-dominated Yugoslav National Army (JNA), to Serbian civilians in Croatia and Bosnia, beginning in the summer of 1990.[39] These hefty purchases of arms were undertaken at a time of deepening economic crisis and fiscal insolvency and without authorization through normal channels.

In summer 1989, the Slovenian Writers' Association and the Serbian Writers' Association began to quarrel about Kosovo. The Slovenian group felt that Serbian abrogation of Kosovo's autonomy and police repression in the province were unconscionable; the Serbian writers defended Belgrade's policy and complained of Slovenian "interference." Within a matter of weeks, this quarrel had reached the governmental level, with growing acerbic exchanges between the Slovenian and Serbian governments. In September 1989, in a bold move, the Republic of Slovenia published a set of draft amendments to its constitution, arrogating to itself the clear right of unilateral secession and declaring that only the Slovenian Assembly was entitled to declare a state of emergency in Slovenia or to authorize the deployment of military forces within the republic. These amendments were promptly attacked in the Serbian press, but the Slovenian Assembly passed them in October all the same.

At this point, Milošević decided to use his grassroots mechanisms to destabilize Slovenia. The aforementioned committee announced its intention to come to Slovenia en masse to "explain the situation" to the Slovenes. The Slovenian government banned any such meeting, and when the Serbs seemed intent on proceeding with it anyway and spoke of bringing 30,000 to 40,000 Serbs to Slovenia, the Slovenian and Croatian railway unions stopped the trains carrying the committee's agitators and supporters and sent them home to Serbia.

This was a turning point. In the wake of this crisis, the Serbian Socialist Alliance (an organizational handmaiden of the League of Communists of Serbia) called on Serbian enterprises (in December 1989) to cut links with Slovenia. Within three weeks, almost all economic contacts and contracts between the two republics had been ruptured. This development signaled the death of Yugoslavia. After this, the chances of "saving" Yugoslavia were very remote.

The following month, the Slovenian party organization announced its withdrawal from the League of Communists of Yugoslavia, and when other regional parties followed suit, the LCY disintegrated. By then, the communists of Slovenia and Croatia had agreed to hold multiparty elections in spring, and the result was the election of noncommunist governments in these two republics. This exerted a pressure on the other republics, which hastily followed suit. In the course of subsequent elections, a noncommunist coalition government was elected in Bosnia, a coalition government with communist and noncommunist participation was elected in Macedonia, and the communists, restyling themselves "socialists," held on to power in Serbia and Montenegro. There were no specific elections in Kosovo and Vojvodina because these provinces had by then lost their autonomy. The upshot was that by the end of 1990, "Yugoslavia" was a two-thirds noncommunist, one-third communist country.

The pervasive discontent which had sharpened and swelled in the course of the 1980s could no longer be tempered—except by radical measures. Unfortunately, the republics, by this point, were already acting like independent states (and in the cases of Slovenia, Croatia, and especially Serbia, already laying the institutional, legal, and military groundwork for separate independence), and these republics did not agree. Slovenia and Croatia thought the Yugoslav federation should be restructured as a full-fledged confederation. Serbia and Montenegro wanted to see the federation recentralized, and the constituent republics shorn of most of their autonomous powers. In one draft reform proposal, the Serbian party suggested, for example, that the republics should hereafter be known only as "federal units"—a proposal that excited a great deal of hostility and anger in Slovenia and Croatia. Macedonia, still infused with Titoist notions, was on the whole content with the constitutional status quo and feared the consequences of change in either the confederal or the centralist direction. And Bosnia-Herzegovina was so internally divided (because of its mixed Serbian-Croatian-Muslim population) that, of necessity, it had to abjure either the confederal or the centralist position. Macedonia and Bosnia tried to play the role of mediators, and suggested a compromise—but to no avail.

There were other disturbing developments afoot, including the cessation by the republics of transfer payments to the federation, resulting in the evanescence of the federal budget (compensated to some extent by the inflationary printing of some of what was needed but resulting all the same in the closure of some agencies, delays of several months in the payment of officials, indeed a backhanded confirmation of Marx's promise that the communist state apparatus would "wither away"). There were also changes and developments in the military sphere. Throughout 1990, various "unreliable" officers, especially Slovenes and Croats, were retired and replaced by Serbian officers, military regions were restructured and reorganized so as to reduce local republic influence, and, beginning immediately after the election of noncommunist governments in Slovenia and Croatia, the JNA terminated all weapons shipments to those republics and in fact confiscated the weapons held by their Territorial Defense Units, thus driving these republics to buy replacement weaponry on foreign markets. The JNA also assisted with the establishment of illegal Serbian militias in Croatia and Bosnia (the recipients of the illegal arms shipments mentioned earlier) and dispatched officers to train these militias for combat.[40] And in summer 1990, the JNA held military train-

ing maneuvers in Bosnia-Herzegovina; the "enemy force" against whom
the army units practiced their mock battle was said to be a joint *Slovenian and Croatian army!*[41] In December 1990, Serbs living in Croatia unilaterally declared the creation of a "Serbian Autonomous
Region—Krajina," signaling the beginning of the conflict in Croatia.[42]

During the early months of 1991, the six republics held a series of
bilateral, trilateral, and multilateral summit meetings in an effort to defuse the crisis. However, only Bosnia and Macedonia showed any willingness to compromise, and they were the least important players in this
act. Ljubljana had issued an unambiguous ultimatum, that if some agreement could not be reached by 26 June, the Republic of Slovenia would
declare its independence. Zagreb promised that if Slovenia seceded,
Croatia would follow. With the JNA and the Serbian militias armed to
the teeth and ethnic hatred and prejudice now spreading like wildfire,
these declarations seemed to promise war.

THE SECOND YUGOSLAV WAR: PHASE ONE

In March 1990, Serbian authorities arrested about 7,000 ethnic Albanians in Kosovo;[43] about the same time, there were confirmed reports of
the mass poisoning of more than 3,000 Albanian schoolchildren.[44] Local
Albanians took to the streets to protest the poisonings and blamed the
tragedy on Serbian machinations.[45] Accompanying these moves were un-
provoked massacres of Albanian civilians in Mališevo and elsewhere, and
an escalating series of armed incidents. Reviewing this record, Shkelzen
Maliqi, a journalist living in Priština, concluded that the Serbian leadership was hoping to provoke an armed rebellion on the part of Kosovo's
Albanians in order to justify the bombing of Albanian villages and systematic slaughter leading to the large-scale flight of surviving ethnic Albanians into Albania or into neighboring Macedonia. In Maliqi's view, the
Serbian leadership was thus hoping to ignite ethnic warfare already in
the spring of 1990, but was prevented from doing so by the Albanians'
spontaneous embrace of a quasi-Gandhian strategy of nonviolent resistance.[46]

Whether Maliqi is right about this must remain uncertain. What is
certain is that the big "prizes," from the Serbian perspective, were the
rich agricultural plains of eastern Slavonia (with their oil wells) and the
timber-rich and mineral-rich stretches of Bosnia-Herzegovina. Moreover,
it was primarily in Bosnia but also in Croatia that the largest numbers of
diaspora Serbs were concentrated. These were, in consequence, the most
dangerous flashpoints. And, in fact, Serbian violence against Croats living on the territory of the Republic of Croatia began on or about 17
August 1990 and, as Anton Bebler notes, immediately betrayed the character of an "organized armed rebellion."[47]

Slovenia and Croatia declared their independence on 25 June 1991, a day before the preannounced deadline. Two days later, the JNA opened hostilities against Slovenia. But within three weeks, the JNA agreed to a truce and began to withdraw from that republic. Milošević announced that he (as president of Serbia, not of Yugoslavia) had no objection if Slovenia wished to secede. By then, inter-ethnic violence within Croatia was escalating.

According to the April 1991 census, 12 percent of the population of Croatia was Serbian, many of these Serbs living in the region adjacent to and surrounding the town of Knin, in southern Croatia. These Serbs provided troops for the militias that had set up roadblocks the previous year, and that were now mobilized for action. As violent incidents between Serbian militias and Croatian police escalated, each side blaming the other, the JNA moved in to reinforce the militias, and carried out aerial bombardment of Croatian positions. By August, Croatia was unmistakably at war. Serbian forces laid siege to several towns in Eastern Slavonia (the eastern tip of Croatia), including Osijek and Vukovar, completely demolishing the latter by October, and driving out the survivors of what had once been a local population of 45,000. The east Slavonian town of Vinkovci was subjected to repeated bombardment by Serbian artillery batteries. The Adriatic pearl, Dubrovnik, also came under siege, and there were aerial attacks on Split, Zadar, and even Zagreb at one point. By the end of 1991, Serbian forces had conquered about 30 percent of Croatian territory and had declared the secession of these conquests (which they called the "Serbian Krajina Republic") from the Republic of Croatia.[48]

The Serbian population was deeply divided about the war, but it is fair to say that the most solid backing that Milošević has enjoyed for his policies (including for the prosecution of the war) has come from the countryside, while Belgrade, on the other hand, has proven fertile ground for opposition politics and pacifism. Interestingly enough, in the first phase of the war (i.e., from June 1991 to March 1992), the Serbian Orthodox Church gave solid backing to the war, and filled the pages of *Pravoslavlje* with lengthy articles purporting to demonstrate the Orthodox, hence Serbian, character of many Croatian cities, including Osijek, Dubrovnik, and Zadar.

Western governments were slow to react, initially confining themselves to admonitions to the warring parties to patch up their differences and restore the Yugoslav federation. It was to take nearly six months (i.e., until December 1991) for the West to accept that Yugoslavia was no more, and to grant diplomatic recognition to Slovenia and Croatia. The two major steps taken by the West within the first three months of the outbreak of hostilities were: first, to convene a Yugoslav peace conference, under EC auspices, in the Hague, beginning on 7 September

1991; and second, to impose an arms embargo, *on Serbia's suggestion,* through a resolution of the UN Security Council, on all the ex-Yugoslav republics.[49] Since Serbia was well armed and had taken the precaution of removing weapons stocks not only from Slovenia and Croatia, but also from Bosnia, the chief effect of the arms embargo was to freeze in place the enormous disproportion in military preparedness between Serbia and Serbian militias in Croatia and Bosnia, on the one hand, and the republics of Croatia and Bosnia, on the other hand. Indeed, at the inception of the conflict, Serbia had in stock some 520 combat aircraft, 2,900 tanks, 2,800 armored personnel carriers, 25,000 mortars, 11,000 artillery tubes, 1,250 short-range surface-to-surface missiles, and 1.2 million rifles.[50] The UN arms embargo gave strong encouragement to the Serbs to continue their war, and to escalate it by expanding the conflict into Bosnia.

EC mediation efforts did produce some results, however, and early in 1992 Serbian and Croatian forces agreed to an EC-brokered truce and to the introduction of UN "peacekeeping" forces along the military frontier. Some 13,500 UN troops took up positions, and despite occasional incidents, hostilities on this front now declined. But neither in 1991 nor subsequently did any Western power or group of powers offer to mediate in the question of Croatia's Serbian minority, leaving it to the Serbs and Croats to settle their differences on the battlefield.

In the meantime, Macedonia, left stranded in a truncated federation, had reluctantly declared its independence in October 1991 only to find that while the EC states were willing to grant diplomatic recognition to Slovenia and Croatia (accomplished in December 1991), they demurred at granting similar recognition to Macedonia, solely because Greece asserted an exclusive claim to that name.

PHASE TWO: THE WAR IN BOSNIA

Bosnia-Herzegovina was a far more complicated problem because of the deep division between its indigenous peoples. Unlike the other republics of socialist Yugoslavia, Bosnia lacked a majority nationality: in Bosnia, there were only minorities, some larger than others. In the 1991 census, the Bosnian population was recorded as 43.77 percent "ethnic Muslim," 31.46 percent Serbian, and 17.34 percent Croatian.[51] These groups were interspersed throughout the republic, and the greatest concentration of Serbs lay in western Bosnia, separated from Serbia by large concentrations of Muslims.

A referendum conducted 29 February–1 March 1992 showed total Muslim and Croatian refusal to remain joined with Serbia and total Serbian refusal to be separated from Serbia. This was a dangerous signal and there was briefly some discussion, within the framework of international mediation, of a "cantonization" scheme which would have divided the republic into more than four dozen ethnic cantons. Of the three political organizations which commanded the support of the largest numbers of each of the three largest nationalities,[52] not one of them responded positively to the initial proposal drawn up by the mediators. Then in early April, talks about "cantonization" or other peaceful accommodations came to an abrupt halt when the militia of Radovan Karadžić's Serbian Democratic Party, backed up by the "Yugoslav" (Serbian) army, began attacking Muslim towns and villages, slaughtering some inhabitants, and setting others to flight. This set the pattern for the coming months.

The ill-prepared Bosnian government of Alija Izetbegović did not even have an army and had made no efforts to import weaponry, although a small amount of weaponry had reached some Muslims by unofficial channels. In these circumstances, Bosnian Serb militias, which continued to benefit from Yugoslav Army aerial bombardment of Muslim-held towns, quickly overran much of the republic. Within two months of the opening of hostilities in Bosnia, Bosnian Serb militias took control of 70 percent of the republic's territory and began the slow strangulation of Sarajevo, a once-majestic city nestled between mountains, a city which for centuries had offered a unique blend of eastern and western culture. Even as tempers rose in the Bosnian countryside, Sarajevo maintained to a considerable degree the friendship and sense of solidarity of its inhabitants who, perhaps alone among Yugoslavia's peoples, understood that they were, first and foremost, *neighbors*. And thus, the siege of Sarajevo found Sarajevo Serbs fighting shoulder to shoulder with Croats and Muslims of Sarajevo to repel these invaders from the countryside who subscribed to the notion that only people of one nationality ought to live in any given state and that, for reasons not spelled out, all conationals had to live in the same state.

A CIA report released in March 1995 concluded that about 90 percent of all atrocities in the Bosnian war had been the work of the Serbian side. Other sources have also documented the orchestrated campaign of mass rape, conducted on orders from Bosnian Serb commanders, of the Muslim women of Bosnia. Some sources estimate that as many as 50,000 Bosnian Muslim women may have been subjected to repeated rape and "forced impregnation" in Serb-run "rape camps" by October 1992 alone.[53]

In the early months of 1993, the British, French, United States, and Russian governments tried to promote the so-called Vance-Owen Peace Plan—a patchwork quilt which many judged to be geostrategically untenable—among the combatants. The Croats readily agreed to it, since the plan gave them more than they had been seeking up to then, and the Bosnian government eventually agreed. But the Bosnian Serbs roundly rejected the plan, after sending out reassuring and ultimately misleading signals to the West over a period of weeks. The Western powers threatened the Serbs with military action, but ultimately did next to nothing. A large part of the problem was that Britain and France actually favored the Serbs, but needed to avoid undue provocation to the United States, the Islamic world, and world public opinion (including much of the British public itself). The result was a hybrid policy of providing humanitarian aid, supporting ineffectual cosmetic military responses (such as the pinprick air strike against the Serb-held airfield at Udbina in November 1994), and invoking empty rhetorical phrases that neither Britain nor France had any intention of backing up with action. The British government at times preferred to look foolish rather than scheming, reminding one of the Serbian phrase, *"igrati Engleski"* (to play English), which is used to mean *to play dumb.*

Apprehending the situation for what it was but forgetting that there is always a price to be paid for aligning oneself with an aggressor, Croatia's Franjo Tudjman gravitated toward a marriage of convenience with Serbia's Milošević, in a move squarely condemned by many Croats. These new partners now devised their own "peace plan" in July 1993 and tried to press the Izetbegović government to agree to it. Ironically, David Lord Owen and his new collaborator in mediation, Thorvald Stoltenberg, endorsed the Tudjman-Milošević plan, proposing only slight revisions. Izetbegović, placed under enormous pressure by Britain and France, initially agreed to the plan, but this plan too died on the table.

Meanwhile, the number of casualties and atrocities escalated steadily in what had become, since the Vance-Owen plan and accompanying Western irresolution, a three-sided conflict, and there were increasing calls in the West for military action to cripple Serbian military strength and force the Serbs to negotiate in good faith, by depriving them of any alternative course of action. Owen spoke for Her Majesty's government in blocking such calls. On 16 November 1993, he told an audience in Dublin:

> We have long been aware of the dangers of simply responding to the cry to "do something." All too often we know that an illness has to work its way through the system. As a protective mechanism the medical profession has developed the skill of masterly inactivity. . . . Politicians need some of the same skills.[54]

Nor was the Russian factor a major concern at the time. During 1992 and well into 1993, Russia was self-absorbed with its own internal problems (including economic conversion and decline, the growth of crime, and ethnic conflicts along its periphery, specifically in Chechnya, Transdniester, Nagorno-Karabakh, Tajikistan, and elsewhere) and would have been in no position to resist a united Western program for the Yugoslav war, had such unity been achievable.

Even though their lack of military hardware exposed the Bosnian Muslims to continued Serbian atrocities, British Prime Minister John Major and British Foreign Secretary Douglas Hurd opposed American and German efforts to lift the arms embargo against the Muslims, on the grounds that there were "enough weapons in the area" and that lifting the embargo would only prolong the war. In fact, as Adrian Hastings has pointed out, the British government systematically reiterated, as if they were facts, many elements of the propaganda line generated by Belgrade.[55] Moreover, even though it was well known that the Serbs had comprised only 31.5 percent of the population of Bosnia-Herzegovina in 1991, when UN and European Union "mediators" returned with their third partition plan in June 1994, they proposed to grant the Serbs 51 percent of Bosnian territory, openly rewarding Serb aggression. Although the Russians (the Serbs' most visible sponsor) urged the Bosnian Serbs to agree to the plan,[56] the Bosnian Serbs rejected it, on the argument that the Muslim-Croat federation had been favored in terms of the distribution of coal and mineral reserves.[57]

In response, and in the face of an escalation of Serb expulsions of Gypsies, Muslims, and Croats from Banja Luka, Bijelina, Janja, and other areas securely controlled by the Serbs since 1992, Western diplomats revealed their real preferences by *rewarding* Milošević. In exchange for the latter's promise to terminate military supplies to the Bosnian Serbs, the Western powers suspended some of the sanctions against the Federal Republic of Yugoslavia (FRY); numerous sources later confirmed that Milošević never carried out his part of the bargain,[58] but for all that, the West did not think to rescind its rewards.

Meanwhile, Croatia and Bosnia found a secure source of arms in Iran,[59] while the FRY signed a military agreement with Russia in February 1995.[60] By then there were increasing rumors that Croatia was strong enough militarily to take matters into its own hands. U.S. Ambassador to Croatia Peter Galbraith tried to dampen the waxing Croatian war fever, issuing a statement on 9 February to the effect: "We state clearly that we shall not support Croatia if it chooses the military option."[61] Galbraith's warning notwithstanding, the Croatian army cleared western Slavonia of Serb occupation forces in early May and liberated the so-called "Krajina" in July–August 1995. Some 150,000 Serbs fled the "Krajina" and headed for Serb-occupied parts of Bosnia.[62] In the meantime, Bosnian Serb forces overran the UN "safe havens" of Srebrenica and Žepa in July, killing up to 10,000 men and boys in Srebrenica and additional numbers in Žepa.[63]

History will record that the limited airstrikes initiated by NATO against certain Bosnian Serb positions in late August 1995 did not go far enough and that the Dayton Peace Agreement which emerged in the wake of those strikes[64] was therefore premised on a level of goodwill and mutual trust which simply did not exist. The Muslim newspaper *Nova Bosna* declared its pessimism quite clearly in July 1996, arguing that there can be "no peace with fascists."[65] Serb and Croat actors made similar statements. Moreover, as of June 1996, Bosnian Serbs were continuing with "ethnic cleansing" in Teslic and Doboj, both areas allocated to their control.[66] In the short run, however, Serbs, Croats, and Bosnian Muslims alike wanted a respite—both to rebuild the areas under their respective control[67] and to build up their military machines in preparation for a new round of fighting. As if anticipating local needs, the UN belatedly lifted the arms embargo against all parties on 19 June 1996.[68] While this move had been preceded by an accord, signed by Bosnian Croats, Muslims, and Serbs, to limit their arsenals for a period of three and a half years,[69] it was not clear what mechanisms would serve to enforce this agreement, let alone extend it beyond its fixed term. Moreover, already in April 1996, Arab states announced that they were pledging about $100 million to train and arm Bosnia's (i.e., the Bosnian Muslims') military.[70] The other sides can be expected to be pursuing similar policies.

Meanwhile, Bosnian Serb leader Karadžić and Bosnian Serb military commander Ratko Mladić, charged with war crimes by the International Tribunal at The Hague, remained at liberty and the Western powers, which had initially insisted on their surrender to international authorities, gradually contented themselves with pressing for Karadžić's resignation from the Bosnian Serb presidency.[71] As reports surfaced that Karadžić might in fact step down, U.S. State Department spokesperson Glyn Davies speculated, "Maybe what we're seeing, and we certainly hope this is the case . . . [is] the marginalization of Radovan Karadžić," adding, in a phrase redolent of Eliza Doolittle, "That would be wonderful."[72]

EPILOGUE AND RETROSPECTIVE

As a result of the war, the post-communist elites of the former Yugoslav republics confront challenges unique in Eastern Europe. By the end of 1995, there were some 215,000 to 220,000 dead in Bosnia[73] as a result of the fighting (plus an additional 50,000 who died in Croatia), more than 2.5 million refugees (some in foreign countries and some within the combat zone), massive damage to infrastructure (in Bosnia and Croatia), staggering unemployment (above all in Croatia and Serbia, with the situation in Bosnia being beyond questions of "unemployment"), and monumental economic dislocation (everywhere except in Slovenia). Moreover, the psychological effects of the war are likely to outlast this generation. As Nicole Janigro notes, already by 1993, 72 percent of the children of Bosnia had witnessed the bombing of their homes, 51 percent had witnessed murder, 39 percent had lost someone close, and 19 percent had even assisted in a massacre.[74] The next generation has already lost its innocence.

For some of Yugoslavia's successor states—Slovenia, Croatia, and the Serb-Montenegrin federation—there are tasks faced in common with some post-communist societies in Eastern Europe. Certainly, economic rehabilitation, privatization, the building of a pluralist system based on the rule of law and notions of fair play, the general challenges of legitimation of new systems, and the need to contain and defuse intolerant nationalism and other strains of chauvinism are tasks which confront all the states in this region, including for that matter Macedonia and whatever government will ultimately rule over Bosnia. But the strains of coping with refugees (affecting Serbia, Croatia, Slovenia, and of course Bosnia) and the destruction of infrastructure are problems which other societies in the region do not face to any comparable degree.

From the vantage point of 1996, looking back over seventy-eight years of Yugoslav history, it is clear that this country has experienced far more turbulence, conflict, and crisis than most countries in Europe, and that the late Tito era was indeed a kind of "golden age" in which people, ever so briefly, had the luxury of being able to forget about big questions and focus on lesser and more mundane matters. Some people will praise Tito for having assured peace for the thirty-five years of his rule and mourn the fact that after Tito there was, in fact, no Tito. Others will criticize Tito for having contributed, at least in part, to laying the groundwork for the present conflict—for failing to leave behind a framework capable of resisting and confounding challenges to the system such as that mounted by Milošević. Most will probably agree, however, that it is too late to think in terms of restoring a unified Yugoslavia, whether constructed on Titoist principles or not.[75] For better or worse, Tito's Yugoslavia is dead and for the foreseeable future Serbia, Croatia, Slovenia, and Macedonia are trying to build a better life by going their separate ways.

Notes

1. For details, see Ivo Banac, *The National Question in Yugoslavia: Origins, History, Politics* (Ithaca: Cornell University Press, 1984), 298–300; and Noel Malcolm, *Kosovo: A Short History* (London: Macmillan, 1998), 267–268, 272–282.

2. Marshall Lee Miller, *Bulgaria during the Second World War* (Stanford: Stanford University Press, 1975), 123–124.

3. A useful study of wartime Yugoslavia is Walter R. Roberts, *Tito, Mihailović and the Allies, 1941–1945* (New Brunswick: Rutgers University Press, 1973). Regarding the Chetniks' collaboration with the Nazis and with the quis-

ling Nedić regime in Belgrade, see Branislav Božović and Mladen Stefanović, *Milan Aćimović—Dragi Jovanović—Dimitrije Ljotić* (Zagreb: Centar za informacije i publicitet, 1985), 94–95.

4. Regarding the *ustashe*, see Bogdan Krizman, *Pavelić i Ustaše* (Zagreb: Globus, 1978).

5. Fikreta Jelić-Butić, *Ustaše i Nezavisna Država Hrvatska, 1941–1945* (Zagreb: Sveučilišna Naklada-Liber and Školska Knjiga, 1977), 167, 169.

6. Milan Borković, *Milan Nedić* (Zagreb: Centar za informacije i publicitet, 1985), 136–137.

7. Vladimir Žerjavić, *Gubici stanovništva Jugoslavije u drugom svjetskom ratu* (Zagreb: Jugoslavensko Viktimološko Društvo, 1989), 61–66.

8. Vojislav Koštunica and Kosta Čavoški, *Party Pluralism or Monism: Social Movements and the Political System in Yugoslavia, 1944–1949* (Boulder: East European Monographs, 1985), 77.

9. Ervin Dolenc, "Culture, Politics, and Slovene Identity," in Jill Benderly and Evan Kraft, eds., *Independent Slovenia: Origins, Movements, Prospects* (New York: St. Martin's, 1994), 84.

10. Ivo Banac, *With Stalin, against Tito: Cominformist Splits in Yugoslav Communism* (Ithaca: Cornell University Press, 1988), 149.

11. For details, see Béla K. Király, "The Aborted Soviet Military Plans against Tito's Yugoslavia," in Wayne S. Vucinich, ed., *At the Brink of War and Peace: The Tito-Stalin Split in a Historic Perspective* (New York: Brooklyn College Press, 1982).

12. Details in Stephen Clissold, *Djilas: The Progress of a Revolutionary* (Hounslow: Maurice Temple Smith, 1983).

13. Boro Krivokapić, *Jugoslavija i komunisti—adresa Jovana Djordjevića* (Belgrade: Niro Mladost, 1988), 55 and 55n.

14. Božo Repe, "Slovenians and the Federal Yugoslavia," in *Balkan Forum* (Skopje), Vol. 3, No. 1 (March 1995), 146.

15. Ibid., 144–145.

16. Quoted in Daniel J. Goulding, *Liberated Cinema: The Yugoslav Experience* (Bloomington: Indiana University Press, 1985), 8.

17. Ibid., 10.

18. Daniel J. Goulding, "Yugolav Film in the Post-Tito Era," in Daniel J. Goulding, ed., *Post New Wave Cinema in the Soviet Union and Eastern Europe* (Bloomington: Indiana University Press, 1989), 249–251.

19. Andrew Horton, " 'Only Crooks Can Get Ahead': Post-Yugoslav Cinema/TV/Video in the 1990s," in Sabrina Petra Ramet and Ljubiša S. Adamovich, eds., *Beyond Yugoslavia: Politics, Economics, and Culture in a Shattered Community* (Boulder: Westview, 1995), 415–416.

20. More details on the fall of Ranković in Sabrina Petra Ramet, *Nationalism and Federalism in Yugoslavia, 1962–1991*, 2nd ed. (Bloomington: Indiana University Press, 1992), 90–91.

21. See the account in Dennison I. Rusinow, *The Yugoslav Experiment, 1948–1974* (Berkeley and Los Angeles: University of California Press, 1977).

22. Savez Komunista Hrvatske, *Izvještaj o stanju u SKH u odnosu na prodor nacionalizma u njegove redove*, Twenty-eighth Session, 8 May 1972 (Zagreb: Informativna služba CK SKH, 1972), 127–128. For further discussion of this period, see also Miko Tripalo, *Hrvatsko proljeće* (Zagreb: Globus, 1990).

23. For more on the Yugoslav rock scene, see Sabrina Petra Ramet, *Balkan Babel: The Disintegration of Yugoslavia from the Death of Tito to Ethnic War*, 2nd ed. (Boulder: Westview, 1996), Chap. 5 ("Rock Music"); and Sabrina Petra

Ramet, "Shake, Rattle, and Self-Management: Making the Scene in Yugoslavia," in Sabrina Petra Ramet, ed., *Rocking the State: Rock Music and Politics in Eastern Europe and Russia* (Boulder: Westview, 1994).

24. Janez Smidovnik, "Disfunctions [Dysfunctions] of the System of Self-Management in the Economy, in Local Territorial Communities and in Public Administration," in James Simmie and Jože Dekleva, eds., *Yugoslavia in Turmoil: After Self-Management* (London: Pinter, 1991), 18, 30.

25. Veljko Kadijević, *Moje vidjenje raspada* (Belgrade: Politika, 1993), as cited in Repe, "Slovenians," 150.

26. *New York Times*, 1 November 1987, 6.

27. Cited in Ivan Kampus, "Kosovski boj u objavljenim najstarijim izvorima i u novijoj Srpskoj historiografiji," in *Historijski Zbornik* (Zagreb), Vol. 62 (1989), No. 1, 3.

28. Ibid., 14.

29. *Pravoslavlje* (Belgrade), 15 May 1982, 1.

30. *Los Angeles Times*, 15 March 1984.

31. *Frankfurter Allgemeine*, 5 February 1986.

32. Staniša Nesić, "Kosovo u novijoj sprskoj poeziji," in *Savremenik*, Nova serija, No. 6 (June 1989), 630–647.

33. For more details about *Pigeonhole* and other similar developments, see Pedro Ramet, "Apocalypse Culture and Social Change," in Pedro Ramet, ed., *Yugoslavia in the 1980s* (Boulder: Westview, 1985).

34. For more on this committee, see Darko Hudelist, *Kosovo—Bitka bez iluzija* (Zagreb: Dnevnik, 1989).

35. *Politika* (Belgrade), 17 June 1988, 5.

36. Dušan Janjić, "National Identities, Movements, and Nationalism of Serbs and Albanians," in *Balkan Forum*, Vol. 3, No. 1 (March 1995), 43.

37. See *Danas*, No. 401 (24 October 1989), 15–16.

38. These purchases, together with Marković's ignorance of them, were admitted in Tanjug (16 July 1991), in FBIS, *Daily Report* (Eastern Europe), 17 July 1991, 31.

39. Details and documentation in Sabrina P. Ramet, "The Breakup of Yugoslavia," in *Global Affairs*, Vol. 6, No. 2 (Spring 1991).

40. Branka Magaš, *The Destruction of Yugoslavia: Tracking Yugoslavia's Break-up 1980–92* (London: Verso, 1993), 267, 311, 333.

41. Ibid., 261.

42. Tanjug (21 December 1990), in FBIS, *Daily Report* (Eastern Europe), 28 December 1990, 44.

43. Janjić, "National Identities," 45.

44. The poisonings are reported in *Süddeutsche Zeitung* (Munich), 1 August 1990, 7, which estimates that "more than 3,000" schoolchildren were poisoned. Shkelzen Maliqi sets the figure at 7,000, in his "Self-Perception of Albanians in a Non-Violent Structuring of National Identity Vis-a-vis Serbs," in *Balkan Forum*, Vol. 2, No. 4 (December 1994), 136. Maliqi attributes the poisoning to a decision taken by Serbian authorities.

45. *Süddeutsche Zeitung*, 1 August 1990, 7.

46. Maliqi, "Self-Perception," 136–137.

47. Anton Bebler, "The Armed Conflicts on the Balkans in 1990–93: Social, Economic, and Political Underpinnings and the International Extraregional Framework," in *Balkan Forum*, Vol. 1, No. 4 (September 1993), 33.

48. It is impossible, in this brief overview, to do full justice to the nuances and vicissitudes of this conflict. For more complete accounts, see Laura Silber

and Allan Little, *The Death of Yugoslavia* (London: Penguin Books & BBC Books, 1995); Reneo Lukić and Allen Lynch, *Europe from the Balkans to the Urals: The Disintegration of Yugoslavia and the Soviet Union* (Oxford: Oxford University Press, 1996); and Norman Cigar, *Genocide in Bosnia: The Policy of "Ethnic Cleansing"* (College Station: Texas A & M University Press, 1995). Regarding the Western response to the war, see Sabrina Petra Ramet, "The Yugoslav Crisis and the West: Avoiding 'Vietnam' and Blundering into 'Abyssinia,' " in *East European Politics and Societies*, Vol. 8, No. 1 (Winter 1994). Also very useful are Magaš, *The Destruction of Yugoslavia*; Jasminka Udovički and James Ridgeway, eds., *Yugoslavia's Ethnic Nightmare: The Inside Story of Europe's Unfolding Ordeal* (New York: Lawrence Hill, 1995); and Viktor Meier, *Wie Jugoslawien verspielt wurde*, 2nd ed. (Munich: Verlag C.H. Beck, 1996).

49. Regarding the arms embargo, see *New York Times*, 26 September 1991, A3.

50. Bebler, "The Armed Conflicts," 33.

51. Tanjug (30 April 1991), trans. in FBIS, *Daily Report* (Eastern Europe), 1 May 1991, 53.

52. For the Muslims, the Party of Democratic Action; for the Serbs, the Serbian Democratic Party; for the Croats, the Bosnian branch of the Croatian Democratic Community.

53. This estimate was made by the Sarajevo State Commission for Investigation of War Crimes, as cited in Slavenka Drakulić, "Women behind a Wall of Silence," in Rabia Ali and Lawrence Lifschulz, eds., *Why Bosnia? Writings on the Balkan War* (Stony Creek, Conn.: Pamphleteer's Press, 1993), 118. For further discussion, see Alexandra Štiglmayer, ed., *Mass Rape: The War against Women in Bosnia-Herzegovina* (Lincoln: University of Nebraska Press, 1993).

54. Quoted in Noel Malcolm, "David Owen and His Balkan Bungling," in *Bosnia Report*, Issue 14 (February–March 1996), 5.

55. Cited with approval in Daniele Conversi, "Moral Relativism and Equidistance: British Attitudes to the War in the Former Yugoslavia," in Thomas Cushman and Stjepan G. Meštrović, eds., *This Time We Knew: Western Responses to Genocide in Bosnia* (New York: New York University Press, 1996), 261.

56. Itar-TASS World Service (29 August 1994), trans. in FBIS, *Daily Report* (Central Eurasia), 30 August 1994, 2.

57. Itar-TASS (25 August 1994), in FBIS, *Daily Report* (Central Eurasia), 26 August 1994, 6.

58. E.g., *New York Times*, 20 April 1995, A3.

59. *Slobodna Dalmacija* (Split), 12 January 1995, 12. Further reports in *Neue Zürcher Zeitung*, 16 April 1996, 3; *New York Times*, 24 April 1996, A4; *Die Welt* (Bonn), 25 April 1996, 7; and *Neue Zürcher Zeitung*, 29 May 1996, 3.

60. Tanjug (28 February 1995), trans. in FBIS, *Daily Report* (Central Eurasia), 1 March 1995, 6.

61. Quoted in *Financial Times*, 10 February 1995, 2.

62. *Neue Zürcher Zeitung*, 7 August 1995, 1.

63. Regarding excavations of mass graves at Srebrenica, see, for example, *Christian Science Monitor*, 19 January 1996, 1, 9; and *Die Welt* (Bonn), 8 February 1996, 6. See also Jan Willem Honig and Norbert Both, *Srebrenica: Record of a War Crime* (London: Penguin Books, 1996).

64. Provisions given in *Bosnia Report—Special Issue*, No. 13 (January 1996).

65. *Nova Bosna*, 2 July 1996, 2.

66. See *New York Times*, 22 April 1996, A3; *Christian Science Monitor*, 30 May 1996, 2; and *New Europe* (Athens), 2–8 June 1996, 29.

67. By April 1996, the international community had pledged to extend almost $2 billion in aid to Bosnia for 1996 alone. See *New Europe*, 21–27 April 1996, 38.

68. *Neue Zürcher Zeitung*, 20 June 1996, 2.

69. *Washington Post*, 15 June 1996, on *AmeriCast*.

70. *New York Times*, 18 April 1996, A6; see also *New Europe* (Athens), 2–8 June 1996, 2.

71. See reports in *Slobodna Dalmacija*, 7 May 1996, 2; *The Times* (London), 3 June 1996, on *AmeriCast*; *Süddeutsche Zeitung*, 6/7 July 1996, 9; and *Neue Zürcher Zeitung*, 27 June 1996, 2.

72. Quoted in *New Europe*, 30 June–6 July 1996, 29.

73. Definitive figures calculated by Vladimir Žerjavić and reported in *Globus* (Zagreb), 9 January 1998, 24–27.

74. Nicole Janigro, *L'esplosione delle nazioni: Il caso jugoslavo* (Milan: Feltrinelli, 1993), 51–52.

75. For an alternative viewpoint, see Flora Lewis, "Reassembling Yugoslavia," in *Foreign Policy*, No. 98 (Spring 1995).

8

Romania

WILLIAM CROWTHER

Romanian political life presents an enigma to the interested observer. Within the past century Romania has been subjected to political upheaval, revolution, and determined efforts to impose social change. During the interwar years its traditional elites struggled with the problems of economic and political modernization. They failed, in the end, to construct viable democratic institutions or a cohesive national community. Even before the appearance of Soviet forces in the country, civil consensus had broken down. Radicals of the right and left clashed over control of state power, and parliamentary institutions fell to military rule. The communist period imposed new turmoil, displacing old elites, altering the population structure, and seeking to create a new socialist culture.

Despite profound and sometimes violent upheaval, distinct strands of cultural and political continuity span the entire period, shaping events that individually find parallels across Eastern Europe. Patterns of interaction between crucial elements of the society recur in the interwar, communist, and post-communist periods. Similar perspectives characterize political discourse throughout the century, despite distinct changes in regime and official ideology. The following account seeks to elucidate Romania's recent political history, beginning with the deterioration of the traditional order and ending with post-communist reconstruction.[1]

INTERWAR ROMANIA

In the years leading up to World War II Romania found itself in a state of turmoil, racked by internal divisions and beset by economic problems.

The fledgling and far-from-perfected democratic system that ruled the country for most of the interwar period was overwhelmed by the associated challenges of the depression and the rise of Nazi Germany. The agricultural economy, long overburdened, fell into collapse as world grain markets failed. Romanian industry, itself badly hit by the failure of international markets, was unable to compensate for the strain caused by the rural crisis.[2]

As incomes dwindled and unemployment rose, the political environment became increasingly unstable. The country's dominant democratic parties, the National Peasant Party and the Liberals, gave way before the advance of right wing extremists. Hostility toward foreigners was apparent in Romanian culture long before the rise of fascism in the 1930s.[3] The Romanian elites' self-perception of being an isolated group under threat (as well as outright anti-Semitism and anti-Hungarian sentiment) was evident in the works of Romanian nationalists as early as the turn of the century. Linked with resentment toward the failed democratic regime and its economic policies in the theories of more extreme intellectual currents, xenophobia became a motive force propelling a powerful indigenous fascist movement in the 1930s.

Romania's interwar left, in contrast, was notably weak. Identified by many in the largely peasant and orthodox population as both atheist and antinationalist, the socialist parties failed to attract a strong following.[4] Communists were also hampered by the success of the Bolshevik revolution and its negative impact upon the peasant population just across their eastern border. Equally detrimental was the dictate of the Comintern that Romanian communists support Moscow's claim to Bessarabia, which had been awarded to Romania in the wake of World War I.

As the Second World War approached, the precarious structure of Romanian political life disintegrated almost entirely. Upon the execution of their leader, Corneliu Codreanu, in late 1938 members of the fascist Iron Guard unleashed a campaign of political terror against an increasingly isolated royalist government. This government's failure to avert territorial concessions in the Second Vienna Award to Hungary, and the loss of Bessarabia because of the Ribbentrop-Molotov Pact led to its fall and King Carol's flight from Romania in September 1940. Power then passed briefly to the Iron Guard, which proved itself both vicious and incompetent. Following this violent and short-lived interregnum, General Ion Antonescu established a military government with the support of the Hitler regime and led Romania through the Second World War linked in a military alliance with Germany.

EARLY COMMUNISM

As the end of World War II approached, Romania's political fate was altered definitively. On 23 August 1944, with Soviet troops occupying

Romanian territory, Marshall Antonescu was overthrown and arrested by forces associated with King Michael, heir to Carol II. While the Romanian Communist Party claimed to have played a decisive part in this event, which they label an "antifascist insurrection," its role appears to have been minor at best. The coup was in all likelihood intended by democratic forces to forestall an immediate and outright takeover by the Soviets and their Romanian communist allies. If so, its success was short-lived. As in other Eastern European countries occupied by the Soviets, an initial postwar coalition government was progressively undermined in favor of increasingly outright communist rule. The end of all pretense came in December 1947, when King Michael was forced to abdicate and steps were undertaken that put Romania openly on the course of so-called "socialist construction."

The transition to communist rule that followed in the wake of World War II was a wrenching experience. Political suppression of those identified as enemies of the country's new rulers was brutal, as were the methods employed to implement the Soviet economic model. Representatives of the prewar political order were exiled or imprisoned and their organizations were banned. As the process of transformation proceeded, the level of political persecution intensified and a relatively moderate "popular front" government was abandoned in favor of open communist dictatorship. The net of repression spread to a wider sphere of the population, sweeping up landholders and prewar intellectuals as well as members of the previous political class.

In Romania introduction of the new order proceeded even less smoothly than elsewhere in the emerging Soviet bloc. One prominent reason for this was the simple lack of an indigenous communist party equal to the task of guiding the process. In blunt terms, the Romanian communists were few, inexperienced, disorganized, and despised. An initial postwar leadership group was formed by merging the so-called Muscovite contingent led by Ana Pauker, and a group of indigenous communist leaders headed by Gheorghiu Gheorghiu-Dej. Georghiu-Dej became the party's general secretary, but unification between these groups was never successfully achieved.

Under this leadership the Romanian Communist Party underwent tremendous expansion during the second half of the 1940s, growing from less than 1,000 members in 1944 to over 800,000 members by the end of 1947.[5] While growth was clearly a primary concern, significant efforts were also undertaken in this period to improve party leadership and control. Recurrent "verification" campaigns led to the expulsion of nearly one-third of the party's total membership, new party schools were established, and cadres were sent abroad to the Soviet Union for training. Finally, divisions at the top of the party were resolved through a series of leadership confrontations. The first to suffer were party moderates, like

Lucretiu Patraşcanu, who fell at the end of the popular front period. Patraşcanu, a long-time communist intellectual who had acted as an intermediary with liberal political forces during the initial Soviet takeover and then served as minister of justice, was purged for insufficient commitment to the Communist Party's policies and for displaying bourgeois tendencies.[6] Open conflict then broke out among the Stalinist faithful themselves. Leaders who had spent the war years in Moscow, Pauker and Vasile Luca in particular, came into conflict with the "workers' faction" that grouped around Gheorghiu-Dej. In 1952 Luca, then serving as minister of finance, was charged with economic improprieties and dereliction in carrying out his duties. Pauker, minister of foreign affairs, had been responsible for party organization and recruitment, and for agricultural collectivization, and was a more formidable opponent. Despite resistance, she was unable to stave off the coalition that Gheorghiu-Dej constructed to displace her. She was charged with complicity in Luca's activities and with improprieties of her own, and purged in 1952. By the mid-1950s intra-party conflict had thus culminated the consolidation of Gheorghiu-Dej's control over the blossoming Romanian communist apparatus.[7]

Romania's early postwar economic transformation, like its political evolution, broadly paralleled events in the rest of Eastern Europe. Physical hardship was widespread. To the substantial damage of the war years was added the burden of postwar Soviet extractions. Initial reform was slow to take hold and ineffective due to the communists' disorganization. Agricultural collectivization, introduced in 1949, was badly managed and extremely coercive. Destabilization of the agricultural sector led to partial abandonment of the initial collectivization effort within two years. In 1951 an intense effort at industrialization was unleashed with the introduction of the First Five Year Plan.[8] But in 1953 the obvious overstress and disequilibrium of the economy, combined with changes in the Soviet leadership associated with Stalin's death, induced decisionmakers to accept the necessity of a period of retrenchment in this effort as well.

THE ORIGINS OF ROMANIAN DEVIATION

While each of the East European communist regimes presents its own unique history, Romania stands apart from the rest on a variety of grounds. Its initial divergence from the mainstream of East European communism resulted from related international and domestic political factors that were evident as early as the mid-1950s. The preeminent external circumstance shaping Romania's political evolution was the deterioration in Romanian-Soviet relations. This in turn can be accounted for, at least in part, by Gheorghiu-Dej's triumph over foes within the Romanian Communist Party more likely than himself to have achieved accord with the post-Stalinist leadership in Moscow.

Gheorghiu-Dej and his colleagues managed to weather the first phase of de-Stalinization by proving both their loyalty and utility to Moscow through maintaining order during the Hungarian crisis of 1956. There was, however, no convincing means through which they could disguise their unmistakable Stalinist origins and disposition. When Nikita Khrushchev renewed his assault on Stalinism during the October 1961 Twenty-second Soviet Party Congress, increased tension became inevitable. Contention arose in the economic realm as well. Bucharest persevered in its commitment to rapid industrialization in the late 1950s after Moscow abandoned this course. Friction was increased by Soviet advocacy of supranational planning and industrial specialization within COMECON. Leaders in Bucharest saw this as a threat to their development priorities and resisted as far as possible.

Taken together these developments set Romania and the USSR increasingly at odds.[9] In response the Romanian communist leaders undertook a series of measures to insulate themselves against Moscow's hostility. Finally, in April 1964, the RCP Central Committee issued its noted "Statement on the Stand of the Romanian Workers' Party Concerning the Problems of the World Communist and Working-Class Movement." This document, often referred to as Romania's "declaration of independence," signalled the Romanians' intention to pursue their own course even in the face of the Soviet Union's express opposition.[10]

THE RISE OF NICOLAE CEAUŞESCU AND ROMANIA IN THE 1970s

Following the death of Gheorghiu-Dej in 1965, Nicolae Ceauşescu moved to assume the leadership of the Romanian Communist Party. The son of poor peasants, Ceauşescu entered the Communist Party youth organization at fifteen years of age, in 1933. His arrest and incarceration soon afterward brought him into contact with Gheorghiu-Dej, who was also in confinement at the time. In 1945 Ceauşescu was elected to the RCP's first postwar Central Committee. From there he rose quickly in the ranks of the new political elite, becoming a deputy minister of agriculture, then deputy minister of defense. In 1957 he was entrusted with responsibility for RCP cadres policy. This broad experience in different sectors of the party organization, as well as his key role in cadres' selection, placed Ceauşescu in an ideal position to compete for the top position on Gheorghiu-Dej's demise. Even so, his success in this endeavor was neither easy nor immediate, but rather required nearly five years to consolidate.

Because of the groundwork laid by his predecessor, Ceauşescu was able to act with some autonomy from Moscow on ascent to leadership of the RCP. He was quick to take advantage of his situation, turning Romanian's independent course to his own ends.[11] A determined "renationalization" campaign was opened almost immediately upon Ceauşescu's assumption of office. The Communist Party was explicitly linked in propaganda communications with the fulfillment of Romanian national aspirations and presented as the highest expression of the national tradition. Party ideologists underscored the link between support for the Communist Party, commitment to Ceauşescu as a national leader, and hostility toward the nation's historic adversaries.

The obvious intent of the broad general shift in the RCP's legitimation strategy was to gain a base of popular support for the new leader by locating the party within the mainstream of the traditional culture. Accommodation with traditional beliefs was necessary in order to counter the perception that the Romanian Communist Party was merely the vehicle through which foreign (Russian) overlords ruled the country.

Highly visible efforts by Gheorghiu-Dej's successors to foster Romania's independence from the Soviet Union added credibility to this strategy.[12] In particular, the 1968 Soviet invasion of Czechoslovakia played a key role in defining Ceauşescu's increasingly nationalist ideological direction. Confronted with the Warsaw Pact forces' action against Prague, Ceauşescu took a strong and public stance in support of national sovereignty and independence. This position gained the regime broad popular approval, including support from a large part of the country's cultural intelligentsia. Many began to see the potential for real independence and reform in Ceauşescu's leadership.

Romania's deviation from the foreign policy line laid down in the USSR also gained a positive response from Western diplomats, who became increasingly willing to provide Romania with support. The possibilities presented by this situation were not lost on Romanian policymakers. Improved ties with the West meant both access to economic resources that would fuel their ambitious industrialization drive, and a degree of increased leverage in their relations with the USSR. Hence Romania's representatives began to vote selectively with the West in forums such as the United Nations, and spoke out publicly in support of national self-determination. The positive response of the United States and its allies was evident in such symbolic acts as President Richard Nixon's 1969 state visit to Bucharest. More pragmatically, Western appreciation was expressed through acceptance of Romania into multilateral institutions such as the General Agreement on Trade and Tariffs in 1971, and the International Monetary Fund in 1972. By 1975 the United States had rewarded the Ceauşescu regime by extending Most Favored Nation trading status to Romania.

In sharp contrast to its nonconformist views with respect to nationalism and its renegade foreign policy positions within the Soviet bloc, the Romanian Communist Party remained markedly dogmatic in regard to its domestic economic and political organization. Once firmly in control, the Ceauşescu faction dropped any pretense of moderation in these policy domains. Like his predecessor, Ceauşescu was firmly committed to rapid industrialization. Despite some early public lip service to liberalization, by the end of the 1960s the RCP held firm to an essentially Stalinist economic course. As the pace of industrialization picked up, moderately reformist tendencies that had appeared during the 1965–1969 period of leadership transition fell prey to the demands of economic "remobilization."

This orientation was evident in the 1971–1975 Fifth Five-Year Plan.[13] The growth rates projected in the final version of the plan were approximately double those of other East European countries, and the accumulation rate rose to between 32 percent and 34 percent, by far the highest within COMECON.[14] In order to facilitate implementation of this ambitious program, the administration of the economy was reorganized in 1973. A "Unitary National Socioeconomic Plan" was introduced by the regime in place of the traditional Soviet style state plan.

Stalinist industrialization, justified as a requisite of national independence, became the cardinal principle that drove Romanian policy throughout the 1970s and the 1980s. Persisting with this course had fundamental implications for the broader political environment. It demanded tighter central control over the economy rather than the devolution of authority that had appeared in other socialist economies. At the same time, capital accumulation at the levels required by the renewed industrialization drive foreclosed the possibility of decreasing popular mobilization and increasing consumer production—the direction taken by the majority of the other East European regimes. The Romanian economic strategy precluded the partial relaxation of political life undertaken in most other post-Stalinist political systems.

On the contrary, in Romania efforts to control all aspects of social life were intensified in the early 1970s. Rather than accepting ideological demobilization, the RCP demanded increased commitment to the goals of socialist transformation. Clearly this was not the course anticipated by party moderates and intellectuals who supported Ceauşescu's rise to power in the mid-1960s. Consequently, as the reality of the situation became apparent, disaffection with the regime grew. In response Ceauşescu broke definitively with the moderates, unleashing the anti-intelligentsia campaign known as the "little cultural revolution" in mid-1971. In the course of the next months thousands of professionals of dubious loyalty to the regime were dismissed or transferred. Moderates were purged from positions in the Communist Party leadership. Among those who

bore the brunt of increased repression were members of the cultural intelligentsia.[15] During the early period of Ceauşescu's consolidation, intellectuals had been encouraged to publicize the excesses of the Gheorghiu-Dej
period, and given freer reign to explore previously forbidden themes in
the national culture. Now, however, writers and artists were attacked for
failing to serve the needs of the Romanian people, and placed under increasingly intense political control. Intellectual freedom was thus limited
to the freedom to criticize the previous leader in the service of the current
one, and to develop national themes in support of Romanian communism. Those who attempted to continue as independent critical voices,
such as Paul Goma, were subjected to increasingly severe suppression.
Many, like Goma, went into exile. Others remained inside the country,
but in conditions of increasing isolation. By the 1980s open expression of
opposition in any form had been muted to the point of near extinction.[16]
    While those who resisted this dictum of subservience to Ceauşescu
were displaced by more compliant voices, figures such as Eugen Barbu
and Adrian Păunescu rose quickly to the top of the cultural establishment
by providing the unrestrained acclaim demanded of them while developing increasingly extreme nationalist themes. These same figures, and
others like them, served equally faithfully in the development of a personality cult which became increasingly exaggerated and disassociated from
reality as the years passed. Literary panegyrics to the dictator became a
notorious aspect of "late-Ceauşescuism." By the end of the decade virtually all progress was attributed to the genius of the communist leader,
while failures were laid at the feet of others.
    Ceauşescu's renationalization efforts were enhanced by the relation-
ship between Romanian communism and the Romanian Orthodox
Church.[17] Beginning in the late 1940s the interaction between Romanian
Orthodoxy and the country's revolutionary elite was less hostile than
were Church-state relations in most of Eastern Europe. Cooperation was
eased by a tradition of close Church-state relations, and by good personal
relations between Gheorghiu-Dej and Patriarch Justinian.[18] When the
Eastern Rite Catholic Church and the Lord's Army, a revivalist movement within the Orthodox faith, were subjected to intense suppression
intended to eliminate them in 1948, the Orthodox Church was left
relatively unscathed. Coercive efforts were directed against Romanian
Orthodoxy in the late 1950s, but the RCP's open shift to a nationalist
legitimation strategy served to salvage the Church's "special relationship" with the Romanian state. Ceauşescu's move toward national independence and emphasis on the Romanian cultural tradition naturally
provided possibilities for enhancing the role of Romanian Orthodoxy.
The Church's obvious nationalist inclination conformed with the emerging ideological tone of the regime. The Church hierarchy took advantage

of the opening thus presented. The leaders of the Orthodox clergy strengthened their position in the country, in exchange for which the Church aided in Ceauşescu's legitimation as a genuine "national" ruler.

Other religious confessions fared much less well under Romanian communism. The main protestant Churches, Lutheran and Reformed, and the Catholic Church drew their members primarily from among ethnic minorities, largely Hungarians and Germans. In a country increasingly dedicated to the nation, defined in ethnic terms, these faiths found themselves in a tenuous position at best. While officially recognized and allowed to function, they were subject to constant official supervision and harassment. Baptist, Pentecostal, and other evangelical Churches were also subject to official disfavor during the Ceauşescu period. While not associated with indigenous ethnic minorities, they were seen as "foreign" and as channels through which alien Western ideas could infiltrate Romanian culture, weakening the regime's hold on the population. Consequently, as Romanian communism became increasingly xenophobic, the evangelicals were subjected to intense harassment and secret police repression.

Romanian communism thus accommodated itself to the Orthodox religious tradition, melding congruent elements of the Orthodox belief system into its nationalist legitimation strategy. Other confessions were in varying degree tolerated or suppressed, but Romanian Orthodoxy, while certainly subject to partial suppression, was equally co-opted and exploited by the regime.

A similar pattern of accommodation to traditional culture, as opposed to outright revolutionary transformation, is evident in Romanian gender relations.[19] The roles of the vast majority of Romanian women prior to the advent of communism were determined by the norms of the traditional peasant society. Women were subordinate members of patriarchal extended families. While playing an important role in the household economy and in decision-making with regard to the family, females were expected to restrict their activities to the family, and to accept the authority of males within it—their fathers before marriage and their husbands afterward.

While formally committed to the elimination of gender inequality, Romanian communists did little or nothing to achieve that end. "Female" household tasks were denigrated as expressions of bourgeois oppression, and a massive effort was undertaken to move women into the workforce. But this effort reflected the regime's appetite for labor to fuel its industrialization drive rather than any commitment to equality. Once included in the urban labor force, women remained largely segregated in specific economic sectors, including services, teaching, health, and textiles. Furthermore, traditional household duties, child rearing, cooking, etc., while denigrated, remained the duties of women, now added to the burden of formal employment.

More generally, the perception of women and their status in the society was little changed. While women did enter high-level positions in greater numbers (largely as a consequence of the preeminent position occupied by Elena Ceaușescu), their actual power, as shown by Mary Ellen Fischer, was limited at best.[20] Norms remained extremely repressive with regard to female sexual behavior. Indeed, Romanian communist culture arguably became more puritanical than the traditional culture, banning virtually any public depiction or discussion of sexual matters. Reproduction was presented as a socialist duty to the nation. In 1966 abortion and contraception were banned in order to promote the growth of the workforce. Over the succeeding decades the use of coercive measures to enforce the regime's pro-natalist policies continually intensified.

With remobilization thus under way, Ceaușescu required an alternative to the formula of grounding his regime on support from a growing socialist middle class and legitimation based on the "socialist social contract" that emerged elsewhere in post-Stalinist Eastern Europe. Romania, in contrast, undertook a mass-oriented political strategy and an intensely populist ideological course. Borrowing from the pre-communist past, RCP leaders played upon ethnic hostility in a manner that could hardly be mistaken for anything less than a purposeful effort to exploit the strain of xenophobia that was evident in traditional Romanian culture.[21] Under the pressure of this policy orientation, relations between the ethnic Romanians and the country's substantial Hungarian minority deteriorated. Ceaușescu increasingly cultivated an intense "siege mentality." Material sacrifice and strict political discipline were justified as requisites of national survival. As part of the same ideological complex, a Ceaușescu "personality cult" which easily rivaled any in the world was deliberately constructed.[22]

Ceaușescu's political skill is attested to by the fact that the 1970s did not find Romania moving along the path to "developed socialism" with its East European neighbors. Rather, in accordance with their leader's grandiose plans for social transformation, Romanians descended into an indigenized reproduction of the Stalinist nightmare from which they had hoped to escape. Unfortunately for his country, while Ceaușescu was sufficiently adept to avoid reform, he provided no means of rectifying the flaws inherent in the Stalinist model. Halfway into the 1976–1980 Sixth Plan, Romania's industrialization drive faltered.[23] In addition to the sheer inadequacy of its planning mechanism, Romania suffered from economic maladies common to other centrally planned economies. Despite heavy investment, improvement in the agricultural sector proved impossible to achieve. Maintaining the continuous influx of new workers which was

essential to extensive industrialization also became increasingly problematic. Finally, from 1975 to 1982 the proportion of expenditure devoted
to consumption grew more slowly than in any other East European
COMECON country.[24] As a result of these difficulties both industrial
output and capital productivity growth rates dropped off in the late
1970s. By the end of the decade economic disaster was imminent. Annual
plan results in 1979 showed production targets under-fulfilled for nearly
every industrial commodity. Income, investment, and labor productivity
goals all went unmet as well.[25]

A final element in the mix of factors that came together to drive
Romania into crisis was the decision by party leaders to borrow the funds
needed to press forward with their strategy in the face of growing difficulties. Net financing flows from Western banks to Romania, which
amounted to $440 million from 1975 through 1977, rose to $4.32 billion
from 1978 through 1980.[26] While virtually all of the East Europeans
made use of this expedient, only Poland's leaders did so in such a way as
to generate an equally adverse effect. In a very real sense, sustaining
growth through borrowing without undertaking serious reform did nothing to improve Romania's long-term prospects, and indeed made an even
greater crisis inevitable in the near future.

ROMANIA IN THE 1980s:
CONTOURS OF DISINTEGRATION

By the close of the 1970s Romania's development program was in serious
jeopardy. Obvious inefficiencies had been sustained by increasing foreign
debt. Reliance on international borrowing in the final analysis merely
made the economy increasingly vulnerable as its own irrationalities continued to grow. The popular support generated by rapid growth and the
novelty of the RCP's nationalist stance during the early Ceauşescu years
was entirely squandered by a regime characterized more than anything
else in the 1980s by its failed promises and increased political repression.

The proximate cause which tipped Romania over the edge into spiraling collapse as the new decade began was a severe international debt
crisis. Disaster descended upon the country abruptly; Bucharest registered a hard currency trade deficit of $2.4 billion for 1980 alone.[27] Its
total hard currency debt increased to $10.35 billion in 1981, and loan
repayment arrears reached $1.1 billion by the end of the year.[28] Ceauşes-
cu's single-minded response to this crisis was consistent with his previous
pattern of behavior. In large part he relied upon an emergency program
to liquidate foreign debt, drastically reduced consumption, and at the
same time intensified efforts to increase production. As official press put
it, Romania would meet the crises with a policy of "adjustment through
growth."[29] This extreme policy did improve the country's international

financial position, generating hard currency surpluses of over $1.5 billion each year in 1982 and 1983. By 1985 net Western debt was reduced to below $5 billion. But reducing debt at this rate imposed catastrophic consequences on the already unstable economy. With respect to consumption, official reports showed a 1.9 percent decline in 1982; but in fact the situation was far worse. Western data indicate that Romanians' consumption probably declined to something in the order of 25 percent below 1980 levels by the middle of the decade.

The privation in the lives of ordinary Romanians that these figures signify bears underscoring. It was typical of Ceauşescu's policy that food exports were increased and imports limited as a quick method of generating hard currency. In 1982 food exports rose by 12.3 percent while imports decreased by 66.8 percent.[30] Rationing was imposed, and shortages of such basics as flour, potatoes, oil, and sugar were endemic. Meanwhile it became practically impossible to obtain gasoline, and during the winters of 1985 and 1986 the use of private automobiles was banned altogether. Most of Romania's cities and towns went unlit at night, and the use of household appliances was limited by law. More than one winter in the late 1980s saw the population coping with sub-freezing temperatures *inside* their apartments. That conditions such as these became a normal part of life in Romania during most of the decade epitomized both the utter bankruptcy of Ceauşescu's strategy of "multilateral development" and the severity of stress under which the Romanian population lived.[31]

Clearly, the decline in material conditions undermined support for the regime in an increasingly broad sector of the population. The Ceauşescu leadership, however, was incapable of taking positive steps to extricate itself from the policy morass that it had created. Party leaders reacted by buttressing their political positions rather than seeking avenues of reform. For Ceauşescu personally one can hardly imagine any alternative. The identification between himself and the obviously failed development strategy was virtually complete. Repudiation of the policy would clearly amount to repudiation of the leader. With reform thus excluded from consideration, the RCP leader's entire energy was directed toward the suppression of the counter-regime tendencies.

This struggle to survive in power fundamentally shaped Romanian politics during the last decade of communist rule. Ceauşescu and his spokesman repeated unambiguous and increasingly dogmatic statements in support of orthodoxy on all fronts.[32] Far from considering decentralization, they pronounced that the difficulties encountered in the national economy "necessitated an intensification and even greater perfection of planned social economic leadership, a growth of the role of the unified national plan as a fundamental instrument in regulating the functioning of the economy."[33] Incredibly, in the midst of growing disaster, Ceauşescu undertook colossal new initiatives to reconstruct Romanian society. The most notorious of these was the planned "systematization" of rural society. "Systematization" was intended to resettle village dwellers into new planned agricultural settlements and to destroy large numbers of traditional villages. In addition to its other catastrophic consequences, this project presented an obvious threat to the existence of Hungarian culture in Romania.

This reactionary course put Romania more and more at odds with the reformist political currents that were becoming dominant in the rest of the Soviet bloc. In a clear reference to the impetus for reform emanating from the Soviet Union during the late 1980s, Ceauşescu contended that alternatives to the existing state of affairs based on reformist ideas were "in complete contradiction with socialist principles" and would never be allowed to manifest themselves in Romania under any circumstances. Stating his position in these uncompromising terms excluded reform from legitimate discourse, placing its potential advocates in jeopardy of being declared treasonous.

Having effectively barred the path to real reform, the Ceauşescu leadership endeavored to create the appearance of reform by calling for improved implementation of the New Economic-Financial Mechanism (a pseudo-reform introduced originally in the late 1970s) but tolerated no real managerial initiative. When the NEFM failed to produce results, enterprise managers and ministry personnel were accused of foot-dragging and evading the law. Workers also came under increased pressure. Labor norms were raised, laws were changed to tie wages more closely to production, penalties for nonfulfillment of production targets increased. This increased pressure on industry, it appears, constituted one of the chief grievances that led to worker unrest in 1987.

As the scope of the disaster facing the country became clear, potential critics were once again purged. No member of the thirteen-member Council of Ministers appointed before 1980 survived in his post past 1984, and only five out of twenty-six members of the government did so.[34] Local party leaders came under sharp attack for their supposed failures to carry out the central government's policies, or to maintain party discipline and morale. Ceauşescu resorted even more than in the past to reliance on family members and cronies to retain control over the political system.[35] The general secretary's wife Elena, the ranking figure in the political hierarchy, and his son, Nicu Ceauşescu, were merely the most obvious examples of this phenomenon. By 1979 Elena was a member of the party's Permanent Buro, first deputy prime minister, and head of the National Council on Science and Technology. Nicu, clearly being groomed as a successor to his father, headed the party's youth organization, was a minister in the government, and in 1984 was named an alternate member of the RCP's Political Executive Committee. Other members of the Ceauşescu extended family accounted for as many as two dozen top positions in party and state institutions.[36]

By the end of the 1980s a decade of state-imposed austerity and continually increasing oppression aroused nearly unanimous hostility. Indications surfaced that organized opposition groups, however embryonic, were becoming active. Despite the vigor with which the regime applied the tactics of political repression, it failed to convince the population that its reform efforts were in any degree genuine. Open letters calling for reform were circulated within the elite. Members of the intelligentsia granted interviews to Western correspondents in the course of which opinions hostile to dictatorship were expressed. Silviu Brucan, ex-ambassador to the United States, was but the most prominent of those who became increasingly willing to publicly express discontent with Ceauşescu's leadership.[37]

On the mass level the growth of political instability was even more apparent. Strikes, work stoppages, and other antigovernment manifestations occurred sporadically beginning with the Jiu Valley miners' strikes of 1977. But the long-term deterioration of conditions caused an unprecedented upsurge in these activities in the late 1980s. In November 1987, workers in Braşov staged what were probably the most significant demonstrations in Romania since the Jiu Valley occurrence. As many as 10,000 workers took to the streets to protest their living conditions and cuts in wages.[38] Student demonstrations were staged in Cluj, Timişoara, Braşov, and Iaşi; and worker unrest occurred in various other parts of the country, clearly indicating an acute breakdown of party control.

A final element in the complex of problems that united to bring down the Ceauşescu regime was the collapse of Romania's carefully nurtured foreign policy position. Worsening relations with Moscow were an inevitable outcome of Romania's intransigence in the face of Soviet reformism. In the past this decline would likely have been balanced by focusing on positive relations with the Western alliance. But Ceauşescu's heavy-handed treatment of dissent had finally provoked a response from Western politicians. In 1987 both houses of the U.S. Congress voted to end Romania's long-standing Most Favored Nation Status because of human rights concerns. Academic and cultural exchanges were brought to a near halt, relations with major multinational lending institutions deteriorated, and Romanian officials were withdrawn from the United Nations.

THE ROMANIAN REVOLUTION

With his conventional techniques of control obviously failing, Ceauşescu relied more and more exclusively on coercive measures alone to retain his grip on power. Workers' demonstrations were put down through a massive deployment of police and militia personnel.[39] Signaling that at last even the party elite was disaffected to the point of open defection, in the spring of 1989 six of the most senior veteran Romania Communist Party leaders circulated an open letter critical of Ceauşescu's leadership. In this context of near absolute domestic delegitimation, the rapid unfolding of events in other East European countries during 1989 spelled the doom of the Romanian dictatorship. Solidarity's victory in Poland, the overthrow of communist rule in Czechoslovakia, and the fall of the Berlin Wall left Ceauşescu without external allies while inspiring his opponents to act.

The spark that touched off mass rebellion in Romania was a confrontation between Hungarian pastor Lászlo Tökés and the representatives of the Ceauşescu regime in the provincial city of Timişoara. Tökés, who had emerged as a local spokesman for anti-Ceauşescu forces, came under increasing pressure from the regime as a consequence of his activities. Finally security police demanded and obtained his agreement to leave his parish. But local supporters attempted to shield Tökés. On 15 December 1989 they came into conflict with the security police. This confrontation rapidly escalated, bringing the entire city into a state of revolt. The lethal use of military force that Ceauşescu ordered in the hope of quelling the Timişoara demonstrations on 17 December served only to spread the unrest to other cities and speed its escalation into an armed uprising. Ceauşescu's final humiliation came on 21 December 1989, when a supposedly well-orchestrated manifestation of popular support in the capital square facing his Central Committee building transformed spontaneously into a mass anticommunist protest.

As the edifice of political repression disintegrated, a diverse coalition formed with the intent of guiding the revolt to a successful outcome.[40] Its main figures were the leaders of the spontaneous uprising, reform communists who had been marginalized by the Ceauşescu dictatorship, and elements of the leadership that abandoned the failing regime for the side of revolutionaries. Organized as the National Salvation Front and headed by former Politburo member Ion Iliescu, these forces announced their assumption of provisional control over the country on 22 December 1989, and began taking steps to stabilize their position. Under what can only be considered extremely irregular circumstances (even by the most charitable observers), Nicolae and Elena Ceauşescu were sentenced to death by a military tribunal and executed on Christmas Day 1989. Members of the National Salvation Front justified this action as necessary to end fighting. Skeptics noted that it also smoothed the road to participation in the successor regime by Ceauşescu associates who would otherwise have been compromised in a public trial of the dictator. The National Salvation Front immediately announced a program of reform, including a call for democratic elections.[41] The Front's spokesmen asserted a nonpartisan position, describing their organization as a non-political umbrella organization. They pledged to act in a caretaker role until a successor regime could be elected.

THE CONTRADICTIONS OF THE EARLY POST-COMMUNIST TRANSITION

Romania was arguably less prepared than any other country in Eastern Europe to undertake democratization. Up to the very end of its existence, the Ceauşescu leadership systematically fostered political alienation and fractured the society along class and ethnic lines. The consequences of this strategy for the post-communist body politic were catastrophic. Romanians' level of political knowledge and the political culture suffered, institutionalized alternatives to the Communist Party simply did not exist, and reformist opposition within the RCP was limited at best. Hence it should come as no surprise that Romanians encountered numerous impediments as they struggled to negotiate the post-communist transition.

Not surprisingly given its provenance, the integrity of the provisional government almost immediately came into question. Adding to the concerns of democrats, both the character of the National Salvation Front and its stated intentions shifted once immediate threats to civil order were reduced. In essence, the two best-positioned elements of the original makeshift coalition (reform communists and representatives of the military) marginalized the less politically experienced leaders of the mass uprising. A dominant core of ex-party leaders formed within the Front's ruling council around the figure of Iliescu. Iliescu himself had been an established member of the RCP elite during the early Ceauşescu period, rising from leadership of the Communist Youth League to the position of RCP secretary for ideological affairs in 1970. But in late 1971 Iliescu fell from grace as a result of his refusal to support Ceauşescu's radical policy line. Progressively marginalized from the country's political processes, he was dropped from the Central Committee in 1984 and placed in charge of a politically irrelevant publishing house. Iliescu thus typified not anticommunism, but rather anti-Ceauşescu reformism within the communist elite. While the Communist Party itself was abolished in early January 1990, Iliescu and his supporters were reinforced by absorption of significant elements of the former RCP network into the structure of the Front. This influx both strengthened the hand of the reform communists and further alienated committed anticommunists from the transition government. On 23 January 1990, the Front reversed its initial nonpartisan position, announcing its intention to participate in the upcoming elections. This decision destabilized an already volatile situation, touching off a series of demonstrations both by the student movement and by anti-Iliescu political parties.

Anti-FSN protests were brought under control only through the use of force. In the last week of January 1990, Iliescu mobilized supportive workers who rampaged through the capital, attacking supporters of anti-Front political parties. At the same time he offered limited compromises to placate the opposition. Most importantly, the Council of the National Salvation Front agreed to dissolve itself as a government and form a new body, the Provisional Council of National Unity, which would rule until elections could be held. The council was broadened to include representation from the opposition political parties.[42] A compromise was also reached on the date for elections, which was moved back to 20 May, 1990.

The efforts by elements of the former elite to assume control of the transition did not go unrecognized by more thoroughgoing critics of the old order. Members of the cultural intelligentsia who had entered the Front's council during the early upheaval of the revolution, including prominent anti-Ceauşescu dissidents Ana Blandiana and Doina Cornescu, resigned with the apparent intention of denying the ruling core the use of their credentials to legitimate the regime as genuinely anticommunist.[43] Several intellectuals, such as Dan Petrescu, Mihai Sora, and Alexandru Paleologu, who initially accepted positions with the transition government, resigned as well.[44] In March 1990 liberal opponents of Iliescu published the Timişoara Proclamation, which denounced the growing power of the former nomenklatura, calling, in essence, for a genuine democratic revolution rather than reform of the previous system and a change in leadership. The Timişoara Proclamation became the focus of an increasingly diverse liberal opposition movement. Seeing less and less hope for cooperation, opposition groups formed outside the National Salvation Front and launched public attacks on Iliescu and his colleagues, charging that the nomenklatura of the old regime had effectively seized control of the revolution. Younger intellectuals, marginalized during the last years of the Ceauşescu regime, along with some members of the older generation, such as Pavel Câmpeanu, coalesced in order to articulate alternatives to the NSF strategy. Most critical in this activity was the Group for Social Dialogue, whose members' views were disseminated through its influential publication "22." In November 1990 a broader grouping, the Civic Alliance, was formed by Romanian intellectuals in emulation of the Czech organization, Civic Forum, and similar broad civil society associations elsewhere in Eastern Europe.

Alterations were also made in the proposed election law. The original version called for a system of single-member districts and for fifteen parliamentary seats to be allocated automatically to the military.[45] This formulation clearly would have been an advantage to the National Salvation

Front in competition with a divided field of opponents. The final law was significantly more favorable to the opposition.[46] It was agreed that elections for the legislative branch were to be held on the basis of proportional representation rather than single-member districts. The assignment of reserved seats to the military was eliminated. The law required inclusion of at least one representative of each ethnic minority group in the Deputies Assembly. According to the law, the president was to be chosen by direct election, held at the same time as the parliamentary vote. First-round victory required that more than 50 percent of the votes be cast for a single candidate. If no victor emerged, a runoff round was to follow.

The key contenders in Romania's first post-communist elections were Iliescu's National Salvation Front, the main historical parties (the National Liberals, the National Peasant Party, and the Social Democrats) and the Democratic Hungarian Union of Romania. In addition a multitude of smaller parties emerged, representing views across the ideological spectrum. Ultimately more than eighty parties participated in the elections. The campaign platform of the National Salvation Front called for the abolition of the most repressive and irrational aspects of the previous dictatorship, and for measured reform. At the same time voters were assured that instability would be avoided. The NSF pledged to protect the population from market forces. It called for a slow transition and avoidance of "major divergences in the accumulation of wealth." In contrast, both of the traditional parties proposed more rapid economic restructuring and failed to provide the population with firm assurances that they would be protected during the transition.[47] Among other points, the National Peasant Party's program called for redirecting investment to the countryside, for decollectivizing within three years, and for promoting Christian values. The National Liberals, on the other hand, launched a strong attack against the legacy of collectivism, echoing the position of traditional European liberal parties.[48] Both of these parties labeled the National Salvation Front "neo-communist" and charged it with hijacking the revolution.

Voters' response to these divergent campaign platforms explains in part the National Salvation Front's electoral success. The historical parties offered programs predicated upon rapid change, but also introduced a greater degree of risk into the economic environment. Iliescu's program promised reform, but accompanied its proposals with strong assurances of continuity. The National Salvation Front was able to identify itself with maintenance of at least existing levels of predictability. Furthermore, Iliescu personally and the Front in general enjoyed a clear identification with the December revolution. Since the leaders of the main opposition parties, Ion Ratiu and Radu Campeanu, were not in Romania at the time of the uprising, their criticisms of the Front were easily painted as criticisms by outsiders against the revolution itself. Attacks on the Front as "neo-communist" were countered by implying that the opposition favored too radical a change.

The first Romanian national election was also shaped by an unofficial struggle for power on the streets. Both the National Salvation Front and the opposition at times incited mass demonstrations in efforts to achieve the political advantage. In late January 1990, when the Front announced its intention to field candidates, for example, mass protest rallies were called by Iliescu opponents in central Bucharest. In response the Iliescu leadership mobilized workers and effectively intimidated the opposition.[49] In the months that followed, campaign offices were attacked, as were opposition candidates in some cases.[50] The Front also abused its near monopoly control over the national media network. While a new press law allowed opposition parties to publish their own journals, there was little time to develop these, and authorities regularly blocked the distribution of the opposition press.

Despite the ongoing controversy, Romania's first post-communist elections were held as scheduled on 20 May 1990. Clearly some irregularities occurred, but the consensus of opinion among observers was that returns accurately reflected popular attitudes.[51] Results confirmed the political dominance of the National Salvation Front and Iliescu. In the presidential race Iliescu won 85.07 percent of the vote. Campeanu of the National Liberal Party took 10.16 percent and Ratiu followed with 4.29 percent. Legislative results were similar. The Front gained 68 percent of Assembly seats, and 76 percent of those in the Senate.[52] Among the most striking results of the election was the strength of support for the Democratic Hungarian Union. With a population of around two million out of the over twenty-four million people in Romania as a whole, the Hungarians gave this party overwhelming support, providing it with 7.23 percent of the total vote. If the Democratic Hungarian Union did better than expected, the historical parties did worse. The third-ranked party nationally was the National Liberal party, with 6.41 percent of the vote. Interestingly, fourth place was not taken by the National Peasants (2.56 percent of the vote), but by the Romanian Ecological Movement, which captured 2.62 percent of the vote. These election results confirmed the main political tendencies that emerged in the first months after the revolution. The National Salvation Front, including significant elements of the previous power structure, consolidated its dominant position, while more militant anticommunist opposition forces remained fragmented.

President Iliescu, with his position bolstered and a National Salvation Front government in place, initiated a program of measured reform. Within months after the election a series of reform laws was passed. Economic initiatives included legislation on enterprise privatization, land privatization, and financial reform.[53] Among other measures, land up to twenty-five acres in collective farms was to be returned to its previous

owners, and 30 percent of the value of state enterprises was to be distributed to the population, with the rest being sold to the state and foreign
investors. Private enterprise was legalized. Over the course of the year
following the elections, price controls were liberalized in stages until market values were reached on most goods. Controls remained in place,
however, for several sensitive commodities.

Extending beyond the economic arena, the Romanian Parliament
undertook general political reform as well. Most significantly, a new constitution was approved on 21 November 1991 and submitted to a referendum.[54] This established a mixed presidential/parliamentary system
based on the French model. While areas of concern remained among both
domestic and foreign critics of the Iliescu regime, the new constitution
did make headway in the construction of a democratic political order.
Some limits on executive power were built into the document, although it
left the president in a strong position. The new constitution also provided
formal guarantees with respect to the provision of basic human rights
and minority rights.

As was to be expected (and as occurred elsewhere in Eastern Europe), once the Romanian successor government shifted from the stage
of early post-communist politics, during which it was possible to focus
on almost universally popular attacks on hated aspects of the previous
regime, consensus began to break down. In a second, postelectoral stage
of transition, politics became necessary to move the country forward, to
undertake concrete and sometimes painful reform initiatives designed to
break down the institutions of the collective economy. As the reform
process took hold, improving conditions in some sectors but imposing
costs in others, competing factions took shape within the National Salvation Front, based on alternative reform strategies. At the same time social
groups impacted by the reform became increasingly active in their opposition. As the year after the election wore on, strike activity increased and
demonstrations by opposition groups became an almost daily routine in
the country's capital.

Reaction against the government and its policies reached a peak in
the fall of 1992, when demonstrations threatened public order in Bucharest for a second time since the revolution. Workers stormed through the
streets demanding the resignation of President Iliescu and Prime Minister
Petre Roman. Iliescu, however, once again proved his political acumen,
shifting the burden of responsibility for the negative consequences of the
reforms onto Prime Minister Roman and engineering his resignation in
mid-September. Differences, however, went deeper than a simple leadership rivalry at the top of the ruling party. Forced from the government,
Roman became the chief representative of those in the National Salvation
Front who considered that reform should proceed both further and
faster. By the spring of the following year Roman's supporters had be-

come sufficiently confident to force a confrontation at the ruling party's congress. In March 1992 Roman was reelected chairman of the party. Iliescu and his supporters responded in May by breaking off to form their own organization, the Democratic National Salvation Front (DNSF).

While the ruling party was thus plagued by internal strife, opposition forces moved in the direction of increased political coherence and cooperation. Putting aside their rivalries, fourteen democratic parties came together to form the Democratic Convention and contest local elections in February 1992.[55] The Civil Alliance Party played a crucial role in construction of the opposition electoral coalition. Formed in June 1991 as the political expression of the Civic Alliance intelligentsia civil society movement, CAP was intended to be an inclusive organization, bringing together a broad range of progressive forces, including elements of the Group for Social Dialogue. It was hobbled, however, by its inability to appeal much beyond the intelligentsia in its search for electoral support. This obvious fact no doubt entered into its leaders' decision to work toward a broad electoral alliance of all liberal forces. The Democratic Convention coalition was initially quite successful. It succeeded in gaining 23 percent of mayoral votes, in comparison with 31 percent for the still unified National Salvation Front. More significantly, the Democratic Convention captured control of seven of the country's largest urban areas, including the capital.

This achievement in local elections raised expectations that a new degree of collaboration had been achieved among regime opponents, and that this would allow them to compete successfully in the upcoming national contest. These hopes, however, were soon dashed. Tensions within the opposition coalition led to public exchanges between its members at least as harsh as those directed against the ruling party. Ultimately the National Liberal Party determined that it could more successfully pursue its goals independently, and withdrew from the Democratic Convention.

The Democratic Hungarian Union of Romania removed itself from the Democratic Convention's electoral agreement for quite different reasons. As the date of the second national elections approached, nationalist rhetoric and xenophobic sentiments in Romania became progressively more intense. Given the probable electoral impact of these attitudes, the Hungarian party's leadership resolved to withdraw from its electoral compact with the Democratic Convention in order to avoid hampering the Convention's chances at the polls. The Hungarians remained within the convention, however. They supported the Convention candidate in the presidential race, and pledged cooperation in the pursuit of common goals in parliament.

Difficulties thus beset the liberal opposition as it entered into Romania's second national election, which was held, after several delays, in September 1992. In general, electoral rules remained unchanged. The

1992 campaign was significantly improved in comparison to the 1990 contest. Less violence occurred, fraud played a smaller role, and access to the media for opposition parties was much improved. The campaign disclosed a strong process of ideological differentiation. At the center of the political landscape was the Democratic National Salvation Front. Following its break with the original National Salvation Front, President Iliescu's DNSF became more overtly an advocate of the status quo. Roman's rump National Salvation Front, on the other hand, assumed a much more reformist stance, contending that Iliescu had "sold out" the 1989 revolution.

Competition to Iliescu's governing DNSF polarized along two ideological dimensions in the 1992 national elections. One group of parties extended to the right of the DNSF on the dimension of nationalism and with it or to its left on the dimension of economic reform. This authoritarian-nationalist grouping included the Party of Romanian National Unity, the Greater Romania Party, the Socialist Workers Party, and the Democratic Agrarian Party. While sharing some common characteristics, each of these parties has unique attributes that distinguish it from the others and make close cooperation difficult to achieve. PUNR, for example, is primarily a regional party of Transylvania (though its national following has grown somewhat), and is closely associated with the nationalist association *Vatra Românească*.[56] Its leader and presidential candidate, Georghe Funar, is the controversial and intensely nationalist mayor of the Transylvanian city of Cluj. A second extreme nationalist party formed in 1991, the Greater Romania Party (*România Mare*), is more national in scope than PUNR. The Greater Romania Party plays upon anti-Hungarian, anti-Western, and anti-Semitic themes. Its leaders characterized economic reform and increasing interaction with the Western economies and international financial institutions as signs of foreign domination. The last two members of the authoritarian-nationalist grouping are best understood as communist successor parties. The PSM, led by Ceaușescu lieutenant Ilie Verdet, is the most direct and least reconstructed successor to the last RCP leadership and thus not surprisingly is staunchly collectivist. The PDAR, staffed largely by cadres of the former regime's agricultural bureaucracy, is closely associated with the FDSN. Cooperation between the successor communist and extreme nationalist elements of this grouping was no doubt eased by the previous association of their leaders. Central figures in both the current nationalist parties played significant roles in the Ceaușescu period cultural apparatus.[57] Included here are such individuals as Greater Romania Party leader Corneliu Vadim Tudor, and Adrian Păunescu, now associated with the Socialist Labor Party.[58]

The second major ideological focus consisted of the parties of the "democratic opposition," and was located at the opposite extreme of these ideological scales. These parties, most of which cooperated in the Democratic Convention, included prominently the Civic Alliance Party (CAP), the National Peasant Party–Christian Democrats, the National Liberal Party, and the Hungarian Democratic Union of Romania. In comparison to the former grouping, these parties were much more favorably inclined to privatization and rapid reform and less attached to Romanian nationalism.[59] Furthermore, the Democratic Convention parties continued to call for a more decisive break with the communist path, and to accuse Iliescu's regime of harboring elements of the former dictatorship.

The outcome of voting in this second contest confirmed that Iliescu had successfully consolidated his position in Romanian political life. With 47.2 percent of the first-round vote and 61.4 percent in the runoff, Iliescu dominated the field. The Democratic Convention's candidate, Emil Constaninescu, was able to attract only 38.6 percent of the final presidential vote. This outcome clearly did not allow the opposition to threaten President Iliescu. But Iliescu's own 23.7 percent decline in support between the 1990 and 1992 elections could not have been comforting to his supporters.

Voting in the legislative elections reflected a similar trend. While capturing a plurality of the vote in the chamber of deputies, the ruling party's support fell to 27.7 percent in comparison to the unified National Salvation Front's 66.3 percent in the previous contest. Roman's faction attracted only another 10.2 percent of the vote, leaving a decline of more than 28 percent to be accounted for. A number of the Front's previous voters clearly shifted to the political right. The Romanian National Unity Party, for example, won only slightly more than 2 percent of the 1990 vote, but more than 8 percent in 1992. Support for the parties making up the Democratic Convention also increased dramatically. From a collective vote of less than 5 percent in 1990, the Convention's combined forces captured more than 20 percent of the vote in 1992.

This second national election represented a decisive step forward for Romania. Significant differentiation occurred within both the elite and the electorate in the years intervening between the first and second contests, fostering a sharpening of distinctions between policy orientations and improved political dialogue. It was thus under very different conditions, and with only approximately 28 percent of the parliament under the control of the Democratic Front for National Unity, that President Iliescu went about the difficult task of organizing a new postelection government. It was ultimately determined that the most expedient course would be the formation of what amounted to a minority government under the direction of a non-party-affiliated prime minister, Nicolae Vacaroiu. Vacaroiu's position on significant issues mirrored those of President Iliescu, who continued to dominate national political life into the mid-1990s.

THE FAILURE OF REFORM
COMMUNISM IN ROMANIA

Following 1992 President Iliescu pursued what was in essence a populist course, striving to consolidate a base of support among peasants and workers. The ruling party, whose name was changed from the FDSN to the Party of Romanian Social Democracy (PDSR) in July 1993, appealed to popular fears concerning rapid marketization and social change. It played up the potential for social dislocation that would follow if liberal reforms were introduced, and promised to provide its constituents with relative stability and continued state protection. President Iliescu and the PDSR also played to nationalist sentiments, forming a de facto legislative alliance with the extreme nationalist parties whose parliamentary delegations supported Prime Minister Vacaroiu's government. In 1994 this coalition became explicit when members of PUNR and the Greater Romania Party entered into the Vacaroiu cabinet.

Two factors were central to the ultimate failure of Iliescu's leadership. The first of these was the nature of the political elite itself. Among the primary considerations that undermined the Vacaroiu cabinet's ability to govern was the continued influential role that holdover elements from the communist regime continued to play in public life. These included both political leaders themselves and managers from the state sector enterprises who benefitted from continued public subsidization. The political elite was embedded in a broader "nomenklatura class" of politically connected individuals who were able to benefit financially from the economy's intermediate stage between market and plan, in essence trading on their access to the state. The interests of these entrenched groups clearly conflicted with efforts to fundamentally reform the Romanian economy.

Second, even assuming a disposition on the part of some elements of the PDSR leadership to transform Romanian society, the Iliescu regime found itself unable to effectively reform or to competently manage the country's economy as a consequence of the constraints imposed by the character of its core constituencies. While the regime's populist strategy was initially expedient from the point of view of electoral politics, it proved unworkable from the point of view of policy formation. Even those limited reforms that were undertaken by the Vacaroiu government during the 1992–1996 period foundered in the face of mass opposition. Repeated rounds of price reform were met by public demonstrations and strikes. In similar circumstances, center-right governments elsewhere in central Europe were able to press forward with rationalization (more or less successfully and more or less completely depending on the case). But given the limited nature of its political base, the PDSR was not in a position to flout popular opposition. Price reforms were followed by wage increases, defeating the original purpose of the exercise and fueling inflation. For similar reasons (and with similar consequences), unproductive enterprises were kept afloat through credits from the National Bank. Privatization efforts under the Vacaroiu government followed a similar pattern. While initial proposals called for decisive change, the implementation of privatization was markedly weak. When resistance was encountered from entrenched interests, reform foundered. As a consequence little progress was made in privatizing large enterprises, most of which remained within the state sector. As of mid-1995 the state sector still accounted for approximately 90 percent of industrial production.[60]

The PDSR's alliance with the extreme nationalist parties also limited the government's ability to maneuver. Initially parliamentary backing from the Greater Romanian Party and PUNR allowed Iliescu's PDSR faction to dominate the legislature and provided critical support to the Vacaroiu government. An obvious but arm's-length relationship with the extremists also worked to President Iliescu's advantage with his mass following, allowing him to garner support from the nationalist constituency, while at the same time avoiding direct association with the most excessive statements of the nationalist leaders. In 1994 the relationship between PDSR and the fringe nationalist parties became explicit through the inclusion of two PUNR ministers in the Vacaroiu government. This was followed by the conclusion of an open agreement on cooperation with PUNR, the Greater Romania Party, and the Socialist Labor Party in January 1995.

While this coalition was thus quite useful to the PDSR in domestic political terms, it became progressively more costly from the point of view of foreign policy. This conflict between domestic and foreign policy goals ultimately caused its demise. As Romania struggled with the problems of transition, the importance of relations with the external environment increased. In addition to the obvious importance of access to multilateral financial institutions such as the IMF and World Bank, the utter collapse of the previous regional alliance system required that Bucharest devise an alternative foreign policy strategy. Integration into European security structures and access to the world market of necessity became priority goals of all mainstream politicians. But progress in the international arena became more and more problematic as the international community increasingly identified the PDSR with nationalist extremism. In an effort to counter this perception and improve relations with the United States and Western Europe, President Iliescu undertook to improve relations with Hungary. This course, however, was unacceptable to the volatile leaders of the nationalist parties, and even as new elections approached, the coalition between them and the PDSR broke down.

Romania's third set of elections, held in November 1996, marked the first definitive change in power to occur since the fall of communism. The change in leadership from successor communists to proponents of reform who had been excluded from power for the first six years of the transition marked a true political watershed. In the initial round of the presidential contest, held simultaneously with the legislative election on 3 November, Iliescu took the first place with 32.2 percent of the vote. This represented a significant decline from his 1992 showing, when he took 47.2 percent of the first-round vote. Second place was once again taken by Democratic Convention candidate Constantinescu, whose vote also decreased slightly between the 1992 and 1996 contests, from 31.2 percent to 28.2 percent of the vote.[61]

The results of the second-round presidential contest, held on 17 November 1996, represented a decisive success for Constantinescu and the opposition parties. Constantinescu's vote in the runoff increased by 26.2 percent, to 54.4 percent of the total vote. Despite President Iliescu's intensified nationalist appeals and efforts to mobilize support on the basis of fear of economic change between the first and second rounds, his vote rose by only approximately half as much, 13.4 percent, to give him 45.6 percent of the vote in the final round.

In the parliamentary elections, the PDSR won only 21.5 percent of the vote and 91 seats in the Chamber of Deputies, and 23.1 percent and 41 seats in the Senate. The Democratic Convention took 30.3 percent of the vote and 122 out of 343 seats in the Chamber of Deputies, and 30.7 percent of the vote and 51 out of 143 Senate seats. With support from the UDMR, which took approximately 6.5 percent of the vote, and the Social Democratic Union with approximately 13 percent, the Democratic Convention was easily able to form a new coalition government under Prime Minister Victor Ciorbea.

These results indicate a massive erosion in support for President Iliescu and the policies that he represented. While rural voters and the elderly continued to favor the PDSR over the Democratic Convention, the margin of their support declined. Working class voters, who had previously supported the ruling party, shifted their allegiance to the liberal opposition. It was this working class vote by the PDSR, along with the strong support of the emerging entrepreneurial class for the opposition parties that, as Michael Shafir points out, best accounts for the outcome of the election.[62]

CONCLUSION

Romanian political life during the past half century has suffered from severe and recurrent discontinuities. The communist transition initially failed to produce a stable leadership group. The Communist Party's unresolved internal factionalism retarded efforts to restructure the country's economy, and (in contrast to events in most other East European countries) enabled a national communist faction to survive the Stalinist period in place. Divergence from the Soviet Union's policy course in the early 1960s caused a second period of upheaval as the ascendant Gheorghiu-Dej leadership undertook an independent "Stalinist" industrialization strategy and took preliminary steps toward a "national" legitimation strategy. The rise to power of Ceaușescu in the second half of the 1960s was accompanied by further turmoil as the new leader purged potential opponents and elevated supporters in order to consolidate his newly won position. Betraying the potential for an independent and more moderate form of communism than many saw in his regime, Ceaușescu, within five years, was moving Romania in a quite different direction, which if even more intensely nationalist than that of his predecessor was also to become even more intensely totalitarian.

The Ceaușescu regime's failure to reach accommodation with, and indeed its increasing isolation from, Romanian civil-society in some ways had the effect of reinforcing important continuities between the communist period and the interwar political tradition. Sharp divisions between elites and the rest of the population, subject rather than participant attitudes with respect to civil-state relations, an abiding distrust of established authority, and intense nationalism were all conspicuous elements in the pre-communist political culture. Thus attitudes were reinforced and in some cases exaggerated to the point of extreme distortion under Ceaușescu's "national communist legitimation formula."

Clearly, this evolution did not lay the groundwork for an easy transition to democracy in the aftermath of communist rule. The framework of organized opposition to the communist dictatorship upon which new civil associations could be based was limited at best. Associations linking liberal elites to the general population (potential electoral supporters in the new environment) were entirely missing. Among peasants and workers deeply ingrained acceptance of authority remained strong.

Short-term circumstances also worked against a smooth democratic transition in 1990. First, Romania's revolution was even more abrupt than others in Eastern Europe, and it was violent. The rapid actions of Iliescu and his supporters simply left no interval in which a democratic opposition could consolidate sufficiently to play an effective role in negotiating the transition to democracy. Second, the hurried termination of Romania's revolution and the quick transfer of allegiance by substantial elements of the communist apparatus to the camp of the transition government created an environment of intense distrust. In the eyes of many, the FSN's ready acceptance of communist cadres discredited the transition. Third, Romania's initial post-communist elections were held with very little preparation and left much to be desired. Nearly constant unrest in the limited period preceding the contest provided little opportunity for opposition parties to organize or for serious debate concerning the country's future.

The 1990 elections represented only a partial political transformation at best, leaving a substantial part of the previous order intact. Yet while recognizing the shortcomings of the 1990 election, it is important to keep in mind the fundamental progress that it exemplified in contrast to the previous situation. Opposition parties were able to organize and to publicize their criticisms of the National Salvation Front. Once the campaign was over, opposition politicians were allowed to play an active role in the parliament and to operate freely. Independent publications flourished, and if large-scale privatization did not proceed swiftly, at least small-scale economic initiative was not hindered. The stage was thus much better set for the 1992 national elections, which proceeded in a relatively calm environment, and which represented a significant step forward in the construction of democratic institutions.

The sum effect of these conditions was a transition situation that was easily exploitable by an aspiring populist leader such as Iliescu. Playing upon the population's insecurities, promising a strong guiding hand, and relying selectively upon the authoritarian-nationalists to counter liberal challenges to his rule, Iliescu was able to effectively assume the reins of power. Democratic electoral politics and freedom of expression and association were established. Yet even given this obvious progress, the extent to which popular interests actually served to determine the outcome of national-level politics remained in some doubt.

In the long term, it was President Iliescu and the PDSR government's own failure to press through reform that produced the 1996 electoral backlash. Economic stagnation, corruption, and maladministration produced increasingly difficult conditions of life for the majority of Romanians, and ultimately eroded support for the Iliescu regime. The significance of the 1996 elections for the consolidation of democracy in Romania can hardly be overstated. As Vladimir Tismaneanu, among others, has underlined, the Democratic Convention victory represented the first time in nearly sixty years that there has been a transition in national level leadership in Romania, through fairly contested democratic elections, without violence.[63] The extreme nationalist parties which were able to play a central role in the early phase of the transition appear to have been effectively marginalized, and liberal elites are now positioned to undertake broad economic and political reforms.

Transition from one form of social system to another is infinitely more complicated than more limited varieties of change, and can only be adequately understood as long-term historic phenomenon. Entire institutions must be dismantled, and others must take shape to replace them, or they must be transformed in order to serve the needs of the new system. Deeply embedded attitudes and patterns of behavior must also be transformed entirely or adapted to new circumstances. Thus it needs to be recognized that the process of post-communist transition in Romania as in the rest of Eastern Europe, far from being complete, is as yet in its early phase.

Even given the difficulties and shortcomings indicated above, however, unmistakable signs of progress are seen in Romania's transition. Free competition for power on the national level has become an accepted aspect of political life. Totalitarian rule has been replaced by competition between several parties representing distinct political positions. Freedom of communication is becoming increasingly well established and, on the local level, individual economic initiative is evident. While daunting problems in areas such as interethnic relations, economic reform, and the construction of a stable pattern of civil state relations remain, Romania has made considerable headway in redressing the heritage of decades of political abuse under communism. As the country prepares to enter the next century, there is good reason to hope that a fuller form of democratic life will in fact be achieved in Romania.

Notes

1. This focuses on the evolution of events up to the conclusion of the first phase of the post-communist transition, at approximately the point of the successful staging of the second set of national elections in 1992.

2. For a thorough treatment of the evolution of Romania's interwar political economy, see Henry L. Roberts, *Rumania: Political Problems of an Agrarian State* (New Haven: Yale University Press, 1951).

3. On the rise of Romanian fascism, see Eugen Weber, "Romania," in Hans Rogger and Eugen Weber, eds., *The European Right: A Historical Profile* (Los Angeles: The University of California Press, 1965) or Nicolas Nagy-Talavera, *The Green Shirts and Others: A History of Fascism in Hungary and Romania* (Berkeley: University of California Press, 1967).

4. On the origins and evolution of the Romanian communist movement, see Ghita Ionescu, *Communism in Romania: 1944–1962* (London: Oxford University Press, 1964).

5. Robert King, *History of the Romanian Communist Party* (Stanford: Hoover Institution Press, 1980), 64.

6. On the entire issue of Patrașcanu and the factional disputes of the early communist period, see Robert Levy's excellent "Did Ana Pauker Prevent a 'Rajk Trial' in Romania?" *East European Politics and Societies*, Vol. 9, No. 1 (Winter 1995), 143–178.

7. For a more complete treatment of the rather intricate conflict with the Romanian Communist Party during this period, see Ghita Ionescu, *Communism in Rumania 1944–1962*, or Michael Shafir, *Romania, Politics, Economics, and Society* (Boulder: Lynne Rienner, 1985).

8. On the economic transformation of Romania during the early period, see John Michael Montias, *Economic Development in Communist Romania* (Cam-

bridge: MIT Press, 1967). For an overview of the process through the late Ceauşescu period, see William Crowther, *The Political Economy of Romanian
Socialism* (New York: Praeger, 1988).

9. While it is obvious that policy tensions need not translate into political
conflict, in the Romanian case serious differences developed concurrently with
opportunities for their expression. Stalin's death and the leadership struggle in
the USSR severely weakened Moscow's leverage in dealing with Eastern Europe.
Simultaneously the Sino-Soviet dispute also provided opportunities for maneuver
that would not have existed otherwise. The confluence of these factors presented
possibilities for the Romanian leaders to assert their independence just as differences with the Soviet Union were beginning to emerge.

10. The "statement" was most remarkable for asserting clearly and firmly
the national sovereignty of Romania, and the "exclusive right of each party independently to work out its political line, its concrete objectives, and the ways and
means of achieving them." For an English translation of the text, see William
Griffith, *Sino-Soviet Relations: 1964–65* (Cambridge: MIT Press, 1967), 269–
296.

11. For more detailed accounts of elite politics during the transition period,
see Mary Ellen Fischer, "Political Leadership and Personnel Policy in Romania:
Continuity and Change, 1965–1976," in Steven Rosefielde, ed., *World Commu-
nism at the Crossroads: Military Ascendancy, Political Economy, and Human
Welfare* (Boston: Martinus Nijhoff, 1980), 210–233; and the same author's "Par-
ticipatory Reforms and Political Development in Romania," in Jan F. Triska and
Paul M. Cocks, eds., *Political Development in Eastern Europe* (New York:
Praeger, 1977), 217–237.

12. For a more complete discussion of his strategy in dealing with the
Soviets at this time, see Shafir, *Romania: Politics, Economics*, 52.

13. Even after the Fifth Plan got under way, a series of reevaluations occurred during which nearly every major production indicator was increased. For
more complete information on the economy during this period, see Andreas C.
Tsantis and Roy Pepper, *Romania: The Industrialization of an Agrarian Economy under Socialist Planning* (Washington: The World Bank, 1979).

14. Thad Alton, "Comparative Structure and Growth of Economic Activity
in Eastern Europe," in *East European Economies Post-Helsinki: A Compendium
of Papers Submitted to the Joint Economic Committee* (Washington: U.S. Government Printing Office, 1977), 214; Marvin Jackson, "Industrialization, Trade,
and Mobilization in Romania's Drive for Economic Independence," in *East
European Economies Post-Helsinki: A Compendium of Papers Submitted to the
Joint Economic Committee* (Washington: U.S. Government Printing Office,
1977), 897.

15. On the role of intellectuals during this period, see Michael Shafir, "Political Culture, Intellectual Dissent, and Intellectual Consent: The Case of Romania," *Orbis*, Vol. 27, No. 4 (Summer 1983), 393–421.

16. For a stark assessment of the role of intellectuals during the Ceauşescu
period, see Doina and Nicolae Harsanyi, "Romania: Democracy and the Intellectuals," *East European Quarterly*, Vol. 27, No. 2 (June 1993), 243–260.

17. For an overview of the various churches active in Romania and their
treatment during the communist period, see Janice Broun with Grazyna Silorska,
Conscience and Captivity: Religion in Eastern Europe (Lanham, Md.: University
Press of America, 1988). For a discussion of the politics of Church-state relations
during the communist period, see Trond Gilberg, "Religion and Nationalism in
Romania," in Pedro Ramet, ed., *Religion and Nationalism in Soviet and East
European Politics* (Durham: Duke University Press, 1984), 170–186.

18. Alan Scarfe, "The Romanian Orthodox Church," in Pedro Ramet, ed., *Eastern Christianity and Politics in the Twentieth Century* (Durham: Duke University Press, 1988), 220.

19. For a more complete discussion of this topic, see Mary Ellen Fischer and Doina Pasca Harsányi, "From Tradition and Ideology to Elections and Competition," in Marilyn Rueschemeyer, ed., *Women in the Politics of Post-communist Eastern Europe* (Armonk, N.Y.: M. E. Sharpe, 1994), 201–224; Doina Pasca Harsányi, "Women in Romania," in Nanette Funk and Magda Mueller, eds., *Gender Politics and Post-Communism* (London: Routledge, 1993), 39–52.

20. Mary Ellen Fischer, "Women in Romanian Politics: Elena Ceauşescu, Pronatalism, and the Promotion of Women," in Sharon Wolchik and Alfred G. Meyer, eds., *Women, State and Party in Eastern Europe* (Durham: Duke University Press, 1985), 120–137.

21. For a complete and fascinating discussion of the place of nationalism in the political life of Romania during the communist period, see Katherine Verdery, *National Ideology under Socialism* (Los Angeles: University of California Press, 1991). For a treatment of the role of nationalism in the cultural life of interwar Romania, see Irina Livezeanu, *Cultural Politics in Greater Romania* (Ithaca: Cornell University Press, 1995).

22. On the Ceauşescu cult, see Mary Ellen Fischer, *Nicolae Ceauşescu and the Romanian Political Leadership: Nationalization and Personalization of Power* (Washington: National Council for Soviet and East European Research, 1983), and "Idol or Leader? The Origins and Future of the Ceauşescu Cult," in Daniel N. Nelson, ed., *Romania in the 1980s* (Boulder: Westview, 1981), 117–141.

23. For the plan period as a whole, Net Material Product growth rates declined despite the fact that the accumulation rate was maintained at 32–33 percent, ultimately equaling the total investment of the preceding three periods combined. Nicolae Ceauşescu, *Raportul cel de al XII-lea Congres al Partidul Comunist Român* (Bucharest: Editura Politică, 1979), 10.

24. Thad Alton, Krzysztof Badach, Elizabeth Bass, and Gregor Lazarcik, "Eastern Europe: Domestic Final Uses of Gross Product 1965, 1970, and 1975–1983," *Occasional Paper No. 82, Research Project on National Income in East Central Europe* (New York: L. W. International Financial Research, 1984), 21.

25. Gabriele Tuitz, "Romania," *East European Economics,* Vol. 64, No. 4 (Summer 1981), 41–46; *Radio Free Europe Research Romania/Situation Report,* No. 3, 18 March 1980.

26. Analysts of the Central Intelligence Agency, "Eastern Europe Faces up to the Debt Crisis," in *East European Economies: Slow Growth in the 1980s,* Vol. 2, Selected Papers Submitted to the Joint Economic Committee (Washington: U.S. Government Printing Office, 28 March 1986). Calculated from figures provided in Table 1, 153.

27. Jan Vanous, ed., *Centrally Planned Economies Current Analysis,* Wharton Econometric Forecasting Associates, 9 November 1982, 7.

28. Romania was forced to negotiate loan restructuring agreements with its Western creditors early in the following year, and in 1983 as well. In all, nearly $2.5 billion was rescheduled during these two years. For details on rescheduling agreements of 1982 and 1983, see Allen E. Clapp and Harvey Shapiro, "Financial Crisis in Eastern Europe," in *East European Economies: Slow Growth in the 1980s,* Vol. 2, Selected Papers Submitted to the Joint Economic Committee (Washington: U.S. Government Printing Office, 28 March 1986), 250.

29. On Romania's international strategy, see Horatiu Dragomirescu's

"Echilibrul economic în Procesul dezvoltării," *Revista Economică,* nr. 6 (7 February 1986), 20–21; "Strategii de politica economică în conditii de criză," *Revista Economică,* nr. 6 (8 February 1985), 25–26.

30. Vanous, ed., *Centrally Planned Economies Current Analysis,* Wharton Econometric Forecasting Associates, 4 April 1983, 4.

31. Austerity efforts had an equally destructive effect on production. The import of Western capital goods declined by an average annual rate of 41.47 percent from 1981 to 1983. The closest comparable figure was nearly half as large, 23.43 percent, for Poland. Zbigniew M. Fallenbuchl, "East-West Trade in Capital Goods since 1970," *Studies in Comparative Communism,* Vol. 19, No. 2, Summer 1986, 137. By 1985 Gross National Product was by far the lowest among East European COMECON members on a per capita basis. Virtually no major industrial indicator in the 1981–1985 Seventh Five-Year Plan was achieved.

32. This "ideological preemption" was particularly evident in the realm of economics. The tone of discourse on this subject was determined by Ceauşescu's elevation of the principle that the accumulation rate should be 28–32 percent of national income to a "law of socialist construction." See, for example, Gheorghe Bistriceanu, "Creştereă venitul national—baza progresului economico-social al patriei," *Revista Economică,* Nr. 18 (19 April 1985), 1–2.

33. Horatiu Dragomirescu, "Conceptie novatoare privînd perfectionareă conducerii economico-sociale planificate," *Revista Economică,* nr. 31 (2 August 1985), 2. Also see Constantin Barbacioru, "Dezvoltarea planificate a economiei, expresie a superiorităţii proprietatii socialiste," *Revista Economică,* nr. 3 (21 February 1986), 19–20; and Viorica Nicolau, "Cresterea unitară armonioasă a tării," *Era Socialistă,* vol. 64 (10 December 1984), 19–22.

34. Of eight party secretaries appointed at the twelfth Romanian Communist Party Congress in late 1979, only one remained in that position by the thirteenth congress in late 1984. *Radio Free Europe Research Romania/Situation Reports,* 16 (2 November 1984), 1–4; and 17 (17 November 1984), 2–5.

35. Nepotism was already well established within the Communist Party, as epitomized by the elevation of Ceauşescu's wife Elena and son Nicu to key positions. Elena Ceauşescu was appointed to the Party Central Committee in 1972, and then to its Executive Committee in 1973. By 1977 she had been appointed to the Permanent Buro of the Political Executive Committee. Nicu was named a candidate member of the Central Committee in 1979, and a full member in 1982. He finally joined his parents at the summit of the party hierarchy when he was made an alternate member of the Political Executive Committee in late 1984.

36. Most prominently, Ilie Ceauşescu, long active as a military historian and regime spokesman on military affairs, was promoted to lieutenant general in 1982, made a deputy minister of defense, and a secretary on the Higher Political Council. Nicolae Andruţa Ceauşescu, who became a lieutenant general in 1978, was released from a diplomatic post in Kiev in 1982 and made rector of the Academy of the Ministry of Interior in 1984. He became a secretary on the Political Council of the Ministry in 1985. See Vladimir Tismaneau, "Ceauşescu's Socialism," *Problems of Communism* (January–February 1985), Vol. 34, No. 1, 50–66.

37. See the account of Brucan's activities in *The Washington Post,* 20 December 1987, A34.

38. *The Wall Street Journal,* 30 November 1987, 22; *The Washington Post,* 15 December 1987, A31.

39. *The Christian Science Monitor,* 16 December 1987, 9; *The Washington Post,* 20 December 1987, A34.

40. The actual course of events leading to Ceauşescu's overthrow and execution, and the nature of the leadership that emerged from Romania's December revolution immediately became the subjects of intense speculation. See, for example, Vladimir Tismaneau, "New Masks, Old Faces," *The New Republic* (5 February 1990), 17–21.

41. For the text of the initial National Salvation Front program, announced on 22 December 1989, see FBIS-EEU-89-246, December 26, 1989, 65–66.

42. See "Iliescu Discusses 1 Feb Roundtable Talks," Bucharest Domestic Service, FBIS-EEU-90-024, February 5, 1990, 63.

43. On the origins of the intelligentsia opposition to Iliescu during the initial transition, see Vladimir Tismaneanu, "The Quasi-Revolution and Its Discontents: Emerging Political Pluralism in Post-Ceauşescu Romania," *East European Politics and Societies*, Vol. 7, No. 2 (Spring 1993), 309–349.

44. Doina and Nicolae Harsányi, "Romania: Democracy and the Intellectuals," *East European Quarterly*, Vol. 27, No. 2 (June 1993), 255.

45. See Michael Shafir, "The Electoral Law," *Radio Free Europe/Radio Liberty Research Reports*, 4 May 1990, 29.

46. Ibid., 28–32.

47. For summaries of the programs of these parties as well as those of the Social Democratic Party and the Ecological Democrats, see Vladimir Socor, "Political Parties Emerging, *Radio Free Europe/Radio Liberty Research Reports,* 16 February 1990, 28–35.

48. In a statement typical of the National Liberal's approach, party Executive Secretary Dinu Patriciu commented in an interview with *Curierul Comercial* on 20 May 1990 that "it is easier to build new structures than to restructure." While possibly true, statements such as this could only raise anxiety among working-class voters, and certainly did not help the liberals' election prospects. "Party Leaders Note Privatization Issues," FBIS-EEU-90-090, 9 May 1990, 43.

49. For the various parties' appeals for popular support during this period, see FBIS-EEU-90-230, 29 January 1990, 92–95.

50. On the use of violence during the campaign, see Dan Ionescu, "Violence and Calumny in the Election Campaign," *Radio Free Europe/Radio Liberty Research Reports,* 25 May 1990, 37–42.

51. See, for example, the following accounts. Adriane Genillard, "Behind Romania's Vote for Ruling Communists," *The Christian Science Monitor,* 23 May 1990, 4; "Press Comments on Fairness, Conduct of the Elections," FBIS-EEU-90-107, 4 June 1990, 53–54; Vladimir Socor, "National Salvation Front Produces Electoral Landslide," *Report on Eastern Europe,* 6 July 1990, 24–31.

52. Thus even if all of the opposition groups voted as a bloc, a circumstance that was virtually unimaginable, the Front would still control both of the new legislative bodies. In fact, on most issues delegates associated with the Alliance for Romanian Unity (AUR), the electoral coalition between PUNR and the Republican Party, and many of the smaller parties could be counted on to act in support of the National Salvation Front, ensuring it of control over both executive and legislative branches.

53. For a more detailed discussion of the early post-communist economic reforms in Romania, see Mugur Isarescu, "The Prognosis for Economic Recovery," in Daniel N. Nelson, ed., *Romania after Tyranny* (Boulder: Westview, 1992), 147–165.

54. See Michael Shafir, "Toward the Rule of Law: Romania," *Radio Free Europe/Radio Liberty Research Report,* Vol. 1, No. 27, 3 July 1992, 34–40.

55. The Democratic Convention included the most significant of the opposi-

tion groupings usually referred to as the "democratic opposition": the National Liberal Party, the National Peasant–Christian Democratic Party, the Civic Alliance, and the Democratic Hungarian Union of Romania.

56. On the origins and character of *Vatra Românească*, see Tom Gallagher, "Vatra Românească and Resurgent Nationalism in Romania," *Ethnic and Racial Studies*, Vol. 15, No. 4 (October 1992), 570–596.

57. It can also be hypothesized that the same "ease through association" argument applies to the relationship developed between the entire authoritarian nationalist grouping and the Iliescu leadership. In the period that falls immediately beyond the time frame of this treatment, these parties developed a covert alliance with the DNSF, and then moved openly into a governing coalition.

58. On the role of these contemporary ideologs of the right during the Ceauşescu period, see Michael Shafir, *Romania: Politics, Economics,* 127–174.

59. Other parties play important roles but were not closely aligned with either of these groups. The Movement for Romania, for example, was extremist on nationality issues, but at the same time its supporters favored economic reform, placing the party in an equivocal position between two opposed blocs. Support for others, such as the Romanian Ecological Movement and the Republican Party, do not need to be determined by the ideological dimensions defined above.

60. For a more detailed treatment of economic reform during this period see A. Ben-Ner and John Michael Montias, "Economic System Reforms and Privatization in Romania," in *Privatization in Central and Eastern Europe,* ed. Saul Estrin (New York: Longman, 1994), 279–310; Yves G. Van Frausum, Yulrich Gehmann, and Jurgen Gross, "Market Economy and Economic Reform in Romania: Macroeconomic and Microeconomic Perspectives," *Europe-Asia Studies* Vol. 46 (1994), 735–756.

61. The apparent decline in Constantinescu's vote was clearly accounted for in large part by the fact that in 1992 the UDMR did not field its own candidate, and its supporters can be presumed to have voted overwhelmingly for Constantinescu in the first round. Constantinescu's first-round vote among non-UDMR voters can thus more accurately be assumed to have increased by approximately 3 percent.

62. Michael Shafir, "Romania's Road to Normalcy," *Journal of Democracy* Vol. 8 (April 1997), 144–158.

63. Vladimir Tismaneanu, "Electoral Revolutions (Romania and the November 1996 elections)," *Society* Vol. 35, No. 1 (November–December 1997) 61–66.

9

Bulgaria

SPAS T. RAIKIN

Bulgaria appeared at the crossroads of European politics, sanctioned by the Treaty of San Stefano, on 3 March 1878, the day of liberation by Russia from a five-hundred-year Ottoman yoke. The treaty was set aside by the Congress of Berlin on 13 July 1878, when England and Austria-Hungary led the other Great Powers to undo the large Bulgarian state which the Russians had created after winning their war in defense of the Balkan Slavs (1877–1878). The Great Powers created two Bulgarian states—the Principality of Bulgaria per se and the autonomous Eastern Rumelia. In 1885, Eastern Rumelia, which is now southern Bulgaria, revolted against the treaty of Berlin and sought union with the principality in northern Bulgaria. In 1912–1913, the Bulgarians fought two Balkan wars in an effort to regain further territory lost in Berlin—first in alliance with Serbia, Greece, and Montenegro against Turkey, and after that alone, against Serbia, Greece, Montenegro, Romania, and Turkey—and lost. In 1915, they joined with Germany, Austria-Hungary, and Turkey, and lost again. The nationalists—whose ranks included the entire spectrum of Bulgarian political parties, except Agrarians and communists—blamed their neighbors and their Western protectors for Bulgaria's woes.

The Nazi-Soviet Pact of 23 August 1939 was welcomed in Sofia. The Bulgarians were relieved of the necessity to choose between Germany and Russia, or between communism and anti-communism. Bulgarian nationalists and revisionists around King Boris and his government could freely subscribe to Germany's revisionism in the interest of Bulgarian justice, confident that Russia would support them. In September 1940, Bulgaria reclaimed southern Dobrudja from Romania. The return of that region was accomplished with German and Soviet help, but Bulgarian luck soon ran out. The evolution of the war situation inevitably brought Bulgaria into a focus where German and Russian strategic interests clashed. The Italian adventure in Greece raised the prospects of Italian-German domination of the Balkans and of Greece becoming a launching pad for British forces. The Soviet Union would not allow the first and the Germans could not tolerate the second. An attempt to deal with the situation was made in November 1940, in Berlin, where Adolf Hitler and Joachim von Ribbentrop tried unsuccessfully to divert Russian interests toward India. Soviet Foreign Minister Vyacheslav Molotov insisted on settling the matter of Bulgaria first. On 26 November 1940, he spelled out Soviet conditions for joining the Tripartite Pact. Bulgaria occupied a central place in his proposals, and he defined with unmistakable clarity the Russian desire to dominate Bulgaria.[1]

But Hitler refused to concede Bulgaria to Stalin. His answer was that it was for the Bulgarians to decide this matter. The Russians sent a special emissary to King Boris, Arkady Sobolev, and the Communist Party in Bulgaria organized a nationwide campaign, collecting signatures in support of the Soviet proposal for a mutual-assistance pact. It was turned down.[2] Only a year earlier Moscow had signed such pacts with the Baltic states, and by August 1940, Estonia, Latvia, and Lithuania were all swallowed by the Soviet Union. At the time, Bulgaria held fast. However, Germany could not be put off so easily. In December Hitler issued his order No. 20, code-named "Marita," directing the German forces in Romania "to move across Bulgaria and to occupy the north coast of the Aegean and . . . the entire mainland of Greece."[3] The Bulgarians were told of the future German operations and after the necessary arrangements were made on 1 March 1941, as the German armies were already crossing the Danube, Sofia signed the Tripartite Pact. When King Boris made his decision to allow the passage of the Germans, he had to consider the 700,000-man German army on the Danube. A few weeks later the Yugoslavs further complicated the political situation by joining the Tripartite Pact on 25 March. On the 27th the Yugoslav government of Prince Paul was overthrown in a sudden coup, in which Serbs marched down Belgrade's streets denouncing the pact. Although the new government quickly offered reassurances to Berlin, Hitler was unsatisfied, and on 6 April 1941, the German armies in Bulgaria moved to wipe out Greece and Yugoslavia. On 17 April, they invited the Bulgarians to occupy Macedonia, which the latter had claimed since 1878 as their own. King Boris was honored with the title "Tsar Unifier."[4] In January 1941, the United States sent Colonel William J. Donovan to try in vain to persuade Boris to stay neutral.[5] The British tried their persuasive powers too, but they also failed. Before leaving the country, their representative in Sofia, George Rendel, tried everything on the king, even threatening that when England won the war Bulgaria might cease to exist.[6] The Western Allies seemed to remember Bulgaria only when they needed the country's support, but by then it was too late. Bulgaria certainly had no good reason to fight the 700,000-man German army on the Danube to protect Greek, Yugoslav, and British interests. Nor was Bulgaria disposed to let the Soviet armies march in.

On 22 June 1941, the German armies attacked the Soviet Union. This ended the euphoria and the sense of false security in Sofia. The unification of the nation under German auspices appeared doomed and the prospects of Bolshevization of the country loomed as its inevitable destiny. After Pearl Harbor, Hitler ordered all his satellites to declare war on the United States and Great Britain. On 13 December 1941, Bulgaria dutifully declared what later was to be called symbolic war against the Anglo-Saxon countries. But, significantly, Bulgaria never declared war on the Soviet Union.

The Germans entered Bulgaria not as an occupying army, but under terms mutually agreed by the two governments. The Germans stayed there, scrupulously observing these terms, even to the point where King Boris could refuse to surrender his Jewish subjects (an estimated 50,000) to be deported to Germany for extermination in the concentration camps.[7] As it turned out, by signing the Tripartite Pact and allowing the German army into the country, Bulgaria had effectively joined Germany and it was inevitable that the Allies would react accordingly.

The Bulgarian communists did not protest the Nazi-Soviet Pact, but like most of the Bulgarians, they never believed in its sincerity. Two days after the German attack on the Soviet Union, on 24 June 1941, the Central Committee of the Communist Party issued its call for "armed struggle against the German invaders and their Bulgarian servants."[8] It was not out of concern for Bulgaria and Bulgarian interests but rather out of concern for the Soviet Union and communism. The Bulgarian communists had never wavered in their loyalty and their support for the Soviet Union. Their political objective was to transform Bulgaria into a socialist country, modeled after the Soviet Union. The Bulgarian communists proceeded to form their partisan units, divided the country into war zones, and established a central military command, challenging the government with their guerrilla forces and terrifying the people. But except for a few skirmishes with the police and the army, no military campaign of any significance ever took place. From the very beginning, the partisan movement was a Communist Party affair, not a national movement for liberation from the Germans. It was an armed rebellion intended to help the Soviet Union and bring about the Bolshevization of Bulgaria. It is quite mistaken to believe that the Agrarians of G. M. Dimitrov constituted the mass of the partisans, as he claimed.[9] They were peasants but they were members and sympathizers of the Communist Party, not of the Agrarian Union. The strength of the movement is placed somewhere between ten and twenty thousand, plus some twenty thousand sympathizers. The maximum numbers may be valid only for the days immediately preceding the fall of the last pre-communist government on 9 September 1944.[10]

It was not the partisan movement and the Communist Party or its Fatherland Front which decided the fate of Bulgaria. It was the defeat of Germany on the Eastern Front which brought the Soviets to Sofia. It has been established that after Stalingrad King Boris made overtures to the opposition to form a new government of the traditional democratic parties.[11] But on 28 August 1943, the king died and those who succeeded him had neither the stature nor the daring to confront the crisis. As the Russian armies were approaching Bulgaria, Prime Minister Dobri Bozhilov was replaced on 1 June 1944. His successor was Ivan Bagrianov, a palace favorite who in the past had attracted national attention with his concerns for the poor peasantry in the country. He attempted to flirt with the communists but was rebuffed by them.

Meanwhile, a Bulgarian delegation was quickly dispatched by way of Ankara to Cairo to negotiate with the Allies, only to be turned away empty-handed. The Bulgarians did not know that in May and June, on the initiative of Winston Churchill, President Franklin Delano Roosevelt had consented, behind the back of his secretary of state, Cordell Hull, to give Stalin a free hand in the Balkans.[12] On 5 September, the Soviet Union declared war on Bulgaria, and as the Red Army was crossing the Danube, the Fatherland Front of communists, "Pladne" Agrarians, "Zveno" politicians, and left-wing Social Democrats, supported by a few independents, in complicity with a few military units and military personnel in the Ministry of Defense, seized power in the early hours of 9 September 1944 in a bloodless coup. All over the country partisan units occupied municipalities, police stations, army barracks, and every other link of the power structure of the government. The German armies had already evacuated Bulgaria and the Soviet army took their place. The government of Konstantin Muraviev ordered the military not to resist the occupation.

SOVIETIZATION OF BULGARIA

A turning point in modern Bulgarian history was 9 September 1944, comparable to 3 March 1878 and 10 November 1989, for it was on that day that the Communist Party unleashed an unbridled reign of terror, which surpassed anything the Bulgarian people had seen. It was ordered by the leadership of the party and was directed by Interior Minister Anton Yugov. The bloody settling of accounts with the political opponents went on for months. Thousands were murdered without the benefit of formal trial and thousands were sentenced to death by People's Courts besieged by mobs shouting "death to the fascists." After the execution squads had done their part, the bodies of the dead were dumped into mass graves. The most prominent victims of this reign of terror were Prince Kiril, Bogdan Filov, and General Nikola Mihov, former regents, Bozhilov and Bagrianov, former prime ministers, along with two dozen former ministers and sixty-eight members of the National Assembly. Muraviev, Dimitar Gichev, Nikola Mushanov, Alexander Girginov, Atanas Burov, and other members of the last Cabinet of Ministers, which ruled only seven days, were spared, but they were given long prison sentences.[13] The nation was intimidated, frightened, and cowed into submission. The only hope for democracy now rested with the bourgeois members of the government of the Fatherland Front, but soon it became clear that communism would stay.

The communists saw the Fatherland Front as a tool to set up a bourgeois coalition government whose real purpose was to allow them to seize power, and then suppress all political parties, including their allies. They used them as camouflage which played well outside Bulgaria, but did not deceive anybody inside the country. As a political coalition, the Fatherland Front was a strange combination of disparate political forces. The "Zveno" leaders had overthrown two Agrarian regimes in the past. The "Pladne" Agrarians, especially their leaders, Dimitrov and Kosta Todorov, were notorious agents of the Serbian government of prewar times and of Western intelligence services. Only four ministers of the first Fatherland Front cabinet were communists, but there was no doubt who was in charge. All physical power in the country was in communist hands and their partners were soon to find out that they were only figureheads.

The test for democracy came quickly as the Fatherland Front was challenged from within its ranks. The challenger was Dimitrov, who was designated representative of the BANU in the National Committee of the Fatherland Front. On 12 October 1944, he signed a declaration of the Front, together with Traicho Kostov of the Communist Party, stipulating that there were no democratic forces outside of the coalition, that all that remained were fascists, including the BANU led by Gichev and the Democratic party of Mushanov.[14] Under the circumstances, the non-communist citizens of the country had no choice but to join the Fatherland Front parties. By October and November the membership of these parties had swelled to enormous proportions. It appeared that the BANU was emerging as a formidable political force, threatening the dominance of the Communist Party. Dimitrov was recognized immediately as a foe who should be destroyed. By mid-January 1945, the leadership of BANU was forced to suspend him and put in his place Nikola Petkov as general secretary of the party. Dimitrov sought refuge in the residence of the American representative in the Allied Control Commission and sometime later was allowed to leave the country.

During the second half of 1945, throughout 1946, and until September 1947, the opposition groups in the country, led by the BANU and its fearless General Secretary Petkov, fought the communists in every possible manner in the framework of limited democracy, but ultimately failed. They managed to elect or rather were allowed 104 deputies in the Grand National Assembly, but after Bulgaria signed the peace treaty with the Allies, the days of the opposition and democracy in Bulgaria were over. One day after the United States ratified the treaty, 3 June 1947, the communist majority lifted the parliamentary immunity of Petkov on 4 June, had him arrested in the hall of the assembly, tried him in August, and on 23 September executed him. Even before that, on 23 August, the BANU was outlawed. The hanging of Petkov marked the end of all illusions for a democratic government in Bulgaria and the beginning of the undisputed rule of the Communist Party. The Western Allies protested but did nothing to prevent the Sovietization of Bulgaria.

The conquest of political power was legitimated by a new constitution, known as the Dimitrov Constitution, which was adopted on 4 December 1947.[15] This constitution legislated, in a roundabout way, the perpetuity of communist power. Article 87 prohibited, under threat of penalty, "the creation of organizations, and membership therein which purpose is to take away or to abridge the rights and liberties obtained in battle by the People's insurrection of 9 September 1944." Even before the document was formally adopted, the party had begun preparing the political climate for the Sovietization of Bulgaria. The first item on the agenda was the liquidation of the multiparty system. This process had already been put in operation with the outlawing of the BANU on 26 August 1947. The Party Plenum of 14 October 1947, having urged a quick adoption of the constitution, also proposed reorganizing the state "in view of the development of the country on the road to socialism." Following these instructions of the Plenum, the National Committee of the Fatherland Front came out with a resolution which initiated the process for a one-party government in Bulgaria. It called for restructuring of its organization where representation of the individual parties would be terminated, thus transforming it into an integral political association.[16] On 3 February 1948, at its congress, the Fatherland Front did just that. One by one the smaller political parties—"Zveno," the Social Democrats, and the Radical Party, which had joined the Front—dissolved themselves.

Quite different was the case of BANU. This organization had deep roots among the peasantry in Bulgaria and the party leadership did not move for its complete annihilation. But the communists were not going to allow it to exist as an independent left party. The question had been debated as far back as 1928, and it had then been resolved that such a policy would be wrong, that the right course for the party would be "to prepare and build a strong alliance of the workers and the peasants under the hegemony of the proletariat as a foundation of the Soviet republic in Bulgaria." In 1922 the communists had proposed this option to Alexander Stamboliyski, but he rejected it. And so did all his successors in the leadership of BANU until 1947, but after January 1945, the Communist Party pressed for its adoption. On its demand Dimitrov was replaced by Petkov, but he too refused to allow party control over the Agrarians. A communist-orchestrated coup in the BANU, on 8–9 May 1945, though retaining Petkov as general secretary, without his consent, did away with the anti-communist leaders. In July he resigned as deputy prime minister and emerged as the most vigorous leader of the opposition forces in the country. In June 1947, he was arrested, tried, and executed. His BANU party was outlawed and the left pro-communist Agrarians, led eventually by Georgi Traikov and Petar Tanchev, subscribed to the policies of the Communist Party. Dimitrov, the communist leader, lectured to the Agrarians against the fallacies in which they had believed. He addressed their congress in December 1947 with the recommendation: "Only by way of Socialism will the Bulgarian peasantry march on the road to economic and social progress." This theme was parroted by Traikov: "All of us will march together with the Workers' party in the Fatherland Front for the building of socialism in our country." In 1948 he asked the executive committee of the BANU to affirm "the reorientation of the Union, recognition of the guiding role of the working class and its avant-garde, the Communist party . . . and for making maximum efforts for the building of socialism in our country." This Executive Committee session changed the bylaws of the organization, defining the Union as an organization which "stands and works for the building of socialism in the village." These decisions were confirmed by the Union's Supreme Council on 1 November 1948.[17] Thus the "independence" and the continued existence of the BANU were preserved, but as an agent of the Communist Party for the implementation of the communist program. Subsequently the Communist Party appropriated to itself the right to determine who could and who could not be a member of the BANU, and ruled that the general membership should never go beyond 100,000 members. The BANU was transformed into a peasant section of the Communist Party, but this did not prevent the latter from claiming a two-party system in Bulgaria. It was a sham coalition, masquerading as democracy.

After adopting the constitution of 4 December 1947, and effecting the political changes assuring themselves of absolute power, the communists moved to implement their program for the socialization of industry and the collectivization of peasant lands. The signal for initiating this process was apparently given at the Warsaw meeting of the nine European Communist Parties in September 1947, by Andrei Zhdanov.[18] Returning from this meeting, the Bulgarians proceeded with the adoption of the new constitution and restructuring of the government. Kimon Georgiev was dropped as prime minister and his place was taken by Dimitrov, the veteran Bulgarian communist leader who had recently returned from the Soviet Union. The party took control of fourteen ministries, while the Agrarians were allotted five, and the Socialists and "Zveno," two seats each. On 23 December 1947, the new government proceeded with the nationalization of industry and all private business, including agricultural technology owned by big farmers (*kulaks*).

The collectivization of Bulgarian agriculture was a far more complex problem, compared to the nationalization of industry and other businesses. The enormity of the task and the far-reaching effects of the change were surpassed only by the limitless faith in communism and Soviet experience professed by Bulgarian Marxists. Here the communists chose to use the highly developed and nationally respected cooperative institutions, but in the process they abused, distorted, and eventually killed the cooperative idea and upon its foundations erected their TKZS, collective farms (*Trudovo kooperativno zemedelsko stopanstvo*), which in English means Agricultural Labor Cooperative Farm. When the process of transition from small private farms was completed, TKZS appeared to be the Bulgarian version of the Soviet *kolkhoz*. For Bulgarians, cooperative farming was not an unknown experiment. Of the fifty or so privately organized cooperative farms prior to September 1944, almost half of them had failed. Almost immediately after taking power on 9 September, the communists pushed for the organization of such new farms and by the end of the year some eighty such units had been formed. The party used every expedient of pressure, of intimidation, coercion, persuasion, and force to make the peasants join in. It was all claimed to be a voluntary process of collectivization. The tactics used suggest something else.

Under the party leadership, a few poor peasants would typically be designated as the "base" of the collective and the land's original owners would be compensated with poor and abandoned lots in distant and mountainous places. Rather than accept such an exchange, the former owners would usually join in. To further advance this process, it was decreed that all peasants should deliver to the state, in the form of requisition, set quotas for agricultural goods—produced or not produced. Unable to meet such quotas, the peasants joined in the cooperatives. Those who were still resisting were branded "enemies of the people" and graffiti denouncing them as such, painted on the walls of their houses, soon appeared all over the country. Most often they were exposed as "Kulaks." Still the process was not moving as fast as desired. A negative reaction to this reform was quick in coming. The newly organized farms were failing, their members threatened with famine, and in no time petitions for their dissolution inundated the Ministry of Agriculture, the office of the regents, the Fatherland Front executives, and even the Allied Control Commission. Hundreds of those protesting were party members. The Politburo reviewed the situation in the spring of 1946, but the relentless pressure continued. All along, BANU leaders, though resisting in the beginning, gave their full support to the program of collectivization. Even so, the progress of the process of building agricultural socialism in Bulgaria was going slowly. Only ninety-eight new farms were organized in 1946 and sixty-nine in 1947. But it all changed after the hanging of Petkov in September 1947, the adoption of the new constitution on 4 December, the dissolution of the non-Communist Parties, and the muzzling of the BANU. No less than 550 new collective farms were organized in 1948. The plan for 1949, 508 farms, was fulfilled in a month and a half. The big push came in the fall of 1949 and 1950, when one thousand more farms were organized. By now, 51.1 percent of the arable land had been collectivized in 2,607 cooperative farms. By the end of 1952, there were 2,747 such farms, representing 60 percent of the arable land. By 1958, 98.4 percent of the land had been collectivized into 3,457 cooperative farms. In 1960, the entire system of collective farms was reorganized, reducing their number to 975, by joining entire districts into one farm. In 1970, they were further reduced to 274 units, now called Agro-Industrial Complexes. Agricultural socialism had become a fact of life in Bulgaria and an integral part of the socialist economy of the country. After 1958 some of the cooperative farms stopped paying rent for the land, and after 1960 all of them followed suit.[19]

The liquidation of the political parties, the nationalization of all business and industry in the country, and the collectivization of the land—fully achieved by 1960—made Bulgaria a carbon copy of the Soviet Union. What the founders of the party had fought for and had written about for decades had now been translated into reality.

SUCCESSES AND FAILURES OF COMMUNISM IN BULGARIA

In 1949 Kostov—number three man in the communist hierarchy after the aging and ailing Dimitrov and Kolarov—was suddenly deposed, arrested, and, after a trial on trumped-up charges as a police agent and a spy for the British and American intelligence services, executed. Kostov had been "exposed" and personally browbeaten by Stalin for having attempted to protect Bulgarian economic interests from (Soviet) Big Brother. He had concealed the prices of precious Bulgarian goods traded on Western markets from his Soviet mentors. Dimitrov and Vulko Chervenkov were present and witnessed Stalin's rage. Somehow the conflict was smoothed out, but two obscure party functionaries in Bulgaria, Todor Zhivkov and Demir Yanev, district party secretaries of Sofia and Plovdiv, respectively, suddenly demanded Kostov's removal from all positions of power, leading to Kostov's downfall. Meanwhile, Dimitrov had died on 2 July 1949, followed by Kolarov on 21 January 1950, a few weeks after the hanging of Kostov. The mantle of leadership passed to Chervenkov, a former immigrant to the Soviet Union, brother-in-law of Dimitrov, who now led the Stalinist forces in Sofia. He lost no time in purging the Kostovites in the party and very soon the leading functionaries on the home front—Yugov, Dobri Terpeshev, Tsola Dragoicheva, and Petko Kunin—were demoted from their party and government positions. The man who benefited most from these changes was Zhivkov. In 1954, after Stalin's death in 1953, Chervenkov, following the example of Georgy Malenkov in the Soviet Union, relinquished the secretaryship of the Central Committee but retained the premiership. Zhivkov was made secretary of the Central Committee. In this capacity he convened the famous April Plenum in 1956. He reinstated the old-guard communists, elevating Yugov to the premiership, and demoted Chervenkov to the post of deputy prime minister. In 1962, he had both Yugov and Chervenkov dropped from the party and government leadership and assumed both positions: secretary of the party and prime minister. Nikita Khrushchev paid a visit to Bulgaria shortly thereafter to endorse Zhivkov's program for the de-Stalinization of the country and demonstrate his support for him. In 1971, after having promulgated a new constitution which created a State Council as the highest government institution, Zhivkov relinquished the premiership and assumed the presidency of the council. This made him head of state. He raised to the premiership first Stanko Todorov, one of his cronies, then dropped him in 1981 in favor of Grisha Filipov. He kept the leaders of the Bulgarian Agrarian Union, Traikov, and after Traikov's death, Tanchev, as his deputies, to maintain the deception of a two-party government.[20]

Judging from the government-sponsored publications, this period in the economic history of Bulgaria, 1948–1989, was truly a period of rapid industrial revolution. In 1944 industrial employment in Bulgaria stood at 100,000. By 1979 it had risen to 1,356,000. By 1971 industrial output had increased seventy-one times as compared to 1939. The national income generated by industry in 1948 amounted to 23.3 percent. By 1979 it had risen to 58 percent. The ratio between industrial and agricultural production in 1948 stood at 40:60, changing to 84:14 in 1979.[21] The economic transformation of Bulgaria began with the first two-year plan in 1949 and continued through eight five-year plans (*petiletkas*), which until 1985 were often fulfilled ahead of time. The country was integrated into the Soviet-sponsored Council of Mutual Economic Assistance (COMECON), the East European counterpart to the Common Market in the West. This greatly benefited the Bulgarian economy. But these spectacular successes came to a halt in the 1980s. In 1987, Zhivkov was constrained to admit that the model of socialism being applied up to then had exhausted all its possibilities. He proclaimed the adoption of a "new model" of socialism.

Much more impressive were the gains of the socialist regime in Bulgaria in the field of national culture. The architects of socialism recognized that their success depended on the new outlook of the people, to be shaped along the lines of Marxist-Leninist philosophy, which was to eradicate the cultural legacy of the capitalist past.[22] This called for a cultural revolution, to be carried out simultaneously with the industrial and the agricultural transformation of the national economy. The first steps of this revolution included a wholesale purge of the intellectual field of "fascists"—fascist ideology, laws, associations, and publications. Many of the nationally recognized scholars, writers, artists, editors, and intellectual leaders were either put in jails or thrown out of their offices. In February 1949, the university was purged of 5,000 "reactionary" students.[23] Many others were allowed to be "reconstructed." At a symposium of historians at the University of Sofia, before an audience of hundreds of faculty and students, an array of academicians marched to the podium and renounced their anti-Marxist views. Chervenkov, sitting beside the lectern, notebook in hand, was writing down his observations. It was a humiliating performance witnessed by this writer. At another symposium of biology scholars, their most prominent scientist, Metodi Popov, literally had to tear out two chapters from his just-published impressive volume *Introduction to Biology*, where he had defended the allegedly "reactionary" theories of August Weissmann (1834–1914). He publicly renounced his position on the universally accepted scientific concepts of heredity and endorsed the new theories of inheritance of acquired qualities espoused by Trofim Denisovich Lysenko, just proclaimed as Marxist orthodoxy.[24]

Marxism-Leninism was enthroned as the official and only permissible ideology permitted in the country, and all national culture was to be tailored according to its precepts. The legacy of the past was reevaluated and the blueprints of the future culture were clearly outlined. The Soviet doctrine of Socialist Realism was made mandatory in literature, art, architecture, and music. Literary works took up officially approved themes such as the struggle against capitalism and fascism (as in D. Dimov's novel, *Tobacco*, published in 1951) and socialist transformation (as in A. Guliashky's novel, *Seven Days of Our Life*, published in 1966). Paintings and sculptures celebrated proletarian and revolutionary themes. In the sphere of classical music, new genres—inspired by Stalinist models in Russia—were introduced, such as the mass song and the oratorio. In 1967 the government staged a congress of Bulgarian culture which elected a Committee of Arts and Culture to carry on and control the cultural revolution. Lyudmila Zhivkova, daughter of the political boss of the country, eventually became chief of this committee.[25] To her credit, she carried out her responsibilities with great zeal. It was under her direction that an impressive Palace of Culture was erected in Sofia.

The cultural revolution focused on extensive reforms and reorganization of the educational system of the country. Numerous higher education institutions were opened. There were five such schools in 1944, with instructional faculty of 453 and about 10,000 students. In 1983, there were thirty schools, with 12,622 faculty and 85,000 students. The government took pride from this record and claimed that Bulgaria offered one of the best educational systems in the world. In 1947, the Bulgarian Academy of Sciences was reorganized. Literature, music, graphic arts, cinema, public libraries (*chitalishta*), and publishing houses registered impressive advances. Table 9-1 documents Bulgarian cultural resources before and under socialism. It suffices to point to one of these activities as an illustration of the progress which the cultural revolution was making. In 1980, Bulgaria had 477 newspapers and 1,014 periodicals, at an annual run of one billion copies. Some 4,681 book titles were published, with fifty-eight million copies printed. Here again the government claimed, with justification, that Bulgaria was "at one of the first places in the world with the number of published newspapers, periodicals, and books per capita of its population."[26]

The Bulgarian film industry registered some important advances, especially during two periods of growth. The first lasted from the late fifties to the early sixties. The second period lasted from about 1971 to 1981, more or less coinciding with the years during which Pavel Pissarev served as general director of Bulgarian film. The Bulgarian film industry became best known internationally for its animation and films for children. But from the standpoint of officialdom, the so-called "partisan film" was perhaps the most important film genre in the early years. But even within this genre there was room for experimentation. An example is the film *Life Flows Quietly By* (1958), which offered a critical depiction of corruption in the ranks of the wartime partisans.[27]

The communist regime claimed also to have advanced the position of women, peasants, and workers. In 1979, Elena Lagadinova, president of the Bulgarian Women's Association and wife of one of the highest officials in the Ministry of Defense, lavished praise on the regime for its care for Bulgarian women and their contribution to the building of socialism. She was addressing the annual congress of the organization. *Zemedelsko Zname* editorialized that the greatest conquest of the socialist revolution had been the liberation of women and the security of their position in socialist society. However, reports in the Bulgarian press during the late 1970s give an indication of what kind of liberation and security of positions was enjoyed by Bulgarian peasant women. In the village of Slavovitsa each woman working for the dairy farm cared for one hundred cows, which produced 400 tons of milk a year. In another village

TABLE 9-1 Statistical Data about the Development of Bulgarian Culture

	up to 1939	1965	1979
Number of library clubs	2,610	4,513	4,249
Newly built premises	485	1,100	2,235
Members of library clubs	160,000	953,000	1,076,000
Public libraries	—	10,813	10,278
Book stock	—	36,035,000	89,606,000
Number of readers	—	3,338,000	3,434,000
Museums	80	133	193
Cultural clubs	—	72	266
Book publishing—total print (volumes)	6,000,000	39,282,000	52,050,000
Number of professional music groups	—	11	26
Number of concerts given	—	806	1,254
Number of amateur artistic groups	—	14,592	18,885
Number of concerts given	—	72,059	114,159
Number of art galleries	—	—	52
Number of exhibition halls	—	—	113
Art exhibitions	—	240	706
Number of exhibited fine arts works	—	16,775	44,721
Number of theaters	13	36	57
Number of performances	4,030	11,550	15,795
Attendance	1,521,000	4,951,000	6,448,000
Number of cinema halls	155	2,403	3,517
Number of film shows	71,328	1,027,506	996,528
Attendance	13,103,000	26,362,000	110,275,000
Number of films made in Bulgaria	3	236	498
Number of newspapers	513	590	495
Total print	130,297,000	602,178,000	934,183,000
Number of magazines and reviews	393	449	1,003
Total print	11,208,000	25,384,000	59,101,000
Number of towns and villages receiving radio programs	—	2,204	2,637

80 percent of the workforce in the dairy division of the cooperative farm was made up of women.[28]

While trying to reshape the cultural outlook of the Bulgarians along Marxist-Leninist lines, alternatively called scientific philosophy, the government was determined to erase any system of thought which did not fit the communist way of understanding the world. Religion was such a system of thought and was, therefore, targeted for destruction. In 1944, the Church was separated from the state de facto, and in 1947, with the introduction of the new constitution, de jure. Religious education in the schools was discontinued, religious rituals accompanying marriages and funerals gradually phased out, and attendance of religious services subjected to mockery and social ostracism. Even the use of traditional Christian names was discouraged and a new list of suggested names was proposed. Leading among the male names given after the 1950s is Krassimir. Few people ventured any longer to name their children Ivan, Georgi, Dimitar, or Nikola. The clergy was subjected to open persecution by arrests, imprisonment, murders, and concentration camps. Two leading metropolitans of the Bulgarian Orthodox Church, Kiril of Plovdiv and Paissiy of Vratsa, were placed under arrest, with the intention of bringing them before a people's court, but they were released and reinstated six months later. Hundreds of priests were murdered without trial, and many others passed through concentration camps. In 1948, Exarch Stefan of Sofia was forcibly removed from his home and sent to a provincial monastery, where he remained a prisoner until the end of his life. The two theological seminaries were abolished although a "priestly school" was allowed to survive. The Theological Faculty was reduced to a Theological Academy, outside of the Sofia University, where it had been since its establishment in 1923.[29]

The Protestant community was hit harder. Fifteen of its leading pastors were tried for espionage and locked in prison for many years. A similar trial of the Catholic clergy for foreign espionage and violations of foreign currency laws led to the execution of Bishop Evgeniy Bosilkov in 1952.[30] In 1949, General Yonko Panov, chief of state security, prepared a memorandum for Yugov, replete with bristling accusations against the Orthodox Holy Synod and its metropolitans, portraying the synod as a nest of counterrevolutionaries and proposing a series of measures to muzzle the Church. Yugov formulated his proposals on the basis of this memorandum to the party Central Committee for seizing control of the Church governing bodies. On 24 February 1949, even before these documents were drafted, Parliament had passed a Law of Confessions which had placed the religious organizations in iron chains. To survive, these organizations, primarily the Orthodox Church, had to accommodate themselves to the new regime and become mouthpieces of communist propaganda.[31] In 1962, a group of scholars, led by Professor Zhivko Oshavkov from the Institute of Philosophy of the Bulgarian Academy of Sciences, on orders from the party, conducted a study of the religious beliefs of the Bulgarian people.[32] Finally, to combat religion the party organized a Society of Atheists, authorizing it to publish a periodical titled *Atheistichna Tribuna* (*Atheistic Tribune*).

An unexpected development of the cultural revolution was the resurrection of Bulgarian nationalism. In pre-communist times nationalism was treated by the party as a mortal sin, as a reactionary philosophy, and was dubbed a "great Bulgarian chauvinism." During the first years after 9 September 1944, the Bulgarian regime went along with a policy of registering residents of Pirin Macedonia as ethnic Macedonians, in conformity with Comintern pronouncements and the respective developments in Yugoslavia since 1943. But after the defection of Tito from the Soviet orbit, it all changed and the Bulgarians repudiated the notion of a separate Macedonian identity and recorded that the residents of Pirin Macedonia were ethnic Bulgarians. The Bulgarian government simultaneously reverted to the position taken by Bulgaria's pre-socialist government and began to insist that the Slavs of Yugoslav Macedonia and northern Greece alike were ethnically Bulgarians. In the beginning in the early 1950s, they moved slowly and cautiously, but in subsequent decades, continuing to this day, they moved with a vehemence and determination. While still pledging their loyalty to internationalism in Zhivkov's era, which was tantamount and limited to loyalty to the Soviet Union, the Bulgarian communists were converted to the views of the Bulgarian nationalists, once called fasicsts, whose views they earlier despised, but vehemently defend even to this day.

REVISIONISM—A GRAVEYARD OF ILLUSIONS

The obituary of socialism in Bulgaria and the funeral oration over its dead body were written by none other than its prophet and messiah, Todor Zhivkov himself. On 28 July 1987, he stood before a stunned Plenum of the Central Committee of the Party and delivered a magisterial address telling them that the old model of socialism had failed and could no longer be used, "because all its possibilities are exhausted."[33] Yordan Yotov, another Politburo official, confirmed: "The old model is definitely exhausted." The failure was blamed on mistakes and "deformations." Zhivkov proposed a "new model" of socialism which, when stripped of his convoluted verbiage, was nothing but a resurrected version of the dead ideal. Zhivkov's speech opened the gates for a revisionist criticism of communism.

Women were in focus under the new glasnost. In 1989 Valentina Stoeva published a scathing article that decried the miserable lot of the working women in Bulgaria. She recalled an incident where while a factory radio was blasting some statistics quoting the accomplishments of the previous Saturday's voluntary work, the women in the ladies lounge were cursing that the next Saturday had also been designated as a working day. She quoted one of the women as saying: "The women in our factory are tired. They have already worked three consecutive Saturdays. They are on the brink of nervous breakdown." The factory was stealing their free time and they were falling far behind in their housework. She indicated that 95 percent of Bulgarian working women were paid less than the average salary and 50 percent of them were assigned to high-risk jobs, contrary to international and national laws. This writer observed that all women in his village, in the month of September 1992, worked in the orchards picking apples. All of these women were over sixty-five years of age and each was paid the equivalent of $1.33 a day. How did the younger women react to this system? Very simple! They refused to have children.[34]

Very often the revisionists would turn to the peasants and the cooperative farms. The peasants, or what was left of them, were described as lonely old men and women in abandoned villages. The writers pointed out that the country had the highest percentage of aging peasant population in the world. The majority of them are still working on the farms to supplement their meager pensions. They were paid twenty stotinki (twenty cents) a day in 1989, while the agricultural produce was purchased by the state at very low prices.

With unusual vehemence the revisionists attacked the social problems afflicting Bulgarian society. Health problems attracted much attention and were handled with candor and concern. In 1979, Minister of National Health Radoi Pop Ivanov had boasted about "the all around spectacular growth of health care in Bulgaria. It is not an accident," wrote Radoi, "that our health care today is rightly matched with that of the developed countries and enjoys a deserved international recognition and prestige." He attributed all these spectacular successes to the advantages of real socialism. But in 1989, Dr. Nikolai Golemanov analyzed available statistical data and arrived at frightening conclusions. Golemanov was alarmed by the increased incidences in death among men of age 15 to 65. Deaths were rising 3 percent annually. And the death rate in the villages surpassed the cities by 30 percent. He further pointed out that 86 percent of the deaths were due to chronic, not infectious diseases. In two years incidences of death from cardiovascular causes among men in active age groups had risen 200 percent, placing Bulgaria at the top of the list for cardiovascular deaths of sixteen European countries. In 1978, Bulgaria led eighteen European countries with strokes—237 per 100,000 population, rising in 1980 to 280. Accidental deaths had increased 360 percent since 1978. Life expectancy had fallen to 68 years during the period 1981–83, in comparison with 1964–66 when it was 69.3. Young men at 15, according to Golemanov, could expect to live, on the average, 44.8 years.

Dimitar Fidanov called attention to the rapid rise of suicide in Bulgaria and attributed it to "high tensions in social life, professional competition, and abnormal conditions for the growth of our children." Mito Bozhkov and General-Colonel Christo Dobrev focused on the progressive physical and mental deterioration of Bulgarian young men of draft age.[35]

The revisionists, however, never crossed the line to renounce socialism as doctrine and as a system of economic organization of society. They mercilessly denounced its failures, its errors, its excesses, but they still held that its alternative, capitalism, was not the answer. For one thing, Zhivkov was still in his residence in Boyana, the party was still in power, and any tinkering with the realities of that power was a risk that only a few would take. They would swing from half-baked liberalism to atavistic lamentations for the old ideas of socialism, but always, even in confusion, would remain loyal to the party. They were not dissidents, nor were they openly advocating glasnost and perestroika Soviet style. They did not attack the government, but they savagely exposed the failures of the system. Zhivkov himself had called for a civil society, which had been swallowed by the state in the Soviet system, but, in his "new model," society was to take charge of the state. Stoiu Stoiev thought that socialist and bourgeois pluralism were complementing, not canceling each other. Professor Ivan Lutzov thought that the cooperative farm was the preferable form of agricultural organization to capitalistic farming. He argued that it generated charge of creative energy, of initiative, of independence and self-development, love of work, love of land, and attachment to animals. He apparently had never seen a cooperative farm. Georgi Petrov went further than any of the other revisionists in advocating a system virtually capitalistic, but still clinging to the old laws, which could just be improved with new legislation.[36]

BULGARIA'S "GENTLE" REVOLUTION

The first glimmers of an awakening political conscience in Bulgaria were noticed in the fall of 1986 when a group of former political prisoners, led by Ilia Minev, began exchanging views for founding a society for the defense of human rights. On 16 January 1988, some forty men gathered at his home in a provincial town and formed the first Independent Society for Human Rights. They attempted to register it with the courts, but ended in jails or were expelled from Bulgaria. They were not men of prominence or with impressive credentials but rather low-level intellectuals, small-time poets, and ordinary workers. They would have remained unknown, but government attempts to suppress their society and the publicity in the official press made them national heroes. On 13 January 1989, the government press opened a venomous attack on them. Minev was called "a Fascist gauleiter, bandit, and terrorist, a criminal and recidivist." But they were soon discovered by Radio Free Europe, BBC, and Deutsche Welle and put in front of the microphones; soon all of Bulgaria was listening to their voices. The dam of silence was broken and an avalanche of organizations sprang up. There appeared an Eco-Glasnost Committee, an Independent Club in Support of Glasnost and Perestroika, a "273 Committee" (named after Article 273 of the Penal Code, incriminating acts of political dissent), Citizens' Initiative Committee, etc. Unlike the first Independent Society for Human Rights, these new committees were made up mostly of university professors and top-level journalists, who eventually emerged as leaders of the democratic forces in Bulgaria.[37]

By contrast with most of the other East European countries, however, the cultural sphere in Bulgaria offered little by way of inspiration to political opposition. On the contrary, in some sectors performers were constantly on the defensive, fending off charges of serving as vehicles of Westernization and bourgeois morality.[38] But for all that, the winds of change would prove irresistible. The collapse of communist regimes elsewhere in the region ensured a reaction in Bulgaria.

On 27 October 1989, reacting to the political maelstrom sweeping Eastern Europe, Zhivkov peremptorily ordered Petar Mladenov, minister of foreign affairs, minutes before a scheduled meeting with United States Ambassador Sol Polanski, to tell the American representative that "the United States is interfering rudely in Bulgarian internal affairs, which is inadmissible," and that "the restructuring in Bulgaria will be effected only with Todor Zhivkov at the helm." Mladenov took offense at the manner employed by Zhivkov and immediately submitted his resignation from the Politburo of the party and as foreign minister.[39] Zhivkov refused to accept his resignation and sent him to China for an official visit, via Moscow, where he met with Mikhail Gorbachev. He returned to Bulgaria on 8 November. By that time Defense Minister Dobri Djourov, Central Committee member Dimitar Stanishev, and Yordan Yotov, a member of the Politburo, had already put into motion a plot to force Zhivkov to resign. They told him bluntly that in view of international and domestic developments, the time had come for him to go. The Plenum accepted his resignation and elected as his successor Petar Mladenov. There were no mass demonstrations and there was no change of government. It was not a revolution. It was a palace coup. In his acceptance speech Mladenov vowed to transform Bulgaria into a contemporary democratic state where the Communist Party would continue to be the vanguard and the guiding force of society, "to build successfully a true socialism." Six days later, 16 November, another Plenum of the Central Committee purged the Politburo of Zhivkovists.

Zhivkovism was subjected to acerbic criticism, but not a single word was said at this point about abandoning one-party rule in Bulgaria. On 17 November, the National Assembly elected Mladenov to succeed Zhivkov as president of the State Council. Again, not a word was said about changing the system, dissolving the assembly, or free elections to revamp the established institutions. Slavcho Trunsky, a veteran partisan leader, bitterly attacked Zhivkov, but he, too, never implied a change of the existing order of things. That same day, 17 November, the Fatherland Front held a rally at the National Assembly, with speeches in support of the changes of leadership, but again, no promises of democratization along Western lines were made.[40] Yet, it was at this rally that the first signals for revolutionary change began flashing. Opposition forces practically took over, shouting the speakers down, raising provocative slogans and attempting to seize the speaker's rostrum. The next day, 18 November, opposition forces called a rally of their own at Alexander Nevsky Cathedral and denounced the regime of the Communist Party. For the first time in forty years the authorities did not intervene to stop it. If there was a revolution in Bulgaria, it started on 18 November, not on 10 November. On 7 December 1989, some of the "informal" organizations, meeting in a basement room of the Department of Sociology of the Sofia University, led by Zhelyu Zhelev, a professor of philosophy, Peter Beron, a professor of zoology, and Konstantin Trenchev founded the Union of Democratic Forces (UDF). By the end of December numerous other opposition groups applied for registration.

In the beginning of January 1990, the Communist Party offered the opposition the option of joining in a national roundtable discussion to negotiate a settlement of the political problems of the country. Only representatives of the UDF were included in these negotiations. Subsequently, the Agrarians in the government, having cut their ties with the communists, formed the third party at the roundtable. After several meetings and some setbacks, the participants signed an agreement on 12 March.[41]

The elections for Grand National Assembly, held in two rounds on 10 and 17 June, brought a disastrous defeat for the UDF and a spectacular victory for the Socialists (on 3 April 1990, the BCP changed its name to Bulgarian Socialist Party, or BSP)—211 Socialists, 144 UDF representatives, sixteen Agrarians (formerly allied with the communists), twenty-three representatives of the Movement for Rights and Freedom (MRF, a party of the Turkish minority), and six seats for sundry political groups.[42] The UDF ineptly tried to challenge the results, but has never been able to make a credible case, even in some of their most recent attempts.[43] The simple explanation for the communist victory and the opposition's defeat is in the indisputable fact that the BSP, on the eve of the elections, still had close to one million members who shared in the privileges and advantages in public life ensured by the old regime. Besides, the administrative infrastructure of Bulgarian society was still under party control and all levers of power and influence had remained intact in communist hands. This may explain why the cities voted overwhelmingly for the UDF candidates, while the countryside backed the BSP. It is not that the opposition failed to make a good case against communism, or that the large masses of people were still in love with the system. It was the fear of losing benefits, fear of suffering reprisals, and the economic dependence of large segments of the population on the established order which ensured the victory of the communists and the defeat of the opposition.

The excitement and the passions vented in the preelection campaign did not subside. Nikolai Todorov, the former ambassador and president of the Academy of Sciences, was elected president of the assembly, but the party suffered several painful blows during the following months. Student and worker strikes, street demonstrations, and protests continued. In the course of these events, in mid-July 1990, it was revealed that Mladenov, president of the republic, had been overheard during a demonstration in front of the National Assembly, on 14 December 1989, suggesting calling the tanks to disperse the crowds. It was and still is claimed that the videotape had been doctored by the CIA for the benefit of the UDF. The tape was now broadcast and Mladenov was forced out of office. On 31 July, the leader of the opposition, Zhelev, was elected by the assembly to succeed Mladenov.[44] Under pressure from the opposition and the general public, the party removed the embalmed body of its hero Dimitrov from the mausoleum in the center of Sofia, incinerated it, and buried his ashes in a cemetery. The leaders of the two leading factions, the BSP and the UDF, reconvened the roundtable and signed a new *Sporazumenie* on 3 March 1991. The new agreement affirmed the irreversibility of the reform process, condemned any illegal pressure on the organs of the state, and set deadlines for adopting the constitution and a series of emergency laws. It also provided for the replacement of the all-communist government of Andrey Lukanov with a government of experts. When the constitution was ready, it was endorsed only by the BSP, the UDF-center, and UDF-liberal groups. Three hundred and ten deputies signed it and celebrated its adoption, while ninety refused to sign the document and left the assembly. The constitution was promulgated on 13 July 1991. The assembly continued in session and adopted a new electoral law. It stipulated that only political parties and groups receiving a minimum of 4 percent of the electoral vote would be entitled to seats in the new parliament. The constitution had prohibited political parties organized on religious and ethnic bases, thus disqualifying the MRF as a Muslim and Turkish party. Members of the National Assembly challenged the status of the MRF as a political party on constitutional grounds, but the court could not muster enough votes to disqualify its elected representatives. Pressure from the United States in support of the Turks caused the matter to be dropped.[45]

The elections for a new National Assembly were held on 13 October. These elections were free, fair, and democratic, but the electoral system produced an assembly which was neither democratic, free, nor representative. Only three of the thirty-eight coalition groups won representation in the parliament: the UDF, 110 seats; the BSP, 106, and the MRF, twenty-four. The UDF won the elections with 1,903,567 votes, or 34.36 percent of the total vote, to 1,836,050 votes for the BSP (33.14 percent), and 418,168 for the MRF (7 percent). But its paper-thin plurality of 1.22 percent, against the 65.64 percent vote against them, was so unconvincing as to be an embarrassment. But in subsequent elections in December 1994, the BSP, the former Communist Party, won a smashing victory over its new rival, the UDF. The political evolution of Bulgaria from 10 November 1989 to 18 December 1994 had turned full circle: from the former Bulgarian Communist Party, to democracy, and then back to the Communist Party, renamed the Bulgarian Socialist Party, now professing a faith in democracy. The same people who once sat in the Politburo and the Central Committee of the party would now preside over the parliament and the government.

LEGACY OF THE POST-COMMUNIST DEMOCRATIC GOVERNMENTS OF DIMITROV/BEROV

It is not too early to pass a definitive judgment on the democratic governments of the UDF, led by Philip Dimitrov, and that of Luben Berov— October 1991–October 1994. If the results of the elections of 18 December 1994 are taken into account, then these governments would seem to have been complete failures. The elections were a referendum on their performance and this referendum was lost by them. The elections for local government, November 1995, brought another crushing defeat for the UDF opposition forces.

The UDF never measured up to the challenges it faced. Its attempt to dissolve the collective farms led to a chaotic disruption and ultimately to the destruction of Bulgarian agriculture, to the point where the Berov government had to slow down the process of disintegration, neither reversing it nor pushing it forward. Berov passed laws to return the land to the peasants, ignoring the fact that the old style small farms were gone forever, that most of the peasants had moved to the cities and would never return to practice the neolithic type of agriculture. The disastrous "reforms" in agriculture brought a bread crisis in May–June 1996, and the shadow of great famine which threatens to plague the country for years to come, no matter who runs the government, unless a massive infusion of investments and a new concept of agricultural organization are found.

In May 1992, a high government official declared the Patriarch of the Bulgarian Orthodox Church Maksim and the entire Holy Synod illegitimate and appointed a new Synod, contrary to the constitutional provisions for separation of Church and state. It was a declaration of war on the Church, which led to arbitrary acts of occupation of church buildings and institutions including the headquarters of the Holy Synod and the Sofia Theological Seminary. The Holy Snyod defrocked the government-appointed Synodal metropolitans and the schism in the ranks of the Church became a national scandal. The act of dismissal of the Patriarch and the Synod was undertaken as a part of a policy of de-communization of the Church, though the government-appointed new Synod was made up of the most pronounced communist stooges of Zhivkov's regime. This schism, orchestrated by the government of Dimitrov, tolerated and indirectly supported by Berov's government, is now on its way out, having failed to attract the clergy of the Orthodox Church and any following among the people, but its legacy of humiliation, intimidation, mockery, and disrespect by high governmental officials of the UDF and its press, as well as the open coddling of foreign-based religious organizations conducting missionary work in Bulgaria, have virtually destroyed the stature of the Church as a national institution of impeccable credentials confirmed by its more than a thousand-year history.[46] The schismatic leader, the former metropolitan of Nevrokop, Pimen, abandoned by the other two metropolitans, convened a Church National Council at the beginning of July 1996 and had himself elected as another Patriarch of Bulgaria. This farcical performance was endorsed by the leaders of the UDF, including State Prosecutor Ivan Tatarchev. The BSP continued and continues to support Patriarch Maksim.[47]

The question of the monarchy in Bulgaria was raised with the fall of the regime of Zhivkov. Sensation-seeking television operators, political manipulators without ideological identity seeking a cause to legitimize themselves, diehard royalists of the past, and the ex-King Simeon himself, promoted the idea with every means at their disposal. In the spring of 1992, the country seemed to be caught in an outburst of monarchism, especially following a May visit to Bulgaria of Princess Maria-Luisa. Even the Grand National Assembly lost its senses and voted for a referendum for monarchy or republic in the beginning of June—only to rescind it a week later. A significant segment of the UDF leadership got involved in this dream and pressed for its realization. This led to a split in its

ranks. The ex-King Simeon did not help matters either. With his Hamlet-
ian indecision, his numerous attempts at ingratiation with the socialists
(communists), and his duplicity on the schism in the Church—engineered
and overwhelmingly supported by the monarchists—he eventually lost
ground in Bulgaria. But he misled the right wing of the UDF and contributed to the dissolution of the broader alliance of the democratic forces.
What is left of the UDF now is a clique of right wing extremists, still
dreaming of a restoration of the monarchy in Bulgaria. The elections of
18 December 1994 wiped out this dream. The elections for local officials,
December 1995, further weakened the chances of the right in Bulgaria to
restore the monarchy. Ex-King Simeon's visit in the country in May–June
1996, though carefully orchestrated by the royalist forces, must have convinced the pretender that Bulgaria has no use for him. He did not articulate any positive program for taking the country out of its present
economic debacle. The only positive note of his visit was his open endorsement of Patriarch Maksim and his public rejection of the schis-
matics.

One of the positive changes in the direction of democracy in Bulgaria
since 1989 is in the sphere of press and media. The printed media in
particular enjoy broad freedom. However, in October 1990, the Bulgarian Parliament voted to restore its rights to exercise control over the national broadcasting media. This was confirmed by the constitution of
1991, and includes, *inter alia,* the provision for parliament's right to
make managerial appointments for national television and radio. The
government of socialist Prime Minister Zhan Videnov used this provision
to make politically motivated appointments. The opposition in turn
charged that the government was engaging in the re-communization of
the media.[48]

The Videnov government experienced difficulties in managing the
economy, however. The Bulgarian lev lost 70 percent of its value against
the dollar between January and May 1996 alone.[49] Meanwhile, Bulgaria's foreign exchange reserves shrank to $650 million by April 1996.[50]
The Videnov government's first good news on the economic front in
1996 came in June with the IMF's announcement that it would grant
Sofia a $460 million standby loan.[51]

And 1996 was also President Zhelev's last year in office. Zhelev was
defeated in primary elections on 4 June, for the nomination of the antisocialist UDF, by a vote of 65.74 percent to 34.26 percent.[52] The victorious UDF nominee, forty-four-year-old Peter Stoyanov, was slated to face
forty-eight-year-old Georgi Pirinski, the Socialist Party candidate, in
presidential elections at the end of 1996.[53]

Historians will, no doubt, debate the nature of the legacies of Zhelev's five and a half years in office. But in my view, by far the most important legacy left by the regimes of Zhelev-Dimitrov-Berov is the alienation
of Bulgaria from Russia—a consequence of a creeping Russophobia, the

experiences of the communist rule under Soviet protection, and a well-pronounced servility and attempts at ingratiation in Paris, London, and Washington, all along accompanied by an uncertain and unconvincing hope for admission into the political and economic structures of Western Europe. But Bulgaria's proximity to Russia cannot be ignored and should be taken into account in assessing prospects for the future.

Videnov's government proved unable to manage the national economy and on 19 December 1996, while the country was in a state of total collapse, he submitted his resignation. President Zhelev asked the BSP to form a new government, but events intervened and the Socialists were thrown out of the political arena. On 10 January 1997, a mass demonstration in Sofia turned unruly and an angry mob invaded the halls of the National Assembly. While the mob vandalized and destroyed the building's interior, police escorted the socialist members of parliament to safety. The scene was reminiscent of the storming of the Winter Palace in St. Petersburg during the October revolution and the assault on the Tuileries of 10 August 1792 during the French revolution. This was the climax of the Bulgarian revolution.

On 21 January, Stoyanov was inaugurated as president and on 4 February the leaders of the BSP, Georgi Parvanov and Nikolai Dobrev, surrendered to him the mandate to form a new government. Had they not done so, the country would have been thrown into a bloody civil war. Stoyanov dissolved Parliament, appointed a service ministry under Stefan Sofiansky, mayor of Sofia and a stalwart of the UDF, and ordered new elections. The UDF and its allies won a smashing victory, while the BSP suffered a humiliating defeat. The new government, led by Ivan Kostov, seems poised to shape the future of Bulgaria, if intraparty rivalries do not undercut it. Kostov has tried to carry democratic reforms further, but his success to this day is meager and unimpressive. However, once venerable Bulgarian institutions, such as the monarchy, which was discredited but still commands considerable respect, the BANU, once the backbone of Bulgarian democracy in the twentieth century, and the Bulgarian Orthodox Church, with long, honorable service to the nation over a millennium, are now in permanent shambles. Rather than rebuild the nation internally, the new government's priorities seem to be focused on the admission of Bulgaria into the European Union and NATO. For now, the economy has stabilized with the help of the International Monetary Fund, but its future is uncertain. Nevertheless, the country seems to be taking tentative steps toward democracy.

Notes

1. Raymond J. Sontag and James Stuart Beddie, eds., *Nazi-Soviet Relations 1939–41: Documents from the Archives of the German Foreign Office* (Washington: Department of State Publication 3023, 1948), 242–252, 258–259.

2. Ruben Avramov, et al., eds., *Istoriya na Bulgarskata koministicheska partiya* (Sofia: Partizdat, 1981), 375.

3. H. R. Trevor-Roper, *Hitler's War Directives, 1939–1945* (London: Sedgwick and Jackson, 1964), 46–48.

4. Stephane Grueff, *Crown of Thorns: The Reign of King Boris III of Bulgaria* (Lanham, Md.: Madison, 1987), 301.

5. Alexander Velichkov, "On Some Aspects of American-Bulgarian Relations immediately before and at the Beginning of World War II," in *Bulgaria, Past and Present: Proceedings of the Second International Conference on Bulgarian Studies, Varna—June 13–17, 1978* (Sofia: Publishing House of the Bulgarian Academy of Sciences, 1982), 207.

6. *Foreign Relations of the United States, Diplomatic Papers, 1943,* Vol. 1 (Washington: Government Printing Office, 1963), 496.

7. After the war, some 45,000 Bulgarian Jews emigrated to Israel. *Washington Times,* 25 February 1993, G4; see also BTA (Sofia), 24 February 1993, in *BBC Summary of World Broadcasts.*

8. Avramov, *Istoriya na Bulgarskata . . . ,* 413.

9. Charles A. Moser, *Dimitrov of Bulgaria: A Political Biography of Dr. Georgi M. Dimitrov* (Ottawa, Ill.: Caroline House, 1979), 169.

10. John D. Bell, *The Bulgarian Communist Party from Blagoev to Zhivkov* (Stanford: Hoover Institution Press, 1986), 63.

11. Grueff, *Crown of Thorns,* 351.

12. Cordell Hull, *The Memoirs of Cordell Hull* (New York: Macmillan, 1948), 1455.

13. Marshall Lee Miller, *Bulgaria during the Second World War* (Stanford: Stanford University Press, 1975), 217.

14. Spas T. Raikin, "Edin znachitelen dokument za politicheskata istoria na bulgarskiya narod ot blizkoto minalo. Deklaratsiata na otechestvenofrontovskite partii, 12 Oktomvri 1944 g." in *Borba* (New York), 1957, No. 3, 14.

15. Veselin Metodiev and Luchezar Stoyanov, *Bulgarski konstitutsii i konstitutsionni proekti* (Sofia: Durzhavno Izdatelstvo "Dr. Petar Beron," 1990), 37; and Avramov, *Istgeriya ne Buigarskata,* 455.

16. Yordan Zarchev, *BZNS i izgrazhdaneto na sotsializma v Bulgaria, 1944–1962* (Sofia: Nauka i izkustvo, 1984), 201, 204.

17. Veselin Hadjinikolov, ed., *Bulgarskiat zemedelski naroden saiuz i sotsializmut* (Sofia: Izdatelstvo na BZNS, 1984), 172, 396–400; Mito Isusov, *Politicheskite partii v Bulgaria, 1944–48* (Sofia: Nauka i izkustvo, 1978), 438; and Zarchev, *BZNS,* 203–205, 208.

18. Zarchev, *BZNS,* 201.

19. Dimitar Kosev, *Istoriya na Bulgaria,* Vol. 2 (Sofia: Nauka i izkustvo, 1955), 942–945; Hadjinikolov, *Bulgarskiat zemedelski,* 376–378, 385–389; Zarchev, *BZNS,* 153, 261; Isusov, *Politicheskite partii,* 273–274; Avramov, *Istoriya na Bulgarskata,* 530; and Petar Tanchev, et al., *The Bulgarian Agrarian Party, a Loyal Ally of the Bulgarian Communist Party* (Sofia: Information Documents and Commentaries, Sofia Press Agency, 1981), 9.

20. Bell, *The Bulgarian Communist Party,* 103–108; Avramov, *Istoria na Bulgarskata,* 479, 480, 490, 501–505; Kostadin Petrov, "Utvurzhdavane na narodnata demokratsia," and Lubomir Ognianov, "Razvitie na sotsialisticheskoto obshtestvo v Bulgaria (1958–1982)," both in Ilcho Dimitrov, ed., *Kratka Istoria na Bulgaria* (Sofia: Nauka i izkustvo, 1983), esp. 435, 440–441, 469, 473–477.

21. Kolyo Kolev, "Profound Transformations in Bulgarian Economy," in

Georgi Bokov, ed., *Modern Bulgaria: History, Policy, Economy, Culture* (Sofia: Sofia Press, 1981), 249–251.

22. Petrov, "Utvurzhdavane," 432.

23. Raikin, *Politicheski problemi pred bulgarskata obshtestvenost v chuzbina, Sbornik statii, eseta, studii i komentari po politicheski, kulturni, ikonomicheski i istoricheski vuprosi publikuvani v emigratsia, 1978–1991* (Sofia: D. Yakov, 1993), Vol. 4, 229–256; and "Bulgarskata kultura v noktite na Bolshevisma," an article written in June 1951, two weeks after this author crossed the border into Greece, first published in *Svobodno zemdelsko zname*, No. 6, June 1980. It touches on all aspects of the communization of Bulgarian culture in all of its branches.

24. Ibid., 237.

25. Lubomir Ognianov, "Postizhenia na Sotsialisticheskata dukhovna kultura," in Dimitrov, ed., *Kratka istoria*, 490; and Bell, *The Bulgarian Communist Party*, 127–128.

26. *Public-State Principle in the Guidance and Management of Culture in the People's Republic of Bulgaria* (Sofia: Sofia Press Agency, 1981), 19.

27. Ronald Holloway, "Bulgaria: The Cinema of Poetics," in Daniel J. Goulding, ed., *Post New Wave Cinema in the Soviet Union and Eastern Europe* (Bloomington: Indiana University Press, 1989), esp. 215–216, 220, 229.

28. *Zemedelsko zname*, 12 May 1979. See also *Zemedelsko zname*, 17 and 19 May 1979 and 8 and 11 May 1979.

29. Spas T. Raikin, "The Communists and the Bulgarian Orthodox Church, 1944–48, the Rise and Fall of Exarch Stefan," in *Religion in Communist Lands*, Vol. 12, No. 3 (Winter 1984), 281–292; Spas T. Raikin, "The Bulgarian Orthodox Church," in Pedro Ramet, ed., *Eastern Christianity and Politics in the Twentieth Century* (Durham: Duke University Press, 1988), 160–182; Spas T. Raikin, "Nationalism and the Bulgarian Orthodox Church," in Pedro Ramet, ed., *Religion and Nationalism in Soviet and East European Politics*, rev. and exp. ed. (Durham: Duke University Press, 1989), 187–206; and Raikin, *Politicheski problemi*, Vol. 3, *Problemi na Bulgarskata pravoslavna tsurkva*, 21–32, 43–49, 73–82, 102–117.

30. *Subversive Activities of the Evangelical Pastors in Bulgaria: Documents* (Sofia: Press Department, Ministry of Foreign Affairs, 1949); Haralan Popoff, *I Was a Communist Prisoner* (Grand Rapids: Zondervan, 1966); Ivan Sofranov, "Muchenik ot nasheto vreme. Episkop Evgeni Bosilkov Nikopolski," reprinted from *Khristianski glas* (Rome), in *Svobodno zemedelsko zname* (Stroudsburg, Penn.), No. 25/26, 1983, 7–11; and Trevor Beeson, *Discretion and Valour: Religious Conditions in Russia and Eastern Europe*, 1st. ed. (London: Collins, 1974), 344.

31. Robert Tobias, *Christian-Communist Encounter in East Europe* (Indianapolis: School of Religious Press, 1956), 352–379.

32. Spas T. Raikin, "Successes and Failures of Atheism in Bulgaria," in *Religion in Communist Dominated Areas*, Vol. 27, Nos. 2–3 (Spring–Summer 1988), 55–58, 88–92.

33. *Zemedelsko zname* (Sofia), No. 180, 29 July 1987.

34. *Zemedelsko zname*, 12 May 1979; Valentina Stoeva, "Izvunrednite suboti," in *Anteni*, No. 6 (February 1989); and *Zemedelsko zname*, 20 March 1989. See also *Zemedelsko zname*, No. 17 and 19, 8 April and 11 May 1979. For further discussion, see Dobrinka Kostova, "Women in Postcommunist Bulgaria," in Marilyn Rueschemeyer, ed., *Women in the Politics of Postcommunist Eastern Europe* (Armonk, N.Y.: M. E. Sharpe, 1994).

250 *Countries*

35. *Zemedelsko zname,* 10 August 1979; Nikolai T. Golemanov, "Zashto umirat muzhete?" *Anteni,* No. 14 (April 1989); Evgeni Petrov, "Opasno izostavane na nezabavno lechenie," *Narodna mladezh* (Sofia), 30 March 1989; *Narodna kultura* (Sofia), No. 19, 5 May 1989; Khristo Dobrev, "Neobkhodimata promiana," *Narodna mladezh* (16 May 1989); *Rabotnichesko delo* (Sofia), 8 May 1989.

36. *Rabotnichesko delo,* 5 July 1989; *Ikonomicheski Zhivot* (Sofia), 24 May 1989; and *Otechestvo* (Sofia), 24 April 1989.

37. Spas T. Raikin, "Glasove ot preizpodnyata. Izyavleniya na Ilia Minev, Dimitar Tomov and Petar Manolov pred BBC." Interview. The text of this broadcast was transcribed from a tape obtained from the London Office of the BBC. See *Politicheski problemi,* Vol. 5, 145–153; *Trud* (Sofia), 13 January 1989; and *Rabotnichesko delo,* 19 January 1989.

38. For example, in the rock scene. For details and documentation, see Stephen Ashley, "The Bulgarian Rock Scene under Communism (1962–1990)," in Sabrina Petra Ramet, ed., *Rocking the State: Rock Music and Politics in Eastern Europe and Russia* (Boulder: Westview, 1994), esp. 146–151.

39. Ashley, "Mladenov's Letter of 27 October to Zhivkov," in *Radio Free Europe Research* (15 December 1989).

40. *Rabotnichesko delo* (formerly *Duma*), 11 November 1989; *Rabotnichesko delo* 25 November 1989; *Rabotnichesko delo* 18 November 1989; and *Uchitelsko delo,* 29 November 1989.

41. *Zemedelsko zname,* 13 March 1990; and *Demokratsia,* 13 March 1990.

42. The popular vote of the major groups was as follows: BSP—2,886,366; UDF—2,216,127; BANU (united)—491, 500; MRF—368,929. See *Duma,* 15 June 1990; *Duma,* 19 June 1990; and *Demokratsiya,* 19 June 1990. On the name change of the BSP, see *Duma,* 4 April 1990.

43. *Demokratsiya,* 24 March 1993; and *Demokratsiya,* 16 April 1993.

44. Mladenov is quoted as having said: "It is best if the tanks come out." See *Demokratsiya,* 25 September 1990. Zhelev was reelected as president in a national election, after the adoption of the constitution of 1991, on 13 January 1992. The popular vote for Zhelev stood at 53.89 percent, as against Velko Vulkanov, backed by the Socialist Party. See *168 Chasa* (20 January 1992). See also *Duma,* 7 July 1990; and *Duma,* 15 July 1990.

45. *Duma,* 23 May 1991; and *Duma,* 18 September 1991.

46. For details, see Spas T. Raikin, "Schism in the Bulgarian Orthodox Church," in *Religion in Eastern Europe,* Vol. 13, No. 1 (February 1993), 19–25; and Spas T. Raikin, "Schism in the Bulgarian Orthodox Church," *Alive in Christ* (Diocese of Eastern Pennsylvania, South Canaan, Penn.), Vol. 8, No. 3 (Winter 1992), 46–49. See also *Politicheski problemi,* Vol. 3, 341–375.

47. Theophila Bogoliubova, "Pimen e noviyat Patriarh," *Demokratsia,* 4 July 1996. Diana Petrova, "Pimen obiaven za Patriarkh 25 godini sled Maxim," *Trud* (Sofia), 5 July 1996.

48. *Duma,* 14 December 1995; *Duma,* 19 December 1995; 24 *Chasa,* 21 December 1995; and *Duma,* 9 January 1996.

49. *Deutsche Presse-Agentur* (Hamburg), 11 May 1996, on *Nexis.*

50. *East European Markets,* 7 June 1996, on *Nexis.*

51. Ibid.

52. *Reuters News Service,* 4 June 1996, on *Nexis;* and *Agence France Presse,* 5 June 1996, on *Nexis.*

53. *Reuters News Service,* 4 June 1996, on *Nexis;* and *Deutsche Presse-Agentur,* 16 June 1996, on *Nexis.*

10

Albania

ELEZ BIBERAJ

Albania, the smallest and the poorest country in Eastern Europe, approaches the beginning of the twenty-first century with great uncertainty. Ravaged by almost half a century of the most repressive communist rule in the region, Albania is in the midst of a painful transition to a post-communist society. Sali Berisha, Albania's first post-communist president, has said that it will take his country up to fifteen years to achieve a full economic recovery and at least a generation to rid itself of the political and societal legacies of communism. Traditionally at the margins of European politics, Albania finds itself competing with other East European countries for Western attention and assistance at a time of declining international interest in the region as a result of the end of the Cold War. In addition to the domestic situation, Albania is faced with an ever-increasing threat of becoming entangled in the Yugoslav conflict, as Serbia continues to pursue a highly repressive policy toward the Albanian majority in the province of Kosova (Kosovo). Albania's relations with its two other immediate neighbors, Greece and the former Yugoslav Republic of Macedonia, remain complicated as a result of disagreements regarding the treatment of ethnic minorities. There is no doubt that Albania is going through one of its most difficult periods since it gained independence in 1912.

Despite its small size and current difficulties, Albania is likely to play an important role in the emerging Balkan order. There are now an estimated seven million Albanians in the region. Albania has a population of about 3.3 million people, but there are almost as many Albanians in neighboring countries. About two million live in the province of Kosova, which since the early 1980s has been under virtual Serbian military occupation. According to Albanian activists, there are some 700,000 Albanians in Macedonia, although Skopje puts the number at 400,000. For now, Albanians in both Kosova and Macedonia seem to have postponed any attempt to unite with Albania. As chances that they can achieve their human and national rights in these countries dwindle, it is likely that they will soon push for unification with Albania, which will provoke strong reaction from their neighbors. Stability and peace in the region will to a large degree depend on how the emerging Albanian question is resolved.

ALBANIA UNDER COMMUNISM

With the exception of their Yugoslav comrades, Albanian communists were the only ones in Eastern Europe to come to power without direct Soviet assistance. Thus they have enjoyed a degree of legitimacy. While communist groups had been created as early as the 1920s, Albania did not have a communist movement until after the outbreak of World War II. Mainly an underdeveloped, agricultural country, Albania lacked a well-developed working class which could serve as the backbone of a communist party. Moreover, King Zog, who had come to power in December 1924, ruled with an iron hand, effectively preventing the creation of opposition parties and thus hindering the country's long-term political growth. It was only after the German invasion of the Soviet Union that Albanian communist groups coalesced into a united party. The Albanian Communist Party (ACP) was created in November 1941 with the assistance of the Yugoslav communists, which accounted for the subsequent Yugoslav domination of the party and the country until the Tito-Stalin break in 1948.[1]

The first European victim of the Axis powers, Albania was annexed by Italy in April 1939 as King Zog fled the country. The Albanians were slow to organize a resistance movement, partly because of the Italian and German decision to attach Kosova and other Albanian-inhabited areas in Yugoslavia to Albania in 1941. For the first time since 1912, the majority of the Albanians lived in one state. After the capitulation of Italy, the Germans moved into Albania, but the Albanians maintained a substantial degree of independence.

Of all political parties created during World War II, the Communist Party was the best organized. With substantial material assistance from the West and guidance from their Yugoslav comrades, Albanian communists organized a resistance movement. Throughout the war period, the communists emphasized the national liberation character of their movement and deliberately downplayed their ideological commitment to the creation of a communist society. On the eve of the liberation of the country, the communists launched a civil war against their opponents. Within a short period of time they were able to defeat Albanian nationalists, grouped around the Legality Movement, which advocated King Zog's return, and the National Front (Balli Kombëtar).

The communists inherited a war-ravaged country. Albania had suffered substantial human and material losses during the war. Some 28,000 Albanians lost their lives in the war against Italian and German occupation and the subsequent civil war, which pitted the victorious communists against the nationalists. Italy, which had announced plans to settle some two million Italian farmers in Albania, had fully integrated the Albanian economy with its own war economy and intensified the exploitation of Albania's substantial reserves of strategic assets, particularly oil, chrome, and copper. The Germans pursued a similar policy during their occupation of the country (1943–44). Before the war, more than 80 percent of the population was engaged in the agricultural sector. In the lowlands, a small landowning class owned large estates worked by tenants, while in the hilly and mountainous regions, independent, small farmers engaged in primitive farming and livestock raising. With the exception of oil and chromium production, which had been intensified during the war, Albania had no industry to speak of. Although the Italians had upgraded Albania's communications network, improved port facilities, and constructed new roads linking mining regions with the ports, these have proved insufficient.

After forming a provisional government in November 1944, the communists moved swiftly to extend and consolidate their control throughout the country. In December 1945, elections were held for a Constituent Assembly, which a month later proclaimed Albania a "people's republic," clearly signaling the determination of the new leaders to forge a close alliance with the emerging communist bloc. The assembly promulgated a new constitution, closely modeled after Yugoslavia's communist constitution. Although the document made no reference to the "special role" of the Communist Party, customarily included in the constitutions of other East European countries allied with the Soviet Union, Albanian communists excluded the possibility of a coalition with other parties and groups. Enver Hoxha, who in addition to serving as party general secretary also simultaneously held the posts of prime minister, foreign minister, and commander in chief of the armed forces, launched a series of political, economic, and military policies designed to consolidate the new socialist order. Through an unprecedented campaign of terror, the prewar political elite was decimated through purges and war crimes trials; leaders of the opposition groups who survived were forced to flee the country. By the end of 1946, the regime had succeeded in eliminating all organized opposition, with the notable exception of small groups in northern Albania which continued their armed struggle well into the late 1940s. From 1945 to 1957, the government also took several economic and social measures intended to destroy the economic base of the country's prewar elite and lay the foundations for a communist command economy. The property of exiled or imprisoned political opponents was seized, and foreign-owned assets were confiscated. The state took over all industrial and commercial enterprises and monopolized domestic and foreign trade. In accordance with the Stalinist economic model, Albania's economic plans emphasized the rapid development of heavy industry over agriculture and light industry. The government announced an agrarian reform, nationalizing all forests and pasturelands, confiscating large estates, and distributing land to landless peasants. Although farmers were urged to join collective farms, collectivization of agriculture gained momentum only in the mid-1950s and was completed a decade later.[2]

Although the constitution adopted in 1946 guaranteed freedom of religion, the communists, from the outset, left no doubt about their objective of destroying all organized religion. The three main religious communities—Muslim, Catholic, and Eastern Orthodox—became the object of a well-coordinated government campaign aimed at discrediting and terrorizing them into submission. Most of the property belonging to religious organizations was confiscated without compensation. By the early 1950s, most prominent religious leaders had been executed, imprisoned, or had fled the country. The antireligious campaign was intensified in the 1950s and the 1960s, climaxing with the government's decision in 1967 to outlaw religion altogether and close all houses of worship.

The cultural sphere was also affected by communist rule. During World War II, a genre of national liberation poetry developed. The theme of partisan struggle continued to figure in Albanian literature for several years after the end of the war. Socialist realism, an aesthetic principle first developed in Stalin's Russia, became the guiding principle of cultural policy in the first decades of communist rule in Albania. In 1945, there was some resistance to the imposition of firm communist control over literature. Specifically, in October of that year, Sejfulla Malëshova, APL Politburo member and minister of culture and propaganda, organized a meeting of Albanian writers in Tiranë for the purpose of creating a writers' union. At this meeting, Malëshova's line was not to prevail and on 21 February 1946, the ill-fated minister of culture was accused of opportunism and deviation to the right and expelled from party leadership bodies and posts.[3]

The cultural sphere was palpably affected by foreign policy priorities. In the first fourteen years of communist rule (1944–58), of approximately 400 works of literature translated into Albanian, about 270 had been authored by Soviet writers. Translations of Soviet authors also predominated in the social sciences. Later, after Albania's break with Moscow in 1961, the Russian influence declined, and Chinese influence expanded to take its place. This influence was manifested in exhibitions of Chinese paintings and sculptures, the staging of Chinese plays, concerts featuring Chinese revolutionary song cycles, translations of Chinese works of literature, and student and sports exchanges.[4]

The new governing elite was young and highly inexperienced in the governing of the country. It blindly copied the Yugoslavs in their domestic and foreign policies and between 1944 and 1948 Albania had for all practical purposes become a Yugoslav colony. But from the inception the ACP, which in 1948 changed its name to the Albanian Party of Labor (APL), was characterized by factional struggles. Hoxha, who was a compromise choice for party leader during the war, was challenged from members of the top leadership who questioned his leadership and feared his dictatorial tendencies. A series of purges in the top leadership during and immediately after the war led to a high turnover in the leading organs of the party. During 1947–1948, Hoxha appeared to be losing the struggle for power, as the Yugoslavs threw their weight behind the party organizational secretary and secret police chief, Koçi Xoxe. The pro-Yugoslav faction became the dominant faction and Albania was about to be swallowed by Yugoslavia when Tito broke with Stalin. Dissatisfaction with Tiranë's alliance with Belgrade had become widespread, which was not surprising given the long enmity between Albanians and Serbs and the fact that at the end of the war Kosova again became part of Yugoslavia. The Yugoslav-Soviet break in 1948 provided the Albanian governing elite the opportunity to break with Belgrade and ally itself with the Soviets. Hoxha moved swiftly to consolidate his power and emerged as the undisputed personality in Albanian politics.

In the wake of the break with Yugoslavia, Albania was fully integrated into the Soviet bloc, becoming a member of the Council of Mutual Economic Assistance and the Warsaw Treaty Organization, becoming the beneficiary of substantial foreign economic assistance. The Albanian governing elite was able to consolidate its power and to embark upon an ambitious industrialization program, adopting the Soviet system of centralized economic planning and abolishing all forms of market mechanism. In 1951 the government drafted the first in a series of five-year plans for the country's economic development. In line with the regime's objective of transforming Albania from a predominantly agricultural country to an industrial-agricultural state, the five-year plans emphasized the rapid development of heavy industry and the mineral sector, collectivization of agriculture, and the expansion of social service.

During the late 1940s and the early 1950s, Albania was at the center of the Soviet Union's Balkan policy, but Soviet interest in Albania declined as Moscow moved to normalize ties with Belgrade after Stalin's death. The Yugoslav-Soviet rapprochement represented a serious threat to Hoxha's regime as it undermined his anti-Yugoslav stand. Hoxha's position was also undermined by the launching of a de-Stalinization campaign throughout the Soviet bloc, which led to the replacement of Stalinist leaders throughout Eastern Europe. In 1956, Hoxha faced the most serious challenge to his leadership since 1948, when senior members of the Politburo demanded a reassessment of the party's policy after the break with Yugoslavia. He was able to weather the crisis partly because his opponents were poorly organized and partly because Moscow had loosened its grip on its allies. Hoxha purged his opponents and took advantage of developments in Hungary and Poland in 1956 to reassert his Stalinist policies. While Stalin was denounced throughout the region, Albania avoided the de-Stalinization process.

By the late 1950s, Albania's ties with the Soviet Union deteriorated, as Tiranë challenged Moscow on a series of issues of a domestic and foreign policy character. In the meantime, Albania moved closer to China, which also had begun to challenge Nikita Khrushchev's leadership of the communist bloc. Hoxha made what was no doubt the most significant decision of his political career in 1960 when he openly challenged Khrushchev, thus precipitating a break with the Soviet Union. Moscow canceled all grants and credits, cut off all trade, expelled Albanians studying in the Soviet Union, withdrew its many advisers, and excluded Albania from the COMECON trading bloc and the Warsaw Pact, with dire consequences for the country.

While Soviet leaders and some observers in the West predicted that Albania would follow Yugoslavia's example in 1948 and move toward a rapprochement with the West, Hoxha's regime embarked upon a policy of total reliance on distant communist China. With this action Hoxha had missed an excellent opportunity to open up his country. The West would probably have invested substantial resources to shore up an Albania independent of the Warsaw Pact. Albania instead entered a long period of political and cultural isolation from the outside world.

Albania's external interactions were almost totally restricted to dealings with China. While Albanian political and cultural elites were traditionally Western oriented, the alliance with China resulted in the severance of even the limited cultural ties that had existed with the West during the 1950s. China considered Albania an important ally—its only ally in the 1960s—and devoted considerable resources to ensure Albania's continued economic development. Thus, the Albanian government was able to pursue its ambitious policies of rapid industrialization, achieving particularly impressive results in extending its hydropower network and constructing oil refineries and ore-processing plants. By the end of 1967, agriculture had been totally collectivized.[5] Between 1962 and 1978, Beijing provided several billion dollars in economic and military aid to Albania. Clearly without such substantial foreign assistance from China, Albania would have been forced to reconsider its anti-Western and anti-Soviet foreign policy orientation. For its part, Albania proved to be an important political ally, serving as China's mouthpiece in the United Nations and other international fora. Relations between the two countries expanded rapidly after China's own break with the Soviet Union in 1963 and reached their climax during the period of the cultural revolution (1966–1969). While evidently there were some differences between the two countries' leaderships even in the 1960s, numerous Chinese delegations, including top leaders, visited Tiranë, expressing strong support for Hoxha's leadership at a time of international isolation. Albania became totally dependent on China for its economic survival. While the Chinese provided considerable help, Albania paid an extremely heavy price for its defiance of the Soviet Union. Distant and underdeveloped China was in no position to offer the assistance, both in terms of the amount and quality, that the Soviet bloc had been providing to Albania. The technology used in some of the projects built with Chinese assistance was from the 1930s and the 1940s. The result was that Albania's overall economic development stagnated, resulting in the further widening of the gap with its immediate neighbors.

The alliance with China affected Albania's domestic politics as well. The Chinese, in contrast to the Soviets in the 1950s, were never able to exert significant influence on Albania's domestic politics, though the upheaval in China during the cultural revolution did influence Hoxha's policies. In 1966, Hoxha launched his own version of a cultural revolution, with the objectives of extending the APL's control over all aspects of life and eliminating any center of potential power which could threaten the party's primacy. Under the guise of attacking deeply rooted traditions of social conservatism which ostensibly were incompatible with communist ideas, the regime initiated well-coordinated campaigns against backward customs and alien foreign influences. In addition, in 1967 all religious institutions were closed down and Albania became the world's first official atheist state. Many mosques and churches, some dating back centuries, were destroyed. Imams and priests were imprisoned or executed. The intelligentsia, long regarded by Hoxha as unreliable, came under severe attack. Prominent writers were chastised for ideological deformations. Intellectuals were ordered to go and live for extended periods of time in the countryside. Through harsh administrative measures the regime succeeded in suppressing all dissent in the ranks of the intelligentsia. For the next two decades, writers and intellectuals faithfully implemented the APL's policies of socialist realism, propagandizing the party's role among the masses. The intelligentsia never really recovered from the onslaught it experienced during the cultural revolution and subsequent purges.

An important aspect of the cultural revolution was the drive for the emancipation of women. From the very beginning of its accession to power, the communist regime had placed great emphasis on improving the status of women in the Albanian polity.[6] Women in Albania had held the status of second-class citizens and had been subjected to a variety of forms of social and economic discrimination. Hoxha's regime had eliminated discriminatory measures and basic transformation occurred in the position of women. The rights of working women were promoted through special legislation, which guaranteed them the right to a job, social security, health care, and education. Evidently distressed with the slow progress in addressing the unequal position of women in the Albanian society, in 1967 Hoxha launched a campaign for the full emancipation of women. The drive was aimed at rooting out the old prevailing customs and traditions. Denouncing the persistence of conservative and patriarchal mentality, Hoxha called for increased women's participation in all sectors of the society. A campaign was launched against arranged marriages, which apparently were particularly widespread in the northern part of the country, the dowry or bride price, polygamy, and other inequalities. The government's drive, which was motivated by ideological, political, and economic considerations, was successful. Women came to play an important role, especially in the economic system. An increasing number of women rose to high positions in the government and the party. But despite the significant gains achieved, there was a gap between the regime's official position of ensuring equality and the actual status of women. By 1980 nearly 46 percent of the workforce was comprised of women,[7] but their representation among the government and managerial elites remained low. Working women bore more than an equal burden of stress and complained that they were taking on more than an equal share of the work that had to be done at home. Moreover, despite the significant increase in women's educational qualifications, the regime was not successful in completely eliminating gender-related differences in employment and education. Most women held unskilled manual jobs. Although by the end of the 1970s women had joined the cabinet and even the party Politburo, their influence on the decision-making process was minimal.[8]

Albania's alliance with China was short-lived.[9] The first signs of problems in Tiranë-Beijing relations emerged in 1971, when China took steps to normalize relations with the United States. The Albanians publicly criticized the Chinese for departing from their previously stated policy of not having any dealings with the two superpowers. The Chinese responded by gradually reducing their economic and military assistance to Albania. With Mao's death in 1976 and the accession to power in Beijing of what Tiranë viewed as a "revisionist" leadership bent on pursuing capitalist policies, Albanian-Chinese relations reached a low ebb. Two years later, Albania broke with China.[10]

With the deepening crisis in relations with China and the obvious costs of isolation, members of the top elite reportedly questioned Hoxha's policies. Hoxha responded by initiating extensive changes in the party and government leadership, bringing in relatively young people who owed their career advancement personally to him. Victims of these purges included longtime members of the Politburo and the Central Committee, and senior government officials. In 1981, Prime Minister Mehmet Shehu, reputedly the second most powerful person in Albania, reportedly committed suicide. It appears that Shehu was pushed to suicide as a result of disagreements with Hoxha. Shehu's demise was followed by extensive purges.[11]

The impact of the widespread purges carried out during the 1970s and the early 1980s was devastating for the country as they resulted in the promotion of inexperienced people to leading positions. By the time Ramiz Alia became party leader following Hoxha's death in April 1985, Albania was faced with a serious economic crisis and a population that had become largely dispirited and apathetic.

Most experts on Albanian affairs agree that Hoxha's regime was one of the most repressive in the region. No East European regime copied more faithfully the Stalinist model than did Hoxha's regime. By the time of the demise of communist rule in the early 1990s, dozens of thousands of Albanians had reportedly vanished in prison and labor camps. An estimated half a million Albanians had been subjected to some sort of government repression. No aspect of life remained outside the control of the APL.[12] With its policies of extreme isolation after the break with the Soviet bloc in the early 1960s, the communist regime distorted the political and economic development of Albania, making it the most impoverished nation in Europe. While the trend in most other socialist countries was toward increased liberalization and a decrease in the party's tight grip over the society, in Albania the opposite occurred.

The main pillars of Hoxha's regime were the military and the secret police, *Sigurimi*. Through a reign of terror, the regime succeeded in eliminating all traces of open opposition to the ruling party. Those who opposed the regime or fell into disgrace faced severe punishment, while those who joined the ranks of the elite enjoyed widespread privileges. Albania reached the point whereby all social groups found themselves in the service of the regime. The intelligentsia, which bore the brunt of the regime's onslaught in the 1940s and the 1950s, had become totally subservient to the ruling party. Intellectuals were not only unable to show any signs of independent activity, but also served as the main advocates of the party ideology. And the many mass organizations became simply instruments of the APL.

Hoxha was concerned that his policies would not outlive him. In the late 1970s, he tried to institutionalize his unique policies with the adoption of a new constitution, which sanctioned the leading role of the APL in the society, prohibited the government from accepting foreign credits and loans, abolished private property, and reaffirmed the 1967 decision abolishing religion.

ALBANIA UNDER ALIA

Among the youngest members of the communist elite that emerged from the partisan war, Alia had skillfully survived Hoxha's violent purges. From the very beginning of his reign in 1985, Alia came under pressure from both the conservative and the more liberal elements of the party. The Old Guard suspected Alia, who had close links with senior officials purged in 1973 on charges of cultural liberalization. The more liberal wing of the party and, particularly, the intellectuals, who had begun to show signs of increased restiveness, had great hopes in Alia and saw him as Albania's Gorbachev.

Alia's public pronouncements reflected a keen understanding of the depth of the political, social, and economic crisis that had engulfed his country. But his responses fell far short of the decisive steps that were required to tackle the nation's problems. Alia lost many opportunities. His main objectives seem to have been to reinvigorate the society by initiating some changes in the highly centralized economic system, loosening the party's grip in the cultural sector, and ending the country's international isolation. He attempted to achieve these objectives while at the same time preserving the party's leading role. But the process of controlled reforms could not keep up with internal demands for changes, which by the end of the 1980s were fueled by a seriously deteriorating economic situation, the revolutions in other East European countries, and developments in Kosova, where ethnic Albanians under virtual Serbian military occupation were able to establish several anti-communist political parties.

The Albanian regime's initial response to the 1989 revolutions in Eastern Europe was to deny that similar events could occur in Albania, which had pursued a different path after the break with the Soviet bloc in the early 1960s. However, events in Eastern Europe, particularly the violent overthrow of Romania's Nicolae Ceauşescu, sent shock waves throughout the Albanian ruling elite. Even before that event took place, in May 1989 some intellectuals called on the state to display tolerance for public criticism of its policies. A few months later a publication by the state publishing house in Tiranë of Neshat Tozaj's searing novel *Knives* took the *Sigurimi* (the state security police) to task for invasiveness and brutality.[13] These straws in the wind provided a clear indication that Albania was not immune to the winds of change sweeping Eastern

Europe and that there might be greater similarities with Ceauşescu's dictatorship in Romania than might at first meet the eye. In order to downplay the striking similarities between Europe's two most dictatorial regimes, the Albanian leadership was among the first to recognize the post-Ceauşescu leadership and to denounce the late Romanian dictator. It was only after Ceauşescu's fall from power in late December of 1989, however, that Alia accelerated the pace of economic reforms, decentralizing the planning system and providing material incentives aimed at improving labor productivity. He also took steps to improve the regime's human rights record and to expand relations with the outside world. While seeking to assuage the concerns of domestic intellectuals and foreign observers of Albania's human rights record, Alia left no doubt regarding his determination to preserve the Communist Party's monopoly of power and excluded the possibility of sanctioning the creation of opposition political parties.

While dissatisfaction with the regime's policies was evidently widespread, no open organized opposition had emerged. Despite a mild relaxation in domestic affairs after Hoxha's death, the government continued to pursue an uncompromising policy against its opponents and critics. As late as the beginning of 1990, border guards were shooting and killing Albanians attempting to flee the country. The secret police remained as powerful as ever. In contrast to the other East European countries where independent centers of power, such as the Church, had begun to operate, none existed in Albania. But despite the absence of an organized opposition, the APL's supremacy was increasingly being challenged. In the beginning of 1990, the regime witnessed the first labor unrest and anti-communist demonstrations. Moreover, disgruntled party members pushed for radical reforms. Many intellectuals, who had faithfully served the party, now concluded that in order to survive, the system had to undergo radical change. Taking advantage of Alia's pro-reform rhetoric, prominent intellectuals advocated greater openness and emerged as the strongest proponents of what the Albanian leader characterized in spring 1990 as a democratization process. The press began to take a more independent stance. While the leadership expressed concern regarding the growing dissipation of APL's ideological parity, it failed to take drastic measures to increase state and party control over the media.

The communist regime suffered its greatest blow to date when in July 1990 five thousand Albanians stormed foreign missions in Tiranë. Although Alia claimed the refugees were in league with foreign forces trying to crush socialism in Albania, he was forced by unprecedented international pressure to allow them to emigrate. But even after this momentous event, Albania did not substantially modify its official line. In August 1990, Alia convened a meeting with the country's most prominent intellectuals. Ostensibly the aim of the meeting was for Alia to acquaint himself with the views of the intellectuals; however, he set the tone of the meeting by ruling out in his opening remarks the idea of a multi-party system. He signaled concern over shrinking support and criticized the media and the intelligentsia for being insufficiently supportive of the regime. Not only did Alia offer no hint that the APL leadership was willing to moderate its stance on political reform, but he reminded the intellectuals of their responsibility to support the APL in the face of growing Western media attacks.

The meeting was held in a tense atmosphere and amid rumors that the secret police had targeted for arrest the nation's most prominent intellectuals. Thus the intellectuals failed to challenge Alia with a common stand. Nevertheless, there were individual confrontations with Alia. Berisha, a prominent cardiologist who six months later would organize Albania's first opposition party, openly confronted Alia with the demand for political pluralism. However, Berisha was not supported by other participants.[14]

Concerned about the widespread popular disenchantment with the regime, Alia in the summer and fall of 1990 announced several measures aimed at appeasing the most dissatisfied sectors of the society. While rejecting calls for the establishment of a full-fledged multiparty system, Alia vowed to permit the free expression of ideas. The mass organizations, which until then had served merely as transmission belts for the ruling party, were declared independent. He also announced a program of economic reforms, termed the "New Economic Mechanism" and modeled after the Hungarian reforms of the 1960s and the 1970s. The parliament approved a new election law, which recognized the mass organizations' right to field their own candidates. For the first time since the communist takeover, independent candidates could run for office with the endorsement of 300 registered voters. The APL also gave up its constitutionally guaranteed monopoly of power, but stopped short of permitting the creation of opposition parties.

With these measures Alia hoped to enlist domestic and international support. However, Albania's failure to be accepted as a full member of the CSCE, at the Paris summit meeting in November 1990, was a serious blow to Alia. A month later, at the Balkan foreign ministers' conference in Tiranë, the first such high-level meeting in Albania since the end of the Second World War, the Albanian government was chastised for its violation of human rights. The implication of these two events was that Albania needed to carry out fundamental reforms in order to be accepted as a full-fledged member of the international community. The West, which throughout the 1960s and the 1970s had pursued a policy of benign neglect toward Albania, premised the strengthening of ties on a major change in Tiranë's human rights policy.

THE END OF COMMUNIST RULE

As late as the thirteenth Central Committee plenum in November 1990, Alia was clearly signaling his determination to combat political liberalization. He continued to gloss over contentious issues and avoided confrontations that could severely strain party unity. He resisted efforts to push reform beyond the boundaries of traditional APL ideological assumptions. His reluctance to carry out radical reforms that might have addressed the country's serious economic and social problems suggested that he still believed the regime could ride out the crisis. Alia's tinkering with cosmetic changes had no discernible effect, and it became increasingly clear that the regime would not be able to stem the growth of dissent. Intellectuals, students, and urban workers were becoming increasingly disenchanted with Alia, apparently believing that the measures he had introduced were aimed at placating international criticism of the regime and not at democratizing the country's political and economic system. While no organized opposition had emerged and the appearance of an alternative reform program seemed a distant possibility, the APL's failure to push for more drastic reform measures in the face of a rapidly deteriorating economic situation inspired a coalescence of opposition, centered around the country's most prominent intellectuals.

The outbreak of student demonstrations at Tiranë University on 8 December 1990 created the most severe crisis since the Alia regime had come to power. Overnight, prominent intellectuals, who had been seen as supporters of Alia's gradual reforms, emerged as leaders of a democratic opposition. After Alia had insisted for months that the creation of other parties would not be permitted, a special meeting of the APL Central Committee sanctioned political pluralism. Student demonstrators supported by a handful of intellectuals, led by Berisha, formed the Democratic Party. Although party organizers did not have adequate time to prepare for the creation of the party, its hastily prepared platform reflected the aspirations of the majority of Albania's population for democracy. It called for the establishment of a multiparty system, full respect of human rights, and the creation of a market economy. Initially, the Democratic Party was careful not to advocate a rapid de-communization of the country for fear of a communist backlash and went so far as to praise Alia, who had come under heavy criticism from hard-liners who saw their power slip away rapidly.

While the APL and the Democratic Party remained the main players in Albania's new political environment, other parties were also formed, including the Republican, Social Democratic, Agrarian, Ecological, and National Unity parties. However, the decree which had sanctioned political pluralism specifically prohibited the revival of nationalist parties of the World War II period whose remnants had survived in exile, such as the National Front and Legality. These parties could not be revived until a new law was adopted in the summer of 1991.

The communists responded to the new situation by taking measures to distance themselves from their Stalinist past. Several Old Guard members of the top party leadership as well as Hoxha's widow, Nexhmije, were replaced. Stalin's name was removed from all institutions. While apparently many APL members were eager to denounce Hoxha and his policies, Alia stopped short of repudiating his former mentor, blaming instead the entire party leadership for past mistakes. The APL also announced a reformist program, which among other things called for the establishment of a free market economy and a pluralist democracy. But Alia's failure to make a clean break with the past caused a massive defection from the APL.

The transition to a post-communist government was prolonged and painful. Before the December demonstrations, parliamentary elections had been scheduled for February 1991. After the Democratic Party and other opposition parties threatened to boycott the election, complaining that they did not have enough time to prepare for them, and following a strike by the miners at Valias, near Tiranë, Alia agreed to postpone the election.

The 31 March elections, the first multiparty elections since the 1920s, were conducted in a tense political atmosphere. The APL had grudgingly agreed to permit the establishment of other parties but made every attempt to ensure its victory in the elections. In addition to administrative impediments to free and fair elections, conservative communist forces attempted to disrupt opposition rallies by attacking and intimidating opposition followers. The situation reached a critical point in late February 1991 with the nationwide communist backlash following the unveiling of Hoxha's monument in Tiranë. There were violent confrontations between Democratic Party and APL supporters and Albania seemed to be on the brink of a civil war. As a result of heightened political tensions during the first three months of 1991, thousands of Albanians fled the country, the majority of them going to Greece and Italy. Less than a month before the elections, Prime Minister Adil Çarçani, a member of the APL's Politburo since 1956, resigned. A new government was formed, led by Fatos Nano, a young economist and a rising star in the communist hierarchy.

In its electoral platform, the Democratic Party called for a radical transformation of the political, economic, and social system. It called for the creation of a state based on rule of law and the full protection of human rights. Moreover, the Democratic Party demanded the depoliticization of the state apparatus, including the secret police and the military. In what at the time appeared as a radical stand, the Democratic Party called for full privatization of agriculture and the return of land to farmers, elimination of state subsidies, and an end to state monopoly over foreign trade.[15]

Not surprisingly, the APL won a landslide victory, capturing 169 seats in the 250-seat People's Assembly. Although opposition candidates won in most urban areas, the Democratic Party won only seventy-five seats. The remainder went to Omonia (five seats), an organization representing ethnic Greeks, and the communist-controlled National Veterans' Organization (one seat). Significantly, several prominent communist candidates, including Alia, Foreign Minister Muhamet Kapllani, and the party secretary representing the liberal wing of the APL, Spiro Dede, were defeated. While the opposition failed to deny the communists the two-thirds of the seats in the parliament necessary to pass major legislation, the Democratic Party carried about 40 percent of the popular vote. This represented a significant victory for an opposition which was less than four months old, had limited resources, could not get its message to the countryside, and had been denied equal access to the state-controlled radio and television.[16]

Following the elections, developments in Albania unfolded very rapidly. The democrats boycotted the opening session of the new parliament to protest the killing of four Democratic Party activists in postelection violence in Shkodër. Democratic Party deputies, supported by liberal communists, succeeded in rejecting the draft-constitution submitted by Alia, which had retained many of the features of Hoxha's 1976 Constitution. Instead, the parliament approved a Law on Constitutional Provisions, pending the promulgation of a new constitution. The communist-dominated People's Assembly elected Alia as president for a five-year term, but with limited powers. Nano created the new government and announced a program of economic reforms.

Although the communists controlled the parliament, Nano's government proved ineffective as the economy continued to deteriorate and labor unrest spread. In early June 1991, Nano was forced to resign, opening the way for the creation of a coalition government led by Ylli Bufi, a relatively unknown communist apparatchik. The new government was dominated by non-communists, with the Democratic Party holding seven ministerial posts, including the economics, finance, and defense ministries. The minister of economics, Gramoz Pashko, also served as deputy prime minister. The opposition, which had rejected Nano's call for a coalition government two months earlier, justified its participation in the Bufi government by arguing that the country was on the verge of descending into total anarchy.

Meanwhile, in the most significant attempt to date to recoup their forces, the communists convened the party's tenth congress in mid-June. The Old Guard was ousted and the party was renamed the Socialist

Party. Nano was elected party chairman and the new leadership moved to distance the Socialist Party from both Hoxha and Alia.[17]

The coalition government, composed of inexperienced officials, enjoyed little authority and proved as ineffective as the Nano government, leading Albania into a deeper crisis. Bufi was unable to initiate any meaningful reforms or arrest the continued economic decline and the country literally came to a standstill. Mounting political tensions and economic difficulties caused another massive exodus, with more than 20,000 Albanians fleeing to Italy. In many parts of the country, the government did not function and the people took matters into their own hands. This was accompanied by massive destruction of state property. By the beginning of autumn, Albania had become totally dependent on foreign humanitarian assistance, primarily from Italy, the European Community, and the United States, to feed its population.

The communists took advantage of the period of the coalition government to block the implementation of meaningful economic and political reforms and to blame democracy for the deepening crisis. Bufi's government collapsed in December 1991, when Berisha withdrew his ministers after the communists refused to meet a series of demands. Minister of Food Vilson Ahmeti was asked to form a caretaker government. The parliament passed a new election law, which reduced the number of seats in the People's Assembly from 250 to 140, and elections were set for 22 March 1992. The collapse of the coalition government was followed by increased political tensions and a polarization of the Albanian society. Communist attempts to blame Berisha for deepening the nation's crisis backfired as there was an unprecedented outpouring of popular support for the leader of the Democratic Party and his calls for a rapid de-communization of Albania.

The 1992 national elections were far more orderly than those of the previous year and probably the only truly free elections in Albania's history. The three main opposition parties (the Democratic, Social-Democratic, and Republican parties), working closely together, were able to conduct a nationwide campaign and enjoyed greater access to the state-controlled media. The Democratic Party's platform called for the implementation of radical political and economic reforms. Leaving nothing to chance, Berisha personally campaigned all over the country. In his public pronouncements he portrayed his party as the only political force that could get the country out of its current predicament and attempted to allay fears that a Democratic Party victory would result in a widespread anti-communist backlash. The opposition was successful in convincing the electorate that international support for Albania was conditioned on a democratic victory at the polls. Prominent ethnic Albanian politicians from Kosova interjected themselves into Albania's election campaign by openly supporting Berisha and his Democratic Party. Under increased domestic and international pressure, the communists appeared resigned to a defeat and were unable to conduct an impressive campaign.

The results of the 22 March 1992 election surpassed the opposition's most optimistic predictions, as the Socialist Party suffered a humiliating defeat, winning only thirty-two seats in the 140-seat parliament. The Democratic Party captured ninety-two seats, the Social Democratic Party seven, the Union for Human Rights (representing ethnic Greeks) two, and the Republican Party one seat. Berisha, declaring that the communist nightmare was over, urged the people to unite around the Democratic Party and build a new Albania. He tried to reassure the communists that there would be no revenge, saying that "the Albanians as a whole are at the same time the accomplices and fellow victims of the regime under which we lived. Our common responsibility and our common suffering must unite us with the ideals of democracy for the construction of a new Albania."[18]

Immediately after the elections, Alia resigned, paving the way for Berisha's election to a five-year term. Enjoying the two-thirds of parliamentary votes necessary for approval of major legislation, the Democratic Party pushed for the revision of the Law on Constitutional Provisions, giving the president enhanced powers to tackle the country's grave crisis. A former APL member, Berisha was born in August 1944 in the northeastern district of Tropojë. A graduate of the Tiranë University Medical Faculty, he was sent to Paris for advanced training. Berisha had caught the public's attention in May 1990, when in an interview with the literary newspaper *Drita* he bitterly attacked the communist isolation of Albania.[19] Following his clash with Alia in August 1990, Berisha showed unusual courage by publishing an article rejecting the official view that pluralism would divide the nation and denouncing what he termed "antidemocratic and conservative elements" that were blocking Albania's democratization.[20] By the time of the outbreak of student demonstrations in December 1990, Berisha had become one of the country's most outspoken intellectuals. He was among the very few who had immediately sided with student demonstrators and played a crucial role in formulating their political demands. A key founding member of the Democratic Party, Berisha was the natural choice for party chairman. A shrewd politician, he was able to unite people with diverse views within the Democratic Party, which in reality was an umbrella organization including various individuals. While his popularity seemed to have declined in the wake of the Democratic Party's decision to enter into a coalition with the communists, he was reelected party chairman at the first convention of the Democratic Party, winning 449 of the 547 votes.[21]

In his inaugural address, the new president acknowledged that his communist-ravaged country resembled a "wasteland," but expressed optimism about the future.[22] Berisha asked Aleksandër Meksi, a prominent archaeologist and a member of the top party leadership, to form the first post-communist government. Reflecting the Democratic Party's immediate priorities of restoring law and order and rapidly reviving the agricultural sector, the minister of public order, Bashkim Kopliku, and the minister of agriculture and food, Rexhep Uka, were also named deputy premiers. Genc Ruli, who had served as finance minister in the coalition government, was put in charge of the new ministry of finances and economy.

POST-COMMUNIST ALBANIA

Of all the former communist countries in Eastern Europe, Albania was least prepared for the painful transition from communist dictatorship to a genuine pluralistic democracy and a market economy. The new government inherited a country in the midst of a serious moral and spiritual crisis, with large segments of the population having lost hope in their country's future and desperately looking for ways to flee abroad. Moreover, the Albanian society had been dangerously polarized by the communist regime's uninterrupted class struggle. The reintegration of a large number of people persecuted and displaced by the communists represented a serious social problem.

By the time the Democratic Party took power, Albania had become totally dependent on foreign assistance to feed its three million people. Two years of widespread political unrest, following decades of communist mismanagement and centralized planning, had led to widespread lawlessness and a virtual collapse of the Albanian economy. Between 1990 and 1992, industrial and agricultural production had declined by as much as 60 percent and 30 percent, respectively. Already Europe's most impoverished country, Albania saw its Gross Domestic Product per capita fall in 1992 to below $400, ranking Albania with the world's poorest countries. Albania had not only completely exhausted its foreign reserves but had accumulated a hard-currency debt of more than half a billion dollars. Inflation had topped 300 percent annually, while unemployment reached alarming proportions as virtually all factories, enterprises, and cooperatives had shut down. In addition to the alarming economic situation, the new government was faced with a serious external threat, with an increasing likelihood of the extension of the Yugoslav conflict to Kosova. Implementing radical reforms aimed at establishing a pluralistic democracy and a market economy would be difficult under the best of circumstances, but doing so in a country as devastated economically and socially as Albania seemed almost impossible.

Nevertheless, having won a clear popular mandate for reform, the Democratic Party moved swiftly to fill the political vacuum that had been created during the last year and a half of turmoil. The immediate priorities of the new government were to arrest the nation's economic decline, restore law and order, begin the difficult task of institution building, and reintegrate the country into the international community after decades of communist isolation. Dispelling hopes for a quick fix,[23] President Berisha skillfully exploited his popularity and the Democratic Party's impressive election victory by building a broad political consensus to help implement economic transformation and recovery programs. He embarked upon an ambitious policy of opening up Albania and developing close ties with the West, particularly the United States. Berisha focused on persuading Western democracies that Albania be treated as a special case because of the very repressive nature of its past communist rule and long isolation from the outside world. Indeed, the international response to the Democratic Party's victory was very positive and Albania became the largest recipient of Western aid on a per capita basis in Eastern Europe. By the end of 1995 Albania had received more than a billion dollars in foreign aid.

Having secured substantial foreign assistance, the government launched a mid-term economic plan, ending subsidies for agricultural and industrial goods and liberalized prices, except for most basic items such as bread and milk. Comprehensive steps were taken to combat inflation and the Albanian currency, *lek,* was made fully convertible. In a bold move only months after assuming power, Berisha repealed a communist decree which provided that workers of enterprises closed for lack of raw materials receive 80 percent of their wages. Albania carried out an ambitious mass privatization program. By 1996, agriculture, transportation, retail trade, and housing had been almost totally privatized. The restructuring and privatization of large state-owned enterprises had also begun and the government was actively seeking foreign partners for the privatization of sectors of strategic importance, including mines, electric power, and telecommunications. Within four years, Albania moved from the ruins of a totally state-owned economy to a market economy, with the private sector accounting for more than 65 percent of the GDP and about 70 percent of the national wealth in private hands.

The implementation of painful austerity measures and determination to stick to tough International Monetary Fund rules, however, caused considerable social dislocations and involved serious political risks for Berisha and his party. The Socialist Party sought to capitalize on discontent caused by austerity measures by condemning the reforms for bringing unacceptable suffering on the public, increasing economic inequality, concentrating wealth in a few hands, and creating a vast mass of poor people. But the president, apparently convinced that Albania could not afford halfway measures, left no doubt that his government was prepared "to sacrifice popularity by pressing ahead with reforms."[24]

Despite serious difficulties, the results of the adjustment program were quick and impressive. Albania achieved one of the highest growth rates in Eastern Europe, exceeding targets set by the IMF.[25] By the end of 1993, consumption returned to and surpassed the pre-1990 level. The precipitous fall in production was arrested, and the GDP grew by 11 percent. The economy showed a strong performance in 1994 and 1995, registering GDP growth rates of 7.4 percent and 13 percent, respectively. In 1996, the economy was expected to grow by about 10 percent. Significant progress was also made in establishing the legal and regulatory framework for a market economy. The parliament passed a series of laws, including bankruptcy and company laws, and a comprehensive banking law which established a two-tier banking system. In an attempt to increase exports and attract foreign capital, export licensing and controls were eliminated. The new Foreign Investments Law, approved in 1993, created a legal framework for foreign investments and provided for compensation for expropriation.

The post-communist government viewed as an urgent policy issue the establishment of the rule of law and the reforming of the judicial system, moribund for decades and abused by those in power to perpetuate their rule while dispensing justice to almost no one. The overwhelming majority of the bench was purged. As Albania lacked qualified lawyers, judges, and prosecutors with untainted records, communist-era holdovers were in many cases replaced by young, inexperienced judges. Arguing that increased corruption, lawlessness, gangsterism, and failure to punish those committing crimes could derail the country's democratic transition, the authorities gave the police emergency powers in a sweeping anticrime crackdown. Under the leadership of Minister of Internal Affairs Kopliku, within a relatively short period of time law and order were restored.[26]

The Democratic Party, having campaigned on the promise of establishing a genuine democracy based on the principle of full separation of powers, an independent judiciary, and full respect for human rights, was expected to give a high priority to the adoption of a new constitution. Once in power, however, the Democrats were faced with more urgent tasks and failed to take advantage of the window of opportunity to secure a speedy approval of the constitution. In retrospect, the procrastination in drafting a new constitution was a serious political mistake. While a special commission chaired by Prime Minister Aleksandër Meksi was given the task of drafting a new constitution, parliament opted to amend and supplement the 1991 Law on the Main Constitutional Provisions.[27] On the eve of Berisha's election as president in April 1992, the Democrats took advantage of the momentum of their electoral victory to push through parliament amendments, enhancing the president's powers. In a reversal of the position they held a year earlier when Alia was elected president, they argued that the new president needed expanded powers to deal with the serious problems confronting the nation and to oversee the political, social, and economic reforms that the Democratic Party had pledged in its electoral platform.[28] The 1991 provisional constitution contained critical deficiencies, the most important of which was the absence of separate chapters on human rights and the judiciary. These deficiencies were corrected with the addition in April 1992 of a Chapter on the Organization of the Judiciary and the Constitutional Court, providing for judicial independence,[29] and in March 1993 with the Charter on Fundamental Human Rights and Freedoms, which contained guarantees of the freedom of speech, religion, conscience, press, assembly, and association as well as assurances on due process of law.[30] These changes set Albania apart from many other East European countries which continued to operate based on their previous communist-era constitutions, and presaged an historic era for Albania as its new leadership faced the task of developing a legal framework for a democratic state, assuring civil liberties and separation of powers.

While lack of consensus between the country's main political forces prevented the adoption of a new constitution, the authorities moved swiftly to dismantle the underpinnings of the communist system. In one of its first actions, parliament approved the removal of communist symbols from the coat of arms and the flag.[31] In May 1992, parliament amended the Law on Labor Relations, allowing the authorities to transfer or dismiss employees of state-owned enterprises and institutions when deemed necessary to further the reform process. Purges were carried out in all the ministries. The security organs, including the once omnipotent secret police, *Sigurimi,* renamed in 1991 the National Intelligence Service (SHIK), were reorganized and purged of pro-communist sympathizers. The foreign ministry bureaucracy, which reportedly had been staffed predominantly by the secret police, also underwent a sweeping purge. More than 50 percent of its personnel were dismissed and all ambassadors replaced. Under Defense Minister Safet Zhulali, the armed forces also underwent radical changes. Despite considerable opposition within the senior ranks of the military, Zhulali carried out a total reorganization of the military, dismissing or sending into early retirement a large number of military cadres. And for the first time in Albania's history, a parliamentary commission was established to oversee the armed forces.

One of the most hotly debated issues was the prosecution of the top leaders of the old regime. Albanians struggled with the legal and moral questions in contemplating who was culpable for communist transgressions. After prolonged internal deliberations, during 1993 and 1994 Nexhmije Hoxha, Alia, and nine former APL Politburo members and senior government officials were tried on charges of corruption and abuse of power. The proceedings were widely criticized as a mockery of justice.[32] Former political prisoners had urged that Alia and his associates be tried on charges of "genocide."[33] But unwilling to hold political trials at this stage, the government ended up charging the former communist officials with what in the opinion of many Albanians were petty economic crimes. Ironically, the proceedings were handled so clumsily that the communists won the propaganda war, as there was a widespread impression of irregularities and substantial legal errors. Virtually all of the Old Guard received only light sentences, which were further reduced on appeal and by several amnesties, or were excused from serving them because of ill health. Nexhmije Hoxha received the longest sentence— eleven years. With the exception of Nexhmije Hoxha, all benefited from the new Penal Code, which went into effect in June 1995, and were released. Alia and his former associates made a concerted effort to capture the public eye, frequently granting interviews and publishing articles belittling human rights transgressions under the old regime and heaping scorn on the Democratic government.

Many Albanians, outraged by the release of former senior communist leaders, criticized the government for not having done enough to make up for decades of dictatorship. They saw this as an inexplicable leniency and a slap in the face of all former political prisoners and urged that the upper echelon from the *nomenklatura* not be premitted to elude prosecution for human rights violations. In late 1995 and early 1996, dozens of former senior communist officials, including Alia and former Politburo members, were arrested. They were charged with crimes against humanity under the new Penal Code, which allowed legal proceedings against crimes committed by the old regime. In May 1996, former Deputy Minister of Internal Affairs and chief of *Sigurimi* Zuliftar Ramizi, the former Chairman of the Supreme Court Aranit Çela, and the former Prosecutor General Rrapi Mino were sentenced to death. Other former officials received long prison sentences.

Albania witnessed significant institutional and legislative transformations. While lack of a political consensus prevented the adoption of a new constitution and voters rejected a draft submitted by the Democratic Party in November 1994, the 1991 Law on Main Constitutional Provisions was completely revamped and a new system was created, with checks and balances, safeguards for fundamental rights and freedoms, and judicial review. The basic constitutional law provided for "the separation of legislative, executive, and judicial powers," and safeguards on presidential powers. Following the example of constitutional arrangements of the newly emerging democracies in the region, the basic law stated that "political pluralism is one of the basic conditions of democracy in the Albanian state." It provided assurances for the protection of the new pluralist character of the state by stipulating a clear separation of political parties from state power and prohibiting party activities in the defense, internal affairs, and foreign affairs ministries, diplomatic representations abroad, attorneys and investigation offices, and in courts. During 1992–1996 there was a remarkable degree of agreement between the presidency, the government, and the legislature on policy outputs and responses to sustain the reform impulse. Political struggles between the executive and the legislature in Albania were less pronounced and acrimonious than in most other East European countries. But this was due more to the Democratic Party's ability to preserve its comfortable majority in parliament than to the practice of accommodation and compromise between the ruling party and the opposition. The fragmentation of the democratic parliamentary group was surprisingly not as deep as many had predicted. The Democratic Party experienced only two splits, resulting in the defection of eight of the original ninety-two deputies. In 1992, Pashko and several other former prominent members of the Democratic Party, who had been expelled from the party, formed the Democratic Alliance. In 1994, right wing deputies Petrit Kalakula and Abdi Baleta withdrew from the Democratic Party parliamentary group, forming their own party.

Berisha's strong leadership qualities and the pivotal role that he played in the downfall of communism helped make him the unquestionable linchpin of Albanian politics. He proved to be an effective president, shaping the nation's agenda during a period of momentous political, economic, and social changes. He emerged as the dominant figure in the policy-making arena and the moving force behind the government's efforts at reform. However, Berisha's dominant role in Albanian politics became the source of considerable debate. His critics accused the president of centralizing the decision-making process, emasculating the government, and marginalizing the opposition in parliment. While these allegations were politically motivated, Berisha's domination of the executive branch at times complicated the decision-making process, undermining good and effective administration and causing unnecessary delays in making decisions on major issues.

The Democratic government displayed both extraordinary persistence in the face of daunting challenges and a willingness to make unpopular and politically risky decisions to further the country's political and economic revival. But the extent to which the new governing elite, with no tradition of democratic problem solving and limited experience in rights and responsibilities, was able to provide transparent and accountable governance remained debatable. A salient feature of decision-makers was lack of responsiveness to citizens' needs, requirements, and wishes, and reliance on commands. The government often failed to draw parliament, the opposition, and the Albanian people into a full and frank discussion and debate of the pros and cons of major decisions before announcing them. The system remained largely closed. Most government officials were reluctant to provide information even to the pro-government media.

Parliament came to play a significant role. While at times it was obstructionist, resembling more a contentious debating club than a lawmaking body, parliament became the most important forum for important deliberations about the country's politics. During 1992–1996, substantial legislation was enacted into law. However, the frantic pace of approval often sacrificed the careful deliberation that many complex issues demanded.

A key element in Albania's efforts to consolidate a democratic system was the establishment of an independent judiciary. Changes were introduced in legal education aimed at imbuing students with a keen sense of ethics, justice, and a lawyer's obligation to society. Law schools in Tiranë and Shkodër began training in new fields such as contract law, commercial law, human rights, property law, ownership rights, etc. But overcoming the weight of half a century of communist rule which had displayed no regard for due process and had considered the judiciary merely as the voice of the ruling party proved to be a daunting task. In practice the judiciary remained weak and subject to considerable executive pressure. While the judiciary came to play a major role in scrutinizing the police and the prosecution and in ensuring due process, Albania had a long way to go to achieve the true rule of law. In a country with an atrocious human rights record and that had seen constitutions repeatedly violated by former communist leaders, cynicism ran deep about the rule of law. Indeed, the implementation of the Charter on Fundamental Human Rights and Freedoms was at times problematic. While there was widespread recognition that Albania had made "tremendous strides in the respect shown for human rights and fundamental freedoms,"[34] there were still significant abuses of human rights, including instances of police abuse, procedural irregularities resulting in denial of fair trial, mistreatment of defendants, and occasional restrictions of the freedom of speech and press.[35] Officials attempted to minimize the significance of such reports by pegging the problems on the misdeeds of a few policemen, focusing attention on the difficulties facing the police, and underscoring the need for better education of police recruits.

While the institutional features of a democratic government were largely in place, civil society as a political force had yet to emerge. With the exception of trade unions, few nongovernmental associations were strong enough to exert effective pressures on state institutions. Lack of sustained political participation on the part of a growing number of Albanians could hamper the development of democracy. The absence of a well-developed civil society sharply limited citizens' ability to influence events.

The drafting of a new constitution stirred extensive political controversy. The country's major political forces failed to put aside their narrow political considerations and to engage in serious bargaining and compromise. Disagreements on the institutional alternatives and the specific powers of each branch of government led to a deadlock. The Socialists, joined by the Social Democratic Party and the Democratic Alliance, advocated reducing the president's powers, essentially confining the head of state to a merely ceremonial role. Berisha's supporters argued that Albania needed strong executive leadership that could make timely decisions. Opposition criticism notwithstanding, Berisha's supporters did not advocate a powerful executive presidency modeled on the French- or American-type presidency, but rather a system that would permit a stable combination of presidential and parliamentary government. Berisha himself came out on the side of a parliamentary system, but he was not willing to go along with the Socialist Party's idea of a figurehead president.

Politics played a major role in blocking agreement on a new constitution. Having failed in its efforts to use popular dissatisfaction with the implementation of radical economic reforms to turn the tide against the government, the Socialists came to view the adoption of a new constitution as an instrument to provoke a parliamentary crisis and thereby force new elections. They actively sought to forge an alliance with other parliamentary parties to block the adoption of the constitution, warning of Berisha's looming dictatorship. The Social Democratic Party, the third-largest party in parliament, had become increasingly despondent over what it considered its meager role in the government coalition. It sought to use the constitution issue to extract concessions from the Democratic Party for greater participation in the cabinet—a demand the Democrats refused. Six former Democratic Party deputies, who had formed the Democratic Alliance, sided with the Socialists.

Under increased domestic as well as foreign pressure, especially from the European Council, which had conditioned Albania's membership on the adoption of a new constitution, Berisha tried to break the constitutional deadlock. Although the Law on Main Constitutional Provisions clearly empowered parliament to adopt and amend the country's constitution, Berisha decided to circumvent the legislature and submit the draft constitution to a national referendum. The referendum, held on 6 November 1994, failed to break the constitutional deadlock, when Albanian voters rejected Berisha's draft. With a high turnout of 84.43 percent, 53.9 percent voted against and 41.7 percent in favor.[36]

The referendum altered Albania's political landscape, ushered in a period of greater partisan competition, and set the stage for months of political turmoil. Although in the final analysis the referendum was a sign of a maturing of the voters, long used to automatically approving their government's policies, the great experiment of Albania's democracy faced its deepest crisis. For the first time after the 1992 elections, the fragile gains of Albanian economic and political reforms seemed at risk. The most spectacular fallout of the referendum was the withdrawal of the Social Democratic and Republican parties from the ruling coalition, and the split between Berisha and his closest confidant, Eduard Selami, who in March 1995 was dismissed as party chairman.

The constitutional referendum had been seen as an indication of the public mood ahead of the 1996 parliamentary election. The Socialist Party was quick to characterize the results as a repudiation of the Democratic Party's policies and a clear signal of voters' inclinations a year before general elections. The Socialists felt emboldened by the referendum results, a development they interpreted as strengthening their position.

In an attempt to regain the political initiative, Berisha called for a determined struggle against corruption and the reinvigoration of the party. The Democratic Party's rank and file were subjected to a widespread and well-coordinated purge, ostensibly aimed at cleansing the party of corrupt officials. With national elections only a year away and a resurgent opposition helped by an anti-incumbent fever, Berisha saw his party faced with a race against time and a tough comeback effort. He argued that the Democratic Party had to regain political equilibrium and prove its ability and effectiveness or face the prospect of losing power in 1996. He began the difficult task of forging new alliances with various political groups and rebuilding bridges with former allies, particularly the right.

By mid-1995, the Democrats were on their way to recovery. The Socialists and other opposition forces were too disparate in outlook to unite behind a plausible alternative to capture the public imagination, sharing no basis to build an alliance other than their distaste for Berisha. While the broader public had showed lack of confidence in the government by rejecting the draft constitution, there was no evidence it was embracing the Socialist Party, the largest opposition force. Despite growing political problems, the government displayed undiminished enthusiasm to stay the course of rapid reforms. The benefits of privatization and other economic changes were gradually, but steadily, filtering through more and more people. A thriving new class of entrepreneurs, who saw their fate clearly linked with continued economic reforms, was rapidly emerging and staking its ground throughout the country. The government also continued to enjoy substantial international support and Albania was seen as a stabilizing factor in the region. And in a clear signal of the recognition of the progress it had made in its difficult transition, in June 1995 Albania was granted full membership in the Council of Europe.

THE 1996 ELECTION

The postreferendum political scene was characterized by increased polarization. Friction and intolerance increased significantly as the 1996 parliamentary elections approached and the government and opposition parties intensified their campaigns for the hearts and minds of the voters, resorting to militant rhetoric and political manipulation. The opposition accused the Democratic Party of using its majority in parliament to rush through controversial legislation before the end of its four-year mandate. The Socialist Party insisted that if it regained power, it would repeal a large portion of legislation enacted during the Democratic Party's government. This only served to intensify calls within the Democratic Party for the intensification of the de-communization campaign. In September 1995, the parliament enacted the "Law on Genocide and Crimes against Humanity Committed in Albania during Communist Rule for Political, Ideological, and Religious Motives," barring former communists and *Sigurimi* collaborators from seeking public office until 2002. Under the law, members of the former APL Politburo and Central Committee, ministers, deputies, district party secretaries, presidents of the Supreme Court and general prosecutors, and former *Sigurimi* agents and informers were prohibited from holding posts in parliament, the government, the judiciary, or the state-run media.[37] The law banned leading opposition politicians, including some leaders of the Socialist, Social Democratic, and Democratic Alliance, from participation in the forthcoming parliamentary election. Opposition parties denounced the law, arguing it was designed to rid the ruling party of opponents before the elections. International human rights organizations also criticized the law for banning people from holding public office based on their past association rather than on individual actions. On 30 November 1995, parliament passed the "Law on Verification of the Moral Character of Officials and Other Persons Connected with the Protection of the Democratic State," regulating the opening of *Sigurimi* files and setting up a screening state commission for those seeking public office.[38]

In January 1996, the Democratic Party–controlled parliament approved changes in the 1992 election law. The number of single member districts was increased from 100 to 115, while the number of proportional seats was decreased from 40 to 25. The small number of proportionally elected seats was designed to reduce overrepresentation among party list candidates. The reduction of proportional seats was viewed as consigning many smaller parties, competing for the same group of voters, to oblivion. The changes also discouraged smaller parties from participating in the election as a bloc. Each party in a potential alliance had to win 4 percent to be eligible for supplementary seats.

Despite the significant institutional and political changes, Albania had yet to see the emergence of a stable system of relatively disciplined and responsible parties. While political participation was concentrated almost exclusively within the realm of the parties, citizens' identification with parties remained relatively weak as these groups sought to develop their positions on the issues amid shifting political allegiances. Most Albanian parties had not developed deep-rooted group loyalties and rested on an uncertain base of popular support. Many overlapped ideologically and in their social appeal, making it difficult to describe their ideological stand in terms of the Western traditional left-right continuum. Moreover, Albania witnessed a tendency toward increasing fragmentation of the largest parties.

The Albanian political scene continued to be dominated by two main actors—the Democratic Party and the Socialist Party. The Democratic Party remained the only party with a clear political and economic program, which strived to appeal to multiple interests. Although the perils and pitfalls of governing the country during a crisis period had taken a significant toll and the Democrats had moved away as an ally of such groups as former political prisoners, followers of right-wing parties, trade unions, and others, the Democratic Party had retained a wide base of support that cut across all segments of the society. The Socialist Party was the most cohesive and powerful opposition force in the country. It rejected Berisha's policy of shock therapy and massive privatization, advocating instead gradual economic reforms and a continued state role in regulating the economy. The Socialists were also wary of Albania's growing military relationship with the United States and NATO. The party leadership was heavily dominated by conservative communists and its claims of renovation were disingenuous. Since its humiliating defeat in 1992, the Socialist Party had displayed little commitment to democratic values and practices and had attempted to block the process of transition every step of the way. But in a bid to prove that they were a moderate force, in the months preceding the elections the Socialists toned down their anti-Western and particularly their anti-American rhetoric. Other important players were the Republican Party, the Social Democratic Party, and the Democratic Alliance. They had gained increased importance, but did not provide real alternatives to the Democrats and the Socialists. Outside parliament there were numerous parties, most of them with small membership.

The campaign focused almost exclusively on domestic issues. Foreign policy issues were far down the list. The issue of Kosova was almost nonexistent in the campaign. Right-wing forces harped on feelings of humiliation by the Serbs, but even among these forces the issue was at best a subdued theme. The Democratic Party ran a vigorous campaign. Berisha paraded tirelessly throughout the country, hammering home the message that voters were faced with a choice between stability and steady growth or another revolution and uncertainty. The president offered a vision for the future and delivered a positive message to voters that went beyond simply branding the Socialists as extremists and appealing to voters to remember the communist past. His strategy consisted of stressing the achievements of four years of Democratic rule, and convincing the electorate of the virtues of reform and the dangers of radically altering the status quo. In their campaign speeches, Berisha and other party officials acknowledged there had been mistakes during four years of Democratic Party rule, but claimed that a Socialist victory would derail market reforms and spark instability. The Socialist Party ran a well-organized campaign. However, it encountered difficulty in convincing the electorate that it had become a bona fide reformist party and was not a proto-Communist Party. The battle did not, as the Socialists had hoped, focus simply on the hardships of reform and governmental political blunders, but on the fear of the communists' return to power. The Social Democratic Party and the Democratic Alliance formed a left-center bloc, but ran an uninspiring campaign, making Berisha the only issue.

Albania's third multiparty parliamentary elections, held on 26 May 1996, were viewed as an important test of its democratic maturity and orientation. However, the elections turned out to be the most controversial in post-communist Eastern Europe. Only hours before the polls were scheduled to close, the Socialist Party, the Social Democratic Party, the Democratic Alliance, and several other minor parties pulled out of the voting, claiming large-scale election irregularities. Opposition parties declared that they would not accept the results or recognize the new parliament. Most foreign observers agreed with the opposition that the elections were marred by widespread irregularities. The ruling party responded by acknowledging that there were some problems with the balloting but rejecting charges of vote fraud and insisting that the results reflected the will of the people. The Democrats accused the opposition of creating problems to mask their humiliating defeat. The second round of elections was held as scheduled on 2 June, and on 16 June balloting was repeated in seventeen electoral districts, in which the Central Electoral Commission said there were irregularities. The Socialists boycotted both rounds.

The final tally showed the Democratic Party had scored a bigger landslide victory than in the 1992 election, winning 122 seats in the 140-seat parliament. This gave it the two-thirds needed to make constitutional changes. The Socialist Party came in second, with ten seats, down from thirty-two seats in 1992. The National Front and the Union for the Protection of Human Rights, representing the ethnic Greeks, won three seats each and the Republican Party two. The Social Democratic Party and the Democratic Alliance were soundly defeated, failing to make the 4 percent threshold necessary to gain entry into the parliament.[39]

In the postelection period, Berisha came under increased international pressure, including from the United States, which had been his staunchest ally. In a 1 June 1996 statement, the U.S. Department of State said the elections were marred by serious irregularities and represented "a significant step backward from the previous parliamentary elections in 1992."

Washington urged Albania to accept an international mechanism for reviewing the elections and recommending appropriate remedial measures.[40] The Organization for Security and Cooperation in Europe urged Albanian parties to consider holding new elections "after a reasonable but limited period of time, under improved conditions and in the presence of international observers. . . ."[41] But despite the harsh criticism, neither the United States nor the OSCE-supported Socialist Party called for new elections or questioned the legitimacy of the newly elected parliament.

In the wake of the controversial 26 May elections, Albania found itself maneuvering through a new political landscape. Berisha quickly moved to reassure the country and the world that the reform process would continue. He also acknowledged the need for domestic healing and tried to bring about a certain degree of reconciliation with the Albanian body politic by opening a dialogue with the Socialist Party, the largest opposition force.

The Democratic Party took the helm at the most turbulent period in Albania's modern history. During the first four years of Democratic rule, Albania attained relative economic and political stability. Pluralistic democracy and market economy were beginning to take root. There was no question that there had been problems and mistakes, but the successes of President Berisha and his government far outweighed their failures. The symbols of a new Albania were everywhere. But the tasks that confronted Albania in fully consolidating its democracy remained formidably ambitious. The ruling Democratic Party needed to take serious measures to restore confidence in Albania's democratic process and allay fears that the country was drifting toward authoritarianism. The road ahead was fraught with the risk of reversion and probably several rounds of elections will be necessary before Albania can build a genuine democracy. But despite all the obstacles, post-communist Albania had come a long way.

Notes

1. Nicholas C. Pano, *The People's Republic of Albania* (Baltimore: Johns Hopkins University Press, 1968); Stavro Skendi, ed., *Albania* (New York: Praeger, 1956); Stephen Peters, "Ingredients of the Communist Takeover in Albania," *Studies on the Soviet Union*, 11, No. 4 (1971), 224–263; Vladimir Dedijer, *Marrëdhanjet jugosllavo-shqiptare, 1939–1948* [Yugoslav-Albanian Relations, 1939–1948] (Belgrade: Prosveta, 1949); and Institute of Marxist-Leninist Studies at the Central Committee of the Albanian Party of Labor, *Historia e Partisë së Punës të Shqipërisë* [The History of the Albanian Party of Labor] (Tiranë: "8 Nëntori", 1968).

2. Pano, *People's Republic,* 58–62; and Peter R. Prifti, *Socialist Albania since 1944: Domestic and Foreign Developments* (Cambridge: MIT Press, 1978), 52–55.

3. Prifti, *Socialist Albania,* 168–169.

4. Ibid., 138–139.

5. Nicholas C. Pano, "Albania," in Joseph Held, ed., *The Columbia History of Eastern Europe in the Twentieth Century* (New York: Columbia University Press, 1992), 45.

6. See John Kolsti, "From Courtyard to Cabinet: The Political Emergence of Albanian Women," in Sharon L. Wolchik and Alfred G. Meyer, eds., *Women, State and Party in Eastern Europe* (Durham: Duke University Press, 1985), 138–51.

7. *Portrait of Albania* (Tiranë: "8 Nëntori", 1982), 155.

8. The communists prided themselves for the success of the drive for the emancipation of women. But after the downfall of communism, observers have noted "the nightmarish reality" of women under Hoxha's regime. Elsa Ballauri, a writer and a human rights activist, wrote in 1991 that, "Albanian women live today caught between a dream and a restless, hard, and nightmarish reality. This physical and psychological terror starts in the milk queue at five in the morning and continues until after midnight—an endless and difficult struggle. Very little has been done for a very long time, nothing to warrant applause, to alleviate the terrible slavery of women in the home." See Elsa Ballauri, "The Joan of Arc Alternative," *Rilindja Demokratike* (Tiranë), 9 January 1991, 5.

9. For background information, see Prifti, *Socialist Albania;* Harry Hamm, *Albania: China's Beachhead in Europe* (New York: Praeger, 1963); and Anton Logoreci, *The Albanians: Europe's Forgotten Survivors* (Boulder: Westview, 1978).

10. Elez Biberaj, *Albania and China: A Study of an Unequal Alliance* (Boulder: Westview, 1986).

11. Elez Biberaj, *Albania: A Socialist Maverick* (Boulder: Westview, 1990), 33–38.

12. See Amnesty International, *Albania: Political Imprisonment and the Law* (London: Amnesty International, 1984); The Minnesota Lawyers International Human Rights Committee, *Human Rights in the People's Socialist Republic of Albania* (Minneapolis, 1990); and Puebla Institute, *Albania: Religion in a Fortress State* (Washington, 1989).

13. Sabrina Petra Ramet, *Social Currents in Eastern Europe: The Sources and Consequences of the Great Transformation,* 2nd ed. (Durham: Duke University Press, 1995), 341.

14. The discussion between Alia and the intellectuals was not made public but it was confidentially circulated to party committees. According to participants, the transcript of the exchange between Alia and Berisha was altered, omitting Berisha's demand for a multiparty system. See Ramiz Alia, *Demokratizim në rrugën e partisë* (Tiranë: The Central Committee of the APL, 1990). The publication is stamped *secret.* See also Ismail Kadare, *Nga një dhjetor në tjetrin* [From One December to Another] (Paris: Fayard, 1991), 87.

15. *Rilindja Demokratike,* 2 February 1991, 1–2.

16. Commission on Security and Cooperation in Europe, U.S. Congress, *The Elections in Albania March–April 1991* (Washington, April 1991); National Republican Institute for International Affairs, *The 1991 Elections in Albania* (Washington, April 1991); and National Democratic Institute for International Affairs, *Albania: 1991 Elections to the People's Assembly* (Washington, April 1991).

17. *Zëri I Popullit* (Tiranë), 14 June 1991, 1–2. See also the Socialist Party's program in ibid., 3 July 1991, 1–3.

18. Radio Tiranë Network in Albanian 1310 GMT, 23 March 1992, trans. in Foreign Broadcasting Information Service [hereafter FBIS], *Daily Report* (Eastern Europe) (Washington), 24 March 1992, 4–5.

19. *Drita* (Tiranë), 20 May 1990, 5–6.

20. *Bashkimi* (Tiranë), 17 September 1990, 2–3.

21. Radio Tiranë Network (29 September 1991), trans. in FBIS, *Daily Report* (Eastern Europe), 30 September 1991, 5.

22. Radio Tiranë Network (9 April 1992), trans. in FBIS, *Daily Report* (Eastern Europe), 10 April 1992, 3–4.

23. In an interview in April 1992, Berisha said that full economic recovery would take between fifteen and twenty years. *Rilindja Demokratike,* 22 April 1992, 1.

24. See Berisha's interview in *The Financial Times,* 21 July 1994, 31.

25. See special survey on Albania in *The Financial Times,* 2 October 1995.

26. See interview with Kopliku in David Binder, "Albania Reported to Move from Brink of Anarchy," *The New York Times,* 29 October 1992, A11.

27. *Gazeta Zyrtare e Republikës së Shqipërisë,* No. 4 (July 1991), 145–160. For background analysis, see Louis Zanga, "A Transitional Constitutional Law," in Radio Free Europe/Radio Liberty, *Report on Eastern Europe,* 2, No. 17, 26 April 1991, 1–4.

28. ATA, 5 April 1992 in FBIS, *Daily Report* (Eastern Europe), 6 April 1992, 2; and Radio Tiranë Network, 9 April 1992, trans. in FBIS, *Daily Report* (Eastern Europe), 10 April 1992, 5.

29. Law No. 7561, dated 29 April 1992, in *Fletorja Zyrtare e Republikës së Shqipërisë,* No. 2 (May 1992), 81–84.

30. Law No. 7692, dated 31 March 1993, in *Fletorja Zyrtare e Republikës së Shqipërisë,* No. 3 (March 1993), 161–171.

31. Radio Tiranë Network, 8 April 1992, trans. in FBIS, *Daily Report* (Eastern Europe), 10 April 1992, 4.

32. Before his sentencing, Alia told the court that he had a clear conscience. Ridiculing the proceedings, the former communist leader said when he looks back at his service to the nation, he has nothing to be ashamed of or any reason to apologize for his actions. For a full text of Alia's statement, see *Zëri i Popullit,* 29 May 1994, 1–2.

33. ATA in English, 6 September 1993, in FBIS, *Daily Report* (Eastern Europe), 7 September 1993, 4.

34. U.S. Commission on Security and Cooperation in Europe, *Human Rights and Democratization in Albania* (Washington, January 1994), 1.

35. Human Rights Watch/Helsinki, *Human Rights in Post-Communist Albania* (New York, 1996). See also U.S. State Department, *Country Reports on Human Rights Practices for 1995* (Washington, March 1996).

36. TVSH Television Network, 10 November 1994, translated in FBIS, *Daily Report* (Eastern Europe), 14 November 1994, 1–2.

37. *Gazeta Shqiptare,* 21 September 1995, 1; *The New York Times,* 24 September 1995, 3; and *The Financial Times,* 25 October 1995, 4.

38. *Fletorja Zyrtare,* No. 26, December 1995, 1139–43. According to the law, files for all other citizens will remain closed for thirty years.

39. *Rilindja Demokratike,* 22 June 1996, 2.

40. Office of the Spokesman, U.S. Department of State, *Albanian Parliamentary Elections,* 1 June 1996.

41. OMRI Daily Digest, No. 123, Pt. 2, 25 June 1996.

PART THREE

❏

Policy Spheres

11

Women and the Politics of Gender in Communist and Post-Communist Central and Eastern Europe

SHARON L. WOLCHIK

The collapse of communism in Central and Eastern Europe and the processes of political, economic, and social transformation it ushered in have had important implications for women in these societies. Changes in the nature of the policy-making process and issues facing political leaders have also had an impact on the way in which women's issues are considered by policy-makers. The end of communist rule created new problems for many women, afflicting them with new hardships. For example, in the Yugoslav successor states, women suffered in some gender-specific ways during five years of internecine warfare, 1991–95. Although less acute elsewhere, ethnic chauvinism has often been associated with elements of misogyny. This chapter will explore these issues, turning first to the changes in women's roles effected during the communist era. Then, the impact of political and economic change on women in the post-communist era and the future of gender relations in the region will be discussed.

THE COMMUNIST LEGACY

When communist elites came to power in Eastern Europe, they adopted the Soviet model of political organization and socioeconomic management. This model included prescriptions for policies to improve the status of women. In harmony with the support provided by Marxism-Leninism for party-guided aspirations to gender equality, communist governments in the region adopted constitutional measures and legal provisions designed to guarantee women equality in all spheres of life. However, women's equality remained a relatively low priority in all of these countries for much of the communist period. Although the ideological support for women's equality did have an impact on public policies toward women, the elites' approach to women's issues and gender role change was determined not so much by any abstract consideration of what such policies would mean for gender equality as by their impact on more important goals. Women's roles were also influenced in important ways by other policies, including broader industrialization strategies, social policies, and demographic policies. The intended and unintended consequences of these policies had an impact on women's roles during the communist period.

There were many important differences in conditions among countries and among regions within countries prior to the establishment of communist systems. However, despite differences in levels of economic development, educational access, religion, political heritages and experiences, and previous traditions in regard to gender roles, women's roles changed in similar ways in all of the countries in the region.[1] This distinctive pattern of change differed in important respects from changes in women's situations that occurred during the same period in non-communist West European countries and in the United States. Differences continued to exist among countries and between urban and rural regions within particular countries, especially in the extent to which women achieved equal access to education, entered the labor force, participated in politics, and in the division of labor within the home. Due to continued differences in development levels, the material situations of women in the northern countries of the region and in many parts of the Balkan countries also differed. But in all countries of the region the pattern of change in gender roles was uneven, and in all, the patterns of change were similar.

During the communist period women's roles changed most in the areas of education and employment. Literacy campaigns in those countries which had high levels of female illiteracy, such as Albania, Bulgaria, and parts of Yugoslavia, led to marked decreases in the number of illiterate women. Women's access to secondary and higher education also increased greatly. Women's educational levels came to equal or exceed those of men in many of these countries. Many girls and women also entered new technical fields of study. Women engineers and technicians became commonplace in many of these countries, as did women doctors, pharmacists, and economists. At the secondary level, girls entered technical training programs in far greater numbers than in the pre-communist period.

However, despite these changes, important differences remained in the educational specializations of men and women. At the secondary level, girls comprised the vast majority of those students who entered teachers' training programs; they also predominated in general academic programs or gymnasia. Far fewer girls than boys entered technical or vocational programs that would have prepared them to obtain jobs as skilled workers. Because most graduates of general secondary schools did not continue their studies but rather entered the labor force directly after graduation, many girls who chose this area of study could only obtain jobs as unskilled workers or low-level clerical or sales employees. Similarly, at the level of higher education, most girls and women continued to choose or be channeled into fields that were traditionally seen as appropriate for women, such as education and culture, or into fields that became feminized, such as medicine, despite the new opportunities for women to enter technical studies.[2] These tendencies had important repercussions on women's wages and positions in the world of work, for they meant that men and women entered the labor force with markedly different skills and levels of preparation.

Similar patterns of continuity and change occurred in the area of work. Women entered the labor force in large numbers. The extent to which paid employment outside the home became an accepted part of the lives of women in the region is evident in the fact that from 60 to 80 percent of all women who were between the ages of fifteen and eighty-four were employed. However, as in the area of education, change in women's economic roles did not mean equality. Women's wages continued to be significantly lower than men's throughout the communist period. Continued inequality in this area in part reflected the fact that most women were concentrated in sectors of the economy with lower-than-average wages. It also reflected the impact of the gender differences in educational specializations discussed above and the fact that women tended to be assigned to the lower ends of qualification and wage ranges and to jobs that did not make use of their qualifications. Central and East European analysts tended to downplay the impact of overt discrimination in perpetuating these wage differentials, but there is no doubt that such actions accounted for part of the persistent gender differences in wages during the communist period.

Women were also much less likely than men to hold important decision-making roles in the economy.[3] Women held higher proportions of leadership positions in areas of the economy in which they predominated, such as education and medicine. As in the area of politics, where women's representation decreased as the level of importance of the office increased, women held more leading positions at lower levels. Even in those areas in which women comprised a large portion of the labor force, the relatively few men who worked in these areas had disproportionately higher chances of occupying top positions.

If one turns to the area of politics and the family, there was much less change in gender roles. Women's roles changed to some degree in both areas after the establishment of communist systems. However, in both, old patterns of gender role expectations and behaviors continued to shape the actions of both leaders and ordinary citizens.

These patterns were clearly evident in the area of politics. In the early communist period in particular communist leaders emphasized the need to draw women into the national political community. Efforts to increase literacy were accompanied by campaigns to teach women as well as other citizens about the fundamentals of the new political system. Women as well as men also found it hard to avoid the large number of political messages and political information that were found in the media as well as in the arts and other areas of culture. Women came to participate in symbolic political activities designed to show support for the regime, such as voting and taking part in mass demonstrations orchestrated by the elites, in numbers approximately equal to those of men.

Women were also well represented in the symbolic governmental elites. However, they played a very limited role in the exercise of real political power within the Communist Party. Women were less likely than men to become members of the Communist Party. They were also less likely than their male colleagues to advance within the party's ranks. Thus, the numbers of women who held leadership positions within the party were lower than those who served in the governmental elites at all levels. Those women who were chosen to occupy political office differed from their male colleagues in terms of social background and previous experience and had, with few exceptions, little influence.[4] As in the Soviet Union, women's direct role in the exercise of political power within the Communist Party appears to have been greatest in many of these countries in the period prior to the party's rise to power and immediately afterward. As the Stalinist system was consolidated in the region, women such as Tsola Dragoicheva in Bulgaria, Ana Pauker in Romania, and Maria Švermová in Czechoslovakia, who played important political roles in their own right, were removed from their positions or fell victim to the purges, and the number of women in high political positions declined.

When the political leadership once again began to be concerned about representation of women in the party elites in many of these countries, the women who were selected differed greatly from this first generation of women Communist Party leaders. In contrast to the first group of women, women who rose to top party posts most often achieved their positions either by virtue of their relationship to a powerful male party leader (as in the case of Elena Ceaușescu in Romania; Zhivkova in Bulgaria; and the wives of several party leaders in Albania) or as the result of work in the mass organizations, often the official women's organization, as in Slovakia, Poland, East Germany, and Hungary in the 1970s and 1980s. Clearly dependent upon the party for their positions, these

women did little to represent the interests of women or direct elite attention to the impact of elite policies on women's situations. In part as the
result of the example of these women, who were perceived to be unfeminine party hacks for the most part, many ordinary women had little interest in politics and sought to avoid the political arena insofar as possible.
Less ambitious than their male counterparts or relatives, in many cases
women were also able to fall back upon the press of domestic duties to
justify their lower levels of political activism. However, while they were
thus able to avoid the irritation and loss of time involved in party meetings, etc., women's low levels of participation in politics also meant that
women had few avenues to use politics to address issues of concern to
them. Women's exclusion from important positions of political leadership and lack of interest in politics also meant that issues of particular
importance to women entered the political arena only indirectly, as the
result of the actions of other intermediary elites, such as social scientists
and public opinion pollsters who perceived the connection between problematic aspects of women's situation and public policy concerns and
brought this connection to the attention of political leaders.[5]

Many of the persisting inequalities in the area of work and politics
can be traced to the lack of change in the divison of labor within the
family. There were important changes in family size and in women's legal
rights within the family under communism. As these countries modernized, family size declined, as did the role of the extended family. The
growth of nuclear, or two-generation families, increased levels of urban-
ization, and improvement in the populations' educational levels were also
accompanied by a shift in attitudes concerning proper relations between
men and women in the family. Legal changes ensured women's equal
rights to inherit and an equal chance to argue for custody of their children in the case of divorce and outlawed some of the most abusive practices in regard to marriage and family life, such as bride price and
arranged marriages. Coupled with the processes discussed above, these
changes led to an improvement in women's situation within the family.
However, many patriarchal attitudes and practices continued. The high
rates of alcoholism found in many of these countries compounded the
situation and led to frequent wife abuse in many cases.

It is also the case that very little changed in the actual division of
labor within the home, despite these changes and changes in women's
educational access and employment patterns. Younger, more educated
men who lived in urban areas did more within the home, but women
continued to bear the main responsibility for the daily work involved in
caring for children and running their households. The state provided
public child care at little expense, although both the availability and quality of these facilities varied greatly from country to country.[6] Women also
benefited from maternity policies that supported them while they stayed

at home with small children and guaranteed their return to the same or equivalent jobs. However, the neglect of the consumer sector for much of the communist period meant that many consumer durables were not widely available, particularly in the early communist period. Due to this fact and the chronic shortages of food and other basic necessities in many of these countries, the running of households was far more time-consuming and tiring for women in these countries than in other developed European countries or the United States. As a result, women had far less leisure time than men and were less interested in increasing their qualification levels or accepting leading economic positions. They were also less likely to want to be involved in politics.

The negative results this uneven pattern of change created for women and their families led to a partial reorientation of the elites' approach to women's issues in many of these countries in the late 1960s. In large part in reaction to falling birth rates, political leaders in a number of these states adopted policies designed to encourage young families to have more children. In addition to longer maternity leaves, low-interest loans for young couples, and greater production of the goods needed to raise young children, the leadership also changed the official model of the ideal socialist woman to fit contemporary circumstances. In countries such as Czechoslovakia, Hungary, and the GDR, officials came to accept the view that women would contribute to socialism differently at different stages of their lives. They also emphasized the social importance of motherhood and of women's maternal roles.[7]

Official recognition of the importance of reproduction was accompanied by a shift in the qualities emphasized in official discussions of women's roles and in official representations of women. One of the most graphic illustrations of this change was the shift from women tractor drivers, scientists, and engineers to smiling young mothers with at least two children on the pages of the official women's magazines. Articles calling for women to remember to cultivate their feminine qualities of empathy, caring, and tenderness further documented the shift in official priorities. During the communist period, the new emphasis on women's maternal roles was coupled with guarantees of women's right to work. Although certain voices raised the issue during periods of reform in several of these countries of whether young women with children should be economically active,[8] political leaders affirmed women's right to be economically active. Officials and experts involved in outlining the pronatalist population policies also argued that such measures should be accompanied by policies that would allow women to maintain their professional qualifications while at home, so as not to fall behind in their occupations.

However, in practice, this reorientation of policy meant that many women stayed out of the labor force to care for their children under the age of three. This reliance on maternal care rather than public child care for the youngest group of children was justified largely on economic grounds, as well as by reference to the benefits for children. Political leaders noted that policies should be adopted to make sure that such extended leaves from the labor force would not lead women to lose their expertise or fall behind in their professions, but in practice, few policies were ever enacted to deal with this aspect of the situation. Pronatalist policies also reinforced the notion, which appears to have prevailed among many groups of women as well, that women were first and foremost defined by their maternal roles. Unfortunately, both policy-makers and women were less likely to see women as suitable candidates for leading positions in the economy or in politics as a result of these views.

Women's roles under communist rule were also influenced by broader political and economic developments. In the early period, these included the consolidation of Stalinist rule and the purge trials and political terror that racked many of these countries. As noted earlier, as the Stalinist system was consolidated, most of the prominent women in the communist parties fell victim to the purges or were removed from office. Ordinary women also suffered the impact of political terror. The consolidation of the Stalinist system also had an impact on the way in which women's issues were considered by political leaders. In the early post–World War II period, the communist parties had women's sections to mobilize women to support party objectives and to be active in politics. Mass organizations for women were also used to provide women with opportunities to be involved in communal life. Although the primary aim of these organizations was to activate women to fulfil elite-determined objectives, many also attempted to take action to benefit women and deal with the very real problems that rapid changes in the structure of economic and social life and women's mass entry into the labor force created for women and their families. Thus, local units of these groups organized "shopping into the bag," or programs that allowed women to turn in grocery orders at their place of work in the morning to find them filled and ready to take home that evening. Others organized communal child-care and laundry facilities.

In the early 1950s, most of these organizations were disbanded. Relying on the argument that women's inequality derived primarily from their economic dependence and the existence of private property and following the Soviet example, Central and East European Communist Party leaders declared that the establishment of communist systems had liberated women. Since women were now equal, there was no longer any need for them to have their own organizations to articulate or defend their interests. As a result, open discussion of problematic aspects of women's situation ceased, and women lost the limited opportunity these organizations had provided to articulate their interests or take action together to remedy their difficulties. Women's issues were seldom considered explicitly by political leaders. Public focus on women's roles came to be limited to a symbolic acknowledgement of women's contributions to the building of socialism on International Women's Day, 8 March, when delegations of members of the national committees of women would meet with political leaders.

Periods of political reform also had their impact on the way in which women's issues were considered, as women as well as men gained greater opportunities during such periods to voice their concerns and call for action on issues of interest to them. With the exception of the reform period in Czechoslovakia in the 1960s, when women intellectuals affiliated with the Communist Party called for a change in the elite's approach to women's issues and more attention to women's needs,[9] women's concerns were seldom articulated in a systematic way by the opposition in the region. In fact, many dissidents shared the view, evident also in official policies, that women's issues were secondary concerns which could only be resolved once broader issues were addressed. Others, including Solidarity activists in Poland, favored more traditional roles for women.[10]

During the last decade and a half of communist rule, chronic if not acute economic and political crises affected the way in which policies toward women were made and implemented. The impact of political and economic crisis on women's issues is perhaps clearest in the case of Poland, where the inefficiencies and corruption of the communist system caused a series of crises in the 1970s and 1980s. As Renata Siemieńska notes in a discussion of this era, crisis in the broader society led many people to retreat to the private realm and strengthened traditional roles within the family.[11] Political leaders, occupied with issues that affected their survival, saw gender issues as secondary. At the same time, because women continued to retain primary responsibility for the running of the household on a day-to-day basis, economic crisis created new concerns and difficulties for many women.[12]

There was a congruence of views, then, of the leadership and many citizens concerning women's roles in many of these countries during the late communist period. Although official policies continued to recognize women's right to work, in practice the policies political leaders adopted coincided with the prevailing view that women's maternal roles were primary.[13] This attitude was shared by many dissidents who were otherwise very critical of these systems.

Attitudes toward gender equality and the way in which women's issues were perceived by leaders and ordinary citizens after the end of communist rule were also influenced by the fact that gender equality was a goal that was imposed from above, rather than one chosen and fought for by women themselves during the communist era. This fact, as well as the difficulties that many women and their families experienced as the result of the uneven pattern of gender role change discussed above, led many men and women to identify gender equality with the communist regime and to reject it as a goal once that regime was no longer in power just as they rejected many other aspects and goals of the system. Once it was no longer necessary even to give lip service to the goals articulated by the old regimes, many groups of men and women openly called them into question.

WOMEN AND THE POLITICS OF TRANSITION

Women's roles and public consideration of gender issues since the fall of communist systems in the region have been influenced by the legacy of communist rule in regard to gender issues noted above. They have also been influenced by the far-reaching economic, political, and social transformations that have occurred since the ouster of communist systems. The end of the Communist Party's monopoly of power, opening of borders, and move back to market economies have brought benefits to many women. At the same time, the transition has created a great deal of disruption for all women and led to economic and other forms of hardship for many women.

Women's roles in the downfall of communist systems varied according to the way in which the systems fell.[14] In those cases, such as Poland and Hungary, in which the end of communist rule occurred as the result of an extended process of negotiation between reformist leaders in the Communist Party and members of the opposition, women played a very limited role. They were seldom represented in the roundtable talks either as dissident leaders or as specialists brought in to provide technical expertise.

In the GDR, Czechoslovakia, and Romania, on the other hand, women played an important role in the mass demonstrations that brought about the rapid end of communist rule. In the GDR, women dissidents were instrumental in organizing the mass demonstrations that grew in size and eventually forced the communist leadership to resign. Similarly, in Czechoslovakia, women dissidents and students were among those beaten by the police on 17 November 1989 as they participated in a peaceful demonstration. Large numbers of other women joined the mass demonstrations of hundreds of thousands of citizens who took to the streets to protest this police brutality and call for the end of communist rule. In Romania, where the end of communist rule came about with far more violence, women were among the protesters and also among the victims of the security forces of the Ceauşescu regime in its last days.

Despite this participation in the events that ended communist rule in the region, women very quickly became marginalized once again from politics. Certain women, including prominent dissident women in

Czechoslovakia and the GDR, as well as in Hungary, served as spokespersons for the new governments that replaced the fallen communist leaderships. A number of others were appointed as advisers, top officials, or ambassadors. However, as the new political leaders moved to take control of the institutions of government and to implement political reforms designed to restore democratic life to their societies, women were for the most part pushed aside.[15]

As the very high turnout rates for the first post-communist elections illustrate, many women were eager to exercise their right to vote for those who would represent them. Many also have joined the plethora of new voluntary associations, interest groups, and charitable and other groups that have developed since the end of communist rule. However, most women play a very small role in politics beyond this level.

Women's marginalization from the exercise of political power is evident in a number of areas. Women's representation in the legislative elites declined in all of the countries in the region. Women were also noticeable by their absence among the leaders of the many new or re-created political parties that formed after the end of the Communist Party's monopoly of political power.[16]

As a number of analysts have noted, the decline in the numbers of women in the legislatures of these countries does not necessarily mean that women exercise less power than they did previously. As discussed earlier in the chapter, women played an essentially symbolic role in politics under the communist system; few of those who were in political roles exercised any real political power. Although they are fewer in number in post-communist legislatures, those women who hold political office now have backgrounds and levels of education closer to those of their male colleagues.[17] At the same time, as the experience of women in other political bodies confirms, numbers do make a difference. The small numbers of women in each of the elected legislatures is one of the factors that makes it difficult for women leaders to articulate women's interests or argue that special attention needs to be given to women's perspectives or to issues that have a particular impact on women.[18]

WOMEN'S GROUPS AND MOVEMENTS

Women's exclusion from the direct exercise of power is paralleled by the lack of a strong women's movement and interest groups that represent women's interests in the political realm. There are feminist groups in all of the countries of the region. In the case of former Yugoslavia, Poland, and Hungary, these date to the 1970s, when women intellectuals, many of whom had contacts with Western feminists, formed women's groups and began doing feminist research.[19] New groups of women organized in many other countries after the end of communist rule. Informal gender studies programs were set up at a number of universities. However, most feminist groups are small, concentrated in urban areas, and have few resources. Most appeal primarily if not solely to young, well-educated urban women.

The majority of the new women's groups formed since the end of communist rule explicitly reject the label feminist. Many focus on what are perceived to have been women's neglected roles as mothers and homemakers. In part a reaction to the previous regime's depiction of feminists as man-hating, antifamily activists, many women in the region, even those who are active on women's behalf, do not see themselves or wish to be seen publicly as feminists. This rejection of feminism also reflects the impact of the activities of the official women's organizations during the communist period on popular perceptions and attitudes. These organizations were seen largely as tools of the regime to mobilize women to fulfil tasks determined by the political leadership, or, at the local level, as knitting societies that provided social opportunities largely for older women. They, and their leaders, who were widely regarded as unfeminine apparatchiki, discredited the idea of women's organizations for many groups in the population. Thus, many women in the region equate feminism or organized activity on behalf of women with the activities and characteristics of these organizations and want nothing to do with them.[20]

Cooperation to further women's interests is also hindered in these societies by partisan divisions. Many of the groups that work to bring to public attention issues of special interest to women do not have the impact that they might, because they cannot cooperate across partisan lines with women who share similar interests. Similarly, many of the newly formed groups are unwilling to cooperate with the successors to the official women's organizations. Unfortunately, it is the latter organizations that have the best-developed local networks and most resources.

Although these new women's groups have little direct political impact at present, their activities in the region are important. Thus, despite the fact that they eschew the label feminist and at times deny that they are engaging in political activities, many of these groups organize lectures, protests, and other actions on issues of interest to women. They also serve, by providing a space for women to meet with others, as a mechanism for women to begin to define their own interests as women and, potentially, as a source of political activism.[21]

Women have also organized, as in Poland, Hungary, and Slovenia, to protest restrictions on access to abortion and to call for action on other issues of current interest to women. In some of the Yugoslav successor states, women's groups formed to call for an end to the war and "ethnic cleansing."[22] With the exception of issues that touch on women's reproductive rights, it is difficult for women to mobilize large numbers of supporters to express themselves on issues of concern to women. It is also difficult for women who do hold leadership positions to raise such issues, because most political leaders do not feel that it is legitimate or important to take action on such concerns.

In this area, then, as in the view that women's roles as mothers need more emphasis, there is a certain degree of continuity in the way in which women's issues are regarded in the communist and post-communist periods. In both time periods, women's issues were seen as secondary to other presumably higher-priority goals. As in the late communist period most political actors after the fall of communist systems regard women's maternal roles as primary. Thus, although many observers argue that there is a backlash at present against women's equality, in fact there are some areas where the policy emphases of communist and post-communist elites are similar. What has changed in regard to attitudes toward women's roles in the economy and at home, then, is the way in which these views can be expressed. It is now possible to be much more open in questioning the value of labor force participation by women with young children; it is also possible to engage in practices that are discriminatory much more openly.

Similar attitudes are evident in regard to women's political participation. Women's low levels of participation in politics in part reflect the impact of transition politics in the region. Thus, a number of aspects of political life at present, including the fluidity of political life, uninstitutionalized party systems, and lack of a well-developed tradition of responsiveness to citizen consensus on the part of political leaders, all increase the costs of political involvement. The time constraints that led many women to eschew political activity during the communist period continue to condition women's potential for involvement in public affairs. Many women, in fact, face greater pressures on their time now than before 1989, as they and their partners must often work two or more jobs to maintain their family's standard of living.

Perhaps most important, though, is the perception that prevails among many women as well as men that politics is somehow not an appropriate area of activity for women. Evident in the statements of many dissidents who became public officials, this view appears to be widely shared.[23] The few women who held top political positions during the communist era continue to condition popular perceptions of women politicians. Many formerly dissident women, who were clearly engaged in political roles in the early post-communist period, did not see themselves as politicians. Those women who have chosen to run for office more recently define their roles somewhat differently, but they are few in number. Given the backlash against the idea of gender equality and its identification with the old regime, they are also handicapped in efforts to raise issues that are of particular concern to women.[24]

WOMEN AND THE MOVE TO THE MARKET

The re-creation of the private sector and efforts to reestablish market economies have had mixed results for women in post-communist Central and Eastern Europe. These changes have created new opportunities for certain women to become entrepreneurs, work in the private sector, and travel abroad to improve their skills and gain new experiences. Many women have also benefited from their newfound ability to practice their professions free of political interference. Other women have seen their living standards increase as the result of their husbands' business activities.

However, for many women the introduction of the market economy has created new hardships. Women's levels of unemployment are higher than those of men in many countries.[25] Women, as well as men, face increased competition and pressure to perform well at work as state subsidies of unprofitable firms have decreased and the private sector has expanded. Women also face increasingly open discrimination in the workplace. Given the identification of policies designed to promote gender equality with communism and the need for enterprises to take profit considerations into account, many enterprise officials appear to favor male employees. Evident in advertisements that specify that they are seeking "engineers (male)," or "technicians (male)," or "pretty, young" women secretaries, these trends have been exacerbated by the behavior of international corporations. Although some of these view women as equally attractive candidates for professional and managerial positions, many appear to recruit women primarily for clerical positions.

Many women as well as men share the view that levels of women's employment were too high during the communist era. This view, which is also held by many women who are active with regard to women's issues, is often coupled with the argument that all women should have the right to choose whether they will join the labor force or stay at home with their children. To some extent a carryover from the earlier reorientation of the elites' approach to women's roles during the communist period, the argument that women should withdraw from the labor force has been expressed more openly and forcefully since the end of the communist era. Prior to 1989, such arguments were most often couched in terms of the benefits for children and families; women's withdrawal from the labor force was also seen as temporary. Since 1989, many groups, including many conservative religious and political groups, advocate a permanent retreat from the labor force for women. Such a course of action is still most often presented in terms of its impact of family life. However, certain advocates of these views also point to the benefits of such choice for women in relieving them of the strain of the well-documented double burden of home and work.

Such views, as well as other aspects of the backlash against women's equality, have been fueled by the activities of conservative religious groups. Such groups, which can now be more active in politics than during the communist period, have also been in the forefront of efforts to restrict women's access to abortion and other reproductive rights in a number of these countries.

Because they continue to bear primary responsibility for running their households on a day-to-day basis, women have also been affected more than men by the impact of the move to a market economy on the standard of living. In this area as in others, the introduction of the market has eliminated certain problems women faced under communism, but introduced new ones. Women no longer have to spend hours a day standing in line, for example, to obtain food or other scarce goods as they did under communism when chronic or acute shortages of many necessities were facts of life. At the same time, while shop windows, particularly in large cities, now are filled with goods, many women cannot afford to buy much of what is available. Time saved standing in line must, in many cases, now be spent in finding bargains or lower-priced goods that are affordable, given constraints on the family budget. In addition to the need to deal with the impact of price liberalization on the family budget, many of the mechanisms women developed to obtain the things their families needed outside of official channels have been disrupted by the market economy.

Women also have experienced the impact of the cutbacks in social services that have followed the end of communist rule and introduction to the market. Many factory child-care facilities have been closed and fees have increased at many public facilities. Changes in children's allowances, maternity leave and payments, and other pronatalist policies are currently under discussion in many countries.[26] Leaders in several countries in the region are also considering introducing or have already introduced tuition payments for higher education.[27]

THE UNDERSIDE OF FREEDOM

The end of tight political control and the opening of borders have brought new social problems to the region and exacerbated existing problems. Thus, drug abuse, crime, prostitution, and AIDS have all increased since 1989. With the end of censorship, social problems such as alcoholism, spouse abuse, rape, and other forms of violence against women that previously were taboo are now subjects of open public discussion. The uncertainty and disruptions that have accompanied the transition have worsened many of these problems.

The end of censorship and increased contacts with the rest of Europe have also resulted in a proliferation of pornography and sex shops. Presented by their advocates as examples of freedom of expression, such developments are seen by traditional groups in these societies as yet another negative aspect of the worst of Western and American popular culture that they see pervading their societies.[28] The activities of organized crime are becoming increasingly evident in these societies as well.

Women have also experienced the impact of ethnic hatred and violence in many of these societies. Women in the former Yugoslav state have felt the consequences of the end of communism most severely. As a result of the violent civil war that accompanied the breakup of the Yugoslav federation many women and children died and thousands of others were forced to leave their homes and become refugees. The impact of war has been greatest in Bosnia, where Muslim Bosnian women suffered most from the ravages of war and the use of rape as a weapon of war. As bearers of the next generation, they were special targets of the policies of "ethnic cleansing," or forced removal of Muslims from areas of Bosnia-Herzegovina by Bosnian Serb troops. Those who remained in their homes faced economic deprivation, if not starvation, and saw their lives and those of their families disrupted. The war also affected Croatian and Serbian women in the areas of conflict.

In addition to the immediate losses of life, the lives of thousands of women in this region were disrupted in fundamental ways. Many struggled daily to try to provide for their families under conditions of siege and near famine. Many women, as well as men, lost the opportunity to study and pursue their careers.

There were several attempts on the part of women in various regions of the former Yugoslav state to organize to stop the war. One of the most important of these was an action organized by women in Zagreb that appealed to women of all national groups.[29] However, the scars of the conflict and its impact on the attitudes of women toward other ethnic groups in the region will remain.

Women have also experienced the effects of renewed ethnic tension in other parts of the region, although with far less serious effect to date. Romany, or Gypsy, women in particular have become targets of the widespread prejudice against Roma in many of these countries.[30] Political leaders' attempts to mobilize citizens around ethnic issues have also affected women in Romania and Slovakia.

CONCLUSION

The end of communist rule created many new opportunities for women. Young, well-educated, urban women are best equipped to take advantage of these changes and benefit from them. For many other women, the shock of moving to the market, the unraveling of the social safety net, and the uncertainty of the transition have created new difficulties.

Due in part to the widespread reaction against the approach to women's issues that prevailed during the communist period, women are seldom found in positions of political power. Those women who hold political office are handicapped in raising issues of particular interest to women by the fact that it is not seen as legitimate to raise such issues. With few exceptions, such as the campaign mounted against the restriction of abortion in Poland, women's groups have not been interested or able to put pressure on political leaders from the outside to attend to the difficulties that the transitions are creating for women. The concentration of political leaders on the issues of "high politics" and the corresponding neglect of local politics and social issues have also contributed to the neglect of issues that are of particular concern to women. As in the communist period, then, women's issues reach the political arena primarily through their connection with other issues that are presumed to be of higher priority. Because women are not well represented, their concerns are often not dealt with by the political system.

It is unlikely that this situation will change in fundamental ways in the near future. Economic austerity and the uncertainty evident in many areas of life are likely to continue for some time to come. Political leaders in this situation are unlikely to see gender equality as a high-priority goal; most women are likely to be too preoccupied with pressing daily issues to be very receptive to efforts to organize them politically.

At the same time, there are several developments that may increase women's willingness to organize on their own behalf. More experience with the workings of a market economy and the more overt discrimination women are facing at work may well mobilize larger groups of women to articulate and defend their interests. The greater exposure of young, well-educated women to feminist ideas through their work for international corporations, travel, and study abroad may also increase support for such activities. Similarly, serious challenges to women's reproductive rights may cause women to band together to fight such restrictions.

Women's current situation also has implications for the success of efforts to re-create democracy and the market economy. Public opinion polls throughout the region indicate that women are somewhat less supportive than men of the move to the market; they are also likely to want the state to retain a larger role in guaranteeing a decent standard of living for all citizens, as well as other social services. Although there were not large gender differences in the Polish elections of 1993, women were somewhat more likely than men to vote for leftist parties that promised to reverse the decline in social welfare that had occurred over the past three years. Many women also supported these parties to protest the greater role of the Church in public life and the restrictive abortion law. In Slovakia, Vladimír Mečiar's Movement for a Democratic Slovakia appears to have garnered support from certain groups of women due to the perception that it would protect women's reproductive rights. These developments raise the possibility, then, that the neglect of women's perspectives and of issues that have a particular impact on women may lead women to support parties that are more receptive to their needs. Unfortunately, in the current context in Central and Eastern Europe, many of these parties are not those that support the move to a market economy or to democracy.

Notes

1. See Sharon L. Wolchik, "Ideology and Equality: The Status of Women in Eastern and Western Europe," in *Comparative Political Studies*, Vol. 13, No. 4 (January 1981), 445–476; and Sharon L. Wolchik, "The Precommunist Legacy, Economic Development, Social Transformation, and Women's Roles in Eastern Europe," in Sharon L. Wolchik and Alfred G. Meyer, eds., *Women, State, and Party in Eastern Europe* (Durham: Duke University Press, 1985), 31–46.

2. See Barbara Jancar, *Women under Communism* (Baltimore: Johns Hopkins University Press, 1978); Alena Heitlinger, *Women and State Socialism: Sex Inequality in the Soviet Union and Czechoslovakia* (Montreal: McGill-Queens University Press, 1979); Sharon L. Wolchik, "The Status of Women in a Socialist Order: Czechoslovakia, 1948–1978," in *Slavic Review*, Vol. 38, No. 4 (December 1979), 583–603; William Moskoff, "Sex Discrimination, Commuting, and the Role of Women in Rumanian Development," in *Slavic Review*, Vol. 37, No. 3 (September 1978), 449–452; Julia Szalai, "Some Aspects of the Changing Situation of Women in Hungary," in *Signs*, Vol. 17, No. 1 (Autumn 1991), 158–161; and Irene Dölling, "Between Hope and Helplessness: Women in the GDR after the 'Turning Point,' " in *Feminist Review*, special issue No. 39 (Autumn 1991), 9.

3. See Sharon L. Wolchik, "Women and Work in Communist and Post-Communist Czechoslovakia," in Hilda Kahne and Janet Giele, eds., *Women's Lives and Women's Work in Modernizing Industrial Countries* (Boulder: Westview, 1993); Jancar, *Women under Communism*, passim; and miscellaneous chapters in section 4 in Wolchik and Meyer, eds., *Women, State, and Party*.

4. See Wolchik, "Status of Women in a Socialist Order," 592–595; Wolchik, "Ideology and Equality," 457–462; Hilda Scott, *Does Socialism Liberate Women?* (Boston: Beacon, 1974), Chap. 1; and Jancar, *Women under Communism*, passim.

5. See Sharon L. Wolchik, "Demography, Political Reform, and Women's Issues in Czechoslovakia," in Margherita Rendel, ed., *Women, Power, and Political Systems* (London: Croom Helm, 1981) for a discussion of this process as manifested in demographic policies in Czechoslovakia. For a discussion as to how this process unfolds during the post-communist period, see Sharon L. Wolchik, "Women's Issues in Czechoslovakia in the Communist and Post-Communist Periods," in Barbara J. Nelson and Najma Chowdhury, eds., *Women and Politics Worldwide* (New Haven: Yale University Press, 1994), 216, 221–222.

6. See Bogdan Mieczkowski, "Social Services for Women and Childcare Facilities in Eastern Europe," in Wolchik and Meyer, eds., *Women, State, and*

Party, 257–269; and Henry David and Robert McIntyre, eds., *Reproductive Behavior: Central and Eastern European Experience* (New York: Springer, 1981), passim.

7. See Heitlinger, *Women and State Socialism*, passim; Scott, *Does Socialism*, passim; and Sharon L. Wolchik, "Elite Strategy toward Women in Czechoslovakia: Liberation or Mobilization?" in *Studies in Comparative Communism*, Vol. 14, No. 2/3 (Summer/Autumn 1981), 123–141.

8. Scott, *Does Socialism*, Chap. 8; Heitlinger, *Women and State*, passim; and Wolchik, "Elite Strategy," 139–141.

9. See Heitlinger, *Women and State*, passim; Scott, *Does Socialism*, passim; and Wolchik, "Elite Strategy," passim.

10. Barbara Jancar, "Women in the Opposition in Poland and Czechoslovakia in the 1970s," in Wolchik and Meyer, eds., *Women, State, and Party*, 168–185.

11. Renata Siemieńska, "Women and Social Movements in Poland," in *Women and Politics*, Vol. 6, No. 4 (Winter 1986), 5–36.

12. For further discussion of these factors, see Sharon L. Wolchik, "Women and the State in Eastern Europe and the Soviet Union," in Sue Ellen Charleton, Jana Everett, and Kathleen Staudt, eds., *Women, the State, and Development* (Albany: State University of New York Press, 1989), 45–65.

13. See Alena Heitlinger, "Pro-natalist Population Policies in Czechoslovakia," in *Population Studies*, Vol. 30, No. 1 (March 1976), 122–136.

14. See Sharon L. Wolchik, "Women's Roles in the Downfall of Communism in Central and Eastern Europe," unpublished paper presented at the Fourth World Congress of Slavic Studies, Harrogate, Great Britain, 1990; and Barbara Einhorn, *Cinderella Goes to Market: Citizenship, Gender, and Women's Movements in Eastern Central Europe* (London: Verso, 1993), passim.

15. Wolchik, "Women's Roles in the Downfall"; and Jiřina Šiklová, "Are Women in Middle and Eastern Europe Conservative?" unpublished manuscript (Prague, 1990).

16. See Sharon L. Wolchik, "Women and the Politics of Transition," paper presented at a conference at the World Institute for Development Research of the United Nations University, Helsinki, Finland, 1991; Ruth Rosen, "Male Democracies, Female Dissidents," in *Tikkun*, Vol. 5, No. 6 (November–December 1990), 11–12, 100–101; and Maria Čermaková and Hana Navarová, "Women and Elections '90," unpublished manuscript (Prague, 1990).

17. See Sharon L. Wolchik, "Women and Politics in Czechoslovakia," unpublished paper presented at the International Research and Exchange Conference (Prague, 1992); and Valerie Moghadam, ed., *Women and Identity Politics* (Boulder: Westview, 1993), passim.

18. Interview with member of the federal parliament in Czechoslovakia (member of the Christian Democratic Party), Prague, June 1991.

19. See Barbara Jancar, "The New Feminism in Yugoslavia," in Pedro Ramet, ed., *Yugoslavia in the 1980s* (Boulder: Westview, 1985).

20. See Reka Pignický, "Why There Is No Feminist Movement in Hungary," unpublished manuscript (Budapest, 1993); Nanette Funk and Magda Mueller, eds., *Gender Politics and Post-Communism: Reflections from Eastern Europe and the Former Soviet Union* (New York: Routledge, 1993); and sources cited in notes 5, 16, and 17. See also Tanya Rennee, ed., *Ana's Land* (Boulder: Westview, 1996).

21. See Wolchik, "Women and the Politics of Transition," passim.

22. Silva Mežnarić, "Gender as an Ethno-Marker: Rape, War, and Identity

Politics in the Former Yugoslavia," in Moghadam, ed., *Women and Identity Politics,* passim.

23. See Wolchik, "Women and the Politics of Transition," passim; and Einhorn, *Cinderella Goes to Market,* passim.

24. See Wolchik, "Women's Issues in Czechoslovakia," 213–214; Wolchik, "Women and the Politics of Transition," passim; and Joanna Regulska, "Transition to Local Democracy: Do Polish Women Have a Chance?" in Marilyn Rueschemeyer, ed., *Women in the Politics of Postcommunist Eastern Europe* (Armonk, N.Y.: M. E. Sharpe, 1994), 47.

25. Einhorn, *Cinderella Goes to Market,* passim; Wolchik, "Women and Work," passim; and Anna Titkow, "Polish Women in Politics: An Introduction to the Status of Women in Poland," in Rueschemeyer, ed., *Women in Politics,* 30–31.

26. See Alena Heitlinger, "The Impact of the Transition from Communism on the Status of Women in the Czech and Slovak Republics," in Funk and Mueller, eds., *Gender Politics,* passim.

27. See Dorothy Rosenberg, "Shock Therapy: GDR Women in Transition from a Socialist Welfare State to a Social Market Economy," in *Signs,* Vol. 17, No. 1 (Autumn 1991), esp. 129–151.

28. See C. W. E. Bigsby, "Europe, America and the Cultural Debate," in C. W. E. Bigsby, ed., *Superculture: American Popular Culture and Europe* (Bowling Green, Ohio: Bowling Green University Popular Press, 1975), 7–8, 10–12, 26–27; Wolfgang Wagner, "The Europeans' Image of America," in Karl Kaiser and Hans-Peter Schwarz, eds., *America and Western Europe: Problems and Prospects* (Lexington, Mass.: D. C. Heath, 1977), 22–25; and John Dean and Jean-Paul Gabilliet, eds., *European Readings of American Popular Culture* (Westport, Conn.: Greenwood, 1996), passim.

29. See Vesna Pusić, "Utopije," in *Erasmus* (Zagreb), No. 6 (April 1994), 31–39; and Vesna Pusić, "Ancien Régime," in *Erasmus,* No. 10 (February 1995), 2–5.

30. For further discussion, see Helsinki Watch, *Struggling for Ethnic Identity: Czechoslovakia's Endangered Gypsies* (New York: Human Rights Watch, 1993); and Zoltan Barany, "Protracted Marginality: The East European Roma," in Sam C. Nolutshungu, ed., *Margins of Insecurity: Minorities in International Security* (Rochester: University of Rochester Press, 1996), 75–98.

12

Religion and Politics in Eastern Europe

PAULA FRANKLIN LYTLE

In early 1949, József Cardinal Mindszenty, archbishop of Esztergom and primate of Hungary, was put on trial on trumped-up charges of antistate subversion and collaboration with foreign security services. He was convicted and, over the protests of Western governments, locked up in a cell, where he remained for seven years, until freed during the tumultuous events of October 1956. He was not alone. Other East European prelates suffered the same fate, whether one speaks of Archbishop Josef Beran of Prague, Archbishop Alojzije Stepinac of Zagreb, or Stefan Cardinal Wyszyński of Warsaw. In each case, the communists combined the imprisonment of leading clerics with the harassment of the clergy, the erection of new tailor-made pseudo-ecclesiastical institutions designed to serve regime ends, and the propagation of an ideology professing that religion had no right to any public role but only the right of existence as "the private affair of the individual." The state structures built by the communists seemed hermetic, solid, and—at least to some—assured of the eternal life to which the Churches themselves laid claim. But when, in 1989, the regimes of Eastern Europe collapsed, crumbling within a matter of weeks, it became clear to all that what the communists had built was no fortress, but only a crystal palace.[1]

Communist hostility to religion was no mere ideological obsession. Quite the contrary. From the very beginning, the communists understood that the Churches posed a unique challenge as value-generating and value-sustaining institutions. Indeed, the rival value systems propounded by the Churches received an especial force from the divine sanction thought to underpin these systems. Thus, to the extent that the communists aspired to complete control over the shaping of society's future development, religion had to be either controlled and manipulated or destroyed outright.

Control took many forms, extending, for example, to efforts to restrict believers' links with coreligionists abroad out of concern for the undermining of state authority. The strategies adopted to implement the policies of control and/or elimination began with initial confiscation and nationalization of Church property. Other methods included establishment of administrative and/or financial control over Churches, secularization of education (including but not limited to encouragement of atheism), creation of parallel organizational structures alongside Church hierarchies, and the development of substitutes for religious rituals and holidays.

The comparative analysis of religion under communist regimes demonstrates the range of responses by institutions to these political pressures and the maintenance of identity over time. These patterns of adaptation to regime pressure also had consequences for the transitions from communism and for post-communist politics. In considering the Church-state relationship in Eastern Europe, the distinction between religion itself and Churches as institutions helps in understanding both the policies toward religion and the responses to them. In her analysis of the relationship between religion and nationalism in this region, Sabrina Ramet employs the following definition for religion which explicitly makes this point. Religion, she urges, may be defined as

> an interrelated set of assumptions about the nature and meaning of human existence, which are thought to have absolute validity, and are actively propagated by an institution or organized sect which locates the legitimacy of those assumptions, and of certain behavioral imperatives derived from them, in the commands of a superior being or group of superior beings, existing in a supernatural realm.[2]

Religion, thus, may be understood as an organizationally controlled pattern of values, symbols, and prescribed behaviors.

PATTERNS OF IDENTITY IN EASTERN EUROPE

The complexity of the Church-state relationship is reinforced by the religious heterogeneity of the region, itself a byproduct of late nation-state formation in Eastern Europe.[3] Poland, Hungary, and Slovakia are predominantly Catholic countries. Prior to World War II, the percentage of the population that was Catholic was about the same in Czechoslovakia

as it was in Poland and Hungary.⁴ After the war, Poland was shorn of
its non-Catholic minorities, while Czechoslovakia and Hungary retained
Protestant minorities. The breakup of Czechoslovakia highlighted this
point, with proportionately more Catholics concentrated in Slovakia.
Yugoslavia included two predominantly Catholic republics—now independent Slovenia and Croatia. Of the other Yugoslav successor states,
Bosnia-Herzegovina has traditionally been divided among Muslims,
Catholics, and Orthodox. Macedonia is Orthodox and Muslim, with
small congregations of Greek-Rite Catholics and Methodists. The remaining successor republics of Yugoslavia, Serbia and Montenegro, are
Orthodox with Muslim minorities. Muslims and Roman Catholics are
the main faiths among the Albanians of Kosovo (a province in Serbia).
Albania is predominantly Muslim with a significant Orthodox minority
(about twenty percent) and a small percentage of Catholics (about 10
percent). Romania is predominantly Orthodox as is Bulgaria. Bulgaria,
however, has a Muslim minority alongside minuscule Catholic and Protestant communities whereas Romania has Roman Catholic, Uniate
(Greek-Rite Catholic), Protestant, and Muslim minorities. The German
Democratic Republic was the only predominantly Protestant country in
the region.

National minorities account for much of the religious diversity in
the region. Members of nations living outside their matrix states (due to
migrations and border changes) have preserved national identity through
their language and religious practices. For example, Hungarians in Romania are generally either Roman Catholic or Protestant. In addition to
the religious minorities mentioned above, Orthodox minorities exist in
Slovakia, Poland, and Hungary.⁵ Orthodox adherents in Poland tend to
be Belarusian, Ukrainian, or Russian, while in Hungary, the Orthodox
community includes Serbs and Romanians as well as a few members of
other nationalities. The April 1991 Yugoslav census recorded that 11.6
percent of the population of Croatia was Serb; most of these are Orthodox. Among the Albanians of Kosovo, most are either Muslims or
Roman Catholics. Bulgaria includes both Slavic converts to Islam and
Turkish Muslims.

The question of religious distribution is further complicated by variations in political saliency within the Orthodox church. Nationality is
often linked to religion in Orthodoxy through the notion of ecclesiastical
autocephaly. Autocephaly in the Orthodox Church refers to its self-gov-
ernance, a status which encompasses concerns ranging from the activities
of Church hierarchy to language use. Granted by one of the ancient patri-
archates of the Orthodox Church, autocephaly implies recognition of na-
tionhood and has at times been associated with the process of state-
building. Thus, the Orthodox Churches in the Balkans have sometimes
figured as the defenders of national identity.⁶

RELIGIOUS POLICY AND REGIME CONSOLIDATION

The consolidation of communist regimes after World War II took place in societies where the religious profiles had been considerably altered by the events of the war. In the Holocaust, the Jewish communities of Eastern Europe were nearly totally destroyed. The numbers of the various minority Churches were also reduced. The Polish Orthodox Church was decimated by both the war itself and the redrawing of frontiers.[7] Similarly, Romania lost some of its Orthodox population. Czechoslovakia lost population through German emigration and territorial changes.[8]

Emigration after World War II further reduced the Jewish population. One estimate placed the number of Jews remaining in Eastern Europe in the mid-1970s as under a quarter million.[9] The institutional presence of Judaism was minimal in the communist states.[10] Regime policy toward Jews was filtered through the foreign policy lens of relations with Israel, usually to the disadvantage of Jews. Anti-Semitism persisted in communist regimes and provided the impetus for much subsequent migration.[11]

Communist religious policy derived both from Marxist-Leninist theory and the practical politics of a hegemonic ideology. Marx considered religious belief as a form of self-alienation in which one ascribes to a benevolent deity the idealized attributes of humanity. His criticism of religion extended to a critique of the conditions which required individuals to engage in these delusions and an assertion of the necessity for revolutionary action to transform their beliefs.[12]

Atheism as a state policy was one component of a more general attempt to negate other sources of values or belief systems. By outlawing religion, the communists believed they could eliminate moral and religious resistance to political ideology. Not surprisingly, the religious policy of communist regimes was closely linked to its nationalities policy,[13] as Marxism posited erasing religious and national differences under communism. The recognition that religious belief often played a powerful role in the maintenance of national identity, however, did not necessarily dictate a unified policy response.

Patterns of policy response tended to be defined and complicated by the character of the given religion in the state rather than by any other factor. Strategies were shaped by the relative status of religions as majority or minority. (These linkages between national identity and religious identity have continued to be apparent in the post-communist era.) Communist regimes were not monolithic, an observation underscored by the circumstances of their collapse. Ramet has identified six factors that determined communist religious policy:

1. size of religious organization in question, 2. the organization's disposition to subordinate itself to political authority and its amenability to infiltration and control by the secret police, 3. the question of allegiance to a foreign authority, 4. the loyalty or disloyalty of the particular body during World War Two, 5. the ethnic configuration of the respective country, and 6. the dominant political culture of the country.[14]

Following from these points, political elites within East European communist states did not necessarily act in concert in their dealings with Churches. Both size and outside contacts could serve as resources for Churches in their interactions with the state. The Vatican was important for Catholic Churches in this respect, although the extent of its role varied. In the GDR, the contacts maintained by the Evangelical-Lutheran Church in the Federal Republic of Germany were crucial. The general tendency toward different policy patterns was further reinforced in the Yugoslav and Soviet cases by federalism, which produced discontinuous religious policies in the republics.[15]

One should not think of the Churches as monolithic. Church hierarchies and clergy were often internally divided on certain issues, even across a number of issues. Some clergy were theologically liberal and politically accommodative toward the communists. Others combined theological liberalism with stiff opposition to communism. Among theological conservatives one could also find diverse orientations toward the communists. Insofar as one could identify diverse orientations also within the political establishments of the communist states, the groundwork was laid for a complex network of Church-state interactions at the factional level.

Only in Albania, however, did party conservatives of the most extreme variant dominate the party apparatus. Here, religion was outlawed as early as 1967. Elsewhere, the communist regimes allowed religious associations to function, albeit always on the condition that they stay out of public debates and eschew all forms of politics.[16]

Insofar as the communists dreamed of creating a "new socialist man" and "new socialist woman," religious identity constituted an obstacle. Socialism was understood to entail atheism. But, at the same time, communists also feared that quite apart from the theological dimension, religious associations had the power to infuse powerful emotions into confessionally associated self-identifications. In certain cases, religious affiliation became associated with national identity, so that one could speak of a linkage of religion and nationalism. The linkage reinforced other opposition currents, contributing something to the construction of other similar alliances.

STRATEGIES AND OBJECTIVES

The strategies used to diminish the Churches' role in post-communist polities can be divided into those targeting the institutional structure and those aimed at influencing individual identification with religious belief systems. There was, however, considerable overlap between these two objectives. The strategies used in the first phase of regime consolidation were also similar to those used to reduce the influence of other societal contenders for power or influence.

Nationalization of Church properties was perhaps the most widely used strategy. In Czechoslovakia, a wave of nationalization of the Catholic Church's schools at all levels occurred in 1945 and again in 1948.[17] In Yugoslavia, Church buildings were seized from Catholic and Orthodox Churches. Hospitals, orphanages, and homes for the elderly were nationalized by the new regimes, removing these traditional functions from the jurisdiction of the Churches.

The charge of collaborationism with the Nazis served as the formal justification for some nationalization of property. Confiscations of Church properties also provided the necessary land for communist governments to undertake agrarian reform programs. In Albania, much of the Church property was confiscated under a law passed in August 1945.[18] Similar laws on agrarian reform were passed with respect to Catholic property in Yugoslavia and triggered a protest from the Church.[19] In Hungary, land reform divided Church property into small plots for redistribution.[20]

Collaborationism was not just a pretext for confiscating property. In Croatia and Slovakia, bishops, priests, and believers were arrested for cooperation with the Nazi puppet regimes. The ex-president of clero-fascist Slovakia, Msgr. Jozef Tiso, was executed. Although in many cases the prosecuted clergy were certainly guilty, such charges also served as a pretext for arresting innocent clergy as well. Show trials of prominent members of the clergy also had a chilling effect on religious practice and left Churches without experienced leadership.

Certain Churches were simply banned. The Uniate (Greek-Rite Catholic) Church in Romania had approximately one and a half million members in 1948, but was proscribed by the state all the same.[21] In the suppression of the Uniate Church, the pattern set in Ukraine of exploiting existing conflicts between Churches was repeated. Despite its relatively small numbers, the Orthodox Church in Czechoslovakia cooperated in the elimination of the Uniate Church.[22] The Orthodox Church also received certain Church buildings, including the monastery at Mukapevo and the cathedral in Uphorod. The Jehovah's Witnesses, Nazarenes, and Christian Scientists were banned in most countries of communist Eastern Europe.

Further institutional control was established through administrative offices responsible for overseeing religious institutions. Yet here one can see differences in how the question of oversight was handled. In Czechoslovakia, this was the State Office of Religious Affairs (within the Minis-

try of Culture) which was created in October 1949.[23] In Bulgaria, the
Orthodox Church was placed under the Ministry of Foreign Affairs. Romania created in 1948 the Ministry of Cults with "unlimited power and
jurisdiction over Church administration and instruction" and required
religious communities to conduct relationships with Churches abroad
through the Ministry of External Affairs.[24] Hungary established the State
Office of Church Affairs somewhat later, in 1951. Later still was the
office administering Church affairs in the GDR, which was not organized
until 1957.[25]

Financial control over the Church was asserted at the same time.
Salaries of clergy were paid by the state in most communist states. While
this arrangement was not unique to the communist era, as a mechanism
it provided a measure of direct control over individuals. Oversight was
also established over religious publications. The extent of censorship varied greatly by state and over time. Commonly, all communications required government approval. The mechanisms of centrally planned
economies could also be used to reduce publications through allocating
only a limited supply of paper for religious publications. The number of
Catholic publications in Poland dropped dramatically through the use of
this mechanism.[26] The nationalization of Church publishing houses and
presses accomplished the same results in Hungary.[27]

One aspect of the nationalization of Church properties—viz., the secularization of religious schools—clearly combined the objectives of
weakening the institutional role with establishing ideological hegemony
of state socialism. In Hungary, 3,150 Catholic schools were nationalized
in 1948. In Poland, the state seized control over Caritas, a Catholic organization which operated nurseries, day-care centers, and boarding
schools as well as other community services.[28] Church-operated elementary and secondary schools were closed in Romania, Yugoslavia, Albania, and Czechoslovakia with no differentiation by religious affiliation.
The attention paid by communist states to education as a crucial aspect
of creating a new society meant that parallel educational systems were
rejected.

The creation of communist-sponsored religious organizations might
seem at first glance to be incompatible with the explicit goals of state
policy. However, the establishment of organizational structures parallel
to those controlled by Church hierarchies was aimed at undermining the
authority of the hierarchy and bringing clergy under more direct supervision of the Communist Party. The formation of such priests' associations
was primarily a tactic used with the Catholic Church, although in Yugoslavia there were Orthodox priests' associations as well. In Yugoslavia,
these organizations were formed in all the republics in the first few years
after the war, and priests were enticed to join by offering members health
insurance, pensions, and other benefits.[29] Membership in Yugoslavia was

relatively high (varying from over 60 percent to over 90 percent by republic) as opposed to a similar organization in Czechoslovakia, Pacem in terris, in which membership was eventually less than 10 percent of the clergy. In Poland, Bolesław Piasecki headed a similar organization, the Pax Association.[30]

Other measures used to control the ranks of the clergy included the closing of theological faculties and seminaries and limiting numbers of students who could enroll. Even in Romania, where the Orthodox Church had reached a modus vivendi with the regime, a number of monasteries lost their original functions and were turned into historical monuments.[31]

Campaigns to encourage atheism in school systems and in public life constituted the principal means of challenging religious belief systems. The Catholic Church was particularly outspoken in its protests against atheism as an element of instruction. In Poland and Hungary, religious instruction remained as an option, but subtle pressures existed to discourage parents from enrolling their children. In Hungary, private religious instruction was illegal, and religious teachers in the schools could be appointed only with governmental consent. These teachers were limited in the contact they could make with students.[32] In Poland, the Ministry of Education required parish priests to submit reports of their religion classes. Available meeting spaces were curtailed by bans. Failure to comply resulted in punitive fines.[33]

Although instruction in atheism was directly intended to counter religious beliefs, the reinterpretation of national history in accordance with Marxist dialectical materialism eliminated the significance of religion in creating national culture. Czech historian Jan Kren refers to the "deformations" in historical scholarship caused by the antireligious bias of the government.[34] The new narratives of state history emphasized elements such as popular uprisings or anti-feudalism as precursors to communism.[35] This invention of tradition by regimes was an attempt to legitimize the existing power relations that were established.[36]

Such efforts did not go unchallenged. The relative strength of the Polish Catholic Church is reflected in its protests against the rewriting of Polish history as educational reform.[37] Pastoral messages addressed this issue, and in a formal protest to the Office of Religious Affairs, Cardinal Wyszyński defended private attempts to address this issue.[38]

Indirect methods existed side by side with the more explicit ideological challenge of instruction in atheism.[39] The substitution of communist ritual for religious ritual has been well documented in the former Soviet Union.[40] These practices took various forms in Eastern Europe, some of which challenged religious calendars through creating alternative, socialist practices.

In Yugoslavia, the substitution of New Year's Day for Christmas began early in the period of consolidation of rule. The campaign to accomplish the shift was explicit in its goals to eliminate Christmas celebrations. Window displays, badges, posters, and appropriate slogans were created for the shift. The propaganda effort included such measures as attempting to ensure that the ministries of trade and forests did not put their products on the market until 26 December. Presents for children persisted as part of the holiday, and the new festival was eventually given the name "Day of Children's Joy."[41]

In addition to engineering a similar shift from Christmas celebrations to New Year's Day, the Bulgarian government encouraged the secularization of saints' days and other rituals, substituting surrogates which celebrated labor and particular professions. In this manner, St. George's Day became Day of the Shepherds, and the ritual content transformed into honoring workers in shepherding cooperatives. Other such transformations were St. Tryphon's Day becoming Day of the Grapekeepers and Grandmother's Day (honoring elderly midwives) becoming the more formal Day of Assistance in Childbirth.[42]

Another form of these practices was the name change campaign in Albania in the late 1970s and early '80s. Although conducted for national reasons as well as antireligious ones, the campaign targeted religious names for elimination.[43] More explicitly national in content were the name change campaigns in Bulgaria in which Muslims in Bulgaria were forced to take Slavic names. At first, the targets of these campaigns were Bulgarian Muslims; the 1984–1985 campaign was the first to include ethnic Turks.

A final example, the youth dedication ceremony (*Jugendweihe*) was developed in the former GDR and reflected a more general tendency of communist parties to emphasize youth mobilization. The specific form of this ceremony, however, was intended to serve as an atheist substitute for confirmation. The ceremony was widely adopted and there was a high degree of compliance.[44]

CHURCH RESPONSES AND THE
DIFFERENCES IN STATE POLICIES

The communists adapted their policies to the specificities of each religious association, modulating their strategies over time. The first phase of regime consolidation involved similar processes of elimination of alternative power bases and contenders, nationalization of property, and the establishment of the educational system. After this consolidation, the specific issues which animated Church-state relations depended more on the Churches themselves than on the regime. Differing degrees and types of accommodation and opposition were reached. Some of the principal features of this process of policy interaction are briefly summarized, illustrating the six factors identified earlier.

One of the strongest national Church organizations in the region was the Roman Catholic Church in Poland. The status of Catholicism as a majority religion with 30 million followers lessened its susceptibility to pressure. On the issue of fascist collaboration, the Church was less vulnerable as the clergy was active in the resistance movement. The significance of the election of Karol Cardinal Wojtyła as Pope John Paul II has been frequently referred to as a crucial factor in the ongoing resistance of the Catholic Church, and he personalized the concern of the Vatican with the circumstances of the Polish Church.[45] Other factors predate his emergence on the political scene and have contributed to the overall profile of institutional strength. The Catholic University of Lublin remained in operation, although operating under a number of governmental limitations aimed at curtailing its activities. By using special collections earmarked for its use, the university was able to meet much of its operating costs and taxes.[46] Finally, the relationship between the Roman Catholic Church and Polish national identity was reasserted by the clergy in response to regime efforts to minimize the role of religion in Polish history.

Like the Polish Catholic Church, the Evangelical-Lutheran Church in the GDR utilized outside contacts to maintain its institutional strength. Due to the anti-Nazi activities of some members of the clergy, the initial measures imposed on the Church between 1945 and 1948 were less stringent than those elsewhere in Eastern Europe.[47] That mediating effect persisted, and the presence of an external ally in the West German Church provided resources and emphasized an all-German identity. Pressure was exerted, however, on the Evangelical-Lutheran Church to break its ties with its sister Church in West Germany, culminating in eventual acquiescence in such a rupture in 1969. The response of the Evangelical-Lutheran Church to state religious policy was perhaps best captured by one of its bishops, Werner Krusche of Magdeburg, who stated in 1976 that his Church sought to occupy "the narrow space between opposition and opportunism."[48] Nevertheless, the stance adopted by the Church was at times interpreted by the ruling Socialist Unity Party (SED) as more confrontational than intended.

In Czechoslovakia, the religious societal profiles were less clear-cut. In contrast to the connections between Polish national identity and Catholicism, Czech national identity and Catholicism exist in greater tension, originating in the experience of the Counter-Reformation in the Czech Lands.[49] Slovak national identity has always maintained a closer connection with the Catholic Church. This division facilitated state efforts to assert control. As mentioned above, through charges of collaborationism against the Catholic Church, the regime sought to undermine the Church but also to discredit Slovak national identity. In addition to the strategies discussed elsewhere of creating divisions in the Catholic Church itself, regime policy deliberately aimed at reinforcing societal divisions by favoring the Czechoslovak (Hussite) Church, the Evangelical Church and the Orthodox Church.[50] The effects of repression in Czechoslovakia seem to have been to force ever more religious activity underground, rather than eliciting a more openly confrontative posture. The steady regime pressure also did not allow for the development of strategies of accommodation as in Hungary.

Hungarian Catholicism does not incorporate any divisions in national identity, but it does not hold the dominant position of the Polish Catholic Church. Approximately a third of religious believers are members of one of the Protestant Churches, divided among the Calvinist Reformed (the largest), the Evangelical-Lutheran, and the Free Churches.[51] The general posture of the Hungarian Lutheran and Catholic Churches can be characterized as having been more accommodating to the regime than many other East European Churches.[52] This policy of accommodation to regime pressure by the Church hierarchy tended to produce splits between the hierarchy and the lower clergy.[53]

Turning to the status of Orthodox Churches in the states in which it has been the majority religion, the co-optation of the Church under communism related more to the reinforcement with national identity. In Bulgaria and Romania, the identification of the Orthodox Church with the respective nation tended to marginalize other confessions (except among minority nationalities). In Bulgaria and Romania, the severe measures taken against the Churches in the period of regime consolidation were combined with the assertion that the Orthodox Churches represented the tradition of the respective peoples. The subsequent developments in both these states includes a later granting of limited sphere of activity which the Church hierarchy feared to jeopardize. Pressure was applied to the Bulgarian Orthodox Church through threatened removal of state subsidies and control over Church appointments.[54] The resulting stance of accommodation by the Church hierarchy meant that the Church advocated the national interests of the regime in exchange for the preservation of an attenuated institutional role.[55]

The relationship of Orthodoxy to Romanian nationality has also helped to preserve the role of that Church in its relation to the regime. Despite the loss of some of their theological faculties, the Orthodox Church was able to preserve much of its seminary training. Religious publications were also maintained.[56] The tolerance of the Orthodox Church may have created a similar split between the younger clergy and the Church hierarchy as in Bulgaria.[57] The status for the Romanian Orthodox Church also came at the expense of other religions in the country.[58]

The relationship between Church and state in multiconfessional Yugoslavia was further complicated by the federal form of the state. Divisions of the state into roughly nation-based republics reflected the attempts of the Yugoslav communists to deal with the national question through political formulae. In the late 1960s, the federal state also decentralized religious policy to the republic level, reinforcing inter-republic differences.

In February 1968, the Central Committee of the League of Communists of Bosnia-Herzegovina issued a resolution recognizing Muslim national identity, and in 1971, the federal census was modified to include Muslim as a nationality.[59] This categorical recognition did not extend, despite pressures by Muslim clergy, to changing the status of the republic of Bosnia-Herzegovina to that of a Muslim republic along the lines of the other republics.[60] In addition, regime support for Macedonian autocephaly was intended to bolster Macedonian national identity against other claims.[61] Concerning the Catholic and Orthodox Churches, their role in the maintenance of Croat and Serb national identity, respectively, necessitated a different policy. After the repressive measures imposed during the period of regime consolidation, more effort was expended in constraint.

As in Yugoslavia, religious policy in multiconfessional Albania was intertwined with nationality policy, but Albanian religious policy aimed at destroying all vestiges of religion through harsh repression of religious identity and efforts to completely dismantle Church institutions. In 1967, a law passed by the Albanian parliament made illegal all displays of religious belief, public and private.[62] Over 2,000 mosques and churches were closed, some destroyed and others converted to secular uses. Churches were transformed into chicken hatcheries, cinemas, grain depots, and stables; religious symbols were removed even from graveyards.[63] In contrast to the other cases, in which religion was given some formal standing as a private matter, the Albanian constitution was amended in 1976 to make constitutional the provisions enacted into law earlier with the following statement:

> The State recognizes no religion whatever and supports atheist propaganda for the purpose of inculcating the scientific-materialist worldview in people.[64]

The revised constitution heralded more suppressive regime measures against religious activity. The approach taken was that of sustained offensive in an effort to reduce possible competing sources of identity. Rather than recognizing and attempting to manage religious and cultural differences, the Albanian government adopted the strategy of elimination, positing that all religious affiliations were products of foreign influence.

The increasingly repressive Albanian regime demonstrates one possible trajectory in which religious policy remained unidimensional. Both Poland and the GDR illustrate the intersection of religious policy and institutions with other issues and factors. The Evangelical-Lutheran Church served as a locus for the independent peace movement in the GDR. Beginning with challenges to the introduction of paramilitary training in the school system in September 1978, the Church expanded to more general mobilization on youth issues and oppositional politics. The Church began to organize "public forums" to discuss this and related concerns (such as conscientious objection), and opposition pacifist cells mushroomed under the Church's protective umbrella. Although the Socialist Unity Party had formed separate peace movements intended to advocate the government's position, the social movement known by its motto "Swords into Plowshares" was loosely affiliated with the Church and grew in strength over the course of the 1980s.[65] The movement as such was without formal organizational structure, but the pressure from below served to influence the stance taken by the Church itself.

The intricate relationship between Solidarity and the Catholic Church requires more space than is possible here. As in the GDR, the Church had become more outspoken in the 1970s, but the advent of Solidarity redirected the debate on the relationship between state and society. Despite providing moral support, the Church hierarchy was wary of the possible severe government response and tended to advocate caution and the avoidance of confrontation.[66] After martial law was declared, activist priests criticized the stance taken by then Archbishop Józef Cardinal Glemp and accused the Church hierarchy of betraying Solidarity for minor concessions by the government.[67] The Church hierarchy tended to play a mediating role between Solidarity and the regime, advocating the cause of the workers but cautious of regime response.

Where factionalization had occurred within the Church, success by the more dissident and/or popular faction forced reassessments of strategy by the Church hierarchy. In Bulgaria, the Committee on Religious Rights, Spiritual Values, and Freedom of Conscience (later the Salvation Christian Union) had issued a list of demands regarding state policy toward religious practice in March 1989. The Holy Synod of the Orthodox Church had protested the formation of the committee, but after Todor Zhivkov's ouster, it adopted these demands as its own.[68]

The strategy of accommodating regime demands maintained certain institutional privileges for less powerful Churches (in Hungary, religious instruction in the schools) that were elsewhere established through greater institutional strength or opposition. Some gains were made at the expense of organizational unity, a unity that was generally reinforced for an oppositional Church. In general, however, resistance and opposition to the measures taken by the regimes grew in the late 1970s and throughout the '80s and should be seen as part of a more general societal trend.

RELIGIOUS ISSUES IN THE TRANSITION
FROM COMMUNISM

A significant dimension of the role of religious institutions in the transition from communism were the coalitions made between those activists engaged in religious resistance with others in opposition to the regimes. Activists in Charter 77 in Czechoslovakia, including Václav Benda, made this element a part of their critique of the state.[69] In Poland, repeated assertions by Church leaders of the right to form independent trade unions supported Solidarity in its struggle for relegalization.[70] Particularly notable in this process was the impetus given to action by the arrest in Timisoara of Hungarian Reformed pastor László Tökés.[71] Demonstrations resulted and the protests spread to Bucharest. The context for these events in December 1989 was Tökés's ongoing protests against the regime's religious policies and the larger East European arena in which Romanians had witnessed the political transformations elsewhere. The intersection of national identity with the issues of opposition can be seen in the July 1989 broadcast by Budapest television of an interview with Tökés in which he denounced the Romanian government's policies against Hungarians in Romania.[72] The incident involving Tökés as a catalyst thus captures the extent to which alliances were formed in regime resistance. This example also highlights the demonstration effects of the events in each country as providing an impetus for political action elsewhere.

In the immediate post-communist period, the abandonment of censorship of religious matters generally preceded structural changes in the institutional status of Churches. Coverage of masses and religious services reappeared on television and radio in countries in which these had been previously banned. New heads of state also attended religious services publicly, and their attendance was covered by the press. In Bulgaria, Petar Mladenov attended a service commemorating national hero Vasil Levski.[73] Croatian President Franjo Tudjman not only attended Mass, but included Franjo Cardinal Kuharić (the Catholic Archbishop of Zagreb) as a key figure in state ceremonies.

With the transitions from communist regimes in Eastern Europe, the status of Churches has altered dramatically. The administrative apparatuses of the old regimes responsible for supervision of religious affairs were dismantled. Some of the earlier forms persisted in new organizations, but the function changed from supervision to coordination.[74] The Romanian National Salvation Front changed the status of the Department of Cults to the Ministry of Cults and removed some of the legal barriers to religious practice. However, the lack of personnel changes in the administrative shift raised concerns that in the Romanian case these changes were superficial.[75] The Croatian constitution made a proviso for a law on religious communities. The law itself had not been enacted by July 1993, although the Commission for Relations with Religious Communities was reestablished at that time.[76]

One exception to the generally benign role of these administrative changes has been the Bulgarian Board of Religious Affairs. Established in 1991 in place of the Committee on the Problems of the Bulgarian Orthodox Church and Religious Cults, the board has been used by reformist politicians and religious activists to challenge the communist-era (and from their viewpoint, politically compromised) religious leadership.[77] The board has challenged both Orthodox and Muslim religious leaders in attempts to revitalize religion there.

The symbolic gestures begun in the transitional period accelerated in the early phase of post-communist rule. Reinstating Church holidays was a relatively painless and popular gesture for new governments to make. The abandonment of the communist ritual calendar has gone hand in hand with the restoration of certain religious holidays as state holidays. Christmas, of course, was a primary focus of restoration, and the difference between the muted, private celebrations in the communist era and the first public celebrations was widely reported by the Western press.

Legislation governing religious freedom also was passed prior to the political transitions as well as early in the first phase. The first of such laws was passed, not surprisingly, in Poland in May 1989. The "Guarantee of Freedom of Conscience and Religion" granted freedom to organize and to spread information. It also permitted Churches to reestablish their institutional framework of schools and hospitals.[78] In Hungary, the Law on Religion of February 1990 guaranteed equal status of Churches and established the terms for official registration.[79] An earlier law had provided formal guarantees of freedom of religion.

Despite the legal guarantees of separation of Church and state established in the constitution-making of the transition period, the establishment of one Church as the official religion of the state became the conscious goal of Church hierarchies in several East European countries after the collapse of communism. The Bulgarian constitution of 1991 grants Orthodoxy this status.[80] Efforts have also been made to establish Catholicism as the state religion of Poland, but they were initially unsuccessful. Ratification of the concordat signed between the Holy See and Poland in July 1993, similar to those signed with Italy and Portugal, was delayed because of the Polish elections. When the concordat was resubmitted to the legislature following the September 1993 elections, the insistence on further delay by the Democratic Left Alliance split its coalition with the Polish Peasant Party.[81] In the parliamentary vote on July 1, 1994, a resolution was passed postponing the ratification of the concordat until after a new constitution is adopted.[82] The Polish Peasant Party advocated quick ratification of the concordat and introduced bills in the Sejm to bring Polish law into line with it. Deputies from the Democratic Left Alliance retreated from the initial demand for renegotiation of the concordat and requested interpretation of certain details.[83]

It is in dealing with issues of restitution of Church property that the euphoria of the transitional period vanished. Reprivatization of state-held property poses difficult legal and logistical issues in post-communist Eastern Europe. Churches are among the many claimants seeking restitution for confiscated and nationalized properties, and Church activists have pressured the states for a resolution of their claims.

As in other areas of the economy, restitution of Church properties has proceeded erratically. It has also provided a test for nascent democratic institutions. After returning 268 monasteries to the Catholic Church, the Czechoslovak Federal Assembly decided that the question of Church property should be handled by special legislation rather than under general privatization.[84] The issue, however, split parliamentary coalition partners in the Czech republic,[85] and had been the subject of executive veto in Slovakia. An initial restitution law by the Slovak parliament was vetoed by President Michal Kovač, and a revised version was passed in October 1993 which omitted the sections he considered unconstitutional because no provision for compensation was made.[86] The original version also did not differentiate between purchased and seized property.[87] Executive veto was also exercised when Serbian president Slobodan Milošević refused to sign into law a bill passed by the Serbian parliament which would have returned property to the Orthodox Church which had been confiscated.[88] In Albania, President Sali Berisha in a speech on 25 December 1995 repatriated all Church properties by decree, but did not provide for the implementation of the policy.[89]

The extent of compensation has proven difficult to resolve, even when it does not trigger conflict between the legislative and executive branches of government. A law signed by Romanian president Ion Iliescu only provided for approximately $18,000 in funds for compensation.[90] In Hungary, opposition parties opposed the draft law on returning Church property and proposed limits for restitution, arguing that the Churches would remain financially dependent on the state. Moreover, a statement by the Hungarian Catholic bishops requested more compensation than allotted by the proposed legislation.[91] By mid-1995, the proposed ten-year transfer (to be accomplished by 2001) was already behind schedule with less than one-quarter of the claims settled. Under the terms of the transfer, the national government paid indemnification either to the relevant Church or religious order or to the local government. State appropriations to meet compensation claims have been insufficient, and this shortfall has also contributed to the delay.[92]

At stake in restitution are several issues. The Churches want to resume their pre-communist institutional functions, particularly schooling.

Control over certain buildings of historic significance has also figured in terms of their symbolic importance. In Prague, St. Vitus Cathedral was declared the property of the Catholic Church through a court ruling.[93] A petition protesting the restitution was, however, signed by approximately 12,000 people, including half of the deputies to Parliament.[94]

Finally, the extent of financial independence from the state is raised by both Church advocates and their opponents. State financing of Churches in Hungary increased exponentially, from 308 million forints in 1990 to 1.1 billion in 1991.[95] With the economies of Eastern Europe in the crisis of transition, the ability of the Churches to support themselves on donations any time in the immediate future is highly doubtful. It seems apparent that some form of state financing will continue, whether it is German-style taxation or direct grants. The issue of financial autonomy has also been raised at a point in which the demands on Church services (including charitable relief) have increased for the same reasons of economic instability.

The educational issue has two aspects—the resumption of Church schooling and the place of religious instruction in state schools. In Hungary, twelve denominational schools reopened in late 1989 and early 1990.[96] However, the above discussed political debate has slowed the pace of restitution there as elsewhere. Unable to keep pace with the growing demand for religious schooling, the Churches submitted priority lists of buildings to government in an attempt to expedite the process.[97] A 1993 law on restitution established a ten-year period in which Churches may request return of confiscated school buildings. A proviso in the law, however, requires that the Church continue to teach in the building. Between 1990 and 1993, the number of students enrolled in Catholic secondary schools grew to 10,000 and in primary schools to 11,000.[98]

In Croatia, Catholic religious instruction was reintroduced in state schools as a subject in fall 1992.[99] An effort to demarcate religious education from regular classes in Slovenia has been established in the form of the necessity of an intervening hour before religious instruction may begin.[100] In April 1992, a policy enacted by the Ministry of Education in Poland expanded the scope of Catholic education in the state schools. Tadeusz Zieliński, the civil rights ombudsman, filed a list of eight objections to the directives with the Constitutional Tribunal. The tribunal asserted that the display of religious symbols in the classroom and prayers before classes did not violate the separation of Church and state. Zieliński's acts in bringing these issues before the tribunal were subjected to intense criticism in the Polish media and by the Catholic Church.[101]

The restoration of Churches as societal institutions has raised the issue of the role of religion in the post-communist state. While guarantees of religious equality and formal Church-state separation have been a feature of new constitutions, many of the Churches in Eastern Europe seek new roles in civil society and politics. A public opinion poll in Hungary in 1991 reflected an acceptance of the role of the Hungarian Churches in "moral and cultural issues" and in "helping to solve social problems" (80 percent), but less support (37 percent) for their role in the political process.[102]

The institutional strength of the Roman Catholic Church in Poland left it well-positioned to advocate its political interests. The Church's agenda included the criminalization of abortion, establishment of Catholicism as the state religion of Poland, restrictions on divorce, and the reintroduction of religious education in public schools.[103] A priority of the Church was to restrict access to abortion.[104] The Polish Senate passed the Unborn Child Protection Bill in 1990 and was praised by the Pope for its stance. The bill provoked a strong debate and was not passed in that form. Subsequently, changes in regulations by the Ministry of Health have required a written application and consultation with four doctors before an abortion can be performed.[105] The changes in administrative regulations effectively limited the number of abortions, and in March 1993, a compromise law was passed which permitted abortion in cases when the mother's health was threatened or the pregnancy was a result of rape or incest.[106]

There are indications, however, that the strong institutional role played by the Polish Catholic Church might produce a reaction against it. In a 1990 opinion poll, 83 percent of the respondents were satisfied with the role of the Church. A year later, this number had dropped to 58 percent expressing satisfaction, with 60 percent agreeing with the statement that the influence of the Church was too great.[107] In the Polish elections of fall 1993, the Democratic Left Alliance had campaigned with the promise (among others) of liberalizing Poland's abortion law, and their dominance in parliament allowed them to achieve some of the liberalization they had proposed. An additional factor has been that the Polish Peasant Party has decided that attitudes on abortion are an individual issue and has suspended party discipline for legislation on abortion, allowing deputies to vote their conscience.[108]

By contrast, the role played by the Evangelical-Lutheran Church in the transition has not translated into strength in the post-communist regime. Part of this is due to German unification; the role of the Church is less significant in the larger arena. However, the Church had expanded its appeal beyond religious issues in the 1980s, mobilizing support on the basis of social issues. In this grassroots mobilization the Church served as an umbrella under which a number of different social issues were addressed. In the post-communist period, this consensus has broken down.

The accommodation achieved in Bulgaria under communist regimes may have hindered the adaptability of Church leadership to the changed circumstances with Church leadership seeking to preserve the status quo ante. The younger, nonsocialist Orthodox and Muslim grassroots have joined to challenge their respective religious leaderships, claiming that the latter have blocked reform. The resultant conflict has perhaps produced more disaffection and widespread religious apathy.[109]

The political spectrum in post-communist regimes is affected by the debate over the role of religion in the state. On the one hand, secular liberals argue for separation of Church and state. On the other, Christian Democrats in Eastern Europe tend to support a more prominent role for the Church as a moral force in politics. The cleavages created and/or manipulated by communist regimes in Eastern Europe have also persisted in altered form. The advent of political pluralism has mapped some of these disputes onto political parties while others remain in the realm of civil society. Furthermore, the alliances created by combined resistance against communist rule have broken down in the normalization of political life.

The divide-and-conquer tactics of the communist regime have produced lingering effects. Communist manipulation of the Uniate/Orthodox conflict has added another dimension of conflict to the issue of restitution. In eastern Slovakia, the Orthodox Church has protested the government's decision to return property of the Uniate Church to the original owners.[110] Although many churches have been returned, debate continues about others. Greek Catholics argue that the original affiliation (prior to confiscation) should determine the status of a church; members of the Orthodox Church counter that the religious practices of the current congregation should be taken into account.[111]

Within the Churches themselves, factionalization persists. The split between grassroots religious organizations and Church hierarchies has persisted, taking on new forms as well. In the former Czechoslovakia, reintegrating underground members of the clergy has posed particular problems for the Catholic Church. Priests who had been secretly ordained but had not received conventional training are now finding their credentials subjected to scrutiny and required to pass theological exams. In addition, some members of the clergy married (sixty priests and four bishops) and were pressured to renounce the priesthood. Eventually a compromise solution was found, however.[112]

Inroads have also been made by neo-Protestant Churches into traditional religious affiliations. Concerns about the growth of "new" religions are particularly marked in states in which the traditional religions had established a modus vivendi with communism. Membership in Protestant Churches is rapidly growing in Bulgaria, perhaps in response to the above-mentioned crisis of Orthodoxy. Politicians have responded to this trend and the appearance of proselytizing religious communities (Unification Church, Hare Krishna, Scientology, Jehovah's Witnesses) by criticizing the state and the Orthodox Church for its failure to respond.[113]

Although already beginning prior to 1989, a similar growth in neo-Protestant Churches has occurred in Romania.[114] In Hungary, the growth of religious sects has been widely covered in the press, and the Hungarian parliament voted in March 1993 to deny four religious sects state subsidies as Churches. A recent legislative proposal has generated fierce debate by specifically targeting sects. Included in its provisions to amend the 1990 Law on Religion are an increase in the number of members required to register as a Church from 100 to 10,000, a requirement that Churches register a summary of their teachings, and an exemption for Churches which have existed in Hungary for more than one hundred years.[115] A similar proposal in Croatia would set the threshold for recognition of religious denominations as high as 30,000 members necessary to register, a provision which has met with Protestant protest.[116] At the other end of the spectrum, voluntary registration in Poland requires only fifteen members, and over one hundred groups have complied. The Council of Ministers' Religious Beliefs Office has suggested that this number be raised to fifty, and other limits could be placed by recognizing only Churches which have been in existence for at least fifty years.[117]

The breakups of Yugoslavia and Czechoslovakia were not without their religious overtones, although neither breakup was motivated by religion. Both dissolutions of multinational states involved the reassertion of national identities which had been muted in the previous state. Secessionism has been associated with increased affirmations of national identity in a variety of arenas. Marked among these manifestations of a heightened sense of national identity are increased religious attendance and a more public role for religion. In the Yugoslav successor states, this phenomenon is not confined to the secessionist states.

In the wars in Croatia and Bosnia-Herzegovina, the intersection of religious and national identity has made religious institutions targets. During the war against Croatia, units of the former Yugoslav National Army and Serb irregulars shelled Catholic churches; in Bosnia-Herzegovina, mosques have been systematically destroyed by Serb forces. The international Muslim community has also organized relief efforts for Bosnia-Herzegovina, and the Organization of the Islamic Conference has also met to discuss the crisis.[118]

The intersection between the institutional role of the Churches and the maintenance of political identities in Eastern Europe had significant consequences for the status of religion under communism. Despite some overall similarities in the initial policies of regime consolidation, policy efforts were shaped by the responses of the Churches themselves and by their institutional resources. The resulting stances varied along a continuum from resistance to accommodation. The experiences of Church-state interaction under communism have also left legacies with which the postcommunist states are now beginning to grapple.

In the post-communist period, Churches confront the state as institutional actors, making demands on the political process and affecting outcomes. Rather than merely the objects of policy, religious organizations have become participants in the process of shaping policy. Yet even as politics of these interactions become normalized, the relationships between Church and state are far from resolved in the new polities.

Notes

1. For an elaborate account of religious-political interactions in the communist era and after, see Sabrina P. Ramet, *Nihil Obstat: Religion, State, and Social Change in East-Central Europe and Russia* (Durham: Duke University Press, 1998).

2. Pedro Ramet [Sabrina Petra Ramet], *Religion and Nationalism in Soviet and East European Politics*, rev. and exp. ed. (Durham: Duke University Press, 1989), 412.

3. The implications of Ottoman religious policy for the successor states are discussed in Charles and Barbara Jelavich, *The Establishment of the Balkan National States: 1804–1920* (Seattle: University of Washington Press, 1977). A companion volume in the same series by Robert A. Kann and Zdeněk V. David, *The Peoples of the Eastern Habsburg Lands, 1526–1918* (Seattle: University of Washington Press, 1984) is invaluable in understanding religious and national diversity in that area.

4. Pedro Ramet [Sabrina Petra Ramet], *Cross and Commissar: The Politics of Religion in Eastern Europe and the USSR* (Bloomington: Indiana University Press, 1987), 56.

5. Suzanne Gwen Hruby, Leslie Laszlo, and Stevan K. Pavlowitch, "Minor Orthodox Churches of Eastern Europe," in Pedro Ramet, ed., *Eastern Christianity and Politics in the Twentieth Century* (Durham: Duke University Press, 1988), 320.

6. Pedro Ramet, "Autocephaly and National Identity," in Ramet, ed., *Eastern Christianity and Politics*, 3–19.

7. Hruby, Laszlo, and Pavlowitch, "Minor Orthodox Churches of Eastern Europe," 326.

8. In Poland and Yugoslavia as well as elsewhere in Eastern Europe, expulsion and emigration of Germans changed the national profile. I am grateful to Sabrina Ramet for bringing to my attention the recent book on this subject by Alfred-Maurice de Zayas, *A Terrible Revenge: The Ethnic Cleansing of the East European Germans, 1944–1950*, John A. Koehler, trans. (New York: St. Martin's, 1994).

9. Joshua Rothenberg, "The Fate of Judaism in the Communist World," in Bogdan R. Bociurkiw and John W. Strong, eds., *Religion and Atheism in the U.S.S.R. and Eastern Europe* (Toronto: University of Toronto Press, 1975), 223.

10. Zvi Gitelman, "Jewish Nationality and Religion in the USSR and Eastern Europe," in Ramet, ed., *Religion and Nationalism*, 73.

11. Ramet, *Cross and Commissar*, 20–22.

12. Robert Tucker, *Philosophy and Myth in Karl Marx* (New York: Cambridge University Press, 1972), 99–100. In his essay, "On the Jewish Question,"

Marx states that "Man emancipates himself politically from religion by expelling it from the sphere of public law to that of private law." See Robert C. Tucker, ed., *The Marx-Engels Reader* (New York: W. W. Norton, 1978), 35.

13. Ramet, *Cross and Commissar*, 38–39.

14. Pedro Ramet, "Interplay of Religious and Nationalities Policy," in Ramet, ed., *Religion and Nationalism*, 9.

15. Ramet, *Cross and Commissar*, 3.

16. Ibid., 5.

17. Sabrina Petra Ramet, "The Catholic Church in Czechoslovakia, 1948–91," in *Studies in Comparative Communism*, Vol. 24, No. 4 (December 1991), 381.

18. Barbara Frey, "Violations of Freedom of Religion in Albania," *Occasional Papers on Religion in Eastern Europe*, Vol. 9, No. 6 (November 1989), 4.

19. Sabrina Petra Ramet, *Balkan Babel: Politics, Culture and Religion in Yugoslavia* (Boulder: Westview, 1992), 125.

20. Leslie László, "The Catholic Church in Hungary," in Pedro Ramet, ed., *Catholicism and Politics in Communist Societies* (Durham: Duke University Press, 1990), 157.

21. Janice Broun, "The Catholic Church in Romania," in Ramet, ed., *Catholicism and Politics*, 207.

22. Ludvik Nemec, "The Czechoslovak Orthodox Church," in Ramet, ed., *Eastern Christianity*, 257–259.

23. Ramet, "The Catholic Church in Czechoslovakia," 378.

24. Broun, "The Catholic Church in Romania," 213.

25. I would like to thank Bob Goeckel for bringing this point to my attention.

26. Vincent C. Chrypinski, "The Catholic Church in Poland, 1944–1989," in Pedro Ramet, ed., *Catholicism and Politics*, 120.

27. László, "The Catholic Church in Hungary," 158.

28. Adam Michnik, *The Church and the Left*, David Ost, trans. (Chicago: University of Chicago Press, 1993), 61.

29. Ramet, *Balkan Babel*, 131.

30. Chrypinski, "The Catholic Church in Poland," 120.

31. Alan Scarfe, "The Romanian Orthodox Church," in Ramet, ed., *Eastern Christianity*, 222–223.

32. Steven Polgar, "A Summary of the Situation of the Hungarian Catholic Church," in *Religion in Communist Lands*, Vol. 12, No. 1 (Spring 1984): 19–21.

33. Michnik, *The Church and the Left*, 76.

34. Jan Kren, "Czech Historiography at a Turning Point," in *East European Politics and Societies*, Vol. 6, No. 2 (Spring 1992), 164.

35. E. M. Simmonds-Duke [Katherine Verdery], "Was the Peasant Uprising a Revolution? The Meaning of a Struggle over the Past," in *East European Politics and Societies*, Vol. 1, No. 2 (Spring 1987): 187–224. Michnik refers to this process in the following terms: "Everything that happened in the past, yet might somehow serve to legitimate the present, is incorporated by the regime and written into a new ideological context." *The Church and the Left*, 160.

36. Eric Hobsbawm, "Introduction: Inventing Traditions," in Eric Hobsbawm and Terence Ranger, *The Invention of Tradition* (Cambridge: Cambridge University Press, 1985), 9.

37. Michnik, *The Church and the Left*, 160–161.

38. Chrypinski, "Church and Nationality in Postwar Poland," in Ramet, ed., *Religion and Nationalism*, 247.

39. The celebration of the Luther Quincentenary in the GDR in 1983 represents another attempt to graft socialist meaning onto events of religious history. Although the celebration was originally organized by the Church, the state set up a parallel committee and sought to redirect the content of it to reflect the perspective of Marxist dialectical materialism and to claim Luther as a kind of forerunner of socialism. See Avran Gordon, "The Luther Quincentenary in the GDR," in *Religion in Communist Lands*, Vol. 12, No. 1 (Spring 1984): 77–85.

40. See Cristel Lane, *The Rites of Rulers: Ritual in Industrial Society: The Soviet Case* (New York: Cambridge University Press, 1981); C.A.P. Binns, "The Changing Face of Power: Revolution and Accommodation in the Development of the Soviet Ceremonial System," in *Man*, Vol. 14, No. 4 and Vol. 15, No. 1; and Richard Stites, *Revolutionary Dreams: Utopian Vision and Experimental Life in the Russian Revolution* (New York: Oxford University Press, 1989).

41. Lydia Sklevický, "The New New Year: Or a Tradition Was Tempered," in *East European Politics and Societies*, Vol. 4, No. 1 (Winter 1990): 4–29.

42. Carol Silverman, "The Politics of Folklore in Bulgaria," in *Anthropological Quarterly*, Vol. 56, No. 2 (April 1983): 58.

43. Frey, "Violations of Freedom of Religion in Albania," 9–10.

44. Sabrina Petra Ramet, "Protestantism in East Germany, 1949–1989: A Summing Up," in Sabrina Petra Ramet, ed., *Protestantism and Politics in Eastern Europe and Russia* (Durham: Duke University Press, 1992), 52.

45. Maryjane Osa, "Resistance, Persistence, and Change: The Transformation of the Catholic Church in Poland," in *East European Politics and Societies*, Vol. 3, No. 2 (Spring 1989): 273–274. See especially footnote 17 for sources on the Vatican's Eastern policy.

46. Chrypinski, "Church and Nationality in Postwar Poland," 249.

47. Ramet, "Protestantism in East Germany," 49.

48. Cited in Ramet, *Cross and Commissar*, 83.

49. Pedro Ramet, "Christianity and National Heritage among the Czechs and the Slovaks," in Ramet, ed., *Religion and Nationalism*, 266–275.

50. Ramet, "The Catholic Church in Czechoslovakia," 385.

51. Joseph Pungur, "Protestantism in Hungary: The Communist Era," in Ramet, ed., *Protestantism and Politics*, 107.

52. Ramet, "Interplay of Religious and Nationalities Policy," 6.

53. László, "The Catholic Church in Hungary," 172.

54. Spas T. Raikin, "The Bulgarian Orthodox Church," in Ramet, ed., *Eastern Christianity*, 173–175.

55. Ibid., 352–377.

56. Scarfe, "The Romanian Orthodox Church," 222–223.

57. Ibid., 229.

58. Trond Gilberg, "Religion and Nationalism in Romania," in Ramet, ed., *Religion and Nationalism*, 348.

59. Sabrina P. Ramet, *Nationalism and Federalism in Yugoslavia, 1962–1991*, 2nd ed. (Bloomington: Indiana University Press, 1992), 177–183. Ramet details the debate which occurred after the census among the republics over the basis for Muslim nationality.

60. Pedro Ramet, "Religion and Nationalism in Yugoslavia," in Ramet, ed., *Religion and Nationalism*, 323–326.

61. Ramet, *Balkan Babel*, 157–159.

62. Nikolaos A. Stavrou, "The Politics of Religious Persecution in Albania," *Religion in Communist Dominated Areas*, Vol. 25, No. 2 (1986): 160–163.

63. Ibid. Also Janice Broun, "The Status of Christianity in Albania," *Jour-

nal of Church and State, Vol. 28, No. 1 (Winter 1986): 54. The Catholic cathedral at Shköder was made into a sports center with a basketball court in the nave and a swimming pool. Its renovation under the new government has taken over two years. Pope John Paul II visited Shköder in April 1993 and was greeted by a crowd of 100,000 people. Patrick Moore, "The Pope Visits Albania," *RFE/RL Daily Report*, 26 April 1993.

64. Quoted in Frey, "Violations of Freedom of Religion in Albania," 8.

65. Ramet, *Cross and Commissar*, 85–94.

66. Chrypinski, "Church and Nationality in Postwar Poland," 255.

67. Tadeusz Kadenacy, "The Church in Poland under Martial Law," in *Religion in Communist Lands*, Vol. 11, No. 2 (Summer 1983), 203–204.

68. Simon Simonov, "Church-State Relations after Zhivkov's Fall," in *Report on Eastern Europe* (27 April 1990), 6.

69. Gale Stokes, *The Walls Came Tumbling Down: The Collapse of Communism in Eastern Europe* (New York: Oxford University Press, 1993), 151.

70. Sabrina Petra Ramet, *Social Currents in Eastern Europe: The Sources and Consequences of the Great Transformation*, 2nd ed. (Durham: Duke University Press, 1995), 191–192.

71. Katherine Verdery and Gail Kligman, "Romania after Ceauşescu: Postcommunist Communism?" in Ivo Banac, ed., *Eastern Europe in Revolution* (Ithaca: Cornell University Press, 1992), 120.

72. Mark Elliot, "Laszlo Tökes, Timisoara, and the Romanian Revolution," in *Occasional Papers on Religion in Eastern Europe*, Vol. 10, No. 5 (October 1990), 24.

73. Ibid., 8.

74. Sabrina Petra Ramet, "The New Church-State Configuration in Eastern Europe," in *East European Politics and Societies*, Vol. 5, No. 2 (Spring 1991): 248.

75. Ibid., 251.

76. *Vjesnik* (Zagreb), 12 July 1993, 2.

77. Kjell Engelbrekt, "Bulgaria's Religious Institutions under Fire," *RFE/RL Research Report* 1:38 (25 September 1992), 60–61.

78. James E. Wood, Jr., "Rising Expectations for Religious Rights in Eastern Europe," in *Journal of Church and State*, Vol. 33, No. 1 (Winter 1991), 4.

79. Edith Oltay, "Religious Sects at Center of Controversy in Hungary," *RFE/RL Research Report* 2:20 (16 July 1993), 37.

80. Engelbrekt, "Bulgaria's Religious Institutions under Fire," 61.

81. Lousia Vinton, "Polish Coalition Divided over Concordat," *RFE/RL Daily Report*, No. 16 (25 January 1994).

82. Vinton, "Polish Sejm Blocks Concordat," *RFE/RL Daily Report*, No. 125 (5 July 1994).

83. Ewa K. Czaczkowska and Eliza Olczyk, "What Divides the Coalition?" *Polish News Bulletin*, 4 April 1996.

84. Peter Martin, "Major Issues Confront the Churches in Czechoslovakia," *RFE/RL Research Report* 1:29 (17 July 1992): 61.

85. Jan Obrman, "Havel Favors Restitution of Jewish Property," *RFE/RL Daily Report*, No. 175 (13 September 1993).

86. Sharon Fisher, "Slovak Parliament Passes Revised Church Restitution Law," *RFE/RL Daily Report*, No. 208 (28 October 1993).

87. Prague CTK (19 October 1993), in FBIS, *Daily Report* (Eastern Europe), 21 October 1993, 12–13. An interesting distinction between Slovak and federal former Czechoslovak laws is that the Slovak law extends the relevant time

frame beyond the 1948 coup (for properties to be considered eligible for restitution) to May 1945 for Catholic properties and September 1938 for Jewish ones.
     88. Gordon N. Bardos, "The Serbian Church against Milošević," *RFE/RL Research Report* 1:31 (31 July 1992): 9.
     89. Fabian Schmidt, "Religious Communities Receive Property Back," *OMRI Daily Digest*, No. 249, Pt. 2, 27 December 1995.
     90. Dan Ionescu, "Romanian President Signs Controversial Restitution Law," *OMRI Daily Digest*, 27 November 1995.
     91. Oltay, "Church-State Relations in the Postcommunist Era," *RFE/RL Research Report* (21 June 1991): 12.
     92. *Heti Vilaggazdasag* (Budapest), 4 March 1995, translated in FBIS, *Daily Report* (Eastern Europe), 14 April 1995, 9.
     93. Jiri Pehe, "Prague Cathedral Declared Church Property," *RFE/RL Daily Report*, No. 239 (20 December 1994). Havel's comments on the restitution marked a difference between "physical and psychological ownership," claiming that "the Czech nation remains the psychological owner."
     94. Steve Kettle, "Czech Deputies Protest Church Transfer," *OMRI Daily Digest*, No. 29, p. 2, 9 February 1995.
     95. Ibid., 10.
     96. Ramet, "The New Church-State Configuration in Eastern Europe," 313.
     97. Oltay, "Church-State Relations in the Postcommunist Era," 11.
     98. *The Irish Times*, 31 August 1993, 9.
     99. *Novi Vjesnik* (Zagreb), 28 September 1992, 4A.
     100. *The Irish Times*, 31 August 1993, 9.
     101. U.S. Department of State, *Poland Human Rights Practices, 1993*, 27 December 1993. Zieliński has also publicly questioned whether the state should pay the salaries of 12,000 religion teachers. See *Chicago Tribune*, 8 November 1992, 23.
     102. Oltay, "Church-State Relations in the Postcommunist Era," 13.
     103. Ramet, "The New Church-State Configuration in Eastern Europe," 318.
     104. The issue of abortion has become a rallying point for the Catholic Church activists in Eastern Europe as well as more generally a reopened social issue. After the compromise position reached during reunification in Germany (which initially preserved access to abortion in the former GDR), restrictions were reimposed when the Federal Constitutional Court declared unconstitutional a June 1992 abortion law. The law had permitted abortion during the first trimester and required counseling. The court's ruling declared that life begins at conception and prevents health insurance plans from paying for abortions unless the mother's life is threatened. It also mandated counseling for women seeking abortions (in a provision similar to the Polish requirement) with the stated objective to dissuade women from abortion. *International Herald Tribune* (Tokyo Edition) 29/30 May 1993, 4. I am grateful to Sabrina Ramet for bringing this to my attention.
     105. Hanna Jankowska, "Abortion, Church and Politics in Poland," in *Feminist Review*, No. 39 (Winter 1991), 177.
     106. Anna Sabbat-Swidlicka, "Church and State in Poland," *RFE/RL Research Report* 2:14 (2 April 1993), 47.
     107. Patrick Michel, "Religious Renewal or Political Deficiency: Religion and Democracy in Central Europe," in *Religion, State and Society*, Vol. 20, Nos. 3 and 4 (1992), 342.

108. Czaczkowska and Olczyk, "What Divides the Coalition?" *Polish News Bulletin*, 4 April 1996.

109. Engelbrekt, "Bulgaria's Religious Institutions under Fire," 60–66.

110. Ramet, "The New Church-State Configuration in Eastern Europe," 314.

111. Martin, "Major Issues Confront the Churches in Czechoslovakia," *RFE/RL Research Report* 1:29 (17 July 1992), 63.

112. Ibid., 64.

113. Engelbrekt, "Bulgaria's Religious Institutions under Fire," 64–65.

114. Earl Pope, "The Role of Religion in the Romanian Revolution," in *Occasional Papers on Religion in Eastern Europe*, Vol. 12, No. 2 (March 1992), 3.

115. Oltay, "Religious Sects at Center of Controversy in Hungary," 37–40.

116. "Croatian Protestants Fear Proposed Law," *Christian Century*, 13–20 September 1995, 841.

117. Grzegorz Kapuscinski and Grzegorz Kasmierczak, "Religious Cults: Oracles of Outrage?" *The Warsaw Voice*, 28 May 1995. The number of members required to register a Church was only fifteen at this point.

118. Patrick Moore, "Islamic Aspects of the Yugoslav Crisis," *RFE/RL Research Report* 1:28 (10 July 1992), 41–42.

13

Eastern European Cinema

HERBERT J. EAGLE

During four decades of communist rule, East European cinema experienced quite different phases in terms of administration of the film industry and the range of themes and styles allowed. From 1948 until the early-to-mid-1950s (what is usually called the Stalinist period), the cinema in most of the countries was strongly centralized, with the official aims and policies of the Communist Party advanced through films subject to strict government control and censorship. A broader range of themes (dealing with personal life, gender issues, national history, philosophy, and religion) and a tolerance for more complex narrative structures and visual style emerged as early as 1954 in Poland and Hungary, by the early 1960s in Czechoslovakia and Yugoslavia, but not until the 1970s in East Germany, Bulgaria, and Romania. Limited critique of contemporary society became possible, as long as it remained in acceptable areas (excessive bureaucracy, individual corruption, Stalinist "errors and distortions") and stayed away from basic tenets of communist belief and the party leaders themselves.

The intensity of admissible critique varied considerably; it was stronger during periods of reform and liberalization (e.g., the ascendance of Władysław Gomułka in Poland in the late 1950s; the period of decentralization and democratization in Yugoslavia in the 1960s; the years leading up to the Prague Spring of 1968 in Czechoslovakia; the reform years of the János Kádár regime in Hungary in the 1970s), much weaker or even nonexistent during periods of Communist Party retrenchment and reaction (Gustáv Husák's "normalization" in Czechoslovakia after the Soviet-led invasion of 1968; the early martial law period under Wojciech Jaruzelski in Poland after 1981). Explicit criticism or exposé of the Communist Party's policies and leaders surfaced only during turbulent political struggles, when the very foundations of strict party control of society were being threatened (the Prague Spring of 1968 in Czechoslovakia; the bid by Solidarity for political power in Poland in 1980–81).

Immediately after World War II, left-wing artists and filmmakers (a number of them members of the prewar avant-garde) had led in rebuilding or founding film industries in all of the countries which the Red Army occupied and which later became communist. For example, Slatan Dudow, who had made the extremely influential proletarian film *Kuhle Wampe* in 1932 (from a script coauthored by Bertolt Brecht), returned to direct films in East Berlin after the war.[1] Prominent members of the interwar Polish avant-garde, including Stanisław Wohl, Jerzy Bossak, and Aleksander Ford, who had pioneered genres of reportage and lyrical documentaries about working people in the late 1930s, returned to Poland.[2] In Czechoslovakia, leftist artistic traditions such as surrealism and Dadaist cabaret satire remained alive for filmmakers even though some of the leading pioneers had emigrated.[3] Eastern Germany (mainly in Berlin), Poland, and Hungary all had extensive prewar film industries which now had to be rebuilt, but skill and talent were available. In Czechoslovakia, the very extensive filmmaking studios at Barrandov in Prague survived the war intact and were among the best equipped on the European continent in 1945. In countries which had very little domestic film production before World War II (Yugoslavia, Bulgaria, and Romania), Soviet help was important in building the industrial base for film production, setting up mechanisms for distribution, and training filmmakers (young filmmakers in these countries not uncommonly went to Moscow or to Prague for their studies).

Film industries were nationalized throughout Eastern Europe, in most cases in 1945; Hungary's industry was the last to be nationalized in 1948. There were important advantages for film in Eastern Europe as a state-supported industry. Major new film academies were established in Berlin, Budapest, Łódź, Belgrade, and Prague within a few years, and somewhat later in Sofia and Bucharest as well. In the established film-producing countries, the academies brought together directors, writers, and cinematographers from the prewar period and put them in a position to train and mentor the next generation. In Bulgaria and Romania, veteran directors were often brought in from the Soviet Union and from Czechoslovakia to teach and to direct productions. Financing was provided for projects which were considered politically, socially, or culturally important and beneficial; thus, filmmakers were not so much captives of the box office as they are in the West. They were considered to be fulfilling a serious mission in society, and they were given greater stylistic leeway than if they had had to cater to popular tastes.

These promising beginnings with respect to the development of individual and national film styles came to a temporary halt with the rather stringent imposition of Soviet-style Socialist Realism by the late 1940s (this was even true in Yugoslavia after the Stalin-Tito rift, only there the style was known as "national realism"). Socialist Realism officially meant "representing reality in its revolutionary development." What this approach to film (as well as to literature, theater, and the visual arts) actually entailed was representing historical and contemporary events as the ruling Communist Party wanted them represented. Thus, films no longer could depict real life or history objectively; they were bound by the idealized party visions of how life had been or should be. The Socialist Realist narrative was also supposed to take the form which had been developed in the Soviet Union. A "positive" hero (who instinctively supported the progressive forces of history, while perhaps lacking a developed communist political "consciousness") battled obstacles in the form of natural forces as well as class enemies. Depending on the plot, these enemies could be German or Fascist soldiers, collaborators, spies, and saboteurs hired by Western governments (so-called "wreckers"), aristocrats or bourgeois bent on retaining or regaining their wealth and power, rich peasants (*kulaks*) who wanted to destroy the collective farms, etc. Irremediable enemies would be defeated, while other characters whose negative actions were perhaps the result of insufficient "consciousness" could be converted and reformed. The positive hero generally required aid from older and more experienced "mentor" figures (members of the Communist Party or even major political leaders in symbolic roles) to discover the correct path to accomplishing his or her goal.

Socialist Realist films were skillfully (and unskillfully!) made by many directors throughout Eastern Europe, intensively from 1949 to 1954 and during many subsequent periods of political reaction. These films can be roughly divided into three generic categories: (1) historical films dealing with the struggle between progressive and regressive forces (e.g., the proletariat struggling against bourgeois factory owners; the peasantry rebelling against the rural aristocracy; indigenous peoples fighting against foreign imperialist oppressors); (2) films about socialist reconstruction, set either in the factory or on the collective farm (in this genre, there was also frequent emphasis on the role of youth in rebuilding the country); (3) World War II films, dealing with communist partisan resistance against the Nazis, the Italian Fascists, domestic neo-Fascist regimes, or those who collaborated with any of these authorities.

The "thaw" in the Soviet Union which followed Stalin's death ultimately meant greater latitude for East European directors, although its effects were felt much more quickly in some countries than in others. Khrushchev's rapprochement with Tito in the spring of 1955 opened the way for advocates of a more humanistic and democratic Yugoslav road to socialism. Like other industries, film production was decentralized in Yugoslavia and the film studios of the six republics and two autonomous regions by the early 1960s had substantial control over their projects and responsibility with regard to profits.[4] In Poland in 1955, the division of the industry into several "Creator's Film Units," each led by a veteran director, also introduced a degree of independence in terms of choice of material. These moves to decentralize decision-making, along with the quite evident public dissatisfaction with Socialist Realist schematism, provided both reasons and opportunities for change.

Film critics in Poland, Czechoslovakia, Yugoslavia, and Hungary began to call for an end to superficiality and ideological simplifications. First in Hungary, Poland, and Yugoslavia, and a few years later in Czechoslovakia (and to a lesser degree in East Germany) films began to change—reflecting greater authenticity in terms of both past events and present situations and greater complexity in portraying character psychology. These transformations were evident both in films about the wartime resistance to the Fascists and in narratives set in the period of "socialist reconstruction." Furthermore, genuine present-day problems began to make their way into the cinema. There was also a considerable expansion in the range of admissible approaches to narrative and style. Such developments began very modestly in Romania as well, where the fledgling industry was still producing fewer than ten films a year, but the interesting new tendencies were almost immediately suppressed by what was then Eastern Europe's most centralized and most orthodox regime.

Change occurred in a differential way, conditioned by the political situation in each country. In the mid-1950s the most dramatic changes were occurring in Polish and in Hungarian film. The rise to power of Gomułka in Poland in 1956 ushered in a period of social critique and cultural liberalization which lasted into the mid-1960s. An analogous movement in Hungary was, however, brought to an abrupt halt with the Revolution of 1956 and its repression by Soviet tanks and troops. The newly installed regime of Kádár had as its principal task the reassertion of communist control over society and this retrenchment affected film considerably. Only in the early 1960s did Hungarian cinema regain the impetus which it had in 1956. Bulgaria also saw only a brief thaw (1956–58) before party leader Todor Zhivkov reasserted a tight state control over the arts. Bulgarian cinema flowered again only in the 1970s. In Czechoslovakia and East Germany, reformist developments were much slower at the outset. There were brief thaws in East Germany in the very early 1960s and again when Erich Honecker first came to power (1971–72), but Socialist Realism remained the governing approach in East German film well into the 1980s.

There was no major challenge to the neo-Stalinist regime of Antonín Novotný in Czechoslovakia until the mid-1960s, but then one of the strongest flowerings in East European cinema brought the "Czech new wave" international attention.[5] Yugoslav "new film" was not far behind, and it was in these two countries that the most daring films were made in the mid-1960s. The Czech new wave ended abruptly with the Soviet-led invasion of August 1968, which put an end to the Prague Spring, but the critical spirit of Yugoslav new film lasted into the early 1970s before it, too, fell victim to Tito's campaign against the country's Marxist humanist philosophers and reformers.[6] Hungarian cinema liberalized again slowly throughout the 1960s and 1970s, whereas in Poland the Gomułka regime's cultural policies became more restrictive. In Romania, Socialist Realist films dominated the scene well into the 1960s, relieved only by ambitious nationalist historical epics and socially innocuous "boulevard" comedies.

During the liberal years of the post-Stalinist 1950s and 1960s in each respective country, films dealing with partisan resistance to the Nazis (as well as with the postwar struggle against anti-communist forces) recognized political and moral ambiguities to a greater extent than previously. Hardship and suffering made a stronger impression than ideological or nationalist posturing, and religious and ethical values were implicitly recognized as crucial. For example, Stole Janković's *Partisan Stories* (Yugoslavia, 1960) brought out the moral anguish and the grief experienced by those who had to kill their own in order to enforce military discipline or ideological directives.[7] In Andrzej Wajda's celebrated Polish films *Kanal* (1957) and *Lotna* (1959), the courage of those Poles who resisted the Germans was secondary to the existential angst of young people facing death.[8] Such films raised the troubling question—what is the value of heroic death when it has no effect on the immediate historical outcomes? Two Bulgarian films exhibited thematic and stylistic affinities with these Polish films: Binka Zhelyazkova and Khristo Ganev's *Partisans* (1958) and Rangel Vulchanov's *On a Small Island* (1957) challenged the idealized image of communist revolutionaries; the former was banned, while the latter barely passed censorship.[9] Aleksandar Petrović's *Three* (Yugoslavia, 1965) focused on the ambiguous morality of the war years. Rather than depicting heroism, patriotism, or devotion to political ideology, Petrović emphasized the fear, suffering, torture, and death which are the actual realities of war.[10]

The persecution of Jews and the complicity of native Fascist movements in their deportation and extermination now also appeared as a theme in a number of films; these films cast a very negative light on ethnic

chauvinism and championed interethnic solidarity. The Slovenian director France Štiglič, in *The Ninth Circle* (Yugoslavia, 1960) told the story
of a young Croatian, Ivo, whose family marries him to a young Jewish
girl, Ruth, in order to save her from deportation. At first, Ivo resents the
restrictions this mock marriage places on him, but, by the end of the film
(after Ruth has been arrested by the Fascist Croatian Ustashe), Ivo sneaks
into the concentration camp and dies in a futile effort to rescue Ruth,
whom he has truly grown to love.[11] In Ján Kádár and Elmar Klos's *Shop
on Main Street* (Czechoslovakia, 1965), set under the Fascist regime in
Slovakia during the Second World War, a handyman, Tono Britko, becomes the "Aryanizator" of a button shop owned by a Jewish widow,
Mrs. Lautmann. Goaded by his status-conscious wife and pressured by
his brother-in-law Markus, head of the Fascist Guardists in the town,
Tono has accepted the position of an expropriator of Jewish property in
the expectation that it will bring him instant wealth. The button business
turns out to be worthless, but Tono's affection and compassion for the
widow grows. Ultimately, however, his fear for his own life prevents him
from acting to save her.

The opportunistic greed, inhumanity, anti-Semitism, and acquiescence to legalized murder which *Shop on Main Street* depicts regrettably
resurfaced in Czechoslovakia during the Stalinist purges of the early
1950s. In the early 1960s, the anti-Zionist campaigns fostered by the
Soviet Union reawakened disturbing memories. Thus, Klos and Kádár's
film made clear allusions to the recent communist past.[12] Other films
worked in this way as well. András Kovács's *Cold Days* (Hungary, 1966)
told the story of the 1942 massacre of thousands of Serbs, Hungarian
Jews, and leftists by Hungarian soldiers in Novi Sad,[13] and Vatroslav
Mimica's *Kaya, I'll Kill You* (1967) pictured, in stark allegorical style,
how the Croatian Fascist *ustashe* murdered their neighbors and destroyed the fabric of civilized life in a once sunny town on the Dalmatian
coast.[14] In Zhelyazkova's *The Attached Balloon* (Bulgaria, 1966) villag-
ers execute a *partisanka* because they are only interested in stealing the
silk material of the military balloon in which she has descended.[15]

Wajda's *Ashes and Diamonds* (Poland, 1956) was much bolder in its
challenge to the official version of history, symbolically criticizing the
entire period of communist rule while ostensibly dealing in an orthodox
way with the postwar struggle for power between communists and anticommunists. Hopes for a democratic and religious Poland are expressed
within the film symbolically, and the film foresees communism's failure
to establish a humane and just society.

Wajda's method of structuring such a broad-based critique is worth
analyzing, because it is one which was mirrored in various ways by other
East European filmmakers. On the day of the German surrender in Europe, two members of the Home Army Resistance (Maciek and Andrzej)

wait in ambush to assassinate the local Communist Party First Secretary Szczuka. By mistake they rather brutally kill two cement factory workers. Maciek (and the Home Army by implication) are portrayed in this sequence as antihuman neo-Fascists, consistent with the prevailing stereotype. When Szczuka and his deputy Podgorski come upon the bodies, the Party First Secretary makes a rather typical "Socialist Realist" speech, urging the workers who have gathered to "fight for what sort of country it's going to be." Szczuka says that he knows "those bullets were meant for me," and stresses his readiness to die for the cause. At the end of the tight narrative, Maciek (by now very ambivalent about his mission because he has fallen in love with Krystyna, the barmaid at the hotel where he has booked a room next to Szczuka's) succeeds in his task, but shortly thereafter is himself gunned down by Polish Security forces. He wanders over a vast field of rubble, finally dying in agony on what might seem to be "the trash heap of history."

Given this seemingly typical narrative featuring a martyred communist hero, however, Wajda proceeds to undercut the genre's usual meanings by carefully crafting structural parallels between the anti-communist Home Army pair and their two principal communist antagonists, using visual symbolism which evokes Polish religious and cultural codes. For example, in one scene Maciek slides a series of filled shot glasses along the hotel bar and then lights them as he recites to Andrzej the names of their fallen Home Army comrades. In the background, a *chanteuse* is singing "The Red Poppies of Montecassino," a song about Polish troops who fought in the British army and perished in large numbers battling the Germans at the battle of Montecassino in Italy. In a later sequence, Szczuka lines up a row of bullets (recovered from the assassination attempt) on his hotel table and reminisces with Podgorski about their comrades who perished in the Spanish Civil War and in the French Resistance (i.e., also fighting the Fascists). On a phonograph in the background we hear the Spanish Civil War song "On the Front at Gandesa," commemorating a battle against the Fascists in which many communists died. Thus, both the Home Army and the communists are paralleled as martyred heroes.

Furthermore, Maciek and Szczuka are surrounded by Christ symbolism. When Maciek finally shoots Szczuka, the latter walks toward him with arms outspread, falling into the embrace of his murderer as he dies. When Maciek is mortally wounded, he hides behind a sheet hanging from a T-shaped laundry post; he reaches his hand around this white "shroud" to discover a bleeding wound in his side, in the place where Christ was speared. Very prominent images associated with fire (flames, candles, matches, smoke, ashes) link the film's title to a stanza by the Polish Romantic poet Cyprian Norwid, a poem which Krystyna and Maciek read from a tombstone during their one-night tryst. This stanza describes the burning of a hemp torch, which consumes itself in a chaotic conflagration; Norwid asks if this tempestuous destruction might lead to the emergence of a diamond, "the morning star of everlasting triumph." Dialogue and imagery are used to establish Krystyna as this "diamond." As both Maciek and Szczuka die at the end of the film, Krystyna is grabbed by the drunken upper-class functionaries of the town (celebrating the end of the war at the bar) and pulled into an off-key Polonaise which Wajda visually transforms into a lugubrious funeral march as a group of political opportunists (the former mayor of the town has already agreed to join the communists in a coalition government) carry the Polish flag into the dawn. The film's ending was a clear comment on the nature of the Poland which was to come—idealists perish and power falls to the corrupt. Wajda's reliance on religious imagery was unusual for its time, but such imagery recurred in Poland and elsewhere during periods of reform and liberalization.[16]

During the late fifties and early sixties, films dealing with topical problems of contemporary life also began to appear. In the context of films about personal life (family relationships, adolescence, courtship, marriage, love affairs) it was possible to raise issues such as lack of housing, other material shortages, bureaucratic red tape, low worker morale, and lack of opportunities for youth.

After 1962, so-called "new film" in Yugoslavia, influenced by Italian neo-realism as well as by the work of a group of Polish documentary filmmakers (whose honest revelations had been characterized by the regime as a "black series" of films), began also to critique social and political aspects of contemporary life with exceptional frankness.[17] In *Days* (1963), Petrović captured the emptiness and sterility of the life of a young working woman; in *The Feather Gatherers* (titled in the West *I Even Met Happy Gypsies*, 1967) he probed the passion, violence, and moral desolation of contemporary Gypsy life. By the end of the decade (a period which the regime's official film commentators dubbed "the black wave") such issues as the political witchhunts of the early 1950s, the abuses of the secret police, and the emptiness of "worker emulation" policies (the creation of so-called "shockworkers") were the topics of films like Žika Pavlović's *Ambush* (1969), Krsto Papić's *Handcuffs* (1969), and Bata Čengić's *Scenes from the Life of Shockworkers* (1972).

In the somewhat more restrictive political environment in Czechoslovakia in the early 1960s, such explicit critique as one finds in the Polish "black series" and in Yugoslav "new film" was still impossible. After getting a number of his satirical filmscripts rejected, Miloš Forman decided to make documentaries which appeared to be simply *cinema verité* (life caught as it is) rather than any attempt to *point* to social problems. Forman's first films, *Competition* (1963) and *If There Were No Music* (1963), dealt with the frustrations felt by young people finding themselves without clear direction and faced by arbitrary authority figures controlling their lives. In his full-length feature films *Black Peter* (1963), *Loves of a Blonde* (1965), and *Fireman's Ball* (1967), Forman and his codirectors Ivan Passer and Jaroslav Papoušek found that ordinary people, asked essentially to play themselves in fictionalized scenarios, *overact* in such a way as to hyperbolize authentic features of their society. Thus, in *Loves of a Blonde*, whose story centers on the betrayal of a young woman, Andula, by a carefree, philandering musician, Mila, Forman was able in a very authentic-looking way to foreground general characteristics of Czech society: the general indifference of bureaucratic planners to the welfare of people (the government places hundreds of young women in dormitories in factory towns, with few young men around); the pathetically inadequate and patronizing attitudes of managers; the widespread male chauvinism in society and in official life; and the general indifference of everyday people to the plight of others. In *Fireman's Ball*, the firemen stage a retirement benefit for their ailing former chief—but they use it as an opportunity to shamelessly ogle girls for a staged beauty contest, while the prizes for a raffle are gradually stolen by guests and firemen alike. When an old man's house burns down because all of the firemen are at this ball, he is offered the now worthless raffle tickets as a gesture of solidarity. Forman's material was not explicitly political, but the portrait of society he painted in his films was not very flattering: people are self-serving, hypocrisy is rampant, and simple human decency is largely absent.

Among the Hungarian films on ostensibly personal subjects some contained clear political commentary as well. István Szabó's *Father* (1966), for example, is about a young boy who attempts to reconstruct, in his imagination, the life of his father based on a few mementoes (glasses, watch, compass, medical instruments) and vague memories. The young boy Takó pictures his father as a partisan who battled the Fascists, as a great surgeon who also hid Jews and saved them from deportation, as the man who succeeded in getting the Budapest trolleys running again after the war, as a charismatic leader whose picture is on posters everywhere—and all of these fantasies are projected for us on the screen. Of course, they are all part of the larger mythology of Socialist Realism which this impressionable young boy has internalized.

In the meantime, in the boy's *real* life, events hardly match these idealized conceptions. Takó is chosen to be a class leader because he has asserted that his father played a major role in the partisan resistance (the fact that we, the audience, know that this partisan "past" is fabricated encourages a very ironic attitude toward the new communist elitism which merely inverted the old hierarchies of class and ideology). Later, Takó defends a friend who is excluded from the Pioneer youth group because of his aristocratic background (there is considerable irony here as well—the boy's father, a count, abandoned his family to poverty and ran off with a German woman at the end of the war). Szabó implies that one must discard the false mythologies of the past, political as well as personal, if society is to develop humanely.

A substantial turn toward everyday life did not manifest itself in East German film until the 1970s, with the films of Łothar Warneke, which dealt with typical surroundings, characters, and problems. The situation faced by young people in an insensitive and restrictive East German society became an acceptable subject only in the 1980s, with such films as Hermann Zschoche's *Island of the Swans*.[18]

Emphasis on philosophical and religious questions continued throughout the 1970s and 1980s, at times tending toward ideological and social criticism of the communist regimes. Zoltán Huszárik's film *Csontváry* (Hungary, 1980) portrayed the Christ-like life of an eccentric nonconformist painter at the turn of the century; the Polish novelist Tadeusz Konwicki's *How Far, How Near* (1972) dealt with the existential *angst* of a man facing death. In Bulgarian film, religious thematics burst on the scene in Todor Dinov and Khristo Khristov's *Iconostasis* (1966, released 1969), a poetic evocation of the life of a woodcarver who, in the depths of despair, draws inspiration from medieval religious frescoes. The film was in many ways reminiscent of *Andrei Rublev* (1964), the masterpiece by the Russian director Andrei Tarkovsky. Like that film, *Iconostasis* used visual poetry to make a powerful statement about art's inspirational role in a stagnant and evil society. Khristov followed this film with *The Last Summer* (1972, released 1974), where he used surreal and fantastic images to convey the thoughts of a villager who refuses to leave his ancestral land even though it is about to be flooded to create a reservoir. Recognition of Bulgaria's religious heritage was strong in the early 1980s, when a number of epic films were made in conjunction with the 1300-year anniversary of the Bulgarian kingdom.[19]

The filmmaker whose oeuvre was largely devoted to philosophical issues over a period of two decades was Poland's Krzysztof Zanussi. His first film, *The Structure of Crystal* (1969), focused on an interaction, almost an extended dialogue, between two men, two scientists—one a confident careerist who is on his way to official success, the other the reclusive friend whom he is visiting, working modestly at a remote meteorological station where he has the time to reflect on life's deeper meanings. Coming to film from a background as a student first of physics and then of philosophy, Zanussi in his later films considered the ways in which science and reason fail to provide answers to life's fundamental questions. There is a strong religious sensibility rooted in Polish Catholicism in his films. His most compelling characters have the qualities of monks, saints, and martyrs—although they often discover these qualities in themselves only in the course of the narratives.[20]

The mid-1960s saw a broadening in permissible styles and structures of a nonrealistic (expressionistic, poetic, surreal, or absurdist) type as well. Philosophical and/or psychological subject matter in particular lent itself to a more abstract or symbolic treatment, as we have seen above. In this regard, Hungary's Miklós Jancsó was a pioneer. His films throughout the 1960s and 1970s focused on political struggle and its psychological and philosophical consequences for individuals and groups. The director's tendency to rely less on dialogue and acting and more on landscape, mise-en-scène, gesture, and choreography accelerated in each subsequent film. *The Round-Up* (1965), for example, was structured around the conflict between rebels loyal to Sándor Rózsa in the abortive Hungarian uprising of 1848 and the Austrian army. The entire film is set in and around a stockade in which a large number of peasants have been rounded up, with the object of forcing the unknown rebels among them to betray themselves. One prisoner, Gajdor, is tortured into confessing, after which he is promised freedom if he can identify other prisoners; even though the authorities realize that Gajdor may be fingering innocent people (for his own reasons), they execute whomever he chooses.

The film elaborates a series of such psychological stratagems. Some prisoners are allowed to battle each other, with the winners, as a reward, being allowed to form a battalion of Rózsa's men within the Austrian army. Rózsa himself is given a full pardon and his men joyously fall out of the ranks of the prisoners to join his unit, singing their revolutionary songs. At this point, the regular army surrounds these men and hoods them for execution. The joy of liberation and the agony of betrayal are captured in this sequence, as in earlier ones, in images of great visual sweep and power. In *The Red and the White* (1967) Jancsó continued to examine historical events using his unique choreographic style, building elaborate tracks on the set so that his camera could move smoothly across large spaces, not only following the action but causing the audience to be caught up in its emotional fervor or frenzy.[21]

Early surrealist films with a progressive "line" involved general condemnation of man's inhumanity to man (and thus could be seen by the authorities to allude to the Fascist past rather than the communist present). Roman Polanski's *Two Men and a Wardrobe* (1958) was about a kindly, gentle pair of men who emerge from the sea with a beautiful wardrobe only to meet with indifference, prejudice, and violence at the hands of the inhabitants of an unnamed city. The film was a broad allegory about the treatment of ideological and ethnic "others" in Eastern Europe. Animated films, particularly those made by Yugoslavia's celebrated Zagreb school, became and remained a treasure-house of allegorical commentary. Personal psychology and memories could also be treated surrealistically, particularly in films based on pre–World War II avant-garde literary works or styles. Thus, Wojciech Has made several films whose visual syntax was highly associative rather than linear; his *Sanatorium under the Hourglass* (Poland, 1974), for example, created a complex visual equivalent to the poetic prose of Bruno Schulz. Jan Němec, in his evocation of unfulfilled desire in *Martyrs of Love* (1966), paid homage to the Czech literary movements of poetism and surrealism. Jaromil Jireš delved into the mysteries of the father-daughter relationship in his adaptation of the Czech Poetist Vitězslav Nezval's *Valerie and Her Week of Wonders* (Czechoslovakia, 1969). Surreal and poetic imagery was to be found in quite a number of Bulgarian films in the early 1970s as well.

During the periods of liberalization, the surreal came increasingly to be used in ways which were inherently subversive to the interests of neo-Stalinist leaders and bureaucrats. This tendency is perhaps best illustrated by film in Czechoslovakia between 1962 and 1968. In 1963, Pavel Jurá-ček and Jan Schmidt made the film *Josef Kilián*, a Kafkaesque tale in which a young man trying to find a certain Josef Kilián runs into countless unreasonable restrictions, procedures, and regulations. The world of corridors and offices through which the young man wanders are a clear allusion to Josef K.'s experiences in Franz Kafka's *The Trial* as well as to the Czechoslovakia of the film's present day. Němec's *About the Party and the Guests* (1966) examined political coercion and acquiescence to it in the manner of the theater of the absurd. By the mid-1960s, the Novotný regime developed a relatively high degree of tolerance for this kind of nonspecific critique, which also inspired the early absurdist plays of Václav Havel.

Later films in Czechoslovakia, like Jiří Menzel's *Closely Watched Trains* (1966) and Věra Chytilová's *Daisies* (1966), did arouse the wrath of the Soviet Union and of the more reactionary elements within the Czechoslovak Communist Party. *Closely Watched Trains* is set during World War II, and its major event is the blowing up of a Nazi ammunitions train. However, the young hero Miloš Hrma (the words in his name suggest "love" and "hymen") who blows up the train not only is not a communist, but he never seems concerned with politics at all. His all-consuming preoccupation is overcoming his problem of premature ejaculation. In fact, sexual fulfillment is what is most important to all of the "positive" characters in the film: the womanizing train dispatcher and casual *partisan* Hubička; the sexy and provocative young telegraphist, Zdenička Svatá; and even the *partisanka* who delivers the bomb, Viktoria Freie ("victory-freedom"). Only the Czech officials who are collaborating with the Nazis, chiefly the stationmaster Lanský and the railway bureaucrat Zedníček, are comically and pathetically repressed. Thematic implications are generated by a dense network of visual matches and puns, most of them sexual. Miloš's railway cap functions, for example, to link the motifs of bureaucratic conformity, heroic action, and sexual success. When Miloš has his hat on (and he wears it very pointedly and inappropriately in certain scenes, such as when he tries unsuccessfully to have sex with his girlfriend Maša), he is conforming to societal expectations—obeying the political regime. When he rebels against authority, when he risks his life, his hat is "off" and its removal is made dramatically visible.[22]

Menzel's *Larks on a Thread* (Czechoslovakia, 1969), also based, like *Closely Watched Trains*, on the prose of Bohumil Hrabal, championed individualism, sexuality, and eccentricity in a more explicitly political way. In this film the irreverent heroes are a collection of political dissidents and unfortunate people framed as perpetrators of what the neo-Stalinist regime considered "economic crimes." Even though they are condemned to forced labor in a junkyard, their spirit is not broken and they ultimately accept an even worse lot (the coal mines) rather than agree to the regime's lies. *Larks on a Thread* was completed only in 1969 (after the Soviet invasion) and was banned. It was not released until after the fall of the communist regime. Absurdism and irony were also used skillfully by the Bulgarian director Georgi Stoyanov in his films of the late 1960s and early 1970s, in particular in his *The Painleve Case* (1969), which mocks military behavior, and in *Birds and Greyhounds* (1969), which creates juxtapositions between regimentation and youth's desire for freedom. Eduard Zakhariev's very successful comedy *The Hare Census* (1973) mocks the functioning of rural officialdom, but invites allegorical application to a larger sphere than just the collective farm.[23] In Romania, only one important film in the tradition of the tragi-comic absurd was made—Lucian Pintilie's *Reconstruction* (1969), in which the reenactment of a tavern brawl by two students (for the benefit of police who continually urge great realism) ultimately results in the death of one of them, as indifferent peasants look on.[24] Further developments in the use of such political allegory were squelched by party leader Nicolae Ceaușescu in 1971.

Freedom and individualism were also opposed to repressive dogmatism in the Yugoslav films of Dušan Makavejev, the most famous and successful of the radical amateur filmmakers who formed Belgrade's film club in the early 1960s. Makavejev pioneered techniques of incorporating actual documentary footage into fiction films. In his *Love Affair or the Case of the Missing Switchboard Operator* (1967), *Innocence Unprotected* (1968), and *W.R.: The Mysteries of the Organism* (1971), Makavejev made this technique the structural basis of his films. In *Love Affair*, the film's fictional "strand" concerns the relationship between Ahmed, a sanitary department official in charge of rat extermination (a Muslim and a loyal communist who was brought up in a state orphanage and the army), and Isabella, an unrestrained, sexually active girl of Hungarian descent, who works as a telephone operator. Into this fictional strand,

Makavejev cuts a great deal of documentary material: lectures by a criminologist and by a self-styled sexologist; clips from Esther Shub's documentary about the Bolshevik Revolution, *The Fall of the Romanovs*; a
pseudo-documentary about rat extermination, which features Ahmed as
participant and narrator (but uses an "authentic" text about the importance of this work).

The story of the love affair, from inception to tragic finale, is intercut
with all of this material. Isabella dies accidentally after a fight with
Ahmed, but the police, guided throughout by the criminologist's point
of view, conclude that Ahmed is her murderer. We see, contrary to the
criminologist's dogmatic certainty, that a human tragedy has resulted
from the collision between Ahmed's rigidity and repressed patterns of
behavior and Isabella's anarchic sense of complete freedom. Many of the
film's documents line up symbolically with Ahmed's attitudes, via clever
visual matches and puns. The film had begun with the following in large
print: "WILL MAN BE REMODELLED? WILL THE NEW MAN PRE-
SERVE CERTAIN OLD ORGANS?" We take the question as referring
to social "organs" and the creation of a new communist "man." However, Makavejev constantly plays on more literal associations through the
film's sexually explicit material. In Shub's documentary, workers who
cut down crosses from the cupolas of churches appear to be castrating
these churches (Ahmed lives in an apartment which resembles one of
these "castrated" cupolas). Through ironic "cuts" and visual rhymes,
Makavejev examines the linked effects of repression on the personal and
political levels. Makavejev continued his brilliant filmic experiments in
Innocence Unprotected and *W.R.*, where he added thematic focus on
ethnic chauvinism and the cult of personality. *Innocence Unprotected*,
which chronicles the making of the first Serbian "talkie" during World
War II, uses the original melodrama, contemporary interviews, and
newsreel footage to make clear the disturbing similarities between Serbian nationalist impulses and their Nazi equivalents. *W.R.* edits filmic
images of Stalin into diverse material, including Wilhelm Reich, thera-
pists who suscribe to his theories and practices, other sexual and political
radicals in the United States, and fictional representatives of Yugoslavia's
supposedly more liberating communism. Makavejev thus explores the
dangers of male chauvinism and the related worship of gurus across a
broad spectrum of cultural and political realities.[25]

Makavejev's films clearly dealt with gender politics as well as the
crisis of communism. In fact, beginning in the 1960s and continuing
through the 1980s a very significant number of films were made in Eastern Europe dealing with the lives of women and with issues of gender
inequality. In *Something Different* (1963), Chytilová exposed the stulti-
fying assumptions of the patriarchy by juxtaposing through alternating
sequences the fictionalized life of a housewife and the actual life of the

gymnast Eva Bosáková. The boredom of the housewife's daily homemaking routine, its failure to lay any claim to larger significance, leads her to distract herself with material things and a romantic fling; Bosáková's regimen is, on its surface, a demanding and not very pleasurable experience, but it produces a stunning aesthetic result. Bosáková's art elevates her life from the mundane, ultimately hedonistic, plane on which the fictional housewife lives.[26]

The poles of female consumption and female creativity also animated Chytilová's cinematic masterpiece *Daisies* (1966). In this film, whose collage style recalls Dadaism, two attractive young women, turned into virtual puppets by their culture, decide that since they are spoiled they will *really* be spoiled. They embark on a series of adventures which poke fun at the assumptions about female existence in a modern patriarchy, while dramatically and physically destroying the typical scenarios and scenery of male desire and power. The young women's binges of seemingly hedonistic destruction are carried out in a highly aestheticized manner, however, aided significantly by the formal experiments of the film's two women creators, Chytilová and set designer Ester Krumbachová. Although in the allegorical narrative the heroines are punished, forced to confess their sins, and symbolically executed by the anonymous agency of patriarchal power (as embodied in clever phallic symbolism), they win our admiration through the dazzling and clever collages they make out of the flotsam and jetsam of male industry, male wealth, and male warfare (there is a strong tendency to conflate the heroines with the film's creators, since they are often seen cutting out images which later appear in the film's collages). *Daisies* and Chytilová's equally surreal *Fruit of Paradise* (1969) led to her banishment from Czech cinema for several years.[27]

Eastern Europe's other major feminist filmmaker, Hungary's Márta Mészáros, made a series of films exploring the situations in which women were finding themselves—among them *Riddance* (1973), *Adoption* (1975), and *Nine Months* (1976).[28] Mészáros's heroines tend to be strong willed, independent, in need of an outlet for their intellectual and creative energies, and at the same time they value intimacy, love, and family. The problem was how to fulfill these various needs in a patriarchal culture which still viewed them primarily as sex objects, housekeepers, and baby machines.

Mészáros's most confrontational presentation of these themes was in the film *Nine Months*. This film begins with a young woman, Juli, going to work in a drab factory where she and other women perform rote tasks under the gaze of male supervisors. One of these, the foreman János, presses his attentions on Juli and quickly proposes marriage. Juli justifiably considers this abrupt offer ridiculous, but she slowly gets involved with János nonetheless. János has traditional expectations. He wants Juli to be the wife and mother in the house which he has just built for his family, and he is very upset to learn that Juli already has a five-year-old son from a previous liaison with a professor. Matters come to a head when Juli becomes pregnant by János; he wants her to stop studying for her exams in horticulture; she refuses. He wants her not to tell his parents about her "bastard" son; she does so anyway. In a fit of temper, János breaks off the relationship, throws Juli out of his house, and forbids her "to have his child." In the final sequences of the film, Juli, though desperately lonely, takes a job as a horticulturalist at a greenhouse and gives birth to her second child alone.

Mészáros uses visual symbolism effectively to reveal underlying realities. On their first date, Juli and János witness a pig being slaughtered with an axe, cut in half from groin to neck; this image becomes a metaphor for the "uses" of women's bodies. János later breaks into Juli's room and rapes her, ripping her nightgown in the same direction as the axe blade had moved earlier ("You treated me like an animal," says Juli). When Juli gives birth at the very end of the film, this image is recalled again. A single shot captures the actress Lili Monori's strained facial expression, her bulging belly, and her vagina as her baby emerges, visually cutting her image in half (Monori consented to having her own child's birth captured on film *before* the fictional narrative itself was filmed). The baby's cries which end the film are testimony to the pain inflicted on women in patriarchal culture, but also to women's strength and courage. The fact that the audience is shocked to realize that they are watching *reality* and not acting underscores the solidarity which Mészáros urges on women, since it is an index of the confidence Monori had in Mészáros—she allowed a very personal moment to become part of a film for mass viewing.[29]

Other filmmakers (male as well as female) devoted films to exploring the lives of women. In *A Hungarian Village* (1974) and *A Commonplace Story* (1975), Judit Elek used a documentary interview style to allow real people in typical situations to speak for themselves. In the process, she revealed the difficult and often tragic circumstances which arise from the collision between traditional expectations for women in a village (marriage for economic rather than romantic reasons, child rearing, menial labor) and the desire of young women to choose their own mates, get an education, and have a significant and useful career. Zsolt Kézdi-Kovács in *When Joseph Returns* (Hungary, 1975), Zanussi in *Balance Sheet* (Poland, 1974), and Khristov in *A Woman at Thirty-Three* (Bulgaria, 1982) also exposed the lack of fulfillment facing women, in the world of work and within marriage. In Georgi Mishev and Lyudmil Kirkov's *Matriarchate* (Bulgaria, 1977), peasant women are left to run the collective farm without their men, who have gone to the city to work in industry; in *Concrete Pastures* (1982) Slovak director Štefán Uher traced the life of an unmarried mother in a remote village.

In the late 1970s, films about the situation of women in society became increasingly important in East Germany as well. In Erwin Stranka's *Sabine Wulff* (1978) the film's heroine is an eighteen-year-old woman just released from reform school. She is a remarkably positive heroine, honest and determined to better her situation. As Sigrun Leonhard writes: "The film transforms Stranka's question of how socialist society reintegrates those individuals who have gone astray into a reflection on how this society deals with creative, energetic individuals whose insistence on their personal visions often proves uncomfortable." Konrad Wolf's *Solo Sunny* (1979) chronicled a nightclub singer's struggles to satisfy her personal need for self-worth, and not only in terms of her professional achievements.[30] The film strongly endorsed the main character's unconventional individualism and, as in Mészáros's films, used an episodic structure and an open ending which provides no easy answers.

Many of the thematic tendencies and trends of the late 1960s continued into the late 1970s and early 1980s: exposés of the errors of the Stalinist past; explorations of religious and philosophical themes; continued emphasis on problems of everyday life, especially as regards young people and women; a more critical attitude toward the shortcomings of socialist society; critique of prevailing morality and social behavior—as well as a broader tolerance of poetic and nonnarrative structure.

Established filmmakers like Menzel and Chytilová in Czechoslovakia, Mészáros and Szabó in Hungary, Zakhariev and Khristov in Bulgaria, and Wajda and Zanussi in Poland constantly pressed to extend the boundaries of the permissible in style and theme. In the late 1970s and early 1980s a group of Yugoslav directors who went to film school at the famous FAMU academy in Prague reinvigorated social criticism with fresh and original styles (they were known collectively as the "Czech School"). Their satirical and sardonic view of contemporary life and its values (or lack of them!) was evident in such films as Goran Paskaljević's *Beach Guard in Winter* (1976), Goran Marković's *Special Education* (1977), Srdjan Karanović's *The Fragrance of Wildflowers* (1978), and Rajko Grlić's *You Only Love Once* (1981).[31] These young directors and others like them in Poland (Feliks Falk, Krzysztof Kieślowski, Agnieszka Holland) and Hungary (Pál Gábor, Péter Gothár) continued their probing social critiques into the late 1980s. Within the parameters of each country's specific political situation, there was a clear tendency toward greater frankness. In addition, more filmmakers were making controversial *political* films in the spirit of the most challenging works of a Wajda or a Makavejev. In the years immediately preceding major political reforms, films emerged which depicted rather directly highly negative aspects of life under communism.

A number of films dealt in particular with the way in which communist ideological training produced distorted human beings. Gábor's *Angi Vera*, set in 1949 at a school for training Communist Party cadres, analyzes the way in which the promise of authoritative approval and career opportunities was used to secure the loyalties of people like the film's heroine, orphaned by the war and badly in need of parental validation. The humane communists who opposed dehumanizing procedures such as "criticism and self-criticism" sessions are expelled, and spartan regimentation and repression of emotions (and sexuality) are the rule. Gábor emphasized the ridiculous excesses of Stalinist puritanical dogmatism and the terrible inhumanity of thought control through the film's lighting patterns. The "beacon of light" which the Communist Party claims to be in the film's rhetoric is transmuted into what seems like an interrogation lamp (in many sequences involving party members) and overexposed whiteness invades scenes where characters conform to this authority (Vera herself, having betrayed her lover and her best friend in the training camp, fades to white at the film's conclusion). Intimacy and humanity occur in this film only in very dark scenes, like those where the students whisper about their romantic escapades in the dormitory darkness.[32] The operation of similar mechanisms in the brainwashing of adolescents at a camp for Young Pioneers in mid-1950s Poland is the subject of Wojciech Marczewski's *Shivers* (1981). Some of the most graphic images of police violence, past and present, were shown in Wajda's *Man of Iron* (1981) and in Ryszard Bugajski's *Interrogation* (1981).

The power of the media, and of course of film in particular, to distort the truth was another prominent theme. Wajda made this a pivotal concern in both *Man of Marble* (1976) and *Man of Iron* (1981). Each film has two main protagonists, one who is part of important historical events (real or fictional), the other a filmmaker or television reporter who is recording those events. In *Man of Marble* the young filmmaker Agnieszka in 1976 is attempting to make a film about Mateusz Birkut, a shock-worker who in 1950 set a record by laying over 30,000 bricks in a single eight-hour shift (both of these characters in Wajda's film are fictional). Among Agnieszka's primary sources of information are films and newsreels she sees about Birkut, films made in the early 1950s: Birkut marries the champion gymnast Hanka Tomczyk (also a construction worker); they move into an apartment which they have built with their own hands, so to speak; Birkut poses for a Socialist Realist statue of himself; he becomes a Worker's Deputy, etc. However, as Agnieszka manages to interview people who knew Birkut, she discovers that much of what she has seen on film is fabrication, events carefully staged and refilmed if necessary to create the "correct" meaning. Agnieszka also learns how the neo-Stalinist government's paranoia and hypocrisy turned Birkut from a genuine, if naive, adherent of communism into a disillusioned political dissident.

A special feature of the film, aside from the story, is Wajda's object lesson in cinematic forgery. The films about Birkut (although they are Wajda's creation for this movie) look like authentic newsreels (*Polska Kronika Filmowa*) of the 1950s and even contain much footage from these newsreels. Through clever editing and matching of film stock, Wajda successfully places his fictional characters into these actual news-reels (for example, when the actual president of Poland in 1950, Bolesław Bierut, visits the construction site at Nowa Huta, he appears to be greeted by Tomczyk, a fictional character—one shot shows Bierut's face and a woman's back as she greets him, the next shows the woman's face—Tomczyk's). Two separate shots, made twenty-five years apart, are made to seem part of one integral event. In many sequences in *Man of Marble*'s "archival" footage, Wajda illustrates in this way the ability of the medium to create its own "reality," falsifying history by mixing the actual and the real in "seamless" fashion. Let the viewer beware!

In *Man of Iron*, which tells the story of the growth of the workers' democratic movement in Poland, Wajda employs an essentially different strategy. Now the mixture of documentary and fiction is acknowledged in the film's opening credits, and Lech Wałęsa, *functioning as a film actor*, plays in some of the film's fabricated sequences in order to create realistic motivation for the plot. Maciek Tomczyk (the son of *Man of Marble*'s Birkut) plays Wałęsa's right-hand man in this film. In the scene of the historic signing of the agreement between the Lenin Shipyard workers and the party, for example, Wałęsa, on his way through the crowded dining hall (the actual location), embraces the fictional Tomczyk; in the very next shot (now from the color newsreel) he makes his way to the podium and signs the agreement. In this way, Wałęsa endorsed the film's version of history by his evident cooperation in the project of making it.[33]

In Yugoslavia, Emir Kusturica's *When Father Was Away on Business* (1985) also uses images to cleverly dramatize the personal consequences of the cult of Tito for a Bosnian Muslim family. The film is narrated by the eight-year-old Malik Malkoć (naively, but with an irony constantly evident to the audience). His uncle Zio, chief of the secret police in the town, has Malik's father Meša arrested for criticizing an anti-Stalin cartoon. Kusturica uses brilliant mise-en-scène to bring out the hypocrisy of this act. In the cartoon, Karl Marx sits at his desk writing *Das Kapital* while an official portrait of Stalin on the wall behind him supposedly gives him inspiration (this cartoon spoofs the Stalin cult and is in accord with Tito's position after the rift with the USSR). When Zio arrests his brother-in-law Meša, similar portraits of Yugoslav party leaders Tito and

Aleksandar Ranković are on the wall *behind him.* Kusturica cleverly shows us that Tito's regime practiced in the extreme the very cult of personality which it condemned in the Soviet Union. The hypocrisy of politics extends to personal life, where it takes the form of marital infidelity. Only the film's children retain any vision of honesty, spirituality, or integrity. Kusturica's film was one of several which treated Yugoslavia's Titoist period with exceptional frankness—in both a tragic mode, as in Lordan Zafranović's *Evening Bells* (1986) and Stole Popov's *Happy New Year, 1949* (1986), and in a satirical vein, as in Božidar Nikolić and Dušan Kovačević's *Balkan Spy* (1984) and in Jovan Ačin's *Dancing on Water* (released in the United States as *Hey, Babu Riba,* 1986).[34]

The opening up of a large number of previously discouraged or forbidden topics in the 1980s was a result of continued pressure by the filmmakers themselves, in some cases led by established directors (e.g., Poland's Wajda) who had attained considerable international prestige and visibility. Progressive forces within the Communist Party of the respective countries began to gain greater influence and were able to pressure the censorship toward a more open policy. As most of these countries sought to increase foreign investment, the political leadership saw the overt repression of ideas in the arts as a potential source of undesirable publicity. The more complex of the dissident films were regarded as less of an internal danger because their principal audience was viewed as being the artistic intelligentsia, not the mass viewer.

Much of the credit for change, however, should go to the individual filmmakers themselves, who continually pressed to make honest and relevant films. The social conscience of this group pressured the industry, which in turn encouraged the tendencies of sympathetic bureaucrats within the cultural apparatus. All of this was in harmony with the increasing frankness in the press and in literature. Filmmakers, like other members of the artistic intelligentsia, functioned as a catalyst, influencing attitudes and helping to prepare the groundwork for the political revolutions of 1989.

The success of those political revolutions, in turn, resulted in tremendous changes within the film industries of Eastern Europe—and not all of these have been beneficial. With the industries now being "privatized," filmmakers have been deprived both of the state's patronage and of their official cultural mission. The influx of the now more popular American films has made it difficult to attract investment for domestic production, since the market for such films has shrunk markedly. Film directors, particularly those who have achieved some measure of international recognition, now seek foreign investment for coproductions in the West, as for example with recent films by Holland (*Europa, Europa; Olivier, Olivier; The Secret Garden; Washington Square*), Kieslowski (*The Double Life of Veronique,* and the film trilogy *Blue, White,* and *Red*) and Szabo (*Colo-*

nel Redl, Meeting Venus). These films have likewise addressed more international or general themes.

Ironically, it is unclear whether the filmmakers of Eastern Europe will be able to function as effectively within their own countries as a force for social critique under the new capitalist production conditions as they did under communist state sponsorship. State support, even when accompanied by some degree of censorship, allowed consideration of serious political and social topics in a relatively direct way. On the other hand, many newly emerging domestic films imitate Hollywood film genres in response to public taste. Willingness to invest in a particular film (on the part of domestic and foreign investors alike) is a function of its perceived box office appeal, as is true in the West. One can speculate that the present phase is only a transitional one, but it makes the shape of filmmaking in Eastern Europe in the future rather difficult to predict.

Notes

1. For a discussion of the role of the German prewar avant-garde in reviving East German cinema, see Mira Liehm and Antonin Liehm, *The Most Important Art: Eastern European Film after 1945* (Berkeley: University of California Press, 1977), 76–84.
2. See Bolesław Michałek and Frank Turaj, *The Modern Cinema of Poland* (Bloomington: Indiana University Press), 1–4.
3. See the fine survey of Czech prewar cinema in Peter Hames, *The Czechoslovak New Wave* (Berkeley: University of California Press, 1985), 11–24.
4. See Daniel Goulding, *Liberated Cinema: The Yugoslav Experience* (Bloomington: Indiana University Press, 1985), 35–43.
5. A detailed treatment of the stylistic and thematic tendencies and major filmmakers of this period can be found in Hames, *The Czechoslovak New Wave*.
6. For a more detailed discussion of Yugoslav "new film," see Goulding, *Liberated Cinema*, 62–84.
7. Ibid., 52–53.
8. These two films are treated in Michałek and Turaj, *The Modern Cinema of Poland*, 132–133, 136–138.
9. See Ronald Holloway, "Bulgaria: The Cinema of Poetics," in Goulding, ed., *Post New Wave Cinema in the Soviet Union and Eastern Europe* (Bloomington: Indiana University Press, 1989), 217–218.
10. Goulding, *Liberated Cinema*, 85–91.
11. Ibid., 49–50.
12. Hames, *The Czechoslovak New Wave*, 49–51.
13. Liehm and Liehm, *The Most Important Art*, 391–392.
14. Goulding, *Liberated Cinema*, 97–101.
15. Liehm and Liehm, *The Most Important Art*, 337.
16. For a more detailed analysis of the film's symbolism, see Herbert Eagle, "Andrzej Wajda: Film Language and the Artist's Truth," *Cross Currents: A Yearbook of Central European Culture* 1 (1982), 339–343.

17. A concise and comprehensive history of "new film" can be found in Goulding, *Liberated Cinema*, 62–84.

18. For an excellent discussion of the films of Warneke and Zschoche, see Sigrun Leonhard, "Testing the Borders: East German Film between Individualism and Social Commitment," in Goulding, ed., *Post New Wave Cinema*, 67–74.

19. On these Bulgarian films, see Holloway, "Bulgaria: The Cinema of Poetics" in Goulding, ed., *Post New Wave Cinema*, 216–224.

20. Michałek and Turaj give a complete survey of Zanussi's films from 1966 to 1984 in *The Modern Cinema of Poland*, 173–195.

21. A complete chapter on Jancsó can be found in Graham Petrie, *History Must Answer to Man: The Contemporary Hungarian Cinema* (Budapest: Corvina Kiado, 1978), 20–105.

22. For a detailed analysis of how objects are used to symbolize repression and freedom in this film, see Eagle, "The Syntagmatic and Paradigmatic Axes in *Closely Watched Trains*," *Film Studies Annual 1977: Part 1 (Explorations in National Cinemas)*, 45–56.

23. See Holloway's article on Bulgarian cinema in Goulding, *Post New Wave Cinema*, 230–234.

24. See Liehm and Liehm, *The Most Important Art*, 354–355.

25. For a more detailed discussion of Makavejev's films, see Eagle, "Yugoslav Marxist Humanism and the Films of Dusan Makavejev," in David Paul, ed., *Politics, Art and Commitment in the East European Cinema* (London: Macmillan, 1983), 131–148.

26. For an extensive discussion of Chytilová's films, see Hames, *The Czechoslovak New Wave*, 206–228.

27. On *Daisies*, see Eagle, "Dada and Structuralism in Chytilová's *Daisies*," *Cross Currents 10* (1991), 223–234.

28. For a fine treatment of these films, see Catherine Portuges, *Screen Memories: The Hungarian Cinema of Márta Mészáros* (Bloomington: Indiana University Press, 1993), 46–58.

29. A more detailed commentary on the film's symbolism can be found in Eagle, "Human Nature and Politics in Contemporary Hungarian Cinema," *Cross Currents 2* (1983), 389–392.

30. For an excellent discussion of East German films dealing with women's lives, see Leonhard's "Testing the Borders," in Goulding, ed., *Post New Wave Cinema*, 60–71.

31. For a discussion of these and other films of Yugoslavia's "Czech School," see Goulding, *Liberated Cinema*, 145–172.

32. For further discussion of *Angi Vera*, see Eagle, "Human Nature and Politics in Contemporary Hungarian Cinema," 401–404.

33. For a more detailed analysis of *Man of Marble* and *Man of Iron*, see Eagle, "Andrzej Wajda: Film Language and the Artist's Truth," *Cross Currents 1* (1982), 343–352.

34. See Goulding, "Yugoslav Film in the Post-Tito Era," in Goulding, ed., *Post New Wave Cinema*, 262.

14

The Economic Challenges of Post-Communist Marketization

ANDREI KUZNETSOV

The most devastating economic crisis ever experienced in Central and Eastern Europe in its postwar history seems to be over now. After five years of market reforms accompanied by hyperinflation, record levels of unemployment, and the most dramatic fall in manufacturing output, the countries of Central and Eastern Europe see their industrial production and GNP figures returning to the level of the last years of communist rule. The politicians who launched reforms early in the 1990s (and their advisers) regard these changes as proof that the approach they had chosen was correct. Paradoxically, they now make their claims as representatives of the opposition, having been ousted from power by a majority vote of the people almost everywhere in the region. Neo-communists have been voted back into office in Poland, Hungary, Bulgaria, Slovakia, and Romania. It is an indication that the reforms, though successful in some respects, have failed to satisfy the majority of the population. Discontent endures because the gains have not been equally spread and living standards and the quality of life are on average below what they used to be.

Back in 1989, experts within and outside the ex-socialist countries were quite unanimous in predicting that the cost of passage to a market economy would involve some temporary deterioration of performance. Some decline in output was even seen as desirable since a considerable part of the output under state socialism had been wasteful.[1] However, the actual scale and persistence of the crisis that followed the initiation of reforms have vastly exceeded earlier expectations. Thus, in 1991, the factual 14 percent decline of GNP in the area overlapped at four levels with the Group of Thirty forecast prepared by an international team of top-quality experts.[2] The problems facing different countries were not absolutely identical. However, a decrease in national output, growing inflation and unemployment, and financial imbalances have been generally recognized as attributes of the initial stage of transition (see Figure 1). As the economic improvement expected from market reforms had been late to materialize, increasing skepticism in respect to the validity of the chosen strategy of change became noticeable by mid-1992. Characteristically, the UN Economic Survey of Europe in 1991–1992 provided the analysis of the economic situation in Eastern and Central Europe with the heading, "Reform results to date: more pain than gain?"

Revitalized optimism occurred in 1993 as data were disclosed, demonstrating that at least one country, Poland, appeared to have turned the corner. In 1994, the economic transformation in Central and Eastern Europe showed further progress. The most striking results have been achieved in such areas as the denationalization of state-owned enterprises, getting budget expenditures under control, and promoting exports. Nonetheless, prudent commentators still talk about years of uncertain transition ahead. Very high inflation persists while the average growth rate of the economy in the former socialist countries remains low at only 1 percent in 1995. Under these circumstances, the impoverishment of the majority of the population has become a major economic and political issue which has led to noticeable social tension in the area. As the social cost of economic reforms remains high, it is not altogether certain that, in the case of quite a few countries, the most difficult stage of transition is behind.

THE CAUSES OF DIFFICULTIES

The erratic development of economic reforms in Central and Eastern Europe has given rise to an extensive stream of publications explaining the difficulties of marketization. They cite a broad variety of reasons for the difficulties, but for the sake of simplicity, they can be grouped into three main categories: (1) the legacy of centrally planned economy and external shocks to it, (2) the cost of systemic change, and (3) the errors and blunders of reformers. Although experts still argue about the relative importance of each factor, it is a widely shared perception that the successes and failures of the process of change have been conditioned by the interaction of factors rather than by any single factor alone.

The legacy of centrally planned economy and external shocks
Long before the cascade of democratic revolutions opened the way for radical political and economic reforms, the European socialist countries

experienced a protracted economic crisis. It existed mainly in repressed and hidden forms owing to overwhelming state control. Its visible features were declining rates of economic growth, wasteful usage of resources including labor and capital, a widening technological gap with more advanced countries, persistent shortages on the supply side, monetary overhang, and serious financial imbalances. Experts on Soviet-style economies were aware of these deficiencies, but their actual scale had not been clear until the change of political regimes and the elimination of central planning had helped to establish the real picture. The economies of Romania, Bulgaria, Eastern Germany, Poland, and to a lesser degree Czechoslovakia suffered from serious structural problems, and remained badly managed, uncompetitive, and unresponsive to technological innovation. Even more devastating was news of the advanced state of environmental pollution in the area. In Eastern Germany, for example, the environment had become a national catastrophe.

While the exact size of macroeconomic disbalances inherited by the region's pluralist regimes from their predecessors is debatable, it is clear that the imbalances alone were serious enough to provoke an economic crisis. Repressed inflation in Poland became hyperinflation under the last communist government, while in Romania stagnation and decay became evident in the early 1980s. However, some experts point out that the economic squeeze in Central and Eastern Europe in the 1990s would not have been so pronounced but for some important external shocks.

The ruinous impact of the elimination of a trade turnover between the European ex-socialist countries must be placed first in sequence of such shocks. For example, intra-COMECON trade was responsible for 40–50 percent of industrial exports. As the COMECON collapsed at the beginning of the 1990s, the region's producers, due to the low competitiveness of their goods and to regulative barriers imposed by the European Economic Community, failed to increase their quotas in Western markets quickly enough to compensate for the shrinkage in traditional markets. Another consequence of the collapse of the COMECON was the erosion of the capital base of the ex-socialist countries which for years had depended on implicit trade subsidies from the Soviet Union. Partially for political reasons and partially owing to the inefficiency of the price mechanism, the Soviet Union sold its energy and nonfood raw materials to Eastern Europe at prices below prevailing world market prices and bought manufactured goods from Eastern Europe at prices above world prices. Experts estimate the sum of transfer in billions of dollars.[3] Finally, the Gulf War in early 1991, which served to disrupt trade with Arab countries and inflate world oil prices, further aggravated the economic situation in the region's countries, all of which depended heavily on imported oil.

The cost of systematic change

Scholars, including Jan Winiecki, Mario Nuti, and Daniel Linotte, stress that serious economic difficulties in the ex-socialist countries were inevitable under the conditions following the introduction of fundamental systemic and structural changes conducive to the development of a market economy. Indeed, marketization in Central and Eastern Europe may be accurately described as a transition from one logic of development and a related set of priorities and ruling principles, institutions, and regulatory mechanisms to a completely different, if not an opposite, logic, determined by its own priorities, institutions, and regulatory mechanisms.

Such a profound qualitative change could not but have provoked some drastic adjustments. Under socialism, the authorities were committed to full employment, stable prices, and the priority development of heavy industry, producing equipment, intermediates, and defense-related output. These and other objectives were sought through administrative measures while prices, interest rates, profit maximization, and cost accounting did not play a significant role. It was typical of the system that the price of a product would not compensate its real cost, making enormous state subsidies inevitable. Constantly increasing share of capacities would be developed to produce machines and materials for the purpose of producing other machines and materials rather than to supply products for personal consumption, for the needs of the social infrastructure, or for exports. The introduction of a market mechanism has induced a radical revision of priorities and stimuli. As a result, about 25 percent of the region's enterprises became "value substractors" in terms of world prices and needed to be closed; indeed, the development of some industries was ill-conceived and some manufactured products were of such low quality that they were a complete waste of limited resources. Hence, a retreat in production, redundancies, and the severing of traditional integrational links.

What makes the systemic change even more dramatic is the development that Nuti has called a "transitional economic non-system." The term designates the period when many institutions and practices necessary for a full-scale market economy are missing (e.g., independent banks, stock markets, regulatory agencies) while the inertia of central planning days is strong, entailing the persistence of structures and rigidities unsuitable for market signals to emerge or to be received and responded to effectively. This precarious situation increases enormously the cost of transition, especially if policy-makers fail to come up with adequate responses.

The errors and blunders of reformers

The complexity of the process of reforms and its so-far-ambiguous results have provoked an extensive criticism of the concepts and policies of reforms. To some extent critics link the difficulties of transition to the policies applied and, respectively, tie their expectations with changes or improvements in these policies. Ideological extremists deny altogether the necessity of a market transition, although the critics may be divided into two camps.

The first camp comprises those who call into question the conceptual principles of ongoing reforms, often labeled "shock therapy" or "the monetarist approach," on the grounds that they only reflect poorly the specificities of the ex-socialist economies. This type of criticism is most vocal in the ex–Soviet Union,[4] but has also surfaced in Eastern Europe (Grzegorz Kolodko) and in the West (Peter Gowan, David Kotz, and John Ross). One of the foremost experts on Polish economic transition, Kolodko, for example, advocated a sixteen-point "new economic policy" for Poland based on the idea of an interventionist, rather than liberal, approach to reforms. The problem with radical critics often is that, while being strong in pointing out the defects of the reform programs under implementation, they fail to be convincing when outlining their own propositions. As for their opponents, they allude to facts from countries in transition and to modern economic and political theory. However, the process of change is exposed to the influence of so many factors that available data can usually be interpreted in more than one way.

The second group embraces those who, while supporting the essential elements of the currently implemented concept of reform, have concerns as to how they are put into action. As there is hardly anyone unconditionally happy with the way the reforms have been developing in Eastern Europe, this is undoubtedly the most populous group. The criticism and advice it provides is usually based on liberal philosophy dominating mainstream economic thinking of late. The debate within this group of scholars has heavily influenced the configuration of economic reforms in the post-communist countries.

STAGES OF TRANSITION

The essence of marketization is the dismantlement of Soviet-style economic mechanisms imposed on Central and East European countries after the Second World War, and the restoration of a capitalist economy, with dominant private property and market-based optimization. This task has proved to be extremely challenging owing to two factors already mentioned, namely the precarious state of the European ex-socialist economies and the difference between the two economic models. Problems involved are not only numerous but also they are interlinked in a very intricate manner. They range from technical deficiencies, such as lack of functional capital markets and credit systems required for efficient capital formation and resource allocation, to a more general issue of changing prevailing behavioral patterns at all levels of society. They involve finding the most efficient way to create jobs with high value-added and wealth-generating capacities, improving labor productivity, and providing sustained technological innovation in order to increase national competitiveness in the face of the growing dependence of the post-communist economies on the international markets.

What made a systemic change of European Soviet-style economies look very much like a chicken-and-egg dilemma was the fact that the reformers could not rely on any of the existing economic factors as the point of rest. Their task was to redesign this mechanism but at the same time to avoid a complete economic breakdown following its progressive decomposition. Under these circumstances the choice of the targets, sequencing of specific policies, and the speed of reform have acquired critical importance.

Although the economies in the countries of Central and Eastern Europe basically imitated a Soviet pattern, the incipient economic conditions for marketization were not equal across the region. The general state of the national economy, the relative share of state-owned enterprises in national output, production efficiency, levels of external debt, dependence on intra-COMECON trade or, conversely, the degree of openness to Western markets were different from country to country. Besides, two countries, Hungary and Yugoslavia, had made some advance toward a decentralized open economy while others stuck to a conventional rigid central planning model. National peculiarities and, in particular, political constraints, which were different in the different countries of the region, conditioned short-term policy choice and to a lesser degree long-term strategies. At the same time, there appears to have been no great difference in opinions among economists and policy-makers in the countries concerned or among those abroad as regards the essential stages of transition toward a market-type economy.

The first stage is *economic stabilization*, which implies the initial adaptation of the existing economic mechanism (prices, credit, money supply, wages) to the standards of the capitalist system. Macroeconomic stabilization is designed to eliminate the most dangerous financial imbalances inherited from central planning (monetary overhang and fiscal deficit) and to kick-start the price mechanism, which under the market economy facilitates an optimal allocation of resources. It is also seen as an important step toward decentralization.

The second element or stage is a radical *institutional reform* aimed essentially at the restoration of private property and economic competition. Privatization in the broadest sense is meant to eliminate the indeterminacy of capital ownership in the former socialist state, which was one of the main reasons for the inefficient employment of capital assets in the period of command economy. Privatization is also expected to induce

changes in entrepreneurial behavior and to make enterprises profit-moti-
vated (under central planning they were output maximizers). Microeconomic reform makes the creation of a market relationship between the
owner of the capital and the manager of the firm conducive to better
performance. This presupposes the adoption of new laws (bankruptcy
legislation, for example) and the creation of an appropriate institutional
environment, including investment banks, capital exchanges, auditing
and consulting firms, which was nonexistent under socialism. Another
important issue was to put an end to the monopolistic position of producers in the market by the direct breakup of large enterprises and to
encourage new business formation.

The third element, which is tightly linked to the second, is *capacity
restructuring*, or the shift of capital and labor from primary and machine-
building industries to those producing consumer goods and high-tech
products, and from industrial production to services. Integrating the ex-
socialist economies in the international market is normally regarded as
an important component of such a restructuring.

TWO APPROACHES TO REFORM

At the start of the transformation period, all the Central and East European countries, with the exception of the ex-GDR which became a special
case following accelerated unification with Federal Germany, faced a difficult choice as to adjustment strategy. It could be either a "big-bang,"
"shock therapy"–type approach, as in Poland, or a more gradual one, as
in Hungary. Both approaches had merits and drawbacks. As it happened,
it was the Polish model of macroeconomic adjustment which has set, by
and large, the pattern for Eastern and Central Europe.[5]

The terms "shock therapy" and "big bang" are quite ambiguous and
sometimes are used loosely. They properly refer to any programs having
as their conspicuous feature a drastic and massive change in key economic parameters.[6] However, it is important to keep in mind that Polish-
style reform programs suggest different tactics at different stages of transition. Leczek Balcerówicz, who as Poland's finance minister supervised
the country's stabilization program until his resignation in December
1991, defined shock treatment as entailing "fundamental shifts in macroeconomic policy using such instruments as exchange rate, interest rates,
and budgetary measures," adding that it needed "especially fast action."[7]
At the same time, institutional reform was conceived as taking a long
time to prepare a necessary and legal organizational framework and re-
train administrators. Thus, the contrast between the two approaches in
question was not so sharp as it might seem and mainly concerned the
speed of stabilization.

The main (theoretical) arguments for gradualism were (a) reforms may be better prepared and (b) cautious reforms would be easier for the population to accept, thus diminishing the threat of a negative social reaction to transition. For some time it seemed that Hungarian experience gave enough justification for these beliefs. In Hungary a reform process was unleashed formally in 1968 with the inauguration of what was labeled the New Economic Mechanism. The process was very slow and inconsistent, and many criticized it as a bureaucratic exercise. Nonetheless, by the end of the 1980s, the Hungarians succeeded in being the first among the socialist countries to establish a relatively competitive and pluralistic economic mechanism similar to a market one, and to create generally better macroeconomic conditions.[8] Also the political system showed stability. Hungary's dedication to market and democratic reforms was recognized by foreign capital. The country has attracted over half of all foreign investment in Eastern Europe. However, the major success failed to come. Industrial production was falling all through the 1990s while unemployment and inflation were on the rise. As a result, the government was forced to contemplate speeding up the economic reforms, whereas the ruling Democratic Forum had to face disappointed voters (according to opinion polls, at the beginning of 1993 only 8 percent of Hungarians supported the government[9]) and a groundswell of nationalist extremism. Consequently, Hungary lost much of its credibility as a success story.

Although other countries in the region have not followed the Hungarian approach to reform, it was probably not because the results were discouraging but because the situation in which they found themselves prompted a different choice. A broad range of economic, political, and social factors were responsible for this. Most importantly, external and internal imbalances in these countries in 1990 were far more critical than in Hungary in 1968. A monetary overhang provoked devastating hyperinflation, growing shortages, and a deteriorating foreign debt position. The challenge was enormous and the response also had to be unprecedented. It was found, paradoxically, in the form of a standard IMF stabilization program similar to stabilization programs this international agency had already sponsored in Latin American countries and elsewhere, including monetary and fiscal restrictions, price liberalization, and the devaluation of domestic currencies and wage guidelines.[10] What made the difference was the speed and the fact that such a program was for the first time applied to noncapitalist economies in the absence of comprehensive banking systems, monetary, labor, and capital markets, and mature tax systems.

It was a bold choice. IMF stabilization programs were often criticized as imposing heavy social costs, especially on the poorest strata of the population, and undermining the long-term developing capacities of the countries.[11] Unlike in most developing countries, however, in Central and

Eastern Europe, stabilization took place in quite a unique situation of social accord as a new polity was enjoying an enormous credit of public confidence, permitting reformers to realize some very daring projects. The following example speaks for itself.[12] Under a communist government in Poland, a modest real wage cut of 8 percent, in early 1988, was followed by successful street protests and overcompensatory wage claims, ending up with the resignation of Zdzislaw Sadowski, the minister responsible for the initiative, and an increase in the (statistical) real wage of 17 percent; in 1990, Balcerówicz achieved, without challenge, a real wage cut of one-third.

Predictably, the consequences of "shock"-type stabilization could not be straightforward. First, stabilization was based on measures of economic atrocity, including those affecting broad groups of the population. Second, a lag between reforms and stabilization results was inevitable. Nonetheless, Polish experience has demonstrated that "shock therapy" was effective in eliminating pervasive shortages of consumer goods, thus putting an end to one of the most notorious defects of Soviet-type economies.

After three years of reforms, one could see that the three East European countries with the best results, or rather, with the best prospects for recovery in the future, included both Poland and Hungary (the third was the Czech Republic). This may be interpreted as suggesting that there are no generally valid recipes for success without reference to the specific country's local conditions. Another consideration on this subject, which appears to find much factual corroboration, is that neither in Poland nor in other transitioning countries was the course of economic austerity implemented consistently enough to endorse the claim that "shock therapy" was fully applied there. The actual practice of reforms, due mainly to social pressures, has been characterized by opportunism and maneuvering not assured by theoretical schemes. The social pressures reflect the growing social stratification in the region's countries. Typically, the extent of poverty has not been diminishing, if not growing, while a relatively narrow group of people with very high incomes has been emerging. The more it became clear that the transformation was going to split the nation into losers and winners, the more important the social and political dimensions of the reforms became. The governments were tempted to postpone unpopular decisions, introducing last-minute changes in already accepted policies, or, on the contrary, to rush into measures favorable to particular interest groups. This often distorted the contemplated effects of reforms and made the process of transformation more uncertain in terms of results.

A STABILIZATION PHASE

Poland started its stabilization plan on 1 January 1990, Yugoslavia a month before, in December 1989, the former Czech and Slovak Federal

Republic on 1 January 1991, Bulgaria on 1 February 1991, and Romania about the same time. The plans were largely similar. In Poland, it included drastic price and trade liberalization, targeting the real money supply and real interest rates, large devaluations and internal convertibility, extreme fiscal pressure on the state sector, rigid budget policy, wage restrictions, and, in the long run, large-scale privatization.

Officials paid particular attention to establishing monetary equilibrium. In Poland, Czechoslovakia, and Yugoslavia the state almost instantly lifted price controls on 85–90 percent of transactions. In Bulgaria and Romania, prices were released in two stages with an occasional temporary restoration of controls, but the effect in terms of price dynamics was eventually the same as in the former three countries. There are some very strong arguments in favor of a price adjustment at an early stage of reform. First, there can be no market allocation leading to internal and external adjustment in the absence of a reliable price signal, but if administrated prices and market prices "coexist" with price indicators, such as enterprise profits, they do not convey much meaning. Second, market-clearing prices are the basis for the evaluation of the industrial assets necessary for an investment process in fixed assets to resume.

The problem with price liberalization is that in order not to allow a switch to market prices to translate into a sustaining hyperinflation, it is necessary to enact very firm anti-inflationary measures with a strong potential for recession. Accordingly, Polish-style stabilization was not restricted to price changes alone but also included regulations aimed against the monopoly of state enterprises, wage inflation, and budget deficits. In practice, this resulted in discrimination against state enterprises and, consequently, against a large sector of the population as over 70 percent of the workforce in Central and Eastern Europe was employed in the state sector. State enterprises were forced to refrain from traditional forms of financing: specifically, centralized subsidies owing to budget austerity and long-term credit owing to sharply raised real interest rates. Besides, they were heavily taxed (in Poland, for example, an average turnover tax of 20 percent plus a new capital tax was introduced). Particularly punitive were the taxes on the increase of wages. This was coupled with deliberately inadequate wage indexation, partial expropriation, due to a disparity between the dynamics of prices and that of interest on bank deposits, and a squeeze on budgetary expenses on social services.

Implemented in this manner, stabilization reforms succeeded in establishing more realistic prices and exchange rates, in eliminating queuing, and in improving the quality of goods and services owing to foreign competition. Nonetheless, inflation was not curbed. A sharp price rise during the initial stage of stabilization had been expected. The problem was, however, that many countries found themselves stuck in this stage for much longer than had been foreseen. Persistent double- to triple-digit inflation had become (with the exception of the Czech and Slovak Republics) a fact of life in the countries of Central and Eastern Europe in the early 1990s. Even in the most successful cases such as Poland, as a dramatic acceleration of inflation in the second half of 1992 has demonstrated, the threat of a recurrence of hyperinflation was not dismissed.

Tight monetary, credit, fiscal, and wage policies forced industry in these countries into deep stagnation as demand collapsed. In Poland, Bulgaria, Romania, and Czechoslovakia real wages dropped 25–30 percent and, at the end of 1992, after over two years of reforms, were still below prereform levels. A rapidly shrinking economy drove up unemployment—which in turn undermined demand even further. Economic shrinkage resulted in falling tax income while rising unemployment inflated social expenditures, thus pushing the government budget deficit to record levels.

The outcomes of sundry stabilization measures gave rise to extensive discussions among economists and policy-makers on their advantages and shortcomings. The deep and persistent fall in output was widely acknowledged as the main setback in the stabilization stage. Whereas some specialists regard a large, sudden, and synchronized drop in output in all sectors as a major theoretical puzzle proposed so far by the process of marketization, others firmly attribute it to the so-called "demand barrier" resulting from a sharp drop in real wages and the erosion of real balances caused by hyperinflation.[13] The monetary surgery was found to have caused both sizable damage to the economy in the form of output and employment losses, and a deprivation of welfare.[14] Clearly, some remission of production would have occurred whatever policies had been followed. However, a bias in monetary stabilization combined with a hands-off policy in regard to industrial enterprises augmented the burden and risks associated with the transition. According to a detailed survey of state enterprises in Poland:

> enterprises have reputedly failed to adjust . . . thereby calling into question a fundamental point of design in the ETP [Economic Transition Program]: that macro stringency alone would suffice to press firms into spontaneous adjustment measures.[15]

The Czech and Slovak Republics have probably experienced the utmost monetarist treatment. The Czech Republic's highly developed industry originally found itself in difficulty when its traditional markets in Eastern Europe and the USSR crashed at the end of the 1980s. As if this shock were not enough, the Czechoslovak government implemented the following set of policies in the aftermath of the January 1991 price liberalization:[16] (a) a cut in the volume of real credit by 30 percent between December 1990 and February 1991; (b) driving real interest rates up an average of 1.5 percent per month from June 1991 onwards; (c) a large budget surplus and an overall current account surplus exceeding initial targets. As a result, the government achieved control over inflation at the price of a drop in retail trade of about 40 percent in real terms and a decrease in industrial production at a rate of 30 percent by the third quarter of 1991. "Such a rate of decline makes the Great Depression pale in comparison," commented the experts of PlanEcon.[17] "We cannot imagine that any democratic government in a Western economy could have implemented the type of policies that have been implemented in Czechoslovakia—it would probably fall within months.[18]

The tolerance shown by the population of Czechoslovakia probably had to do with an early turnaround in real wages and a relatively beneficial overall situation in the labor market. These developments, however, provoked a mixed reaction among experts. Some of them fear that an early recovery in the Czech Republic has an unreliable basement which can mean more problems in the future. They find the explanation of the rise in wages and the reduction of employment at a rate below the decline of output, in 1992, in the "preprivatization" type of expectations on the part of enterprise managers who preferred to increase prices and pay higher salaries from the money normally destined for investment rather than put painful restructuring into effect.

Unlike Czechoslovakia, in Poland first-generation reformers were ousted from the cabinet following the October 1991 elections when the opposition headed by the Democratic left captured 25 percent of the vote. The subsequent governments could not ignore public resentment with the policies of economic austerity and endorsed the expansion of public spending on social needs and other expenditures meant to cushion the outcomes of "shock therapy." In 1992, the government of Jan Olszewski announced that priorities would be to stimulate the economy with tax cuts and provide more subsidies to state-owned enterprises. This resulted in a heavy budget deficit in 1992, well above the 1991 level, thus canceling one of the most important achievements of 1990 reforms, i.e., getting a deficit/GDP ratio within 5 percent. With a deficit as huge as that, the threat of hyperinflation is always real.

The troublesome coexistence of skyrocketing inflation and a devastating industrial slump was also characteristic of Bulgaria, Romania, and the Yugoslav successor states. Unfortunately for these economies, they seem not to have been able to find a way out of this trap. Of course, in Serbia, Croatia, and Bosnia the war made any serious stabilization effort impossible, at least until after the Dayton Peace Accords. Of the five countries, Bulgaria appeared to have the brightest prospect (at least until recently) after it had made considerable progress in reducing the rate of inflation during the course of 1992. However, the government budget deficit rose dramatically thereafter, with unemployment exceeding 14 percent, putting it on the top of the list of the East European countries most affected by unemployment. The way out for Bulgaria may be in the activation of microeconomic policies aimed at privatization.

As for the Romanian economy, *PlanEcon* (13 November 1992) described its state on the eve of 1993 as a free fall with no sign as yet that this fall was about to end. The detailed analysis of this phenomenon, due to its complexity and a relative absence of reliable data, presents a big problem. It would not be incorrect, however, to point to the particularly disastrous state of the Romanian economy at the time the Nicolae Ceauşescu regime was overthrown and the social and political implications it brought about as factors making successful transition very difficult. In 1990–1992, two subsequent cabinets pursued liberalization policies but failed to keep their promises to achieve economic recovery. In November 1992, Nicolae Vacariou was appointed prime minister. He declared that his main concern was to implement an emergency "anticrisis program" in the fields of energy and food distribution aimed to "get [Romanians] through the winter under normal conditions." In terms of long-term strategy, Vacariou appears to be an advocate of extensive state intervention in the economy in the period of transition to a market. The liberal opposition accused the government of trying to restore the command economy. Vacariou considers his approach to be only pragmatic and promises to halt the decline of production by the second half of 1993 and turn around the economy in 1994.[19]

In 1992, in Slovenia the economic situation was very much similar to other European ex-socialist countries, though with some important reservations. Estimates of the main macroeconomic aggregates indicate, on the one hand, a decline of 6.5 percent in real GDP and of 20 percent in gross fixed investment, an 11 percent rate of unemployment, and a major setback of 16 percent in private consumption and of 13.2 percent in industrial production.[20] On the other hand, a significant reduction in the annual inflation rate was coupled with a rapid buildup of foreign currency reserves, from about US$400 million at the end of 1991 to around US$1.3 billion at the end of 1992.

The dramatic reduction in Slovenia's trade with the other Yugoslav successor states was the central factor behind the persistent economic depression of this small export-oriented economy. Another striking problem was the financial crisis, reflected in large financial losses, insolvency, and lack of discipline in public finance. The government applied a tight monetary and fiscal policy coupled with the control over prices of nontradables in order to secure a decline in the rate of inflation. Together with fiscal reform, this has been seen as the main pillar of a stabilization policy. These efforts have brought some results which are expected to translate into more stable macroeconomic conditions in 1993. Nonetheless, real GDP is likely to decrease further by 1 percent. As previously, much will depend on the development of foreign trade as exports have always had a leading role in economic developments in Slovenia.

THE PRIVATIZATION CHALLENGE

The privatization of a huge public property is universally regarded as another big issue of a post-communist transition. Mass privatization would mean that Eastern Germany would have to tackle 8,000 firms, Poland about 7,500 firms, Bulgaria 5,000 firms, former Czechoslovakia 4,800, Romania 4,000, and Hungary 2,500, accounting in each case for no less than 80 percent of national value added.[21] For comparison, in Great Britain the much-heralded privatization program of the first Thatcher government involved only about 20 firms, accounting for a mere 5 percent of value added.

Unlike stabilization programs, from the very beginning there was less unanimity at a government level as to a conceptual framework for privatization. The disastrous impact of the price adjustment on the industrial sector has only increased controversy. There is no hesitation about whether to privatize. The questions yet to be answered are how to privatize, to what extent, and how to treat the state sector in the meanwhile.

To start with, modern economic theory is split into two camps on the issue of relative property efficiency.[22] There is a school of thought which does not consider that private ownership is inherently superior to public on the basis that there is no difference in "allocative efficiency" between private and public firms in competitive markets. "As regards big industrial or commercial firms, the core of modern economy under both capitalism and socialism, the question of ownership is not so important after all," claims, for example, John Kenneth Galbraith.[23] "What matters . . . is to recognize the right of the firm to decide on its own performance and to benefit from right decisions." Galbraith also maintains that modern capitalism has nothing to do with "free enterprise" orthodoxy and that it has survived only owing to a mixed composition of its economy where state enterprises are no less important than private firms.

In the 1980s, however, it was scholars arguing that the form of ownership did matter who commanded general attention. They strongly asserted that only private owners can escape the inefficiencies imposed by state control. Four efficiency-related advantages were specifically underlined: (1) private firms should be less subject to political interference; (2) private firms should be more capable of offering decent incentives to attract good managers; (3) private enterprises should be more subject to the discipline of commercial financial markets; and (4) private ownership should mean that the interests of capital are better represented.

Both points of view appear to have influenced reformers in Eastern Europe. Czechoslovakia is a good example. While the political leadership in the Czech Republic put all its trust in the invisible hand of the market and started a landslide privatization, next door, in Slovakia, the government was much more cautious in its approach and showed willingness to preserve a considerable state presence in industry. Not unimportantly this latter approach was predetermined by the fact that industrialization in Slovakia took place in the postwar period and was implemented according to a socialist doctrine, giving priority to large and very large enterprises with a bias toward heavy industry.

In fact, a high concentration of production and employment in big enterprises was a general feature of socialist economies. In 1990, the share of enterprises employing more than 500 people in industry was 43 percent in Czechoslovakia, 86.9 percent in Poland, 74.5 percent in Romania, and 72.1 percent in Bulgaria. In addition, the enterprises were more narrowly specialized than was usual in the West; there was often just one national producer of a particular product. In addition, these gigantic structures were created in accordance with the perception of efficiency as it was seen under central planning (i.e., the enabling of direct control from the center) which makes them vulnerable in a market environment. The gigantic scale of many state-owned companies aside, it was typical of state enterprises to be overstaffed and to have a vast array of supporting productions and social services, including kindergartens, medical centers, and holiday homes. It was obvious that they could not survive unchanged under any other conditions than those of a centrally planned economy. The economic recession of 1990–1992 only made things worse as the enterprises lost markets, squeezed production, accumulated debt, and discontinued a normal investment process. As a result, many properties seemed to be unsalable unless a prior streamlining and financial restructuring had been undertaken first. However, the dominating belief has been that if enterprises remain in the hands of the state, they would not adapt themselves to market conditions.

Poland and Hungary were the first to adopt privatization programs in 1990. The intention was to privatize fast, but both countries have been unable to keep their programs on track.[24] Small enterprises such as shops and restaurants were easy to turn private, and thousands of them have been sold by public offerings and tenders. Problems began when it became the turn of big firms. Only foreign investors could raise enough money to buy them, but these investors did not show any interest in doing so except for some "crown jewels" of national industry with an established share in the international market, such as the lightbulb company Tungsram in Hungary.

The way the fate of the public sector is decreed is crucial for the livelihood of millions of employees as well as for the competitiveness of the national economy. Every decision entails great responsibility. However, as Nuti once remarked, Central and East European governments tended to confuse "their potential ability to privatize with the realization of that potential and pretend that the state sector does not exist" contrary to the evidence that until progress in privatization changed the balance between private and public property, the activities of state- and municipally owned companies would still determine the national economic performance.[25] It cannot be ignored that big public enterprises have remained the competitive core of national industry while their relative share in production has shrunk. In 1992 Poland had a trade surplus with the West and figures show that the private sector was responsible for at least 45 percent of the GDP (31 percent in 1990). These facts may appear to suggest that private business was the driving force behind Polish export success, but, according to a recent World Bank country report, 80 percent of export revenue, in 1992 as well as in 1990, was being earned by the state sector.[26]

Already at the early stage of stabilization public enterprises found themselves deprived of traditional state subsidies while the clear provisions of how the state sector was to be financed were generally missing. It was assumed that the enterprises would try to adjust to hard budget constraints by bringing down costs. The actual reaction was different: they started raising prices and accumulating debt between companies. Managers appeared reluctant to streamline their businesses, partially because of old habits, but also owing to expectations associated with the eve of privatization and an inadequate financial system in which credit flows did not go to the most efficient producers but rather to those enterprises with the best connections with banks. As a result, macroeconomic measures failed to bring about desirable responses at the enterprise level. This had made the need for privatization even more urgent.

There are two principal fashions of handling this problem in the former socialist countries. One reflects the perception that the duty of the government is to speed up the process while a market mechanism is to be entrusted with the task of restructuring the national property. According to the other, microeconomic restructuring should precede or accompany the privatization of state companies in order to increase their value and attractiveness as an asset and then to submit them for public offerings.

Czechoslovakia (the Czech Republic after 1 January 1992) chose the first approach. There the voucher scheme proved to be the most intriguing part of a large-scale privatization program. Each adult citizen was entitled, almost for free, to a voucher booklet allowing him or her to bid for a share of privatized entities at public auctions. More than eight million persons became owners of vouchers. In the first round of auctions alone, in 1992, corporate assets with a "net book value" of about $9.3 billion were distributed to millions of new shareholders.[27]

Nobody has had a chance up to now to evaluate the full impact of voucher privatization on the Czech economy. Certain implications of the scheme raised some skepticism.[28] Probably the main problem with this scheme is that it does not provide any visible evidence that the change in ownership will promote profit maximization and business efficiency. No new capital or expertise will be introduced into troubled companies. Furthermore, the individuals receiving a share in privatized enterprises, if ownership is broadly spread, will not have any influence over the specific competitiveness of the companies they come to own. Since, with so little information available, the acquisition of assets will comprise a considerable chance element, new owners may soon discover their property to be uncompetitive and unprofitable. In other cases enterprises competitive in their operations may fall into the hands of entrepreneurially incompetent individuals who could ruin the business. As a result, business conditions in the country may become even more precarious.

About 17.5 million Romanians received voucher booklets for assets estimated to be worth Leu 1,500 billion. The Romanian mass privatization program, nonetheless, did not copy the Czech one. Two-thirds of property was to be sold by conventional methods by means of auctions and sell-offs, and 30 percent was intended for voucher transfers to be put in five Private Ownership Funds with the object to maximize its value.

The idea of prior restructuring in necessary cases is implicit in the privatization programs proclaimed in Poland, Hungary, and Bulgaria. However, financial and organizational restructuring takes time and money, and extends the period of a transition during which public bodies continue to interfere with economic processes. To many this seems unacceptable. The authorities of Poland and Hungary are reported (at this writing) to be considering a Czech-style voucher scheme. In the meantime, the desire to speed up the privatization process dominates the ongoing decision-making. Hungary has paved the road by having adopted in January 1992 a new bankruptcy law which made it possible for creditors to force companies into bankruptcy if they did not pay their debts within ninety days. Such enterprises or their assets may then be bought for bargain prices. This law was inspired by an understandable desire to liberate the economy (and the budget) from inefficient enterprises and, moreover, to do so in the best traditions of neoliberalism, leaving it to the market to decide winners and losers. The problem with this law, however, was the timing and the way it treated, or mistreated, the specifics of the current situation. A payments crisis resulting from the misfunction of the monetary and financial system, the low performance of existing market structures, and contradictory state regulations have put at the brink of bankruptcy almost every third state-owned industrial enterprise in the country.[29]

According to one point of view, to let state enterprises in Central and East European countries go bust, pay ex-employees unemployment benefits, and sell the physical assets piecemeal so that new owners might start from scratch would be the least of evils. According to another, the increase in social security payments and the fall in tax revenues resulting from the bankruptcy of state firms would far exceed the cost of trying to restructure them. Paul Reynolds, director of the British research group Adam Smith Associates, says: "If it is the case that increasingly [state] enterprises are being allowed to go bust, the social and unemployment consequences will be terrible. Suppose half of them go under—an economy cannot sustain that. It will bring down the successful private companies as well."[30] Such a spread of opinions is, on the one hand, the evidence of the complexity of the problem. On the other hand, it demonstrates how little objective knowledge we still have about one of the most important aspects of transition.

The only example of privatization based on prior comprehensive macroeconomic restructuring demonstrated so far has been by Germany. In July 1990, 10,500 East German enterprises employing four million people were put under the management of a government agency called Treuhandanstalt, entrusted with a mandate to maximize the returns on the sales of state assets while ensuring optimum employment. The stated policy of Treuhand was to privatize quickly. However, if a company could not be sold, Treuhand's policy was to attempt to restructure it to salvage at least the core business or any other viable part. By June 1992, 4,803 companies had been privatized, 1,209 had been closed down, and 5,435 were still owned by Treuhand.[31] None of the other Central and East European governments has been able to spare the resources and expertise that Treuhand could lavish on state property in Eastern Germany. The apparent dilemma of macroeconomic adjustment is that case-by-case privatization by a central agency cannot accomplish much, granting the available amount of resources to be applied to this end, while speedy mass privatization, as was argued, may prove to be a shaky alternative.

By the mid-1990s, apart from Eastern Germany only the Czech Republic, in which the domination of one party, Václav Klaus's ODS, provided a unique environment for reforms, had found a definitive solution to the issue of privatization. In other countries of the region large state-owned enterprises still present a challenge. Some economists have begun to question the obsession with mass privatization.[32] It is described as time-consuming. It delays restructuring and does not clarify the ownership structure or create a system of economic incentives characteristic of a market economy. It is recommended that the government should follow a more balanced approach instead by concentrating on creating a favorable economic environment, benefiting the emerging entrepreneurship of the region.

THE INTERNATIONAL ASPECT
OF MARKETIZATION

As previously mentioned, international factors have had a great impact on the dynamics of post-communist transition. The collapse of the intra-COMECON market in 1989–1990 was responsible for much of the decline of industrial and agricultural output in the area. Foreign debt was and still is another major issue. In the 1970s, the communist governments of Eastern and Central Europe received from the West loans totaling $49.8 billion. These resources were generally misallocated and did not generate the flow of income in hard currency sufficient to pay back the loans. As a result, in 1988 the area had a cumulative debt of $103.1 billion, putting a great strain on the economy, with Poland and Yugoslavia being in particular difficulties.

Unfolding marketization boosted demand for foreign capital. Transitional countries sought financial credits to support structural adjustments in the monetary sphere and foreign direct investments to start up privatization and modernization of national industry, and to make up for chronic undercapitalization typical of centrally planned economies.

This situation gave Western political governance structures, international organizations, and transnational corporations considerable leverage over East and Central European governments. The IMF and the EEC insisted on measures leading to the accelerated opening of the markets of the formerly socialist countries to Western products.[33] The argument was that an end must be put to a situation in which Central and East European countries were protected from competitive pressure of international trade which, in market economies, provided a strong incentive to improve efficiency. Transitional economies were called upon to lift or restrict foreign trade control and facilitate access to foreign exchange resources for the residents by introducing internal convertibility of the national currency.

As a result, already at the initial stage of transition the post-communist economies made a great stride toward openness—when industrial slump was at its peak. Furthermore, although exports to the West increased, they could not compensate for the collapse of intra-COMECON trade because Western governments and transnational corporations were not ready to open Western markets to East European goods. When Poland volunteered to drop all import restrictions, the EC did not reciprocate. Now Poland has one of the lowest tariff regimes in the world, but half of Poland's exports to the EC confront some kind of restraint. The most Poland, Hungary, the Czech Republic, and Slovakia have been able to obtain is a grant of associate status with the European Community (EC), now European Union (EU), amounting largely to a promise of a ten-year transition to free trade. In the meantime, the steel lobby in the EC has set an extremely low ceiling on East European imports—1 percent of total EC raw steel capacity. The EC has also refused to relax restrictions on imports of food, textiles, clothing, and chemicals. Together with iron and steel, these are the most competitive (they account for 33–46 percent of exports to the EC from the Czech and Slovak Republics, Poland, and Hungary) and the most suffering industries in Eastern Europe.

The West appears to be putting more emphasis on the restoration of trade within Central and Eastern Europe. The immediate challenge, however, is not to let it collapse even further. To stimulate intraregional trade an infusion of financial resources is necessary. The G-24 countries and international institutions have made a commitment to the East and Central European countries in the amount of $100 billion including food and medical aid, economic restructuring and technical assistance, export credit and investment guarantees, debt relief, and balance-of-payments support.[34] However, only a meager share of what the West promised has actually been delivered. Besides, just a fraction of these funds was in grant form; the rest was loans and credit guarantees. As a result, according to the Institute for East-West Studies, levels of disbursement were disappointingly low, from 3 to 27 percent, as recipient governments were reluctant to assume extra financial burdens for their countries.

The inflow of private capital was below expectations and far below levels that regional policy-makers considered desirable. The largest amount of foreign investment was recorded in Hungary. There, by the end of 1992, foreigners owned 3 percent of productive assets, far below the planned 20–25 percent. Private investors were mainly discouraged by high political and policy risks. In turn, the barriers in the way of product exportation to the EC were important in deterring those foreign investors, including firms from North America and the Far East, who wanted to exploit the location and cost advantages of the region's countries to compete in Western European markets.

Experts within and outside Central and Eastern Europe have called upon Western governments to take a more responsible approach with regard to the transitional countries and help them carry the weight of change. The EC is accused of providing an example of protectionism, undermining liberal economic reforms in the post-communist European countries. The Institute for East-West Studies Task Force on Western Assistance to Transition[35] has summarized the maxi agenda for Western governments: (1) abandon the use of tied assistance to Central Europe, particularly in the form of export credits; (2) provide a higher proportion of assistance in grants as opposed to loans; (3) open markets progressively to Central Europe; (4) provide incentives for private investment in Central Europe.

After the first three years of marketization in Central and Eastern Europe, it seemed that whatever economic policies were applied, the result was a depression. Presently the recent upturn of industrial production, a considerable growth of the small-scale private sector, and quite a strong increase in trade turnover with the West in Poland, the Czech Republic, and Hungary demonstrate that efforts to reshape the post-communist economic systems are working. It is very tempting to speculate about the lessons of marketization in Central and Eastern Europe. Moreover, there is growing demand for good advice from the newly emerged states of the Commonwealth of Independent States (CIS) in which a quick transformation is badly needed. However, probably one of the most clear lessons from the experience of Central and Eastern Europe is how risky it is to generalize from this experience. Now more than ever, economic policy-making should be liberated as much as possible from any ideological dictate, whether it is an oversimplified market orthodoxy or the old orthodoxy of central planning, in order to provide the particular flexibility in approaches that the post-communist transition requires.

Notes

1. Jan Winiecki, "Post Soviet-type Economies in Transition," in *Weltwirtschaftliches Archiv* (Tübingen), Vol. 126, No. 4 (1990): 781–783.

2. The reader should be warned from the outset about possible inconsistency and approximateness of the data concerning economic transition in Central and Eastern Europe. In particular, long-term comparisons raise problems because national accounts under communist governments are suspect. Screening later economic developments also is not easy because different sources often cite different figures.

3. See, for example, Michael Marrese and Jan Vanous, *Soviet Subsidization of Trade with Eastern Europe: A Soviet Perspective* (Berkeley: Institute of International Studies, University of California, 1988).

4. The discussion in academic circles in Moscow on the fundamental multi-volume report *A Study on Soviet Economy* (1991) prepared by the IMF, the World Bank, the OECD, and the EBRD is representative in this respect. Giving praise to the objectiveness and the thoroughness of the authors of the report, experts of two leading economic institutes of the national Academy of Sciences were unanimous in noting its "cognitive, analytical rather than practical value." All objections summarized, the practical value of the report was dismissed on the grounds that it did not account for the principal differences between the content of monetary, budgetary, credit, and other relations in the Soviet economy and a capitalist economy. Hence, the recommendations of the report, quite predictably biased toward exactly monetary, budgetary, and credit instruments, were found inadequate for a situation in which the market was both underdeveloped and overmonopolized, the production of consumer goods was marginal in comparison to the output of heavy industries, the weight of a military-industrial complex

was enormous, agriculture was in a deep structural crisis, and the population was poor. The "program of the four" was criticized as too radical and painful, as putting too much emphasis on purely market measures whilst the specifics of the Soviet system and the necessity to preserve the integrity of the economy required gradualness and the preservation of the elements of the centrally planned system at least in the initial stages of transition (see *Voprosy ekonomiki* [Moscow], No. 4 [1991]: 37–47 and No. 5: 3–27). However, in Russia itself, within only one year some of the most radical proposals of the agenda outlined in the "program of the four" have materialized in the governmental economic policy.

5. See *ECE Economic Survey for Europe*, 1992; and Maxwell Fry and Domenico Mario Nuti, "Monetary and Exchange Rate Policies during Eastern Europe's Transition: Some Lessons from Further East," *Oxford Review of Economic Policy*, Vol. 8, No. 1 (Spring 1992).

6. *Economic Survey of Europe in 1991–1992* (New York: UN Economic Commission for Europe, 1992), 41.

7. *Transition: The Newsletter about Reforming Economies* (Washington), Vol. 3, No. 8 (1992): 4.

8. See *Hungary: OECD Economic Survey 1991* (Paris: OECD, 1991).

9. *The Economist* (London), 30 January 1993, 30.

10. *Economic Survey of Europe in 1991–1992*, 41; and *The Economist*, 23 January 1993, 21.

11. Peter Körner, et al., *The IMF and the Debt Crisis* (London: Zed, 1986).

12. Nuti, "Economic Inertia in the Transitional Economies of Eastern Europe," paper presented at the 1992 conference "Impediments to the Transition: The East European Countries and the Policies of the European Community," (Florence: European University Institute, 1992), 8.

13. Brian Pinto, Marek Belka, and Stefan Krajewski, *Microeconomics of Transformation in Poland: A Survey of State Enterprise Responses*, Poland Resident Mission, The World Bank, Working Paper Series, 1992, 4.

14. See for example Guillermo Calvo and Fabrizio Coricelli, "Stabilizing a Previously Centrally Planned Economy: Poland 1990," *Economic Policy*, No. 14 (1992).

15. Pinto, Belka, and Krajewski, *Microeconomics of Transformation in Poland*, 1.

16. *PlanEcon Report* (New York), No. 40–41 (1991).

17. Ibid., 7.

18. Ibid., 11.

19. See Dan Ionescu, "Romania's Cabinet in Search of an Economic Strategy," *RFE/RL Research Report* (Washington), Vol. 2, No. 44 (1992): 45–49.

20. *Financial Times* (London) (30 March 1993): 33–36.

21. *The Economist* (21 September 1991): 10.

22. For a recent overview of the debate, see Aidan Vining and Anthony Boardman, "Ownership versus Competition: Efficiency in Public Enterprises," *Public Choice*, Vol. 73, No. 2 (1992): 205–239.

23. *La Lettera del Venerdi* (Milan) (31 May 1991): 22.

24. In Hungary, the government originally set a target of 70–75 percent privatization of all state assets by the end of 1994. In 1991, of the total of 400 enterprises (about 20 percent of the book value of state assets) only five had been sold by the end of the year, twenty turned into limited companies in preparation for privatization, and another 200 started. By the end of 1991, both the First Privatization Program and the Second Privatization Program were considered failures. In 1992, a goal of privatizing 50 percent of state assets by the end of

1994 was set. Marvin Jackson, "Practical, Equity, and Efficiency Issues in the Privatization of Large-scale Enterprises," *Leuven Institute for Central and East European Studies Working Paper*, No. 1 (1992): 17.

25. Nuti, "Economic Inertia in the Transitional Economies of Eastern Europe," 17.

26. *The Guardian* (London), 9 January 1993, 7.

27. The firms most popular with voucher holders were almost exclusively banks, hotels, breweries, ceramics works, and foreign trading companies. *Transition: The Newsletter about Reforming Economies*, Vol. 3, No. 7 (1992): 11.

28. See for discussion Franz Lang, "Short-run Effects of Economic Reforms in Eastern Economies," *Intereconomics*, Vol. 26, No. 5 (1991): 223–229; "Survey on Eastern Europe," *The Economist*, 21 September 1991, 17–18; *Newsweek*, 16 March 1992, 40–41; and *The Economist*, 16 May 1992, 91–92.

29. The Tungsram story helps to convey the idea of the business environment in the country. A showcase of successful privatization, Tungsram, in which the transnational giant General Electric owns 75 percent of stock, was constrained to stop production for two weeks in the spring of 1992, despite injections of capital and managerial skill from its powerful parent company. Tungsram American manager George Varga cited general economic recession and stifling government fiscal policy as the causes of the closedown of the enterprise. *Izvestiia* (Moscow), 12 May 1992.

30. *Central European*, November 1992, 14.

31. *East European Markets* (London), 26 June 1992, 15.

32. See, for example, Krzysztof Ners, "Privatisation (from Above, Below, or Mass Privatisation) versus Generic Private Enterprise Building," *Communist Economies and Economic Transformation*, Vol. 7, No. 1 (1995): 105–116.

33. As the disappointing results of reforms piled up, the IMF, in the person of its executive director, was compelled to accept that under certain conditions "it might not be as heretical as it looks to maintain import tariffs, keep production in some sectors under government control . . . , implement a rigorous income policy, and avoid massive price increases. . . ." *External Economic Relations of the Central and East European Countries: NATO Colloquium 1992* (Brussels: NATO, 1992), 69.

34. *Transition: The Newsletter about Reforming Economies*, 12.

35. Ibid.

15

Democracy, Markets, and Security in Eastern Europe

DANIEL N. NELSON AND GEORGETA V. POURCHOT

Where there is no security, democracy and markets will not long survive. Paradoxically, where there is no democracy or free markets, the resources needed to create and maintain security are too meager and too undependable. Democracy, free markets, and new bases for security constitute the principal goals of post-communist nations in Eastern Europe. At risk is the continuance of democratic development in Europe's eastern half, as well as the stability of Western Europe. Were post-communist Europe to lose the battle for democracy and free markets, the rise of an antidemocratic right-wing extremism in Western Europe could not be discounted—generated in large part by a visceral fear of immigration and an increased economic burden.[1]

During the Cold War, security came to be equated with fear. Alliances for common defense, especially the North Atlantic Treaty Organization (NATO), were created to shield Western democracies from Soviet and communist military aggression. Security, however, involves more than simply warding off peril. Peace and prosperity are core attributes of security; they are obtained by maintaining a dynamic balance between threats and capacities. An equilibrium is essential. A security dilemma is born when a state, perceiving a threat, enhances its armaments, thereby endangering neighboring states that, in turn, intensify their military preparations. Arms races begin whenever security is believed to reside merely in greater capacity.

Another dangerous consequence of equating capacity with security is to condemn those with less power and wealth to a life of peril. The rich have greater capacities to balance whatever threats might appear, thereby ensuring their well-being. The rich get more secure, and the secure have the best chance to be rich and democratic.

That democracies tend not to go to war against other democracies is often attributed to constitutional processes, civic culture, and values that transcend power politics.[2] Yet, part of the explanation must be that democratic countries are likely to be those in which economic strength, social cohesion, and political consensus have been an adequate counterbalance to threat, thus enhancing physical and material security. Democracy, however, cannot be nurtured in an insecure environment.

To see democracy as the key to producing a peaceful world order is far too simple; the requisites of democracy should not be ignored. Should peace among democracies be attributed to their democratic condition and related values or should the advent of stable democracies be seen as an attribute of a stable peace?

Which political systems become democratic is the most basic issue as free governments seek to achieve free markets and national security simultaneously. States that become democratic may be those with the capacity to counterbalance threats and thus obtain security; pluralism, tolerance, and rule of law can then be nurtured. Although security is not sufficient for democratic development, an equilibrium between threats and capacities may be necessary.

What happened in Czechoslovakia in 1938 illustrates one kind of danger that may confront even a well-established and prosperous free-market democracy. When external demands clearly outstrip indigenous capabilities—when a severe disequilibrium between threats and capacities exists—no political and socioeconomic system will be up to the task. The Czechs of 1938 had no one on whom to rely, given the weakness of the French-inspired "Little Entente" and the vapid rhetoric of Neville Chamberlain.

Democracy's susceptibility to internal threats is even greater. In political systems in which nascent democracy has begun to take root, interests that fear its public legitimation have frequently sought to create an atmosphere of threat. Such politicians encourage voters to infer that economic or social conditions exhibit dangerous trends that require a vote for their party. Demagogues go further, however, by insisting that democracy is an expensive luxury in the face of peril to the nation. Scapegoats are identified. For Jean-Marie le Pen's *Front National* in France, the threat is immigration, and the scapegoats are North African Muslims. Germany's right-wing Republican Party and others focus on immigration as well, demonizing Gypsies, Turks, Serbs, Poles, Romanians—almost anyone from the eastern half of Europe. Russian extremists have embraced anti-Semitism. When intolerance takes root, democracy is the final casualty. Lies and exaggeration foster perceived threats, and those threats are then used as crude tools with which to chip away at commitments to democratic institutions and constitutional guarantees.

The relationship among democracy, free markets, and security is extraordinarily fragile; it can be endangered by both external peril and internal demagoguery. This interdependence cannot be ignored. The loss of security, even if accompanied by renewed sovereignty and personal liberties, can have devastating consequences for individuals, groups, states, and regions. The cost of insecurity is a weakened prognosis for both democracy and free markets. Where security is assured—through the good fortune of geographic isolation or through a guarantee provided by a stronger ally during the critical years of institutional infancy—democracy has its best chance.

These preliminary observations lead to a prescription for the foreign policy of the West. During the Cold War, the West sought to contain dangers with a perimeter defense. The West's new aim—a world of stable democracies—requires a more productive United States and West European policy. What kind of productive policy should this be?

Western efforts in post-communist Europe after 1989 were intended to insist on free market economics, while providing some help in organizing new political parties and media outlets. Each East European country's agreement with international financial institutions framed a path toward an economy of a Western sort, while campaigns were funded, elections monitored, and interest groups, polling, and media outlets organized under the tutelage of Western granting agencies. The umbrellas of "democratization" and "privatization" have been very wide, encompassing many U.S. and West European efforts to mold new political and economic infrastructures in Eastern Europe.

However, the provision of security to post-communist Europe cannot lag behind free and fair elections, rule of law, freeing prices, or selling off state assets. None of these far-reaching political and economic reforms will survive unless new paths to security are found for the eastern half of Europe. Raising industrial or military capacities to defeat enemies will be far less important than managing threats through conflict resolution and arbitration, confidence- and security-building measures, and peacekeeping deployments. Not surprisingly, these endeavors cannot be easily accomplished with the same institutional tools used by the West during the Cold War. NATO, for instance, has taken on peace-enforcement duties in Bosnia; but even there, NATO's military strength was employed because of the *absence* of other capable institutions, and its role was recast as the "Implementation Force," or IFOR (later SFOR, or "Stabilization Force"), that included non-NATO countries and institutions.[3]

Democracies and free markets cannot be created overnight from the rubble of authoritarianism. Without substantial indigenous political, socioeconomic, or military capacities, the internal and external threats confronting post-communist Europe (discussed below) will be more than adequate to retard, if not defeat, fledgling democratic institutions.

SECURITY LOST

Almost as soon as velvet revolutions and popular coups pushed aside decrepit communist rulers in Eastern Europe, the leaders of post-communist Europe quickly began to sense the exposed nature of their regenerated sovereignty. Being held for decades in Moscow's grasp, with national command structures subsumed within Soviet "theaters of military operations," had always been abhorrent to national dignity. However, Moscow's presence did create a forty-five-year moratorium on interstate disputes in the region.

The specifics of all internal and external threats—tangible or perceived—to states, governments, or peoples of post-communist Europe extend well beyond the scope of this chapter. Nevertheless, some general outlines can be sketched.

The Internal Dimension

Building new political and socioeconomic structures in countries long ruled by one-party authoritarian regimes required first, the demolition of Leninist economic, political, and social institutions. This deconstruction implies, as can be seen in almost every place in Europe and Central Asia once ruled by communists, a perilous but utterly unavoidable transit across potentially disastrous waters. Five principal domestic obstacles have endangered post-communist systems during their first decade of proto-democracy, including the political apathy of the populace toward authority; political and bureaucratic opposition from the residual communist *nomenklatura* and secret police; the political costs of marketization; uncertain civil-military relations; and nationalism.

POLITICAL APATHY

Lurking beneath all of the perils to proto-democracies in Europe's eastern half is the yawning gap between popular trust and political power. The abject failure of Communist Party governments did not bequeath legitimacy to post-communist politicians; dissidents were popular only until they became bureaucrats and parliamentarians. Thereafter, they soon became indistinguishable from "the authorities" of the past communist years.

During the early 1990s, the popular enthusiasm that followed the collapse of the communist regimes in 1989 and 1990, to culminate with the disintegration of the bastion of communism—the Soviet Union—started to wane. By 1993, signs of public apathy and alienation from political institutions prevailed across the region. Dissatisfaction was high and confidence in parliamentary and executive institutions was low and falling. Almost all national political figures were perceived negatively by citizens. In Russia, a 1993 nationwide sample survey found that 93 percent of the respondents distrusted the political parties and 67 percent did not trust President Boris Yeltsin.[4] The same situation prevailed in the other former communist countries: Public trust in parties and political movements was 20 percent in the Czech Republic, 20 percent in the Slovak Republic, 10 percent in Hungary, and 8 percent in Poland. A similarly low percentage of trust was maintained with regard to parliaments: 19 percent trusted their parliament in the Czech Republic, 24 percent in Slovakia, 20 percent in Hungary, and 12 percent in Poland.[5] By 1994, the mean of popular trust in institutions across Eastern Europe was 13 percent for political parties and 20 percent for parliaments.[6]

In the years immediately following 1989, peoples of Eastern and post-Soviet Europe were tired of politics because political leaders and institutions were performing poorly, and appeared only to make things worse. Integral to the struggle against communist dictatorships had been an effort to expand the public political sphere in Eastern Europe. However, the realm of public politics was tainted by years of corrupt Communist Party rule, and nascent post-communist governments confronted decades of doubt, distrust, and distancing between authorities and the populace. This sentiment was reflected in countless public opinion polls throughout post-communist Europe. For example, in mid-1991, after a year and a half in power, Poland's Solidarity government was already being called a "new dictatorship" by 23 percent of a national sample.[7] In Russia, a majority of respondents were looking for qualities such as honesty and dignity in their choice of a candidate before the 1993 parliamentary elections.[8] In Hungary, despite an increase of public confidence in the national government after the 1994 elections, in which the Hungarian Socialist Party won a majority of seats, the public did not think that the new democratic political system was any less corrupt than the former system. One in three Hungarians expressed the belief that there was more political corruption under the new regime than before, and another third believed that the level of corruption had remained about the same.[9]

Having taken great risk to insist on the expansion of debate about politicians and policies during communist dictatorships, populations in Europe's eastern half now doubt that much has changed. Private wealth, public squalor, withdrawal to self and family, and rejection of community—these dichotomies characterize the internal threat of purposeful apathy that pervades Eastern Europe.

Although these sentiments are not unique to one world region, nowhere is there a greater need for citizens' engagement in public life than in Europe's eastern half. Creating a legitimate, self-sustaining public political sphere not dependent on mobilization is a daunting task. In the part of Europe ruled for so long by one-party authoritarianism, populations believe that political authority is corrupt and irrelevant; individuals learned that "the system" would not respond to their needs and could not solve their problems.

The result was a rejection of involvement in public life and decrease in participatory politics. In Hungarian by-elections during 1991 and 1992, many results were declared void because of turnouts as low as 17 percent.[10] In Russia, the turnout went from 74 percent for the June 1991 presidential elections, to 65 percent for the April 1993 referendum, to 55 percent for the December 1993 parliamentary elections. In the December 1995 parliamentary elections, turnout went slightly upward (64 percent), but much of this seeming rejuvenation of public interest in the political life of the country was, instead, a protest vote for extremists against those who now govern.[11]

Increased disinterest in politics was also signaled by high percentages of respondents who, prior to elections, did not know for whom to vote, or whether they would vote at all. In 1991, 34 percent of a national sample of Hungarians said that they were unlikely to vote, and another third said that they might or might not vote.[12] In 1995, another poll found that 26 percent of Hungarians would not vote and 15 percent would not have known for whom to vote if elections had been held the following weekend.[13] In Russia, in a preelection poll held in St. Petersburg, about 50 percent of respondents said they would not vote in the upcoming elections of 1995 for one of two reasons: They either did not believe the election results would affect their lives, or they saw not voting as a means to protest against the system.[14] This level of alienation was reached after only a few years of post-communist parliamentary government.

As time passed in countries where market reforms engendered higher productivity and expanded output, some popular confidence began to regenerate. By 1996, nostalgia for the old communist systems had receded in Slovenia, the Czech Republic, and Poland. In these countries, prior wealth and/or earlier starts to the transition have made change less threatening. Nostalgia for communism in these three cases has been lower due both to the passage of time *and* to macroeconomic improvements that offered hope about the benefits of free-market democracy.[15]

Such hopeful attitudes, however, have not made their way into countries where conditions of socioeconomic threat remain high. By 1996, this was true of Bulgaria, Hungary, Slovakia, and Romania, but also of post-Soviet parts of Europe, including Russia. In Russia, for instance, the gloom had deepened, with a third of the population desiring communist rule of some kind, and another 12 percent and 10 percent asking for military or monarchical rule, respectively.[16]

Throughout post-communist Europe, indeed, optimism (where it exists) rests precariously on the expectation that economic growth will lead to trickle-down benefits to the entire population. Thus far, the expansion of Poland's economy, for example, has led to more inequality in incomes and accumulated wealth while leaving behind many workers and farmers. Were growth to slow or the bubble to burst, an undertow of resentment and mistrust would return with a vengeance.

POLITICAL BUREAUCRATIC OPPOSITION

Each proto-democracy has been challenged from within, by the stratum of *nomenklatura* who occupied significant local and national posts during the communist period, as well as by the secret police establishments that underpinned every communist regime. People who were active in the administration of these regimes have retained positions of influence in the new systems and will probably continue to do so for some time to come. In many critical jobs, there are still too few adequately trained substitutes available, and with the preservation of old bureaucrats comes the preservation of old power relations.

Considerable debate always existed about the size of the *nomenklatura* in Eastern Europe. No one disagrees that, in the Communist Party of the Soviet Union (CPSU), the elite was a small subset of the 18,000,000 or more who were party members in the early 1980s. Definitions and estimates of the elite core ranged from slightly greater than 1 percent to almost 8 percent of the total CPSU membership.[17] It is clear, in any event, that the *nomenklatura* had tremendous influence in critical posts in industry, the military police, and trade unions. In the late 1970s, perhaps 17,000 industrial managers in the USSR were part of the *nomenklatura*, a staggering number whose removal or whole-hearted conversion would have been necessary for any kind of transition to a market economy.[18]

Many of these individuals have not been anxious to implement market-oriented policies. The transformation of ministries, local governments, research institutes, courts, and other institutions has been slowed down or hindered by the recalcitrance of the *nomenklatura*.[19] In addition, quite apart from foot-dragging, there have also been concerted efforts by extremists of the right and left to bring about the failure of democratic experiments.

When communist *apparatchiks* do engage in reform, it is for their own benefit. Data are beginning to be collected in post-communist Europe that show a discomfiting association between membership in the former communist *nomenklatura*, on the one hand, and business ownership and high income in the new market environment, on the other.[20] It is too early to tell how lasting this link will be, but if anyone thought that the demise of communist regimes meant that the leadership positions would change hands quickly and completely, that person was mistaken.

Many Communist Party officials had created a cash reserve through petty corruption, had the greatest opportunity to learn about the West through travel, information, and education, and had the best contacts with European and North American sources of grants, loans, and investments. These advantages, although waning over time, remain powerful.

POLITICAL COSTS OF MARKETIZATION

A rapid and fundamental shift toward free market economies in Eastern Europe placed many enterprises and a high proportion of the workforce in economic peril. The cumulative economic contraction after 1989 was extraordinary. Declining production, inflation, and unemployment were evident from 1989 to 1995 in most cases. Even in 1995–96, a large gap remained between 1988–89 output and wages vis-à-vis the mid-1990s.[21] Only in 1997 did countries of the Northern tier—Poland, the Czech Republic, and Hungary—decisively exceed 1989 output levels.

Freeing prices, selling state-owned property, and making currency convertible were part of the shock therapy imposed by Poland's government in January 1990. The government's enormous legitimacy quickly waned as the economic pain mounted before any gain was evident. Tadeusz Mazowiecki's government, and his effort to defeat Lech Wałęsa for the presidency, had both failed by late 1990. In 1991, positive assessments about Poland's economic future evaporated and expectations sagged; almost three-fifths of those surveyed in early 1992 felt that the situation in the country was moving in a "bad direction."[22] Although some objective indicators of the economy began to show improvement by the end of 1992,[23] Poland's electorate continued to be pessimistic about the future development of the country and about their personal standard of living. In 1993–94 surveys, a cumulative 75 percent of Poles thought that the economic situation of their families was unsatisfactory, and a total of 56 percent thought that the situation of their households would either remain the same or get worse in five years' time.[24] The expectation that further hardship would accompany the way to a completely free market economy was probably heightened by the rising rate of unemployment.[25]

The somewhat encouraging signs of economic recovery were obscured by the political crisis that began to consume Poland in 1992. Of particular harm was the destructive debate about politicians' contacts with the Polish secret police during the communist years, with Wałęsa's enemies at first hurling charges at the president about collaboration. The year 1992 saw the fall of two prime ministers and their cabinets, and considerable doubt about the roles of the presidency and the parliament raised serious constitutional issues that remained unsettled four years later. The Polish political crisis continued unabated even as aggregate economic growth returned, inflation was held in check, and unemployment showed modest improvement.

In the early post-communist years, in Hungary and the Czech and Slovak Federal Republic, fears of inflation and unemployment were much stronger than might have been warranted, given the mixed economic signals in both countries in 1992. Inflation rates in these countries—22–25 percent in Hungary and 10–12 percent in the Czech and Slovak Republic—were then the lowest in the region. Relatively high unemployment in Hungary (14 percent) was offset by a rapid increase in private employment growing out of new foreign investments. In public opinion polls, however, 47 percent of those Hungarians surveyed thought that things were moving in a bad direction economically, with only 32 percent believing that things were moving in the right direction.[26] Czechs and Slovaks were about evenly divided (38 percent "bad," 43 percent "good").[27]

As economies in Hungary and the Czech Republic improved in 1994–1995,[28] the public mood seemed to alter. In October 1994, a USIA-commissioned poll in Hungary found a large increase in public trust in institutions, with 58 percent trusting the direction of the new government, up from 24 percent the previous fall. This increase, however, was a consequence of the Hungarian Socialist Party's victory in May 1994, rather than of economic improvement. Respondents thought that the new government "more closely reflected public values."[29] When the new Socialist government led by Gyula Horn announced an austerity package in March 1995, public opinion shifted significantly. In April 1995, a public poll revealed an increase in the popularity of the politicians who had been most critical of the austerity measures,[30] and Horn's standing continued to erode in 1996–97.

None of the East European countries is yet willing to reject market reforms entirely, and that applies to Russia as well. After initial public rejection of the Gaidar program of 1991, public attitudes evolved. Despite a prevalent public perception that the economic direction pursued by the government did not respond to the interests of the majority,[31] surveys indicated that the efforts of the Russian government to carry out reforms were evaluated positively by a majority in 1992.[32] In 1993, Russian respondents still said they would favor some type of market reform rather than a return to the old economic system.[33] Yet other surveys indicated that Russians were simultaneously worried by the expenses of living in a market economy.[34] As the gap between surging prices and a much slower increase in wages continued to grow into 1995, Russians' average real income remained substantially lower than in 1991.[35] Voting for a party that promised public assistance to those who had been most disadvantaged by the current reform process seems, in light of such trends, to be based on self-interest.[36]

Every post-communist market economy is experiencing difficulties, and the intensity and breadth of conflict grow as economic transitions are accelerated. Broadly consensual movements that had opposed communist rule have broken down into competing groups and strata, now that the adversary has been defeated and narrow economic interests are emerging. Although people generally continue to support the notion of a free-market economy, they also reject individual responsibility for individual well-being. In short, they favor cautious change.

UNCERTAIN CIVIL-MILITARY RELATIONS

How well do armies and post-communist governments coexist? In the years since the demise of communist regimes in Eastern Europe, there have been no military coups in the East European corridor from the Baltic to the Bosphorus. Farther to the east, however, the assertiveness of the Russian military, in alliance with conservative nationalists, has created independent policy lines. Former Russian Defense Minister Pavel Grachev and other senior officers articulated views sharply at odds with those expressed by the Foreign Ministry while Andrei Kozyrev was minister. Yevgenni Primakov, Kozyrev's successor, may be more compatible with military views of the world, but will still find it difficult to accept the general staff's autonomy.

No one should forget that every East European army—with the sole exception of the Czech military—has a history of participating in coups in the twentieth century. For the Bulgarian Army, coups or plots became routine prior to World War II.[37] During the communist period, armies were either at first indistinguishable from the party (as in Yugoslavia and Albania) or were compromised by access to material resources.[38]

Where army loyalty now lies, however, is less certain. On the surface, force reductions and restructuring, the empowerment of a new generation of senior officers, and doctrinal reorientation have been proceeding. Yet military leaders and defense ministers have also opposed budget reductions and drastic cuts in their order of battle, coming into open conflict with civilian policy-makers. Former Polish Defense Minister Jan Parys, former Bulgarian Defense Minister Dimitur Ludzhev, former Chief of the Hungarian General Staff László Borsits, and many others were early political casualties after 1989. These cases were by no means identical; rather, they illustrate the tensions that existed regarding the proper role of defense establishments in larger decisions about post-communist politics.

Such tensions persisted into the mid- and late nineties, as the search for renewed defense doctrines and civil-military relations throughout Eastern Europe was paralleled by the crisis of identity of the defense industries. Efforts by these industries to stay alive have been considerable. With a legacy of overgrown military-industrial complexes, notoriously inefficient, and employing large proportions of the communist-era workforce, these industries could not survive under the conditions of a market economy. By 1991, arms production in the former Czechoslovakia had fallen to 50 percent of its 1987 record level.[39] After the breakup of the Federation, arms production continued to decline until 1993, when it stabilized. In Slovakia, the defense industry output declined to 10 percent of the 1988 production peak and approximately 50 percent of the employees lost their jobs.[40] In Poland, the industry's output fell by 80 percent between 1988 and 1993.[41]

The behemoth industries of the former Warsaw Pact states still exist and have contributed greatly to the difficulties experienced as countries in Eastern Europe moved toward market economies. The often unclear nature of government policy toward the defense sector, with no specified guidelines for privatization, left enterprise managers confused about the criteria of their enterprises' performance. By the end of 1993, 70 percent of a sample of defense enterprises in the Czech Republic, Slovakia, Hungary, and Poland were trying to survive, following a strategy of "semi-active survival." In addition to reducing costs (oftentimes by lay-offs), these enterprises started to generate new revenues with new products and/or services. An estimated 20 percent of the sampled enterprises seemed to await bankruptcy, unless their respective governments rescued them.[42] It is not overstatement to argue that the relation between civilian governments, the officer corps, and the defense industries in post-communist Eastern Europe greatly affects the prospects for internal stability in each of these countries. NATO admission, for Poland, Hungary, and the Czech Republic, will *require* accelerated change in civil-military relations; for others, the pace of change may well recede.

NATIONALISM

Although an explosive union of ethnic identity and intolerant chauvinism is found in many places, nationalist unrest is particularly intense in Southeastern Europe and the Caucasus.

Yugoslavia's violent death began long before 1989. From the defeated Austro-Hungarian and Ottoman empires following World War I was cobbled a fragile and fractured state. After World War II, only wartime partisan leader Josip Broz Tito's charisma, fear of the Soviet Union, and the close integration of the army and the Communist Party kept Yugoslavia alive. When Tito died in 1980, economic deterioration, corruption, and increasing inequities exacerbated schisms between nationalities. Communist Serbian President Slobodan Milošević was willing and able to use these schisms for political ends; his inflammatory rhetoric was first directed in particular against the large Albanian population in the province of Kosovo. When Serbs, Croats, and others began their war in

1991, the violence that ensued became a harbinger of things to come throughout the region.

Romania and Bulgaria also have a potential for nationalist unrest. An organization of ill repute—*Vatra Româneasca*—operates in Romania, fomenting anti-Semitism, antipathy toward Hungarians and violence against Gypsies. *Vatra* was born in 1990, but its roots appear to be those of the pre–World War II Fascist Iron Guard. Its composition is Romanian—largely, but not exclusively, from Transylvania—with strong links to the former secret police (*Securitate*) members. In Bulgaria, the Bulgarian Socialist Party and other more extreme groups propagate strongly negative views about the Turkish minority and Islam generally. Macedonia contains a mix of ethnic and religious groups and has a potential to become a catalyst of a Balkan war. Macedonia involves almost every nation and state within the Balkans, and it remains the oldest and most intractable of Eastern Europe's nationalist disputes.

Joining the Balkans as a center of nationalist warfare has been the Caucasus—particularly, of course, the vicious war between Armenians and Azeris, a civil war within Georgia, and a brutal Russian attempt to extinguish Chechen autonomy through unrelenting air attacks and artillery bombardments. Moldova's simmering tensions pit an ethnically Romanian state against the holdouts of old-line Russian communism in Tiraspol and other cities across the Dniester River.

Even in this cursory survey, one finds ample reminders of nationalist fury. From 1991 to 1996, perhaps several hundred thousand people were killed as a result of combat from the Adriatic to the Caspian Sea—an arc of death and destruction unparalleled in Europe since World War II.

The External Dimension

A grave menace to both democratic systems and free-market economies in Eastern Europe lies in the dissemination of weaponry and in the proliferation of uncertain or weak *ententes*. Both trends provide nutrients for demogogues who destroy from within the rule of law, pluralism, and free-market principles.

ARMAMENTS IN ABUNDANCE

The disintegration of the Soviet Union generated an array of new, well-armed players in Eurasian security. Large "under-employed" conventional force structures, sales of deactivated weapons, and military assistance grants have emboldened rival nations and ethnic groups and enabled them to confront one another. In a part of the world that for decades has exhibited the largest proportionate military effort of any region, an abundance of arms allows grievances to escalate to deadly combat.[43]

When the Conventional Armed Forces Treaty (CFE) was signed in

1990, much was known about the disposition of military equipment in Europe. It is no longer. A great deal of Warsaw Pact weaponry has been redistributed, much of it coming from the poorly disciplined militaries in Russia and Ukraine, often involving criminal elements in both states. Corruption within the Commonwealth of Independent States (CIS) forces while they were still stationed in Germany was documented, and pilfering of weapons described in detail.[44] From Belarus, tank parts and firearms of all sizes and lethality have been marketed with the open admission by high-ranking officials, such as Former First Deputy Minister Aleksandr Tushinski.[45] The temptation to resell military equipment is in part a function of the problem of destroying or converting the massive quantities of military hardware that were in Warsaw Pact inventories. Ukraine, for example, faced the immense task of destroying or converting more than 2,000 main battle tanks; it simply did not have the capacity to rapidly carry out this task. Having a few or many of these tanks slip through the cracks of the CFE verification system eases a dismantlement problem and is, of course, to Ukraine's economic advantage.

Weapons, and the technologies that went into building them, are being distributed widely to China (Mig-29s, Mig-31s, and Su-27s), Iran (three Kilo-class submarines), and other buyers. In post-communist Europe, devastating conventional wars have been fought in the Balkans and Caucasus with these arsenals. When combat first broke out in the former Yugoslavia in mid-1991, the sides were poorly prepared. The Yugoslav "People's Army" (JNA) had large stocks of weapons, but was ill-trained, while the Serbs' opponents lacked armaments. In the following years of war, however, multiple rocket launchers, radar-controlled artillery, antiaircraft missile systems, and much more effective antitank weapons have been deployed on the ground, while Croatia built up a credible, if small, air force. These rising combat capabilities bode poorly for a stable truce. Huge economic dislocations and mass migrations could result, driven by renewed or enlarged conflicts over irredentist issues and maltreated diasporas.

ACCORDS, *ENTENTES,* AND SIGNS OF INSTABILITY

Governments caught within this web of growing uncertainty are grasping for safe havens. Since 1989, there has been a reconstruction of intraregional *ententes* and alliances, a redistribution of military equipment, and a desperate reach for Western support and guarantees through NATO, the European Union (EU), and large powers. For Poland, Hungary, and the Czech Republic, NATO has "arrived." For others, the search goes on. Albania's desperation was painfully evident when it became the first country in the region to make a formal application for NATO membership in early 1993; this application, as expected, was received without commitment. Nevertheless, Albania's former Defense

Minister Safet Zhulali was very busy with bilateral meetings throughout the region, trying to strengthen ties and guarantees.[46]

Yet, bilateral treaties and regional organizations have accomplished little. A few states have modernized their force structures while reducing their active forces. Others have participated in officer training opportunities in Western military institutions and Partnerships for Peace (PfP) exercises that imply closer ties with NATO. Some countries have gained a modicum of reassurance about the intentions of their neighbors through negotiations, while most states in post-communist Europe have been busily signing accords with as many near and distant countries as possible, hoping to insulate themselves from a hostile environment.

Ironically, these efforts served only to reinforce old cleavages. When Europe's eastern half was divided and held captive by the Soviet Army, the goal of a Europe whole and free was only imagined. Now, it cannot be consummated.

THREATS AND DEMAGOGUES

There are no massed armies pressing on the borders of East European states today, although the residual presence of Russian troops is discomfiting to those in the Baltic republics, Moldova, and elsewhere. Neither has there been truly bellicose rhetoric, save for the rabid pronouncements about Moldova, the Baltics, and other former Warsaw Pact states by Russian extremists such as Vladimir Zhirinovskii.

The real danger arising from external threat perceptions lies in their contribution to already insecure domestic conditions. Because of nationalism, the pain of marketization, and other internal matters, new governments are less than sanguine about their own prospects for survival. External threats can be used as political bludgeons by antidemocratic opposition groups. Added uncertainty created by mass migration or an influx of arms makes the pursuit of a free-market democracy all the more perilous.

Europe's eastern half will end the twentieth century with a widened and intensified perception of insecurity even though it faces no proximate military dangers. Unlike the prelude to the two world wars, when expectations of military invasions were palpable, armies no longer hold center stage. Nevertheless, a prevailing climate of mistrust and suspicion exists, denying security to proto-democracies that are extraordinarily in need of safety.

Instead, a crescent of wars—from the Adriatic to the Caucasus, and to Central Asia—may have claimed 300,000 lives (200,000 in the former Yugoslavia, 25,000 in Tajikistan, and perhaps 75,000 in the Caucasus) from 1991 to 1996. From Albania, Kosovo, and Macedonia, through Bosnia, Croatia, east through Transylvania into Moldova and the Crimea, and farther to Georgia, Armenia, Azerbaijan, and Chechnya, horrific fighting and thousands of deaths have led to reassessments of military cutbacks, and prolonged the political survival of reactionaries opposed to fundamentally plural, tolerant societies.

In the north, from Central Europe to the Baltic states, where armed clashes have not occurred, cooperation has gone further, and economic capacities are greater. Yet it would be a great error to assume that these early, positive signs insulate nascent democracies, such as Hungary or Poland, from internal or external peril.

SECURITY PURSUED

Europe's eastern half will not obtain security through national armed forces. Surplus weapons and a militarily skilled people are not sources of security. Even for a state with notable resources—Poland, for example—maintaining a credible conventional defense is doubtful, given current budgetary constraints. Plans for the Polish armed forces reflect a movement toward smaller units, with less densely armored mechanized regiments being the mainstay of Poland's order of battle.[47]

Restructuring, redeploying, reducing, professionalizing, depoliticizing, developing new sources for arms, and inaugurating educational exchanges and joint training exercises with advanced democracies through NATO and PfP are part of a new face of East European military organizations. In addition, a substantial effort has been devoted to articulating new military doctrines: "circular defense," and "limited defense." Lacking money, however, few of these ideas guide procurement, training, or deployment. Poland's armed forces may be relatively potent due to the country's homogeneity, the size of its armed forces (more than 200,000 troops), and more training opportunities. Few of the region's other militaries, however, exhibit much that would give a strong aggressor any pause. No one should expect the armed forces of post-communist Europe to provide the capacities needed to deal with perceived threats.

The main source of East European security, instead, will be through tightly interwoven bilateral, regional, and multilateral guarantees. At the bilateral level, individual states and their neighbors must continue to take small steps, such as the "Open Skies" Accord between Romania and Hungary, which inaugurated four flights by both sides over the other's territory per year; the first took place in January 1993. Multiple bilateral confidence- and security-building measures can do much to constrain the violence against diasporas and claims on the territory of others. Demilitarized zones, regions of military transparency, exchanges of military officers and defense planners, and other innovative steps can reduce uncertainty and were, for example, built into the Dayton Accord that ended the Bosnian conflict. Such bilateral agreements are difficult to maintain, however, given neighbors' conflicting interests.

Regional networks will be a second vital component of East European security. The Baltic State Council, a Black Sea Economic Zone, the Central European initiative and other regional efforts enhance the prospects for regional cooperation as these groups are small enough for direct communications. Security will not be found easily among these regional *ententes* however. Visegrad (originally a trilateral process for cooperation among Poland, Hungary, and Czechoslovakia), for example, would never have sufficed as a security guarantee because it involved small, relatively weak countries that do not necessarily share interests. Indeed, it is no longer a real actor. Subregional pacts run the risk of becoming second-class associations. Denied closer affiliation with the EU, for example, the Black Sea Economic Zone had become a kind of "common bazaar" of states, each with some connection to the Islamic world. However, assembling several weak states into one organization does not necessarily create a strong entity.

At the multilateral level, the momentum toward a monetary union and a common defense and foreign policy in the European Union waned after the Maastricht Treaty. Other organizations that might help fill the security vacuum in Eastern Europe include NATO's 1999 extension east and, in the background, the underdeveloped Organization for Security and Cooperation in Europe (OSCE). NATO's desultory initial response to the needs of the continent's eastern half, however, included creating (at the 1991 Rome NATO summit) the North Atlantic Cooperation Council (or NACC) and, in December 1993, the Partnership for Peace program (PfP). Not until 1995 did a firm commitment to enlarge receive political backing. OSCE's inability to stop the fighting in Yugoslavia suggested that such an amorphous body will require major upgrading before it can meet its rhetorical claims. Problems within the OSCE process are easily recognizable: they include its consensual or near-consensus decision rules and the fragmented and limited staff, among others. The constrained institutionalization of the OSCE after the Brussels summit in 1994 may now have reached a plateau beyond which little can be done unless bold political decisions are taken.[48]

Such political decisions will first require a shift in Western ideas about security, as well as expectations about OSCE's role. Security in post-communist Europe is critical to the peace and prosperity of the West. In the eastern half of Europe, indigenous military forces will be unable to shoulder the burden of national security no matter what leaders insist or hope. Multilayered security links hold most promise because bilateral arrangements can break down easily, while regional efforts often add weakness to weakness.

Such an approach has been the preferred vision of East European security, as first enunciated by then Polish Foreign Minister Kszysztof Skubiszewski, former Romanian Foreign Minister Adrian Nastase, and former Czech and Slovak Foreign Minister, Jiři Dienstbier. Their visions of security, although not always consistent with those of their militaries, were important markers in 1990–91. They understood quickly that the United States and their other allies vastly preferred NATO as the comfortable, familiar alliance system. NATO is the foremost institution of transatlantic security by virtue of U.S. insistence and European indecision, and post-communist countries had no choice but to acknowledge the importance of being closer to NATO. Politicians like former Prime Minister Václav Klaus in the Czech Republic, or former President Zhelyu Zhelev in Bulgaria, were vocal proponents of joining NATO. Others have taken a more cautionary tone but still advocate steps that would make their countries more attractive for eventual EU or NATO membership.

Multinational collective security organizations such as the OSCE have been dismissed by most as impractical because of their size and unwieldy decision-making rules. Yet only the inclusivity of the OSCE can provide adequate coverage for all of Eastern Europe's security needs. From the Baltic to the Bosphorus, organizational membership must not be an issue in the degree to which international support is available to fledging democracies. NATO ought not metamorphose itself out of business by enlarging membership and functions to be all things to all people. Further, NATO's accession of former Warsaw Pact states involves a potentially disruptive admissions process that raises expectations only to be later frustrated; more, not less, insecurity may follow should Eastern Europe become divided between those first allowed to join NATO and those excluded.

The present OSCE, however, is also unable to metamorphose further. A few small institutional components with minuscule budgets, pursuing conflict resolution, human rights for national minorities, and democratic motivations, leave much to be desired. Even among such organizations, the OSCE is likely to have little efficacy as long as its resources are so limited and its discussions are based on consensus or the "consensus-minus-two" possibility (whereby decisions are made without involvement of two disputing states).

These limitations can be remedied, however. Although opportunities to enhance collective security at the Helsinki and Budapest Summits in 1992 and 1994 were lost, the lessons of warfare in the Balkans and the Caucasus may generate a greater urgency for institutions that help *prevent* conflict.

Essential for the development of an effective collective security organization will be a permanent, fully staffed secretariat. At the moment, the OSCE has only a rudimentary office in Prague, a small staff in Vienna, and a democratic initiatives office in Warsaw; many administrative and agenda-planning tasks are thus absorbed by the state serving in the rotating post of "chair-in-office." An invigorated collective security organization would also need two permanent commissions, with adequate staff in the principal areas of OSCE activity: human rights and security matters. In the latter domain, where the Helsinki process produced significant accords on confidence and security-building, Europe needs more. Specifically, it needs a permanent peacekeeping garrison, on which the OSCE could draw quickly before wars break out. Euro-Atlantic security and the fragile peace in some East European locales should not depend on cobbling together peacekeeping forces while conflict spreads.

That such measures rest on political will and old leadership is self-evident. Yet, these proposals need to be considered in light of persistent insecurities in post-communist Europe that will not recede. One cannot foresee an environment in which diasporas and irredentist issues will fade. Therefore, the conditions that will constrain these problems must be created. Only a system of collective security offers this opportunity, and, thus, it must be the West's principal concern for the immediate future.

Notes

This is a substantially revised version of an essay that first appeared in *Survival*, Vol. 35, No. 2 (Summer 1993), 156–171.

1. For a report on such volatility, see *The Washington Post* (12 July 1991) and *Christian Science Monitor* (26 November 1991). William Drozdiak (in *The Washington Post*) cites data indicating that 42 percent of the French admitted to hostility toward immigrants. The appeal of anti-immigration rhetoric continued to propel the extremist political party of Jean-Marie le Pen, *Front National*, supported by roughly a tenth of the popular vote in the December 1995 elections.

2. J. D. Singer and Melvin Small, in "The War-Proneness of Democratic Regimes, 1816–1965," in *Jerusalem Journal of International Relations*, No. 1 (Summer 1976), 50–69. For broad confirmation of the "democracies are more peaceful" hypothesis, see Steve Chan, "Mirror, Mirror on the Wall . . . Are the Democratic States More Pacific?" in *Journal of Conflict Resolution*, Vol. 28 (1984), 617–648. The most recent opus devoted to the democratic peace theme is Bruce M. Russett et al., *Grasping the Democratic Peace: Principles for a Post-Cold War World* (Princeton: Princeton University Press, 1993).

3. For a summary of international collective initiatives to end the conflict in the former Yugoslavia, see Lori Fisler Damrosch, *Enforcing Restraint: Collective Intervention in Internal Conflicts* (New York: Council on Foreign Relations Press, 1993). For an update on the role of the United Nations, from the beginning of the conflict to present, see "The United Nations and the Situation in the Former Yugoslavia," reference paper DPI/1312 rev. 4, available on the Internet. Regarding IFOR's potential role, see Daniel N. Nelson, "To Make Peace in a Year, IFOR Must Do More," *The Christian Science Monitor* (9 February 1996).

4. Richard Rose, I. Boeva, and V. Shironin, *How Russians Are Coping with Transition: New Russia Barometer II* (University of Strathclyde Studies in Public Policy, No. 216, Glasgow, 1993), question 144, 152–161. Nationwide represen-

tative sample survey conducted by means of face-to-face interviews with 1,975 respondents, between 26 June and 22 July 1993.

5. Rose and Christian Haerpfer, "Mass Response to Transformation in Post-Communist Societies," in *Europe-Asia Studies*, Vol. 46, No. 1 (1994), 3–28, Table 6.

6. Rose and Haerpfer, *New Democracies III: Learning from What Is Happening* (University of Strathclyde: Center for the Study of Public Policy, SPP No. 230, 1994), Fig. 2, 17.

7. See the text of a Warsaw TV report from 25 July 1991 trans. in Foreign Broadcast Information Service (FBIS), *Daily Report* (Eastern Europe), 26 July 1991, 19.

8. Institute of Socio-Political Research (ISPR), *Sotsial'naya i sotsial'no-politicheskaya situatsiya v Rossii: Analiz i prognoz* (Moscow: Russian Academy of Sciences, 1994), 127.

9. *USIA Opinion Analysis*, memorandum M-290-94, "Public Confidence in Democratic Institutions Rises in Hungary" (27 December 1994), 3.

10. For election turnout, see *RFE/RL Daily Report*, No. 150 and No. 152 (8 and 12 August 1991).

11. For the 1991 and 1993 elections, see International Republican Institute, *Russia. Election Observation Report* (12 December 1993), 32 and Table 2, 33. For the December 1995 elections, *Keesing's Record of World Events*, News Digest (December 1995), 40871-2. The percentage for 1995 was compiled by the authors.

12. *RFE/RL Daily Report*, No. 150 and No. 152 (8 and 12 August 1991).

13. Magyar Nemzet (Budapest) (10 October 1995), 1, 6, trans. in *Daily Report* (Eastern Europe), 19 October 1995, 23–25.

14. "1995 Elections to Reflect Different Voting Behaviors," in *Open Media Research Institute (OMRI), Special Elections Report*, No. 12 (8 December 1995).

15. See *New Democracies Barometer IV* (Paul Lazarsfeld Society, Vienna, March 1996).

16. For Bulgaria, Romania, Slovakia, and Hungary, see *New Democracies Barometer IV*. For Russia, see *New Russia Barometer* (Center for the Study of Public Policy, University of Strathclyde, March 1996).

17. See a summary of differing estimates in Maria Hirszowicz, *The Bureaucratic Leviathan* (New York: New York University Press, 1980), 90–92.

18. Estimate is the authors', from data in Mervyn Matthews, *Privilege in the Soviet Union* (London: Allen & Unwin, 1978), 31.

19. Bulgarian Radio, 4 August 1991, accused "middle level, communist *nomenklatura*" of having encouraged price increases in order to "hamper economic reform." See *RFE/RL Daily Report*, No. 149 (7 August 1991), 3.

20. In Russia, with the initiation of market reforms, the so-called "Gaidar Program" of 1992, the privatization process took the form of *nomenklatura* privatization, with managers of the former state enterprises buying off these enterprises. The widespread public frustration with this phenomenon was mirrored by opinion polls which found that 39 percent of Russian respondents were against putting up state enterprises for sale (as compared to 29 percent in favor) because of their belief that the sale merely favored former members of the Communist Party, who had the resources and the information required to capitalize on such assets. See John Tedstrom, "Russia: Progress Report on Industrial Privatization," *RFE/RL Research Report*, Vol. 1, No. 17 (24 April 1992), 46–50; and Mary Cline, "Attitudes toward Economic Reform in Russia," *RFE/RL Research Report*, Vol. 2, No. 22 (28 May 1993), 43–49. Similar processes of acquisition of

state assets were signaled in Hungary and in Poland. See Gabor Bakos, "Hungarian Transition after Three Years," in *Europe-Asia Studies*, Vol. 46, No. 7 (1994), 1189–1214; and Mark Kramer, "Polish Workers and the Post-Communist Transition, 1989–1993," in *Europe-Asia Studies*, Vol. 47, No. 4 (1995), 669–712.

21. Many statistical estimates are imprecise and contradictory. The structural changes in the economies of Eastern Europe basically shocked the established systems of data collection. New methods had to be found, and in many cases the measurement of concepts had to be modified. Consequently, even data from one country may not be comparable over time, and cross-national comparisons become questionable. Nevertheless, one early attempt at offering a compendium was Hieronim Kubiak's data on "symptoms of communism's post mortem disintegration"—data distributed at the Stockholm International Peace Research Institute's conference on East European Security, Stockholm, May 1991.

22. *Gazeta Wyborcza*, No. 42 (19 February 1992), 1, citing a Gallup Institute poll.

23. After an initial decrease of 9.8 percent in GNP between 1990 and 1991, economic indicators showed a 14.5 percent increase in GNP and a 13.7 percent increase in GNP/per capita between 1991 and 1993. Authors' computations of indicators (adjusted for inflation) released in *World Military Expenditures and Arms Transfers, 1993–1994* (U.S. Arms Control and Disarmament Agency, February 1995), 79. Also, the inflation rate decreased by 2.58 percent by the end of 1993.

24. Rose and Haerpfer, *New Democracies Barometer III*, Appendix questions No. 25 and 27.

25. Poland's rate of unemployment remained on the rise, with 11.8 percent in 1991, 13.6 percent in 1992, and 16.4 percent in 1993. See *Życie Gospodarcze*, No. 5 (1995), 9. The unemployment rate eventually stabilized in 1994–1995.

26. "A Review of Economic Performance in 1992," *RFE/RL Research Bulletin*, Vol. 10, No. 1 (5 January 1993), 1.

27. Rose and Haerpfer, *New Democracies Barometer III*, Appendix.

28. According to the Czech Statistical Office, in 1994, the Czech Republic's GDP grew by 2.7 percent in real terms. See "Klaus on Czech Economic Prospects," *Open Media Research Institute*, No. 44, Part 2 (2 March 1995). In Hungary, the GDP grew by 1.5 percent in 1995, and a 1 percent growth was projected for 1996. See "Hungarian Economic Growth Expected to Slow," *Open Media Research Institute Daily Digest*, Vol. 87, Part 2 (3 May 1996). The Hungarian projections are based on the report published by analysts at the Postabank and economic research firm GKI Gazdasagkutato Rt.

29. *USIA Opinion Analysis*, M-290-94, 3.

30. "Popularity of Hungarian Opposition Party Grows," *Open Media Research Institute Daily Digest*, No. 86, Part 2 (3 May 1995).

31. ISPR (1993), 69.

32. In March 1992, a total of 55 percent rated the government's efforts positively, as compared to 35 percent who rated then negatively. Muscovites and city-dwellers were more likely to show satisfaction with the reform, while rural residents were more likely to be dissatisfied. Surveys were conducted by Vox Populi between 13 February and 3 March 1992. In Amy Corning and Jill Chin, "Critical Evaluations of the Russian Government," *RFE/RL Research Report*, Vol. 1, No. 25 (19 June 1992), Fig. 4.

33. In a survey conducted by the Media and Opinion Research Department of Radio Free Europe/Radio Liberty in May 1993, 58 percent of respondents were in favor of some free-market type of economic system, with only 20 percent

favoring a planned economy. In Mary Cline, Amy Corning, and Mark Rhodes, "The Showdown in Moscow: Tracking Public Opinion," *RFE/RL Research Report*, Vol. 2, No. 43 (29 October 1993).

34. In November 1993, the greatest worry of Russian citizens was the cost of living (69 percent). In ISPR (1994), 124.

35. "Wide Gap between Basic Prices and Wages in Moscow," *Open Media Research Institute Daily Digest*, Vol. 86, Part 1 (3 May 1995). Also "Average Russian Income Drops," *Open Media Research Institute Daily Digest*, Vol. 95, part 1 (17 May 1995).

36. In the Duma elections of December 1995, the revived Communist Party of the Russian Federation (founding congress in February 1993) ran on a platform of restricting privatization, holding a referendum on the restoration of the Soviet Union, reestablishing order and security, and providing public assistance to the disadvantaged groups. With some 30 percent of the Russian population living on a monthly wage below the subsistence minimum, such promises may have raised the public's support for the communists. See *Keesing's Record of World Events*, News Digest (December 1995), 40871-2; and "Average Russian Income Drops," *Open Media Research Institute* (17 May 1995).

37. See John Jaworsky, "Bulgaria," in Teresa Rakowska-Harmstone, Christopher Jones, et al., *Warsaw Pact: The Question of Cohesion*, Phase II, Vol. 3 (Ottawa: Ministry of Defense, ORAE, 1985), 9.

38. For East European defense expenditures and socioeconomic trade-offs during the communist period, consult Thad P. Alton, "East European Defense Expenditures, 1965–1982," in U.S. Congress, Joint Economic Committee, *East European Economies: Slow Growth in the 1980s* (Washington: U.S. Government Printing Office, 1985).

39. *Hospodarske Noviny* (Prague) (1991), 20.

40. These figures were reported by Pavel Cech, technical manager, and Karel Droppa, head of department of special production with the Slovak Ministry of Economics, in personal interview with Yudit Kiss. Reported in Yudit Kiss, "Sink or Swim? Central European Defense Industry Enterprises in the Aftermath of the Cold War," in *Europe-Asia Studies*, Vol. 47, No. 5 (1995), 787–812.

41. Ibid.

42. Ibid.

43. For an empirical portrait of this military effort, see Daniel N. Nelson, *Alliance Behavior in the Warsaw Pact* (Boulder: Westview, 1986).

44. See a report on this matter in *RFE/RL News Briefs*, Vol. 2, No. 5 (5 January 1993), 5.

45. See Tushinski's comments in *RFE Daily Report*, No. 19 (29 January 1993), 5.

46. For example, Defense Minister Zhulali went to Budapest to confer with Lajos Fur, in January 1993—one in an endless round of sojourns and pilgrimages by Albanian officials.

47. One early authoritative statement was *The Polish Army: Facts and Figures* (Warsaw: Ministry of National Defense, 1991). For more on governmental directions for the defense industry, see Douglas L. Clarke, "Eastern Europe's Troubled Arms Industries: Part I," *RFE/RL Research Report*, Vol. 3, No. 14 (8 April 1994), 35–43.

48. A review of the achievements and difficulties of CSCE is "Beyond Process: The CSCE's Institutional Development, 1990–92," (Washington: Commission on Security and Cooperation in Europe, U.S. Congress, 1992), 37–39.

16

Democracy, Tolerance, and the Cycles of History

SABRINA P. RAMET

I

The ancient Greeks were torn between two rival interpretations about the movement of history. On the one hand were partisans of a linear approach, who believed that people could build on the past and that political development was tantamount to progress (Heraclitus). Arrayed against them were those who held for a cyclical view of history, in which no achievement is permanent, and civilization is condemned to retrace parallel curves endlessly (Parmenides). The debate between Heraclitus and Parmenides shook the ancient Greek world, not the least because the stakes were anything but negligible: at issue was a choice between diametrically opposed orientations toward politics, political change, and political possibility. Plato, who belonged to the younger generation, accepted Parmenides' judgment on this point, and became subsequently the most famous advocate of the cyclical approach to history. Where Heraclitus saw a historical movement in a direction which was for the analyst to determine, but which was, in any case, determined by fixed historical laws, Plato argued that systems evolve from oligarchy to democracy, disintegrate into chaos, embrace despotic rule as a solution to widespread chaos, gradually divide power and reestablish the oligarchy, and begin the cycle anew. The cyclical view essentially triumphed among the ancients. The Enlightenment changed all this. The moderns, beginning with Hobbes and Locke, and continuing with Hegel, Comte, and Marx, have preferred a linear view of history, which is seen as pushing toward some final ultimate stage sometimes called Absolute Knowledge, sometimes Absolute Freedom, sometimes pure communism, sometimes the Triumph of Democracy, and sometimes the End of History.[1] But within this school there are differences. For Frank Fukuyama, thus, the achievement of democracy is seen as the universal aspiration and eventual tendency of all nations, and as a stage beyond which no further evolution is possible. For Barrington Moore,[2] by contrast, democracy, while valued as the ideal end-stage, is nonetheless seen as only a possible final stage, one of many and one which entails the passage through some specific previous developmental phases. In Moore's view, these phases, which are political, economic, and cultural in character, constitute alternative paths of transition. States which bypass the harsh winter of these transitions, in his view, cannot attain the warm summer of democracy.

It is, thus, one thing to enumerate alternative developmental routes, one of which must be traversed if democracy is to be attained. It is quite another thing, at least if we are to believe Moore, to identify those historical movements or processes which need to have occurred before institutions of a nominally democratic type have any chance of fulfilling their promise. (If, for example, a civil war may function to draw a country together—as Moore suggests—how serious does this war have to be in order to function in this way? And how can we recognize which wars are sufficient for this purpose and which are not?) Following Moore's line of thinking, one could only conclude that just as one cannot establish a despotic regime in any country at any time, so too one cannot establish a democratic government anywhere one fancies. Plato, for all his differences about the nature of history, would have understood.

The differences between these two understandings of history are not inconsequential. For those who see history as linear, it becomes extremely difficult to imagine a return to political forms which were discarded earlier, or even to political tasks which were undertaken earlier. Hence, it was commonplace in the 1970s and 1980s for "linearists" to write off currents of disaffection[3] in Eastern Europe, to portray communism as secure for the indefinite future, and to take it as a given that there could be no second attempt to build pluralist systems, except conceivably in a watered-down compromise fashion within the basic framework of the socialist system.[4] For "linearists," historical moments, once surpassed, can never be revisited. As Heraclitus once said, "You cannot step in the same river twice."

But for those who see history as cyclical, the return to earlier forms (perhaps with some variations) is not at all unexpected. On the contrary, the adherents of a cyclical view see the struggles over equality, over human dignity, over tolerance, and over political participation as fixtures, in which no side is ever able to achieve a complete and final victory.

Adherents of this school tended to take currents of disaffection seriously, understanding them as reflections of the points of weakness in the communist system. And hence, adherents of this school became aware, as early as 1986, that communism's days were numbered.[5] And hence, too, there was no reason for surprise on seeing that the renewed effort to construct pluralist systems in Eastern Europe should be accompanied by new depths of social and economic uncertainty, furnishing, in turn, the psychological space in which the radical right has reappeared and festered.[6]

II

The effort to construct pluralism—or if one prefers, democracy—is by no means assured of success. A key ingredient for success in this enterprise is that the elites take appropriate steps to foster a democratic political culture. It is, in a word, essential to the project of democratization that the predominant values in a system be in accord with the parameters of that system and, more specifically, that political elites foster values supportive of and in accord with democratic institutions.

It may be useful to set forth a definition of *democracy*. By the term, I shall mean *any system based on the principles of political choice and social tolerance*. At first glance, it may seem that this definition is unduly lean, indeed perhaps that I have used Occam's razor not merely to shave Plato's beard, but indeed to lob off the Greek philosopher's head altogether. To this I reply that in implementing this view of democracy, one necessarily seeks to expand political choice and social tolerance—the latter value constituting the only necessary check on the former. Party pluralism, alternative media, and universal suffrage for elections based on secret ballots are all measures that address the value of political choice in a serious way, while the separation of Church and state is a common measure adopted in the quest for social tolerance.

If this definition may be accepted, then it follows that the more political choice and the more social tolerance found in a given society, the more democratic is its system. And further, the less political choice or the less social tolerance is found in a society, the less democratic it is in practice, and the more its institutions, in whatever spirit they may have been designed, will function in an undemocratic and even antidemocratic way. Hannah Arendt is among those who have pointed to the essential connection between toleration and democracy, showing how the festering of anti-Semitism paves the way for totalitarian and authoritarian ideologies.[7]

The Western liberal tradition, which served historically as the midwife of democratic systems in their modern sense, held that the values of choice and tolerance are mutually inclusive. More specifically, as Joseph Raz notes, classical liberalism held that political choice is meaningless unless those to whom choice is granted are able to exercise their choice autonomously, and that autonomy, in turn, presumes toleration.[8] And in fact we find that authoritarian parties typically subvert democratic systems by conducting propaganda which, among other things, seeks to narrow the space for acceptable political discourse, typically by manipulating images of "us" and "them," i.e., by fostering stereotypes, prejudice, inter-group hatred, and intolerance.

Many post-Enlightenment societies have sought to maximize yet a third value—equality. There may in fact be only three routes to equality: (1) the homogenization of the population, on the argument that if people can be made the same, then they can be treated the same; (2) genocide and/or expulsion of "undesirables," on the argument that if people are not the same, they should be removed from society; and (3) tolerance, which argues that if people are different, equal treatment should be nuanced only to the extent necessary to assure an equal result (e.g., providing special paths for wheelchairs is a means to enhanced equality, not to discrimination). Homogenization has been attempted in this century by Josef Stalin and by Romania's Nicolae Ceaușescu, among others. Genocide and expulsion have been the favored policies of Adolf Hitler, Croatian fascist leader Ante Pavelić (1941–45), and contemporary Serbian leaders Slobodan Milošević (president of rump Yugoslavia) and Radovan Karadžić (former president of the Bosnian Serb Republic); for that matter, Bulgaria, Greece, and Turkey conducted a massive population exchange after World War I on the logic of this strategy. Tolerance, the third alternative, is, however—and I think this much is only obvious—the only acceptable option for societies valuing both democracy and equality.

Furthermore, equality without tolerance turns out to be just as spurious as choice without tolerance. It is clear enough that Hobbes and Locke, the *Urvater* of classical liberalism, were motivated by the desire to assure political order and the security of person and property, and that they were concerned to elaborate the rights enjoyed by people in the defense of person and property. Writers as diverse as Leo Strauss[9] and Heinrich von Treitschke[10] have recognized that these "natural rights" are traced, by these early liberals, back to Natural Law, i.e., to the notion that human logic must necessarily trace some common paths in the moral sphere, that some actions are demonstrably "reasonable" and others demonstrably "unreasonable." One may also call this the notion of Universal Reason, without intending any Hegelian implications. As understood by classical liberalism, Universal Reason was, by definition, universal, and Natural Law and natural rights, similarly, applied to all humans, regardless of sex, race, or religion. Universal Reason simultaneously establishes both the reasonableness of morality and the foundations of the claim of human equality.

This identifies yet another pressure point of democracy. Now it may happen that a group, whether a political party or a religious organization or a racist-supremacist cabal, may declare that morality is somehow "not reasonable"—usually by claiming that there is nothing inherently moral or immoral and that we need X party, Y Church, or Z race to set the rules by which we can live. But such a claim strikes at the foundation of classical liberalism, and, in consequence, at anything we might call liberal democracy, including anything which could be subsumed under a category of democracy as I have defined it here. In essence, the hinging of morality on revelation or regulation moves us away from Universal Reason and toward moral relativism.

Moral relativism is beguiling—first because it is so compatible with the exaggerated individualism which has taken hold in the United States and much of Europe, and second, because it even seems, to many, to be implied in the very notion of toleration. But tolerance is not the only value worth protecting. If it were, as J. Budziszewski warns us, then tolerance would "hardly be anything more than good conscience in our continuing lack of convictions."[11] On the contrary, tolerance, to be worthy of the name, must be informed by Universal Reason, i.e., by regard for the principles of Natural Law.

The classical liberal notions of Natural Law and Universal Reason already presume the universal extent of the moral field, i.e., that all living persons are moral subjects with the same broad rights and duties, and moral objects entitled to the same general treatment. Any creed or ideology which narrows the moral field, by defining some persons as lying outside the moral field, relativizes morality and subverts democracy at the most basic level. Simić explains the concept in these terms:

> Within a moral field, members are expected to act towards each other with reference to a common set of shared ideas by which behavior is structured and evaluated. In contrast, behavior outside the moral field can be said to be amoral in that it is primarily idiosyncratic, and as such may be purely instrumental or exploitative without being subject to sanctions.[12]

Nationalism is a particularly powerful ideology which routinely works to narrow the moral field, so that for the Serb nationalist, it is "honorable" to massacre Muslims, for the Armenian nationalist, it is "honorable" to shoot Azeri, for the Slovak nationalist, it is "only right" to take down Hungarian street signs in purely Hungarian villages in southern Slovakia and to replace them with signs in the Slovak language. Slovakia for the Slovaks. Armenia for the Armenians. Serbia for the Serbs.[13]

III

I have argued above that liberal democracy is founded on four central values, two of which I have chosen to highlight as primary. These are: political choice; social tolerance; order and security of person and property; and Universal Reason. The foregoing argument suggests that in order to have liberal democracy, one must safeguard these four values (and most especially the values of choice and tolerance). To want liberal democracy is to want these values as well. From this conceptual promontory, certain propositions can be derived: (1) When the values of the existing system are discordant with the mainstream values of society, the system will decay. (2) Changes in social values lead to changes in political organization.[14] And (3) when the real values of a society are discordant with the nominal nature of the system being built, the values will predominate, either subverting or diluting the goal system. This triad of propositions provides an important key to understanding both the reasons for the decay and ultimate collapse of communism in Eastern Europe and the challenges presently confronting the new systems in that region. Communism, we may say, was built up in Eastern Europe on the foundation of three central values: control, social justice, and equality (understood in class terms). In the 1950s and 1960s, the East European Communist Parties could count on a basic cadre which was dedicated to these values (on a Marxist understanding of them) and which viewed the state as a mechanism for their realization. By the early 1980s, if not before, the communist elites no longer retained their earlier belief that the system was fostering justice and equality, and that left only sheer control to sustain and "inspire" the elite. Moreover, sizable sections of the intelligentsia, the religious bodies, and in Poland, at least, even the working class were redefining their understanding of justice and equality in non-Marxist ways, and in many cases, subordinating these either to the more traditionally liberal values, or to yet other values (nation and faith being the typical alternatives). The shift in values played a critical, indeed central role in the erosion of communism in the region.[15]

But the discord between the decaying communist system and emergent alternative values presupposes neither a consensus on values in these post-communist societies nor the predominance of values favorable to democracy—regardless of the rhetoric of 1989. What is presently occurring in Eastern Europe is, in fact, remarkably similar to what occurred in the region after World War I, viz., the erection of institutions conforming to notions of political pluralism ("democracy") alongside the promulgation and proliferation of values in tension with or even incompatible with democracy. In particular, one may say that with the sole exceptions of the Czech Republic and (in part) Slovenia, the post-communist societies of Eastern Europe are heavily oriented to the values of nation, tradition, and prosperity. I shall examine these one by one.

If the nation is the highest good, that already narrows the moral field and relativizes morality, as we have seen. Nationalism also potentially subverts all four liberal values, whether directly or indirectly. The claims of tolerance are eroded by nationalism, by construing some persons as having greater moral value than others, and the constriction of the moral field is itself logically incompatible with the notion of Universal Reason. It may appear less obvious how nationalism may subvert political choice and personal security. But quite apart from the "inconveniences" associated with the conflicts in Bosnia-Herzegovina and Moldova, which have been sustained in each case by rabid strains of nationalism, even loyal and obedient citizens may find themselves unable to keep their jobs, to publish articles, or even to shop in safety unless they demonstratively affirm whatever may be the shibboleths of the day (e.g., that Croatia is threatened and entitled to the retrieval of all land lost since June 1991, or that Serbia is threatened and that all Serbs are entitled to have the areas in which they live attached to Serbia).[16]

By tradition, I mean everything that is normally understood by "traditional values," but most especially the subordination of women on the principle *Kinder, Küche, Kirche* (children, kitchen, Church). Numerous writers have attested to the fact that powerful social forces in the postcommunist societies of Eastern Europe are energetically reasserting these traditional values. The agents of these values are typically the Christian Churches, Christian Democratic parties, fascist parties, and nationalist/racist organizations.[17] "Traditional values" strike a potentially deadly blow at Universal Reason, by excepting half the human race from full inclusion here, and have direct consequences for social tolerance by raising up narrow values to which all are expected to conform (and in conjunction with nationalism, by expecting the "good Slovak mother," for example, to bear a full complement of Slovak children). As Katherine Verdery has noted, ". . . postsocialist Eastern Europe reveals how tightly interwoven are 'socialism' and 'capitalism' with specific—and variant—organizations of gender: and these in turn are bound up with the national idea."[18]

Finally, there is *prosperity*, a particularly insidious value, because classical liberalism (except arguably in the specific derivation associated with the name of Adam Smith) was not designed with an eye to assuring economic prosperity and efficiency. Neither Hobbes nor Locke nor J. S. Mill nor even Jeremy Bentham thought of prosperity and efficiency as the motivating purposes of democracy. Some scholars argue that democratic systems presume the prior achievement of some modicum of economic prosperity; others argue that economic prosperity is a consequence of democracy; still others (including the present author) argue both positions. But no one has ever suggested that the purpose of democracy was to maximize economic prosperity. Insofar as the desire for prosperity is a prime motivator in contemporary Eastern Europe, it is a spurious motivator. There is nothing inherent in democracy that guarantees, for example, that a true democracy has a prosperous economy; this does not follow at all, although one might, more reasonably, argue that a true democracy affords meaningful political choices. This in turn suggests that to the extent that these new systems are unable to deliver prosperous economies, popular support for them may be all too easily eroded. An established democracy has a record on which to fall back in times of duress; a new democracy has no such record to reinforce its claim to legitimacy.

These considerations lead me, in turn, to the following conclusion: In order to weather the stresses of the post-communist transition and consolidate liberal democracies, it is essential that the political values of classical liberalism gain preeminence over the competing claims of nation, tradition, and prosperity. But ironically, while there are sundry political parties and religious organizations consciously and systematically promoting these latter values, there has been no systematic effort made anywhere in the region to foster and disseminate the democratic values of tolerance, security, and Universal Reason, and even the value of political choice has been construed narrowly. And this leads me to conclude that unless elites in the region start to give this agenda priority soon (making use of schools and media as the chief vehicles of resocialization), the instability in the region may grow, subverting most of the new democracies, and potentially condemning Eastern Europe to retrace the same path it took in the 1930s.

Notes

An earlier version of this essay was originally published in T. Hara, ed., *Slavic Eurasia in Transition: Multiple Analyses* (Sapporo, Japan: Slavic Research Center of Hokkaido University, 1994). Reprinted by permission.

1. Francis Fukuyama, "The End of History?" in *The National Interest*, No. 16 (Summer 1989). For an interesting "inversion" of Fukuyama's argument, see Shoji Ishitsuka, "The Fall of Real Socialism and the Crisis in the Human Sciences, with Implications for Social Justice," in *Social Justice*, Vol. 21, No. 4 (Winter 1994).

2. Barrington Moore, Jr., *Social Origins of Dictatorship and Democracy: Lord and Peasant in the Making of the Modern World* (Boston: Beacon, 1966).

3. I have explained the concept of disaffection in Sabrina Petra Ramet, *Social Currents in Eastern Europe: The Sources and Consequences of the Great Transformation*, 2nd ed. (Durham: Duke University Press, 1995), Chap. 3.

4. Examples of this approach and set of conclusions include Zygmunt Bau-

mann, "Social Dissent in the East European Political System," in *Archives Euro-péenes de Sociologie*, Vol. 12, No. 1 (1971); Andrzej Korbonski, "The Prospects for Change in Eastern Europe" and "Reply"—both in *Slavic Review*, Vol. 33, No. 2 (June 1974), especially 238–239, 254–255; and Korbonski, "Soviet-East European Relations in the 1980s: Continuity and Change," in Marco Carnovale and William C. Potter, eds., *Continuity and Change in Soviet-East European Relations: Implications for the West* (Boulder: Westview, 1989), especially 22.

5. I have enumerated the various predictions made by observant scholars beginning in 1987 in my *Social Currents*, 2nd ed., Chap. 1. The Helsinki Watch book *Reinventing Civil Society*, published in 1986, is the first writing of which I am aware which clearly pointed to the proximate demise of communism. See *Reinventing Civil Society: Poland's Quiet Revolution, 1981–1986* (New York: Helsinki Watch, 1986).

6. For details, see Ramet, *Social Currents*, 2nd ed., Chap. 18 ("Civil Society and Uncivil Chauvinism"); also Anita J. Prazmowska, "The New Right in Poland: Nationalism, Anti-Semitism and Parliamentarianism" and Jill A. Irvine, "Nationalism and the Extreme Right in the Former Yugoslavia"—both in Luciano Cheles, Ronnie Ferguson, and Michalina Vaughan, eds., *The Far Right in Western & Eastern Europe*, 2nd ed. (Harlow, Essex: Longman Group, 1995).

7. Hannah Arendt, *On the Origins of Totalitarianism*, rev. ed. (London: A. Deutsch, 1986).

8. Joseph Raz, "Autonomy, Toleration, and the Harm Principle," in Susan Mendus, ed., *Justifying Toleration: Conceptual and Historical Perspectives* (Cambridge: Cambridge University Press, 1988).

9. Leo Strauss, *Natural Right and History* (Chicago: University of Chicago Press, 1953).

10. Heinrich von Treitschke, *Politics*, Vol. 1, trans. from German by Blanche Dugdale and Torben de Bille (New York: Macmillan, 1916), 71.

11. J. Budziszewski, *True Tolerance: Liberalism and the Necessity of Judgment* (New Brunswick: Transaction, 1992), xiii.

12. Andrei Simić, "Obstacles to the Development of a Yugoslav National Consciousness: Ethnic Identity and Folk Culture in the Balkans," in *Journal of Mediterranean Studies*, Vol. 1 (1991), No. 1, 31.

13. I have discussed the dangers of nationalist and religious zealotry at greater length in my book *Whose Democracy? Nationalism, Religion, and the Doctrine of Collective Rights in Post-1989 Eastern Europe* (Lanham, Md.: Rowman & Littlefield, 1997). See also Thomas Martin, "The End of Sovereignty," in *Democracy & Nature*, Vol. 3, No. 2 (Issue No. 8, 1995).

14. Plato went even further and wrote, "Any musical innovation is full of danger to the whole State, and ought to be prohibited; when modes of music change, the fundamental laws of the State always change with them."—Plato, *The Republic*, Book 4.

15. As I have argued in my *Social Currents*, 2nd ed.

16. Renata Salecl, "Nationalism, Anti-Semitism, and Anti-Feminism in Eastern Europe," in *New German Critique*, No. 57 (Fall 1992).

17. See Slavenka Drakulić, "Feminism Is a Dirty Word in Hungary," in *The Utne Reader* (January–February 1990); and Jiřina Šiklová, "Sind die Frauen der Ost- und Mitteleuropa Konservativ?" in *Die Neue Gesellschaft, Frankfurter Hefte*, Vol. 38, No. 11 (November 1991).

18. Katherine Verdery, *What Was Socialism, and What Comes Next?* (Princeton: Princeton University Press, 1996), 81.

FOR FURTHER READING

The following bibliography is a guide to additional sources in English.

Chapter 1: Introduction
Berend, Ivan T., and György Ranki. *Economic Development in East-Central Europe in the Nineteenth and Twentieth Centuries* New York: Columbia University Press, 1974.
Brzezinski, Zbigniew K. *The Soviet Bloc: Unity and Conflict*, rev. and enl. ed. Cambridge: Harvard University Press, 1967.
De Zayas, Alfred-Maurice. *A Terrible Revenge: The Ethnic Cleansing of the East European Germans, 1944–1950* New York: St. Martin's, 1994.
Golan, Galia. *The Czechoslovak Reform Movement* Cambridge: Cambridge University Press, 1971.
———. *Reform Rule in Czechoslovakia: The Dubček Era, 1968–1969* Cambridge: Cambridge University Press, 1973.
Hitchins, Keith. *Rumania, 1866–1947* Oxford: Clarendon, 1994.
Hockenos, Paul. *Free to Hate: The Rise of the Right in Post-Communist Eastern Europe* New York and London: Routledge, 1993, rev. 1994.
Rothschild, Joseph. *East Central Europe between the Two World Wars* Seattle: University of Washington Press, 1974.
———. *Return to Diversity: A Political History of East Central Europe since World War II*, 2nd ed. New York: Oxford University Press, 1994.
Skilling, H. Gordon. *Samizdat and an Independent Society in Central and Eastern Europe* Columbus: Ohio State University Press, 1989.
Sugar, Peter F., et al. *A History of Hungary* Bloomington: Indiana University Press, 1990.
Vali, Ferenc A. *Rift and Revolt in Hungary: Nationalism versus Communism* Cambridge: Harvard University Press, 1961.

Chapter 2: Fault Lines
Chirot, Daniel, ed. *The Origins of Backwardness in Eastern Europe: Economics and Politics from the Middle Ages until the Early Twentieth Century* Berkeley: University of California Press, 1989.
Hupchik, Dennis. *Culture and History in Eastern Europe* New York: St. Martin's, 1994.
Jelavich, Barbara. *History of the Balkans*, 2 Vols. Cambridge: Cambridge University Press, 1983.
Lampe, John R., and Marvin R. Jackson. *Balkan Economic History, 1550–1950* Bloomington: Indiana University Press, 1982.
McNeill, William H. *Europe's Steppe Frontier, 1500–1800* Chicago: University of Chicago Press, 1964.
Stokes, Gale. "Eastern Europe," in Mary Beth Norton and Pamela Gerardi, eds., *The American Historical Association's Guide to Historical Literature* New York: Oxford University Press, 1995, 1025–69.

Subtelny, Orest. *Domination of Eastern Europe: Native Nobilities and Foreign Absolutism, 1500–1715* Kingston: McGill-Queens University Press, 1986.

Sugar, Peter F. *Southeastern Europe under Ottoman Rule, 1354–1804* Seattle: University of Washington Press, 1977.

Szucz, Jeno. "The Three Historical Regions of Europe," in *Acta Historica Academiae Scientiarum Hungaricae*, Vol. 29, Nos. 2–4 (1983): 131–184.

Tihany, Leslie C. *A History of Middle Europe: From the Earliest Times to the Age of the World Wars* New Brunswick: Rutgers University Press, 1976.

Walters, E. Garrison. *The Other Europe: Eastern Europe to 1945* Syracuse: Syracuse University Press, 1987.

Wandycz, Piotr S. *The Price of Freedom: A History of East Central Europe from the Middle Ages to the Present* London and New York: Routledge, 1993.

Chapter 3: Czechoslovakia

Jancar, Barbara Wolfe. *Czechoslovakia and the Absolute Monopoly of Power: A Study of Political Power in a Communist System* New York: Praeger, 1971.

Jelinek, Yeshayahu. *The Parish Republic: Hlinka's Slovak People's Party, 1939–1945* Boulder: East European Monographs, 1976.

Johnson, Owen V. *Slovakia, 1918–1938: Education and the Making of a Nation* Boulder: East European Monographs, 1985.

Korbel, Josef. *Twentieth-Century Czechoslovakia: The Meanings of Its History* New York: Columbia University Press, 1987.

Mamatey, Victor S., and Radomir Luza, eds. *A History of the Czechoslovak Republic, 1918–1948* Princeton: Princeton University Press, 1973.

Mastny, Vojtech. *The Czechs under Nazi Rule: The Failure of National Resistance* New York: Columbia University Press, 1971.

Myant, Martin. *The Czechoslovak Economy 1948–1988* Cambridge: Cambridge University Press, 1989.

Skilling, H. Gordon. *Charter 77 and Human Rights in Czechoslovakia* London: Allen & Unwin, 1981.

———. *Czechoslovakia's Interrupted Revolution* Princeton: Princeton University Press, 1976.

Suda, Zdenek. *Zealots and Rebels: A History of the Ruling Communist Party of Czechoslovakia* Stanford: Hoover Institution Press, 1980.

Taborsky, Edward. *Communism in Czechoslovakia, 1948–1960* Princeton: Princeton University Press, 1961.

Wolchik, Sharon L. *Czechoslovakia in Transition: Politics, Economics, and Society* London and New York: Pinter, 1991.

Chapter 4: Hungary

Berend, Ivan T., and György Ranki. *Hungary: A Century of Economic Development* New York: Barnes & Noble, 1974.

———. *The Hungarian Economy in the Twentieth Century* London: Croom Helm, 1985.

Braham, L. Randolph, ed. *The Tragedy of Hungarian Jewry: Essays, Documents, Depositions* New York: Columbia University Press, 1986.

Fel, Edit, and Tamas Hofer. *Proper Peasants: Traditional Life in a Hungarian Village* Chicago: Aldine, 1969.

Felkay, Andrew. *Hungary and the USSR, 1956–1988: Kadar's Political Leadership* New York: Greenwood, 1989.

Gati, Charles. *Hungary and the Soviet Bloc* Durham: Duke University Press, 1986.

Kecskemeti, Paul. *The Unexpected Revolution: Social Forces in the Hungarian Uprising* Stanford: Stanford University Press, 1961.

Király, Bela, and Paul Jonas, eds. *The Hungarian Revolution of 1956 in Retrospect* Boulder: East European Monographs, 1977.

Kopacsi, Sandor. *In the Name of the Working Class: The Inside Story of the Hungarian Revolution* New York: Grove, 1988

Pinter, Istvan. *Hungarian Anti-Fascism and Resistance, 1941–1945* Budapest: Adademiai Kiado, 1986.

Szelenyi, Ivan. *Socialist Entrepreneurs: Embourgeoisment in Hungary* Madison: University of Wisconsin Press, 1988.

Szent-Miklossy, István. *With the Hungarian Independence Movement, 1943–1947* New York: Praeger, 1988.

Chapter 5: The German Democratic Republic

Bentley, Raymond. *Technological Change in the German Democratic Republic* Boulder: Westview, 1984.

Childs, David. *East Germany* New York: Praeger, 1969.

———. *The GDR: Moscow's German Ally*, rev. ed. Cambridge: Cambridge University Press, 1988.

Hamalainen, Pekka Kalevi. *Uniting Germany: Actions and Reactions* Boulder: Westview, 1995.

Philipsen, Dirk. *We Were the People: Voices from East Germany's Revolutionary Autumn of 1989* Durham: Duke University Press, 1993.

Pike, David. *The Politics of Culture in Soviet-Occupied Germany, 1945–1949* Stanford: Stanford University Press, 1992.

Shingleton, A. Bradley, Marian J. Gibbon, and Kathryn S. Mack. *Dimensions of German Unification: Economic, Social, and Legal Analyses* Boulder: Westview, 1995.

Sontheimer, Kurt, and Wilhelm Bleek. *The Government and Politics of East Germany* London: Hutchinson, 1975.

Tate, Dennis. *The East German Novel* New York: St. Martin's, 1985.

Verheyen, Dirk, and Christian Soe, eds. *The Germans and Their Neighbors* Boulder: Westview, 1993.

Chapter 6: Poland

Bethell, Nicholas. *Gomulka: His Poland, His Communism* Harlow: Longmans, 1969.

Bielasiak, Jack, and Maurice D. Simon, eds. *Polish Politics: The Edge of the Abyss* New York: Praeger, 1983.

De Weydenthal, Jan B. *The Communists of Poland: An Historical Outline*, rev. ed. Stanford: Hoover Institution Press, 1987.

Gross, Jan Tomasz. *Polish Society under German Occupation: The Generalgouvernement, 1939–1944* Princeton: Princeton University Press, 1979.

Kurski, Jaroslaw. *Lech Walesa: Democrat or Dictator?* Boulder: Westview 1993.

Ludwikowski, Rett R. *Continuity and Change in Poland: Conservatism in Polish Political Thought* Washington: Catholic University of America Press, 1991.

Pasini, Rebecca. "Piety amid Politics: The Roman Catholic Church and Polish Abortion Policy," in *Problems of Post-Communism*, Vol. 43, No. 2 (March–April 1996): 35–47.

Sanford, George. *Military Rule in Poland: The Rebuilding of a Communist Power, 1981–1983* New York: St. Martin's, 1986.

Schatz, Jaff. *The Generation: The Rise and Fall of the Jewish Communists of Poland* Berkeley: University of California Press, 1991.

Torańska, Teresa. *"Them": Stalin's Polish Puppets* New York: Harper & Row, 1987.
Touraine, Alain. *Solidarity: Poland, 1980–1981* Cambridge: Cambridge University Press, 1983.

Chapter 7: Yugoslavia

Banac, Ivo. *The National Question in Yugoslavia: Origins, History, Politics* Ithaca: Cornell University Press, 1984.
————. *With Stalin, against Tito: Cominformist Splits in Yugoslav Communism* Ithaca: Cornell University Press, 1988.
Benderly, Jill, and Evan Kraft, eds. *Independent Slovenia: Origins, Movements, Prospects* New York: St. Martin's, 1994.
Djilas, Milovan. *Wartime* New York: Harcourt Brace Jovanovich, 1977.
Koštunica, Vojislav, and Kosta Čavoški. *Party Pluralism or Monism: Social Movements and the Political System in Yugoslavia, 1944–1949* Boulder: East European Monographs, 1985.
Magaš, Branka. *The Destruction of Yugoslavia: Tracking Yugoslavia's Break-up 1980–1992* London: Verso, 1993.
Meier, Viktor. *How Yugoslavia Was Lost*. Trans. from German by Sabrina Petra Ramet. London and New York: Routledge, forthcoming in 1999.
Pleština, Dijana. *Regional Development in Communist Yugoslavia: Success, Failure, and Consequences* Boulder: Westview, 1992.
Ramet, Sabrina Petra. *Balkan Babel: The Disintegration of Yugoslavia from the Death of Tito to Ethnic War*, 2nd ed. Boulder: Westview, 1996.
————. *Nationalism and Federalism in Yugoslavia, 1962–1991*, 2nd ed. Bloomington: Indiana University Press, 1992.
Roberts, Walter R. *Tito, Mihailović and the Allies, 1941–1945* New Brunswick: Rutgers University Press, 1973.
Rusinow, Dennison I. *The Yugoslav Experiment, 1948–1974* Berkeley: University of California Press, 1977.
Tomasevich, Jozo. *The Chetniks: War and Revolution in Yugoslavia, 1941–1945* Stanford: Stanford University Press, 1975.

Chapter 8: Romania

Almond, Mark. *Decline without Fall: Romania under Ceaușescu* London: Alliance, 1988.
Crowther, William E. *The Political Economy of Romanian Socialism* New York: Praeger, 1988.
Fischer-Galati, Stephen. *Twentieth Century Rumania* New York: Columbia University Press, 1991.
Gilberg, Trond. *Nationalism and Communism in Romania: The Rise and Fall of Ceaușescu's Personal Dictatorship* Boulder: Westview, 1990.
Ionescu, Ghita. *Communism in Rumania, 1944–1962* London and New York: Oxford University Press, 1964.
Jowitt, Kenneth. *Revolutionary Breakthroughs and National Development: The Case of Romania, 1944–1965* Berkeley: University of California Press, 1971.
King, Robert. *History of the Romanian Communist Party* Stanford: Hoover Institution Press, 1981.
Lungu, Dov B. *Romania and the Great Powers, 1933–1940* Durham: Duke University Press, 1989.
Nelson, Daniel N., ed. *Romania after Tyranny* Boulder: Westview, 1992.

Roberts, Henry L. *Rumania: Political Problems of an Agrarian State* New Haven: Yale University Press, 1951.

Saiu, Liliana. *The Great Powers and Rumania, 1944–1946: A Study of the Early Cold War Era* Boulder: East European Monographs, 1992.

Verdery, Katherine. *National Identity under Socialism: Identity and Cultural Politics in Ceauşescu's Romania* Berkeley: University of California Press, 1991.

Chapter 9: Bulgaria

Bell, John D. *The Bulgarian Communist Party from Blagoev to Zhivkov* Stanford: Hoover Institution Press, 1986.

Bokov, Georgi, ed. *Modern Bulgaria: History, Policy, Economy, Culture* Sofia: Sofia Press, 1981.

Bonev, Vladimir. *For a United, Popular Fatherland Front* Sofia: Sofia Press, n.d.

Brown, J. F. *Bulgaria under Communist Rule* New York: Praeger, 1970.

Crampton, R. J. *A Short History of Modern Bulgaria* Cambridge: Cambridge University Press, 1987.

Dellin, L. A. D., ed. *Bulgaria* New York: Praeger, 1957.

Groueff, Stephane. *Crown of Thorns: The Reign of King Boris III of Bulgaria* Lanham, Md.: Madison, 1987.

Hristov, Hristo. *Bulgaria 1300 Years* Sofia: Sofia Press, 1980.

Kostov, Vladimir. *The Bulgarian Umbrella* New York: St. Martin's, 1988.

McIntyre, Robert J. *Bulgaria: Politics, Economics and Society* London: Pinter, 1988.

Miller, Marshall Lee. *Bulgaria during the Second World War* Stanford: Stanford University Press, 1975.

Nikoloff, Assen. *The Bulgarian Resurgence* Cleveland: published by the author, 1987.

Chapter 10: Albania

Biberaj, Elez. *Albania: A Socialist Maverick* Boulder: Westview, 1990.

———. *Albania and China: A Study of an Unequal Alliance* Boulder: Westview, 1986.

Costa, Nicholas J. *Albania: A European Enigma* Boulder: East European Monographs, 1995.

Griffith, William E. *Albania and the Sino-Soviet Rift* Cambridge: MIT Press, 1963.

Hall, Derek. *Albania and the Albanians* London: Pinter, 1994.

Jacques, Edwin E. *The Albanians: An Ethnic History from Prehistoric Times to the Present* London: McFarland, 1995.

Logoreci, Anton. *The Albanians: Europe's Forgotten Survivors* London: Gollancz, 1977.

Pano, Nicholas C. *The People's Republic of Albania* Baltimore: Johns Hopkins University Press, 1968.

Prifti, Peter R. *Socialist Albania since 1944: Domestic and Foreign Developments* Cambridge: MIT Press, 1978.

Sjoberg, Orjan. *Rural Change and Development in Albania* Boulder: Westview, 1991.

Vickers, Miranda. *The Albanians: A Modern History* London: I. B. Tauris, 1995.

Zickel, Raymond, and Walter R. Iwaskiw, eds. *Albania: A Country Study* Washington: Federal Research Division, Library of Congress, 1994.

Chapter 11: Women

East European Feminist Conference. *What Can We Do for Ourselves?* Belgrade: Center for Women's Studies, 1994.

Einhorn, Barbara. *Cinderella Goes to Market: Citizenship, Gender, and Women's Movement in East Central Europe* London: Verso, 1993.

Funk, Nanette, and Magda Mueller, eds. *Gender Politics and Post-Communism: Reflections from Eastern Europe and the Former Soviet Union* New York and London: Routledge, 1993.

Heitlinger, Alena. *Women and State Socialism: Sex Inequality in the Soviet Union and Czechoslovakia* London: Macmillan, 1979.

Jancar, Barbara. *Women Under Communism* Baltimore: Johns Hopkins University Press, 1978.

Rueschemeyer, Marilyn, ed. *Women in the Politics of Postcommunist Eastern Europe* Armonk, N.Y.: M. E. Sharpe, 1994.

Schaffer, Harry G. *Women in the Two Germanies: A Comparative Study of a Socialist and a Non-Socialist Society* New York: Pergamon, 1981.

Scott, Hilda. *Does Socialism Liberate Women? Experiences from Eastern Europe* Boston: Beacon, 1974.

Turlakova, Eleonora. *Bulgarian Women* Sofia: Sofia Press, 1976.

Wolchik, Sharon, and Alfred G. Meyer, eds. *Women, State, and Party in Eastern Europe* Durham: Duke University Press, 1985.

Wrochno-Stanke, Krystyna. *Woman in Poland* Warsaw: Interpress, 1969.

Yedlin, Tova, ed. *Women in Eastern Europe and the Soviet Union* New York: Praeger, 1980.

Chapter 12: Religion

Alexander, Stella. *Church and State in Yugoslavia since 1945* Cambridge: Cambridge University Press, 1979.

Beeson, Trevor. *Discretion and Valour: Religious Conditions in Russia and Eastern Europe*, rev. and enl. ed. Philadelphia: Fortress, 1982.

Broun, Janice. *Conscience and Captivity: Religion in Eastern Europe* Washington: Ethics and Public Policy Center, 1988.

Goeckel, Robert F.. *The Lutheran Church and the East German State: Political Conflict under Ulbricht and Honecker* Ithaca: Cornell University Press, 1990.

Michnik, Adam. *The Church and the Left*, trans. from Polish by David Ost Chicago: University of Chicago Press, 1993.

Mojzes, Paul. *Religious Liberty in Eastern Europe and the USSR: Before and After the Great Transformation* Boulder: East European Monographs, 1992.

Monticone, Ronald. *The Catholic Church in Communist Poland, 1945–1985* Boulder: East European Monographs, 1986.

Ramet, Pedro, ed. *Catholicism and Politics in Communist Societies* Durham: Duke University Press, 1990.

Ramet, Sabrina P. *Nihil Obstat: Religion, Politics, and Social Change in East-Central Europe and Russia* Durham: Duke University Press, 1998.

Ramet, Sabrina Petra, ed. *Protestantism and Politics in Eastern Europe and Russia: The Communist and Post-Communist Eras* Durham: Duke University Press, 1992.

Solberg, Richard W. *God and Caesar in East Germany: The Conflict of Church and State in East Germany since 1945* New York: Macmillan, 1961.

Weigel, George. *The Final Revolution: The Resistance Church and the Collapse of Communism* New York: Oxford University Press, 1992.

Chapter 13: Cinema

Goulding, Daniel J. *The Liberated Cinema: The Yugoslav Experience* Bloomington: Indiana University Press, 1985.

————, ed. *Five Filmmakers: Trakovsky, Forman, Polanski, Szabo, Makavejev* Bloomington: Indiana University Press, 1994.

————, ed. *Post-New Wave Cinema in the Soviet Union and Eastern Europe* Bloomington: Indiana University Press, 1988.

Hames, Peter. *The Czechoslovak New Wave* Berkeley: University of California Press, 1985.

Holloway, Ronald. The *Bulgarian Cinema* Rutherford, N.J.: Fairleigh Dickinson University Press, 1986.

Liehm, Antonin J. *Closely Watched Films: The Czechoslovak Experience* White Plains: International Arts and Sciences Press, 1974.

Liehm, Mira, and Antonin J. Liehm. *The Most Important Art: Eastern European Film after 1945* Berkeley: University of California Press, 1977.

Michalek, Bolesław, and Frank Turaj. *The Modern Cinema of Poland* Bloomington: Indiana University Press, 1988.

Nemeskurty, Istvan. *Word and Image: History of the Hungarian Cinema* Budapest: Corvina Press, 1968.

Paul, David W., ed. *Politics, Art and Commitment in the East European Cinema* London: Macmillan, 1983.

Petrie, Graham. *History Must Answer to Man: The Contemporary Hungarian Cinema* Budapest: Corvina Press, 1978.

Portuges, Catherine. *Screen Memories: The Hungarian Cinema of Márta Mészáros* Bloomington: Indiana University Press, 1993.

Chapter 14: Economics

Admiral, P. H., ed. *Economic Transition in Eastern Europe* Oxford: Blackwell, 1993.

Amsden, Alice, Jack Kochanowicz, and Lance Taylor. *The Market Meets Its Match: Restructuring the Economies of Eastern Europe* Cambridge: Harvard University Press, 1994.

Brada, Josef C., Ed A. Hewett, and Thomas A. Wolf, eds. *Economic Adjustment in Eastern Europe and the Soviet Union* Durham: Duke University Press, 1988.

Ellman, Michael, and Bladimir Kontorovich, eds. *The Disintegration of the Soviet Economic System* London and New York: Routledge, 1992.

Fallenbuchl, Zbigniew M., ed. *Economic Development in the Soviet Union and Eastern Europe* New York: Praeger, 1975–1976

Frydman, Roman, Andrzej Rapaczynski, and John Earle. *The Privatisation Process in Central Europe* London: Central European University Press, 1993.

Havlik, Peter, ed. *Dismantling the Command Economy in Eastern Europe* Boulder: Westview, 1991.

Kaser, M. C., and E. A. Radice, eds. *The Economic History of Eastern Europe, 1919–1975,* 3 Vols. Oxford: Clarendon, 1985.

Kornai, Janos. *The Socialist System: The Political Economy of Communism* Oxford: Clarendon, 1992.

Nelson, Joan, ed. *A Precarious Balance: Democracy and Economic Reforms in Eastern Europe* San Francisco: International Center for Economic Growth, 1994.

Poznanski, Kazimierz, ed. *Stabilization and Privatization in Poland: An Economic Evaluation of the Shock Therapy Program* Boston: Kluwer, 1993.

Welfens, Paul. *Market-Oriented Systematic Transformations in Eastern Europe* Berlin: Springer-Verlag, 1992.

Chapter 15: Security
Cowen-Karp, Regina, ed. *Central and Eastern Europe: The Challenge of Transition* Oxford and New York: Oxford University Press, 1993.
Haglund, David G. *NATO's Eastern Dilemmas* Boulder: Westview, 1994.
Lampe, John, and Daniel N. Nelson, eds. *East European Security Reconsidered* Washington: Woodrow Wilson Center Press, 1994.
Larrabee, F. Stephen. *East European Security after the Cold War* Santa Monica: Rand, 1993.
Moens, Alexander, and Christopher Anstis. *Disconcerted Europe: The Search for a Security Architecture* Boulder: Westview, 1994.
Nelson, Daniel N. *Alliance Behavior in the Warsaw Pact* Boulder: Westview, 1986.
Siccama, Jan, and Theo Van den Doel. *Restructuring Armed Forces in East and West* Boulder: Westview, 1994.
Van den Doel, Theo. *Central Europe: The New Allies?* Boulder: Westview Press, 1994.

Chapter 16: Democracy and Tolerance
Diamond, Larry, and Marc F. Plattner, eds. *The Global Resurgence of Democracy* Baltimore: Johns Hopkins University Press, 1993.
Di Palma, Giuseppe. *To Craft Democracies: An Essay on Democratic Transitions* Berkeley: University of California Press, 1990.
Huntington, Samuel P. *The Third Wave: Democratization in the Late Twentieth Century* Norman: University of Oklahoma Press, 1991.
Mendus, Susan, ed. *Justifying Tolerance: Conceptual and Historial Perspectives* Cambridge: Cambridge University Press, 1988.
O'Donnell, Guillermo, and Philippe C. Schmitter. *Transitions from Authoritarian Rule: Tentative Conclusions about Uncertain Democracies* Baltimore: Johns Hopkins University Press, 1986.
Rabusha, Alvin, and Kenneth Shepsle. *Politics in Plural Societies: A Theory of Democratic Instability* Columbus, Ohio: Merrill, 1972.
Ramet, Sabrina Petra. *Social Currents in Eastern Europe: The Sources and Consequences of the Great Transformation*, 2nd ed. Durham: Duke University Press, 1995.
Sartori, Giovanni. *The Theory of Democracy Revisited* Chatham, N.J.: Chatham House, 1987.
Schöpflin, George. "Nationalism, Politics and the European Experience," in *Survey*, Vol. 28, No. 4 (Winter 1984): 67–86.
Verdery, Katherine. *What Was Socialism, and What Comes Next?* Princeton: Princeton University Press, 1996.
Vladislav, Jan, ed. *Václav Havel: Living in Truth* London and Boston: Faber and Faber, 1986.

ABOUT THE EDITOR

SABRINA P. RAMET is a Professor of International Studies at the University of Washington. She is the author of seven books, among them: *Whose Democracy? Nationalism, Religion, and the Doctrine of Collective Rights in Post-1989 Eastern Europe* (Rowman & Littlefield, 1997) and *Nihil Obstat: Religion, Politics, and Social Change in East-Central Europe and Russia* (Duke University Press, 1998). She is editor or co-editor of a dozen previous books.

ABOUT THE CONTRIBUTORS

GALE STOKES is a Professor of History at Rice University. His publications include *Politics as Development: The Emergence of Political Parties in Nineteenth Century Serbia* (Duke University Press, 1990) and *The Walls Came Tumbling Down: The Collapse of Communism in Eastern Europe* (Oxford University Press, 1993), which won the AAASS Wayne Vucinich Prize as an outstanding book in the field of Russian, Eurasian, and East European Studies for 1993. His most recent book is *Three Eras of Political Change in Eastern Europe* (Oxford University Press, 1996).

SHARON L. WOLCHIK is a Professor of Political Science and International Affairs at George Washington University. For five years she served as the Director of the Russian and East European Studies program at George Washington University. She is the author of *Czechoslovakia in Transition: Politics, Economics, and Society* and coeditor of *Women, State and Party in Eastern Europe, Foreign and Domestic Politics in Eastern Europe in the 1980s,* and *The Social Legacy of Communism.* Her latest book, which she coedited with Jane Jaquette, is *Women and Democracy,* which will be published in 1998.

LÁSZLÓ KÜRTI teaches political science at the University of Miskolc in Hungary. He was Assistant Professor of Anthropology at American University in Washington, D.C., before returning to his native country in fall 1992. Kürti has contributed articles to *East European Quarterly, Journal of Communist Studies, Anthropological Quarterly,* and other journals, and is editor of *Beyond Borders: Remaking Cultural Identities in the New East Central Europe* (Westview, 1997).

BRIGITTE H. SCHULZ is an Associate Professor of Political Science and Coordinator of the Comparative Development Studies Program at Trinity College, Hartford, Connecticut. She is coeditor of *The Soviet Bloc and the Third World* (1989) and author of *Development Policy in the Cold War Era* (1995). She has written extensively on East and West German foreign policy behavior. She is currently working on an edited volume, *Unified Germany: Domestic Problems and Global Challenges.*

JACK BIELASIAK is a Professor of Political Science and a member of the Russian and East European Institute at Indiana University, Bloomington. He is the author of numerous articles on political elites, working-class movements, political institutions, and electoral processes in Eastern Europe appearing in *The American Political Science Review, Communist and Post-Communist Studies, Economic and Industrial Democracy,* and other journals. He is also the editor of *Poland Today* (1981) and *Polish Politics: Edge of the Abyss* (1984). He is currently at work on a book on the development of political party systems in the formerly communist states of Eastern Europe.

WILLIAM CROWTHER is an Associate Professor of Political Science at the University of North Carolina at Greensboro, and is codirector of the Parliamentary Documents Center. He is the author of *The Political Economy of Romanian Socialism* (Praeger, 1986), coauthor (with Helen Sedor) of *Belarus and Moldova Country Study* (U.S. Federal Research Division, 1995), and contributor of articles to *Russian Studies, Comparative Politics,* and other journals, and has a chapter on Moldova in *Democratization and Political Participation in Post-Communist Societies* (Cambridge University Press, 1997), edited by Karen Dawisha and Bruce Parrott.

SPAS T. RAIKIN is an Associate Professor Emeritus of History at East Stroudsburg University. He is editor of *The Free Agrarian Banner.* He has published several books in Bulgaria, and has contributed essays to *Religion in Communist Lands, Religion in Eastern Europe,* and other journals, as well as to two edited books, *Eastern Christianity and Politics in the Twentieth Century* (1988) and *Religion and Nationalism in Soviet and Eastern Europe,* revised and expanded ed. (1989).

ELEZ BIBERAJ is Chief of the Albanian Service at Voice of America in Washington, D.C. He is author of *Albania in Transition: The Rocky Road to Democracy* (1998), *Albania: A Socialist Maverick* (1990), and *Albania and China: A Study of an Unequal Alliance* (1986). He has also contributed articles to *Conflict Studies, Problems of Communism, Survey,* and *East European Quarterly* on Albania and Yugoslavia.

PAULA FRANKLIN LYTLE is an Assistant Professor of Political Science at Lewis and Clark College. She recently completed a manuscript on peasant mobilization by the Communist Party in Yugoslavia during World War II. Her recent work focuses on the symbolic dimensions of power in the Yugoslav successor states.

HERBERT J. EAGLE is an Associate Professor of Slavic Languages and Literatures at the University of Michigan, where he teaches courses on Russian and East Central European film. His works on cinema include *Russian Formalist Film Theory* (1981), and articles on filmmakers Dusan Makavejev, Jiří Menzel, Vera Chytilová, Andrzej Wajda, Roman Polanski, Peter Gothar, Sergei Eisenstein, Alexei German, Karen Shakhnazarov, Vasily Pichul, and Pavel Lungin, in journals such as *Film Studies Annual, Wide Angle, Michigan Quarterly Review,* and *Cross Currents,* as well as in anthologies, including (most recently) Daniel Goulding's *Five Filmmakers: Tarkovsky, Forman, Polanski, Szabo, Makavejev* (1994).

ANDREI KUZNETSOV is a Senior Lecturer in the Faculty of Management and Business at Manchester Metropolitan University. He coauthored and coedited a number of books in Russian. His most recent book is *Foreign Direct Investment in Contemporary Russia: Managing Capital Entry* (Macmillan, 1994). He has contributed articles to *Communist Economies and Economic Transformation, Europe-Asia Studies, Russian and East European Finance and Trade,* and other journals.

DANIEL N. NELSON is a Professor of International Studies at Old Dominion University in Norfolk, Virginia, and President of Global Concept, Inc., an international consulting firm. His most recent books are *After Authoritarianism* (1995), *East European Security Reconsidered,* coedited with John Lampe (1993), *Romania after Tyranny* (1992), and *Balkan Imbroglio* (1991).

GEORGETA V. POURCHOT is Project Coordinator for the U.S.-Romania Action Commission at the Center for Strategic and International Studies in Washington, D.C. She has worked as an editorial assistant for *International Politics,* and has contributed a chapter in a forthcoming book entitled *Romania in Transition.* She was elected to the Romanian House of Representatives in May 1990.

INDEX

References that include a T (e.g., 25T) indicate tables.